OXFORD
UNIVERSITY PRESS

Complete
Economics
for Cambridge IGCSE® & O Level

Second Edition

Sir Dan Moynihan
Brian Titley

Oxford excellence for Cambridge IGCSE® & O Level

OXFORD

OXFORD
UNIVERSITY PRESS

Great Clarendon Street, Oxford OX2 6DP

Oxford University Press is a department of the University of Oxford.
It furthers the University's objective of excellence in research,
scholarship, and education by publishing worldwide in

Oxford New York

Auckland Cape Town Dar es Salaam Hong Kong Karachi
Kuala Lumpur Madrid Melbourne Mexico City Nairobi
New Delhi Shanghai Taipei Toronto

With offices in

Argentina Austria Brazil Chile Czech Republic France Greece
Guatemala Hungary Italy Japan Poland Portugal Singapore
South Korea Switzerland Thailand Turkey Ukraine Vietnam

Oxford is a registered trade mark of Oxford University Press
in the UK and in certain other countries

© Brian Titley 2012

The moral rights of the author have been asserted

Database right Oxford University Press (maker)

First published 2007
Second edition 2012

All rights reserved. No part of this publication may be reproduced,
stored in a retrieval system, or transmitted, in any form or by any means,
without the prior permission in writing of Oxford University Press, or as
expressly permitted by law, or under terms agreed with the appropriate
reprographics rights organization. Enquiries concerning reproduction
outside the scope of the above should be sent to the Rights Department,
Oxford University Press, at the address above

You must not circulate this book in any other binding or cover
and you must impose this same condition on any acquirer

British Library Cataloguing in Publication Data

Data available

ISBN: 978-0-19-839941-4

10 9 8 7 6 5 4 3 2 1

Printed in China by Golden Cup

Acknowledgments

® IGCSE is the registered trademark of Cambridge International Examinations.

The publishers would like to thank Cambridge International Examinations for kind permission to reproduce past question papers.

Cambridge International Examinations bears no responsibility for the example answers to questions taken from its past question papers which are contained in this publication.

Text acknowledgements

We are grateful to the following for permission to reproduce extracts from copyright material:

Extracts and statistical data from publications produced by the Office of National Statistics (ONS), are Crown copyright material and are reproduced under the terms of the Click-Use Licence No. C2007001380, with the permission of the Controller of OPSI and the Queen's Printer.

The Associated Press via The YGS Group for (p 404) Jean-Marie Godard and Sylvie Corbet: 'France to raise retirement age from 60-62', Associated Press, 16.6.2010; and (p 414) 'China faces major gender imbalance', Associated Press, 12.1.2007.

Bangkok Post, Post Publishing plc for (p 33) 'Government policies fail the poor', *Bangkok Post*, 12.7.2009.

The Chartered Institute of Taxation for (p 90) Mark Schofield and Tonia Theodosiou: 'Green Taxes in other Developed Countries' in *The Green Tax Report 2009*.

Copyright Agency Ltd, Australia (CAL) for (p 395) Steve Lewis and Nic Chistensen: 'Tens of millions in foreign aid wasted on salaries and commissions', *The Courier-Mail*, 24.5.2011, copyright © News Ltd/ Courier-Mail, 2010

Deutsche Presse Agentur (DPA) for (p 145) Bill Smith: 'China's Rising Wages push Investors Inland', 2.8.2010, copyright © DPA 2010.

Elizabeth C Economy, Director of Asia Studies, Council on Foreign Relations for (p 373) E Economy: 'Economic Boom, Environmental Bust', 2.10.04, www.cfr.org.

Gamepro for (p 274) Dave Rudden: 'Canada boasts the third-largest video game industry', GamePro.com, 4.6.2010.

Daniel Griswold, Cato Institute for (p 463) D T Griswold: 'Is the US trade deficit really bad news?', www.cato.org, 15 .5.1998.

Guardian News and Media Ltd for (p 33) David Adams: 'Supermarket suppliers "help destroy Amazon rainforest"' *The Guardian*, 21.6.2009, copyright © Guardian News and Media Ltd 2009 for (p 290) Polly Curtis: 'UK plans skills academies to close productivity gap', *The Guardian* 22.3.05, copyright © Guardian News and Media Ltd 2005 (p 402) Ian Sample: 'World faces "perfect storm" of problems by 2030', *The Guardian*, 18.3.2009, copyright © Guardian News and Media Ltd 2009; (p 386) David Smith 'The food rush: rising demand on China and West sparks African land grab', *The Guardian*, 3.7.2009, copyright © Guardian News and Media Ltd 2009; and (p76) Jonathan Watts 'China's worst oil-spill threatens wildlife as volunteers assist in clean-up', *The Guardian*, 21.7.2010, copyright © Guardian News and Media Ltd 2010.

The Independent for (p 386) Sarah Arnott: 'Beijing's billions buy up reserves', *The Independent*, 2.10.2010, copyright © The Independent 2010; (p 33) Kunal Dutta: 'Turks and Caicos quits after corruption inquiry', *The Independent*, 24.3.2009, copyright © The Independent 2009; and (p 371) Brett Young: 'Finland suffers double-dip', The Independent, 10.10, copyright © The Independent 2010.

International Labour Organization (ILO) for figures (pp 346, 348) from *Global Employment Trends* 2011, copyright © International Labour Organization, 2011.

The Irish Times for (p 395) Paul Cullen: 'Overseas aid is funding human rights abuses', *The Irish Times* 20.1.2011, copyright © The Irish Times 2011; and (p 17) Irish Times Reporter: 'Choice of higher taxes or spending cuts urged', *The Irish Times*, 21.9.2010, copyright © The Irish Times 2010.

MSN New Zealand for (p 73) 'Romania tackles obesity with fatty foods tax', 19.2.2010, www.health.msn.co.nz

News International Group via the Newspaper Marketing Agency for (p 87) 'Today is the day we start to eat Earth' by David Brown, *The London Paper*, 9.10.06.

OECD for extracts from OECD Statistics , www.oecd.org (pp162, 299), and for tables, graphs and charts from *Taxing Wages 2010*, (OECD, 2011) (p 310); OECD *Factbook 2010:Economic, Environmental and Social Statistics* (OECD, 2010) (p 35); and *OECD Family Database*, (OECD, 2010) (p 144).

Solo Syndication for (p 357) James Chapman: 'Is the REAL cost of unemployment £61 bilion per year?', The *Daily Mail*, 3.1.2007; and (p 33) Daily Mail Reporter: 'Vets accused of overcharging by up to 500% for some pet medicines!', *The Daily Mail*, 27.9.2010.

Telegraph Media Group Ltd for (p 395) Gordon Rayner: 'Millions in overseas aid to African embezzled' *Daily Telegraph*, 5.2.2011, copyright © Telegraph Media Group Ltd 2011.

Voice of America (VOA) for (p 425) 'Tens of Thousands protest at G20 Summit in Seoul', 7.11.2010.

World Federation of Exchanges (WFE) for (p 123) *2010 WFE Market Highlights* (January, 2011).

World Trade Organization (WTO) for global trade figures (pp 431, 432, 445)

The publisher would like to thank the following for permission to reproduce photographs:

t=top b=bottom m=middle l=left r=right

P3: Leo Francini/Shutterstock; P4: Ssguy/Shutterstock; P5tl: TonyV3112/Shutterstock; P5tr: xtrekx/Shutterstock; P5bl: Richard Jones/Rex Features; P5br: makspogonii/Shutterstock; P6t: Vasiliy Ganzha/Shutterstock; P6b: Maksim Toome/Shutterstock; P7t: Monkey Business Images/Shutterstock; P7b: Jorge Fernandez/Alamy/Photolibrary; P9t: JHershPhoto/Shutterstock; P9bl: Sugar0607/Dreamstime; P9bm: Ifong/Shutterstock; P9br: Drozdowski/Shutterstock; P11l: Jeff Dalton/Dreamstime; P11m: Yangchao/Dreamstime; P11r: Paul Vinten/Dreamstime; P12: Oliver Hoffmann/Shutterstock; P14t: DV/Photolibrary; P14b: Janine Wiedel Photolibrary/Alamy/Photolibrary; P15: Maynard Case/Shutterstock; P25: Sergey Kelin/Shutterstock; P30l: Marmaduke St. John/Alamy/Photolibrary; P30r: Joel Stettenheim/News Archive/Corbis; P40: Nigel Cattlin/Alamy/Photolibrary; P76: SkyTruth/NASA; P80t: Michael Kemp/Alamy/Photolibrary; P80b: Ian Bracegirdle/Shutterstock; P84l: Elena Elisseeva/Shutterstock; P84m: Photofusion Picture Library/Alamy/Photolibrary; P84r: Kevin Eaves/Shutterstock; P85t: Imagebroker/Alamy/Photolibrary; P85m: PhotoStockFile/Alamy/Photolibrary; P85b: Masterfile; P86t: Stuwdamdorp/Alamy; P86b: Keith Morris/Alamy/Photolibrary; P89t-b: Planetobserver/Science Photo Library, steve estvanik/Shutterstock, Steve Estvanik/Shutterstock, Christopher Waters/Fotolia; P112: R. Peterkin/Shutterstock; P113: Ria Novosti/Science Photo Library; P117: Bazuki Muhammad/Reuters; P119tl: Kevpix/Alamy/Photolibrary; P119tm: Justin Kase zsixz/Alamy/Photolibrary; P119t: Andrew Walters/Alamy/Photolibrary; P119b: Crack Palinggi/Reuters; P123t: Tupungato/Shutterstock; P123b: Mark Thomas/SPL/Photolibrary; P126: Kevin Kallaugher; P133l: Ton Kinsbergen/Science Photo Library; P133r: Doug Martin/Science Photo Library; P150: Bela Szandelszky/AP Photo; P157t: Keith Morris/Alamy; P157b: John Hart/Creators Syndicate; P184l: J van der Wolf/Shutterstock; P184r: Tweetlebeetle/Shutterstock; P199l: Geoffrey Robinson/Rex Features; P199r: Steven Senne/AP Photo; P203l: Norman Pogson/Alamy; P203r: Cooperative Central Bank Ltd; P205tl: David Pearson/Rex Features; P205tr: Ted Aljibe/AFP; P205m: Stale Edstrøm/Dreamstime; P205b: Sergei Telegin/Shutterstock; P207: Keith Morris/Alamy; P212l: AFP; P212r: Alex Segre/Rex Features; P214tl: Patrick Landmann/Science Photo Library; P214tr: Jeanma85/Fotolia; P214bl: Nick Stubbs/Dreamstime; P214br: David Parker/Science Photo Library; P215t: David Pearson/Rex Features; P215b: Monkey Business Images/Shutterstock; P216l: Interfoto/Alamy; P216r: Greenpeace; P219: Rodger Whitney/Shutterstock; P221l: Natasha Owen/Fotolia; P221r: Rainer Plendl/Shutterstock; P241l: © Copyright 2003-2011 Exxon Mobil Corporation; P241r: Tim Sloan/Stringer/Getty Images; P250t: Chris Whitehead/Photolibrary; P250b: Glow Images, Inc/Photolibrary; P254l: Sutton-Hibbert/Rex Features; P254r: Kevpix/Alamy/Photolibrary; P255l: Brook/Shutterstock; P255r: MB Pictures/Rex Features; P258: Justin Sullivan/Getty Images; P264: Enrique Marcarian/Reuters; P269l: Christopher Parypa/Shutterstock; P269r: Stephan Zabel/Istockphoto; P277l: Rob/Fotolia; P277m: Pedro Jorge Henriques Monteiro/Shutterstock; P277r: Richard Lord/Photolibrary; P278l: Dewayne Flowers/Shutterstock; P278m: U.S. Army Spc. Breeanna J. DuBuke; P278r: Budda/Dreamstime; P291t: Colin Cuthbert/Science Photo Library; P291b: Mykhaylo Feshchur/Shutterstock; P293b: © Crown copyright; P30l-r: Blend Images/Alamy/Photolibrary, wrangler/Shutterstock; P308l: Hung Chung Chih/Shutterstock; P308m: Andre Joubert/Alamy/Photolibrary; P309r: JTB Photo Communications, Inc./Alamy; P313tl: Macana/Alamy/Photolibrary; P313tr: Xavier Lhospice/Reuters; P313bl: Dr Juerg Alean/Photolibrary; P313br: Simon C Ford/Photolibrary; P316: Luke MacGregor/Reuters; P327: National Photo Company Collection/Library of Congress; P332: OUP; P366t: Maksim Dubinsky/Shutterstock; P366m: Fred Guerdin/Reporters/Science Photo Library; P366b: Digital Vision/Thinkstock; P372t: Tim Graham/Alamy; P372b: Paper Girl/Fotolia; P383tl: Joanna Zielinska/Fotolia; P383tr: Bruder/Fotolia; P383bl: Akhtar Soomro/Reuters; P383br: Jitendra Prakash/Reuters; P401t: Mark Edwards/Photolibrary; P401b: Mark Edwards/Still Pictures/Photolibrary; P403t: Paulaphoto/Shutterstock; P403b: Gilles Lougassi/Shutterstock; P410l: Kyodo/XinHua/Xinhua Press/Corbis; P410r: Bazuki Muhammad/Reuters; P416: Peter Treanor/Alamy; P425: Park Jin-hee/XinHua/Xinhua Press/Corbis; P427l-r: Paul Weatherman/U.S. Air Force, Photoshut/Shutterstock, Photoshut/Shutterstock, Turumtaev Ildar/Shutterstock; P429l: Gary/Fotolia; P429b: Cobalt/Shutterstock; P430t: Vario Images GmbH & Co.KG/Alamy; P430b: EmiliaU/Shutterstock; P435: AFP; P444l: S_oleg/Shutterstock; P444r: Justin Kase zsixz/Alamy/Photolibrary; P453: Wiklander/Shutterstock.

Cover Image: Robert Clare/Getty Images

Illustrations: Spike Gerrell and HL Studios

Introduction

Learning about economics will provide you with the knowledge, understanding and skills you will need to succeed

Whether you want to one day start your own business, work for a major international company or a government, become a teacher or doctor, or run a charity, the study of economics will provide you with the knowledge, understanding, critical thinking and skills you will need to succeed.

The newspapers often describe complicated economic problems such as inflation, unemployment, balance of trade deficits, anti-competitive behaviour, changes in exchange rates, recessions, speculative bubbles in stock market prices and supply shortages. It is sometimes difficult to understand these and what impact they could have on our daily lives without an understanding of economics.

People who have studied economics are good at problem solving because they learn to identify problems, to suggest alternative solutions, to determine what information is relevant, and to weigh up different costs and benefits in decision making.

Knowledge of economics also helps us understand what determines the prices of different products, why people earn different amounts in different jobs and why these can change over time, why some countries are poor and others are rich and how and why governments influence the behaviours of different groups of consumers and producers. But above all, the study of economics makes us realize that we are all dependent upon one another and that the decisions we make will affect others.

By studying for the Cambridge International Examinations IGCSE or O Level in Economics you will therefore develop valuable lifelong skills including:

- an understanding of economic theory, terminology and principles
- the ability to apply the tools of economic analysis to real-world situations
- the ability to distinguish between facts and personal judgements in real economic issues
- an understanding of, and an ability to use and interpret, basic economic data, numeracy and literacy
- the ability to take a greater part in decision-making processes in everyday life
- an understanding of the economies of developed and developing nations
- an excellent foundation for more advanced study in economics.

Complete Economics will help you to build these skills quickly. It contains everything you need to master the content of the Cambridge IGCSE and O Level Economics courses in an enjoyable and exciting way by providing real insight into how different markets and entire economies work.

Final examinations will assess your skills and knowledge of economics

At the end of your Cambridge IGCSE or O Level course in Economics you will take two papers (from May 2014):

Paper 1 Multiple choice	45 minutes
Candidates answer 30 multiple choice questions.	
30% of total marks.	
Paper 2 Structured questions	**2 hours 15 minutes**
Candidates answer one compulsory question that requires them to interpret and analyse previously unseen data relevant to a real economic situation, and three questions from a choice of six.	
70% of total marks.	

Those students studying for the Cambridge IGCSE in Economics who will sit their exams in 2012 or 2013 will take three papers:

Paper 1 Multiple choice	45 minutes
Candidates answer 30 multiple choice questions.	
20% of total marks.	
Paper 2 Structured questions	**2 hours**
Candidates answer one compulsory question and three questions from a choice of six.	
50% of total marks.	
Paper 3 Analysis and critical evaluation	**1 hour 30 minutes**
Candidates answer two compulsory questions and are required to interpret and analyse previously unseen data relevant to a real economic situation.	
30% of total marks.	

The following key skills will be assessed in all the examination papers.

Knowledge and understanding	Analysis
Show your knowledge and understanding of economic facts, definitions, concepts, principles and theories Use economic vocabulary and terminology.	Select, organize and interpret data Apply your economic knowledge and understanding in written, numerical, diagrammatic and graphical form Use economic data, to recognize patterns in such data and to deduce relationships.

Critical evaluation and decision making
Distinguish between evidence and opinion, make reasoned judgements and communicate them in an accurate and logical way Recognize that economic theory has various limits and uncertainties Evaluate the social and environmental implications of particular courses of economic action. Draw conclusions from economic information and critically evaluate economic data Communicate conclusions in a logical and concise manner.

The requirement to demonstrate evidence of the key skills in the different examination papers varies. The importance placed on each skill in each examination paper from May 2014 is as follows:

Assessment objective	Paper 1 (%)	Paper 2 (%)
A: Knowledge with understanding	45+/-5	20+/-5
B: Analysis	55+/-5	35+/-5
C: Critical evaluation and decision-making		45+/-5

So, for example, up to 50% of the marks in paper 1 will be allocated to evidence of your knowledge and understanding and up to 60% for evidence of your analytical ability. (Note that this applies to examinations from May 2014 onwards.

Complete Economics contains a wealth of real examination questions for you to practise and develop these key skills. Model answers to help you attain top marks for all the examination questions in this book are provided on the support website. The website also contains additional examination papers for you to complete, and sample answers.

Best of luck with your studies and examinations!

Note
Unless otherwise reported all $ figures quoted in the text are US dollars. In many cases the $ sign is used simply to denote a unit of money and could therefore represent any currency. However, real world examples of values quoted in $ are always actual US dollars unless otherwise stated. This is because many other countries use a dollar sign to denote their currency, such as the Australian dollar, the Bahamian dollar and the Canadian dollar.

Wherever you see an arrowhead symbol followed by numbers at the end of a paragraph they are referring you to look at other units in the book that contain related information and further explanation on the concepts you have just covered. For example, ➤ **4.2** suggests you should look at Unit 4.2 on Organizing Production.

Contents

Introduction iii

1 The basic economic problem: choice and the allocation of resources — 1

1.1 The basic economic problem — 2
- What is the economic problem? — 3
- Factors of production — 4
- The satisfaction of human wants — 7
- Opportunity cost: the cost of choice — 10
- Assessment exercises — 19

2 The allocation of resources: how markets work; market failure — 21

2.1 Economic systems — 22
- What is an economy? — 22
- How economies determine what, how and for whom to produce — 23
- Different economic systems — 25
- The market economic system — 26
- The mixed economic system — 31

2.2 How markets work — 39
- What is demand? — 39
- What is supply? — 48
- Market price — 55
- Price elasticity of demand — 59
- Price elasticity of supply — 66
- The impact of taxes and subsidies on market outcomes — 70

2.3 Social costs and benefits — 75
- How the decisions of firms can affect others — 75
- Market failure and government intervention — 81
- Opportunity cost revisited — 84
- How consumers' decisions can affect others — 85
- Conservation or commercialization? — 87
- Assessment exercises — 95

3 The individual as producer, consumer and borrower — 101

3.1 Money and finance — 102
- Why do we need money? — 103
- The functions of money — 105
- What makes a good money? — 108
- The history of money — 110
- What is money? — 112
- The money market — 114
- The stock market — 122

3.2 Occupations and earnings — 129
- Why do people work? — 130
- What is the labour market — 134
- The market wage for a job — 136
- Why do the earnings of employees differ? — 139
- Why do governments intervene in labour markets? — 146

3.3 The role of trade unions — 150
- What is a trade union? — 150
- How trade unions are organized — 153
- Collective bargaining — 154

3.4 Spending, saving and borrowing — 161
- Consumption — 161
- Saving — 168
- Borrowing money — 170
- Assessment exercises — 177

4 The private firm as producer and employer — 181

4.1 Types of business organization — 182
- Starting a business — 183
- The sole trader — 186
- Partnerships — 187
- Joint-stock companies — 190
- Multinational corporations — 198
- Cooperatives — 202
- Public sector organizations — 205

4.2 Organization of production — 210
- Production — 211
- The aims of production — 215
- Productivity and factor demand — 217
- Calculating costs and revenues — 225
- Profit, loss or break-even — 232

4.3 The growth of firms — 237
- The size of firms — 238
- How firms grow in size — 240
- Increasing the scale of production — 242
- Can firms grow too much? — 245

	The relationship between costs and productive scale	247
	Why some firms remain small	249
4.4	**Competition**	**252**
	Why do firms compete?	252
	Pricing strategies	257
	Market structures	260
	Monopoly and opportunistic behaviour	263
	Controlling monopolies and regulating competition	268
	Assessment exercises	271

5 Role of government in an economy — 275

5.1	**Government economic policy**	**276**
	The role of government in a mixed economy	277
	Macroeconomic objectives	279
	Demand-side policies	284
	Supply-side policies	290
	Policy conflicts	294
5.2	**Taxation**	**298**
	Financing public expenditure	299
	Tax systems	304
	Direct taxes	308
	Indirect taxes	312
	Balancing the budget	316
	Assessment exercises	321

6 Economic indicators — 325

6.1	**Price inflation**	**326**
	What is inflation?	327
	How to measure inflation	329
	What causes inflation?	333
	The costs of inflation	337
	What is deflation?	340
6.2	**Employment and unemployment**	**345**
	Employment trends	346
	The causes and consequences of unemployment	351
6.3	**Output and growth**	**360**
	Measuring output	360
	Economic growth	364
	Growth cycles	369
	Economic growth or economic welfare?	372
	Assessment exercises	378

7 Developed and developing economies: trends in production, population and living standards — 381

7.1	**Developed and less-developed economies**	**382**
	Economic development in different economies	382
	Development indicators	386
	Measures to reduce international poverty	392
7.2	**Population**	**398**
	The global population	399
	Causes of population change	406
	The structure of populations	411
	Assessment exercises	420

8 International aspects — 423

8.1	**International specialization and trade**	**424**
	Globalization and trade	425
	International specialization	426
	International trade patterns	430
	Free trade or protectionism?	434
8.2	**Balancing international payments**	**443**
	Exports and imports	444
	The balance of payments	447
	Exchange rates	451
	Correcting a trade imbalance	462
	Assessment exercises	469

Index — 472

What's on the website?

- Guidance and answers to all the activities and exam preparation exercises in this book
- Answers to all the end of chapter assessment exercises in this book
- Printable versions of all the crosswords in this book along with their solutions
- An economics dictionary containing definitions for all the essential terms used in the course
- Further exam preparation in the form of two practice papers with sample answers provided

www.oxfordsecondary.com/9780198399414

1 The basic economic problem: choice and the allocation of resources

1.1	The basic economic problem
Assessment	Multiple choice
	Structured questions

The resources available to produce goods and services are scarce compared with our limitless wants. Land (natural resources), labour (human effort), capital (man-made resources) and enterprise (the knowledge and skills people need to organize production) are all scarce resources. They are factors of production because they are organized into firms by entrepreneurs to produce goods and services to satisfy our needs and wants as consumers.

Resources are inputs to productive activity and products (goods and services) are outputs from productive activity. However, because there are not enough resources to produce everything we need and want we must make choices. For example, if we choose to use up scarce resources in the production of cars those same resources cannot be used to produce food. This opportunity is foregone.

Making a choice between alternative uses of scarce resources therefore always involves a cost in terms of what we have to give up in return. The benefit of the next best alternative foregone is the opportunity cost of that decision.

Scarcity of resources relative to human wants is the central problem in economics. The study of economics therefore involves examining and informing decisions about how best to use scarce resources in an attempt to satisfy as many of our needs and wants as possible to maximize economic welfare.

Unit 1.1   The basic economic problem

AIMS

By the end of this unit you should be able to:

▶ define the nature of the economic problem (limited resources and unlimited wants)
- appreciate that people's wants for goods and services are unlimited

▶ define the factors of production (land, labour, capital and enterprise)
- understand that the resources used to make goods and services are scarce

▶ define opportunity cost and analyse particular circumstances to illustrate this concept
- explain why scarcity of resources leads to choice
- understand how economics can be used to help increase choice

▶ demonstrate how production possibility curves can be used to illustrate choice and resource allocation

▶ evaluate the implications of particular courses of action in terms of their opportunity cost.

The basic economic problem: choice and the allocation of resources

SECTION 1 — **What is the economic problem?**

Oil runs out

World News — Tuesday 24th May 2127

Today the world's oil supply has dried up. A crisis meeting of world leaders took place in Washington last night.

Yesterday the top oil-producing companies of the world declared that the world's supply of oil was now exhausted. The last barrel of oil has been filled and the oil rigs will drill no more. The world now faces an energy crisis. No more oil will mean no more petrol for transport or machinery. There can be no more plastic for components in many household products like televisions, microwave ovens, cars and telephones.

Energy ministers from around the world are meeting today in Switzerland to discuss the crisis and try to find a solution. Coal deposits are low and nuclear power stations are already overworked to meet the demand for electricity.

The newspaper article above paints a gloomy picture of what might happen in the future. It is hard to imagine a world without oil but even now there is only a limited amount of oil left in the ground. In other words, it is **scarce** and as more and more is used up there will come a time when no oil remains. The world's oil took many millions of years to form – we may use it all up in a few hundred years.

However, it is not just oil that is scarce. Some forecasters suggest if we continue to consume goods and services in the future at the same rate as we do today many natural commodities, such as aluminium, copper, lead, tin, zinc, and timber from the last remaining rainforests, will all be used up within the next 50 years. Even the clean air we breathe and the water we drink are limited and may eventually run out. If you imagine the world as a round ball then it is possible to see that only a limited amount of these **resources** can be squeezed from it.

The basic economic problem

This is because our wants for many different goods and services are growing all the time but there are just not enough resources in the world to satisfy them all. As you will discover in the next few pages, this is the central problem in the study of economics.

SECTION 2

▲ Production

Factors of production

Resources are important because they are used to make **goods** such as bread, televisions, cars, fruit and vegetables, and to provide **services**, including banking, insurance, transport, health care, policing and cleaning.

Production therefore involves using resources to make and sell goods and services to satisfy our wants. Resources are the **inputs** to productive activities and goods and services are the **outputs**. ➤ 4.2

Any activity that fails to satisfy a want is not a productive activity according to economists. So, for example, if resources are used to make clothes nobody wants to wear, televisions that fail to display moving images, clocks that cannot keep time or any other good or service that fails to satisfy a want then those resources have not been used productively.

The people who make and sell goods and services are known as **producers**. They can be business owners, managers or employees. ➤ 4.1

Resources are used to produce goods and services

Scarce resources used up in the production of goods and services to satisfy our wants are known as **factors of production**. In addition to natural resources, such as timber, coal and many crops, they include the people who go to work or run business organizations and the buildings, machinery and equipment they use.

All these resources or factors of production are scarce because the time people have to spend working, the different skills they have and the land on which factories, shops and homes are built are all limited in supply relative to our wants. Not convinced? Just take a look at some of these real newspaper headlines.

Microchip shortage slows smart-phone, computer production

Factory jobs return, but employers unable to fill them because of skill shortages

New entrepreneurs lack financial and other skills needed for success

Equipment shortage limits oil exploration

Companies forced to idle their heavy equipment due to impact of large tyre shortage

The basic economic problem: choice and the allocation of resources

> **PROBLEM 1: RESOURCES ARE SCARCE**

▼ Factors of production include natural resources, people, machinery and land

How resources are classified

Economists group together different factors of production under four main headings.

Land

The fertile soil vital to the growth of plants, minerals such as coal and oil, and animals for their meat and skins, are known as **natural resources**, but to simplify economists call all of these **land**. Land therefore includes the seas and rivers of the world, forests and deserts, all manner of minerals from the ground, chemicals and gases from the air and the earth's crust.

Labour

Nothing can be produced without people. They provide the physical and mental effort to make goods and services. People who work with their hands and use their brains to help make goods and services provide **human resources**, or what is termed **labour**.

The basic economic problem

The size and ability of an economy's labour force are very important in determining the quantity and quality of the goods and services that can be produced. The greater the number of workers, and the better educated and skilled they are, the more an economy can produce.

Enterprise

While most people have the ability to contribute to the production of goods and services, not everyone could be a successful business person and be able to employ and organize resources in a **firm**. A firm is an organization that owns a factory or a number of factories, offices, or perhaps even shops, where goods and services are produced. Business know-how, or the ability to run a production process, is known as **enterprise**. The people who have enterprise and can control and manage firms are called **entrepreneurs**. They are the people who take the risks and decisions necessary to make firms run successfully.

Capital

To make the task of production easier, man has invented many tools: pens to write with, computers to calculate, screwdrivers, spanners, hammers, rulers, and many more. On a grander scale, turbines drive engines, tractors plough the land, ships transport goods, lathes shape and refine metals and wood, and factories and offices have been built to house many man-made tools and machines. These **man-made resources** which help to produce many other goods and services are known as **capital**.

Economists tend to talk of **units** of factors of production. For example, an economist might say that 'a firm has employed 30 more units of capital'. This simply means that it has bought 30 new identical machines. Similarly, if an economist talks of units of land, it could mean tonnes of coal, barrels of crude oil, or acres of land. Likewise, employees or the individual hours they work are units of labour for an economist.

ACTIVITY 1.1

Classifying resources

1. Below is a list of many of the scarce resources that are used to produce cartons of orange juice. Draw three columns and label them **natural resources, human resources** and **man-made resources**, and then in pairs decide in which column each item should go.

Telephones	Oil	Shops
Advertising people	Lorries	Ship's crew
Cotton for clothing	Printing machines	Factory buildings
Fertile soil	Orange trees	Insecticide sprays
Squeezing machines	Bank clerks	Oranges
Orange pickers	Power stations	Roads
Package designers	Coal	Accountants
Calculators	Warehouse workers	Shop assistants
Water	Lorry drivers	Wood

2. Now try to produce a list of resources you think are used to produce cars. Compare your list with the rest of the class, and again sort them out into natural, human and man-made resources.

6 The basic economic problem: choice and the allocation of resources

SECTION 3

The satisfaction of human wants

Any resources that are not scarce are called **free goods**. The air that we breathe seems without limit and so is considered to be a free good. However, with increasing pollution in the world, fresh, clean air may become scarce!

At first sight it may seem that although there is only a limited amount of resources in the world, the world is such a big place that these things might not be so scarce. Before you agree with this view, look at Activity 1.2.

ACTIVITY 1.2

Needs and wants

A

B

Look at the two photos A and B. Photo A represents modern city life; photo B shows a group of people living in a poor African village.

1. What needs have the two families in common?
2. Which family will not be able to satisfy all its needs?
3. What do you think are the wants of the family in picture A?
4. What do you think are the wants of the family in picture B?
5. Why can't the wants of either family be satisfied?
6. What do you think are the main differences between **needs** and **wants**?

The basic economic problem

Needs and wants

All people have the same basic needs. Whether rich or poor, we all need food, clean water and some shelter from the extremes of weather in order to live safely and to survive. However, people usually want far more than they need. We want fashionable clothes, big televisions and music players, cars, overseas holidays, insurance and banking services, and much more.

Just imagine if we could list everything that everyone in the world wanted. The list would go on forever and would grow longer as the world population expands. Our wants are without limit and many of them cannot be satisfied. As we now know, this is because there are simply not enough resources in the world to make all the goods and services we want and need.

PROBLEM 2: HUMAN WANTS ARE UNLIMITED

ACTIVITY 1.3

What do we need and what do we want?
Below is a jumbled collection of different goods and services. Draw a table like the one below and sort them into needs and wants, giving reasons for your choice.

You should now understand the difference between needs and wants. Write a sentence to explain what these two words mean.

Needs	Wants	Reason
Eggs	LCD – TVs	Eggs are food
		Televisions bring pleasure – but not essential for survival

The basic economic problem: choice and the allocation of resources

What is consumption?

▲ Consumption

Goods and services are the outputs or **products** of productive activity using scarce resources. Goods and services are also referred to as economic goods because they are not freely available.

We use up goods and services or products to satisfy our needs and wants. This is called **consumption**.

When we eat we are consuming food. When we watch television we are consuming electricity, the television set and the services of a television company. When we go to schools and colleges, we are consuming the services of teachers. We are consuming when we read books, sit on chairs, sleep on beds, put money into a bank account, ask a policeman the time, listen to the radio and use up any other goods and services in order to satisfy our wants.

The people who buy goods and services to satisfy their wants are known as **consumers** and their spending is called **consumption expenditure**.

What is exchange?

People can satisfy some of their wants by producing a number of goods and services for their own consumption. For example, keen gardeners may grow some vegetables to eat to satisfy part of their need or want for food. Others may make furniture from wood for their families to use. However, very few people can make all the things they want. In order to obtain the goods and services they cannot produce themselves they must engage in trade or **exchange**. In modern economies most people are able to do this by going to work to earn money. They then exchange this money for the goods and services they want that are produced by other workers. ▶ **3.1**

Goods and services

Different goods and services satisfy different needs and wants. Economists group together different products into four main categories.

Consumer goods and services

A **consumer good** is any good that satisfies consumers' wants. Some of these consumer goods are called **consumer durable goods** because they last a long time, for example cars, washing machines, televisions, furniture and computers. **Non-durable goods** are perishable or used up quickly, for example food, drink, matches, petrol and washing powder.

▼ Durable and non-durable goods

Sometimes our wants are satisfied by someone doing something for us. These are called **consumer services**. Examples include the services of a doctor, banker, insurance agent, window cleaner, teacher or policeman.

Capital goods

Man-made resources which help to produce other goods and services are known as capital goods. For example, screwdrivers, drills, ploughs, lorries,

The basic economic problem | 9

roads, power stations and factory buildings are **capital goods** because they are not wanted for themselves, but for what they can help to produce. Capital goods are bought by producers. The buying of capital goods is known as investment. Therefore, we can talk of a firm investing in new machinery and buildings to allow them to produce other goods and services. Investment in capital goods, like factories and machines, will increase production and help an economy grow. ▶ **6.3**

Public goods and merit goods

Imagine that someone came to your door and asked you to pay $20 towards the cost of powering the street lamp out in the street for another year. The collector argues that the street lamp provides you with light to help you see at night when you are driving or walking home. It also benefits your neighbours and the people across the street. You know that if they all give $20 to the collector this will be enough to keep the street lamp on at night, whether you pay or not. That is, you can still enjoy the benefits of street lighting even if you pay nothing towards it. In this case consumption cannot be confined to those who have paid for it.

However, if all your neighbours thought in the same way as you, the collector would be unable to get $20 from anyone and the street light could not be kept running. The only way that street lighting can be provided is if the government provides it and forces everyone to pay for it by collecting taxes.

Goods and services which are provided by a government because everyone benefits from them, even if they do not pay for them, are called **public goods**. A government provides these goods and services as no private firm would wish to produce them, because nobody would pay for their use. Examples of public goods include defence, the police, law and order, protection of the environment, lighthouses, and of course, street lighting.

Sometimes a government will also provide goods and services because it thinks that people ought to benefit from them, even if they cannot afford to buy them, and to benefit the economy. Such goods and services are called **merit goods**. Examples of these goods are health care and education. ▶ **5.1**

SECTION 4

Opportunity cost: the cost of choice

Choosing what we want

We have learned that wants are unlimited but the resources used to produce the goods and services to satisfy our wants are limited. That is, there is **scarcity**. Nobody can have sufficient goods and services to satisfy all their needs and wants, so people must choose which wants they will satisfy. Choice is necessary because scarce resources can be used in lots of ways to make many different goods and services. Scarce resources have alternative uses.

> **PROBLEM 3: SCARCE RESOURCES HAVE ALTERNATIVE USES**

For example, many football clubs have spare land next to their grounds. The problem facing these clubs is to choose what to do with this land. They could build a sports complex or leisure centre to serve the community, or a supermarket, or an apartment block or even an office complex. Whatever they do, they can only choose one of these options because land is a scarce resource.

▼ For example, a piece of land can be used for agriculture or to build a motorway on:

People, nations and the world must therefore choose how scarce resources are to be used. That is, they must choose which goods and services to make because they cannot make everything that they want.

ACTIVITY 1.4

Alternatives

Below is a list of resources. See how many alternative uses you can find for them. That is, list as many different goods and services as you can that you think the resources can be used to produce.

1 An area of farmland.
2 A person who is good at maths.
3 A spade.
4 An egg.

The economic problem

So, we have now discovered the central problem in economics: resources are scarce and have alternative uses, but our wants are without limit. Therefore not all of our wants can be satisfied. We must therefore choose what goods and services to produce and therefore which of our many wants to satisfy.

PROBLEM 4: WE MUST CHOOSE WHICH WANTS TO SATISFY

To make sure we make the right decisions it is important that we consider what our options are before we choose the best ones.

▲ The economic problem

The basic economic problem 11

ACTIVITY 1.5

The next best thing

Choosing between goods and services involves a very special cost. Imagine that you have just bought the list of items below. But now imagine that you were unable to buy these and therefore had to buy your second-best choice instead. Copy and complete the table.

What I have just bought	What could I have bought instead?
Large flat-screen television	
Four-bedroom house	
Cakes and sweets	
A ticket to the World Cup Final	

Opportunity cost

In the second column in Activity 1.5 you have listed your second-best choices, or your next best alternatives to the products in column one. For example, if you had bought a large flat-screen television, you may be going without the benefit of a holiday. The benefit of the holiday given up is the real cost of owning the large flat-screen television.

The true cost of something is what we have to give up to get it. This is known as the **opportunity cost**. It is the benefit we could have enjoyed from the next best alternative we choose to go without.

Opportunity cost arises not only when we choose to buy things but also when we choose how to allocate scarce resources to the production of different goods and services. For example, in deciding to use a piece of land to build a new sports complex, we may be going without the benefit of new houses, or farmland to grow food. The problem of resource allocation therefore involves evaluating the 'trade-offs' of alternative uses. Choosing one use means going without another.

ACTIVITY 1.6

The cost of making choices

A factory employs 10 people and has 2 machines able to produce and pack 300 glass bottles each day. The same employees and machines could instead be used in the same factory to make and pack 400 glass jars each day.

The same 10 employees used to work on a farm and were very skilled at growing and harvesting corn until the farm was sold and the factory was built on the farmland. Compared to the farm the factory is noisy and pollutes the air with smoke.

1 What is the opportunity cost to the factory owners of using the 10 employees and 2 machines to make 300 bottles each day?

2 What is the opportunity cost to the employees of working in the factory?

3 What is the opportunity cost to society of the factory?

Opportunity cost in production

Because resources are scarce and have alternative uses, a decision to devote more resources to producing one product means fewer resources are available to produce other goods. A useful way to show this is by using a **production possibility curve (PPC)**, also called a production possibility frontier or boundary.

The basic economic problem: choice and the allocation of resources

For example, the diagram below shows a PPC in a firm producing cars and trucks. Using its existing resources and technology efficiently the firm can produce 100 cars per week (where the PPC touches the vertical axis) or 120 trucks (where the PPC touches the horizontal axis). The PPC therefore shows that the firm has to give up 120 trucks to produce 100 cars each week. However, it is more likely that the firm will choose to produce some cars and some trucks with its resources. Combinations of cars and trucks the firm is able to produce are plotted along the PPC.

▼ A PPC for a firm producing cars and trucks

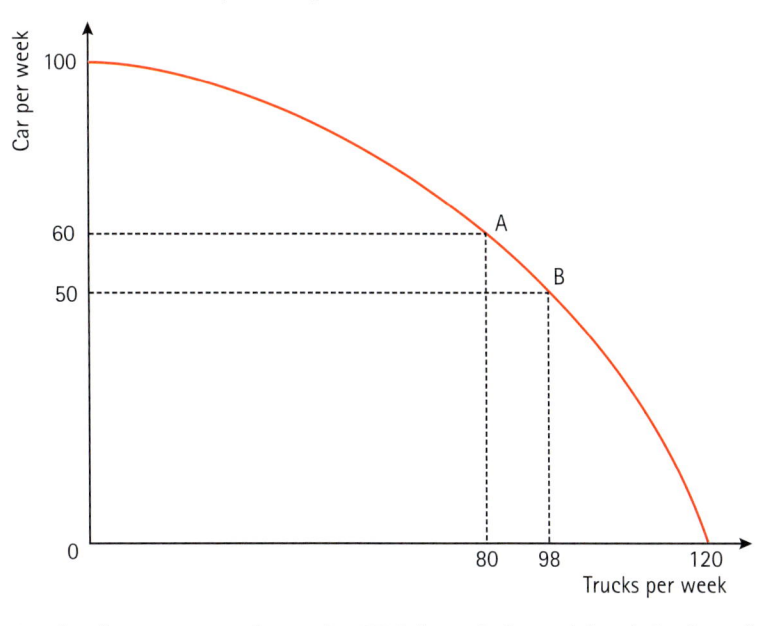

▼ A PPC for an economy

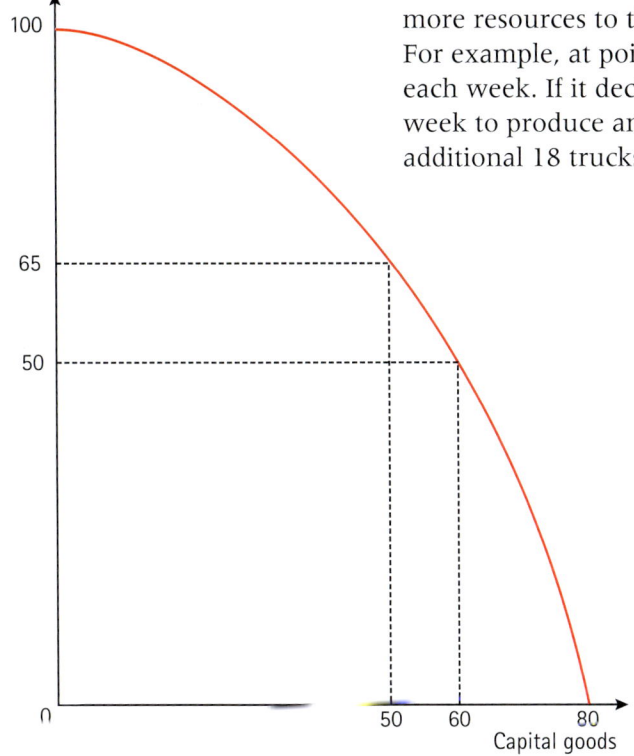

As the firm moves along the PPC from left to right, it is therefore allocating more resources to the production of trucks and giving up some car production. For example, at point A the firm has decided to produce 60 cars and 80 trucks each week. If it decides to move to point B it will be giving up 10 cars per week to produce an additional 18 trucks instead. The opportunity cost of the additional 18 trucks to the firm is therefore the lost output of 10 cars.

Now imagine we can draw a PPC for an entire economy. The economy can choose to allocate its scarce resources to the production of consumer goods or capital goods, such as factories, machinery and equipment for other firms. The economy can produce 100 tonnes of consumer goods or 80 tonnes of capital goods with its resources per period of time.

The economy may decide to produce 65 tonnes of consumer goods and 50 tonnes of capital goods. If it then decides to increase production of capital goods by 10 tonnes it will have to move resources away from the production of consumer goods. The PPC diagram above shows this will result in a reduction of 15 tonnes of consumer goods. The opportunity cost of an additional 10 tonnes of capital goods is therefore the 15 tonnes of consumer goods foregone.

The basic economic problem

A PPC therefore shows the combined maximum possible output of two products or groups of products a firm, or even an entire economy, can produce efficiently with existing resources and technology.

More examples of opportunity cost

But it is not just firms or entire economies that face tough choices about how to allocate scarce resources. Here are some more examples of opportunity costs:

- A household decides to save $500 in a bank account so that it can afford to go on holiday next year. This means the household is giving up the benefit of spending that money now on other goods or services that will give the householders satisfaction.

- A 55-year-old employee has been offered a new job or the chance to retire early. He will earn $20,000 per year in the new job and will no longer have to work weekends, which means he can spend more time with his family. However, if he chooses to retire early he will benefit from having much more leisure time but will receive a small monthly pension of just $1,000.

- A group of business owners choose to invest $5 million in building a new hotel. They could have invested their money in a car hire business instead but thought the hotel venture would earn them more profit.

- A government decides to raise an additional $10 billion in taxes to fund the building of new motorways. The roads will improve journey times for many motorists. However, the money could have been used to provide new schools instead. Taxpayers will also have to give up more of their income to pay the increased taxes.

Some people have more choice than others.

ACTIVITY 1.7

Free to choose?

1 Look at the photographs and copy the table below. Put a tick in the first column if you think the Bangladeshi children in the first photograph are free to choose. Tick the second column if the European boys are free to choose.

Free to choose? ✗ or ✓	Children in Bangladesh	European children
Can go to a soccer match.		
Can eat in a restaurant.		
Can catch their own food.		
Can drive a car.		
Can visit foreign countries.		
Can own their own house.		
Can obtain medical help when needed.		
Can receive an Economics education.		
Can receive a daily paper.		
Can be independent.		
Can receive radio and television.		

▲ Children in Bangladesh

▲ European children

2 Which group of children has more choice and why?

14 The basic economic problem: choice and the allocation of resources

The boys in the second picture have a greater choice of goods and services to enjoy than the children in the first picture. This is because the boys in the second picture live in a country which has far more resources to produce more of the goods and services people want.

The children in the photograph from Bangladesh have far less choice. There are fewer resources in their country that can be used to produce goods and services to satisfy their wants.

In some countries, many people may have very little choice. For example, in the poorest countries of Africa, not even basic needs for food can be satisfied with the available resources. This great difference in choice is caused by the relative lack of resources in the poorer countries. Yet in both rich and poor nations people want more resources than are available. ➤ 7.1

The purpose of economics involves advising how best to use scarce resources in order to make goods and services to satisfy as many wants as possible. In other words, economics attempts to increase people's choice and maximize their economic welfare. When people have more goods and services to choose from, they are better off. For example, the Western boys are better off than the children in Bangladesh simply because they have the ability to choose between more goods and services.

However, the satisfaction of wants by the making of goods and services has also brought with it the problems of pollution and the destruction of the environment. ➤ 2.3

EXAM PREPARATION 1.1

a   Explain the terms scarcity and opportunity cost. [4]
b   Describe the factors that affect an individual's choice of occupation and show how the idea of opportunity cost might be relevant to that choice. [6]

Cambridge IGCSE Economics 0455/02 Q3 May/June 2006
Cambridge O Level Economics 2281/02 Q3 May/June 2006

Conflicts of interest

▼ A motorway cutting through farmland

Recall from the examples of opportunity costs on page 14 how a decision by a government to invest $10 billion in the construction of new motorways was at the expense of building new schools. The motorways will benefit motorists but will fail to satisfy the wants of students and their families for improved educational facilities. The same decision will also conflict with the wants of many taxpayers to pay lower taxes. Similarly, the building of motorways on scarce farmland will be to the dissatisfaction of farmers and nature lovers, and to nearby residents who will suffer traffic noise and pollution once the motorways are in use.

Choosing between alternative uses of scarce resources therefore involves conflicts of interest. People cannot always get what they want and some will be dissatisfied or adversely affected by the choices made by others.

ACTIVITY 1.8

Anytown conflict: a case study

The local government of Anytown is under pressure from its local taxpayers. This is because the Anytown government has $10 million remaining of its budget to spend on resources.

The local social housing development is in urgent need of repairs and the residents are angry.

'It is inhuman that we should have to live in such conditions; damp and dirt are everywhere. The local government should build some new properties.'

But in the north of the town, the old hospital has been forced to close due to lack of funds for repairs. People who live in the north have to travel to the southern Anytown hospital for treatment.

'It is intolerable that people like me have been forced to travel such a long way to receive health care. The local government should modernize and re-open the old hospital.'

The local government faces a choice. It can either build a new housing development or modernize the old hospital. Each scheme would cost an estimated $10 million but whatever choice the local government makes, only some of the local people's wants will be satisfied.

Your task

The people living in the north of Anytown and the people living on the housing development are locked in disagreement. They both want the local government to satisfy their wants, but only one of them can win.

Split up into an even number of groups of three or four students. Half of the groups are to represent the people in the north of Anytown and the other half are to represent the people from the housing development.

1. In your group write a speech to be read to the class outlining why your group's wants should be satisfied by the local government.

2. Choose one pair of opposing groups. These groups now read their speeches to the whole class and are then given five minutes to argue their case. The rest of the class will be the local government which then decides by majority vote how it will spend the $10 million.

Questions

1. Why is there disagreement or conflict in Anytown?
2. To avoid all conflict in Anytown, what is needed?
3. If there were enough resources to produce everything everybody wanted, would there be any opportunity costs? Explain your answer.

ECONOMICS IN ACTION

What opportunity costs and conflicts of interest are illustrated in these news articles?

HP cuts 9,000 jobs

Computer systems and software provider Hewlett-Packard is spending US$1 billion to create new automated networking and data centers for its business customers. But as a result of this increased streamlining and automation, HP expects to eliminate around 9,000 jobs, or about 3 per cent of its work force, over the next few years.

People must choose between higher taxes or spending cuts

PEOPLE IN Northern Ireland should be given an opportunity to vote on whether to accept spending cuts or pay higher taxes to save public services, according to a leading Northern Ireland economist.

Mike Smyth, president of an influential European Union economic think tank, believes the scale of the public expenditure cuts proposed by the UK government will result in a 'severe decline in living standards' in Northern Ireland.

However, government officials have argued the tax rises needed to continue paying for current levels of public service provision would also cause hardship for many people and businesses across the region.

WEBSITES

These websites contain some helpful definitions and discussion of opportunity cost:

- www.referenceforbusiness.com
- www.wikipedia.org/wiki/opportunity_cost

KEYWORDS

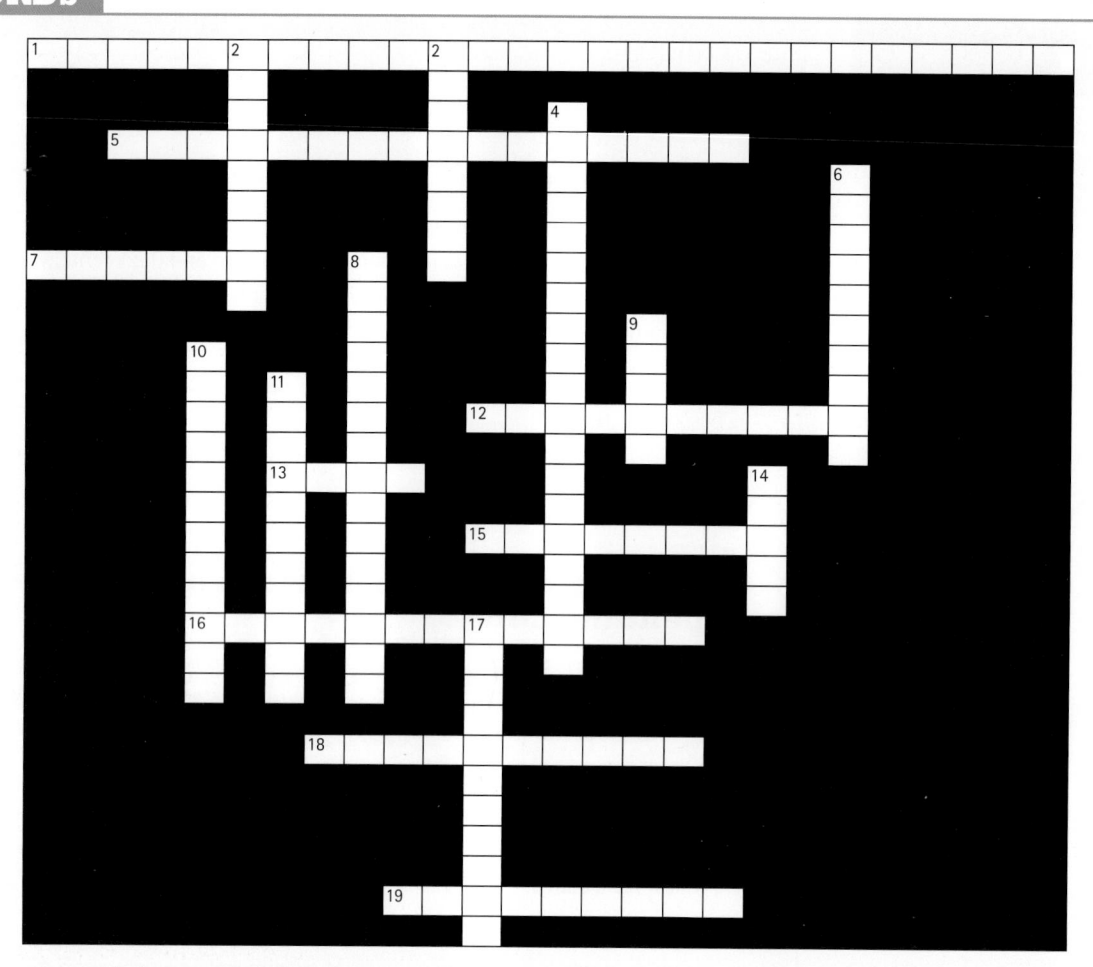

Clues across

1. A curve that shows the combined maximum possible output of two products an economy can produce efficiently with existing resources and technology. It shows how much of one product must be given up to produce more of the other (10, 11, 5)
5. A term used to describe goods that are consumed or used up by people over a relatively long period of time such as a washing machine, computer and mobile phone (8, 8)
7. A term used by economists to describe human effort used in the production of goods and services (6)
12. Goods or services, such as education and health care, usually provided by a government because they can benefit everyone in society (5, 5)
13. A term used by economists to describe all natural resources used in production (4)
15. Trade in goods and services between producers and consumers (8)
16. Another term used to describe products that require scarce resources to produce them to satisfy human needs and wants and are therefore limited in supply (8, 5)
18. Using scarce resources to make and sell goods and services that satisfy the needs and wants of consumers (10)
19. People – workers and entrepreneurs – involved in productive activities (9)

Clues down

2. People and organizations who are willing and able to buy goods and services to satisfy their needs and wants (8)
3. The outputs from productive activities, and an economics term also used to describe all goods and services (8)
4. Scarce resources available for use in productive activities (7, 2, 10)
6. The skills and willingness to take the risks required to organize productive activities (10)
8. The benefit foregone by giving up the next best alternative use of scarce resources (11, 4)
9. Human desires for goods and services. They are unlimited (5)
10. A person with enterprise and the willingness to take the risks and decisions necessary to organize scarce resources into firms to produce goods and services (12)
11. Goods or services, such as street lighting and sea defences, that are provided for free by a government because all consumers will benefit from them whether they pay for these products or not. It is therefore impossible to charge different individuals or firms different prices for the amounts they consume (6, 5)
14. Human requirements for life and survival (5)
17. The using up of goods and services to satisfy human needs and wants (11)

The basic economic problem: choice and the allocation of resources

Assessment exercises

Multiple choice

1 Which of the following is not included in the study of economics?
   - A Scarce resources
   - B Choice
   - C What people should buy
   - D Opportunity cost

2 According to the meaning of opportunity cost, what is sacrificed when a decision is taken?
   - A An identical alternative
   - B Any alternative
   - C The least valuable alternative
   - D The next best alternative

3 A new dam is built in Turkey to provide hydroelectric power and a water supply. What is the opportunity cost to the economy of building the dam?
   - A The cost to households and businesses of consuming the water supply
   - B The benefits foregone from other uses of the money used to pay for the dam
   - C The cost to consumers of using hydroelectric power
   - D The money used to pay for the construction and running of the dam

4 A firm can produce a number of possible combinations of two goods. It can either produce 500 of good *x* and 300 of good *y*, or 600 *x* and 250 *y*. What is the opportunity cost of producing an extra 100 of good *x*?
   - A 100 y
   - B 250 y
   - C 50 y
   - D The extra wages paid to the workers

5 In the study of economics, resources are also known as:
   - A Workers and machines
   - B Raw materials
   - C Factors of production
   - D Profits

6 Production can be defined as:
   - A Any activity that turns raw materials into finished goods
   - B Any activity that makes and sells goods and services
   - C Any activity that is designed to satisfy wants
   - D Any activity that makes a profit

7 An entrepreneur is someone who:
   - A Owns a factory
   - B Takes the risks and decisions necessary to organize resources to produce goods and services
   - C Is a supervisor in charge of workers
   - D Is a producer

8 The basic economic problem faced by all economies is:
   - A Rising prices
   - B Unemployment
   - C Scarcity of resources
   - D Low economic growth

9 In the diagram below what is the opportunity cost of increasing the output of wheat from 300 tonnes to 400 tonnes per month?

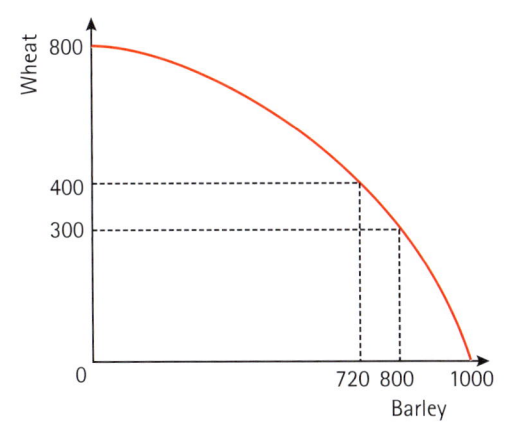

   - A 800 tonnes of barley
   - B 80 tonnes of barley
   - C 120 tonnes of barley
   - D 720 tonnes of barley

10 A social club has sold raffle tickets at US$10 each. The owner of the winning ticket received a prize of US$250. A student bought a ticket, but did not win. What is the opportunity cost to the student?
   A US$10
   B US$250
   C What could have been bought with the US$10
   D What could have been bought with the US$250

11 Which statement best explains why drought is an economic problem?
   A Rainfall cannot be predicted easily
   B The effects of drought require government action
   C Droughts cannot be prevented
   D Water is a scarce good

Structured questions

1 Many governments have increased their spending on police and armed forces but there is an opportunity cost of this policy.

   (a) Explain the term opportunity cost and discuss why an increase in spending on police and armed forces may result in an opportunity cost. [4]

   Cambridge IGCSE Economics 0455/02 Q5(a) May/June 2009
   Cambridge O Level Economics 2281/02 Q5(a) May/June 2009

2 Protestors often oppose large companies that wish to erect large buildings on open rural land rather than in more expensive city centres. The protestors regard this as a destruction of the environment rather than the use of natural resources.

   Explain the concept of opportunity cost and illustrate it by using the above statement. [5]

   Cambridge IGCSE Economics 0455/04 Q6(a) October/November 2002
   Cambridge O Level Economics 2281/02 Q6(a) October/November 2002

3 In the UK the Royal Society for the Protection of Birds (RSPB) has recently bought land around the coast to prevent building on the area where rare birds breed. It has received donations from the public towards the cost. The RSPB plans to set up special visitor centres in the area.

   Explain which factors of production are involved in the above action by the RSPB. [4]

   Cambridge IGCSE Economics 0455/02 Q3(a) October/November 2003
   Cambridge O Level Economics 2281/02 Q3(a) October/November 2003

2 The allocation of resources: how markets work; market failure

2.1	Economic systems
2.2	How markets work
2.3	Social costs and benefits
Assessment	Multiple choice
	Structured questions

Choosing what goods and services to produce, how to produce them and who to produce them for, involves making decisions about the allocation of scarce resources. How these decisions are made is called an economic system.

Every country has an economic system or economy involving decisions about the production, consumption and exchange of goods and services. In a market economic system, the spending decisions of consumers determine what, how and for whom to produce: private sector firms seeking to earn profits will allocate scarce resources to the production of goods and services for consumers with the greatest willingness and ability to pay for them.

In a free market the price of a good or service will be determined by the decisions of consumers to buy that product and the production decisions of firms. Effective demand is the willingness and ability of consumers to buy goods and services. In general, as prices rise demand will tend to contract. Supply refers to the willingness and ability of producers to provide goods and services. In general, as prices rise producers are willing to supply more.

The market price for a good or service will be determined when consumer demand for it matches supply. Demand may increase, thereby pushing up the market price, if consumers' incomes rise, the product becomes fashionable and tastes favour it, or if other similar products become more expensive. The supply of a good or service may increase, thereby pushing market price down, if the cost of producing it falls, for example due to technological change.

However, some producers and consumers in a market economic system may allocate scarce resources to activities that are wasteful, inefficient or even harmful to other people, the economy and the environment. This is because private sector firms and consumers will usually only be concerned with their own private costs and benefits. They may fail to take account of the external costs of their decisions and actions on others, including pollution and the rapid depletion of natural resources and habitats. In a mixed economic system a government can also organize resources and productive activities to help correct market failures that may otherwise reduce economic welfare.

Unit 2.1 Economic systems

> Unit of Capital, piece of land,
> The minds of labour and their hands,
> Stir and stir my magic broom,
> And answer the questions
> What, How and for Whom?

AIMS

By the end of this chapter you should be able to:

▶ describe the allocation of resources in **market and mixed economic systems**
  - understand the problem of **resource allocation** and describe the functions of an **economic system**
  - explain why a mixed economic system has a **public sector** and a **private sector**

▶ describe the concept of **market failure** and explain the reasons for its occurrence
  - understand and describe the concept of a **market** in economics
  - explain why markets can sometimes allocate scarce resources to uses that are wasteful, inefficient or even harmful to people, an economy and the environment

▶ evaluate the merits of the **market economic system**
  - assess and contrast the advantages and disadvantages of different economic systems
  - appreciate why and how a government can intervene in a market economy to correct market failures.

SECTION 1

What is an economy?

People and firms produce, exchange and consume goods and services in an **economy**.

An economy can be of any size, with any number of people and firms involved. For example, a village or small town will have a small local economy, but may be part of a much larger regional or even national economy.

22 The allocation of resources: how markets work; market failure

For example, Nairobi is the capital city within the national economy of Kenya. In turn, the Kenyan economy is part of the African economy in which all other African countries are included, such as Algeria, Cameroon, Egypt, Mauritius, Swaziland and South Africa. Similarly, all African national economies form part of the global economy.

Some economies have access to more resources than others but all have far fewer resources than they require to satisfy all the needs and wants of their populations. All economies must therefore choose which wants to satisfy and how with their available resources. For example, an economy may choose to satisfy a want for energy but will it do so by generating electricity from coal-fired power stations, nuclear power plants or from renewable sources such as solar panels or wind turbines?

Every economy must therefore decide what goods and services to produce, how to produce them, and who to produce them for. Economists refer to this as the problem of **resource allocation**. That is, every economy must choose how, and how much, land, labour, capital and enterprise to assign to different productive uses.

ACTIVITY 2.1

Tropical trouble

Divide into groups of three or four people. Now read on . . . you are part of the crew of a cargo vessel. After weeks at sea a violent storm lashes against your ship. It is forced on to rocks and a group of you are shipwrecked on a desert island. You salvage what little you can from the ship but most of your supplies are lost in the storm.

In the bright tropical sunlight of the next day you take stock of your available resources. You realize that the wreck of the ship provides metal and wood, and the natural vegetation of the uninhabited island provides a valuable source of food.

In your group discuss and provide answers to the following questions.

1 What is the central economic problem facing your group of survivors?

2 What is the best way of organizing and using the resources available to you?

Write down how your group has decided to overcome the problems facing it.

SECTION 2

How economies determine what, how and for whom to produce

The problem of resource allocation involves answering three key questions.

What to produce?

One problem facing people when there is scarcity is deciding exactly **what** goods and services to make. This involves choosing which wants to satisfy. Every society, no matter what its size, is faced with the same choice. In the case of the desert island in Activity 2.1 the choice may be between food, clothing and shelter. In a more advanced country its society may have to decide between more nuclear weapons or more hospitals.

How to produce? Once it has been decided exactly what goods and services to produce there is the problem of deciding **how** to make them. What tools are needed? How many workers? How much land is needed? In addition, there are many different ways of making things. For example, when producing corn a lot of machinery could be used to plough the land, plant seeds and eventually harvest the crop with relatively few workers. Alternatively, a lot of workers could be used to physically plough, plant and harvest, with very little machinery.

For whom do we produce? When the questions of what to produce and how to produce have been answered a final problem remains. Because of scarcity not every person's wants can be satisfied so whose wants to satisfy must be determined. In other words, it must be decided **who** gets the goods and services that have been made. Some people are stronger than others, while some people may work harder than others – perhaps they should obtain more goods and services? Others may be weak and be unable to work at all – should they get any goods and services? Or should everybody receive an equal share of all the goods and services produced, even if some people are in greater need than others? How did your group decide who to produce for on the tropical island? The question of who should get the goods and services must be answered by society as a whole. Economists cannot tell us what is best because the answer depends on people's opinions. That is, it involves making a value judgement.

ACTIVITY 2.2

Problem solving

Remember your solutions to the problems you faced as a group of survivors on a desert island.

1 Copy out the table below and write down your solutions to the problems posed in each column.

2 If you can think of any other ways to solve these problems include these in your table.

3 Compare your answers with those of another group in your class and make a note of any other ways they have thought of to answer the three questions.

How to decide what to produce?	How to decide how to produce?	How to decide for whom to produce?
Build shelter	Everyone helps using large palm leaves	Everyone shares a shelter

There are many different solutions to the problem of resource allocation. How an economy decides what goods and services to produce, how to produce them and who to produce them for is called its **economic system**.

An economic system for deciding how scarce resources are used will depend on the decisions and actions of people in that economy, just as you did on the imaginary island economy in Activity 2.1. Some people may be very caring and want everyone to have an equal share of scarce resources, while others may want to be rich and powerful by keeping most of the available resources for themselves. They may even exploit less fortunate people.

An economic system will therefore develop from the way people think and behave, and may also change over time. However, without an economic system few decisions will be made about the allocation of resources, fewer goods and services will be produced and many resources could be left idle.

SECTION 3

Different economic systems

In the study of economics there are three main types of economic system depending on how much government involvement there is in making decisions about how resources are used, what goods and services are produced and who they are produced for.

Market economic system

In a **free market economic system** all decisions are taken by **private sector** organizations and individuals. There is no role for government or a public sector and therefore no taxes or public spending.

Planned economic system

In a **planned economy** most decisions about how resources are used, what is produced, and how goods and services are priced and allocated, are taken by **public sector** organizations. These are organizations owned, controlled and accountable to the government. There may be very few private sector businesses in planned economies and very little consumer choice.

The main problem with the planned economic system is that all the goods and services produced are those the government wants people to have and not necessarily what people want. In planned economies such as the old Soviet Union there were often shortages of many consumer goods and services and product quality was poor. This was because public sector firms were not required to make a profit and therefore did not have an incentive to compete for sales or to keep their costs as low as possible.

Since the 1990s the governments of many planned economies, including China and Russia (then as part of the Soviet Union), have therefore introduced policies that have increased the role of the market economic system in their economies. For example, in 2001 the Chinese government stopped setting the prices of sugar, silk, natural rubber, gold jewellery, coal, tea and many other products and allowed these instead to be determined by private sector producers. Many price and other controls still remain but private enterprise and businesses in these economies are now expanding rapidly.

Mixed economic system

In reality there are no totally free market or planned economies. All economies are mixed to some degree.

In a mixed economy ownership of scarce resources and decisions about how to use them are split between the private sector and a public sector.

In some mixed economies like Iceland, Slovakia and Romania, the public sector is large and controls significant resources. In others, including the USA, Hong Kong, the Philippines and Brazil, the private sector is large and the role for government is relatively small.

0% ← less government involvement   more government involvement → 100%

| MARKET ECONOMY | MIXED ECONOMY | PLANNED ECONOMY |

Economic systems 25

SECTION 4

The market economic system

What is a market?

A market is a very important concept in economics, as we will discover later in this chapter.

Very simply a **market** is any set of arrangements that brings together all the producers and consumers of a good or service so they may engage in exchange. The market for any good or service is therefore made up of all the producers willing and able to make and supply that particular product and all those consumers willing and able to buy it.

For example, the market for computers consists of all producers and all consumers of computers. Similarly, there is a market for every different type of food, for clothes, televisions, cars, holidays, insurance and all other goods and services.

In economics, therefore, a market does not refer to a particular location where goods and services might be traded, such as Billingsgate fish market in London, the famous Khan el-Khalili market in Cairo in Egypt, or the local market in the town or village where you live. For an economist, any organization or any person who wants to buy or sell a particular good or service, wherever they are in the world, is part of the market for that good or service. Markets can therefore be spread over a small area or a very large area. For example, the market for a local newspaper or the services of a particular hairdresser at a beauty salon will both tend to be very localized. The markets for national daily newspapers such as *El País* in Spain, *The Times* in the UK, or *L'Express* in Mauritius will be national domestic markets. Some goods and services, however, are exchanged all over the world. For example, the markets for crude oil, aircraft and computers are **international** or **global markets**.

In most markets, producers exchange their goods or services with consumers in return for money. However, many years ago many producers would often be willing to accept other goods or services they needed or wanted in exchange for their own. This is called **barter** and it still exists in some places today. ➤ **3.1**

Deciding what, how and for whom to produce

All the resources in a market economy are privately owned by people and firms. Every firm will aim to make as much **profit** as possible. Profit is the amount of money a firm makes from selling goods and services less the money it costs to buy or hire the resources required to make them. However, a firm will only be profitable if it uses the scarce resources to make those goods and services that consumers will buy. ➤ **4.2**

In a market economic system all firms aim to make a profit and they do this by moving scarce resources away from producing things consumers are unwilling or unable to buy into the production of goods and services that they will buy. That is, firms will move out of markets that are shrinking as consumers are buying less and into markets which are expanding because consumers are buying more. ➤ **3.4**

What is produced in a market economy depends therefore on what consumers want and are willing to pay for. Firms will produce what consumers want in the cheapest possible way so as to to maximise their profits. Those consumers who are able to enjoy the goods and services produced, however, are only those with enough money to buy them.

ACTIVITY 2.3

An introduction to the workings of a market system

Savita Shah has employed 30 people to work in her firm or business organization. She owns a patch of land, a factory building and hires 15 machines. Savita wants to make as much money or profit as possible for herself. This is the aim of her firm. At present she uses her scarce resources to make pairs of bright multicoloured boots.

The latest fashion among young people is pastel-coloured shoes and Savita notices that sales of her boots are falling. That is, the market for boots is shrinking. Younger people are no longer willing to use their money to buy brightly coloured boots, but will instead pay a high price for pastel-coloured shoes. In other words, the market for shoes is expanding.

As her profits begin to fall, Savita realizes there is more money to be made from the production of shoes and so switches her scarce resources away from making boots into the production of pairs of pastel shoes to satisfy the wants of fashion-conscious young people.

Savita now faces a problem. There are two ways of making the shoes. The first method only requires 20 of her 30 workers and 10 of her machines, and each pair of shoes will cost $6 to produce. The second method requires all 30 workers with only 7 machines, and each pair of shoes will cost $10 to produce. Savita decides to use the first and cheapest method because she wishes to make as much profit from the sale of her shoes as possible.

After only a short time, Savita's profits have increased dramatically and are far greater than her profits when she made boots. Eager young people who can afford to pay for the pastel-coloured shoes can now satisfy their wants.

Questions

In a market economy there are often many thousands of firms all behaving like Savita's.

1. What is the main aim of a firm producing goods and services in a market economy?

2. How do firms in this type of economy decide **what** to produce? *Hint* Why did Savita decide to produce shoes instead of boots?

3. In a market system how do firms decide **how** to produce goods and services?

4. Once the goods and services have been produced who are they for? *Hint* Which teenagers could not satisfy their wants for shoes?

5. In deciding to produce shoes Savita chose the cheapest method which meant she needed only 20 of her 30 workers. What will happen to the 10 workers who are not needed?

How do firms know what is profitable?

If consumers are spending more and more on a product, firms producing that product may be able to increase their prices and earn more profit without reducing sales.

For example, sales of Savita's shoes are rising rapidly. She therefore decides to increase the prices of all her shoes by 10%. This will help cover the costs of buying more materials and using more electricity, but will also increase her profit on each pair of shoes sold. The rise in consumer demand for Savita's shoes and the increase in their prices will be noticed by other firms. For example, sales and profits of the Charvi Clothing Company have been falling and so its owners and managers decide the business will make more profit in future by making and selling shoes to satisfy the increasing consumer demand for them. As a result, the clothing company stops producing clothes and moves its resources into the production of shoes. Many other firms may also decide to enter the market to supply shoes if they are more profitable than other products.

Economic systems

In a market economy, high or rising **market prices** therefore provide firms with important signals about what consumers want and are willing to pay for, and therefore which products will be profitable to make and sell. In the same way, if the market price and profitability of a product is falling because consumer demand for it is shrinking, this will act as a signal to firms to move their resources into other, more profitable uses.

In a market economy therefore it is this **price mechanism** that guides the many decisions taken by different producers and consumers about how scarce resources should be allocated between competing uses. That is, the desire by private sector firms to make profits and the preferences and spending patterns of consumers will determine what goods and services are produced, how they are produced, and who they are produced for. ➤ **2.2**

How good is the market economic system?

Advantages of the market economic system

1 **A wide variety of goods and services will be produced**

   This is because different firms will compete to satisfy consumers' wants and to make profits.

2 **Firms will respond quickly to changes in consumer wants and spending patterns**

   In a market system if people want a good or service and can afford to buy it, then it becomes profitable to make it and resources are quickly moved to the market to produce such goods and services. On the other hand, if the good is not wanted it becomes unprofitable and resources are directed away into more profitable uses.

3 **The profit motive of firms encourages them to develop new products and more efficient production methods**

   Most firms in a market economy will aim to make as much profit as they can. Firms therefore have an incentive to develop new products and product designs to increase sales. The research, development and use of new materials, production equipment and methods can also help to reduce the cost of making and selling goods and services and therefore boost profits.

4 **There are no taxes on incomes and wealth or on goods and services**

   In a totally free market economy there is no public sector and therefore no need for a government to raise tax revenue to pay for public sector spending.

ACTIVITY 2.4

Mustard

Unlike in a market economy, a government takes decisions on how to allocate resources to different productive activities in a planned economy. However, as the article below from the late 1980s explains, government planning was often a very poor substitute for the price mechanism in former planned economies such as the Soviet Union.

1. How were resources wasted in the economy of the former Soviet Union?

2. In a market economy why are mustard producers unlikely to make mustard in three-litre jars for the general public?

3. Apart from weight, what other instructions should the government planners in the former Soviet Union have given to the mustard producers for them to produce a suitable product for consumers?

4. What problem does the article illustrate about government planning of production in an economy? Explain your answer in full.

Soviet mustard glut
Spicy scandal in giant jars

The recent acute shortage of mustard thoughout the Soviet Union – it was classified as an unavailable product – has been rectified with a vengeance in the Ukrainian industrial region of Krasnadon, where shoppers are now able to buy it only in giant three-litre jars.

This latest example of the bizarre by-products of the Soviet system has been disclosed by the Moscow weekly *Literaturnaya Gazeta* (Literary Gazette), whose editors explained that they thought protest letters from readers in the Ukraine were a hoax.

As the complaints continued to pour in from many towns in Krasnadon, the magazine questioned Mr G. Stelyanko, the Ukrainian Minister of Trade, who admitted that the Krasnadon food factory had indeed taken to bottling mustard in such impractical jars.

The magazine, the official publication of the Soviet Writers' Union, decided to investigate whose idea it was to sell mustard in such enormous jars.

The results pointed to a long list of bureaucratic problems in the Soviet system. At first it appeared that the answer was simply that the factory had decided to make the change to cut its workload, by reducing from 10,000 to 333 the number of jars produced from each ton of pungent Soviet mustard.

Then the investigators discovered the irony went further. Mr Stelyanko, after further questioning, explained that the Krasnadon factory was suffering an acute shortage of small glass jars because state shops were refusing to refund money on empty jars.

The magazine concluded, with a note of despair, the as a result mustard in the giant jars would soon go off, forcing every family to throw it away. Then, once again, the Soviet Union will have another mustard deficit.

Disadvantages of the market economic system

A free market economic system can have major drawbacks, or **market failures**. These occur when free markets fail to produce goods and services that are worthwhile and when the decisions of producers or consumers result in wasteful or harmful activities. As a result, market failures will reduce economic welfare. This means other resource allocations or market outcomes may be more beneficial and economically worthwhile.

1. **Firms will only produce goods and services if they are profitable**

    Some services, such as street lighting, sea and flood defences and national parks, are unlikely to be provided by private sector firms because they will be unable to charge consumers a price according to how much they use them or benefit from them. Similarly, postal services or roads to rural areas may not be provided because too few people will use them and fail to cover the cost of their provision. ➤ 4.2

2   Firms will only supply products to consumers who are able to pay for them

People with the most money have the most freedom to choose and buy what they want. People who have very little money, like many unemployed or elderly people, have much less freedom and spending power. For example, private sector firms in a market economy will not provide education or health care for people who cannot afford to pay for these services.

3   Resources will only be employed if it is profitable to do so

If a profitable use cannot be found for some of the scarce resources then they will be left unemployed. Labour is just another factor of production, and one reason why some people are unable to find paid employment in modern economies is because there is no profitable use for them.

4   Harmful goods may be produced if it is profitable to do so

For example, dangerous drugs and weapons may be freely available to consumers who want them and can afford to buy them.

ACTIVITY 2.5

Freedom of choice in a market economy

The two pictures below show two different groups of people who live in a market economy.

▼ A casino

▼ An unemployment queue

1   Which group of people has more freedom to choose to buy a foreign holiday, a new car and a new home?

2   Explain why this group of people has greater freedom of choice.

5 Some producers and consumers may ignore the harmful effects of their decisions and actions on others and the environment

For example, some consumers may drop harmful litter, play music very loud to the annoyance of their neighbours or smoke cigarettes in public places where other people can inhale their smoke. Some firms may pollute rivers and oceans causing damage to nearby farms and to marine life, thereby increasing costs to agricultural and fishing activities. ➤ **2.3**

6 Some firms may dominate the market supply of a particular good or service

Firms able to dominate or control the market supply a good or service are described as **monopolies**. They may use their market power to restrict competition with other firms and to charge consumers high prices ➤ **4.4**

SECTION 5

The mixed economic system

Because of the disadvantages of the free market economic system almost all national economies in the world have a **mixed economic system**.

A **mixed economy** combines government planning and ownership of resources with use of the free market economic system to determine the allocation of resources.

Why have a mixed economic system?

In a mixed economy a government can intervene in different markets in an attempt to correct the worst market failures. It can organize resources to provide essential goods and services and also introduce laws and regulations to control harmful activities. Recall the market failures we considered on pages 29 and 30 and consider how a mixed economy can respond.

In a market economic system	In a mixed economic system
Firms will only produce goods and services if they are profitable	A government can provide **public goods** such as street lighting, public parks and national defence that are in the public and economic interest. Private sector firms will not provide public goods because it is impossible to charge individual consumers according to how much they use and benefit from them. Instead a government can raise the money necessary to pay for their provision from tax revenues. ➤ **1.1**
Firms will only supply products to consumers who are able to pay for them	Many public sector organizations employ resources to deliver **merit goods** and essential **public services**. These may include education, health care, and public transport and postal services especially in hard to reach rural areas. Because merit goods benefit so many people and organizations a government will often provide them free of charge or at a low cost to those who need them the most. ➤ **1.1**
Resources will only be employed if it is profitable to do so	A government can provide jobs in public sector organizations and provide welfare payments to people out of work or on low incomes. It may also provide financial help to prevent the collapse of important private sector firms during economic recessions, for example major employers or producers of strategically important products such as defence equipment, energy and foodstuffs. ➤ **6.3**

Economic systems

In a market economic system	In a mixed economic system
Harmful goods may be produced if it is profitable to do so	Because some people may want to buy dangerous goods, such as drugs and weapons, private sector firms may find it profitable to supply them. A government can use laws to make the production of dangerous and harmful goods illegal, and it can impose high taxes on others, such as cigarettes, to discourage their consumption because they are harmful. ➤ 2.2
Some producers and consumers may ignore the harmful effects of their decisions and actions	Some firms and consumers in the private sector will only consider their own private costs and benefits. For example, a private firm dumping chemical waste into a river will be ignoring the cost of this decision on the environment and other firms and people who use the river. A government can introduce laws and regulations to protect the natural environment, other organizations and consumers from harmful activities. ➤ 2.3
Some firms may dominate the market supply of a particular good or service	A private sector firm that is large and powerful enough to control the supply of a good or service to consumers may be tempted to abuse its market power by forcing any competing firms out of the market and charging consumers high prices because they have few or no alternatives to buy instead. A government can regulate or break up monopolies so they cannot behave in these ways. ➤ 4.4

A mixed economy therefore overcomes many of the problems of a free market economy through government ownership and control of some scarce resources and government interventions to control or regulate the decisions of private sector firms and consumers in some markets. However, a mixed economy may also combine many of the disadvantages of both a market economic system and planned economic system.

Government interventions may introduce new problems

Government interventions can create problems in mixed economies. By correcting failures in some markets a government may distort the allocation of resources and cause problems in others.

1 **Taxes can distort market price signals and reduce work incentives**

   To pay for public sector resources and provision of goods and services, a government will need to raise tax revenue from the incomes, profits or wealth of people and business organizations. However, if tax rates are too high they may reduce incentives among people to work hard or set up and run business organizations because the rewards from doing so will be reduced after taxes have been deducted from their earnings or profits.

   Consumers will also have less disposable income after income taxes have been deducted to spend on the goods and services they want, while taxes on the value of goods and services will increase their market prices. ➤ 5.2

2 **Laws and regulations can increase production costs and reduce the supply of goods and services**

   Complying with health and safety, employment, environmental, consumer protection and other regulations or laws used to control the activities of firms can increase the costs of producing goods and services. As a result, fewer goods and services may be produced and market prices will be higher. ➤ 2.2

ACTIVITY 2.6

Mixing it up

All the newspaper headlines and articles below are real. What problems do they describe about resource allocation in a mixed economic system?

New research from the British Chambers of Commerce (BCC) reveals that new employment regulations and taxes will cost UK businesses a staggering £25.6 billion over the next four years, which could reduce future job creation.

Veterinary surgeons accused of overcharging by up to 500% for some pet medicines!

Government policies failing the poor

Despite all the public spending initiatives, the very poor in Bangkok are still trapped in poverty.

A 25 per cent corporate tax on the profits of local businesses is too high, local business representatives have argued. Fewer small businesses are starting up as a result.

Supermarket suppliers 'helping destroy Amazon rainforest'

Government authorities in Brazil investigating illegal deforestation have accused the suppliers of several major supermarket chains of selling meat and leather linked to massive destruction of the Amazon rainforest. Prosecutors are seeking hundreds of millions of dollars in compensation.

The move follows a three-year investigation by Greenpeace into the trade in cattle products traced to illegal farms across the Amazon region.

Cattle farming is now the biggest threat to the remaining Amazon rainforest, a fifth of which has been lost since 1970.

Turks and Caicos PM quits after corruption inquiry

The premier of the Turks and Caicos Islands has resigned after an investigation found 'clear signs of corruption'.

Michael Misick, who denies selling Crown land for personal gain, quit a week earlier than expected. His departure follows allegations that his government misused public funds and profited from the sale of government-owned land in controversial deals, including one to build a Dubai-style luxury resort off the coast of the islands in the West Indies.

Customers warned energy bills are to stay high despite skyrocketing profits at power companies

---

Economic systems 33

3 **Public sector organizations may be inefficient and produce poor-quality goods and services**

Most public sector organizations are not required to make a profit from their activities. As a result, managers of these organizations may place less importance on controlling costs. Resources may not be used efficiently and the quality of goods and services provided may be poor. ➤ **5.1**

4 **Some government spending may be for political or even personal gain**

Many governments and government officials in mixed or planned economies want to be popular, but some may go further and pump public money into projects that may be more popular than necessary to improve the popularity of the ruling government, especially ahead of elections.

Some government officials may even misuse public money by over claiming travel and other expenses, or even by awarding contracts to private sector firms to undertake public projects in return for bribes.

ECONOMICS IN ACTION

Why and how have these governments intervened in their economies? What problems have these interventions caused?

Cyprus, Latvia and Macedonia joined a growing list of countries to ban smoking in public places such as restaurants and bars to protect the health of customers and employees. However, many owners of restaurants and bars have complained to their governments that the introduction of the smoking ban has led to a sharp drop in consumer demand and put jobs at risk.

Environmentalists have argued that financial help given to firms by the US government to boost the production of biofuels is damaging the environment and increasing food prices globally.

The US government claims the production of fuel from arable crops such as corn and soybeans will cut environmental damage because it reduces the need to drill for crude oil and because emissions from biofuels used in vehicles and energy production are less harmful than those from fossil fuels.

In contrast, environmentalists point to food prices worldwide having risen dramatically in the past few years due in part to more corn and soybean crops being diverted from use in animal feed and foodstuffs to the production of biofuels. More and more forests and woodlands are also being cleared to grow crops for the biofuels industry in the USA.

> **EXAM PREPARATION 2.1**
>
> a Explain what is meant by a market system. [5]
>
> b Discuss when it might be desirable for a government to act as a producer of goods or services. [6]
>
> c Sometimes the government does not act as a producer of goods and services but still influences private producers. Explain how it might do this. [9]
>
> *Cambridge IGCSE Economics 0455/04 Q6 May/June 2005*
> *Cambridge O Level Economics 2281/02 Q6 May/June 2005*

Public vs private expenditure

Although most economies today are mixed economies some planned economies continue to exist in a very few including Cuba, North Korea and Myanmar. However, even within these and all mixed economies, the size of the public sector relative to the private sector can vary greatly. For example, the public sector in Iceland accounted for almost 58% of the total expenditure on goods and services in the Icelandic economy in 2008, while public sector spending in Peru was just over 17 % of total spending.

▼ Public sector expenditure as a percentage of total spending, selected countries 2008

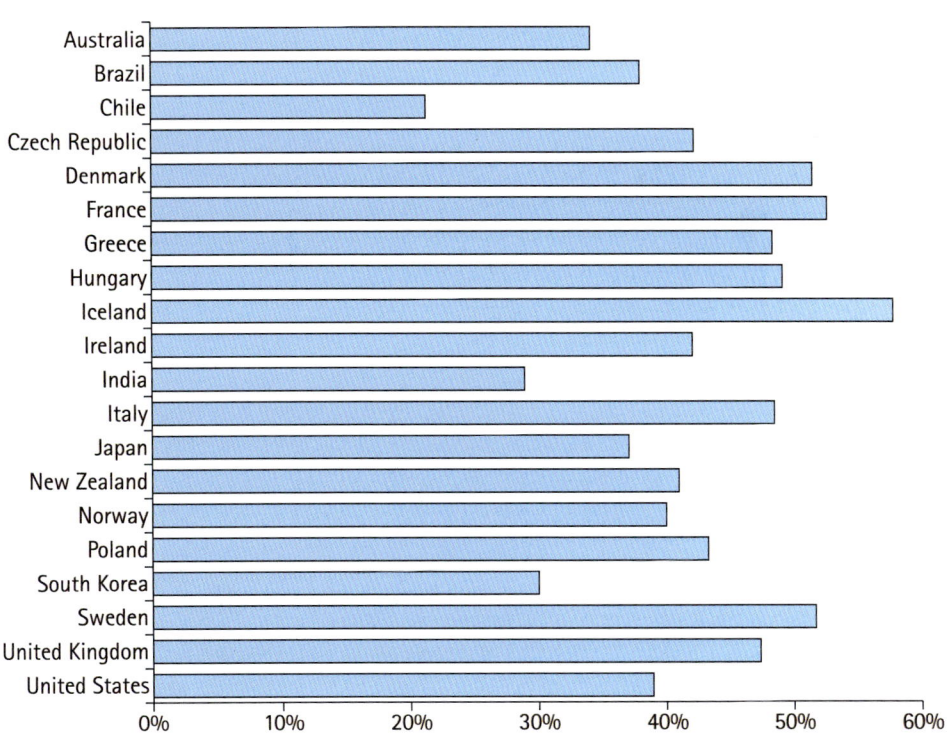

Country	%
Australia	~34
Brazil	~38
Chile	~21
Czech Republic	~42
Denmark	~51
France	~52
Greece	~48
Hungary	~49
Iceland	~58
Ireland	~42
India	~29
Italy	~48
Japan	~37
New Zealand	~41
Norway	~40
Poland	~43
South Korea	~30
Sweden	~52
United Kingdom	~47
United States	~39

Source: 'Public sector expenditure as a percentage of total spending, selected countries 2008' reproduced from *OECD Factbook 2010: Economic, Environmental and Social Statistics* (OECD, 2010), copyright © OECD 2010

ACTIVITY 2.7

A taxing time

> **Food shortages and higher prices likely, argue farmers as government cuts agricultural subsidies**

> **Microsoft, the world's largest software company, threatens to move some jobs overseas if US taxes on profits are increased.**
> 'It makes US jobs more expensive' said a company spokesperson.

> French consumers can expect a three-fold increase in taxes on electricity to pay for government subsidies for solar energy, according to the energy watchdog.

> Britain has outlined sharp cuts to public spending by slashing welfare benefits for the unemployed and cutting 490,000 public sector jobs.
> The government confirmed there would be £81 (US$131.5) billion in public spending cuts through to 2015 in order to reduce public sector debt. In addition, value added tax on many goods and services will rise from 17.5% to 20% and an additional £2 billion will be raised each year from a new tax on banks.

> - A range of measures to raise additional tax revenue will be announced by the government today to pay for increases in welfare payments and public sector pay.

> **Cuba to cut 1 million public sector jobs**
> Analysts say it is the biggest private sector shift since the 1959 revolution. As many as one in five of all workers could lose their jobs.
> Cuba's communist government currently controls almost all aspects of the country's economy and employs about 85% of the official workforce of around 5.1 million people.

1. Who are the 'winners' and 'losers' from the tax and public expenditure changes described in the above headlines and articles?
2. Using examples from the articles suggest why public expenditure decisions by a government may create conflicts of interest in a mixed economy.

The size of a mixed economy is measured by the sum of its public sector and private sector output, income or expenditure. ➤ **6.3**

Because public sector spending must be funded from taxes paid by private sector individuals and organizations it follows that the more the public sector spends, the higher taxes must be and therefore the less the private sector will have left over from its own income to spend. That is, the opportunity cost of more public sector expenditure in a mixed economy is foregone private sector expenditure. ➤ **5.1**

Public expenditure includes the spending of all government-owned and government-financed organizations, including central and local government departments and state-owned firms. It includes public spending directly on goods and services but also **transfer payments** such as welfare payments to people on low incomes and **subsidies** and grants to firms. ➤ **5.1**

Current public expenditure includes transfer payments and the wages of public sector employees, payments for electricity and telephones and other consumables, while public sector **capital expenditure** includes investments in new roads, schools, medical equipment, machinery and other productive man-made resources that can increase the future capacity of the economy to produce goods and services. That is, capital expenditure can help to boost output and **economic growth**. ➤ **6.3**

Changing the total amount and types of public expenditure and taxes at the expense of private sector expenditures can therefore create conflicts of interest.

WEBSITES

The following websites contain some helpful definitions and discussion of economic systems:

- www.referenceforbusiness.com/encyclopedia/Ca-Clo/Centrally-Planned-Economy.html
- www.referenceforbusiness.com/encyclopedia/Man-Mix/Mixed-Economy.html
- economics.about.com/od/howtheuseconomyworks/a/mixed_economy.htm
- en.wikipedia.org/wiki/Market_economy

Economic systems

KEYWORDS

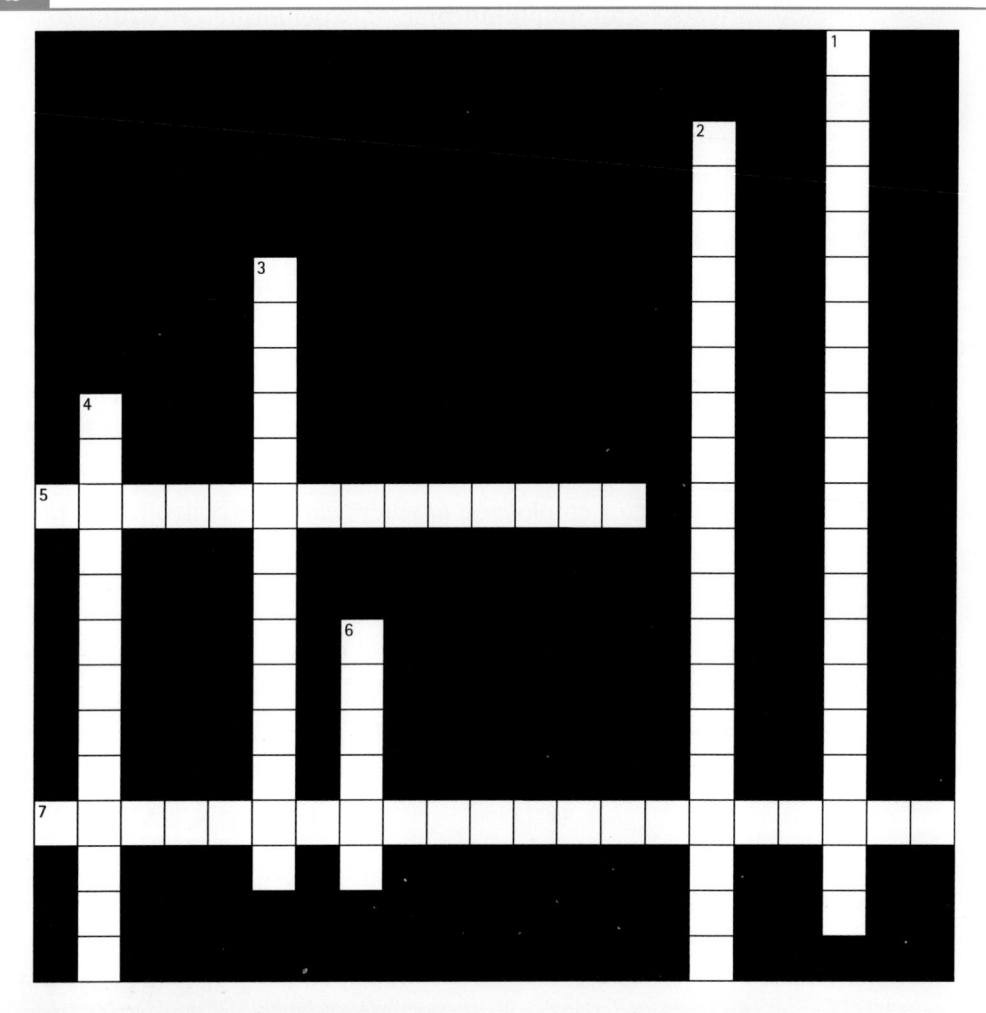

Clues across

5. The system or means by which decisions taken by different producers and consumers are guided about how scarce resources should be allocated between competing uses (5, 9)
7. An economic system in which the government determines what goods and services to produce, their prices and how they are allocated (7, 8, 6)

Clues down

1. An economic system in which decisions about how resources are used, what goods and services they produce and how they are allocated, are taken by private sector firms and consumers (6, 8, 6)
2. An economic system that combines a market economy with government planning and the public sector ownership of resources and provision of goods and services (5, 8, 6)
3. How an economy allocates resources to competing productive activities and assigns the outputs or products of these activities to different consumers (8, 6)
4. These occur when market outcomes are inefficient because the decisions of producers or consumers fail to allocate resources to the production of goods and services that are worthwhile or result in wasteful or harmful activities (6, 8)
6. Any set of arrangements that allows producers and consumers to exchange a particular good or service (6)

The allocation of resources: how markets work; market failure

Unit 2.2   How markets work

PRODUCERS   CONSUMERS

AIMS

By the end of this unit you should be able to:

▶ demonstrate the principle of **equilibrium price** and analyse simple market situations with changes in demand and supply

- understand how consumer **demand** and producer **supply** can determine the **market price** and quantity traded of a good or service
- derive and draw a **market demand curve** and a **market supply curve** for a product and use them to determine its equilibrium price

▶ describe the causes of changes in demand and supply conditions and analyse such changes to show effects in the market

- use **demand and supply analysis** and diagrams to show the impact on the market price and quantity traded of different products following shifts in their market demand and supply curves

▶ define **price elasticity of demand and supply** and perform simple calculations

▶ demonstrate the usefulness of price elasticity in particular situations such as revenue changes and consumer expenditure

- explain how a government can use **taxes and subsidies** to influence the market prices and quantities traded of different products.

SECTION 1

What is demand?

Consumers' demand for goods and services has a key role in determining the allocation of resources in a market or mixed economy. **Demand** is the want or willingness of consumers to buy goods and services. However, to be an **effective demand** consumers must have enough money to buy the goods and services they need and want. Producers in the private sector will only supply those goods and services consumers are willing and able to pay for, and at prices that exceed their costs of production.

From the previous unit we know that changes in prices provide firms with important signals about what consumers want and are willing to pay for, and therefore which products will be profitable to make and sell. A rising market price for a product may signal that consumer demand for that product is rising and becoming more profitable to make and sell. As a result, firms may allocate more resources to the production of that product. In contrast, if the market price and profitability of a product is falling, firms may decide not to produce it anymore. This unit looks at how this **price mechanism** works. ➤ **2.1**

ACTIVITY 2.8

Food for thought

HEALTHY FOODS MEAN HEALTHY PROFITS AT SAINSBURY'S

A growing range of premium and healthy food has boosted profits at Sainsbury's by 42 per cent.

Rising consumer demand for healthier foods has led the supermarket chain to expand its range of organic food products to more than 1,000 lines. Sales of organic foods rocketed by 450 per cent last year.

Wal-Mart goes for organic growth

Wal-Mart, the world's biggest retailer, has announced its stores will sell more organic food products and has asked its suppliers to increase their range of products to meet rising consumer demand.

Although organic foods still only make up around 2.5% of total Wal-Mart sales, the prices of organic foods are around 20 to 30% more than non-organic varieties and demand is forecast to grow strongly by over 15% a year.

1 Who makes up the market for food products?
2 How are consumers' wants changing in the market for food products?
3 Why do you think more consumers now want and are able to buy healthier food products?
4 What has happened to the prices and profits of healthy foodstuffs as a result of the change in consumer demand for them?
5 What has happened to the allocation of resources in the food industry as a result of changes in the pattern of consumer demand?

Demand curves

The amount of a good or service consumers are willing and able to buy is known as the **quantity demanded** of that product. Economists measure the quantity demanded of a particular good or service at a certain price over certain periods of time, say the number of oranges bought per week, litres of petrol per month, or the amount of electricity consumed per year.

Individual demand is the demand of just one consumer, while the **market demand** for a product is the total demand for that product from all its consumers.

The allocation of resources: how markets work; market failure

ACTIVITY 2.9

What is your individual demand?

1 Imagine your favourite chocolate bar was on offer at a number of possible prices. How many bars of chocolate would you be prepared to buy each month at each possible price?

Price of a chocolate bar (cents)	Your demand per week
200	?
150	
100	
50	
25	

2 Copy and complete the table. You have now completed your **demand schedule** for the chocolate bar, that is, a table of figures relating quantity demanded to price.

Use this information to plot a line graph below to show your individual **demand curve** for the chocolate bar.

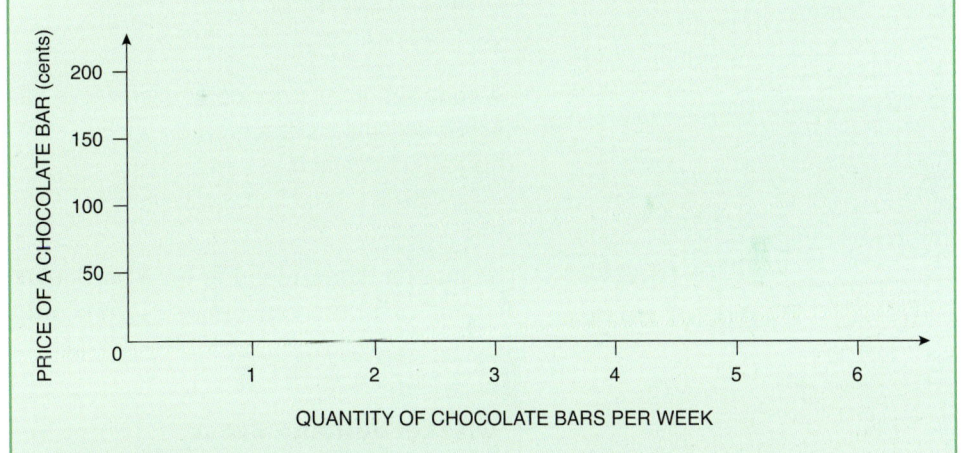

3 Which of the following statements applies to your demand curve?
   a It shows that as price rises, quantity demanded falls, and as price falls, quantity demanded rises.
   b It is downward sloping.
   c Price and quantity demanded move in opposite directions.

Don't be surprised if all three statements apply to your demand curve. For the great majority of goods and services experience shows that quantities demanded will rise as their prices fall. In general, demand curves will be downward sloping when plotted against price.

How markets work

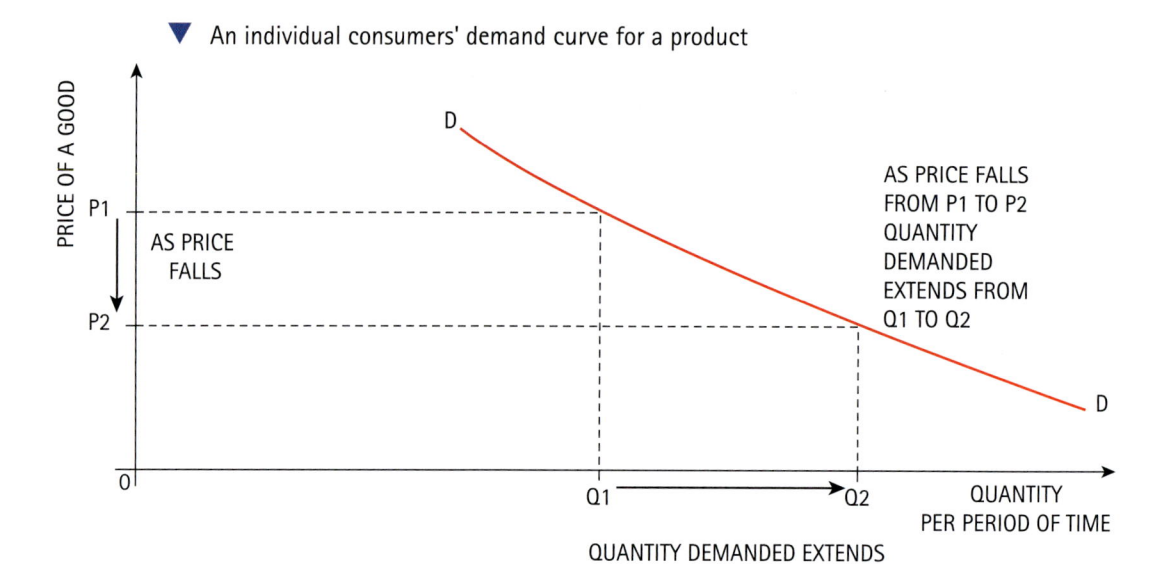

▼ An individual consumers' demand curve for a product

[Graph: Price of a good on vertical axis (P1 above P2), Quantity per period of time on horizontal axis (Q1 before Q2). Downward sloping demand curve DD. Annotations: "AS PRICE FALLS" (vertical arrow from P1 to P2), "AS PRICE FALLS FROM P1 TO P2 QUANTITY DEMANDED EXTENDS FROM Q1 TO Q2", "QUANTITY DEMANDED EXTENDS" (horizontal arrow from Q1 to Q2).]

So, as the price of a product changes consumers *move along* their demand curve. That is, their demand extends as price falls, or contracts as price rises.

> **An extension of demand** or increase in quantity demanded refers to the way in which demand rises with a fall in price, with no change in any other factor that could affect demand.

> **A contraction of demand** or decrease in quantity demanded refers to the way in which demand contracts when price rises, with no change in any other factor that may affect demand.

The market demand curve

The market demand curve for a particular good or service will display the demand of all the consumers of that commodity given a set of possible prices.

ACTIVITY 2.10

Market demand curve

Producers of orange light bulbs have the following information about the amount of orange light bulbs consumers *will* buy each *month* given a number of possible prices. The market demand schedule is as follows.

Price of an orange light bulb (cents)	Market demand per month
50	100,000
40	150,000
30	200,000
20	260,000
10	370,000
5	450,000

1. With price on the vertical axis, and quantity per month along the bottom axis, plot the market demand curve for orange light bulbs and label it DD.

> 2 Use the graph to work out how many orange light bulbs would be demanded at a price of:
>
>   a 35 cents   b 15 cents.
>
> 3 If orange light bulb producers together wished to sell the following amount of bulbs each year, approximately what price should they charge?
>
>   a 225,000   b 400,000
>
> 4 Explain why the market demand curve for orange light bulbs slopes downwards.
>
> 5 Explain the difference between individual demand and market demand.

In general the **market demand curve** for any good or service will be downward sloping, showing the relationship between quantity demanded and price, assuming that nothing else changes that will affect how much consumers demand.

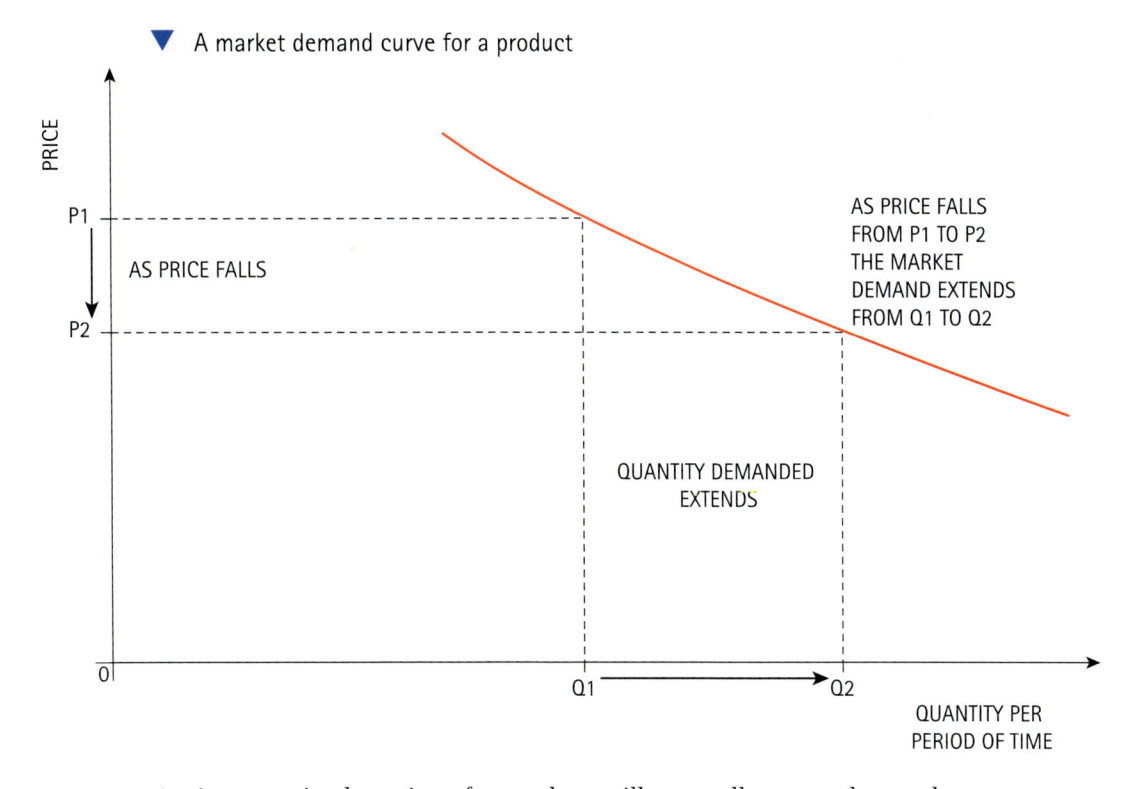

▼ A market demand curve for a product

[Graph showing downward-sloping demand curve with axes PRICE (vertical) and QUANTITY PER PERIOD OF TIME (horizontal). Points P1 and P2 marked on price axis, Q1 and Q2 on quantity axis. Labels: "AS PRICE FALLS", "QUANTITY DEMANDED EXTENDS", "AS PRICE FALLS FROM P1 TO P2 THE MARKET DEMAND EXTENDS FROM Q1 TO Q2"]

An increase in the price of a product will normally cause demand to contract. However, this assumes that no other factor affecting consumer demand changes. Demand curves are drawn based on the assumption that nothing else changes other than price so only changes in the price of the product will cause a movement along a demand curve. This is called the **ceteris paribus** assumption, meaning 'all other things remaining unchanged'.

Shifts in demand curves

However, what happens to the demand for particular goods and services when factors other than price do change? For example, will a fall in people's income cause them to demand less of a product whatever its price? What effect will an advertising campaign for a product have on demand, regardless of the price of the product?

An increase in demand

For example, let's take the market demand for chocolate bars:

Price (cents) of a chocolate bar	Original demand per month	Increased demand per month
50	100,000	200,000
40	150,000	250,000
30	200,000	300,000
20	260,000	360,000
10	330,000	430,000
5	400,000	500,000

▶ An increase in market demand

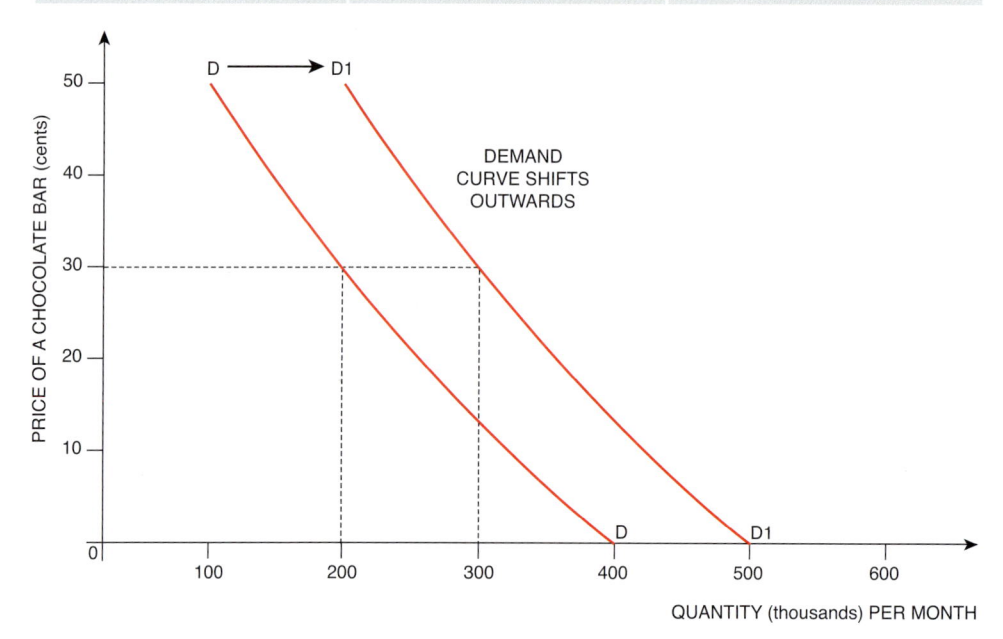

The diagram above shows an increase in demand for chocolate bars, but it could be any other good or service because the same rules apply. At each price consumers are now willing to buy more chocolate bars than they did before. The whole demand curve has shifted outwards from DD to D1D1.

> **An increase in demand** means that consumers now demand more of a product at each and every price than they did before. The market demand curve will shift out to the right.

A fall in demand

For example, let's look at the market demand for rechargeable AAA batteries.

Price of a battery (cents)	Original demand per week	Decreased demand per week
100	10,000	5,000
80	15,000	10,000
60	20,000	15,000
40	25,000	20,000
20	30,000	25,000

The allocation of resources: how markets work; market failure

▶ A fall in market demand

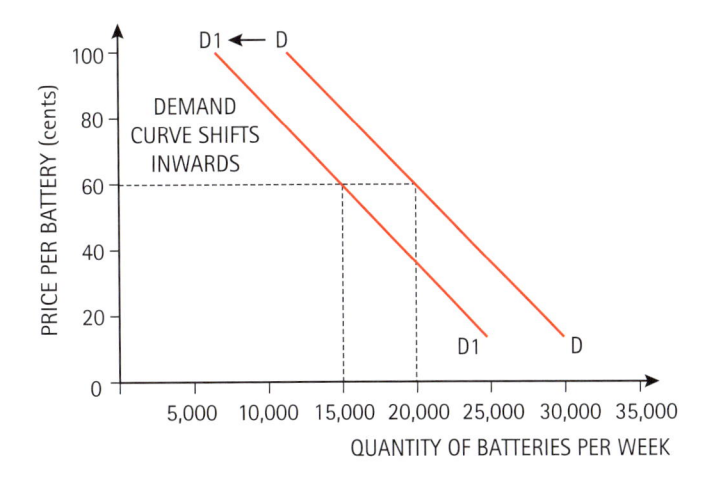

A fall in demand at all prices will cause the demand curve to shift to the left, or inwards, from DD to D1D1.

A fall in demand means that consumers now demand less of a product at each and every price than they did before. The market demand curve moves in towards the left.

A rise in market demand

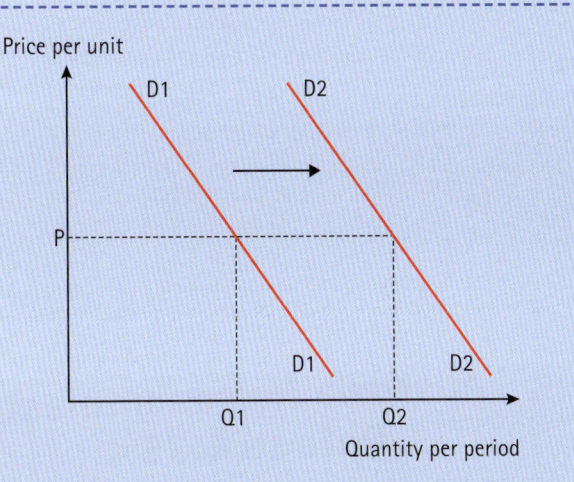

A rise in the market demand for a product may be caused by:

- an increase in consumers' incomes, for example due to rising employment
- a reduction in taxes on incomes
- a rise in the price of substitutes
- a fall in the price of complements
- consumers' tastes or fashions changing in favour of the product
- increased advertising of the product
- a rise in the population
- other factors, for example, a hot summer can boost demand for cold drinks and summer clothes.

A fall in market demand

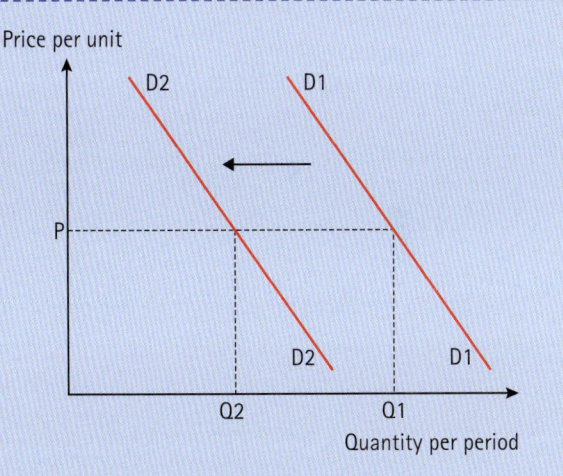

A fall in the market demand for a product may be caused by:

- a fall in consumers' incomes, for example due to rising unemployment
- an increase in taxes on incomes
- a fall in the price of substitutes
- a rise in the price of complements
- consumers' tastes or fashions changing in favour of other products
- product advertising being cut back or banned
- a fall in the population
- other factors, for example, a ban on smoking in public places may reduce demand for cigarettes.

How markets work 45

ACTIVITY 2.11

What causes a shift in demand?

Income tax cut in Malaysian Budget

The Prime Minister of Malaysia yesterday announced a series of new tax measures and incentives. Among these was a cut in income tax rate charged on the highest individual annual incomes above MYR100,000 from 27% to 26%. The amount of income an individual is able to earn each year before paying tax was also raised from MYR8,000 to MYR9,000.

'These tax cuts will increase the disposable income of Malaysian taxpayers, make working more attractive and improve the international competitiveness of Malaysia's tax system', said a spokesperson for the Government.

Demand for online music services soars

The falling price of personal music players, such as the Apple iPod and Sony Walkman, able to download music, video and other files from the internet has boosted demand for such online content while sales of CDs and DVDs continue to fall.

According to new projections released by the United Nations, the World population is forecast to grow from 6.9 billion in 2010 to 8.9 billion in 2050.

India tries to keep its cool

Soaring temperatures across India are boosting the sales and prices of ice-cream and beverages, including Coca-Cola and Pepsi. As a result demand for sugar from food and drink manufacturers has also been rising rapidly.

The hot weather is also likely to benefit makers of lassi, a sweetened yogurt served on street corners in Northern India in the summers.

1. Look at the articles above and for each one suggest
   a. What factors have changed that could affect consumer demand for different goods and services?
   b. Will consumer demand increase, fall or remain unchanged given the changing factor?
2. Now draw a diagram to show the market demand curve for soft drinks such as Pepsi and Coca-Cola, before and during the hot weather in India described in the article above and to the right.

Australia Raises Interest Rate to 4.75%

Concerns over accelerating price inflation have forced the Central Bank of Australia to raise the interest rate by 0.25% to 4.75%. The move will increase the cost of borrowing money for many consumers and businesses.

The allocation of resources: how markets work; market failure

The following factors are likely to cause changes in demand and shifts in market demand curves.

1 Changes in consumers' incomes

Because effective demand is the willingness to buy a product backed by an ability to pay, it is clear that as incomes rise consumers will be able to buy more, while a fall in incomes will cause demand to fall. However, the precise nature of the relationship between income and demand will depend on the type of product considered and the level of consumers' income. For example, a rise in income is unlikely to make most consumers want to buy more salt or newspapers each day or week, but it might allow them to travel less by bus and take a taxi more often, or even buy a bigger car.

In general, if the demand for a product tends to rise as incomes rise the product is said to be a **normal good**. On the other hand, if demand tends to fall as incomes rise the product is said to be an **inferior good**. For example, as incomes rise people can afford to travel longer distances by plane rather than by train. Long-distance train journeys might therefore appear to be an inferior good in consumer preferences as incomes rise.

2 Changes in taxes on incomes

Disposable income refers to the amount of income people have left to spend or save after taxes on their incomes have been deducted. Any change in the level of income tax rates and allowances are therefore likely to result in a change in the quantity of goods and services demanded. ➤ 5.2

▼ Complementary goods

▼ Substitute goods

3 The prices and availability of other goods and services

Some of the goods and services we buy need other things, or accessories, to go with them. For example, cars need petrol, DVD discs need a DVD player, bread is often consumed with butter or margarine. These **complementary goods** are said to be in **joint demand**.

If the prices of new cars rise, consumer demand for them may contract and in turn reduce the demand for petrol. A fall in the price of DVD recorders may lead to a rise in the demand for recordable DVD discs and shift their market demand curve outwards as demand for the recorders expands.

On the other hand, some goods and services are **substitutes**. A product is a substitute when its purchase can replace the want for another good or service. For example, margarine is considered a close substitute for butter. A rise in the price of one may therefore result in a rise in demand for the alternative. Different makes of car are also close substitutes: a fall in the price of Toyota cars may cause a fall in the demand for cars made by Ford.

A firm will find it useful to gather information on changes in the prices and quality of competing and complementary products from rival producers because any changes in them can affect the demand and, therefore, the sales revenues and profits of that firm.

4 Changes in tastes, habits and fashion

The demand for goods and services can change dramatically because of the changing tastes of consumers and fashion. For example, many consumers all over the world are now demanding goods that are kinder to the environment and animals, and foods that are healthier.

Change in fashion can cause a shift in demand

Carefully planned advertising campaigns based on market research information about consumers can also help to change tastes and shift demand curves for the advertised products out to the right. ➤ **4.4**

5 Population change

An increase in population will tend to increase the demand for many goods and services in a country. For example, the population of India has expanded rapidly over time and is forecast to grow to around 1.7 billion people by 2050. In contrast, population growth in many Western countries is now negligible. Birth and death rates have fallen and this has resulted in a rise in the average age of their populations and the growing number of middle-aged and elderly people has resulted in a changing pattern of demand. ➤ **7.2**

6 Other factors

There are a great many other factors that can affect demand. The weather is one example. A hot summer can boost sales of cold drinks and ices. A cold winter will increase the demand for fuel for heating. Higher interest rates can increase the demand for savings schemes but reduce the amount of money people want to borrow, including mortgages for house purchases. ➤ **3.4**

Changes in laws may also affect demand for some products. For example, it is illegal in many countries to ride a motorbike without a crash helmet, and an increasing number of countries are outlawing smoking in public places.

ACTIVITY 2.12

Competing or complementary?

Below is a list of goods and services. Think of some possible complements and substitutes for each of them.

Goods and services	Possible substitutes	Goods and services	Possible complements
Electric oven	?	Flat-screen televisions	?
Woollen jumpers		Fountain pens	
Gas supplies		Guitars	
iPods		Toothbrushes	
Passenger rail journeys		Computers	

SECTION 2

Supply curves

What is supply?

Supply refers to the amount of a good or service firms or producers are willing to make and sell at different prices. The amount of a good or service producers are willing and able to make and sell to consumers in a market is known as the **quantity supplied** of that product, measured per period of time, say each week, month or year.

Clearly a private sector firm interested in profit will only make and sell a product if it can do so at a price over and above what it cost the firm to make. The higher the price of the product, the more the firm will supply because the more profit it will expect to make. This can be applied generally to the supply of all goods and services. As price rises, quantity supplied tends to rise.

The **market supply** of a product will consist of the amount supplied by all the individual producers competing to supply that product.

In general, the supply curve for any product will slope upwards, showing that as price rises, quantity supplied extends.

As price falls, quantity supplied contracts. This is because as price falls firms will expect to earn less profit as revenue will exceed costs by a smaller margin.

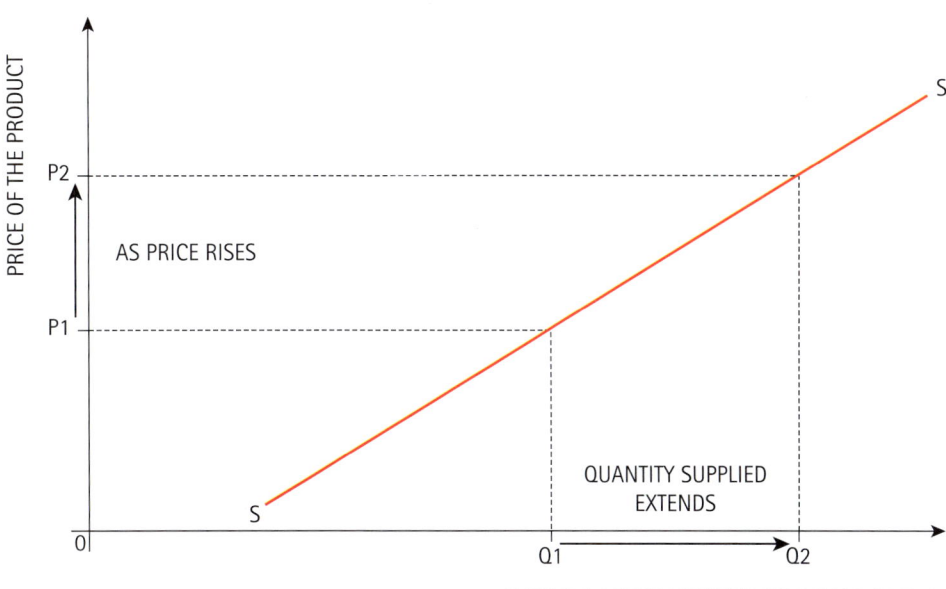

▼ A market supply curve for a product

As price rises from P1 to P2 the market supply extends from Q1 to Q2. That is, a change in the price of the product causes a **movement along** the supply curve.

> An **extension of supply** refers to how supply increases with a rise in the price of a product, given that no other factor affecting supply changes.

> A **contraction of supply** refers to how supply contracts with a fall in the price of a product, without a change in any other factor that may affect supply.

A change in the price of a product will normally cause its supply to extend or contract. Changes in things other than the price of a good can cause its market supply curve to move. A movement of the supply curve for a good reflects either an increase or decrease in supply.

How markets work

ACTIVITY 2.13

The market supply curve

The following table represents the market supply schedule for silver-plated tankards. Copy the graph axis below, plot this information on the graph axis and label your curve the market supply curve (SS).

Price of tankards $	Market supply per month
20	1,600
16	1,100
12	700
8	300
6	100

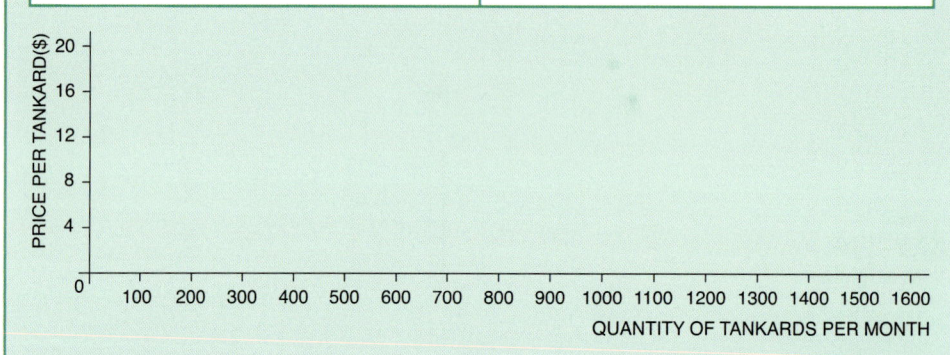

1. How does the quantity supplied change as price changes if all other factors that could affect supply do not change?

2. What will cause an extension in supply?

3. What will cause a contraction of supply?

4. Use your graph to work out how many tankards will be supplied at a price of:
   a. $14
   b. $10

5. a. If consumers wished to be able to buy 700 tankards each month how much must they be prepared to pay for them?
   b. What will be the tankard producers' total revenue?

6. The following table displays the costs and revenues involved in the production and sale of tankards by all the producers in the market. Using the market supply schedule complete the table and explain why the market supply curve for tankards slopes upwards from left to right.

Output of tankards per month	Total cost ($)	Total revenue ($)*	Profit ($)
100	600	600	500
300	1,800		
700	4,000		
1,100	6,200		
1,600	9,000		

* at lowest price

Shifts in supply curves

An increase in supply

For example, let's take the market for disposable razors.

Price of a razor (cents)	Original supply per month	Increased supply per month
50	10,000	12,000
40	8,000	10,000
30	6,000	8,000
20	4,000	6,000
10	2,000	4,000

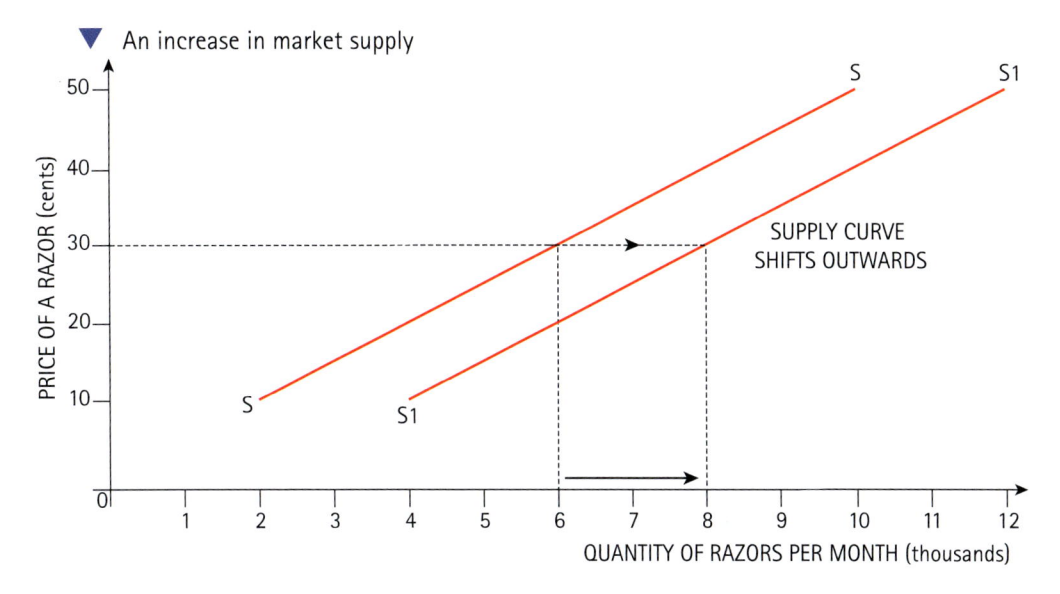

▼ An increase in market supply

The diagram above shows an increase in the supply of disposable razors, but it could be any other good or service. At each and every price, razor producers are now willing to make and sell more razors than they did before. The whole supply curve has shifted outwards from SS to S1S1.

> **An increase in supply** means that producers are now more willing and able to supply a product than they were before at all possible prices. The market supply curve shifts out to the right.

A fall in supply

For example, let's take the market supply of potatoes.

Price per kg of potatoes (cents)	Original supply per month (kg)	Supply per month (kg)
100	50,000	40,000
80	40,000	30,000
60	30,000	20,000
40	20,000	10,000
20	10,000	0

How markets work 51

▼ A fall in market supply

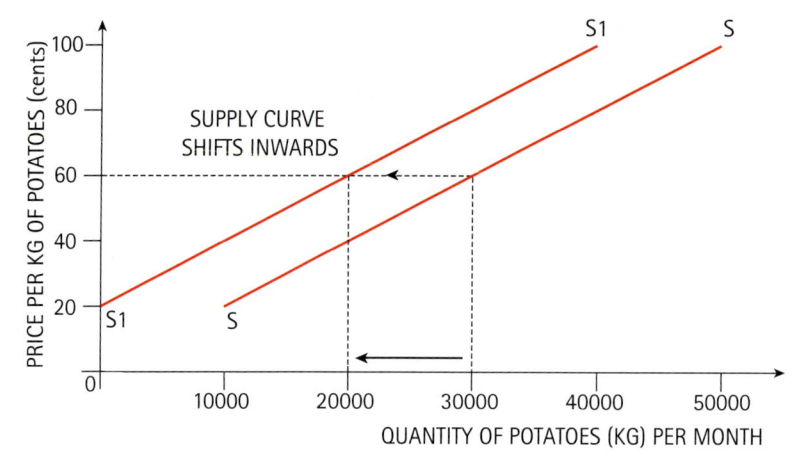

A fall in supply at all prices will cause the supply curve of a commodity to shift inwards from SS to S1S1.

> A **fall in supply** means that producers are now less willing and able to supply a product at each and every price than they were before at all possible prices. The market supply curve shifts in to the left.

ACTIVITY 2.14

What causes a shift in supply?

Read the following passage and try to pick out all the factors that have caused a change in the supply of potatoes and cabbages.

Farmer Bumpkin plans to plant five fields of potatoes and three fields of cabbages each year. The price he can usually get for a kilogram of potatoes is 30 cents, while the price of a kilogram of cabbages is 50 cents. Farmer Bumpkin has estimated that his time, effort, machinery and fertilizer costs add up to an average 12 cents per kg of potatoes and 20 cents per kg of cabbages.

- Which crop is the more profitable one to grow?

However, in the following season the price of potatoes rises to 45 cents per kg.

- What would you advise Farmer Bumpkin and farmers like him to do? Given your advice what will happen to the supply of cabbages?

In the very next growing season, Farmer Bumpkin discovers a new 'Speedo' cabbage harvester is available, and at a very reasonable price. He used to pay some boys and girls from the nearby village to help pick his crops each year, but now he can pick them all by himself using the machine. He estimates that this saving has reduced the average cost per cabbage grown to only 10 cents per kg.

- If the price of potatoes and cabbages have remained unchanged what would you now advise Farmer Bumpkin and farmers like him to do? How will this affect the supply of potatoes and cabbages?
- In the very next season the landowner who rents her land to Farmer Bumpkin decides to cut the rent of land from $500 per year to $300. That is, from $100 per field to $60 per field. Farmer Bumpkin wonders if he should rent an additional field now that it costs much less to produce potatoes and cabbages. If he decides to do this what will be the likely effect on the supply of his potatoes and cabbages?
- A farmer's year is not without its problems. Towards the end of the season an early but very hard frost damages Farmer Bumpkin's entire cabbage crop.
- What will happen to the supply of cabbages now?
- What factors have caused changes in the supply of potatoes and cabbages?

Changes in the following factors will cause changes in supply and shifts in the market supply curve for a product.

1 Changes in the cost of factors of production

By far the largest determinant of supply is the cost of resources for production, such as payments made for raw materials and power supplies, wages for labour, and rents or leasing costs for buildings and machinery.

A rise in the costs of production, for example due to workers winning generous wage rises or a shortage of raw materials, will tend to reduce profits. Producers affected by these costs will tend to cut back their demand for labour and raw materials in an attempt to save money and will therefore be less willing and able to supply as much of their particular goods or services as they did before. An increase in the costs of land or payments for capital will also tend to have the same effect. ➤ 4.2

In contrast, a fall in the costs of land, labour and capital will tend to increase profits and market supply. This was the case in Activity 2.14 as Farmer Bumpkin enjoyed a cut in the rent he paid for the land he uses to grow cabbages, encouraging him to increase production.

Governments may also try to influence the supply of goods and services by private sector firms through taxes and subsidies, as we will see in Chapter 6. Taxes can be regarded as an additional cost of production while subsidies help offset costs.

2 Changes in the price and profitability of other goods and services

Price changes act as the signals to private sector firms to move their resources to and from the production of different goods and services. In a free market, resources are allocated to those goods and services that will yield the most profit.

In Activity 2.14 a rise in the price of potatoes will cause Farmer Bumpkin to move his resources out of the production of cabbages into the production of potatoes. As a result, the supply curve for cabbages will shift inwards at every possible price as farmers are now less willing to grow them.

The same will apply to almost all other goods and services. A fall in the price of one may cause producers to cut production and supply more of another, more profitable product.

3 Technological advance

Technical progress can mean improvements in the performance of machines, employees, production methods, management control, product quality, etc. This allows more to be produced, often at a lower cost, regardless of the price at which the product is sold. For example, advances in deep water mining technology and rig design have helped a number of countries to drill for oil in deep oceans once thought too costly to exploit.

In the case of Farmer Bumpkin his new 'Speedo' cabbage harvester will allow him to shift the supply curve of his cabbages outwards.

4 Business optimism and expectations

Fears of an economic downturn may cause some firms to move resources into the production of goods and services they feel will be less affected by a fall in consumer incomes and demand. For example, high-cost, luxury items such as cars and overseas holidays often fare badly during economic recessions. Conversely, expectations of an economic recovery may result in a reallocation of scarce resources into new markets, thereby shifting their supply curves out towards the right. ➤ 6.3

5 Global factors

The supply of goods and services can be affected by many factors that cannot be controlled by producers. For example, sudden climatic change, trade sanctions, wars, natural disasters and political factors can have a material impact on the supply of many goods and services.

On the Bumpkin farm the weather will be a major factor affecting the supply of the farmer's crops. A good summer growing season will help increase supply.

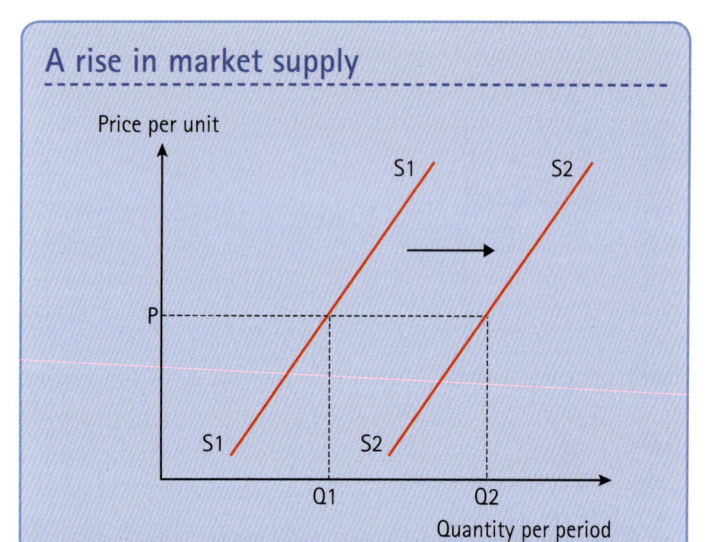

A rise in market supply

A rise in the market supply of a product may be caused by:

- other products becoming less profitable
- a fall in the cost of employing factors of production, for example due to falling wage costs or lower prices for materials
- an increase in resources, for example from new sources of raw materials
- technical progress and improvements in production processes and machinery
- an increase in business optimism and optimistic expectations of profit
- the government paying subsidies to producers and/or cutting taxes on profits
- other factors, such as a good summer to boost crops of fruit and vegetables.

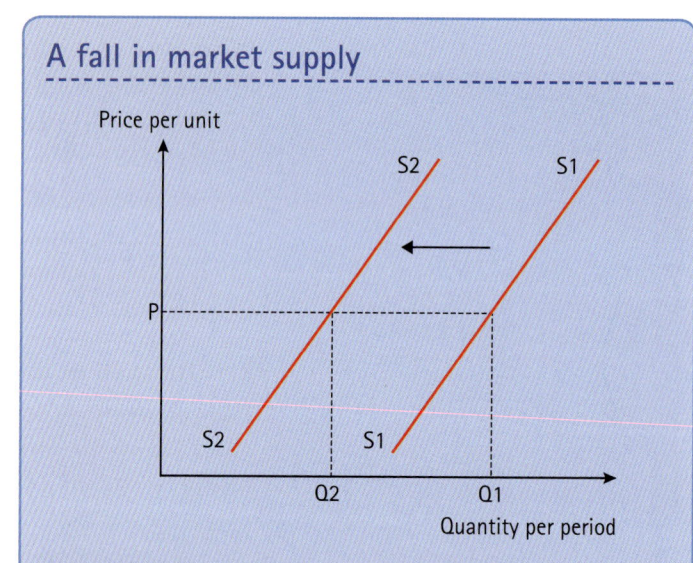

A fall in market supply

A fall in the market supply of a product may be caused by:

- other products becoming more profitable
- a rise in the cost of employing factors of production, for example due to increased hire charges for machinery
- a fall in the availability of resources, for example a shortage of skilled labour
- technical failures, such as a cut in power supplies or mechanical breakdowns
- a fall in business optimism and profit expectations becoming more pessimistic
- the government withdrawing subsidies and/or increasing taxes on profits
- other factors, such as wars and natural disasters.

54 The allocation of resources: how markets work; market failure

SECTION 3

Reaching an equilibrium

Market price

We have now looked at the two market forces that determine the price of a product. For each good and service there is a market supply schedule and a market demand schedule. If the two are combined we will find that the quantity demanded and quantity supplied will be equal at one price. This is the market price at which the product will be exchanged in the market. The market price can also be found using the market demand and supply curves.

ACTIVITY 2.15

Finding the market price

Consider the market demand and supply schedules for chocolate bars.

Price of a chocolate bar (cents)	Quantity demanded per month	Quantity supplied per month
50	100,000	420,000
40	150,000	300,000
30	200,000	200,000
20	260,000	120,000
10	330,000	60,000
5	400,000	40,000

On graph paper plot the demand and supply curves for chocolate bars on one graph with 'Price of a chocolate bar' on the vertical axis and 'Quantity per month' along the bottom axis.

1. Using the above table state at which price demand equals supply.

    This will be the **market price** for chocolate bars because at that price producers are willing to make and sell just as many bars as consumers are willing to buy.

2. a Find the market price of chocolate bars using your demand and supply curves.

    b What is the quantity of chocolate bars traded at this price in the market?

3. a When the quantity demanded is greater than the quantity supplied economists say there is an **excess demand**. At which prices in the table is there an excess demand for chocolate bars?

    b Similarly, when the quantity supplied exceeds the quantity demanded there is said to be an **excess supply**. At which prices in the table is there an excess supply of chocolate bars?

4. a If there is excess demand what do you think will happen to the price of chocolate bars?

    b If there is excess supply what do you think will happen to their price?

    c At which price will there be no excess demand or supply?

How markets work

▼ Equilibrium in the market for chocolate bars

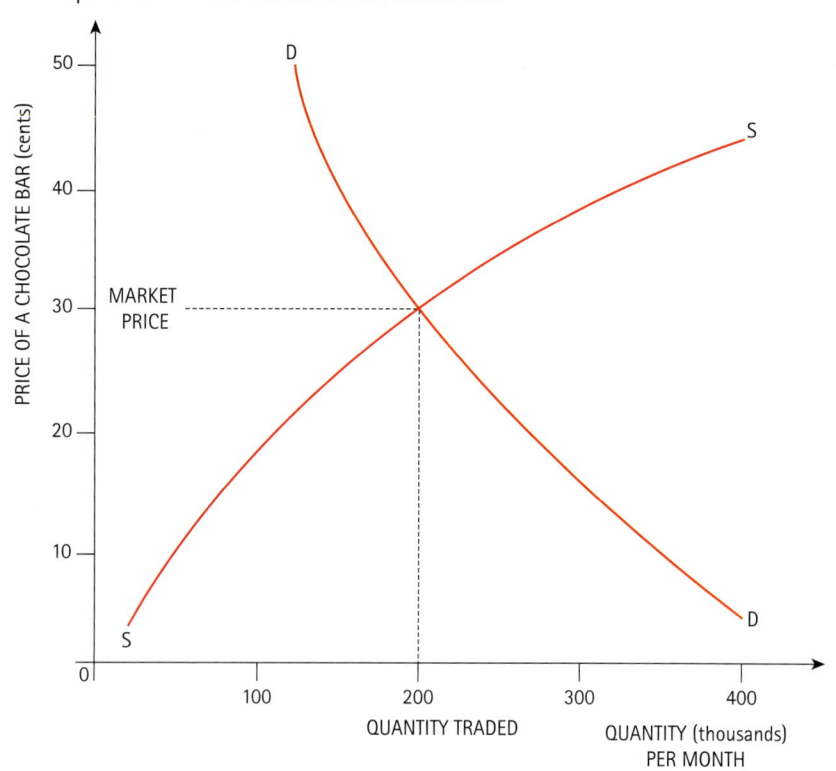

In the above exercise it should be clear that a market price will be determined at 30 cents per chocolate bar. Only here will market demand equal market supply. Another name for market price is **equilibrium price** because it is the price at which the amount supplied equals or satisfies the amount demanded.

In a graph equilibrium is found where the demand and supply curves cross, as in the diagram to the left. At this market price of 30 cents 200,000 chocolate bars will be traded each week.

At prices higher than the market price (for example 40c) firms will supply more than consumers demand and so there will be an excess supply. In order to persuade consumers to buy up this excess supply, the price will have to fall.

At prices lower than the market price (for example 20 cents) the quantity demanded by consumers exceeds what firms will supply. There will be an excess demand. As a result, the price will rise.

When demand does not equal supply this is known as a **disequilibrium**.

▼ Disequilibrium in the market for chocolate bars

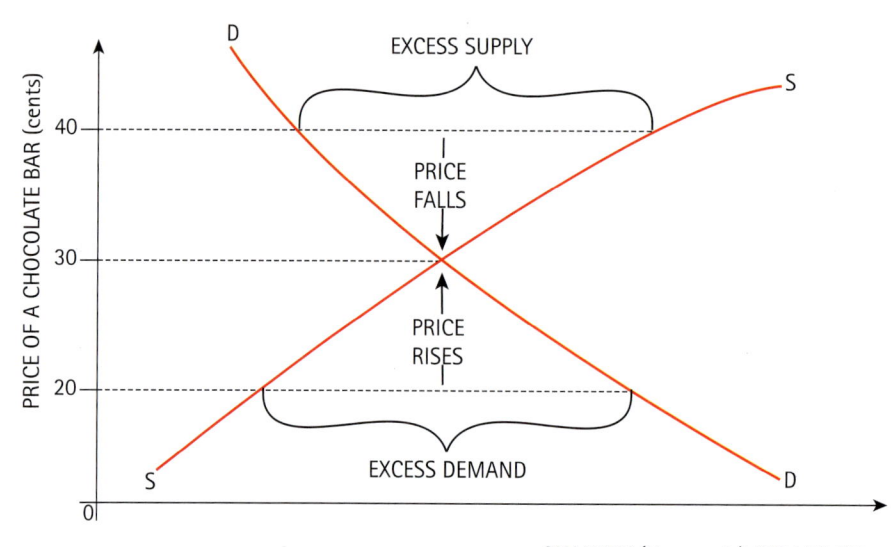

Only when a market is in equilibrium, where the market supply matches the market demand, will there be no pressures to change the market price. That is, there will be no excess demand or supply and the equilibrium market price will be stable unless there is change in the market demand or market supply of the product.

The allocation of resources: how markets work; market failure

Changes in market prices

Changes in market prices will occur as a result of changes in demand and/or supply.

1 A shift in demand

An increase in demand for a product, because people's incomes have risen, or the price of a substitute good has gone up, will cause the demand curve to shift outwards.

In the diagram below it shifts from DD to D1D1. As a result, the market price rises from P to P1.

Producers extend the supply of the product to meet the higher level of demand because they are willing to supply more at higher prices.

▼ An increase in demand and market price

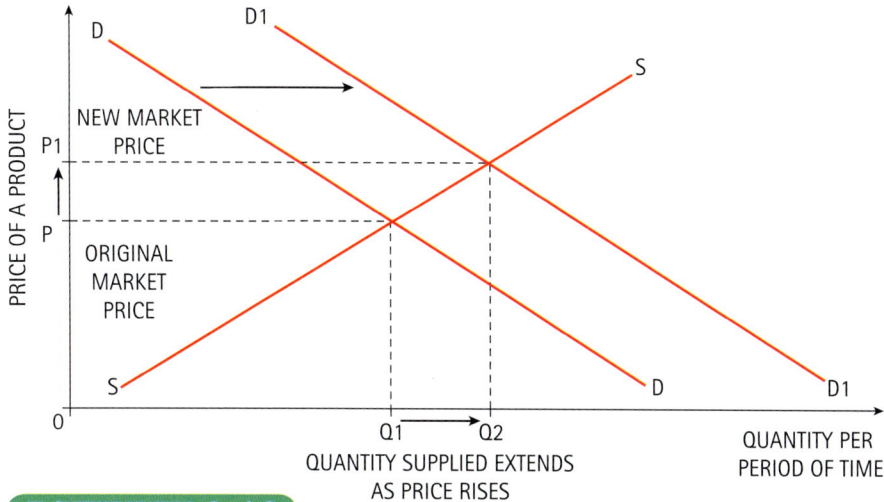

ACTIVITY 2.16

A fall in demand and market price

Below is a market demand and supply schedule for ballpoint pens.

Price per pen (cents)	Original demand per week	Original supply per week
300	100	500
250	200	400
200	300	300
150	400	200
100	500	100

1. Plot and label the demand curve (DD) and supply curve (SS) for ballpoint pens.
2. Mark in the market price (P) and the quantity traded (Q) at this price.
3. Imagine now that demand falls by 200 units at each and every price. Draw and label the new demand curve (D1D1).
4. What is the new market price (P1) and the new quantity traded (Q1)? Show these on your graph.
5. What has happened to supply and why?
6. Suggest four reasons why demand for ballpoint pens might fall.

How markets work

An increase in supply of a product because workers have accepted lower wages, or technical progress has increased the performance of capital equipment, will cause a movement outwards in the supply curve from SS to S1S1. As a result, market price will fall from P to P1 as a greater supply is available. As the market price falls so consumers will extend their demand for the product from Q to Q1.

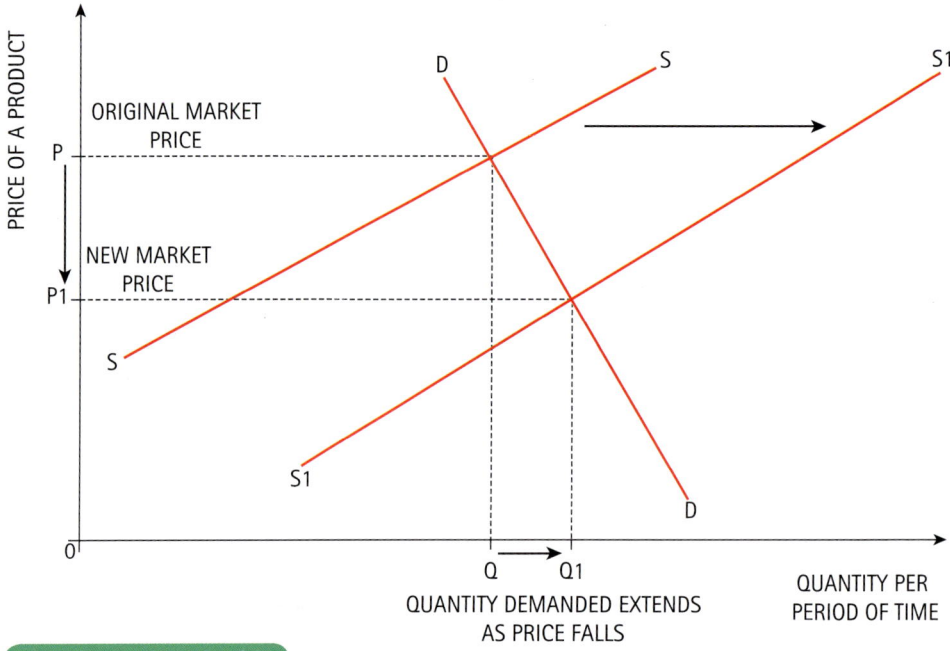

▼ An increase in supply and market price

ACTIVITY 2.17

A fall in supply and market price

Below is the market demand and supply schedule for wheat (tonnes per year).

Price per tonne (dollars)	Original demand per year	Original supply per year
500	100,000	500,000
400	200,000	400,000
300	300,000	300,000
200	400,000	200,000
100	500,000	100,000

1 Plot and label the demand curve (DD) for wheat and its supply curve (SS).

2 Mark in the market price (P) and the quantity traded (Q) at this price.

3 Imagine now that supply falls by 200,000 tonnes at each and every price. Draw and label the new supply curve (S1S1).

4 What is the new market price (P1) and the new quantity traded (Q1)? Show these on your graph.

5 What has happened to demand and why?

6 Suggest four reasons why the supply of wheat may fall.

58 The allocation of resources: how markets work; market failure

A fall in the supply of a product will cause its supply curve to shift inwards and market price will rise. Consumers' demand contracts along their demand curve as market price rises until demand equals supply once again.

We have now looked in detail at how the **price mechanism** works in a free market. The forces of demand and supply establish the market price of a product. Changes in demand and supply will cause changes in price.

An increase in the demand for a good or service will raise market price. This will be the signal to producers to use more resources to supply more. This way consumers get what they want as firms compete for their demand. An increase in the supply of a product lowers market price and enables more people to share the increased supply.

ACTIVITY 2.18

Families count cost of rush for a flat-screen TV

FAMILIES who paid out for the latest in flat-screen TVs might be wishing now that they had waited a little longer.

Manufacturers have produced so many that there is a worldwide glut. Retailers are admitting that prices for state-of-the-art LCD and plasma sets, which originally cost in the thousands, are now 'dropping every day'.

Manufacturers and retailers launched a big push on the sets over the last six months, tied to the World Cup and the launch of high definition services promising much sharper pictures and sound.

During the build-up to the football World Cup, major retailers were selling a high value flat-screen television every 15 seconds. But even during the busiest periods retailers warned that there would be a lull in sales immediately after the tournament, which has now led to rival stores having to slash prices to clear stocks.

In the meantime, so many flat-screen TVs have been produced that the glut has forced manufacturers to slash their premium prices.

A flat-out market

1. What happened to the demand for large flat-screen televisions in the run-up to the World Cup?

2. What impact do you think the change in demand for flat-screen televisions has had on demand and supply in the market for ordinary (cathode ray tube) televisions?

3. What happened to the supply of large flat-screen televisions? What affect did this have on the prices of these products?

4. What is likely to happen to the quantity traded of flat-screen televisions following the increase in their supply?

5. Draw a diagram to illustrate the movements in demand and supply curves in the market for large flat-screen televisions.

SECTION 4

Price elasticity of demand

What is price elasticity of demand (PED)?

When prices rise we can assume that the quantity demanded will contract for most goods and services. However, firms and economists would like to know by how much consumer demand will contract or expand as prices change.

For example, a train company would like to know what would happen to demand for its services, and therefore the revenue it earns from tickets, if it increased its fares. Increasing fares in peak periods when many people have to travel by train to and from work in busy cities may have very little impact on demand because many people have few or no alternative means of travel. Journeys by road by car or bus may take too long, the traveller may not own a car, or car parking in the city is too expensive. However, raising train fares for journeys off-peak and at weekends may cause demand, and therefore revenue, to fall significantly because people may decide against travelling and spend their leisure time doing something else or travelling by car or bus instead because the roads are not so busy.

Similarly, a government would want to calculate how much tax revenue it could expect from a tax placed on a particular good or service. For example, many governments levy excise taxes on cigarettes to discourage people from smoking. However, despite the tax many people continue to smoke which in turn provides the government with a stream of tax revenue from the sale of cigarettes. ➤ 5.2

Consider the two diagrams below.

The demand curve is quite steep. As price rises by 25% from $2.00 to $2.50 demand contracts very little from 1,000 to 900 units per period, a fall of just 10%. This might be very similar to the demand for train journeys during busy peak periods.

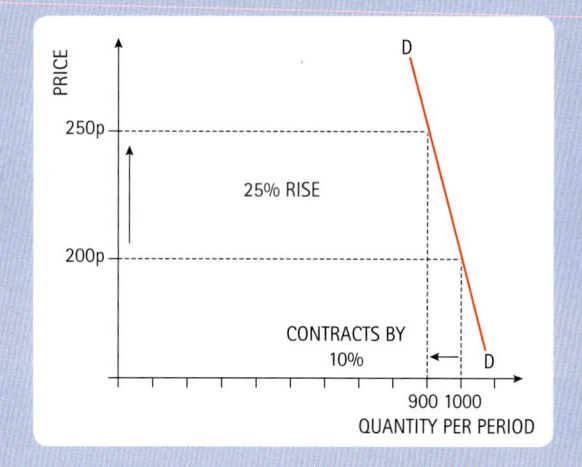

In this case **demand** is said to be **price inelastic** as the percentage change in price is much larger than the percentage change in demand.

The demand curve is quite flat. As price rises by 25% from $2.00 to $2.50 demand contracts significantly, from 1,000 to 500 units, a fall of 50%. This could be what the demand curve for off-peak travel by train looks like.

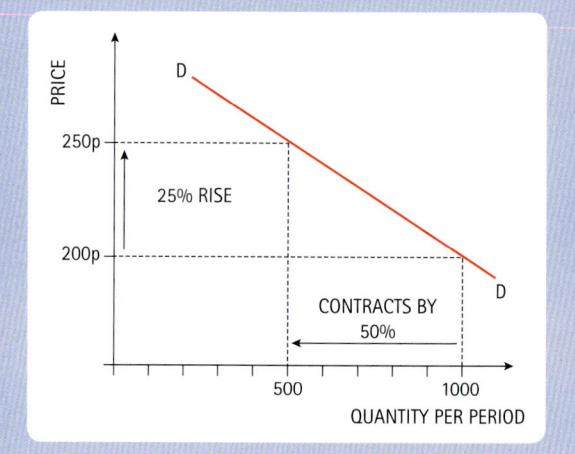

In this case **demand** is said to be **price elastic** as the percentage change in price is less than the percentage change in demand.

The responsiveness of quantity demanded to changes in the price of a good or service is known as the **price elasticity of demand (PED)** of that product.

If a small change in the price of a product causes a big change in quantity demanded, the demand for that product is said to be price elastic. That is, quantity demanded stretches (expands or contracts) significantly when the price is changed.

On the other hand, if a small change in the price of a product causes only a very minor change in quantity demanded, the demand for that product is said to be price inelastic. That is, quantity demanded stretches very little when price changes.

ACTIVITY 2.19

A problem to 'stretch' you

Assume there is a rise of about 10% in the prices of the following goods. State whether there is likely to be large, small or no change in the quantity demanded. Then state whether you think demand is price elastic or inelastic, and why.

Product	Small or large change in quantity demanded	Price elastic or price inelastic	Why?
Electricity			
Luxury holiday			
Bread			
A Toyota car			
A newspaper			

Products such as electricity and bread are essential items for many consumers. An increase in price may only have a very small impact on the quantity demanded. Demand for these goods therefore tends to be relatively price inelastic. Similarly, purchases of newspapers only account for a relatively small amount of many people's incomes and this tends to make demand for them price inelastic. In contrast, demand for more luxurious, high-value products such as holidays and cars may contract significantly if their prices rise. Demand for these types of products tends to be price elastic.

How to measure PED

PED compares the percentage change in quantity demanded with the percentage change in price that caused it. For example, imagine personal hi-fi producers raise their prices from $20 to $25, that is, by 25%. If the quantity demanded contracted from 1,000 per week to 500 per week then this represents a 50% reduction in quantity demanded, which is double the percentage change in price. As demand has changed by a greater percentage than price, demand is price elastic. That is, each 1% change in price will cause a 2% change in the quantity of personal hi-fis demanded.

If, on the other hand, the percentage change in price caused a much smaller percentage change in quantity demanded, demand would be price inelastic.

The PED for a product is calculated as follows:

$$PED = \frac{\% \text{ change in quantity demanded}}{\% \text{ change in price}}$$

Percentage changes are worked out as follows:

$$\% \text{ change in quantity demanded} = \frac{\text{change in quantity}}{\text{original quantity}} \times \frac{100}{1}$$

$$\% \text{ change in price} = \frac{\text{change in price}}{\text{original price}} \times \frac{100}{1}$$

How markets work

For example, look at the following demand schedule.

Price of the good	Quantity demanded per week
$5	100
$4	110

Taking $5 as the original price and 100 as the original quantity, the change in price is $1 and the change in quantity 10.

1. % change in quantity demanded = $\frac{10}{100} \times \frac{100}{1} = \frac{1,000}{100} = 10\%$

2. % change in price $\frac{\$1}{\$5} \times \frac{100}{1} = \frac{100}{5} = 20\%$

3. PED = $\frac{\% \text{ change in quantity demanded}}{\% \text{ change in price}} = \frac{10\%}{20\%} = \frac{1}{2} = 0.5$

Demand is price inelastic because the percentage change in price of 20% is greater than the percentage change in quantity demanded of 10%. The PED is 0.5.

ACTIVITY 2.20

Using the formula

Below is the demand schedule for tins of beans.

Price of beans per tin (cents)	Market demand per week
40	1,000
30	1,500

1. Calculate the PED. (*Hint:* Use 40 cents as your original price.)
2. Comment on its value.
3. What will the demand curve for beans look like? Draw a simple diagram to show this.

The demand for baked beans in the above example is price elastic because the percentage increase in quantity demanded of 50% is greater than the 25% fall in price that caused it (PED = 2). The demand curve for beans will therefore be quite flat.

In general when PED is **greater than 1**, demand is price **elastic**. If PED is **less than 1**, demand is price **inelastic**.

Price elasticity and total revenue

A firm will wish to know if an increase in price will cause its total revenue to rise. However, if quantity demand contracts significantly, revenue is likely to fall.

ACTIVITY 2.21

What happens to total revenue?

Below are two demand schedules, one for bread and one for passenger flights between two US cities.

Price per loaf	Quantity demanded per month
*25 cents	10,000
20 cents	10,500

Price per airline ticket	Quantity demanded per month
*$500	1,000
$400	1,800

* original price and quantity

1. In each case calculate the PED. Comment on their values.

2. Calculate the total revenue (price × quantity demanded) for bread and for airline tickets at each price.

3. a. Would you advise bread-makers to cut the price of a loaf from 25 cents to 20 cents? Explain your answer.

   b. Would you advise the airline to cut the air fare from $500 to $400? Explain your answer.

4. Using the information above, decide which of the words in italics below does not apply in each case.

   a. Demand is price elastic when the percentage change in quantity demanded is *more/less* than the percentage change in price. A fall in price will cause a *large/small* extension in quantity demanded so that total sales revenue *falls/rises*. If price is increased, total revenue would *fall/rise*.

   b. Demand is price inelastic when quantity demanded changes by a *greater/smaller* percentage than price. A fall in price will cause a *small/large* extension in quantity demanded so that total sales revenue *falls/rises*. A rise in price therefore causes total revenue to *fall/rise*.

PED and firms' revenues are closely linked.

In the case of bread, because demand is price inelastic (PED = 0.25), when the price is lowered, there is only a very small extension in demand and so total revenue falls. An increase in price would therefore raise revenue. In the case of airline tickets it is advisable for the airline operators to lower the fare from $500 to $400. Because demand is price elastic (PED = 4) sales expand proportionately more than the change in price and revenue will rise. An increase in price would therefore reduce revenue if demand is price elastic.

What affects PED?

1 The number of substitutes

When consumers can choose between a large number of substitutes for a particular product, demand for any one of them is likely to be price elastic.

Demand will be price inelastic when there are few substitutes. For example, many foods, such as milk and medicines, have few substitutes.

2 The period of time

If the price of a product rises consumers will search for cheaper substitutes. The longer they have, the more likely they are to find one. Demand will therefore be more price elastic in the long run.

3 The proportion of income spent on a commodity

Goods such as matches or newspapers may be price inelastic in demand because they do not cost very much and any rise in their price will only take a little bit extra out of a person's income. If the price of cars was to rise by 10% this could mean paying an extra $500 or more for a car. This is a considerable part of a person's income. Demand for cars is more likely to be price elastic.

Some special demand curves

If a rise or fall in the price of a product causes no change in the quantity demanded of that product, demand is said to be **perfectly price inelastic**. That is, PED is 0.

If a product is only demanded at one particular price, demand is said to be **infinitely price elastic**. That is, a small change in price will cause quantity demanded to fall to zero, that is, quantity demanded will change by an infinite amount.

If PED is 1 then demand is said to be of **unitary elasticity**. A percentage change in the price of a product will cause an equal percentage change in the quantity demanded. The result will be that the total amount spent on that product by consumers will remain the same whatever its price.

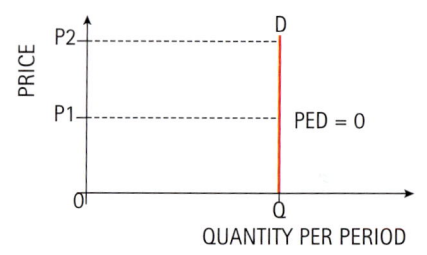

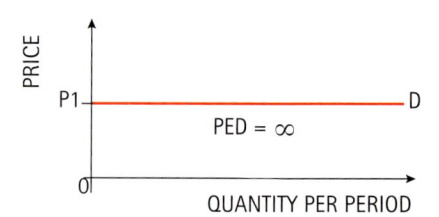

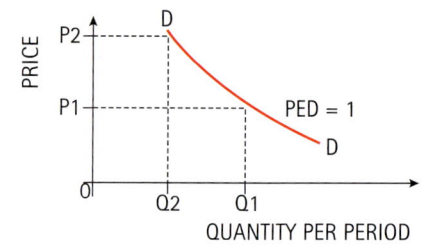

ACTIVITY 2.22

Elastic brands

Modest rise in sales of *Daily Star* after price cut

The decision to slash the price of the *Daily Star* newspaper by 50% helped to boost month on month sales of the tabloid newspaper by 0.27% to 864,315 copies.

A study by health economists in Japan found that the price elasticity of demand for influenza vaccinations was very low at just 0.0441 to 0.0187 nationally.

In contrast, a study of Australian livestock grazing industries found price elasticities of demand for beef, lamb and pork were between 1.4 and 1.6. There was also evidence that the meats were strong substitutes for each other in consumer demand.

Toyota sales surge after slashing prices

The world's biggest carmaker saw US sales of its vehicles rise by 41% in March from a year earlier, having fallen 16% year on year in January and 9% in February.

Toyota attributed this increase in sales to providing buyers with discounts of up to $2,250 a vehicle last month. The price incentives, including interest-free loans and discount leases, were worth an average of 10% on each new vehicle.

1. Why do you think the PED for flu vaccinations was much lower than the PEDs for different meats?
2. What is meant by beef, lamb and pork being strong substitutes in consumer demand?
3. Calculate the PEDs for Toyota cars and the *Daily Star* newspaper suggested by the data in the articles. For which product is consumer demand more price elastic and why?

EXAM PREPARATION 2.2

a. Explain the difference between an equilibrium price and a disequilibrium price. [4]

b. Many more people travel by aeroplane today than ten years ago. With the help of a demand and supply diagram, explain what might have happened in the market for travel to cause this increase. [6]

c. Define price elasticity of demand and suggest why different goods have different price elasticities. [5]

d. Discuss whether knowledge of price elasticity of demand is of use to a company selling holiday tours. [5]

Cambridge IGCSE Economics 0455/04 Q2 October/November 2006
Cambridge O Level Economics 2281/02 Q2 October/November 2006

ECONOMICS IN ACTION

How can knowledge of the PED of different consumer groups help firms to plan their pricing strategies? Why do you think advertising may reduce the price sensitivity of consumers?

FLAT PACKED AND PRICED

IKEA, the Swedish home products company that designs and sells ready-to-assemble furniture, appliances and home accessories, is the world's largest furniture retailer with more than 300 stores in over 35 countries. It opened its first store in China in 1998 and now has a number of outlets across the country including in Shenyang, IKEA's second largest store in the world with 47,000m^2 of floorspace.

Whereas in most areas of the world IKEA products are considered 'good value' by most consumers, in China its products were thought to be aimed at consumers with high incomes. However, this also meant that many Chinese consumers were very sensitive to price and a small reduction could persuade many more to buy IKEA products because they also wanted to be associated with a high income 'lifestyle' created by the IKEA brand. After cutting all its prices by 10% IKEA's China sales rose by 35% that year and 50% the following year.

It all Ads up!

Market research carried out by the Neilson Company and Arbitron in the USA using a panel of 11,000 people across 5,000 households found that it is possible to identify consumer groups whose sensitivity to price depends on their exposure to advertising.

Their analysis found that increased exposure to advertising appeared to reduce the sensitivity of consumers' demand to price changes: there was a negative relationship between price elasticity of demand and advertising exposure. Audiences with the highest exposures showed the least sensitivity to price changes.

SECTION 5

What is price elasticity of supply (PES)?

Price elasticity of supply

We have seen how the price mechanism works whereby an increase in demand will cause the market price of a product to rise. As a result, supply extends so that consumers get what they want. However, as economists we would wish to know by how much quantity supplied will change in response to the price change. **Price elasticity of supply (PES)** is a measure of the responsiveness of quantity supplied to a change in price.

The allocation of resources: how markets work; market failure

Price elasticity of supply (PES)

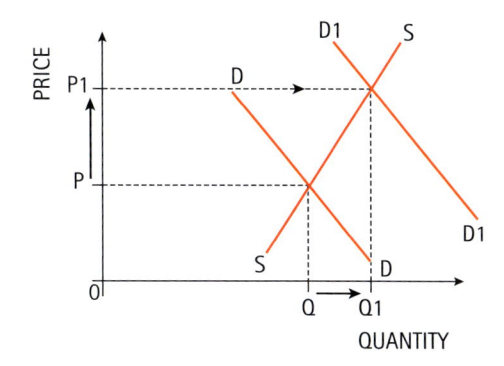

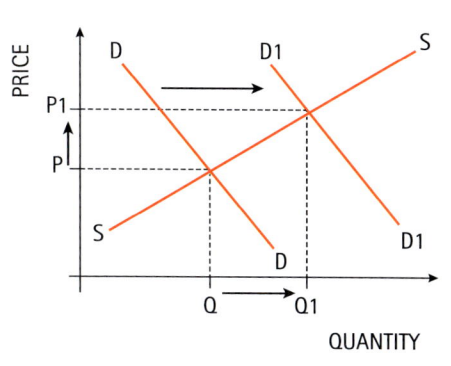

In the above diagram the increase in demand from DD to D1D1 has caused market price to rise from P to P1. However, despite this large rise in price the extension in supply is only small from Q to Q1. Supply is price inelastic.

In this diagram the increase in demand from DD to D1D1 has caused only a small increase in price from P to P1 but a large extension in supply from Q to Q1. Supply is price elastic.

To measure PES we use the following formula:

$$PES = \frac{\% \text{ change in quantity supplied}}{\% \text{ change in price}}$$

If the percentage change in price is greater than the percentage change in quantity supplied, supply is price inelastic and the value of PES will be less than 1.

If the percentage change in price causes a much larger percentage change in quantity supplied, supply is price elastic. PES will therefore be greater than 1.

Below is the supply schedule for carnations, a popular cut-flower, in the springtime.

Price per bunch of five carnations	Quantity supplied per month
100 cents	10,000
200 cents	12,000

$$\% \text{ change in quantity supplied} = \frac{\text{change in quantity}}{\text{original quantity}} \times \frac{100}{1} = \frac{2,000}{10,000} \times \frac{100}{1} = 20\%$$

$$\% \text{ change in price} = \frac{\text{change in price}}{\text{original price}} \times \frac{100}{1} = \frac{100c}{100c} \times \frac{100}{1} = 100\%$$

$$PES = \frac{\% \text{ change in quantity supplied}}{\% \text{ change in price}} = \frac{20}{100} = 0.2$$

How markets work

The PES of carnations is less than 1, that is, supply is price inelastic. This is because even if there is a large rise in price more carnations cannot be grown very quickly.

What affects PES?

1 Time

The carnations example illustrates how the PES can vary over time. Supply of most goods and services, including carnations, will be fixed at any one moment in time. For example, a shop will only have a certain amount of newspapers, books or joints of beef. A market stall will only have a fixed amount of carnations to sell. It will take time to get more of these things. In this special case the supply curve is a vertical line showing that whatever the price the quantity supplied will be the same.

▼ Supply at any given moment is fixed

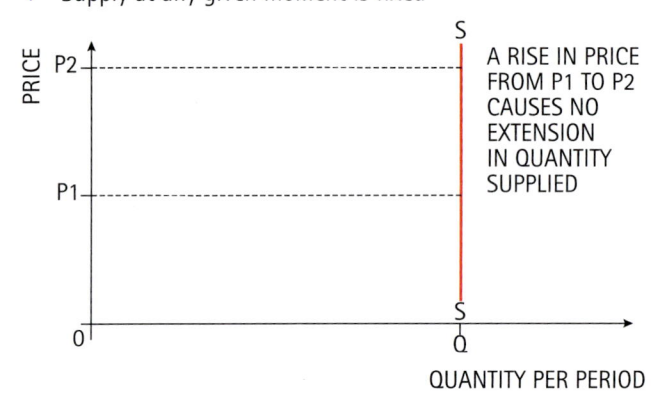

A RISE IN PRICE FROM P1 TO P2 CAUSES NO EXTENSION IN QUANTITY SUPPLIED

In the short run, firms can produce some more goods for sale, but only by using more labour, that is, by working overtime or employing more workers. More carnations can be picked and sent to the market as price rises. However, supply can only rise a little because the amount of land, seeds and the season needed to grow the carnations will soon run out.

▼ Supply is price inelastic in the short run

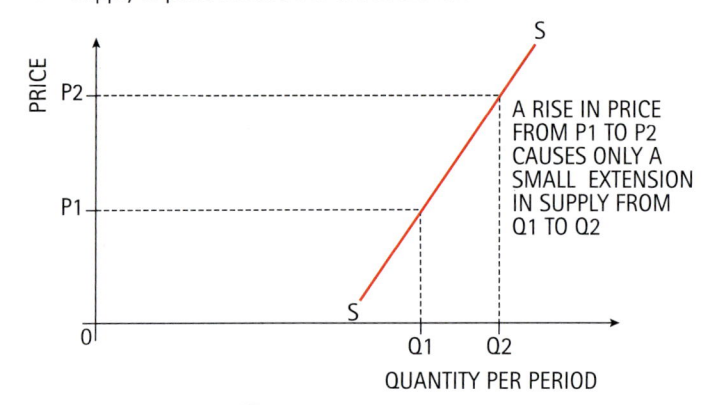

A RISE IN PRICE FROM P1 TO P2 CAUSES ONLY A SMALL EXTENSION IN SUPPLY FROM Q1 TO Q2

In the long run, firms can obtain more labour, land and capital to expand their scale of production, so in the long run the supply of most products becomes more price elastic.

68 The allocation of resources: how markets work; market failure

▼ Supply in the long run is price elastic

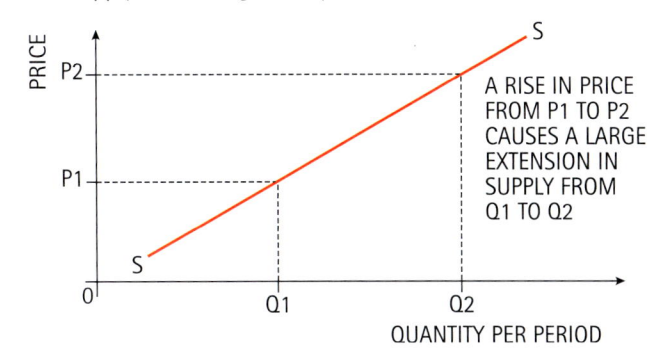

A RISE IN PRICE FROM P1 TO P2 CAUSES A LARGE EXTENSION IN SUPPLY FROM Q1 TO Q2

2 The availability of resources

If a firm wishes to expand production it will need more of the factors of production of land, labour and capital. If the economy is already using most of its scarce resources then firms will find it difficult to employ more to expand their output. The supply of many goods and services will therefore be price inelastic when an economy is at or near full employment.

If, however, there is a large supply of unused or unemployed resources, such as labour, then firms will be able to use them when they want to raise output and supply will be more price elastic. ➤ **6.2**.

ACTIVITY 2.23

Stretching supply

Below are imaginary supply schedules for natural rubber and man-made rubber.

Price per kg (cents)	Quantity supplied of natural rubber per month
80	1,000
100	1,100

Price per kg (cents)	Quantity supplied of man-made rubber per month
80	2,000
100	2,800

1 Calculate the PES for natural rubber and man-made rubber.
2 Comment on their values and suggest reasons why they differ.

Some special supply curves

If the quantity supplied of a commodity remains the same whatever its price, supply is said to be **perfectly price inelastic**, that is, PES = 0.

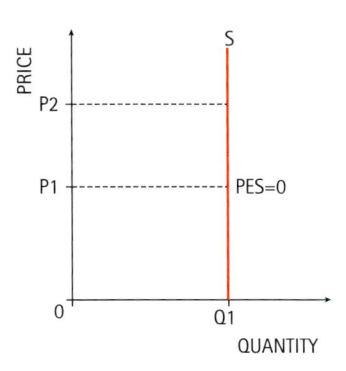

If producers are willing to supply as much as they can at one particular price and supply nothing at any other price then supply is said to be **infinitely price elastic**.

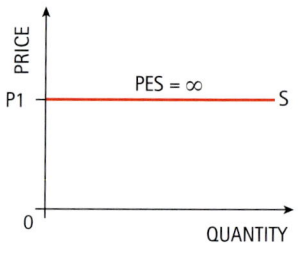

If the PES = 1, then supply is said to be of unitary elasticity. A percentage change in price will cause an equal percentage change in quantity supplied. This will be the case for any straight line supply curve that passes through the point of origin of its graph.

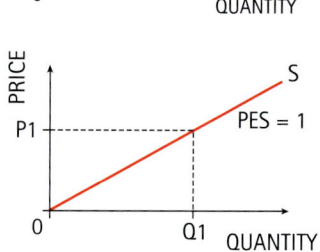

SECTION 6

The impact of taxes and subsidies on market outcomes

In a mixed economy a government may intervene in different markets to influence the market price and quantity traded of certain goods or services to achieve different market outcomes. ➤ **2.1**

Tax and supply

A tax can be used to raise the market price of a product, either directly to reduce consumer demand for that product or by making production more expensive so producers reduce market supply. This will in turn increase market price.

Taxes levied on goods and services are called **indirect taxes**. Examples include ad valorem taxes such as value added tax (VAT) and other sales taxes that are levied as a percentage of the selling price of a good or service, and specific **excise duties** such as those on petrol, alcohol and cigarettes, which are often a fixed tax mark-up on price. Such taxes have the effect of increasing market prices and thereby contracting consumer demand, especially if demand is price elastic. ➤ **5.1**

Taxes can be regarded as an additional cost of production that has to be paid by the producer to the government. They have the effect of moving the market supply curve vertically upwards by the amount of the tax.

▼ A tax on petrol

Price per litre ($)	Litres demanded per month (millions)	Litres supplied per month (millions)	Litres supplied per month after $0.40 per litre tax (millions)
$1.60	100	900	700
$1.40	200	800	600
$1.20	300	700	500
$1.00	400	600	400
$0.80	500	500	300
$0.60	600	400	200
$0.40	700	300	–
$0.20	800	200	–

The allocation of resources: how markets work; market failure

The imaginary figures on page 70 show how much producers of petrol are willing to supply and how many litres consumers are willing to buy at each possible price before and after an excise duty of 40 cents per litre is applied. For example, before the tax was imposed producers were willing to supply 600 million litres of petrol per month if the market price per litre was $1.00. At this price they would earn revenues of $600 million per month (that is, 600 million litres × $1).

However, if $0.40 per litre was taken in tax from producers their revenue after tax would be just $0.60 per litre or $420 million per month. Therefore, in order to continue to earn $600 million each month after tax from the sale and supply of 600 million litres of petrol, producers would need to obtain a price of $1.40 per litre.

Clearly, at a price of just $0.40 per litre revenues after the excise tax would be zero, so producers will no longer be willing to supply any petrol at $0.40 per litre or below.

In fact, whatever the amount of petrol the producers were willing to supply before the tax was applied, they will now only do so at a much higher price to offset the impact of the tax on their total revenue. As a result, the entire market supply curve shifts up by the amount of the tax. That is, the supply curve shifts upwards by $0.40 at each level of supply against each possible price per litre.

▼ The effect of an indirect tax on market price

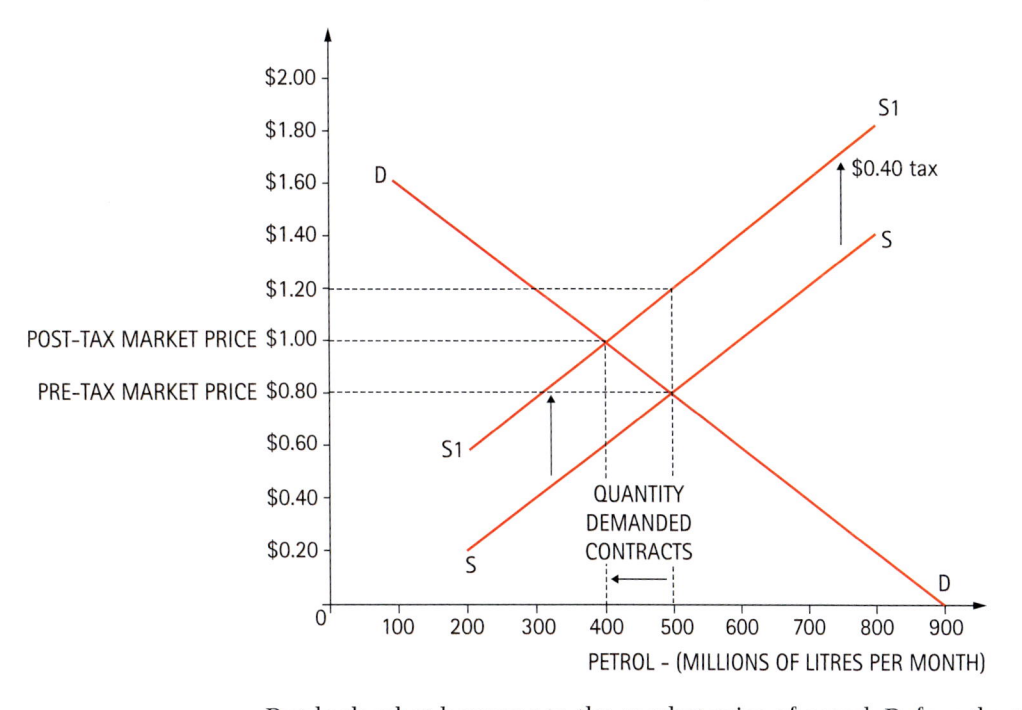

But look what happens to the market price of petrol. Before the tax of $0.40 per litre the market price for a litre of petrol was $0.80. After the $0.40 tax the market price has risen by just $0.20 per litre to $1.00. This might appear odd at first but remember as price rises consumer demand contracts because normal demand curves are downward sloping. So as producers of petrol try to pass on the full amount of the tax to consumers, demand for petrol contracts and producers earn less revenue. As a result, the $0.40 tax per litre of petrol is shared

▼ The effect of an ad valorem tax on supply

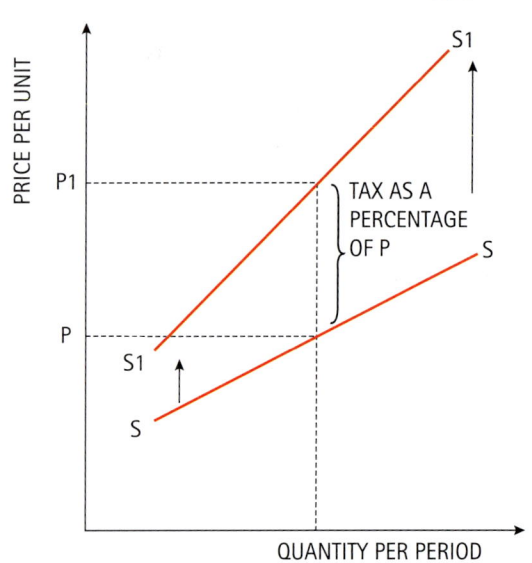

between the petrol producers who earn less revenue after tax and the consumers of petrol who must pay a higher market price per litre consumed. Only in an extreme case if demand was perfectly price inelastic would producers be able to pass on the full amount of the tax to consumers, because the quantity demanded would not change.

The effect of an ad valorem tax such as VAT is very similar. The supply curve will shift up by the amount of the tax as producers try to offset the tax by seeking to charge higher prices. The only difference is that the supply curve shifts up by more, the higher the price. This is because an ad valorem tax is levied as a percentage of the selling price. So, a tax of 15% would add $1.50 to the price of a good selling for $10 and $3 if the price was originally $20.

A **subsidy** is a payment made to producers to help reduce their costs of production. As a result, producers will tend to increase supply at every given price. As supply increases, the market price will tend to fall, to the benefit of consumers.

Subsidies and supply

Subsidies are often used in agriculture to support the incomes of farmers to encourage them to produce more essential foodstuffs. For example, in the diagram below a subsidy paid per tonne of maize produced has shifted the supply curve of maize down from SS to S1S1. The increase in supply at every possible price will result in a fall in the market price of maize so consumers can afford more and demand can expand.

▼ The effect of a subsidy on market supply

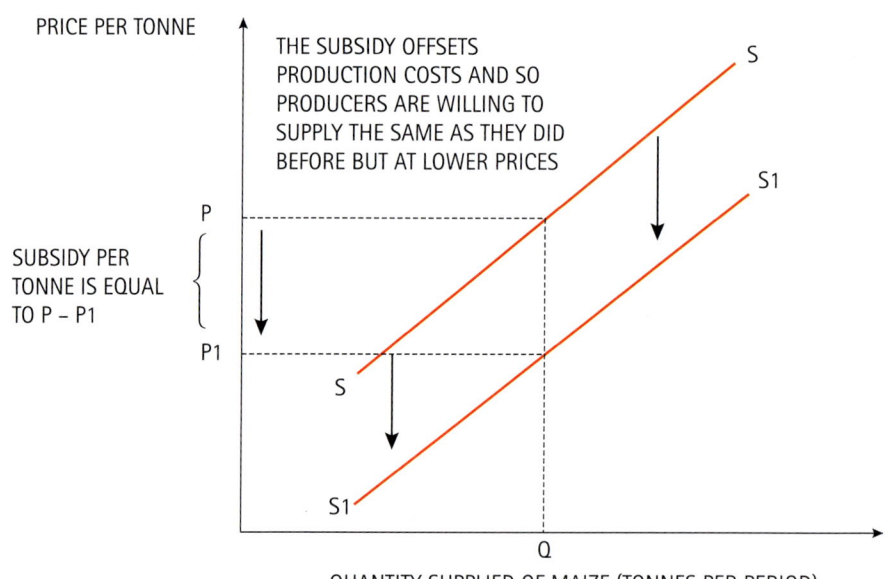

Subsidies are also used to encourage the production of new innovative goods and services, which private sector firms might otherwise find too costly and risky to produce initially.

Subsidies are also being used in many countries such as China, the USA and in Europe, for example to help expand the production and lower the market price of solar panels and wind turbines. It is hoped this will encourage business and households to generate renewable energy and so reduce the need for oil, coal and gas-fired power stations which produce harmful greenhouse gases. ► 2.3

However, subsidies can often distort competition. For example, a country may subsidize its industry because it is inefficient and needs to lower its costs of production relative to countries with more efficient producers. As a result, more efficient producers may lose customers and be forced out of business. For example, the USA has been accused by many other countries of subsidizing its inefficient steel industry at the expense of more efficient overseas producers. ▶ **8.1**

Further, subsidies designed to encourage production can result in excess supply, causing market prices to collapse which in turn causes producers to move their resources out of that market and thereby defeat the aim of the subsidy. For example, generous subsidies to many European farmers in the past resulted in butter mountains and milk lakes which could not then be sold in Europe because market prices would have fallen and cut farmers' incomes significantly, forcing many of them to consider closing.

ECONOMICS IN ACTION

How and why have the governments of Romania and India, like many others, used taxes and subsidies to alter the market prices of the products in the articles?

India sails into the wind

At the end of 2009 the Indian government announced it was to invest 3.8 billion rupees (Rs) in a new programme to encourage greater use of cleaner, renewable energy.

Producers of electricity from wind turbines are expected to receive a subsidy of Rs 0.5 per unit of electricity they produce against an average cost of Rs 3.0 per unit. The subsidy is intended to promote increased investment in wind turbines and use of renewable energy by lowering the costs of production and final energy prices for consumers.

Romania introduces a fat tax

Romanian people love their food, so much so that more than half of the population of 22 million people is overweight. Poor diets among both adults and children are blamed, with instances of obesity having doubled among 10-year-olds.

Growing concerns about the rising cost of health care and to the economy of the obesity epidemic has prompted the Romanian government to introduce a tax on fatty foods in an attempt to reduce the problem. The new tax means it will cost far more to buy burgers, chips, fizzy drinks and other fast foods with high fat and sugar content.

Romania joins a long list of other countries also trying to tackle rising obesity in their populations.

Taiwan has introduced a tax on fast food, Norway taxes sugar and chocolate, and Denmark and Austria have made artery-clogging trans-fats illegal. New York City and California in the USA have also banned the use of trans-fats.

How markets work

KEYWORDS

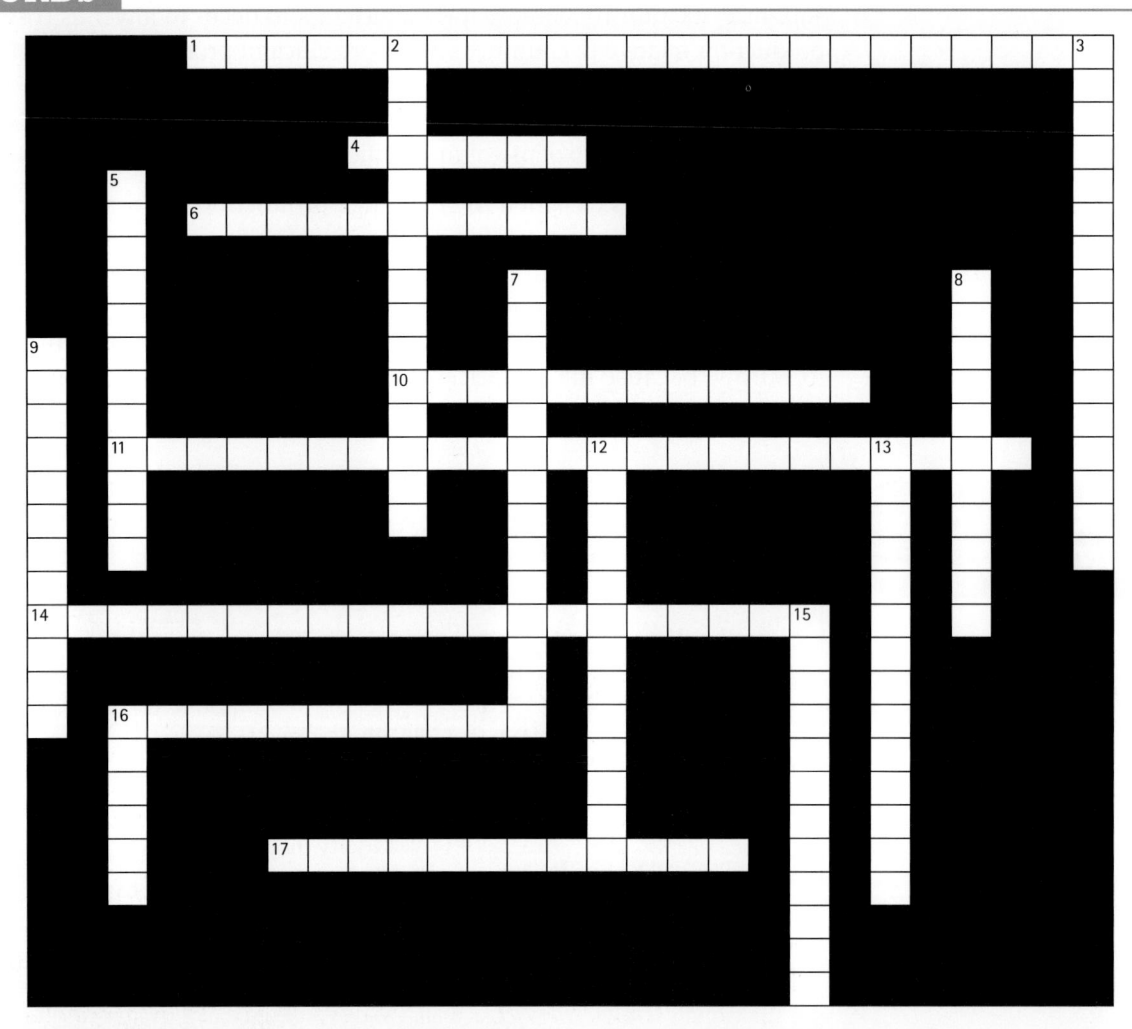

Clues across

1. The responsiveness of consumer demand for a product to a change in its price (5, 10, 2, 6)
4. The want or willingness of a consumer or group of consumers to buy a good or service (6)
6. The equilibrium price for a product in a market, determined where market demand exactly matches market supply (6, 5)
10. When the market demand for a product exceeds its market supply so there is upward pressure on its market price (6, 6)
11. The responsiveness of producer supply of a product to a change in its price (5, 10, 2, 6)
14. A market outcome, in terms of price and total quantity traded, which is unstable and liable to change because market demand and market supply are unequal (6, 14)
16. Products which compete to satisfy the same consumer demand, such as butter and margarine (11)
17. Consumer demand for a product is described as this if a small change in its price causes a much larger demand response (5, 7)

Clues down

2. A consumer want for a product backed by an ability to pay for it (9, 6)
3. Personal income remaining to spend or save after direct income taxes have been deducted from it (10, 6)
5. When the market supply of a product exceeds market demand so there is downward pressure on its market price (6, 6)
7. A Latin phrase used in economics meaning 'all other factors being unchanged' (7, 7)
8. Products for which demand rises as consumer incomes rise (6, 5)
9. The total demand for a product from all its consumers (6, 6)
12. Products for which demand tends to fall as consumers, incomes rise (8, 5)
13. Consumer demand for a product is described as this if a small change in its price causes a much smaller demand response (5, 9)
15. The total volume of value of a product supplied to a market by all its producers (6, 6)
16. The willingness and ability of a producer or group of producers to make a product available to consumers (6)

The allocation of resources: how markets work; market failure

Unit 2.3   Social costs and benefits

AIMS

By the end of this unit you should be able to:

▶ define **private and social costs and benefits** and discuss conflicts of interest in relation to these costs and benefits in the short term and long term through studies of the following issues:

- conserving resources versus using resources
- **public expenditure** verses **private expenditure**.

This will involve:

- recognizing how decisions to use scarce resources can result in **private costs and benefits** for those people or organizations taking these decisions as well as **external costs and benefits** incurred by others
- understanding why the total cost to society of an activity, or its **social cost**, includes all the private and external costs caused by that activity
- evaluating whether or not a decision to use scarce resources will increase **economic welfare**, comparing the social costs and benefits of that decision
- understanding that only an **economic use of resources** will generate more social benefits than social costs.

SECTION 1

Positive and negative externalities

How the decisions of firms can affect others

When many hundreds of thousands of gallons of thick, toxic oil gushed from ruptured pipelines in China in July 2010 it had a devastating impact on marine and wild life, and many communities and businesses located around the Dalian coastline of the country.

A man was killed during the clean-up operation while many businesses in the fishing and tourism industries were unable to continue operating and significant revenue was lost. The loss of life, the damage to the natural environment and wildlife and the losses suffered by other organizations represent the **external costs** of the oil spill.

China's worst-ever oil spill threatens wildlife and local industries as volunteers assist in clean-up

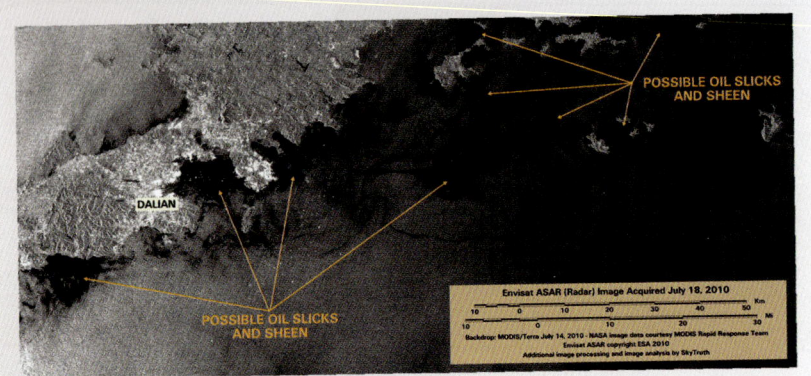

Chinese officials have warned of a severe threat to wildlife from one of the country's worst reported oil spills as an army of volunteers was dispatched to beaches to try to head off the black tides.

Five days after two pipelines exploded at the north-east port of Dalian, oil had reportedly spread over an area of 430 square kilometres, prompting a dispersal mission along the coast.

Hundreds of local volunteers are spreading absorbent matting along the Yellow Sea shoreline in an attempt to stop the slick from damaging beaches enjoyed by an increasing number of tourists each year on which many local hotels, restaurants and tour companies rely heavily for revenue.

Out at sea, authorities have started to use oil-consuming bacteria to try to disperse the slick, along with chemical agents and lengthy floating barrages.

The fishing industry has also suffered a major blow as fishing in the waters around Dalian has been banned for at least a month but local fisherman are worried that fish stocks may take many years to recover.

'The oil spill will pose a severe threat to marine animals and water quality, and sea birds for some time,' the deputy bureau chief for the city's Maritime Safety Administration told a regional TV station.

In contrast, Chinese oil companies, like many other oil companies all over the world, spend many millions of dollars each year using resources to explore and drill for new sources of oil, and on pipelines and petrochemical factories. These are their private costs. The revenues they earn from the sale of oil and petroleum products to consumers are their **private benefits**.

However, despite the precautions taken by oil companies and many other firms, a society can be left worse off as a result of their activities if they create serious negative externalities, including pollution and destruction of the natural environment.

A **negative externality** imposes external costs on other people and organizations that did not agree to the action that caused it. An **external cost** is a cost incurred by another party but not by those responsible for the harmful activity. A negative externality is therefore something bad and will therefore reduce satisfaction and lower economic welfare.

Because most private sector firms are motivated to make a profit they may overlook any negative externalities their resource allocation decisions may cause.

However, many uses of resources are clearly beneficial. They create goods and services to satisfy our needs and wants, provide employment and incomes, and therefore increase our living standards and economic welfare.

For example, many firms invest in technological advances and the training of their employees. These investments represent additional financial costs to those firms but they can in turn create **positive externalities**.

For example, Swiss multinational Roche Pharmaceuticals recently invested around $182 million in two European production facilities to manufacture a patient-friendly device that will allow people to administer their own cancer-fighting drugs at home and therefore reduce the time they need to spend in hospital.

Roche is a profit-making company but its investments in the advance of medicine and health care can help improve the health and life expectancy of many people, reduce the costs of sick leave and lost production due to staff illness in many other firms and reduce the cost to governments of providing public health care.

In the same way, private sector investments in early laser technologies many years ago, initially by AT&T (American Telegraph and Telephone) now benefit many millions of other firms and consumers worldwide because different types of lasers are now used in DVD players, for laser light shows, to measure distances accurately, in the cutting and welding of metals, for fingerprint detection, in surgical procedures, and for much more. These are all examples of positive externalities or spillovers from the investment in early laser development to other uses and organizations.

A **positive externality** therefore produces external benefits for other people and organizations that were not involved in the decision or action that created it. An **external benefit** is a benefit enjoyed by another party without that party having paid for it. Positive externalities are therefore good things to have and encourage. They increase satisfaction and improve economic welfare.

▼ The production of new drugs can produce positive externalities

▼ But the production of drugs may also produce negative externalities

Now let's apply what we know about externalities and private and external costs and benefits to a particular use of resources to examine whether or not that use is economically worthwhile.

River life dead!

The river Eden today is a dead river. Over the last year nearly all the fish and plant life in the river have been destroyed. In the past month cattle grazing along the banks of the river have been poisoned. Fears are growing that local children will be next.

A report has found that the river has been highly polluted by the nearby Chemix plastics plant. Chemix has, for the past two years, been dumping chemical waste into the river. The waste is pumped into the river along an underground pipeline from the Chemix plant.

Scientists estimate that it will cost $2 million to clean up the damage caused to the river each year unless the dumping of chemical waste is stopped.

Social costs and benefits

In the news article above, the estimated $2 million cost to clean up pollution in the River Eden each year is not the only cost of the decisions by Chemix about how to use resources to produce plastics and how to discharge its waste chemicals. All the costs and benefits arising from its activities have been estimated in the tables below.

Plastics production	$m per year
Private costs	**$10 m**
- wages	
- purchases of chemicals and materials	
- equipment charges	
- factory and office rent	
- costs of electricity, insurance, transport, etc.	
Private benefits	**$15 m**
- sales revenue	
Profit	**$5 m**

External costs and benefits	$m per year
Lost revenues to farming and costs of restocking	$5 m
Lost revenue from fishing and tourism	$2 m
Cost of cleaning up the polluted river	$2 m
Total external costs	**$9 m**
Benefits to other people and firms who use plastics	$2 m
Value to other firms of employees trained by Chemix	$1 m
Total external benefits	**$3 m**

Local farmers use water from the River Eden to irrigate their land and for their animals. They have suffered a loss of cattle and crops as a result of pollution from Chemix. As news spreads of the poisoning, all farmers in the area, regardless of whether their produce has been affected or not, may be unable to sell their output to fearful consumers. Local fishermen have also lost their livelihood because the waste has killed all the fish in the River Eden. In addition, tourists no longer visit the area to stay in waterside inns and hotels that have developed along the riverbanks.

The lost revenue to the farming, fishing and tourist industries are estimated to be worth $7 million each year Chemix continues to pollute the river, meaning the total external cost incurred by others as a result of the activities of Chemix are $9 million per year. Chemix does not pay for the external costs it creates, nor does it compensate the other people or firms affected by them.

The costs to the people, farms and other organizations near to the Chemix plant are significant, yet Chemix as a private sector firm may be uninterested in these costs. Chemix is likely only to be concerned with its own **private costs** of plastics production, including the hire of equipment and machinery, factory and office rent, the purchase of chemicals, the payment of wages, insurance and electricity charges, etc. ▶ **4.2**

The private costs of Chemix plus the external costs to the rest of society is the total **social cost** ($19 million) of the firm's decision to use resources to produce plastics, that is,

private costs + external costs = total social cost

The price Chemix charges consumers for its plastic is greater than the private costs of producing them. Chemix is therefore able to earn a profit from using resources to produce plastics. However, the market price of the plastic does not cover the external costs of the firm's production. If it did, price would be much higher and consumers may buy less plastic as a result. Sales and therefore the profits of Chemix would be much lower.

Chemix earns revenue of $15 million each year from the sale of its plastics to consumers compared to its private costs of production of $10 million each year. Producing plastics is therefore a profitable use of resources for Chemix. The difference between its private benefits and private costs is an annual profit of $5 million. If this amount of profit is more than Chemix could earn from using the same resources in their next best use then Chemix would conclude it is using its resources in the best possible way. The problem is, however, that many other people and firms think it is not the best use of these resources because of the widespread pollution Chemix has caused. Despite a profit of $5 million from the production of plastics, Chemix has imposed external costs on the rest of society of $9 million.

However, the management of Chemix argues that the company also creates many external benefits worth an estimated $3 million each year. Plastics are used in many modern, labour-saving products such as microwave ovens and cars and many other firms would be unable to make these products if Chemix did not supply them with plastic. The firm also trains its workers in specialist moulding techniques, computer assisted design and production and in management and financial skills. These skills may benefit other firms in the future when workers leave Chemix and take jobs elsewhere.

These external benefits should also be taken into account when deciding whether or not using resources to produce plastics is worthwhile for society and the economy as a whole.

Taken together, therefore, the private benefits of Chemix and the external benefits it creates for the rest of society gives the total **social benefit** ($18 million) of the firm's decision to use resources to produce plastics, that is,

private benefits + external benefits = total social benefit

So, we now know that the total social cost of the decision by Chemix to use resources to produce plastics is $19 million each year and exceeds the total social benefit of that same decision of $18 million each year. This means society could be better off if those resources were used in the production of other goods and services, despite the profit made by Chemix. That is, economic welfare could be higher if the resources employed by Chemix are used in productive activities that are less harmful to other people, firms and the natural environment and/or create more external benefits.

An economic or uneconomic use of resources

▼ An economic use of resources?

▼ An uneconomic use of resources?

Whenever the social costs of an activity exceed its social benefits, as in the case of Chemix, society as a whole is made worse off even if some people and firms enjoy profits and external benefits.

A use of resources is **uneconomic** if its total social cost exceeds its total social benefit. Society will be better off – and economic welfare higher – if the same resources are allocated to another use.

Only an **economic use of resources** will raise economic welfare because the social benefit created by that use will be greater than its social cost. It follows that if a productive activity creates significant social benefits then a society will be better off allocating more resources to it. For example, society may benefit from having access to more parks and open spaces, more health care and investments in medical advances, but private firms will not allocate resources to these uses if it is not profitable for them to do so.

ACTIVITY 2.24

Not painting a pretty picture

The Non-drip paint company is considering whether or not to locate a new factory near the town of Greensville. The company estimates that the new plant will cost $5 million a year to run, but should add $6 million to revenue from the sale of the paint it produces.

The people of Greensville are worried that the new factory will release smoke, containing harmful chemicals, into the air. These chemicals will pollute the air and even get into the soil and water supplies as rain will bring the chemicals back down from the air.

The local health authority estimates that over many years this smoke will damage people's health and increase the need for medical care at an estimated cost of $4 million a year.

The local authority believes that the smoke will blacken the walls of historic buildings in the area and cause their eventual erosion. Regular cleaning will therefore be needed at an estimated cost of $2 million each year.

On a more positive note, it estimates that the paint factory will encourage other firms to locate in the area as suppliers of materials, providers of transport, etc., and that this will reduce local unemployment and help other local businesses. These external benefits are valued at $3 million.

1. What does the Non-drip paint company take into account when deciding whether or not to produce paint with its resources?
2. From society's point of view should the firm take other factors into consideration?
3. Which of the following statements do you think are correct?
    a. From the point of view of the paint company, resources are being used in the best way if:

The allocation of resources: how markets work; market failure

      i   Private benefits are greater than private costs.
      ii   Private benefits equal private costs.
      iii Private benefits are less than private costs.
      iv External benefits are greater than external costs.

  b From the point of view of society, scarce resources are in their best use when:
      i   Social benefits exceed social costs.
      ii   Social benefits equal social costs.
      iii Social benefits are less than social costs.
      iv Private benefits are greater than private costs.

4 Using the figures presented in the case study calculate:
  a The paint company's estimated yearly profit.
  b Whether or not paint production at the factory is worthwhile for society.

5 A conflict of interest between the paint company and the local community has arisen. How does this illustrate the central economic problem?

Group exercise

Divide into groups of eight or nine. One half of each group will play the role of the directors of the Non-drip paint company, while the other half are local community representatives.

1 The directors of the company prepare a report stating why they feel they are right to go ahead with the paint factory even if it does mean producing smoke. For example, the aim of the company is to make a profit because it has a duty to its shareholders.

2 The local community group prepares a report stating why they feel the paint factory should not locate in their area.

3 The company directors and local community representatives in each group now meet to read and discuss their reports. They must attempt to reach a solution to the conflict. If no solution is reached, the teacher may act as an arbitrator.

4 Each group's recommendations and findings are then reported back to the teacher.

In the above exercise, the location and production decisions of the Non-drip paint company ignore any external costs and benefits. The company is only interested in making a profit, or **commercial return**, from producing paint. The result is that because social costs are greater than the social benefits of paint production, society will be worse off. In fact, private and external costs ($5 million + $6 million) exceed private and external benefits ($6 million + $3 million) by $2 million each year.

SECTION 2

How the market can fail

Market failure and government intervention

In the example we looked at earlier, the Chemix plastics company found it profitable to use resources to make plastics at a location next to the River Eden. The production process involved discharging waste chemicals into the river. In a market economic system the most profitable use of resources should be the best use of those resources, but because of the significant external costs of this production it clearly is not the best use for everyone else. Chemix and the market system have therefore failed to use resources in the most efficient way possible because the external costs of plastics production have been overlooked. If the market price of plastic was much higher in order to cover the external costs, consumers would buy less plastic and less would therefore need to be produced.

In fact, whenever a use of resources creates external costs or external benefits, the market economic system will fail to allocate resources efficiently. This is because private sector firms will only decide what, how and for whom to produce by considering their own private costs, benefits and profits. Government intervention may be required to ensure that firms take account of the external costs and benefits their decisions or actions create. ➤ **2.1**

Laws and regulations

Now imagine many local people and other firms affected by the river pollution have complained to their government to ban the production of plastics at Chemix and force the company to close. However, the government, the employees of Chemix and other firms that rely on supplies of plastic are worried that the closure of the factory will result in too many local jobs and external benefits being lost.

The government therefore decides instead to introduce legislation to ban Chemix from dumping its waste in the river. If Chemix breaks the law it will be fined many millions of dollars.

To comply with the new law Chemix must change its production process to reduce waste. It will need to install new equipment to filter and clean the waste that remains after each batch of plastics has been produced. These measures will increase the private costs of Chemix by $1 million per year and therefore reduce its profits. However, as a result, there will be no further discharges of untreated waste into the River Eden and no more external costs imposed on others.

Laws and regulations can be introduced by governments to ban or control activities that create serious negative externalities and external costs. For example, many countries have introduced anti-pollution laws to control the contamination of land and the release of untreated waste and chemicals into water supplies and into the air. Planning regulations can also be used to stop homes and offices being built with hazardous materials and where they might spoil the landscape and views enjoyed by others

The European Union and some other countries have also introduced laws to remove from sale and stop the production of light bulbs that are not energy efficient. The owners and managers of firms who break laws and regulations may be fined or even imprisoned if the breach is very serious.

Taxation

If market prices fail to reflect the external costs of a productive activity then it may be possible to impose a tax on product prices to make sure they do. ➤ **2.2**

Raising the prices of products that are themselves harmful, such as cigarettes, or outputs of a production process that creates significant external costs, should reduce consumer demand for those products and make them less profitable for private sector firms to produce.

Many countries have introduced 'green' taxes, including taxes on waste disposal, energy use and petrol. Firms can avoid paying these taxes if they cut

The allocation of resources: how markets work; market failure

their waste, energy and petrol consumption. Cars and petrol are also taxed in many countries to reduce demand for large vehicles and to encourage producers to develop and produce 'greener' alternatives.

However, in some countries these taxes are still considered relatively modest and further increases may be required to stop firms consuming so much energy and producing so much waste. Some governments are reluctant to do this or to introduce further taxes because they argue it will make their firms less competitive than overseas firms who do not have to pay such taxes. If consumers switch to buying the goods and services of these overseas firms then domestic firms may go out of business and workers will be made unemployed.

Subsidies

Private sector firms are not interested in producing external benefits for others because they are not paid for them. For example, a bus company may find it unprofitable to provide buses for people after the rush hour because not enough people use the service then. However, for those people who do use the buses at these times they benefit from a means of transport. Many old people and schoolchildren travel at off-peak times. The bus service also helps to reduce road congestion and pollution because people may use their cars less as a result. To help the bus company provide buses it could be given a subsidy. A **subsidy** is a payment of money given by a government to a firm to offset or reduce production costs. Subsidies may be given to firms in order to encourage them to produce goods and services that result in external benefits.

Some industries produce large external benefits. By taking over the ownership and running of a whole industry a government can allow nationalized industries to act in the public interest, and take account of any external costs and benefits they might give rise to. ➤ **4.1**

For example, in many countries bus and train services are nationalized and run by a public corporation. Bus and train fares may be be kept low to encourage people to use these services for travel instead of using their cars that may otherwise cause traffic congestion and harmful exhaust fumes and air pollutants. However, because low fares fail to generate enough revenue to cover their costs of provision, taxes will have to be raised to pay for these services.

Government policy and conflicts of interest

Taxes, subsidies, laws and regulations can also be used not just to influence the production decisions of firms but also the decisions of consumers where these may have external costs and benefits. For example, these may include taxes on cigarettes, free or subsidized vaccinations against infectious diseases and regulations such as speed limits on roads and a ban on smoking. We shall consider these further in the following sections.

However, in deciding to introduce policies to control firms and consumers to reduce the harmful impacts their decisions may have on others and the environment, a government may simply create other conflicts of interest. Higher taxes will reduce the amount of income people and firms have left to satisfy their wants, and regulations can curb their freedom of choice. This can create conflict between people who, for example, want higher taxes to pay for subsidized transport, and people on high incomes who may have to pay more tax but who may benefit very little from low-cost bus and train travel. Similarly, higher taxes on electricity and gas use to try to conserve energy consumption and the release of harmful emissions may hit the poor and most vulnerable people the hardest.

Now consider a decision by a government to spend $50 million to build a new motorway. To pay for the construction the government intends to raise taxes on incomes. Many people argue they cannot afford to pay more in taxes while many private sector firms have suggested they will have to reduce the number of people they employ if they have to pay higher taxes.

However, government officials have undertaken a cost benefit analysis and estimated that the motorway will improve journey times, reduce costs and cut accidents on other roads for a great many people and businesses. Building and maintaining the new motorway will also create new jobs in the construction sector. The officials believe that, together, these external benefits could be worth as much as $600 million over the next 20 years.

There will, however, be some external costs from additional noise nuisance and air pollution to nearby residents over the next 20 years. These external costs are estimated to total £150 million, but because the estimated social benefits of the motorway ($600 million) exceed the social costs of the motorway ($50 million plus $150 million) the government decides to go ahead.

Nevertheless, protestors against the new motorway point out that the government has failed to consider the loss of agricultural land on which the motorway is to be built and the destruction of wildlife habitats. They also accuse the government of ignoring the impact of increased vehicle emissions on global climate change and argue the government should use $50 million of taxpayers' money to fund public transport alternatives instead.

So who is right? Do the social benefits of the new motorway exceed its social costs? This will be difficult to answer because external costs and benefits are often difficult to value accurately.

SECTION 3

Opportunity cost revisited

In Unit 1.1 we discovered that because of scarcity we must choose what to do with scarce resources, and in choosing one use we must give up another. The benefit of the next best alternative given up is known as the opportunity cost.

For example, if we use land, labour and capital to build a motorway we may have to go without 10 new schools. In Unit 1.1 we would have said that the opportunity cost of the motorway is the 10 schools given up.

▼ Choice?

But the real opportunity cost of the motorway is not just the 10 schools foregone, it is also the peace and quiet, fresh air and attractive countryside that have also been given up. The opportunity cost, or the benefit of the next

The allocation of resources: how markets work; market failure

best alternative foregone, therefore, always includes any external costs that occur. If opportunity cost did not include these costs, it would not be a true measure of what has been gone without.

> ### ACTIVITY 2.25
>
> **Belt up!**
>
> Amiya Bundhun was an economics student at college and now works for a bank. She was injured in a car accident and has just spent six months in a hospital paid for by the government.
>
> Amiya decides to work out the opportunity cost of not wearing her seat-belt. She values the wages she has lost over six months at $12,000 and she values her lost social life at $4,000. Amiya calculates that the opportunity cost of not wearing her seat-belt is $16,000.
>
> The police and ambulance driver that attended to her at the scene of her accident said that Amiya would not have been hurt had she been wearing her seat-belt.
>
> 1. What is meant by opportunity cost?
> 2. What has Amiya missed out in calculating the opportunity cost of not wearing her seat-belt?
> 3. 'Wearing a seat-belt is up to me to decide. It's my life and if I get hurt in an accident it affects nobody else.' This is often said by car drivers, but would an economist agree with them? Explain your answer.

SECTION 4

▼ Vaccinations

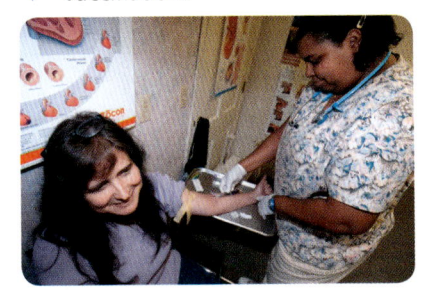

▼ Loud music

How consumers' decisions can affect others

So far we have only considered how firms' decisions to produce goods and services can affect society as a whole. However, we will now look at how people's decisions to consume goods and services can affect others. Consider the following examples.

The girl in the first picture is looking forward to her holiday in a hot, foreign country. However, before she can go she must protect herself from some of the diseases she may catch in that country. In the picture she is seen having a vaccination.

It also protects a great many other people because if the girl had caught a disease she would pass it on to others when she returned from her holiday. Her decision to have a vaccination has therefore protected the rest of society from the disease. This consumption has resulted in an external benefit.

The boy in the second picture likes playing music very loudly. The only problem is that his neighbours don't like loud music and are upset by the noise. The boy's decision to consume noisy music has imposed an external cost on other people.

Social costs and benefits

▼ Litter

The man in this picture has just finished eating a banana. Instead of placing it in a bin he has carelessly discarded it on the road. Litter is unsightly to many people. This is an external cost resulting from others' consumption. Furthermore, society must bear the cost of cleaning up the rubbish.

ACTIVITY 2.26

Smoking

Look at the picture of a man smoking in a café.

1. Give three private costs that a cigarette manufacturer will have to pay.
2. How will the manufacturer calculate the total revenue from the sale of cigarettes?
3. How are other people in the café affected by the man's decision to consume a cigarette?
4. Many countries have introduced laws to ban smoking in public places. What sort of things will a government have to pay for in order to make sure the ban is observed?
5. Research has shown that smoking can damage your health.
    a. What is the opportunity cost of increased health spending on treating smokers?
    b. Who will bear the cost of increased health spending?
6. Imagine that the government decides to increase the tax payable on a packet of cigarettes. What affect may this have on:
    a. The number of cigarettes consumed?
    b. The revenue of cigarette-makers?
    c. The workers in cigarette factories?

But perhaps the biggest concern facing us all today is how our ever growing wants and rising consumption of goods and services is creating ever increasing mountains of waste, global climate change through rising pollution and the depletion of increasingly scarce resources. As a result, our individual consumption decisions will not just have an impact on people living nearby but on people and the environment all over the world, and not just on today's society but on future generations for years to come.

The allocation of resources: how markets work; market failure

ACTIVITY 2.27

Living on borrowed time

Today is the day we start to eat Earth

THE Earth reaches an ecological tipping point today as we start officially to live beyond the means of our resources.

Experts at a British think-tank have calculated that we are now plundering natural resources faster than they can be replaced.

Rapid population growth, climate change and rising living standards are all placing huge strains on nature.

The doomsday scenario was spelt out by the new economics foundation (nef) after analysing research by the US academic group, Global Footprint Network, which says humans are over-using resources by 23 per cent.

The group warned that the world's six billion inhabitants must start facing up to the problem now or face the bleak consequences. Nef researchers worked out how quickly man is using the resources of farming land, forest, fish, air and energy. Mathis Wackernagel, executive director of Global Footprint Network, said: 'Humanity is living off its ecological credit card and can do this only by liquidating the planet's natural resources.'

Global warming, falling farm production, over-fishing and deforestation are all stark signs of how grim the outlook is, according to nef.

The grim warning will spark further fears of battles for resources among the world's nations. The British military has recently admitted it is already planning for resource wars later this century.

In groups discuss the article above. How does it illustrate, or provide examples of, the following economic concepts:

- resource allocation
- opportunity cost
- social costs and benefits
- economic conflicts of interest.

What actions do you think consumers, firms and governments could take to conserve resources and reduce the external costs of their individual production and consumption decisions?

SECTION 5

Conservation or commercialization?

To satisfy our growing wants for goods and services we are using up scarce natural resources at an ever increasing rate. In addition to the already huge demand for goods and services from consumers in developed countries, global population growth and increasing wealth in newly industrialized countries such as China and India are also now fuelling much of this increased demand. ▶ 7.1

Social costs and benefits

Resource depletion refers to the exhaustion of natural resources through the economic activities of production, consumption and exchange. Many natural resources, such as crude oil and iron ore, are **non-renewable**, meaning they are not replaced as they are used up. Similarly, many animal, bird, marine and plant species have become extinct because of increasing human activity.

ACTIVITY 2.28

Conserve or consume?

- Should we cut down forests to grow more crops to feed people in less-developed countries?
- Should we build more reservoirs to provide drinking water by flooding areas of natural land?
- Should we devote more resources to buying weapons to defend our countries or spend more on developing new forms of energy that do not harm the environment?
- Should we build more nuclear power stations to meet energy demands or spend more on conserving energy instead?
- Should developed countries pay less-developed countries to protect their natural environments, including tropical rainforests?
- Should we build homes, instead of nature reserves to protect endangered species and habitats?
- Should the government raise taxes to help protect the environment or lower taxes to allow consumers to choose how to spend that money?

1 Copy out a table like the one started below. In the column headed 'Conflict', write down the questions listed above.

2 Answer these questions on your own in the second column, explaining your answer.

3 Compare your answers with those of your neighbour and make a note in your table of which answers you agree on and which cause disagreement. Why is there disagreement?

4 For the questions upon which you agree with your neighbour, can you prove that your choices are the correct ones? Explain why you may not be able to prove this.

5 For the questions upon which you disagree is it possible for you to prove definitely that you are correct? Explain.

CONFLICT	MY CHOICE AND REASON	DOES MY NEIGHBOUR AGREE AND WHY?	DOES MY NEIGHBOUR DISAGREE AND WHY?

As more and more food is needed, more and more land is being converted to farmland or used to build homes and roads. The burning of oil and gas to generate power for energy use is also rising as consumers buy more and more electrical goods, and industries around the world increase their production in response to this growing demand.

As a result, many people are now calling for greater efforts to conserve scarce resources and to protect the environment.

Evidence of the depletion of the earth's resources

The Aral Sea between Kazakhstan and Uzbekistan was once the world's fourth largest inland lake, but over the last 40 years it has shrunk by 90 per cent. This devastation was caused by intensive cotton farming in central Asia.

▼ Battery farming

▼ Deforestation

▼ Smog

Conservationists argue we must slow the pace at which we consume resources for the following reasons:

- The burning of fuels for energy and in production of petrol and chemicals releases harmful emissions and pollutants. These cause acid rain which has harmful effects on plants, aquatic animals and infrastructure, and contribute to global warming.

- Deforestation to clear land of trees for farming and building has destroyed habitats for animals and plant species, and changed local climates.

- Over-farming of land has used up all the goodness in the soil, resulting in areas where nothing will grow.

- The use of pesticides and chemical fertilizers to increase crop production has polluted rivers and water supplies and killed wildlife.

- Intensive farming techniques, such as battery farming and the use of drugs to increase animal reproduction and growth rates for meat consumption are cruel and have helped spread diseases.

- Over-fishing has depleted fish stocks and harmed other marine, bird and animal populations.

- Many animals and fish species have been hunted into or close to extinction, and many more will die out due to the destruction of their habitats and climate change.

- Growing air pollution, especially in increasingly congested cities and growing urban areas, has increased breathing problems for many people.

- Oil spills, and the dumping of waste into rivers and the sea, has destroyed the marine habitat in many areas, killed many fish, birds and animals, and contaminated the food chain for humans.

- Clean water supplies and air are in short supply in an increasing number of areas.

- Global warming is already having a dramatic effect on the planet and climate change is causing more violent storms, droughts and floods.

Social costs and benefits

For example, a report commissioned by the World Wide Fund for Nature says heat waves, droughts, rising sea levels, flash floods, forest fires and disease 'could turn profitable tourist destinations into holiday horror stories' including the Maldives, the Seychelles, the European Alps, the eastern Mediterranean, southern Spain, the European lakes, South and east Africa, Australia, Florida and Brazil. Many businesses based on tourism in these areas will lose customers and their livelihood due to global warming.

Global warming may also affect food production. It will become possible to grow new crops in areas that are currently too cold to support them. However, more pests and diseases may offset any benefits higher temperatures may have. For example, researchers have looked at the impact of rising temperatures on irrigated rice production in China, India, Indonesia, the Philippines, Thailand and Vietnam and found that rising temperatures over the past 25 years have already cut rice yields at several key farming locations by 10–20%.

The speed at which global warming is expected to occur is faster than most plant and animal species will be able to cope with. Some species may adapt but others will suffer and may become extinct.

ECONOMICS IN ACTION

How and why are governments around the world using taxes to reduce waste?

Every year billions of tonnes of waste bottles, cans, paper and foods are discarded all over the world. Scarce resources have been used up producing these products, and scarce land then has to be used to bury the waste.

Waste therefore involves a significant opportunity cost. If firms used fewer packaging materials or more were recycled then fewer natural resources would be used up in their production and could be used in other ways.

Many governments levy taxes on the disposal of waste materials, particularly those that are harmful to the environment. Here are some examples.

China levies a tax on the disposal of household and commercial waste, together with a separate tax on the disposal of waste water; at the same time companies that preserve water and reduce their consumption are offered reductions in taxes on their profits.

Sweden also levies taxes on both domestic and commercial waste and has successively reduced the amount of waste going through landfills and increased recycling.

Some provinces of Canada use taxes to transfer the cost of waste disposal from local governments to firms that introduce packaging waste or hazardous products. Annually, these taxes raise over CAN$100 milllion in the various provinces and are causing businesses increasingly to look at ways of reducing their environmental footprint, and therefore the amount of 'green tax' they must pay.

ACTIVITY 2.29

Where have all the polar bears gone?

Climate change could cause serious problems. Although there is still much uncertainty, climate researchers who have prepared reports for the Inter-governmental Panel on Climate Change (IPCC) suggest there could be some very serious implications.

Sea levels rise as ice caps melt	Agricultural change
At present some 46 million people live in areas at risk of flooding due to storm surges. A one-metre rise could put 118 million in peril. If the global ocean level went up by one metre, Egypt would lose 1% of its land area, the Netherlands would lose 6%, Bangladesh would lose 17.5%, and on the Majuro Atoll in the Pacific Marshall Islands some 80% of the land would disappear under water.	Over time, total global crop production could be unchanged but effects on regions could vary widely. Those most at risk from famine would be peoples who rely on isolated agricultural systems in arid and semi-arid regions. Populations particularly under threat live in sub-Saharan Africa, south east Asia and tropical areas of Latin America. Climate change could also alter market conditions and the range of agricultural pests.
The spread of disease	**Changes to ecosystems**
Warmer temperatures could increase the spread of diseases like malaria, dengue fever and yellow fever. If the temperature increases by 3–5 °C the number of people potentially exposed to malaria could go up from 45% to 60% of the world population and result in an extra 50–80 million cases a year. Air pollution and exposure to greater extremes in temperature could lead to a greater frequency of asthma and respiratory diseases.	The composition and range of many ecosystems will shift as species respond to climate change. Possibly up to two-thirds of the world's forests will undergo major changes. Some forests may disappear altogether. Deserts are likely to become more extreme and result in increased soil erosion. Mountain glaciers could retreat and inland wetlands would be affected by global warming with resultant changes in habitat for the current species.

Researchers suggest that there could be many other changes but both the scientists and environment campaigners agree a number of measures could be used to reduce the impact humans are having on the climate.

So what can we do?

- Make more use of low-carbon fossil fuels such as natural gas, and decarbonize exhaust gases from power plants.
- Switch to renewable and clean sources of energy such as solar, wind and wave power.
- Use more nuclear power, although this produces radioactive waste.
- Recycle more waste, and generate less waste by using less packaging.
- Make fewer car journeys by using buses and trains instead to reduce emissions.
- Insulate our homes, to help reduce the burning of coal and oil for heat and electricity.
- Plant more trees and practise better land management.

Investigate how global warming could affect your country. What impact could it have on the environment, the amount and allocation of scarce resources, consumers and employees? Suggest measures, including taxes, subsidies, and regulations, your government could introduce to change the behaviour of firms and consumers to reduce the impact they are having on the environment. What will be the likely private and external costs and benefits of these measures? For coursework, write up your findings and arguments in a report to your government.

Arguments for and against conversation

Conservation, and protection of the environment and wildlife, involves choice and inevitably gives rise to conflict. For example, should 'green' taxes rise to discourage production or consumption that damages the environment? Should resources be used or conserved to protect the environment or should they be used to help reduce poverty?

When attempting to answer important questions like these and also the issues raised in Activity 2.29, it is difficult to avoid using our opinions. The problem is that opinions differ because what is thought to be fair and right for one person or group of people may not be so for another. For example, there are many people who argue that humans, the environment and wildlife will simply adapt to climate change and so we should not do anything to conserve resources now. Some areas and species may be wiped out but many will adapt and this is an entirely natural process that has been happening ever since life first appeared on the earth. This may be a scientific fact but economics is not concerned with this fact or with people's opinions.

As economists we cannot answer whether protecting the environment is more important than reducing poverty, but we can analyse the implications of using resources in these different ways and the economic effects of different actions undertaken by consumers, firms or governments. For example, we might analyse the economic implications of introducing measures to conserve resources as follows.

▼ Should government measures be introduced to conserve resources?

NO	YES
▸ The free market encourages the most efficient allocation of resources through the price mechanism. Firms that waste resources will face higher costs and will not be able to compete with more efficient firms. ▸ Conserving resources will mean resources are left idle. If we use fewer resources to produce fewer goods and services, there will be fewer jobs and less income. More people will be worse off. Rather than conserving resources we should be using resources more efficiently to achieve environmental goals.	▸ If the prices of goods and services are too low to cover the external costs of their production in terms of the damage they do to the environment then demand for them will be too high. Taxes on these goods and services can be used to raise their price and cut demand to an economically efficient level. ▸ Measures designed to conserve resources will not result in less food, nor will fewer goods and services be produced, just different and more efficient methods of production which do not deplete resources or damage the environment.

NO	YES
▸ In a free market, prices will rise as resources are used up and this will discourage their consumption and encourage conservation and waste reduction instead. ▸ As some resources run out and their costs rise, we will develop or find cheaper alternatives, such as the use of plants and animal waste to produce biofuels instead of using oil.	▸ Resources will be reallocated from the production of goods and services with high external costs to those with low or zero external costs. More jobs will be created in organic farming, energy-saving devices such as wind machines and solar panels and the production of other environmentally friendly products. As their production expands so their costs of production and prices will tend to fall, encouraging consumers to change their consumption patterns.

EXAM PREPARATION 2.3

In China, the State Council has ordered a reduction in urban development projects in Beijing. This is because, as developers clear land, people's homes are destroyed. It will also support the government's aim of reducing total demand in the economy.

a   Explain what is meant by the conservation of resources. [4]

b   Urban development is often thought to be beneficial. Consider who might benefit from an urban development project. [6]

c   Explain how a government might control private companies that wish to develop an area. [3]

d   Discuss why the development and exploitation of an urban area might be disadvantageous. [7]

Cambridge IGCSE Economics 0455/04 Q5 October/November 2006
Cambridge O Level Economics 2281/02 Q5 October/November 2006

WEBSITES

The following links provide some useful information on private and social costs and benefits:

- en.wikipedia.org/wiki/Externality
- en.wikipedia.org/wiki/Environmental_economics
- www.bized.co.uk/reference/glossary/Social-costs
- www.talktalk.co.uk/reference/encyclopaedia/hutchinson/m0031914.html
- www.absoluteastronomy.com/topics/Resource_depletion

KEYWORDS

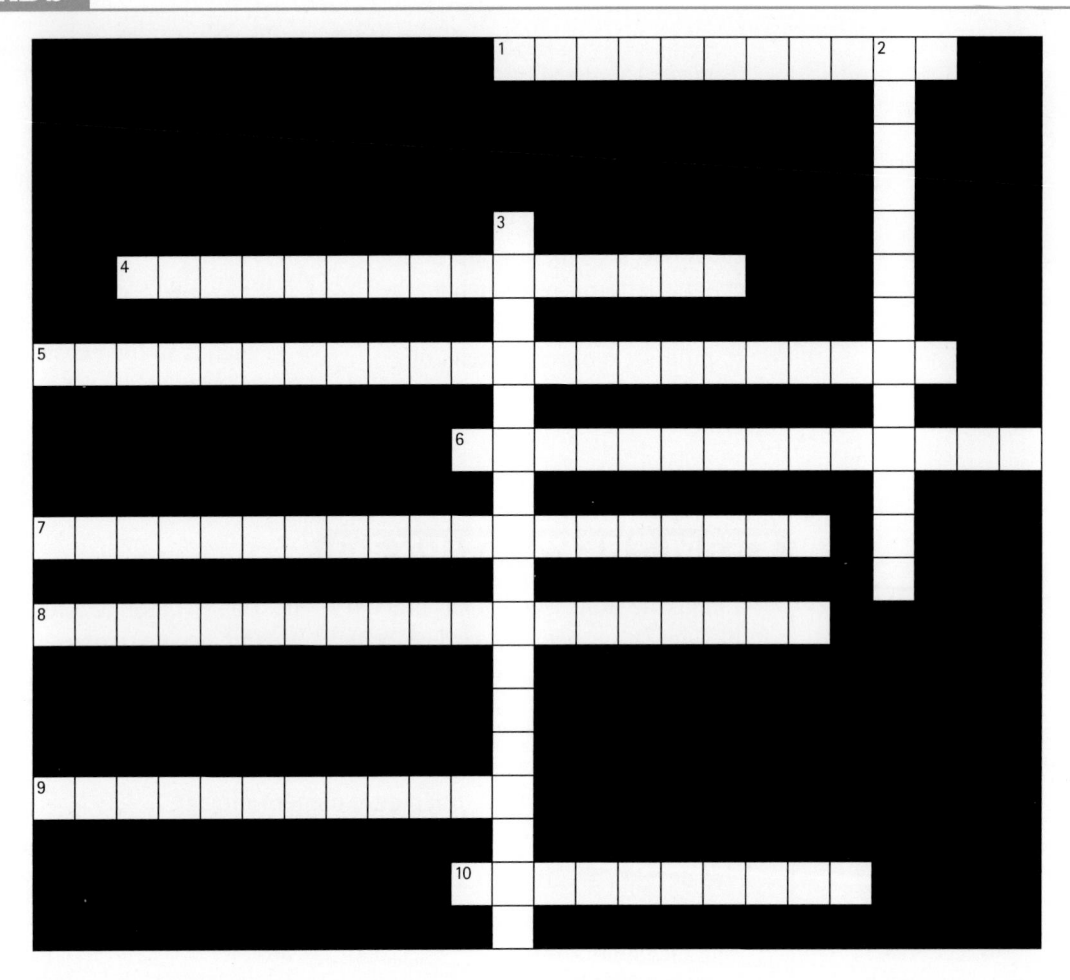

Clues across

1. The financial cost, such as the purchase of a new computer, incurred by the person or firm responsible for the action or decision that caused it (7, 4)
4. A benefit, such as improved health care, resulting from the actions or decisions of a consumer or producer but enjoyed by other people or organizations without having had to pay for it (8, 7)
5. An allocation of resources that yields a total social benefit in excess of its total social cost (8, 3, 2, 9)
6. A financial benefit, such as sales revenue, enjoyed by the person or firm responsible for the action or decision that created it (7, 7)
7. An external benefit enjoyed by people or organizations resulting from the actions of others (8, 11)
8. An external cost imposed on other people and organizations that did not agree to the action that caused it (8, 11)
9. A cost, such as pollution, that is incurred by other people or organizations but not by those responsible for the action or decision that caused it (8, 4)
10. The total cost to society of an activity, including both its private and external costs (6, 4)

Clues down

2. The total benefit to society of an activity, including both its private benefits and external benefits (6, 7)
3. The exhaustion of natural resources through increasing production, consumption and exchange (7, 9)

The allocation of resources: how markets work; market failure

Assessment exercises

Multiple choice

1. The basic economic problem faced by all economies is:
   - A Rising prices
   - B Unemployment
   - C Scarcity of resources
   - D Low economic growth

2. A government decides that an economy should make more use of the market. Which policy might help to achieve this?
   - A A decrease in controls on imported goods
   - B An increase in government ownership of land
   - C An increase in subsidies to industry
   - D The fixing of minimum wage levels for workers

3. A mixed economy is one that has:
   - A Farms and factories
   - B A public and a private sector
   - C Capital and consumer goods
   - D Goods and services

4. In a free market economy the price mechanism:
   - A Helps the government to provide services
   - B Measures the total value of wealth
   - C Makes profits for firms
   - D Determines the allocation of resources

5. During the 1990s the economies of Eastern Europe changed from planned economies to market economic systems. Which of the following best describes the change that took place?
   - A More centralized government planning to allocate resources
   - B Fewer price controls
   - C Increased dependence on the price mechanism to allocate resources
   - D Increased resource unemployment

6. Which of the following is an advantage claimed for the market economic system?
   - A It responds quickly to consumer wants
   - B It provides public goods
   - C Unemployment can rise rapidly
   - D It relies on traditional methods of production

7. The diagram shows a shift in demand for product Z.

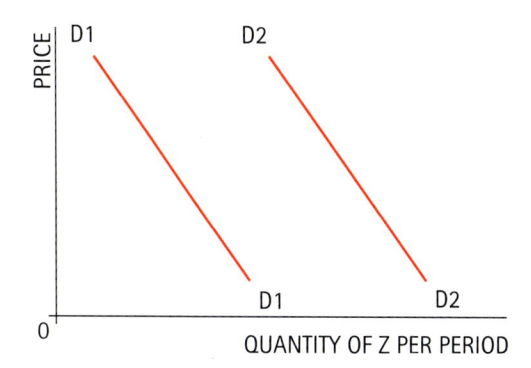

   Which of the following may have caused the shift in demand curve D_1 to D_2?
   - A A fall in incomes
   - B A rise in the price of a substitute
   - C A rise in the price of a complement
   - D A rise in the supply of Z

8. Demand for a product is likely to be price inelastic:
   - A The smaller the number of substitutes
   - B The smaller the number of complements
   - C The higher the price
   - D The greater the fraction of income spent on it

9. The best explanation of the shift in the supply curve from SS to S_1S_1 would be:

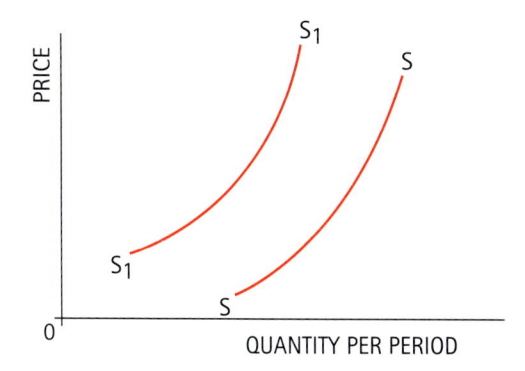

   - A A rise in the price of the product
   - B A fall in the price of raw materials
   - C Technical progress
   - D A rise in wages paid to labour

Assessment 95

Questions 10–12 are based on the following diagram.

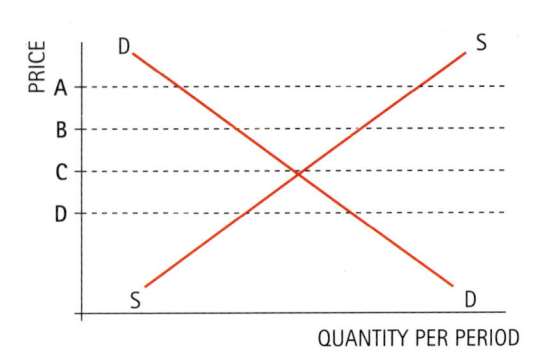

[Diagram: Price-Quantity graph with Demand curve (D) sloping down and Supply curve (S) sloping up, with price levels A, B, C, D marked on the price axis from highest to lowest, where C is approximately at equilibrium.]

At which price will there be:

10 A market equilibrium?

11 The greatest excess demand?

12 The greatest excess supply?

13 If a rise in price from $1 to $1.10 caused supply to extend by 27%, PES would equal:

   A   17
   B   1.7
   C   2.7
   D   3.7

14 Which of the following pairs of commodities is an example of goods in complementary demand?

   A   Beef and lamb
   B   Coffee and tea
   C   Butter and margarine
   D   Quilts and quilt covers

15 Other things unchanged, an increase in demand for a product will cause:

   A   Market price to rise and supply to contract.
   B   Market price to fall and supply to extend.
   C   An increase in supply as market price rises.
   D   An increase in market price and an extension of supply.

Questions 16 and 17 are based on the following terms:

   A   A contraction of supply
   B   A contraction of demand
   C   A fall in demand
   D   A fall in supply

Which of the above best describes a situation where:

16 Crop disease leads to a poor harvest of corn?

17 An increase in air fares reduces the number of passenger flights?

18 An external cost is:

   A   A cost created by a firm which it pays for
   B   A cost created by a group of people, or a firm, that others pay for
   C   A cost created by society, that private firms pay for
   D   A cost paid for by government

19 Which of the following is likely to be an external cost of building a new airport?

   A   The price paid for the land
   B   The cost of materials
   C   The noise caused by construction
   D   Wages paid to workers

20 A particular use of resources is said to be economic if:

   A   Social benefits are greater than private benefits
   B   Social costs are greater than social benefits
   C   Private costs are less than private benefits
   D   Social costs are less than social benefits

21 If the production of a good or service results in high external benefits, but low private benefits, then:

   A   Private firms will produce more than society wants
   B   Private firms will produce just enough to satisfy the wants of society
   C   Private firms will produce less than society wants
   D   Private firms will use resources to produce something else

96   The allocation of resources: how markets work; market failure

22 Which of the following represents an external benefit?

  A A firm that obtains a discount for buying materials in bulk
  B A historic building blackened by traffic pollution
  C An increase in a firm's revenue resulting from the success of its advertising
  D A bigger supply of honey than usual for a bee-keeper thanks to his neighbour's garden flower display

23 A large supermarket applied to build on protected woodland. Despite the loss of the woodland and its recreational value, local government allowed the building because many jobs would be created and much needed income would be brought to the local community.

Which economic ideas are NOT involved in the above statement?

  A Public sector and external costs
  B Free market and the conservation of resources
  C Opportunity cost and economic growth
  D Private enterprise and external benefits

24 Why is knowledge of price elasticity of demand useful?

  A To monitor the rate of price inflation
  B To calculate changes in disposable incomes
  C To estimate the effects of changes in production costs
  D To forecast the impact on revenues of different pricing strategies

25 Many cities have introduced additional charges for drivers using their vehicles in the city during peak traffic periods. What is a possible external benefit of this policy?

  A Increased traffic on other roads
  B Increased government revenues
  C Reduced air pollution
  D Reduced economic activity

Structured questions

1 Alcohol and government policy

In the UK, the National Health Service often has to deal with the consequences of drinking alcohol. It is said that there is less trouble in other countries which have more relaxed licensing laws. In the UK, accidents caused by drinking alcohol result in 150,000 hospital admissions every year. Time taken dealing with these admissions prevents other treatment. There are about 22,000 deaths linked to alcohol-related illnesses every year.

There are also other consequences. Very many working days are lost each year because of alcohol abuse which, it is estimated, cost employers £6.4 million in lost production. There is also the cost of policing the city centres particularly at night and at weekends, when excessive drinking causes riotous behaviour. It is argued that while police are controlling this behaviour it leaves property more vulnerable to burglary. Property owners, as a result, may have to pay extra insurance premiums and protect their property by paying for burglar alarms to be fitted. Then there are legal costs. If people are prosecuted for drink-related offences it involves court costs, lawyers' costs and costs for the witnesses to attend court. There are also the costs of establishing centres that treat people who drink excessively and the costs of social workers who care for those who are victims of drink-related incidents.

One of the difficulties of trying to calculate the cost of alcohol use is how to estimate figures such as those above. How do we measure the cost of police time? How do we measure the costs of an emotional upset when someone is injured by a drink-related driving accident? How do we measure the effect of violence in the home caused by excessive drinking?

Yet there are benefits from alcohol. People gain pleasure from drinking: it is a social activity. Some alcohol is said to give health benefits. The government places a tax on alcohol and gains a large amount of revenue as a result. Many people are employed in the manufacture and distribution of drinks. Others are employed in clubs and bars that serve alcohol.

a (i) Define opportunity cost. [2]

    (ii) Identify and explain **one** example of opportunity cost from the above extract. [2]

b You are asked to investigate the economic arguments for and against a ban on the sale and consumption of alcohol. Discuss how helpful you would find the above extract and what further information you would seek. [10]

c The government decides not to introduce a ban on alcohol. Instead it considers either raising the existing indirect tax on alcohol or banning the advertising of alcohol. Discuss which of these two approaches you would favour. [9]

Cambridge IGCSE Economics 0455/06 Q1 October/November 2006

2 Fishing in the UK

Cod is a fish which is very popular as a food in the UK. By 2002, only 7% of the 240,000 tonnes bought each year was caught in the seas around the UK. This was because during the 1960s and 1970s intense fishing almost wiped out the stocks of cod in those seas. By 2002 the UK had to rely on imports of cod from Iceland, Norway and Russia.

To overcome the need to import so much fish it was proposed in 2002 to breed cod on fish 'farms'. A Norwegian-owned company began to develop a farm by constructing cages. Local people complained because they said the cages would destroy an area of natural beauty. The farm was intended to employ 25 people. The plan was for the farms to be developed slowly so that eventually they would be able to supply 24,000 tonnes of cod a year and employ 1,600 people in an area where the rate of unemployment was high. The UK government saw this as an important move towards maintaining independence in the supply of the fish.

Those who wanted to develop the farms saw them as a way to increase profitability in the fishing industry. Previously most of the farming of fish had been concentrated on salmon. Salmon is another fish which is popular in the UK. The farming increased output and, as a result, the price of salmon had fallen. This had caused profits to decrease.

The developers of the cod farms also said that the farms would allow the stocks of cod in the oceans to recover and that, therefore, the farms would be a benefit to fishermen. The fishermen did not agree. They said that all farmed fish need to be fed and the food would have to be found in the fishing grounds that supplied other fish. This would cause problems because the food is limited. A spokesperson said 'There is no point in talking about a recovery in the fishing industry if there is not enough food for the fish to eat.'

a Calculate the amount of fish bought in 2002 that was caught in the seas around the UK.

Show how you calculated the figure. [2]

b What proportion of the UK total demand for cod would be produced by the fish farms if they produced all that was planned? [1]

c Explain **two** advantages of establishing the fish farms. [4]

d Explain with the help of a demand and supply diagram what has happened in the market for **salmon** in the UK. [4]

e Explain what is meant by opportunity cost and identify an example of opportunity cost from the article. [4]

f Discuss whether the cod farms would necessarily increase the profitability of the fishing industry as a whole. [9]

Cambridge IGCSE Economics 0455/06 Q1 May/June 2004

3 A company produces cigarettes which it believes have a low price elasticity of demand.

    a Explain what is meant by price elasticity of demand. [4]

    b How might knowledge of price elasticity be of use to a producer? [6]

    c Some countries have now prohibited smoking in public areas in buildings. Use the concepts of private and social costs and benefits to explain this policy. [6]

    d Discuss what effect the policy of prohibiting smoking in public areas might have on the manufacturers of cigarettes. [4]

Cambridge IGCSE Economics 0455/02 Q2 May/June 2009
Cambridge O Level Economics 2281/02 Q2 May/June 2009

4 Many governments have increased their spending on police and armed forces but there is an opportunity cost of this policy.

    a Explain the term opportunity cost and discuss why an increase in spending on police and armed forces may result in an opportunity cost. [4]

    b Discuss whether such government spending could be a result of market failure. [6]

    c Sometimes governments do not provide goods and services but they still influence the activities of private firms. Analyse how they might do this. [10]

Cambridge IGCSE Economics 0455/02 Q5 May/June 2009
Cambridge O Level Economics 2281/02 Q5 May/June 2009

5 In Ghana local farmers manage small plots of land for subsistence farming. However, some have benefited by selling pineapples at an agreed, fixed price to an exporter. The exporter provides finance, training, fertilizers and machinery and even building materials for the farmers' homes.

    a Identify and explain which factors of production are mentioned above. [4]

    b In 2005, European supermarkets changed their demand to a new, sweeter pineapple not grown in Ghana. Use demand and supply diagrams to explain what happened in the market for both types of pineapple. [6]

    c Explain why farmers might benefit from an agreed, fixed price. [3]

    d The Ghanaian Government has launched an Action Plan to provide farmers with more finance, better transport and storage facilities to help them compete. Discuss whether governments should always subsidize the production of goods and services. [7]

Cambridge IGCSE Economics 0455/04 Q3 May/June 2008
Cambridge O Level Economics 2281/02 Q3 May/June 2008

3 The individual as producer, consumer and borrower

3.1	Money and finance
3.2	Occupations and earnings
3.3	The role of trade unions
3.4	Spending, saving and borrowing
Assessment	Multiple choice
	Structured questions

Individuals are both owners of factors of production and consumers of goods and services. They exchange their labour for money to buy the goods and services they need and want. Money is a good that is generally accepted in exchange for other goods and services.

The banking system in any modern economy ensures that there is enough money in circulation to finance production, consumption and exchange. At the heart of any banking system in most economies is a central bank. The central bank in an economy will maintain the supply of money and stability of the national currency.

Firms demand labour and other productive factors to use in the production of goods and services and will need money to pay for these resources. Companies can raise money from borrowing or by selling shares through a stock exchange.

Many people supply their labour to firms in return for wages. The wage rate for an occupation is determined by its labour market conditions. The equilibrium wage rate tends to rise if the demand for labour increases or the supply of labour falls. Workers with particular occupational skills that are in short supply relative to the demand for them will often command a high wage rate compared to other groups of workers.

Most people will specialize in the same occupation for all or much of their working lives. Differences in wages and non-wage factors such as hours of work, holiday entitlements, the provision of training and job security, attract people to different occupations and industries. Changes in the net advantages of different jobs can therefore cause changes in the supply of labour.

Labour employed in different private and public sector organizations may organize trade or labour unions to seek improvements to wages and working conditions. Negotiation between trade union representatives and employers is known as collective bargaining. However, during negotiations, trade unions may undertake industrial action that disrupts productive activities.

Governments will often intervene in labour markets to restrict the bargaining strength of some powerful trade unions, to protect the rights and responsibilities of employees and their employers, to influence total employment in their economies and sometimes to set minimum wages for the lowest paid workers.

People with low incomes tend to spend all or most of their income on satisfying just their basic needs for food and shelter. Some may also get into debt by borrowing money so they can spend more on goods and services to satisfy more of their needs and wants. Unless they are confident that their incomes or wealth will rise in future to cover loan and interest repayments then borrowing might not be a wise decision. If interest rates rise faster than their incomes they may run into financial difficulty. High interest rates may discourage borrowing but encourage greater saving in an economy.

Unit 3.1   Money and finance

I hate to hurry you along Mr Smythe, but the first payment is nearly due.

AIMS

By the end of this unit you should be able to:

▶ describe the **functions of money** and the need for **exchange**

- understand why a generally accepted **medium of exchange** is needed in a modern economy
- list the main functions a **money** must perform
- critically assess the suitability of different commodities for use as money
- describe the main forms of money in existence today

▶ describe the role of **central banks**, **stock exchanges** and **commercial banks**

- understand the importance of a well-functioning **banking system** in a modern economy
- distinguish between different types of **bank** and the financial services they provide
- evaluate the role of a central bank in an economy in supervising the banking system and managing the government's **monetary policy**
- describe how some firms are able to raise **share capital** to finance their activities through a stock exchange.

The individual as producer, consumer and borrower

SECTION 1

The need for specialization and exchange

Why do we need money?

Just imagine how different life would be today if there was no money. How could we buy all the different goods and services we need or want? How would people be paid for the work they do?

For example, when you have finished your studies and go out to work would you want to be paid in oranges or tea for your labour? Or perhaps you'd prefer to start your own business in the future. If so, would you be happy to exchange the good or service of your firm with consumers in return for olives or shoes or meat?

Your answer to both these questions will probably be no, but many years ago before the widespread use of money you would have had no choice. You would either have had to accept other goods or services as payment or be **self-sufficient** by producing everything you needed or wanted for yourself.

Many of our ancestors had to be self-sufficient. All individuals or small communities would produce all the things they needed or wanted for themselves, for example by growing and hunting their own food supplies, building their own shelters, weaving materials to produce clothes from cotton and wool, making cooking pots from clay and so on.

However, it is difficult to produce everything you need or want for yourself. People have different skills. Long ago some people were better at making spears and pottery while others were more skilled at hunting and fishing. Similarly, some villages were located on good farmland while others were in woodland areas able to supply timber for building materials and spear rods. People and also entire communities therefore began to specialize in those productive activities they were best able to do.

ACTIVITY 3.1

How specialization began

The cartoon tells a simple story of how a caveman named Og discovered the benefits of **specialization** over self-sufficiency by growing and exchanging tomatoes for other products.

Write a story to go with the pictures and include as many advantages and disadvantages of self-sufficiency and specialization as you can think of.

THE TALE OF OG... The First Economic Caveman!

1. Once upon a time
2. On the very next day
3. And then...
4. When suddenly he thought...
5. And so...
6. And they all lived happily ever after.

Money and finance

Specialization was the first step towards a wealthier society. A community that practised specialization was able to produce more than enough food, clothes, pots and other things that it needed. The increased production achieved by specialization is the result of the **division of labour**, whereby each worker specializes in doing a particular task rather than being a 'Jack of all trades'. ➤ 3.2

However, with specialization people need to exchange or trade. If people specialized in producing one particular good or service, like Og and his tomatoes, then they must swap any they have left over for goods or services produced by others in order to obtain a variety of goods and services to satisfy their wants.

Overcoming the problems of barter

Exchanging one good or service for another is called **barter** but it has many problems. For example, if a farmer had some spare corn and needed an axe he or she would travel to a local market to find someone who was willing and able to exchange an axe for the corn. But how much corn would need to be exchanged for an axe? And what if the axe maker wanted apples in return rather than corn? Perhaps the farmer could travel to other markets to find an axe maker who wanted corn in exchange, but the farmer would have to be quick because eventually the corn would turn bad and rot.

ACTIVITY 3.2

Imagine there is no money and we have to rely on swapping goods with each other. In groups of three, each member of the group acts out the role of either a ruler-maker, a pencil-maker or an eraser-maker.

ye olde swap shop

1 Firstly, the pencil-maker wishes to exchange some pencils for some rulers. Try to arrange a swap on the best possible terms for yourself. What problems do you encounter?

2 Now the eraser-maker wants to exchange erasers for some pencils. But the pencil-maker is not interested in obtaining erasers. Your only hope is to involve the ruler-maker in the swap.

3 Imagine now that the goods being traded are eggs, milk and cheese. What problems would arise if you could not find anyone to swap your goods with? (Imagine fridges have not been invented yet!)

You may have discovered from the activity that **bartering** is a very inconvenient way to conduct economic activity. In fact three main problems arise.

1 Fixing a rate of exchange

Look at the diagrams on the next page. How many pencils are worth one ruler? How many pencils are worth one apple? How many oranges are equivalent in value to one ruler? Indeed, how many rulers could Farmer Giles get for a cow? And so it goes on.

In a barter system the value of each and every good must be expressed in terms of every other good.

2 Finding someone to swap with

Miss Swap may want some apples from Mr Trade and in return may be prepared to offer him some cheese. If by chance Mr Trade would like some cheese they can barter. But if Mr Trade does not like cheese no deal can take place. In this case an economist would say no **double coincidence of wants** exists. In other words, before two people can barter they must both want the good that the other person has.

3 Trying to save

A final problem is how to save under a barter system. A carpenter could store tables and chairs but would need a large room, but imagine trying to save some meat or cheese for a long period of time without the help of a refrigerator.

Barter is therefore a very inefficient method of exchange. No wonder many years ago people had to produce most of the basic goods and services they needed for themselves and go without many others. Clearly it would be much easier if there was a single commodity or good that everyone was willing to accept in exchange for their labour and all other goods and services. This commodity is called **money** and it overcomes the problems of barter.

SECTION 2

The functions of money

Having money enables people, communities and firms in modern economies to specialize in the production of those goods or services they are best suited to, and then to use the money they earn to buy all the other goods and services they may need or want from other producers. Without money, specialization and exchange will be difficult and therefore far fewer goods and services will be produced and far fewer wants will be satisfied.

Money and finance 105

Money overcomes the problems of barter by performing the following functions.

Money is a medium of exchange

Because money is a good that is generally acceptable in exchange for all other goods we do not have to search for a person who is willing to barter. That is, money overcomes the problem of needing a double coincidence of wants. Now, Miss Swap can sell her cheese to anyone who is prepared to buy it with money. In turn Miss Swap can use this money to buy the apples she wants from Mr Trade, or anyone who is willing to sell her some apples. Therefore, trade is brought about by two transactions with money being used in each.

Money is a measure of value

Just as a thermometer measures temperature and a ruler measures length, so money measures value. Using money helps those producers and consumers engaged in trade to avoid the problems of fixing prices of goods and services in terms of all other goods and services.

Instead of arguing and attempting to remember how many pencils you can get for one ruler, all goods have a price expressed in terms of one single product called money. That is, money is a unit of account used to measure and compare the value of different goods and services, and used to express their prices.

Remember that the measure of value function means the same as the unit of account function.

Money is a store of value

One of the problems with barter is that many goods are difficult to save either because they take up too much space or they lose their value over time because they perish.

Money is usually a good store of value. Unless prices are rising rapidly, money tends to hold its value over time. In other words, it allows people to save in order to make purchases at a later date.

Some people save by storing valuable antiques and works of art, things that we do not regard as money but which can be exchanged for money in the future. People may save in this way because as the prices of goods rise over time, the purchasing power of money, or what it will buy, is reduced. When prices rise rapidly due to **inflation**, money will fail to be such a good store of value. ➤ **6.1**

Money is a means of deferred payment

When a person buys goods on credit the consumer has the use of the goods but does not have to pay for them immediately. The consumer can pay some time after he or she receives the goods. In the case of hire purchase, payment is made by instalments spread over a number of months or years.

Credit in a barter system would be very confusing and open to cheating. For example, imagine a person who trades a box of nails for a dozen apples to be paid one month later. Would the apples be fresh? Would they be large or small apples? Using money to pay later overcomes these problems and therefore encourages people to engage in trade, reducing the worry of giving credit. ➤ **3.4**

ACTIVITY 3.3

Funny money

How fake money saved Brazil

IN 1994 BRAZIL replaced its currency, the Cruzeiro, with a new money called the Real. This was part of an economic stablization plan to designed to rid the economy of crippling hyperinflation, restore confidence in the economy and reduce poverty. For many decades Brazil had one of the most unequal income distributions in the world and the lack of economic growth coupled with rampant price inflation in prices was causing widespread hardship.

During the 1980s and early 1990s, Brazil's runaway inflation rate peaked at an annual rate of 2,439 per cent, or just under 92 per cent per month. This meant products such as eggs that cost just $1 at the start of a year, would cost almost $2 just one month later and a staggering $2,439 by the end of the year. Shops would have to raise their prices almost every hour of every day just to keep up. In turn consumers would need to go to the shops with more and more cash each day simply to buy the same amount of products they did the previous day. Many would try to run ahead of shopkeepers just to avoid the latest mark-ups in prices. More and more people were forced into poverty as a result. Eventually confidence was lost in the currency, in the economy as place to invest and do business, and in the government's ability to control inflation.

So in 1992 the new finance minister invited Edmar Bacha, an economist, to advise the Brazilian government. Bacha started by telling it to slow down the rate at which it was creating new money. Without growth in Brazil's output of goods and services to match, the additional money simply forced up prices.

Bacha also knew it was vital to restore people's confidence in the currency. The Cruzeiro had become worthless. Nobody held on to it or wanted it because in fell in value every minute of every day as prices continued to soar. People would trade in US dollars or other stable currencies. A new currency was therefore needed that people could trust to hold its value. Bacha therefore advised playing a trick on people by introducing a fake money called the URV or Unit of Real Value. The URV didn't actually exist but every product would be priced in URVs. Similarly all wages and taxes were expressed in URVs.

Prices, wages and all other monetary values listed in URVs were kept stable over time. The only thing that changed was the exchange rate between Cruzeiros and URVs. So, for example, eggs now priced at say 100 URVs one month would be the same price the next month and the month after that and so on, but 100 URVs might be worth 100 Cruzeiros one month and 200 the next.

Bacha argued that eventually people would get used to prices in URVs being stable and stop expecting prices to rise so rapidly. In turn they would become used to paying for goods and services in URVs and stop thinking about the Cruzeiro and how much it was worth. This was despite the URV or what had become known as the 'real' not being a real currency. However, once this had happened it did in fact real. New notes and coins were printed and the Real became the new currency of Brazil in 1994.

And the magic trick worked! By 1996 the monthly inflation rate had fallen to less than 1 per cent from over 45 per cent in 1994. Economic activity had increased strongly during the second half of 1994 and thereafter, led by a boom in domestic demand that was fuelled by lower inflation and higher real wages including for many of the country's poorest workers. Since then Brazil has emerged as a rapidly developing economy and major exporter, and some 20 million people have been lifted out of poverty.

1. Why did the Brazilian government replace the national currency, the cruzeiro, with a new currency called the Real as a measure of value in 1994?

2. Which of the following functions of money was the cruzeiro failing to perform before it was replaced by the Real?
   a   a medium of exchange
   b   a measure of value
   c   a store of value? Give reasons for your answer.

Money and finance

SECTION 3

What makes a good money?

A vast range of objects have been used as a medium of exchange at one time or another in the past in different countries. These have ranged from beads used by the American Indians to large stone discs used by the inhabitants of Yap, a small island in the Pacific Ocean.

Money, as we know it today, has been the product of a long period of development. Man has slowly discovered, by a process of trial and error, that some objects fulfill the functions of money better than others.

dog's teeth — Stone Money (Yap) — Manillas (Africa) — knife money (China)

ACTIVITY 3.4

What is a 'good' money?

In groups discuss which of the items shown below would make a good money. Appoint a spokesperson for your group to record your views and to present your arguments to the class.

Cigarettes, Gold, Mountains, Cheese

Your discussion may have led you to the conclusion that characteristics such as the following are important for a good money to possess.

1 Acceptability

Anything can be used as money as long as it is generally acceptable. This is why a worthless piece of paper can be used as money, for example, a 10 dollar or a 50 euro note. It is only worth this amount in spending power because everyone accepts it as such. Thus our present money is a **token money** – as a piece of paper or metal coin it is worth much less than the face value printed upon it.

2 Durability

Any good used as money must be hard-wearing. Money would be useless if it just melted away in your pocket. Coins and notes must be strong and durable so that they may act as a store of value.

3 Portability

Money should be easy to carry around. A house would clearly be far too heavy to move. A cow would be reluctant to go shopping with you, and even more reluctant if you tried to squeeze it into your wallet or purse. Paper notes are lightweight and can be folded into a wallet or purse, while a handful of small metal coins can be carried easily in your pockets.

4 Divisibility

If cars were used as money a problem would arise if you tried to buy something priced at half your car. Sawing the vehicle into half would reduce its value. One whole working car is worth much more than two halves. Therefore it must be possible to divide money of a large value into smaller values to make small purchases or to give change, without it losing value. This is why we have notes and coins with different face values to buy goods and services with different prices and to give change.

5 Scarcity

A good money must be limited in supply or scarce if people and firms are to value it. For example, small stones or pebbles would not be a good money because people could simply pick up as many as they liked from the ground whenever they wanted to. A shopkeeper would not exchange her goods for pebbles that were freely available. Only if money is scarce will people value it as a good that can be used in exchange.

So why is money so important?

In Section 1 we learnt how people living in a self-sufficient society began to specialize in the jobs they were most able to do. Specialization was the first step towards a wealthier society and people in a community that practised specialization were for the first time able to produce more than enough food, clothes, pots and other things that they needed. They had some left over – a surplus.

If people specialize they must trade. A man concentrating on making pins could not satisfy his need for food by eating pins or his need for clothes by wearing pins. Therefore trade is a necessity for individuals to obtain those things they cannot make on their own.

But in a barter system trade is difficult. There is no guarantee that an expert pin-maker will be able to find people willing to swap their goods for his or her pins at a fair rate of exchange. The result is the pin-maker and others will be unable to specialize to their full potential. They would have to spend their time and effort producing a range of goods and services in order to increase their chances of trading successfully for the things they needed.

This would mean that much less would be produced by whole economies than if they had specialized in the production of those goods and services they were best able to produce.

Money therefore encourages specialization by making trade easier. This enables an economy to increase its national output and income and allows people to enjoy a much higher standard of living. In turn, the more an economy specializes the more money it needs to finance an increasing amount of production and trade. ▶ 6.3

Money is needed by consumers, firms and governments to make payments to hire labour and buy other resources, and goods and services. The banking system can provide this money and make it easier to make payments. Therefore, as the output of an economy grows and more trade takes place, so the banking system must develop and create more money.

SECTION 4

The history of money

There have been five main stages in the development of money, with each stage being the result of mankind's attempt to find objects that display the characteristics of a good money.

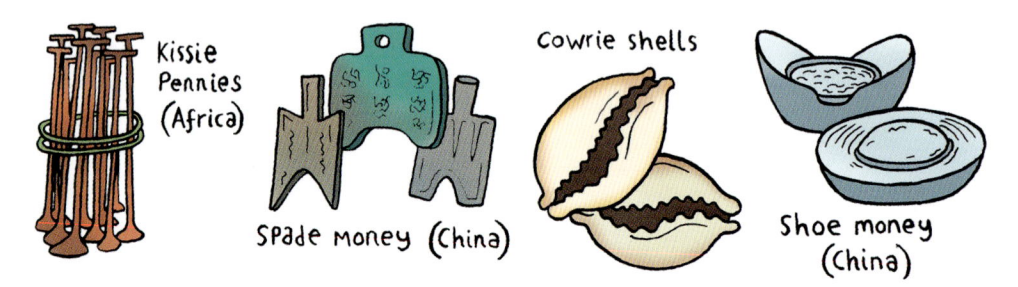

Stage 1

The earliest form of money was goods. Knives, beads and shoes among other objects were used as money because many people were willing to accept these in exchange for their produce. However, such commodity money was quickly abandoned because many of the goods did not possess the essential characteristics of a good money: acceptability, divisibility, portability, durability, scarcity.

Stage 2

Precious metals, such as gold and silver, have always been scarce enough to make them a possible money. However, trading with metals involved carrying around a weighing scale and tools to cut the metals.

Stage 3

The problem of portability that cursed metals led to the natural development of coinage. Precious metals in predetermined weights were often stamped with the face of the king or queen, and with another stamp to show their value.

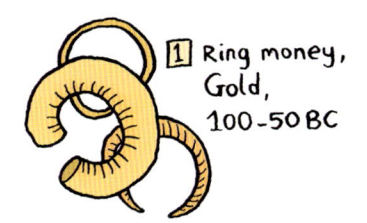

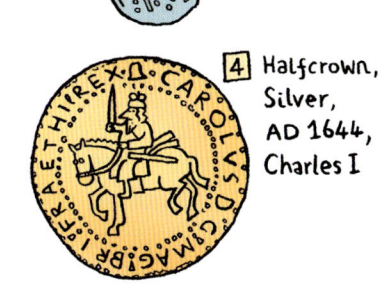

1. Ring money, Gold, 100-50 BC
2. Sceat, Silver AD 734-766, Anglo-Saxon
3. Silver AD 802-839, King Eegerht, Anglo-Saxon
4. Halfcrown, Silver, AD 1644, Charles I

▲ Early coins of the UK

But one problem remained. Throughout history the temptation to 'clip' coins, trimming a fine filing of the precious metal from the edges, has been greater than the fear of being caught.

The invention of the ribbed edge on coins overcame the problem of 'clipping'. Another problem with early precious coins was that the rulers of countries often debased them. Coins would be called in for re-minting on a special occasion. The rulers would then mix cheap metals with gold or silver, producing perhaps six coins for every four received, cleverly keeping two for themselves. The result of this today is that the metal content of coins is virtually worthless, yet people still accept such coins in exchange for goods because they know they are generally acceptable.

Stage 4

The first paper money was issued by early goldsmiths who accepted deposits of precious metals for keeping in their safes. In return they issued a paper receipt to the owner. It was quickly realized that these paper claims to gold were far easier to exchange for goods than spending time and effort withdrawing the gold only for it to be given to someone who would then re-deposit it with a goldsmith for safe keeping.

Stage 5

Goldsmiths' receipts for deposits of precious metals were to become the first paper money, and goldsmiths the first banks. In most countries today only the central bank has the right to issue notes and coins, but this money can no longer be converted into gold. Below is an example of an early paper note issued by the Bank of England in the UK.

Money and finance

SECTION 5

What is money?

We now know that money is a generally acceptable medium of exchange. However, we also know that to be money a commodity must also act as store of value. Given this, our savings in banks and other financial institutions can be classified as money because one day we may withdraw these deposits so that they may be exchanged for the goods and services we want.

Notes and coins circulating in an economy and deposits with banks and other financial institutions make up the **money supply**.

ACTIVITY 3.5

Mrs Mint's money

Mrs Mint is tempted by a luxury cruise advertised in the local travel agency. The only problem is the cost of $3,000. At home she tries to figure out just how much money she has.

Emptying the contents of her purse she finds that she has $50 in notes and coins. The jar on her sideboard contains $100 in crisp notes. But not nearly enough for that cruise!

Remembering that she has a savings account at the bank which allows her to withdraw any cash immediately, Mrs Mint calculates that another $300 can be added to her list. But still not enough to pay for that cruise!

After waiting seven days Mrs Mint can withdraw her savings from another account she also keeps at the bank. This account contains $400. It appears that she will have to withdraw her long-term savings. In 90 days she can obtain $600 from a government savings scheme. In 120 days $700 can be withdrawn from a credit union that she saves with each month. Mrs Mint also has $800 tied up for two years in a government bond. Finally, she considers selling some of the jewellery she has kept for several years to enable her to sail away on the luxury cruise liner for the holiday of a lifetime.

In the above passage Mrs Mint has a variety of ways by which she can raise the necessary money to pay for the luxury cruise.

1 If money is purely a medium of exchange, list those items included in the passage that you consider would be money and give reasons for your choice.

2 If instead we focus upon money being a store of value, which other commodities would you also class as money, giving reasons for your choice?

It is not an easy task to decide exactly what is money. **Cash** or notes and coins with different face values are generally accepted and recognized as money in all economies. However, cash can lose its value over time as prices rise.

In contrast, many **financial assets** can provide a good store of value and may therefore be a good form of money, especially if they can be converted easily and quickly into cash in order to make payments. If they can they are **liquid assets** and may be thought of as **near money**.

For example, personal savings can be withdrawn quickly from an instant access savings account held at a bank. However, savings tied up in a bond for two years will not become a medium of exchange until the bond has matured at the end of the two-year period. So although different savings accounts and other **financial assets** can perform all of the functions of money, some do so better than others and at different times.

Jewellery, valuable antiques and other **physical assets** may also provide a good store of value but are not generally acceptable in exchange for other goods and may be difficult to sell quickly to raise cash. That is, they are not near money. Physical assets may also go down in value over time if they become less collectable or damaged.

In summary therefore, some assets are nearer money than others for three main reasons.

1. Some assets fulfill the functions of money better than others. For example, cash is a good medium of exchange, but antiques are not.

2. Some assets can be converted to cash more quickly than others. For example, financial assets held in a bank deposit account can usually be withdrawn instantly or within a few days, whereas assets in some other saving schemes cannot be converted into cash for many months or longer.

3. Some assets retain their value on conversion to cash better than others. For example, those in savings accounts hold their value because banks reward people who save with them with periodic payments or interest, whereas cars lose their value over time.

Bank deposits held at banks and other financial institutions are most easily converted into cash, usually for little or no cost. Bank deposits have therefore become the most important form of money in most modern economies. For example, look at the table below for the US economy at the end of 2010. Banks are able to create deposit money by constantly re-lending any cash that returns to them in the form of bank deposits.

▼ Two ways of creating money are printing notes and coins, and bank loans

▼ The supply of money in the USA, 31 December 2010

	Amount ($ billion)	Percentage share of total
Notes and coins	917.6	8.6
Bank deposits	9,731.1	91.4
Total	10,648.7	100.00

Source: US Federal Reserve, 20 January 2011

The national income of an economy is not the same as its supply of money. This is because notes and coins can be exchanged many times each year. For example, imagine you have just received one dollar in return for some work. You use the dollar to buy a magazine. The shopkeeper then uses the dollar to buy some petrol. Already this one dollar has been used three times and created $3 of income.

The number of times notes and coins are exchanged, or circulate in an economy over a given period of time, is called the **velocity of circulation** of money. This can vary over time but in the US economy was around 16 during December 2010. That is, every $1 of currency exchanged hands in payment for goods and services on average 16 times over that month and therefore created $16 of income in the US economy.

Money and finance

SECTION 6

The money market

In a modern economy people, firms and government need somewhere they can keep their money safely and need easy ways to make payments to others. They may also want to borrow money, make investments and exchange the money used in their country for the currency used in another so they can make payments overseas. Business organizations that specialize in providing these services are called **financial institutions**. Without financial institutions, specialized production and trade on the scale enjoyed today would not be possible, costs of production would be much higher, economies would be less developed and economic growth would be much slower. ▶ **6.3**

What is the market for money?

The **money market** is really no different from any other market. It is made up of all those people and organizations that want money, and all the people and organizations willing and able to supply money, namely a banking system that creates deposit money, and a central bank that issues notes and coins.

What is a bank?

The main types of financial institutions in the market for money are **banks**. They are just like any other business except the product they supply is money, in the form of loans and other financial products.

A bank is a **financial intermediary** because it brings together customers who want to save money and customers who want to borrow it.

▶ Banks are financial intermediaries between customers who want to deposit money and customers who want to borrow money

Most but not all banks are large, profit-making companies. Banks are among some of the world's largest corporations in terms of their revenue, profit or number of employees. They earn revenue in a number of ways.

114 The individual as producer, consumer and borrower

Charging interest on loans

Banks accept deposits of money and savings from their customers and make loans from this money. They attract deposits and savings by paying customers interest on their money or a share of banking profits.

A bank will not keep all their customers' deposits and savings in its vaults. It will lend most of this money to other customers, including individuals and firms, for example to buy cars, overseas holidays, machinery and property. In turn, these people and firms will use the borrowed money to pay others for goods and services. People and firms receiving payments will then deposit or save money they receive, with a bank. In this way, banks create money in an economy in the form of additional bank deposits.

A customer who borrows money from a bank must repay the loan with interest over an agreed period of time. The interest charge is calculated as a percentage of the amount of a loan. So, for example, a customer who is loaned $1,000 repayable over one year in 12 monthly instalments and is charged interest at 5% of the loan value will repay the bank $1,050 in total.

The percentage of interest charged on a loan, or **interest rate**, represents the cost of borrowing money. Interest rates can vary over time and by different types of loan and customer. For example, a large loan over 10 years to a new, small business may be charged a higher rate of interest than a smaller loan to be repaid over 2 years to a person in regular, paid employment. This is because banks may consider there to be a greater risk of non-repayment of loans made to small businesses. Many small businesses fail and may be unable to repay their debts.

Making loans is inherently risky, so the greater the risk the higher the interest rate a bank will charge. Also, over time, price inflation may rise and reduce the value of the loan in terms of what the money will be able to buy after it has been repaid. Interest charges will help to compensate a bank for any reduction in value of the money it has tied up in loans due to rising price inflation.

As long as loans are repaid and interest charges on loans exceed interest payments on savings, a bank will make a profit from making loans.

Charging fees for the provision of other financial services

For example, a bank may charge its customers fees for the following services:

- withdrawals from automated cash machines
- exchanging and transferring foreign currencies
- buying and selling shares in public limited companies
- providing life, property and travel insurance
- issuing debit and credit cards
- storing valuables
- organizing customer payments in the form of cheques or electronic transfers to the bank accounts of other people, businesses or government authorities
- telephone and Internet banking services.

Making investments

A bank can use money deposited by its customers to invest in the shares of other public limited companies. If the shares it holds increase in value the bank will make a gain from selling them. It will also receive a share of any profits made by these other companies. ➤ **4.1**

▼ The 10 biggest banks in the world by market value

Banking group	Profit 2010 US$ billion	Market value US$ billion
Industrial and Commercial Bank of China	16.3	210.3
China Construction Bank	15.6	192.6
HSBC	6.0	171.8
JP Morgan Chase	11.7	143.7
Bank of China	11.9	127.1
Bank of America	6.3	127.0
Wells Fargo	12.3	123.5
Citigroup	-6.1	106.6
BCO Santander	12.8	93.5
Itaú Unibanco	5.8	83.7

ACTIVITY 3.6

Why do we need banks?

Digital Dreams is a small but rapidly expanding company manufacturing digital video equipment. It has recently received a $200,000 loan repayable over 20 years to buy new business premises.

Digital Dreams sells much of its equipment online to customers who use credit and debit cards and so it accepts all these forms of payment. It also accepts cheques from customers.

The company keeps most of its sales revenue in a savings account. The balance is kept in a deposit account to pay wages to employees and other costs, including electricity, gas and local taxes, by direct debit.

If there were no banks:

1 How would Digital Dreams make and receive payments?
2 Where could it store its sales revenue safely?
3 How could it finance its new business premises?
4 What would be the likely impact on the costs of running Digital Dreams?

Types of bank

There are several different types of bank in a modern economy. They all offer very similar services, but each type tends to specialize in particular financial products and groups of consumers.

▼ Maybank is the largest commercial bank in Malaysia with over 380 branches

1 Commercial banks

Commercial banks are often called 'high-street banks' because they have retail branches located in most cities and towns. However, many banks provide telephone and online banking facilities for their customers so there is no need to visit a branch.

Commercial banks were originally set up to provide financial services for small businesses but now they provide services for everyone from private individuals to both large and small businesses. These services will include:

- accepting deposits of money and savings
- helping customers make and receive payments
- making personal and commercial loans
- buying and selling shares for customers
- providing insurance
- operating pension funds
- providing financial and tax planning advice
- exchanging foreign currencies.

Types of account

A **deposit account** is a current account, savings account or another type of bank account which allows money to be deposited and withdrawn by the account holder.

A **current account** or **checking account** is used by the account holder for everyday transactions. Most people will have their weekly or monthly wages or salaries paid directly into their current account. Payments from a current account can be made using cheques (or checks) or via electronic transfers of money to the bank accounts of other people or organisations.

A **savings account** is a safe place to store your savings. Interest will usually be added to your savings by a bank depending on how much you have saved and how often you can make withdrawals. The more you have saved, and the fewer times you are able to make a withdrawal, the better the rate of interest paid to you.

Types of loan

An **overdraft** allows bank customers to overdraw their account by an agreed amount. It provides a convenient short-term loan, for example to pay unexpected bills. Interest is charged.

A **personal loan** is repaid with interest over a fixed period, usually for more than 6 months and up to 10 years.

A **commercial loan** is a loan to a business to pay for operating costs and the purchase of materials and machinery. The loan is repayable with interest over a fixed period of time.

A **mortgage** is a long-term loan, often up to 25 years, used by people or firms to buy property. The loan is secured against the property, meaning that if the loan cannot be repaid the property has to be sold to repay the debt.

Methods of payment

Using **cash**, or notes and coins, is the easiest way of paying for goods and services in person. Many banks allow account holders to withdraw cash from their accounts at any time of the day, from many different locations, using ATMs.

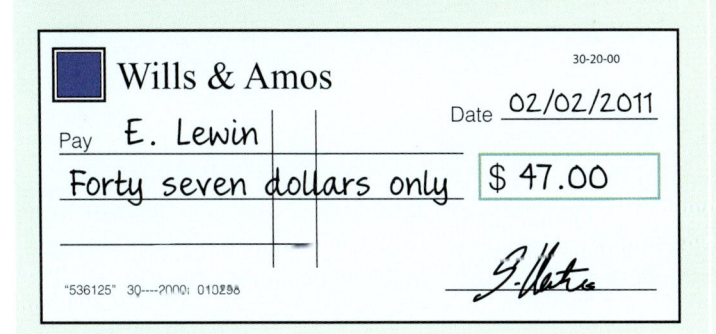

A **direct debit** is an easy way to make regular payments of varying amounts to the same organization from your account, for example to pay monthly bills from an electricity or telephone supplier. Once set up, the supplier will simply provide your bank with its account details, the amount to be paid each month, and your bank will make these payments on your behalf.

A **cheque** (or check) is a written promise to pay cash to, or transfer money into the account of, another person or organization. If you write a cheque it must show your name, your account number, the amount you are promising to pay, and to whom it is to be paid. The person or organization receiving your cheque will pay it into their bank account. Once received the amount written on the cheque will be transferred into their bank account from your bank account.

Money and finance 117

Methods of payment

A **debit card** is an electronic method of making payment to another business organization. It means you do not have to use cash or write a cheque. Once your card is 'swiped' through a payment machine, your bank details and the amount to be withdrawn from your account, and the details of the account to receive your payment, are transmitted electronically to your bank headquarters and the transfer is made instantaneously.

A **credit card** can be used to make payments in much the same way as a debit card except it allows the card holder up to a month or longer to pay for purchases made using the card. A credit card therefore provides a short-term loan. Interest is payable if the amount on the credit card is not repaid in full in the specified period.

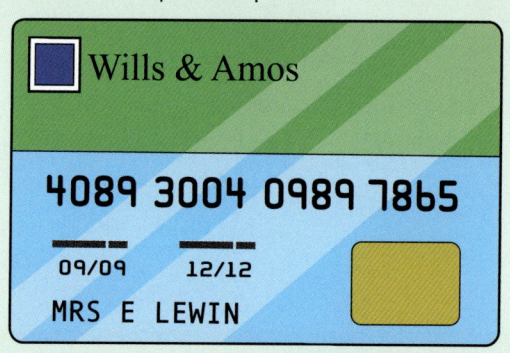

2 Credit unions

A credit union is a cooperative, not-for-profit organization, owned by and for its members. Credit unions were started by people who worked or lived together to provide low-cost loans to members who were on low incomes and unable to borrow money from other banks, for example to help with home repairs, school fees and medical expenses. Credit unions are popular in the USA, and many have now expanded the range of services they offer to include checks, credit cards and loans to small businesses.

3 Mutual societies

These are also known as savings and loans associations or building societies in some countries. They are owned by and run on behalf of their members or customers. Traditionally they specialized in providing mortgages to buy property but now offer many commercial banking services.

3 Investment banks

These banks specialize in helping large business organizations raise finance to fund their operations and expansion, usually through helping them to issue and sell stocks and shares on the stock market. They can also provide advice on company mergers and takeovers. Today, most large commercial banks also provide investment banking services.

Merchant banks are a type of investment bank. They were originally set up to help merchants finance the sale and transportation of goods overseas. Today, they provide finance for large companies through the purchase of their shares rather than providing loans.

4 Islamic banks

Islamic banking is based on principles of Islamic Sharia law, which forbids interest charges and payments. Instead, an Islamic bank can earn a profit from the fees it charges customers for banking services including making loans, and people who deposit their money will earn a share of the bank's profits rather than be paid interest.

Many multinational banking organizations, such as HSBC, also provide Sharia compliant banking services in many countries.

Islamic banks do not charge or pay interest to customers.

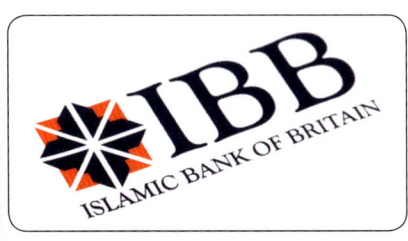

EXAM PREPARATION 3.1

The euro replaced the national currencies of many European countries in the European Union in 2002 to become the sole legal tender in the eurozone.

a List **four** functions euro notes and coins should perform. [4]
b Explain how consumer price inflation in Europe may affect these functions. [6]
c Describe two ways commercial banks could lend euros to individuals and firms. [4]
d Why is a central bank often described as the lender of the last resort to the banking sector in an economy? [6]

The role of a central bank

The central bank is the centre of the banking system in most economies. The main function of a central bank is to maintain the stability of the national currency and the money supply.

In many countries the central bank is owned by the government and run by a public corporation. The oldest central bank in the world is the Bank of Sweden, which was opened in 1668. This was followed in 1694 by the Bank of England in the UK.

A central bank usually performs the following functions:

- **It issues notes and coins for the nation's currency**

The central bank in a country will normally have the exclusive right to print and issue new notes and coins and to replace old worn out ones in that country.

- **It manages payments to and from the government**

The tax and other revenues of the government of a country will be held in an account at the central bank. Government payments, including for contracts to build roads and the wages of government employees, will also be made from the government's account.

- **It manages the national debt**

A central bank can issue and repay public sector debt on behalf of the government. ▶ 5.2

Money and finance

- **It supervises the banking system, regulating the conduct of banks, holding their deposits and transferring funds between them**

A central bank can set rules to make sure banks conduct their business properly and to determine which organizations can become banks. It will also hold the deposits of commercial and other banks, and transfer funds between their accounts to settle the many millions of cheque, debit card and other payments made by their customers to the accounts of other people and firms or even to the government.

- **It is the 'lender of the last resort' to the banking system**

A central bank will lend money to the banking system if one or more banks run into difficulties meeting payments. It does this to prevent banks from running out of money and going bankrupt.

- **It manages the nation's gold and foreign currency reserves**

These reserves are used to make payments overseas and to stabilize the value of the national currency. For example, if the value of the national currency is falling against other world currencies the central bank can use these reserves to buy up the national currency on the global foreign exchange market. As a result of this increase in demand for the national currency, its foreign exchange value will tend to rise. ➤ **8.2**

- **It operates the government's monetary policy**

Governments will use monetary policy in an attempt to influence price inflation, employment and growth in their economies. Monetary policy involves changing the interest rate to influence the level of borrowing, saving and spending by individual and business consumers. For example, price inflation can be caused by people and firms spending too much money on goods and services. Raising the interest rate in the economy will make borrowing money more expensive and reduce demand for loans. It will also make saving more attractive and increase demand for savings. The central bank can increase the interest rate in the economy by raising the interest rate it charges the banking system in the economy when it loans it money. ➤ **5.1**

It is usually the job of the government finance minister to decide what the interest rate should be, but some central banks are able to set interest rates without political interference from government ministers. For example, a government may lower interest rates for political reasons before an election simply to boost its popularity rather than for economic reasons to control inflation. Lowering interest rates too much may increase borrowing and, as a result, increase the problem of inflation in an economy. In contrast, a central bank can decide what the interest rate should be to control inflation over time by observing wage increases, raw material costs, house prices and other economic variables that provide an early warning of inflationary pressures in the economy. ➤ **6.1**

Examples of 'independent central banks' include the US Federal Reserve, the Bank of England (since 1997), the Reserve Bank of India (1935), the Bank of Mexico (1993), the Bank of Japan, the Bank of Canada, the Reserve Bank of Australia and the European Central Bank.

ACTIVITY 3.7

You can bank on it!

Compare and contrast the functions and activities of a commercial bank with the central bank in your country.

1. What are the main functions of the two banks?
2. What services do they provide and to whom?
3. How are they organized, controlled and financed?
4. What are their relationships with other banks in your country and globally?
5. What role do they play in your economy?

ECONOMICS IN ACTION

How and why did the Central Bank of Nigeria intervene to save its banking sector from collapse? Why did the Central Bank of Chile buy US dollars?

Central Bank acts boldly to stabilize banking sector

In 2009 the Central Bank of Nigeria announced a N400 billion (US$2.5 billion) bailout for five of the country's banks – Oceanic Bank, Intercontinental Bank, AfriBank, Finbank and Union Bank. The CEOs and executive directors of the five banks were also suspended and immediately replaced.

The Central Bank said the injection of money was necessary because the banks were running out of cash and other liquid assets that could be converted easily and quickly into cash. The decision to inject N400 billion into the troubled banks would be sufficient to enable them to continue their normal business and would protect the savings of their depositors.

According to the Central Bank the banks had loaned too much money to organizations in financial difficulties and had too many bad loans with repayment arrears. This was due it said to poor governance and credit control in the banks.

Chilean Central Bank to intervene to stop slide in value of US dollar

According to a media statement, the central bank said it expects to buy US$12 billion from national reserves.

The fall in the value of the US dollar has caused problems for Chile's fruit growers and exporters who have suffered a fall in their export earnings from the USA. Over the last six months the US dollar has fallen in value from 520 Chilean pesos to just 465 pesos, its lowest exchange rate in 32 months.

After the announcement, the dollar shot up to become worth 490 pesos.

SECTION 7

The stock market

Stock is the name used to describe money raised by a joint stock company or corporation, or a government. ➤ **4.1**

A company is owned by its shareholders. Companies issue and sell stocks in the form of shares. A **shareholder** is any person or organization that buys and holds shares in a joint stock company. The market value of all shares or equity issued by a company is called its **market capitalization**.

Many investors buy and hold stocks in companies because they hope the market prices of their stocks will rise over time so they can sell them at a profit. Shareholders are also entitled to a share of any profits made by the companies they own. They will receive a **dividend** paid from any profits in a company for each share held. The more shares held in a company the larger the total dividend paid from any profits.

Unlike loans, a company will not have to repay the money it raises from the sale of its shares. Money raised from the issue and sale of shares is therefore called **permanent capital**. If shareholders want their money back they must sell their shares to other investors and they can do this through a stock exchange such as the New York Stock Exchange (NYSE) or the National Stock Exchange of India. A **flotation** involves a new company issuing shares for the first time for sale through a stock exchange. ➤ **4.1**

Similarly, governments can raise money to finance public expenditure through the sale of government loan stocks or **bonds**. ➤ **5.1**

▼ Types of stock that can be bought and sold through a stock exchange

Type of stock	also known as:	
Preferred stock	preference shares	These are issued by joint stock companies. Holders of preference shares in a company will receive a share of any profits before the holders of other types of shares. That is, a preferred stock or preference share is given preference in the payment of dividends from profits. The dividend paid is usually a fixed percentage of the face value printed on the share. Dividend rights are often cumulative, so that if a dividend is not paid in one year it accumulates to be paid in future years. Preference shareholders, however, are not usually allowed to vote on company policy or in the election of directors to run their company at annual general meetings (AGMs).
Common stock	ordinary shares	Most shares held in joint stock companies are common stock. Ordinary shareholders receive a dividend from any profits remaining after preference shareholders have been paid. If no profits remain, ordinary shareholders will not receive a dividend. Holding ordinary shares can therefore be more risky than holding preference shares. However, ordinary shares carry one vote per share at AGMs. So, a person or organization that owns 10,000 ordinary shares in a company has 10,000 votes. The person or organization with the most ordinary shares in a company is the majority shareholder and can determine company policy and who sits on the board of directors.

Type of stock	also known as:	
Government stock or securities	government bonds	These are loan stocks issued by a government to borrow money over a fixed period of time. This means they are repaid with a fixed rate of interest at the end of their term, or on 'maturity'. For example, UK government gilt-edged securities often mature after 20 or 25 years. Within this time they can be bought and sold many times over by different investors. The final holder of the stock at maturity gets repaid its face value plus interest, but investors who buy and sell the stocks before they mature can make a profit from changes in their market price over time.

Functions of a stock exchange

A **stock exchange**, or bourse, is a business organization that enables individuals, companies and governments to buy and sell shares on the global stock market. It is the most important source of finance for most companies.

A stock exchange is able to do this because:

- it brings together buyers and sellers of new and second-hand stocks
- it provides up to the minute information on the market prices of different stocks and quantities traded
- it supervises the conduct of firms of brokers that buy and sell shares on behalf of investors.

The **stock market** is the global market for the buying and selling of new and second-hand government stocks and company shares. It therefore consists of all those individuals and organizations willing and able to buy stocks and shares and all those individuals and organizations willing and able to sell them.

▲ An ordinary share certificate

▲ Inside the New York Stock Exchange (NYSE)

▼ The world's largest stock exchanges, 2010

Stock exchange	Total value of stocks traded, US$ billion
NYSE	17,795
NASDAQ	12,659
Shanghai Stock Exchange	4,496
Tokyo Stock Exchange	3,788
Shenzen Stock Exchange	3,572
London Stock Exchange	2,741
Frankfurt SE (Deutsche Börse)	1,628
Korea Exchange	1,607

Source: 'Largest Exchanges by value of share trading in the *Electronic Order Book* in 2010 and 2009', reproduced from *2010 WFE Market Highlights* (January 2011)

The largest stock exchange in the world is the New York Stock Exchange (NYSE). In 2010 the total value of all the stocks and shares traded through the NYSE was just under US$17.8 trillion.

Most trading in stocks and shares is now conducted electronically. The NASDAQ was the first fully electronic stock exchange, founded in 1971. NASDAQ stands for National Association of Securities Dealers Automated Quotations.

Money and finance

Without stock exchanges, companies would find it very difficult to raise the finance they need for their productive activities. Think of how difficult it and costly it would be for a new company to search for thousands, sometimes millions, of different people and other companies who were willing and able to buy its shares. Even if it could, other people and companies might be reluctant to buy its shares because if they ever wanted to get their money back they would, in turn, have to search for other people and companies to sell them to. A stock exchange will buy and sell shares on their behalf through the global stock market.

How a stock exchange works

Stock exchanges are not open to the general public. This means that if a person or company wants to buy or sell some shares they must contact a share dealing firm (or **broker**) that is a member of a stock exchange.

The global market in shares is huge and growing. This means that brokers must have very large sums of money in order to buy and sell shares on the stock market. Because of this, many professional share dealers work for major banks and other large financial institutions such as pension funds.

A member of the public or a company that wants to buy or sell shares can either contact a broker or simply go to a major bank. It is very easy nowadays to simply buy and sell shares over the Internet through online brokers and banks.

Brokers will buy and sell shares for a fee known as commission. For example, a customer might wish to buy 1,000 shares in Google at no more than $10 a share. The broker and the customer will agree a commission to be paid to the broker for undertaking the work. For example, this might be a charge of 1% of the total cost of the shares.

The broker will now attempt to buy shares in Google at the lowest possible price from other firms of brokers called **market makers**, usually by placing an order on a stock exchange's computerized share-dealing system. Market makers are special brokers or dealers who create the market in shares. They do this by always being willing to buy and sell shares with other brokers or dealers. These market makers make their profit by selling the shares they hold at a higher price than the price they paid for them.

Share price indices

Like the price of any other product, share prices reflect changes in the market demand for them and how many are supplied. ➤ 2.2

For example, if a company announces poor profits, shareholders may want to sell their shares because they will receive a poor dividend. However, a company that wins a big customer order or announces a merger with another company to form a larger, more profitable company may cause demand for its shares to rise. Changes in the market prices of shares can, therefore, reveal much about how well different companies are performing.

Investors in shares can watch how share prices are changing over time either by monitoring the prices of shares in individual companies or by tracking a share price index. For example, the S&P Global 100 tracks the average price of shares traded in 100 of the largest multinational companies that are traded on different stock exchanges around the world. ➤ 4.1

Most share price indices, however, are national indices. A national index tracks the average prices of shares traded on one or more of a country's stock exchanges. For example, the Dow Jones Industrial Average Index provides an up-to-date average market price on the NYSE of the shares in 30 of the largest and most widely held public companies in the USA. The most regularly quoted stock market indices also include the S&P 500 Index in the USA, the French CAC 40, the German DAX and the Japanese Nikkei 225.

The chart below shows the movement in the FTSE 100 index (the 'footsie') over a 12-month period. It charts the movement in the average price of shares in the top 100 companies traded on the London Stock Exchange in the UK. The index is recalculated every minute relative to a base value of 1,000 set in January 1984. At midday on 30 December 2011 the index value was 5,572.28, which means the average share price in the top 100 companies had increased by just over 557% since 1984.

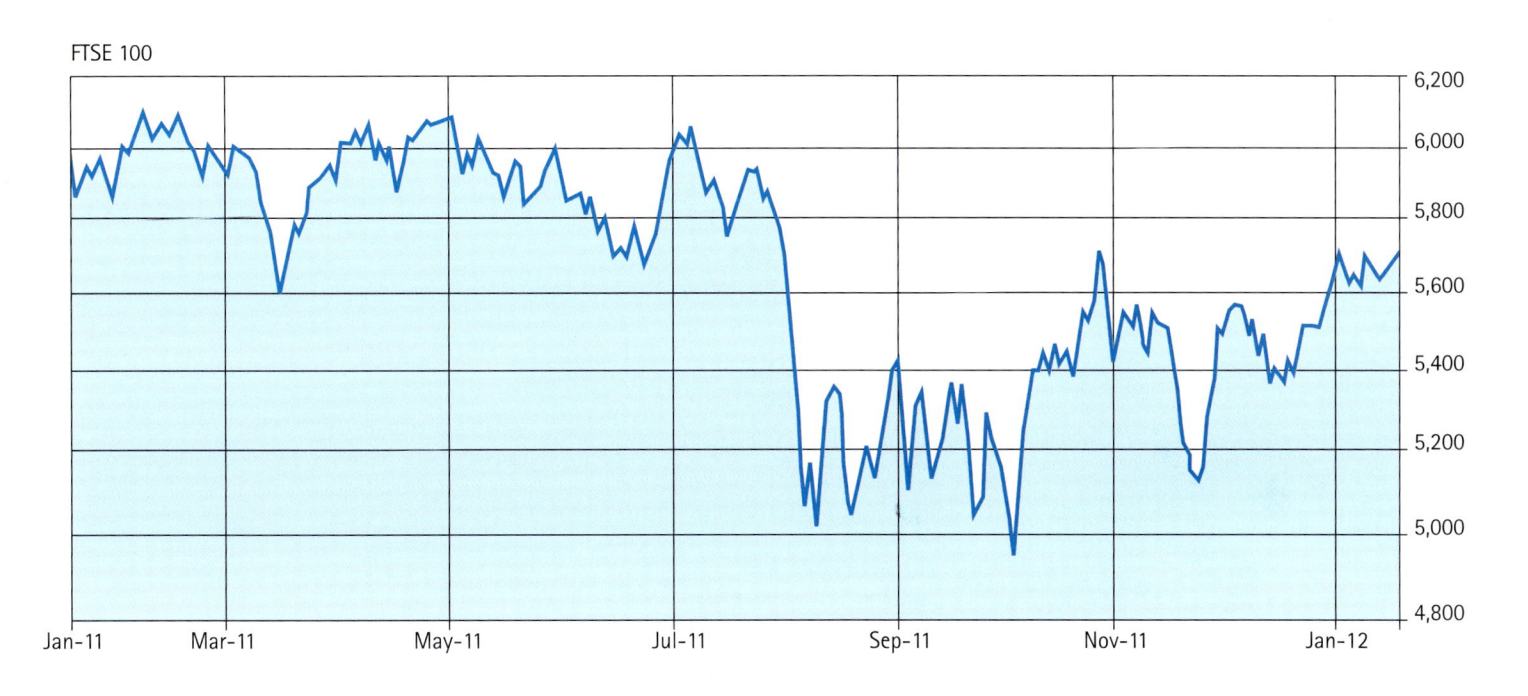

The FTSE 100 chart shows how the market price of shares can change rapidly over time. It is possible for people and companies, including financial institutions, to make money on the stock market by guessing which way share prices are likely to move in the future. Attempting to make money from buying and selling shares in the hope their prices will change is called **speculation**.

Speculating on changes in share prices

People and firms who buy shares in the hope their price will rise so that they can sell them at a profit are called **bulls**. The stock market is called **bullish** if share prices are rising in general.

Money and finance 125

People and firms who sell shares in the hope their price will fall so that they can buy them back later at much lower prices are called **bears**. When share prices are falling the stock market is called a **bear market**. Bears buy the shares back despite their falling prices because they believe their prices will rise again in the long run and that dividend payments from company profits could be good.

People and firms who apply to buy up newly issued shares in the hope their price will rise quickly after dealing begins are called **stags**.

ACTIVITY 3.8

Floating away

Saudi Arabia's Al-Khodari to sell shares at $12.80 each

Saudi Arabia's construction and manufacturing company Al-Khodari will sell individual shares to the public at SR48 ($12.80) each for its forthcoming flotation of a 30 per cent stake in the company.

Established in 1966, Al-Khodari announced the planned initial public offering (IPO) on 1 July. It will float a total of 12.75 million shares on the Saudi Stock Exchange (Tadawul) but only Saudi nationals and Saudi-registered financial firms will be able to buy the shares in the company.

Riyadh-based GIB Financial Services, a wholly owned subsidiary of Bahrain's Gulf International Bank (GIB), has been appointed as financial adviser, lead manager and underwriter for the share offering.

1. What is a stock market?
2. Explain how the Saudi Stock Exchange provides a stock market.
3. Why do you think the company in the article wants to sell shares through the Saudi Stock Exchange?
4. How many shares will the business issue, and how much in total is it hoping to raise from their sale?
5. Why might the market price of shares traded in Al-Khodari exceed their face value of SR48 (or $12.80) per share?

ACTIVITY 3.9

Share your success

Imagine you have $50,000 to invest in shares through a stock exchange. Use company news and financial pages of newspapers and websites to choose the shares of up to 10 companies you want to buy, how many shares you will buy in each company and the market price you will have to pay.

Record this information in a table or on a spreadsheet. For example:

Name of company	Where are the shares traded?	Market prices per share ($)	Number of shares bought	Total value (week 1)
Cadbury Schweppes plc	NYSE	$42.95	100	$4,295
PT Indosat Tbk	NYSE	$24.74	50	$1,237
Bancolombia S.A	NYSE	$28.40	75	$2,130
...				

Check and record the market prices of your shares at the end of every week over a three- to six-month period and calculate the gain or loss you have made in the value of your shares. Also add in and record any dividends you would be paid. As you do so, use financial newspapers and online reports to record reasons why the market prices of your shares may have changed.

WEBSITES

Learn more about the functions of money at:

- www.bized.ac.uk/virtual/bank/economic/money/worksheet.htm
- laborsta.ilo.org
- www.wikipedia.org/wiki/money

There are also a great many useful and interesting websites providing news and information on banking, financial products, stock markets and share prices. Here are just a few:

- Bloomberg markets magazine www.bloomberg.com
- Financial Times markets www.ft.com/markets
- Fortune business and financial news money.cnn.com/magazines/fortune/
- central banks www.bis.org/cbanks.htm; www.centralbanksguide.com/
- links to stock exchanges www.tdd.lt/slnews/Stock_Exchanges/Stock.Exchanges.htm
- list of websites on stock markets and prices www.rba.co.uk/sources/stocks.htm

KEYWORDS

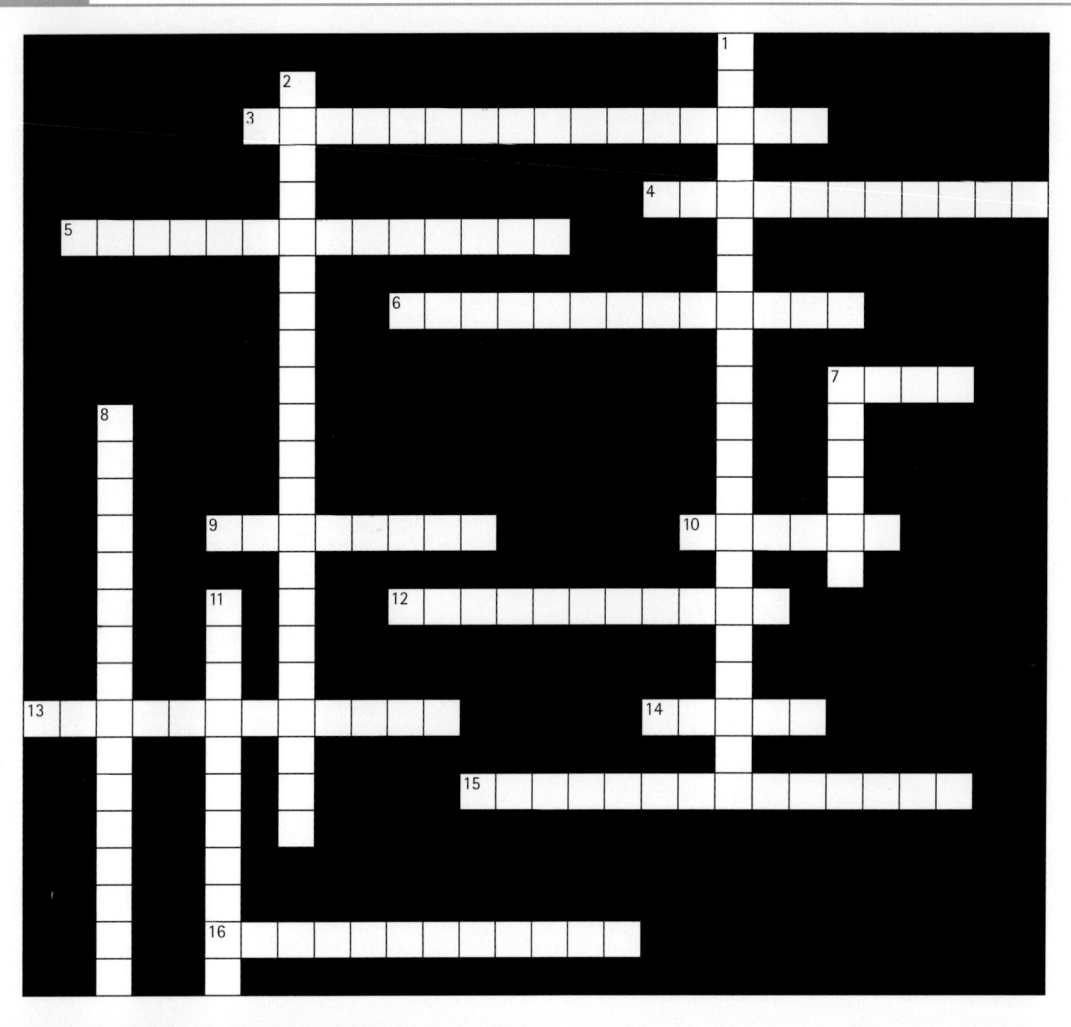

Clues across

3. A good money must fulfill this function (6, 2, 8)
4. The main bank in an economy responsible for managing the stability of the national currency and the money supply (6, 4)
5. A type of bank with retail branches in many towns and cities (10, 4)
6. An organization that brings together buyers and sellers of shares (5, 8)
7. The name given to a speculator who buys shares in the hope their price will rise quickly so they can sell them for a profit (4)
9. A long-term loan for buying property (8)
10. A share dealer, able to buy and sell shares on a stock exchange (6)
12. A person or organization who owns shares in a joint stock company (11)
13. The cost of borrowing money (8, 4)
14. Another term used to describe the exchange of goods and services, usually for money (5)
15. Another name for common stock with voting rights issued by a company (7, 5)
16. The term used to describe financial assets that can be converted into cash easily and quickly (6, 6)

Clues down

1. The name used to describe an organization, such as a bank, that brings together customers who want to save money and others who wish to borrow it (9, 12)
2. The number of time notes and coins are exchanged on average in an economy in a given period of time (8, 2, 11)
7. Trading or swapping goods and services without money. This form of exchange requires a double coincidence of wants (6)
8. Money raised from the sale of shares that a company never needs to repay (9, 7)
11. The total of bank deposits and notes and coins in an economy (5, 6)

The individual as producer, consumer and borrower

Unit 3.2 — Occupations and earnings

AIMS

By the end of this unit you should be able to:

▶ identify the factors affecting an individual's choice of occupation (**wage factors** and **non-wage factors**)

- compare the **net advantages** of different occupations and understand how they affect **labour supply** decisions

▶ describe likely changes in the **earnings** over time for an individual

- demonstrate how **wage rates** are determined by the demand for labour and supply of labour to different occupations

▶ describe the differences in earnings between different **occupational groups** (male/female; skilled/unskilled; private/public; agricultural/manufacturing/services)

- distinguish between **labour markets** for different occupations and skills
- explain how and why governments may intervene in labour markets

▶ describe the benefits and disadvantages of **specialization** for the individual.

SECTION 1 — Why do people work?

ACTIVITY 3.10

Just the job

Restaurant and Bar Manager
To lead, manage and operate a restaurant and bar with cutting edge cocktails and global cuisine. 50 hours per week. Late evenings and shift-working required.

Labourer Wanted
General labouring and odd jobs. Hours 8am – 5pm. Monday to Friday. Must be willing to travel.

Hair stylist
To wash and cut hair. Part-time. Mornings only.

Warehouse staff
You could be earning instead of looking!
WAREHOUSE STAFF – We've found the way to make temporary assignments more interesting for YOU.
You'll have the opportunity to select from a variety of assignments locally or in city locations offering excellent rates of pay, holiday pay and other benefits.
If you're available for a week or more we can put you to work.

Economist
An international oil company is looking for an Economist to join their Business Environment Division, initially on a 2-year contract.
The successful candidate for this unusual opportunity to experience the oil industry at first hand is likely to have a degree and postgraduate degree in economics, a strong quantitative background including familiarity with PCs and a high level of analytical, written and oral communication skills.
The post can be filled at various levels of previous experience, with a remuneration package to match, but preference will be given to those whose understanding of the economy within a global environment can be readily acknowledged.
The planning team is responsible for analysing and identifying economic trends and developments, in particular those relating to energy demand and supply.

Fruit picker wanted
for busy farm for three months during summer. Must be prepared to work long hours and outdoors in all weathers.

Security guard required
We require a security person for the reception area at our Group Head Office.
The hours of work involved are Monday to Friday 10pm to 7am and duties include dealing with all overnight visitors and deliveries to the building, whilst maintaining an effective security presence.
Applications are invited from mature persons who are confident and alert, and of a smart appearance.
We offer a good rate of pay for this responsible position.

Book Shop Assistant
A great opportunity for a bright, enthusiastic person interested in literature, art, music and foreign languages to gain valuable experience in bookselling and publishing. 5 days per week. 10 am till 7 pm

In groups, look at the job advertisements above.

1. For each job, discuss with your group what you think the monthly wage or annual salary for the job is likely to be.
2. Which job do you think offers the highest wage or salary, and which one offers the lowest? Why do you think this is the case?
3. Which job do you think is likely to get the most applicants and why? Try to think of reasons other than just the wage or salary.
4. Which of the jobs above would you most like to do and least like to do, and why? Again, try to think of reasons other than the wage or salary the job may offer.
5. Which job would you most like to do when you leave school or college, and why? Try to find out what the job currently offers in terms of pay and other monetary and non-monetary benefits. Are you still attracted to this job?

The decision to supply labour

Most people will supply their labour to firms to earn an income. Firms pay **wages** to workers to supply their labour to produce goods and services. Paid employment therefore provides people with money to buy the goods and services they need and want and cannot produce themselves.

However, some people may supply their labour for free, for example by undertaking voluntary work to assist charities. So money may not be the only reason people go to work.

In addition to a desire for money, working satisfies many more of our different wants and needs. For example, working makes us feel useful, it provides the opportunity to meet new people and make new friends, and it teaches us new skills and ideas. Combinations of all these different reasons, both financial and non-financial, therefore motivate people to supply their labour and be productive in work.

Payments for labour

Firms will advertise a **wage rate** for each job to attract people to supply their labour. The wage rate for a job can be paid in many ways:

- **A time rate** is a rate of pay per hour worked, so the more hours an employee works the more he or she will earn. For example, if an employee is paid $20 per hour and works 35 hours each week the employee's **gross weekly wage** will be $700. Workers who work additional hours during evenings or weekends, may receive an **overtime rate** at 1.5 times or even twice the normal time rate.

- **A piece rate** is paid to an employee of a firm per unit of output produced, for example for each article of clothing made or kilogram of apples picked, so the more output produced by an employee the more he or she will earn. Piece rates are often paid in addition to time rates to workers in manufacturing firms to give them the incentive to increase their productivity.

- **A fixed annual rate** or **salary** for a job will be divided into 12 equal monthly payments regardless of the number of hours actually worked by the jobholder each week over and above an agreed amount of time, often between 35 to 40 hours per week. Salaries are often paid to managers, office staff and other employees in non-manual occupations.

- **Performance-related payments** may be offered to individual employees or teams of workers who are highly productive. For example, commission may be paid to retail employees and others involved in sales, such as financial advisers and travel agents. The more sales they make or revenue they earn for the organization they work for the more they will earn, usually as a percentage of their sales. Some firms may also pay their employees a share of an increase in their profits.

The total or **gross earnings** of an employee each week or month may therefore vary and be made up of many different payments, including a basic wage or salary, overtime payments, commission and a performance-related bonus.

All of these forms of payment are referred to as **wage factors** and are clearly very important in the decision of a person whether to supply his or her labour.

In addition to wage payments, firms may attract a supply of labour by offering workers other benefits that nevertheless have monetary value such as free medical insurance, use of a company car, price discounts, pension contributions and free membership and use of a gym. These are often referred to as perks or **fringe benefits**.

Occupations and earnings

Choosing an occupation

Most people specialize in a particular activity or occupation for all or most of their working lives. So how do people choose an occupation to supply their labour to?

Clearly differences in wage factors between occupations will be important. However, as already mentioned, in addition to a desire for money, working satisfies many more of our different wants and needs. For example, working makes us feel useful, it provides the opportunity to meet new people and make new friends, and it teaches us new skills and ideas.

For example, a job that offers few promotion prospects, involves repetitive and uninteresting tasks and working long unsociable hours may be unattractive to many people even if that job offers a high wage rate.

In contrast, some people may be attracted to occupations that pay relatively low wages because they offer interesting careers, generous holiday entitlements or are considered to more worthwhile and satisfying, such as nursing or charity work. These are all **non-wage factors** that can attract people to different occupations.

A person seeking employment may therefore accept a lower wage if a job offers attractive non-wage benefits. However, a person may only accept a job that has unattractive non-wage features, for example, dangerous work or working late nights and weekends, if the wage rate is high enough to compensate for them (see Section 4 below).

People will therefore choose between different occupations and employers by comparing their wage factors and non-wage factors.

Non-wage factors include:

- hours of work
- holiday entitlement
- promotion prospects
- flexible working arrangements
- qualifications required
- quality of working environment
- how secure the job is
- how satisfying the work is
- fringe benefits
- training opportunities
- pension entitlement
- opportunities for promotion
- interesting and varie tasks
- distance or time it takes to travel to and from work.

All the wage and non-wage factors that affect the attractiveness of a particular job or occupation are called its **net advantages**. A person will compare and select jobs or occupations by comparing their advantages and disadvantages. Choosing between different occupations will therefore involve trade offs. For example, the opportunity cost of choosing a job with high wages may be a loss of leisure time because of the need to work longer hours or to travel further to and from the place of work.

For example, a person hoping to become a medical surgeon will have to complete up to eight years of study at university and medical school before training can begin in a hospital. It may take a further three to seven years before that person can eventually become qualified as a surgeon. During this time medical students may have to borrow money to pay their fees, while subsequent training at a hospital will often involve further study and long hours of work, including during evenings and weekends, often for relatively low pay. However, qualified surgeons are among the highest paid workers in the world and have rewarding careers saving the lives of many people. Those thinking of becoming a surgeon will have to weigh up all these factors before they decide to specialize in this occupation.

In contrast, very little training is required to become an office cleaner. The job does not require long periods of study to gain qualifications so a person can start earning an income immediately they leave school. However, the wage rate for cleaners is often very low, the work can be uninteresting and dirty, and the job offers little chance of promotion or advancement.

Occupational specialization

People will usually make career choices while they are still at school or college according to their interests and abilities and some view of the net advantages of different jobs. They may choose subjects to study that will help them develop the skills and obtain the qualifications they will need for the occupation they want to pursue.

Specializing in particular occupational skills sets, such as engineering, marketing and sales, art and design, tourism and hospitality, accounting, construction or medicine, can have both advantages and disadvantages for a working person. For example, people with skills that are in demand will tend to attract much higher rates of pay than unskilled labour. However, people who have skills that are no longer in demand will find it difficult to find a job and may have to retrain.

▼ Some specialist skills may become outdated and unwanted due to modern technology

The introduction of modern technology, especially in agriculture and many manufacturing industries, has had and continues to have a major impact on many employees. Many have lost their jobs because their skills have become out of date and are no longer required. For example welders in car manufacturing and typesetters in printing have been replaced with new advanced machines, industrial robots and computer equipment able to carry out their tasks quicker and more efficiently. Replacing labour with capital equipment in production is known as **factor substitution**. ➤ **4.2**

However, changes in consumer demand for different products and the development of new industries and technologies are also creating a demand for new skills. For example, demand for labour skilled in computer programming, video game and website design, solar and wind energy engineering, biotechnology and many other new occupations is rising rapidly.

Occupations and earnings | 133

The benefits of specialization for an individual

- Specialization allows individuals to make the best use of their skills and abilities.
- Employees can improve further on their skills by repeatedly carrying out the same or similar tasks or duties.
- Skilled employees will often earn more than unskilled employees because they are more productive and there is greater demand for their labour from firms.

The disadvantages of specialization for an individual

- Individuals must rely on others to produce the goods and services they want but cannot produce themselves.
- Doing the same job for many years can become boring and stressful.
- Skills and occupations can become outdated and unwanted if consumer demand or technology changes. This means people with unwanted skills may lose their jobs and be unable to find new ones unless they retrain. For example, many manufacturing workers in developed economies have lost their jobs in the last few decades due to competition from manufacturing firms in low-wage economies overseas and the introduction of industrial robots and computer-aided manufacturing equipment and processes. ➤ **4.2**

SECTION 2

What is the labour market?

There is a **labour market** for every type of occupation just as there are markets for all other goods and services. Firms will demand labour with the right skills to do the jobs available and people willing and able to do those jobs will supply their labour. We can therefore use demand and supply analysis to examine the economics of labour markets, including what causes changes in the demand for labour and the supply of labour to different occupations, what determines the amount people earn, and why wage rates differ. ➤ **2.2**

Markets for labour can also be local, national or even international if people are willing and able to migrate overseas to work. There will also be labour markets for different skills and occupations. For example, there are labour markets for bricklayers, doctors, train drivers, accountants, soldiers, shop assistants, nurses and even economists. We can also distinguish between labour markets for young workers who may have little work experience and older workers with more experience, and between labour markets for temporary, part-time and full-time employees.

The demand for labour

The demand for labour is a **derived demand** because firms want labour to produce goods and services that consumers want and are willing to pay for. It follows that the more goods and services demanded, the higher their market price will be and therefore the more revenue is generated from their sale, so the greater the demand for labour is likely to be.

However, private and public sector organizations are only likely to employ additional workers if they add more value than they cost to employ. In a private profit-making firm this value is measured by how much extra revenue and profit each worker creates. So, for example, a worker will be worth employing if he or she generates an additional $5,000 in revenue each month but only costs $3,000 per month to employ. If, however, this employee would only generate extra output worth $2,000 each month he or she would not be worth employing. The demand for labour is therefore closely related to the wage rate workers receive for their employment and how productive they are. ➤ 4.2

In general, therefore, the higher the wage rate in a particular labour market the more expensive it is to employ workers and the fewer will tend to be demanded. This is shown in the diagram below. We use the symbol n to denote labour and w to represent the wage rate. The demand curve for labour (DnDn) is downward sloping so that as the wage rate rises from w to w1 the demand for labour contracts from n to n1.

▼ The demand for labour with specific occupational skills

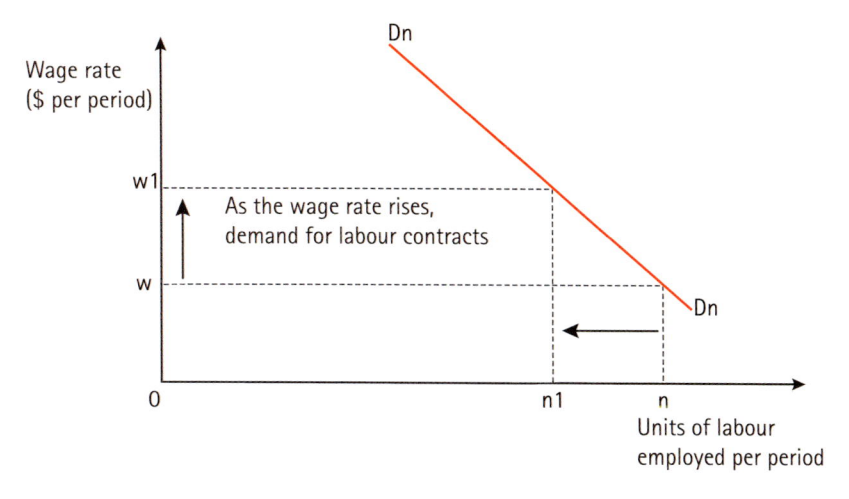

The supply of labour

The total supply of labour in an economy is its working population or labour force. ➤ 7.2

However, the supply of labour to a particular occupation will depend on how many people are willing and able to do the jobs on offer. So, for example, the market supply of train drivers will consist of people currently employed as train drivers, people employed in other occupations who want to become train drivers, and people who are unemployed but are also willing and able to be train drivers.

It is likely that as the wage rate for train drivers increases, so more and more people will want to be train drivers. The market supply curve for train drivers will therefore slope upwards. Indeed, this is generally the case. The higher the wage rate in a particular labour market the more labour will be supplied. This is shown in the next diagram. The supply curve for labour (SnSn) is upward sloping so that as the wage rate rises from w to w1 the supply of labour extends from n to n1.

▼ The supply of labour with specific occupational skills

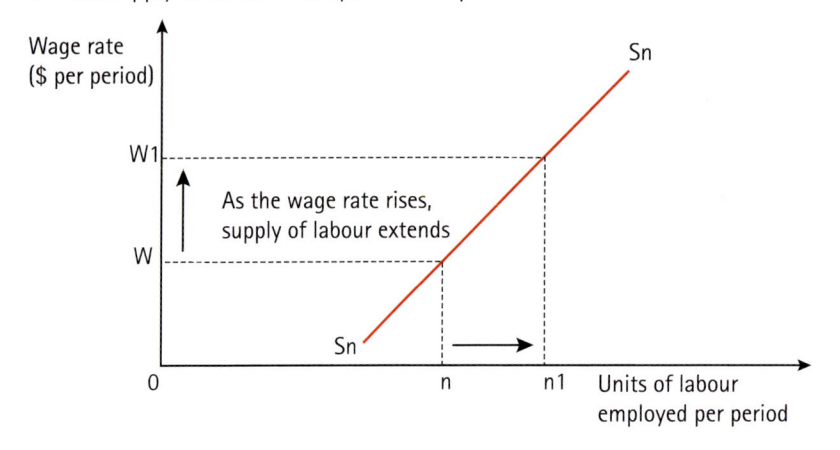

(Graph: Wage rate ($ per period) vs Units of labour employed per period. Supply curve Sn slopes upward. At wage W, labour = n; at wage W1, labour = n1. Label: "As the wage rate rises, supply of labour extends")

However, while the positive relationship between labour supply and wages holds in general, it may not always be the case that an individual will be willing to work more and more hours as the wage rate rises. At some point individuals might decide they earn enough and would like to take more leisure time. For example, consider a builder currently earning $7 per hour. At this wage rate he might choose to work 35 hours each week and earn $245. If the wage rate rises to $10 per hour he may work 40 hours and earn $400. But at $15 per hour he may only work 32 hours and choose to spend more time relaxing because he is still better off with earnings of $480 each week. As a result, the supply curve of our individual builder, and many other workers like him, will be backward bending. At very high wage rates it is possible to have both more wage income and more leisure.

▼ A backward bending supply curve for our builder

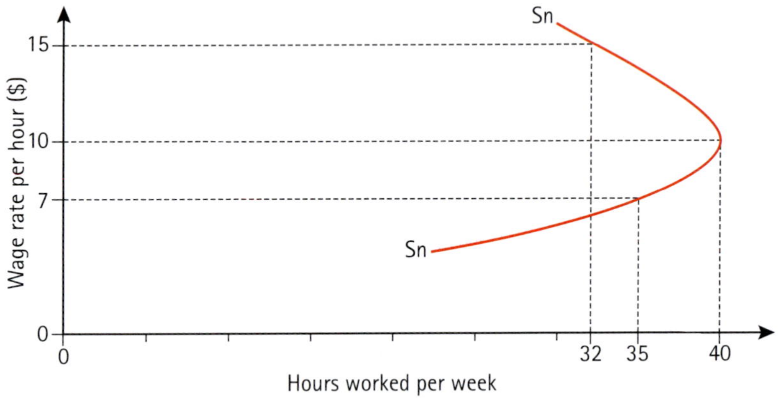

(Graph: Wage rate per hour ($) vs Hours worked per week. Backward-bending supply curve Sn. At 35 hours, wage $7; at 40 hours, wage $10; at 32 hours, wage $15.)

Although most people do work a fixed number of hours each week, there is still evidence to suggest that the total supply curve of labour is backward bending. This is evidenced by trade unions' attempts to reduce working hours as living standards have improved, and in the reduction of the working week in many developed countries from 60 hours at the start of the century to an average today of around 41 hours or less per week.

SECTION 3

The market wage for a job

Just as in a market for any good or service, the market price of labour, or **equilibrium wage rate**, for an occupation will be determined where the demand for labour is matched by a supply of labour.

The equilibrium wage rate for a particular job can be illustrated graphically. At this wage we find how much labour will actually be employed by firms.

The individual as producer, consumer and borrower

▼ Equilibrium in an occupational labour market

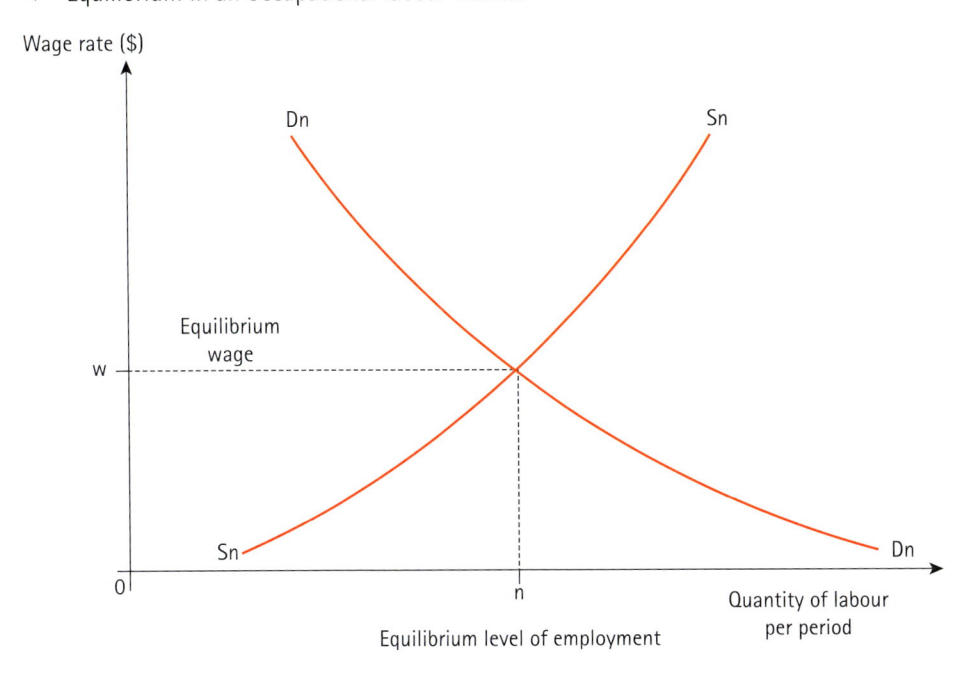

The equilibrium wage rate and the amount of labour employed by firms will change if there are changes in labour demand and supply conditions.

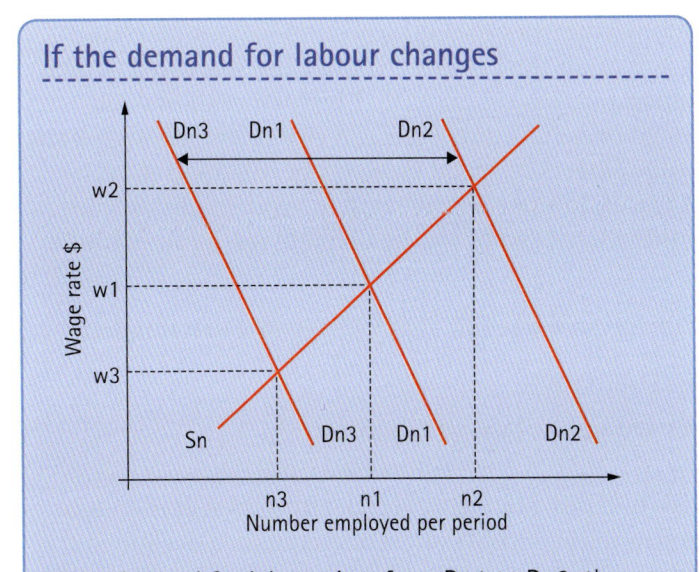

If the demand for labour changes

If the demand for labour rises from Dn1 to Dn2, the wage rate rises from w1 to w2 and employment increases from n1 to n2.

If demand falls from Dn1 to Dn3, the wage rate falls from w1 to w3 and employment falls to n3.

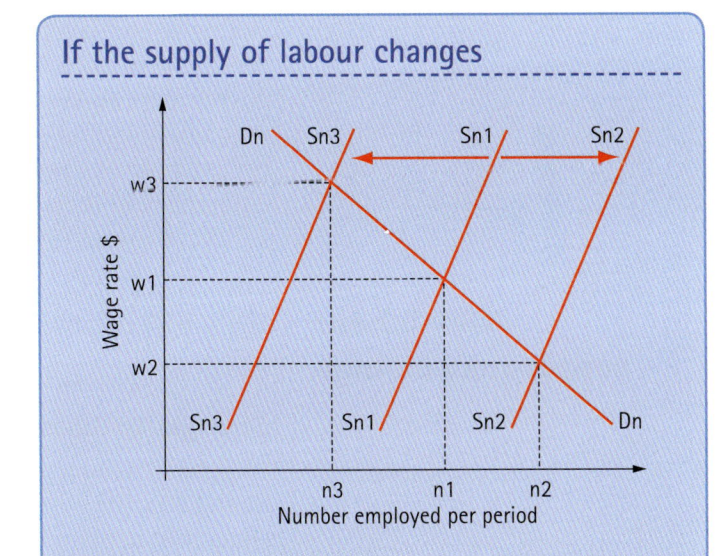

If the supply of labour changes

If the supply of labour rises from Sn1 to Sn2, the wage rate falls from w2 to w1 and more people are employed at n2.

If supply falls from Sn1 to Sn3, the wage rate rises from w1 to w3 and employment falls.

Occupations and earnings

Why firms may change their demand for labour

The following factors may cause firms to change their demand for labour.

Changes in consumer demand for goods and services

If consumer demand rises, firms may expand output in response. To do so they will tend to increase their demand for labour. This may initially mean asking their existing workers to work additional hours, but may also involve hiring more workers if the increase in consumer demand is permanent. Changes in the pattern of consumer demand over time, due to population changes and changing tastes, can therefore mean demand for some types of labour will be increasing while demand for others is falling. ➤ 2.2

Changes in the productivity of labour

If labour becomes more productive and increases the value of output it can produce over and above the cost of wages, then firms may demand more labour. New technologies and working methods, and training programmes, can help increase the productivity of labour. ➤ 4.2

Changes in the price and productivity of capital

If machinery and equipment becomes cheaper or more productive than labour, then a firm may replace labour with more capital-intensive production methods.

Changes in non-wage employment costs

Wages are not the only cost to an organization of employing people. For example, employers in many countries have to pay employment taxes and welfare insurance for each worker they employ. If these are increased by the government then the demand for labour may fall. Employment laws and regulations may also change over time and affect the cost of employing labour, for example by requiring employers to spend more on health and safety equipment in their workplaces in order to protect their workers. In contrast, a fall in non-wage employment costs can boost the demand for labour by firms.

Why labour supply may change

The supply of labour at any given wage rate may change due to a number of factors.

Changes in the net advantages of an occupation

We know that people are attracted to different jobs by their net advantages. Changes in the advantages and disadvantages of different jobs will therefore affect the supply of labour to those occupations. For example, a decline in the promotion prospects or holiday entitlement of school teachers relative to other occupations is likely to result in a fall in the supply of school teachers at every possible wage rate, from SnSn to Sn1Sn1 in the diagram to the left.

In contrast, a cut in required hours of work and the introduction of free medical insurance for airline pilots will tend to increase the supply of labour to airline operators.

▼ A fall in the supply of teachers

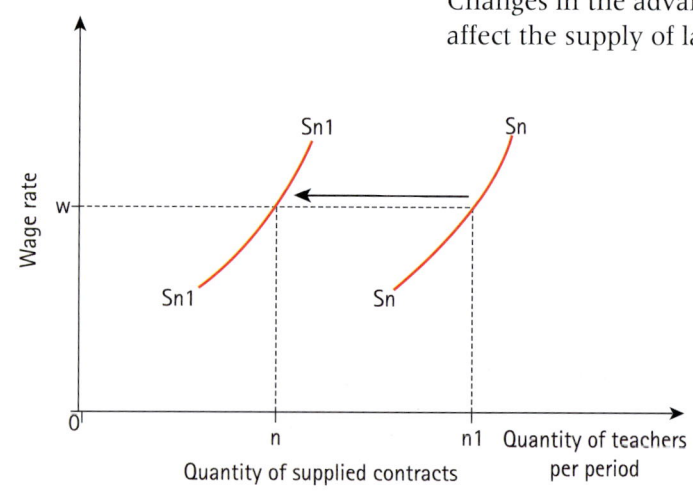

[Diagram: Wage rate on y-axis, Quantity of teachers per period on x-axis. Two supply curves Sn and Sn1, with Sn1 shifted left from Sn, showing movement from n1 to n at wage rate W. Quantity of supplied contracts labelled on x-axis.]

138 The individual as producer, consumer and borrower

Changes in the provision and quality of education and training

Changes in the level and type of education and training courses offered can increase the supply of workers with different skills. For example, the introduction of courses in computer programming and cellular engineering has increased the number of people able to supply these skills to occupations that require them.

Demographic changes

Changes in the size and age distribution of the population in an economy will also cause changes in the supply of labour to different occupations. ➤ 7.2

For example, inward migration to many developed economies has helped boost the supply of labour to many occupations. In contrast, the increasing average age of their populations because birth rates are low means that more people are leaving the labour market due to old age. Others are moving from full-time employment in industry to part-time jobs in services as they get older and want to enjoy more leisure time.

ACTIVITY 3.11

The rise and fall of labour

Look at the factors listed below that could affect labour market outcomes. In each case indicate whether you think there will be an increase or decrease in the demand for labour, an increase or decrease in the supply of labour and whether the equilibrium market wage rate for each occupation will tend to rise or fall as a result.

What has changed?	Impact on labour demand	Impact on labour supply	Impact on market wage rate
• Nurses are offered new contracts with shorter working weeks			
• Consumer spending on flat-screen televisions increases significantly			
• The government raises the retirement age of public sector workers			
• Overtime payments for airline employees are to be scrapped			
• Computerized assembly lines boost labour productivity in car plants			
• A major retail chain announces it will remain open 24 hours each day			
• Assaults on police increase			
• The government announces it will tax tips received by restaurant and hotel staff from next April			
• A survey finds more people are working part-time and flexible hours			
• Statutory maternity leave and pay are to be increased			
• New technology allows more office workers to work from home			

SECTION 4 — Why do the earnings of employees differ?

What are wage differentials?

Differences in wages between different occupations and employees in the same occupations are called **wage differentials**. For example, an experienced doctor may earn over $200,000 per year while a farm labourer in the same country may earn less than $10,000 each year. Differences in the wages and earnings of workers are common in all countries. For example, the average weekly earnings of full-time female employees in the USA were $657 in 2009, or about 80% of the average weekly earnings of $819 of full-time male employees. Wages can also vary significantly between countries.

What explains occupational wage differentials?

Clearly two people with similar skills and experience doing the same job for the same hourly wage but working different hours each week will have different earnings at the end of each week. However, in economics we are interested in explaining differences in wage rates between different occupations and groups of employees using demand and supply analysis.

We know the demand for labour is derived from consumer demand for goods and services and depends on how productive labour is. We also know that labour supply decisions are related to the net advantages of different occupations. We can therefore use our knowledge of these factors to explain wage differentials.

1 Different abilities and qualifications

Workers do not all have the same education, training and ability. For example, an accountant is a more skilled worker than a cashier. If both workers were paid the same amount, very few people would be willing to undertake the many years of study necessary to become an accountant.

Because the training period is so long for some jobs the supply of these particular workers may be very low and, as a result, their wages may be very high. For example, it takes doctors over six years to qualify to do their job and up to 15 years, perhaps more, to become a skilled surgeon.

People with skills that are in very short supply relative to the demand for those skills will tend to command very high market wages. This explains why skilled footballers like David Beckham, and famous actresses such as Katrina Kaif and Cameron Diaz, are able to command huge salaries.

2 'Dirty' jobs and unsociable hours

Some jobs are dirty or dangerous and so workers must be paid more in order to attract a supply of labour. Some people have to work nights or other unsociable hours and may be paid more to compensate for this. These are called **compensating differentials**.

3 Job satisfaction

The satisfaction provided by undertaking a job can compensate for relatively low wages for some people. Some occupations, such as nursing, are considered more worthy than others by some people and this makes these occupations more attractive. Because of a large supply of labour to such occupations market wage rates may be low.

4 Lack of information about jobs and wages

Sometimes workers work for less than they could earn in other roles simply because they do not know about the availability of better-paid jobs elsewhere. Lack of information about job availability can restrict the supply of labour to those jobs and can therefore help explain some differences in earnings between different jobs in different areas.

5 Labour immobility

The ease with which workers can move between different occupations and different areas of a country is known as **labour mobility**. If workers are very mobile, they can move easily to those jobs that offer them the most pay, and they will also move from places with high unemployment to areas with more job vacancies. High labour mobility or willingness to move can help to increase the supply of labour to different occupations in different areas and reduce regional differences in unemployment and wage rates in a country.

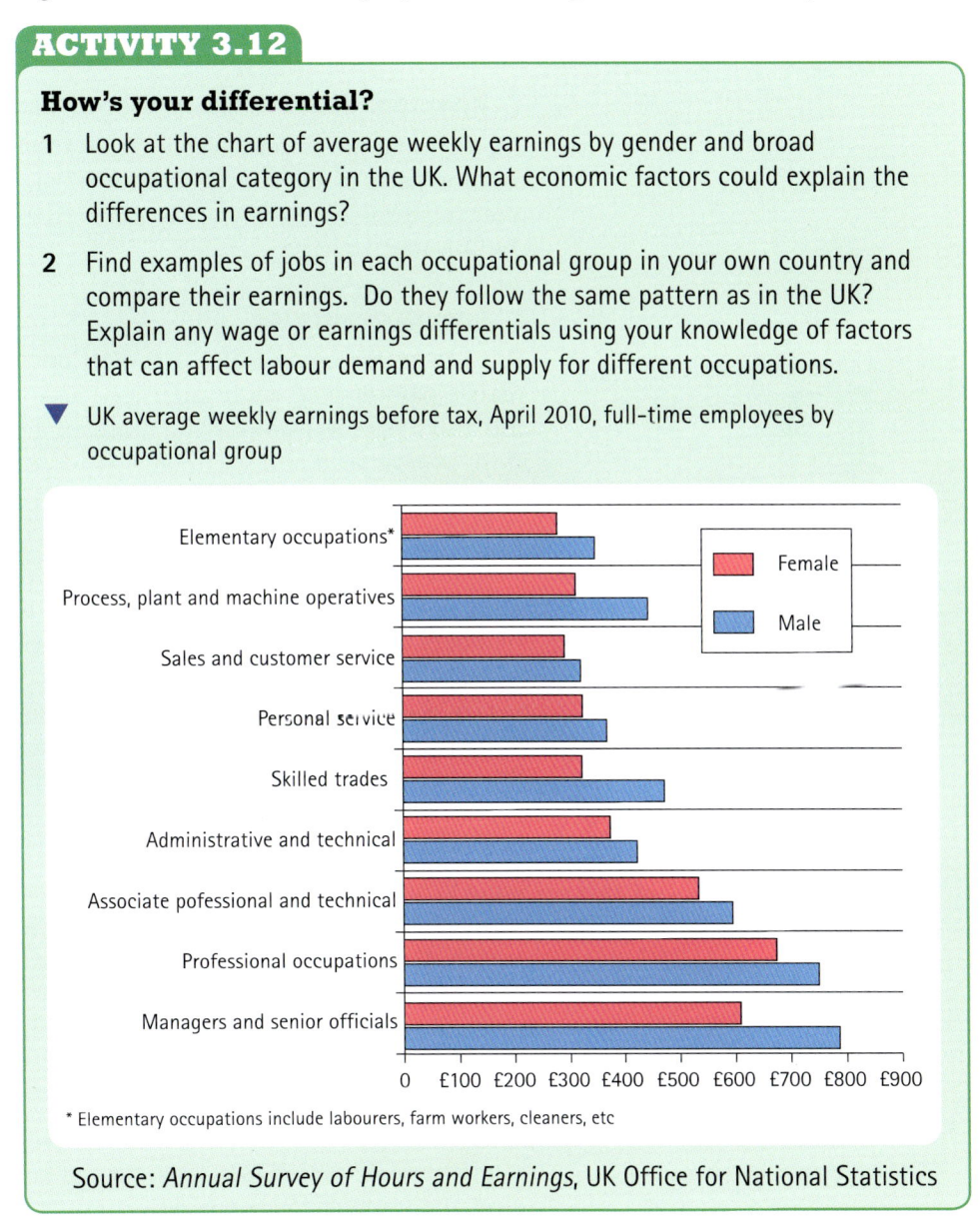

> **ACTIVITY 3.12**
>
> **How's your differential?**
>
> 1. Look at the chart of average weekly earnings by gender and broad occupational category in the UK. What economic factors could explain the differences in earnings?
>
> 2. Find examples of jobs in each occupational group in your own country and compare their earnings. Do they follow the same pattern as in the UK? Explain any wage or earnings differentials using your knowledge of factors that can affect labour demand and supply for different occupations.
>
> ▼ UK average weekly earnings before tax, April 2010, full-time employees by occupational group
>
> * Elementary occupations include labourers, farm workers, cleaners, etc
>
> Source: *Annual Survey of Hours and Earnings*, UK Office for National Statistics

However, because many people are not very mobile large differences in wage rates for different occupations and even for the same jobs but in different areas can persist. For example, some workers may not wish to leave their families and friends in order to move to better-paid jobs elsewhere. Even if they wanted to move to a better-paid job elsewhere they may not be able to afford housing in the new area or the cost of retraining in new occupational skills. For example, the length of time and costs involved in training to be a surgeon restricts the **occupational mobility of labour** and therefore the supply of labour to that profession.

6 Fringe benefits

Some jobs may offer lower wages than others because they offer more perks instead, such as company cars, free life insurance or cheap travel. However, it is usually the higher-paid jobs that also tend to offer the most perks in order to attract the most skilled workers.

Why do earnings differ between people doing the same job?

People in different occupations can earn different amounts of money, but even people in the same jobs can earn very different amounts. This can happen for the following reasons.

1 Regional differences in labour demand and supply conditions

For example, there may be shortages of workers with particular types of skills in some parts of the country. Firms in such areas needing these workers may offer higher wages to attract workers from rival firms or from elsewhere in the country.

2 Length of service

Many firms have pay scales that offer pay increases linked to the number of years a worker stays with the firm. This extra pay is both a bonus for loyalty and also a payment for having more experience and skill. Firms reward their more experienced and productive workers with higher pay because they want to keep them.

3 Local pay agreements

Some national trade unions may agree a national wage rate for all their members through collective bargaining with employers. All workers belonging to the union with similar work experience and levels of skill will therefore receive the same wage wherever they work in a country. However, many workers and employers can often agree their pay locally, so regional differences in pay in the same occupation can occur. ➤ **3.3**

4 Non-monetary rewards differ

Some firms may offer their workers more fringe and other benefits than rival firms, such as longer holidays, free medical care and enhanced pension contributions, instead of higher rates of pay. In some countries non-pay rewards are not taxable so they may offer a worker better value than paying higher wages from which income and other payroll taxes will be deducted.

5 Discrimination

Workers doing the same job may be treated differently by different employers simply because of their sex, age, race or religion. Personal discrimination unrelated to the skills and productivity of different workers is a non-economic reason why wage differentials may exist between different workers doing the same jobs. Such personal discrimination is outlawed in many countries.

Investigating wage differentials

Economists, social researchers, trade unions, employers' groups and governments often monitor the following key earnings differentials.

Public–private sector pay gap

Governments are major employers in many countries. The public sector therefore competes with private sector firms to attract many of the same types of workers with the same skills and so governments need to be aware what private sector firms are paying.

> **US president imposes public sector pay freeze to cut budget deficit**
>
> Barack Obama tonight imposed a two-year pay freeze on all non-military employees of the federal government. Obama said the pay freeze would save approximately $2bn over the current fiscal year and up to $28bn over the next five years.
>
> Public sector unions have warned that a pay freeze will hurt some of the lowest paid workers in the public sector. 'It's unfair that executives can keep their juicy salaries while nurses and other staff get squeezed in a two-year pay freeze' said a union spokesperson.

Yet some people argue because the government is such a big employer it has the power to hold down the wages of public sector workers relative to those paid in the private sector. However, lower public sector pay might be explained by many of its employees having more secure jobs and, in some cases, better pensions. For example, civil servants, the police and teachers are not at risk of losing their jobs due to falling consumer demand like many private sector workers.

But data is mixed. While there are many relatively low-paid workers in public sector jobs, others appear to earn as much if not more than private sector workers in very similar jobs. For example, a recent study in Pakistan suggested its public sector workers earned on average 49% cent more. This was explained by public sector workers generally having higher levels of education and productivity. A similar study in the UK also concluded there was very little difference in the pay of public sector and private sector workers once differences in their levels of education and qualifications were taken into account.

Skilled and unskilled workers

Wage inequality has been increasing between skilled and unskilled workers in many developed and developing economies. This is partly explained by the increasing globalization of production. Less-developed economies have many low-skilled workers who work for relatively low wages compared with workers in other economies. It is therefore cheaper for many firms to produce goods and services in the less-developed economies. In addition, the demand for skills is rising and firms competing for skilled workers are offering higher wages to attract them. Trade union power has also decreased in many developed economies as manual labour-intensive industries have declined in importance. ➤ **6.2**

Industrial wage differentials

Differences in wage rates between different industries will normally reflect differences in the labour market demand and supply conditions of the different occupations they employ and also regional labour market conditions depending on where different industries tend to be concentrated. Expanding industries will tend to offer higher wages to attract workers with the skills they need, especially if the supply of labour with these skills is relatively low. In contrast, the demand for labour in old, declining industries will be falling.

▼ Average gross hourly earnings by industry, Canada 2009

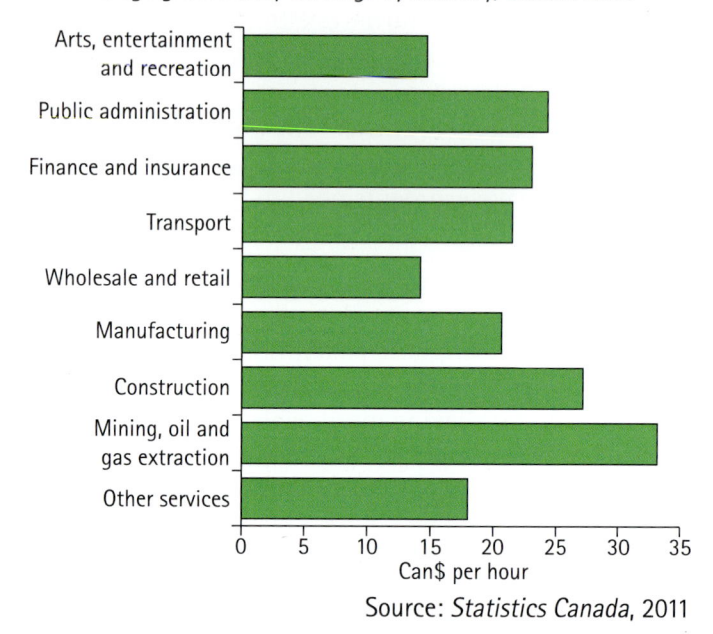

Source: *Statistics Canada*, 2011

▼ Hourly earnings in manufacturing, selected countries 2007 (US$, adjusted for differences in exchange rates)

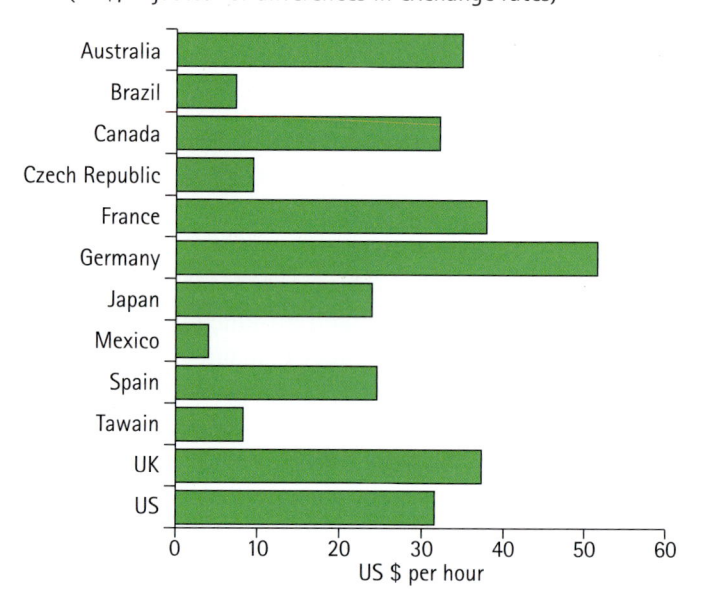

Source: US Bureau of Labour Statistics, 2011

▼ Gender pay gap, selected countries 2006: diference between male and female earnings as a percentage of male earnings, all industries

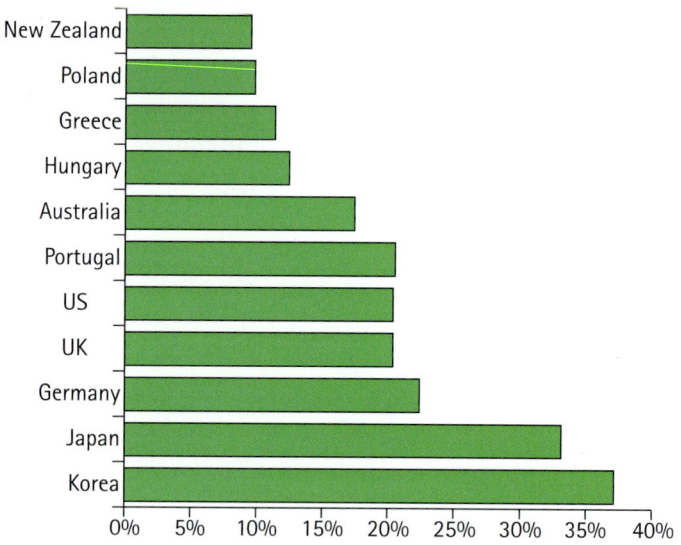

Source: 'Gender pay gap, selected countries 2006' reproduced from *OECD Family Database*, (OECD, 2010), copyright © OECD 2010

However, changes in some occupational and industrial wage differentials may be resisted by powerful trade unions that want to maintain the same differences in their members' pay relative to other groups of workers, regardless of changing labour market conditions. They are, therefore, not only concerned with wage differentials between members of other unions, but also wage differentials between unionized and non-unionized labour. ➤ 3.3

Gender pay gap

The average earnings of men usually exceed those of women the world over. For example, female earnings in 2010 were on average 82% of male earnings across 27 countries of the European Union (EU) according to research by Eurobarometer. Much of the difference in earnings can be explained by the following factors:

- There are differences in the occupational distribution of men and women. More women tend to work in occupations such as teaching, nursing and retailing than men. Market wage rates for these occupations are often below many those for many other occupations

- Women often take career breaks to raise children, and therefore may build up less work experience than males and have less career progression.

- More women work part-time than full-time compared to men.

However, the pay gap between men and women has declined during the past two decades in most developed economies. This change reflects more women joining the labour force and entering paid employment, and changes in attitudes in society towards women working and men sharing family responsibilities more. Many countries have also introduced equal pay laws.

The individual as producer, consumer and borrower

International wage differentials

Making international comparisons of wages and earnings is difficult. Data is not always available. However, it is clear that there are significant pay differentials between countries. Wages on average are higher in developed economies than in developing and less-developed economies even after adjusting for prices and living costs which are often much higher in developed economies. ▶ **7.1**

Real income and consumer spending on goods and services is far higher in developed economies. Remember that labour demand is related to the level of demand for, and revenue from, goods and services. In less-developed economies incomes are generally low and consumer spending is, therefore, also low. Hence, countries with low economic development tend to have few industries and generally low demand for labour. Most people in the least developed economies are employed in agriculture. ▶ **7.2**

However, less-developed economies have large potential labour forces but skill levels are relatively low. The combination of an abundant supply of labour with low demand for labour means wages will tend to remain low in many less-developed economies. In contrast, wage levels are now starting to rise rapidly in fast-developing economies such as China and India as the demand for goods and services, both at home and from overseas, grows rapidly and, consequently, the demand for labour from a growing number of industries increases.

ECONOMICS IN ACTION

Why are wage rates in China rising rapidly? Why might this cause some firms to relocate overseas? What are the possible implications of rising wages on inflation in China and countries that import Chinese goods and services?

China's labour pains

A series of high-profile strikes by Chinese workers and double-digit wage rises have highlighted China's rapidly changing labour market, prompting some to predict the imminent end of the country's status as a powerful magnet for inward investment from Western economies.

But despite a trickle of manufacturing operations now leaving China, many analysts say it is too soon to expect a flight of firms relocating to countries with even cheaper labour.

Lu Zhengwei, chief economist at the China Industrial Bank, forecasts an initial shift of industrial activity from China's booming coastal areas to its relatively poor, overpopulated inland provinces in the next few years where the supply of labour is more abundant and wage costs lower.

'Moving to inland areas will decrease costs. We calculated that salary levels in population-intensive areas inland are less than 70 per cent of those in Dongguan, one of southern China's biggest manufacturing bases.'

SECTION 5

Why do governments intervene in labour markets?

The government is a major employer in many countries, often employing the labour of many thousands of teachers, doctors, civil servants, army personnel and other public sector workers. Because it is such a major source of demand for labour it is able to exert a big influence over the market wage rates for different occupations in different areas.

However, governments also often intervene in labour markets for other reasons. Here are some examples.

1 To protect the rights of employees and employers

Employment laws and workplace health and safety regulations have been introduced in many countries not only to give employers and workers certain rights, but also to make them responsible for observing the rights and responsibilities of each other. In a totally free labour market, a powerful employer may not provide a safe working environment for employees or a powerful trade union may not deliver levels of labour productivity expected by employers. For example, the table below lists some of the key legal rights and responsibilities of employees and employers in the EU.

▼ Key legal responsibilities and rights (EU)

Employees	Employers
▶ to comply with the terms and conditions of their employment, for example, on hours of work, holidays, dress codes, maternity leave, disciplinary procedures, etc.	▶ to comply with the terms and conditions of their contract with an employee
▶ to comply with health and safety regulations, such as observing no-smoking signs and wearing protective clothing	▶ not to discriminate against any worker because of their sex, marital status, race, religion, disability, union membership or because they work part-time
▶ to receive at least the legal minimum levels of sick and maternity pay, and redundancy compensation	▶ to provide a healthy and safe working environment and any necessary equipment
▶ to receive at least four weeks of paid holiday per year and take minimum rest periods each day	▶ to comply with the legal rights of employees to minimum daily rest periods, paid holiday entitlements, maximum weekly working hours, payments for sickness, maternity and redundancy
▶ not to have to work more than 48 hours each week, except for jobs involving the driving of goods and public service vehicles	▶ to have the right to legally terminate employment and to defend their actions at an employment tribunal and the European Court of Justice
▶ to have protection from unfair dismissal and the right to defend their actions at an employment tribunal and the European Court of Justice	

2 To outlaw and regulate restrictive practices that may be used by powerful trade unions and major employers

In a free market, wage rates will be set by the interaction of labour supply and demand decisions. However, a powerful employer may be able to set a low market wage while a trade union may use its power over the supply of labour to a firm or occupation to force up market wages without similar gains in labour productivity.

Laws have been introduced in a number of countries to control the power of employers and trade unions over wages and working conditions. For example, in the UK employers must observe the legal rights of their employees, and trade unions no longer have the right to strike without first conducting a full ballot of their members. A trade union may also be liable for any damages or losses suffered by an employer from industrial action.

3 To raise the wages of the lowest-paid workers

Many countries have minimum wage legislation designed to protect vulnerable and low-paid workers from exploitation by powerful employers. The first national minimum wage law was introduced in New Zealand in 1896, followed by Australia in 1899 and the UK in 1902, and again in 1999. In 2006 in the EU, 18 out of 25 member states had national minimum wages. Apart from raising the pay of low-paid workers, it is argued that favourable minimum wages will make them work harder and achieve higher levels of productivity. However, some employers argue that minimum wages set above free market wage levels will simply raise production costs and reduce the demand for labour.

ACTIVITY 3.13

The minimum wage debate

Minimum wages do create some jobs – for economists. In the USA and the UK economists have been studying whether setting a floor under pay destroys jobs or reduces poverty.

A study by the OECD suggests the policy is ill suited to dealing with the problem of poverty. In most countries, many low earners have well-paid partners or affluent parents. Since most low-paid workers are not in poor households, most of the income gains that might come from a minimum wage would benefit families which are not poor.

Critics of minimum wages frequently argue that a government-mandated pay level reduces total employment because firms will scale back hiring rather than adding employees who must be paid more than they are worth. Those in favour argue an imposed wage minimum could have an opposite effect where the employer is large and powerful in relation to the pool of suitable workers. A powerful employer may be able to hold down wages by restricting its demand for labour. If a government sets a higher minimum wage, the employer no longer has this incentive. Because the employer must pay the higher wage there is no point any longer in restricting its demand for labour.

The OECD study – which considered data from nine countries, including the USA, Japan, France and Spain – found that a 10 per cent rise in the minimum wage reduced teenage employment by around 3 per cent in both high and low minimum wage countries.

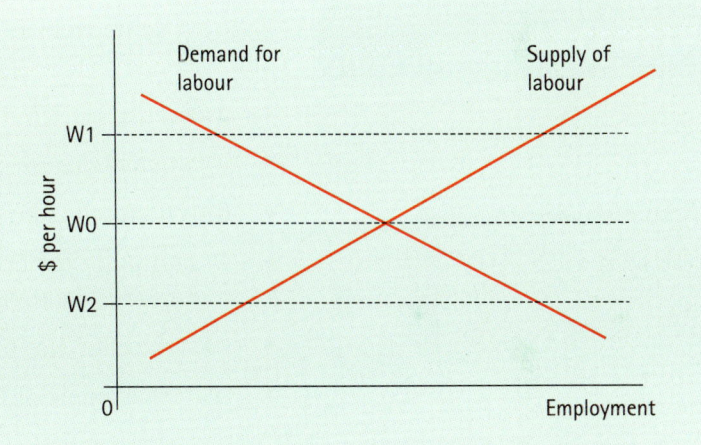

1 From the article, what are the arguments for and against a minimum wage? Does it matter what level the minimum wage is set at? Explain your answer using diagrams where possible.

2 How could you try to monitor the impact of a minimum wage over time?

3 In the diagram, what will be the impact of a minimum wage set at (a) W1 (b) W2?

4 Calculate the wage elasticity of demand for teenage labour suggested by the findings of the study.

4 To reduce unemployment

Governments may often provide unemployed workers with help re-training in the new skills required for employment in new growing industries and occupations. A government may also provide financial assistance to firms to encourage them to locate in areas of high unemployment. ➤ **6.2**

A government may also provide an employment service to help people look for jobs and prepare people for job interviews. In this way, a government can reduce the costs of searching for employment and increase the mobility of labour.

5 To outlaw unfair discrimination

While it is perfectly legal to discriminate between people in work according to their experience, performance and ability, it is unlawful in many countries to discriminate against people because of their sex, race, religion or disability, and also their age in some countries. For example, the Equal Pay Act in the UK makes it unlawful for employers to discriminate between men and women in terms of their pay and conditions where they are doing the same or similar work of equal value.

WEBSITES

Here are some websites to help you find out more about labour markets and wages:

- www.bized.co.uk/learn/economics/wages/index.htm
- www.tutor2u.net/revision_notes_economics_gcse.asp (select How We Work)
- International Labour Organization *laborsta.ilo.org*
- Organisation for Economic Co-operation and Development (OECD) – select Statistics then Labour) www.oecd.org
- UK Office for National Statistics (select Labour market) www.statistics.gov.uk
- US Department of Labor: Bureau of Labor Statistics www.bls.gov

KEYWORDS

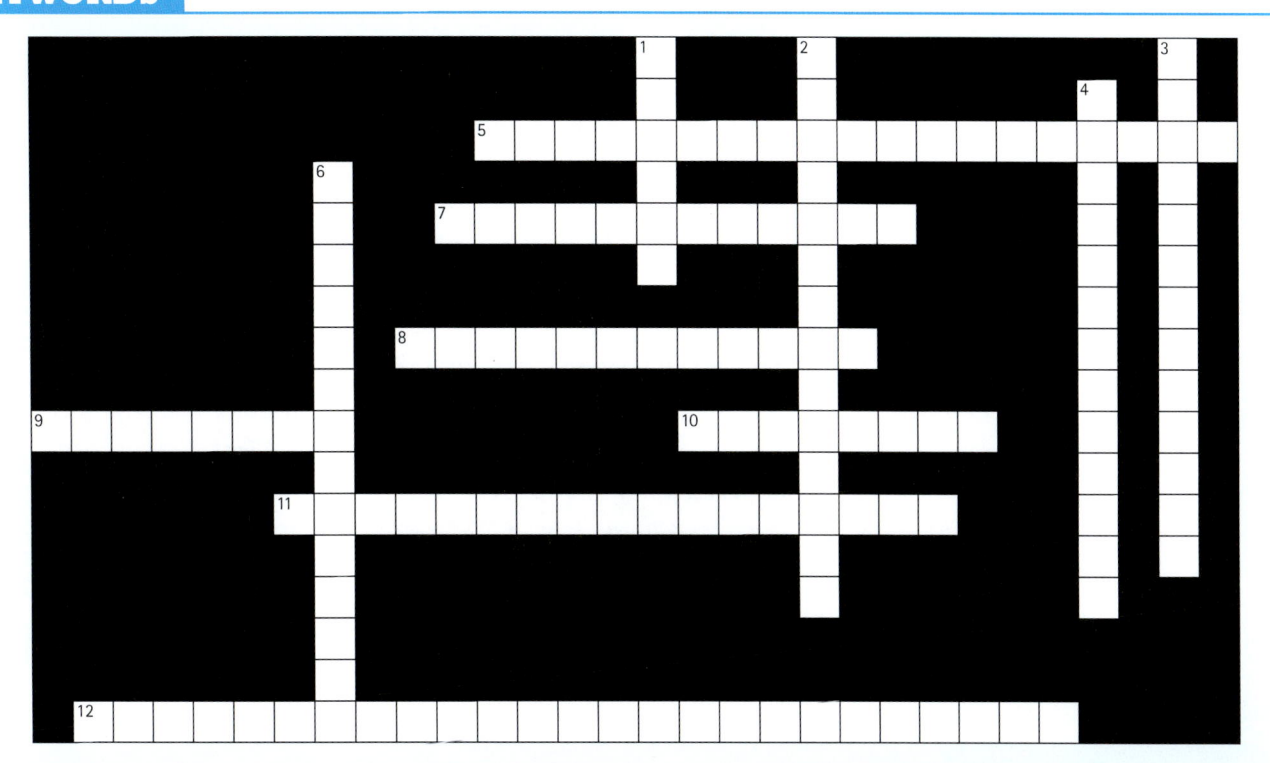

Clues across

5. The market clearing rate of pay at which the amount of labour demanded by firms will match the amount supplied (11, 4, 4)
7. The term used to describe the differential in average earnings between male and female employees (6, 3, 3)
8. Any set of arrangements that brings together all those people willing and able to supply their labour with organizations that want to hire labour (6, 6)
9. A wage rate for additional hours worked, usually during evenings or weekends, over and above agreed hours (8)
10. The amount paid to an employee per period of time worked or per unit of output produced (4, 4)
11. Differences in rates of pay between different occupations, industries, locations and group of workers (4, 13)
12. Higher rates of pay offered to workers to attract their labour to unpleasant, unsociable or dangerous jobs (12, 13)

Clues down

1. An annual rate of pay, often paid to employees in professional and other non-manual occupations (7)
2. Perks or rewards for employees, such as free medical insurance or use of a company car, that have monetary value (6, 8)
3. The balance of all the advantages and disadvantages of a particular job or occupation that people will consider when deciding whether or not to supply their labour (3, 10)
4. The total pay received by an employee for his or her labour per week or month. This may consist of wages or a salary, a piece-rate payment and other performance-related payments (5, 8)
6. Features of a job other than wage factors, such as hours of work and holiday entitlement, that make it attractive (3-4, 7)

Occupations and earnings

Unit 3.3 — The role of trade unions

AIMS

By the end of this unit you should be able to:

▶ describe **trade unions** and analyse their role in an economy

- distinguish between different types of **trade union** or labour union
- describe how trade unions are organized
- understand the role of **collective bargaining** in setting wages and other employment conditions
- explain factors that can affect the bargaining strength of a trade union
- analyse why **industrial disputes** occur, their impacts on employees, firms and an economy, and how they are settled.

SECTION 1

What is a trade union?

Many workers belong to labour unions or **trade unions** all over the world. Trade unions promote and protect the interests of their members with the purpose of improving their wages and working conditions. In return, members will usually pay a union membership fee to help fund the union organization.

Trade unions first developed in European countries during the Industrial Revolution in the 18th and 19th centuries following the development of factories and mass production. During this time the structure of the UK and other Western economies changed rapidly from ones based on farming and craft industries, to industrialized economies in which manufacturing industries produced most of the total output and provided most of the jobs. Work in factories was often poorly paid and undertaken in appalling conditions. Workers therefore began to organize themselves into unions to challenge the owners of factories to improve their conditions.

ACTIVITY 3.14

Why I'm part of the union!

Training Courses

Through the union stewards, health and safety (H&S) representatives, branch officials and active members can benefit from an extensive range of training courses to improve their skills. These include

- Bargaining issues and negotiating skills
- Company information and accounts
- Human resource management
- New technology and change at work
- The law at work
- Communication and tutoring skills
- Trade unionists and the environment
- Organization and recruitment

Union movement asks government for tougher regulations of health and safety to reduce industrial injuries and accidents in the workplace

The union centre at the coast offers premium holiday accommodation to members looking for reduced rate holidays and short breaks. Convalescent patients can enjoy up to two weeks' free accommodation, subject to conditions. In addition, the centre boasts professional, state-of-the-art conferencing and seminar facilities.

South African Truck Drivers to Strike Over Wages

South African truckers plan to go on strike next week in a dispute over wages.

The South African Transport and Allied Workers' Union is demanding a 20 per cent increase for 2011 and 2012, while the Road Freight Employers' Association is offering 15 percent. The strike will be joined by the Transport and Allied Workers' Union of South Africa and the Professional Transport Workers' Union.

Public sector unions reacted angrily at the government announcement of 'significant' job cuts across public sector organizations over the next 3 years. They are demanding the government abandons its plans and improves pay and pensions for millions of low-paid workers

1. From the above articles what do you think are the aims of trade unions?
2. What do you think are the possible benefits or problems for a business that has a high level of trade union membership among its workforce?
3. Would you join a trade union? What would be the possible costs and benefits of your membership?

The trade union movement worldwide has helped fight and bring to an end child labour in many countries; it has improved workers' safety, increased wages for both union and non-unionized workers, reduced hours of work and improved education and other benefits for many poor and working class families.

The functions of trade unions

Trade unions have a number of aims regarding the welfare of their members. These include:

- negotiating improvements in and other non-wage benefits with employers
- defending employees' rights and jobs
- improving working conditions, such as securing better hours of work and better health and safety policies
- improving pay and other benefits, including holiday entitlement, sick pay and pensions

- encouraging firms to increase workers' participation in business decision making
- supporting members who have been dismissed or who are taking industrial action
- developing the skills of union members, by providing training and education courses
- providing social and recreational amenities for their members
- influencing government policy and employment legislation.

Before trade unions existed, a worker had to negotiate on his or her own for increased pay and better working conditions with his or her employer. With few rights, a worker could face being sacked for asking. Trade unions, however, can negotiate with and put pressure on employers on behalf of all their members to secure these aims. Trade unions therefore helped to reduce the power employers had over their workforces.

However, trade unions do not have the legal right to represent workers in some countries, or this right may not be recognized by employers and politicians. Unions are even outlawed in some countries and union officials can be jailed.

In contrast, in some countries unions work closely with, and even help to fund political parties. They can also use their power to influence government policies and employment laws to be more favourable to their members or to workers in general. In addition, many trade unions offer their members education and training to improve their skills and provide their members with recreational amenities including social clubs.

Types of trade unions

Trade unions are often grouped into four main types.

1 **General unions** represent workers from many different occupations and industries. For example, Unite in the UK represents all sorts of clerical, manufacturing, transport and commercial workers in both the public and private sector.

2 **Industrial unions** represent workers in the same industry, for example, the Turkish Union of Defence Workers (TÜRK HARB-˙IS¸), the National Union of Mineworkers in South Africa (NUM) and the Overseas Telecommunications Services Employees Association of Mauritius (OTSEA).

3 **Craft unions** are often small and relatively few in number today. They usually represent workers with the same skills across several industries, such as the Union of Operators and Technicians in Cinema and Video Projection in Spain and the United Brotherhood of Carpenters and Joiners of America.

4 **Non-manual unions** and **professional associations**, sometimes called white-collar unions, represent workers in non-industrial and professional occupations, such as the Association of Iranian Journalists (AOIJ), All India Bank Officer Association (AIBOC), German Police Union (GDL) and the National Union of Teachers (NUT) in the UK.

SECTION 2

How trade unions are organized

A union will consist of its members from different workplaces who belong to the union and full-time officials who are employed by the union at all levels in the organization to run and manage the union. Typically a union will be organized as follows:

General secretary	The head of a union. The person who takes on this role will normally be elected by members
National executive	This is the management tier of the union with executive members elected by union members to run the union nationally. It will decide union policy and strategy, consider and respond to government legislation that may affect members' interests, and be responsible for union finances
District committee	Branches can belong to a district or regional committee of elected union officials to run the union and look after union affairs in a region
Branch	All members in a local area will be part of a local branch and can attend branch meetings to discuss union business and issues that affect workers in different workplaces
Shop stewards	These are employees who, in addition to their normal job, also represent union members in their workplace, help with any issues they have and carry out day-to-day tasks on behalf of the union
Members	These are employees who belong to the union

Each year a union will usually hold an annual general meeting (AGM) or annual congress where delegated members and shop stewards from different workplaces can attend to discuss common issues with the union's **national executive** and vote on union policies.

Individual unions may also unite with, or affiliate to, a national union organization – a trade union congress or federation – which provides coordination and national representation for the union movement. These organizations can speak up on behalf of unions and their members to powerful employer associations, the media, and national and international governments to ensure that union members' interests are taken into account. Examples include the Trades Union Congress in the UK (*www.tuc.org.uk*), the Malaysian Trade Union Congress (*www.mtuc.org.my*), the Indian National Trade Union Congress (*www.intuc.net*), and the Canadian Labour Congress (*www.canadianlabour.ca*).

International cooperation

National and regional trade unions representing workers in specific industries or occupations can also join global union federations, such as the International Transport Workers' Federation Union and the International Federation of Journalists. They can also join together to cooperate in pan-regional labour organizations such as the European Trade Union Confederation (ETUC), the International Confederation of Arab Trade Unions (ICATU) and the Organization of African Trade Union Unity (OATUU).

The largest organization of trade union members in the world is the International Confederation of Free Trade Unions (www.ictfu.org). In 2006 this had over 230 affiliated organizations in 150 countries and territories, with a combined membership of over 150 million. Other global trade union organizations are the World Confederation of Labour (www.cmt-wcl.org) and the World Federation of Trade Unions (www.wftucentral.org).

Union membership

Union membership in some countries has been rising while others have experienced falling membership. For example, union membership has been rising in countries such as Argentina, Bahrain, China, India and Nigeria. In contrast, union membership has been falling for many years in the USA, Germany and the UK, and in a number of Eastern European countries including Bulgaria, Estonia and Latvia. In the USA union membership fell from a peak of 22.5 million workers in 1975 to just 15.3 million workers in 2010, around 12% of the total US workforce.

The decline in the number and membership of unions in many developed economies is often attributed to the decline in the manufacturing industry and the growth of the service sector in these countries. For example, in the UK around 80% of the total workforce is employed in service industries. Union membership in services tends to be lower than in manufacturing industries. Men are also more likely than women to be union members, but in some developed and developing economies the number of women union members is growing.

Unions also tend to be much stronger in the public sector than the private sector. The decline in the size of the public sector in many former planned economies in Eastern Europe may also help to explain falling union membership in some of these countries.

> **EXAM PREPARATION 3.2**
>
> In 2002 in the UK and in Germany trade unions supported strikes in some public sector occupations.
>
> a   Explain what is meant by the public sector and give **one** example of a public sector occupation. [3]
>
> b   Describe the functions of trade unions and explain which function you consider to be the most important. [7]
>
> c   State **three** factors that might determine an individual's choice of occupation. [3]
>
> d   Discuss why some occupations receive higher wages than other occupations. [7]
>
> *Cambridge IGCSE Economics 0455/04 Q2 October/November 2004*
> *Cambridge O Level Economics 2281/02 Q2 October/November 2004*

SECTION 3

Collective bargaining

What is collective bargaining?

The process of negotiating over pay and working conditions between trade unions and employers is known as **collective bargaining**.

Trade unions will often argue for improved wages and other working conditions if:

- price inflation is high and rising
- other groups of workers have received pay rises
- new machinery or working practices have been introduced in the workplace
- the labour productivity of their members has increased
- the profits of the employing organization have increased.

Depending on how collective bargaining is organized, negotiations between a union and employers can determine the pay and conditions for all workers in all firms in a particular industry in the economy, or they will reach local area agreements between individual firms and their workforces.

How collective bargaining is organized depends on the relationship between a union and the firms that employ the union's members. One or more trade unions can represent employees in a firm or a workplace. For example, there may be several trade unions present in one organization representing workers with different occupational skills, such as engineers or clerical workers. Alternatively, a single trade union may represent all the workers in a particular business or even an entire industry regardless of their occupations and skills.

Union representation in the workplace	
Closed shop	Trade union membership is made a compulsory condition of a taking a job in an organization. The closed shop is outlawed in many countries because it gives a union too much power to dictate who a firm should employ and to call all the workers in that firm out on strike
Open shop	A firm can employ both unionized and non-unionized labour
Single union agreement	An employer agrees to a single union representing all its employees

Single union agreements are increasingly popular because they offer an employer a number of advantages:

- Time is saved by negotiating with only one union.
- It avoids disagreements arising between different unions.
- It is easier to implement changes in working practices through one union.
- A closer working relationship with the union should develop and help to reduce industrial disputes.

The main problem with a single union agreement in a workplace is that it gives the trade union significant bargaining power. Because of this most firms will only agree to single union representation for their employees if the trade union agrees to commitments on improved levels of productivity, maintaining skill levels in the workforce and not to take strike action.

What determines the bargaining strength of different trade unions?

> **Public sector electricity workers in Nigeria launch an indefinite strike over wages**

> **Nigeria's National Union of Electricity Employees (NUEE) called off its nationwide strike today after reaching an agreement with the federal government**

Look at the two headlines below to your left. How long do you think it took for the second headline to be published in a Nigerian newspaper after the first one appeared announcing a strike by electricity workers? The answer is just one day!

An indefinite strike by all 40,000 employees of the government-owned Power Holding Company in Nigeria would have left many people and businesses in the country without power, causing hardship and halting production. As a result, the government of Nigeria held urgent talks overnight with union representatives and together an agreement on wages was reached.

In contrast, when 1,500 cleaners at Dutch Railways went on strike to highlight the poor wages and working conditions of all 150,000 cleaners employed in the Netherlands, it took nine weeks to resolve with employers. So why did reaching an agreement take so long in this case? Much depends on the bargaining strength of the workers' trade union.

The National Union of Electricity Employees in Nigeria was in a strong bargaining position to negotiate higher wages because its members strike was supported by all of Nigeria's electricity workers and because they were responsible for providing an essential service to a great many people and businesses. In contrast, only 1% of cleaners in the Netherlands went on strike over improved pay and conditions. Most cleaners continued providing useful but non-essential cleaning services to different firms in the Dutch economy. Other Dutch railway employees were also able to help keep railway stations and trains clean when the cleaners took strike action.

The bargaining power of a trade union to secure improved pay and other working conditions from employers is therefore stronger when:

- the union represents most or all of the workers in that firm or industry
- union members provide products and public services consumers need and for which there are few close substitutes, such as electricity, public transport, health care and education
- the union is able to support its members financially during strike action to compensate them for their loss of earnings.

Unions and employers will also negotiate over employment levels and other benefits such as pension rights, holiday entitlement, training and the introduction of new technology and working practices.

Why do industrial disputes occur?

Collective bargaining between trade unions and employers can sometimes fail to reach an agreement. For example, if a union demands a wage increase for its members not matched by higher productivity, then production costs will rise. Firms will either face trying to pass on higher wage costs to consumers in higher prices, or the profits of the owners of the firm will be reduced. Demand for more holidays, better pensions and sick pay, and resistance to new working practices, will also tend to raise costs and could mean that a firm becomes uncompetitive. As a result, a firm may try to reduce its costs by reducing its demand for labour and making some workers unemployed. ▶ 3.2

Disputes over demarcation can also arise. These occur when a union insists that its members can only carry out certain jobs and will not take on new tasks, or when a firm employs non-union members to carry out the same or similar tasks instead.

Industrial actions

When negotiations between employers and unions fail to end in agreement, workers may take disruptive **industrial action** to put pressure on their employers to address their demands or grievances. **Official action** has the backing of their trade union, and other unions may also take action in support. **Unofficial action** means that workers taking the industrial action do not have the support of their union.

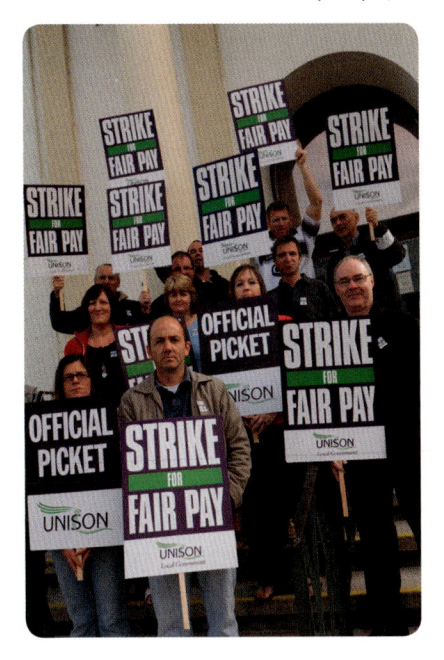

▼ Workers on strike over equal pay

Forms of industrial action	
Overtime ban	Workers refuse to work more than their normal hours
Work to rule	Workers deliberately slow down production by complying rigidly with every rule and regulation
Go-slow	Workers carry out tasks deliberately slowly to reduce production
Strike	Workers refuse to work and may also protest, or picket, outside their workplace to stop deliveries and prevent non-unionized workers from entering

Industrial action can increase the bargaining strength of workers to force employers to agree to their wage and other demands. However, union action also has major implications:

- **Businesses** suffer higher costs and lose output, revenues and profits during industrial action. If the action goes on for a long time a business may also lose important customers to rival firms.

- **Union members** will not be paid their wages or salaries during a strike although some may receive income support from their union's strike fund. Some workers may also lose their jobs if employers cut back their demand for labour because the industrial action has lost them customers and profits.

- **Consumers** may be unable to obtain the goods and services they need and may also have to pay higher prices if firms pass on their increased costs.

- The reputation of **an economy** as a good place for business may be damaged by frequent and widespread industrial action. Firms may decide to invest and set up businesses elsewhere. This will increase unemployment and lower incomes.

The role of trade unions

Arbitration may be necessary to settle industrial disputes. This involves employers and unions agreeing to let an independent referee, often a senior government official or lawyer, help them reach agreement. This normally means both sides in the dispute accepting a compromise – something that is satisfactory to both parties but rather less than they had initially wanted.

Because industrial action can be so damaging some employers and unions have reached 'no strike' agreements. In return, employers may agree to more generous wages and improved working conditions. Alternatively, both sides agree to accept the judgement of an independent arbitrator who will determine what a fair wage increase or change in working conditions should be, based on evidence and recommendations presented by the union's and employer's representatives.

Laws have also been introduced in many countries relating to the power of trade unions to take industrial action. For example, an employer in the UK can seek legal damages from a union for lost profits if industrial action is taken without first balloting its members. Mass picketing is also unlawful. Only a handful of strikers are allowed to picket outside their workplace.

ACTIVITY 3.15

A tough negotiation

In groups of four, act out the following roles in an industrial dispute between an employer and a trade union. Your job is to try to find a settlement that both sides in the dispute are willing to accept. The roles in the dispute are shown opposite.

Union representatives
- the shop steward
- a machine operator

Employee representatives
- the managing director
- the work study engineer

Union threatens action over new machinery

The Association of Metalworkers is today threatening to take industrial action if the decision to install new computer-assisted metal shaping and grinding machinery in PK Metals plc is taken without assurances on pay and redundancies. The local branch of the union has asked for a 5% wage increase for members to operate the new machinery.

'Any strike action could damage the company considerably,' said Mr Graham Stone, managing director of PK Metals. 'A major new order from an overseas customer has recently boosted the company's prospects and we must deliver on time and to quality.'

Any disruption could threaten the international reputation of the company. The management are also keen to avoid any increase in wage costs that may make the firm uncompetitive.

Workers are claiming that the new technology requires a higher level of skill and concentration, and compensation is sought. They are also seeking management assurances that there will be no redundancies as a result of the new machines.

The two sides in the dispute have agreed to meet and negotiate today.

The union brief

The machine operators want a pay rise for operating more complex and demanding machinery. You also want to set an example for the future. You do not want your employer to think that every time it introduces new ways of working it can overlook its workforce. What you want is a share in the increased profits that can come from the increased output of the new machines.

You also fear that redundancies may follow as machines replace workers, and you want to limit the number of jobs lost.

You both know that the firm has recently received a large order from overseas, so you need to be careful that you do not cause the firm to lose the order. This could mean losing jobs.

Your task before negotiations

Before you enter negotiations write a brief report for all your union members to read, pointing out your demands and the management's position. This should include answers to questions such as:

- What is your pay claim?
- Why have you made this pay claim?
- What has been the management response?
- What forms of action could the union take if necessary?
- Why are both you and the management keen to avoid a strike?

Your tasks after negotiations

Write a report highlighting the results of negotiations, that is, what agreements, if any, were reached.

If no firm agreement was reached, do you advise your members to accept or reject the management's offer? If no agreement was reached, what will the union do next?

The employer's brief

The work study engineer has concluded that the machines require no more effort to operate than the old ones. In fact, you feel that they ease pressure on the skilled operator. No pay rise is necessary to compensate.

As the managing director you fear that any cost reductions from the increased output from specialist machinery may be lost if workers push for higher wages. It may even allow lower-cost competitors to undercut your prices. If you are also unable to cut the number of jobs your plant will be over-staffed and wage costs will be much higher than they need to be.

However, you do not want to lose the goodwill of the workforce at a critical time for the company with an overseas order to fulfill.

Your task before negotiations

Write an information sheet for the management team including answers to such questions as:

- What wage claim has the union made?
- What are the implications of accepting or rejecting this claim?
- Why you are keen to avoid a strike?
- What will be discussed with the union?

Task after negotiations

Prepare another management document to report on agreements reached and their effects on the company and the action that will be taken if negotiations break down and no firm agreement is reached.

The negotiations

The four people in the role-play should try to negotiate an agreement acceptable to both sides. If you cannot reach an agreement perhaps your tutor can join in to act as an independent commentator, or ask for the meeting to take a short break while you work out what to do next.

WEBSITES

Sources of information to help you with your coursework include:

- the biz/ed education online service www.bized.ac.uk/compfact/tuc/tuc11.htm
- European Industrial Relations Observatory www.eurofound.europa.eu/eiro

KEYWORDS

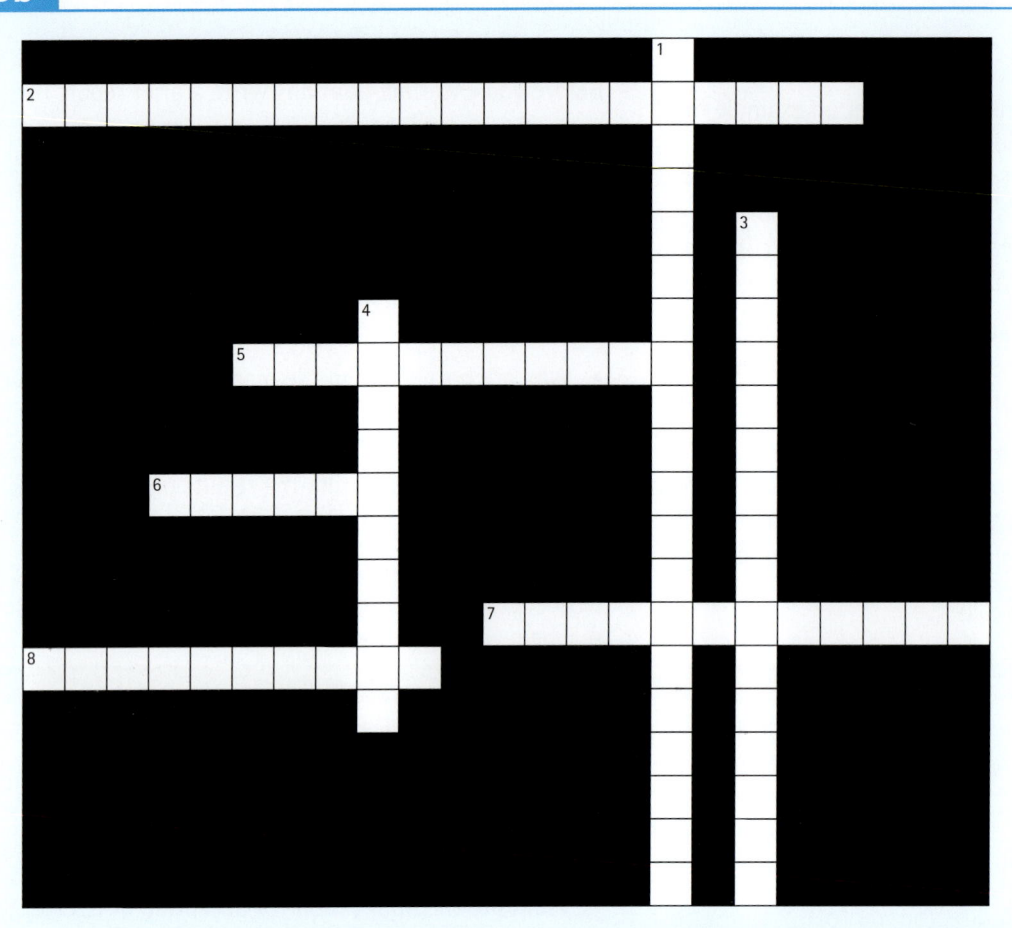

Clues across

2. The process of negotiating pay and working conditions between trade union representatives and employers (10, 10)
5. An industrial action that involves workers refusing to work more than their normal hours (8, 3)
6. A disruptive action taken by a group of workers who refuse to work (5)
7. A type of trade union with members drawn from many different industries and occupations (7, 5)
8. This exists when trade union membership is made a compulsory condition of a taking a job in an particular workplace or organization (6, 4)

Clues down

1. An agreement between an employer and a single trade union to represent all workers at a particular workplace. The arrangement saves time by negotiating with only one union and avoids disagreements arising between different unions (5, 5, 9)
3. The term used to describe all disruptive activities, such as a strike or work to rule, that workers carry out to support their wage or other demands (10, 6)
4. An association representing employees in a particular workplace or industry with the aim of improving their pay and working conditions (5, 5)

The individual as producer, consumer and borrower

Unit 3.4 — Spending, saving and borrowing

AIMS

By the end of this unit you should be able to:

▸ analyse the different motives for **spending, saving and borrowing**
  - understand how age, tastes, **consumer confidence** and other factors affect our spending, saving and borrowing patterns
  - appreciate how saving involves a choice between **current consumption** and future consumption
  - analyse the impact changes in **interest rates** and the **availability of credit** can have on decisions to borrow money
▸ discuss how and why different income groups have different **expenditure patterns**
  - define **disposable income** and understand why it is a key determinant of how much different people spend, save or borrow.

SECTION 1

Consumption

People hire out their services as labour in return for wages and other earnings. Some people also invest in companies and earn dividends from profits, while others invest in savings and other investment schemes and earn interest on their money. Other people may rent out land and buildings they own to other people and firms. But what do people do with all the income they earn?

People are owners of factors of production and also consumers of goods and services. They earn money to buy the goods and services they want and need but do not produce themselves in their work. Any income they do not spend, and which is not taken in tax, can be saved.

Disposable income

Wages and salaries, dividends from company profits, rents and interest from savings are all forms of taxable income in most countries. The income a person has left after income-related taxes and charges have been deducted is called **disposable income**, because that person can dispose of it how he or she wants, i.e. people can choose to spend it or save it how they like. A rise in income taxes will therefore reduce disposable income and the amount people have to spend or save. Some people may, however, simply choose to save less if taxes rise rather than to cut their spending. ▶ 5.2

The more disposable income a person has, the greater their potential **consumer expenditure** on goods and services, and the more they will be able to save. But how much people can buy with their disposable income will also depend on prices. Increasing prices will reduce the real purchasing power of income.

Spending, saving and borrowing 161

Therefore, the amount individuals can choose to spend on goods and services depends on their **real disposable income**. Some people with very low real disposable incomes may only be able to afford to satisfy their basic needs for food and shelter, while others with high disposable incomes may chose to consume a vast array of different goods and services mainly for pleasure.

Global economic growth has increased real incomes and, with it, consumer expenditure over time. For example, the charts below demonstrate how closely income and consumer expenditure are related in Australia and Mexico. The same is true in all countries. ➤ 6.3

▼ Real income and consumer expenditure are closely related in all countries

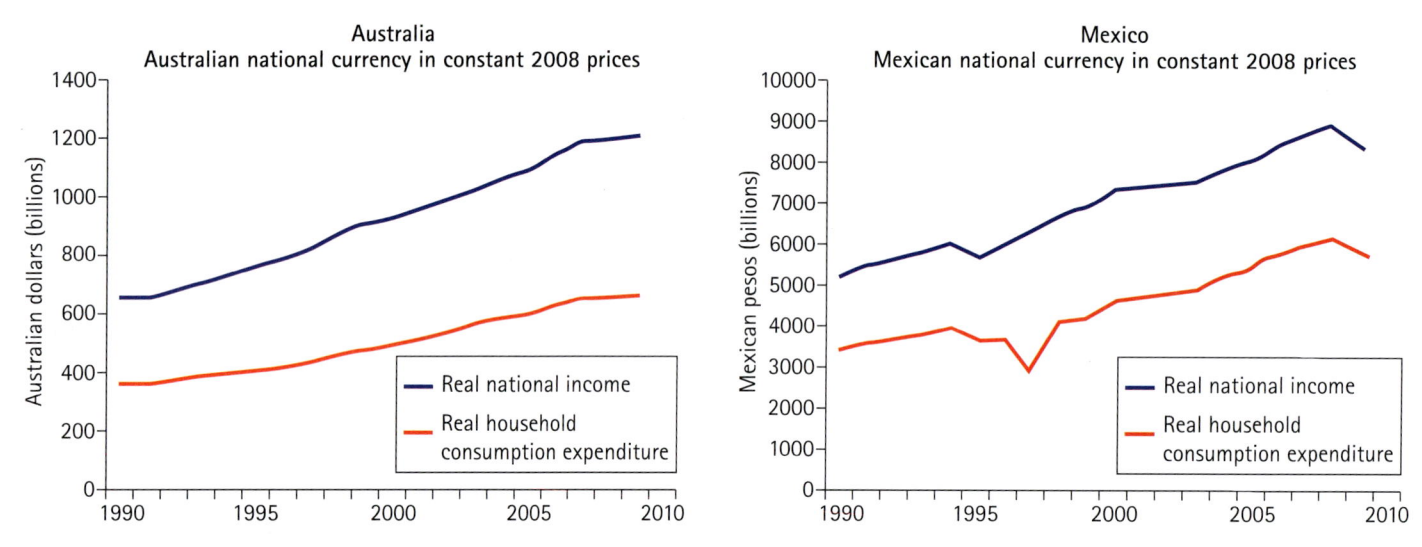

Australia
Australian national currency in constant 2008 prices

Mexico
Mexican national currency in constant 2008 prices

— Real national income
— Real household consumption expenditure

Source: 'Australian national currency in constant 2008 prices' and 'Mexican national currency in constant 2008 prices' reproduced from OECD Statistics, www.oecd.org, copyright © OECD 2011

Why do people consume goods and services?

People buy goods and services to satisfy their wants and needs. Consumption involves the using up of goods and services to satisfy wants.

In general, people will choose to spend their disposable incomes on consuming those goods and services that provide them with the most satisfaction or **utility**. That is, a person with a given disposable income, and faced with a set of prices and places to buy different goods and services, will consume those goods and services that maximize his or her total utility.

Consider a simple example of a boy eating cakes. He likes cakes but if he buys too few to eat he will not maximize his utility. However, if he buys and eats too many at once he may start to feel sick and his utility will start to fall. Let's say he does buy too many cakes. He should have bought fewer and instead spent money on things that would have given him more pleasure than those extra cakes, such as a music CD or a visit to the cinema to watch a film. The same will apply to the consumption of shoes, holidays, cars and all other goods and services, hence the saying 'you can have too much of a good thing!'

The individual as producer, consumer and borrower

Patterns of consumer expenditure can vary greatly even between people with similar incomes, simply because people have different tastes. Tastes may vary between different groups of consumers according to their age, sex and family circumstances, for example whether they are married and have children. ➤ **2.2**

People's tastes can also change over time and may be influenced by the views of other consumers. For example, we might change our mind about going to the cinema to watch a particular film or visiting a local restaurant, because we have heard bad reports from other people who have seen the film or eaten at the restaurant. Similarly, we might use a car mechanic or hairdresser and really like their services, in which case we will tend to use them again and again. All of these types of products are called **experience goods and services**, because it is difficult to judge how much we might like them until we have consumed them, and because we can also tell other people about our experience of them. ➤ **7.2**

After income, the following are the three most important factors that affect the level of consumer expenditure in an economy:

Wealth

The more wealthy people feel, the greater their spending on goods and services is likely to be. Private **wealth** consists of a stock of goods that have a money value. It includes assets such as houses, jewellery and shares in companies, many of which can be sold for cash. Wealth also includes money saved in bank accounts and other investment schemes that can easily be withdrawn. ➤ **3.1**

Consumer confidence

If consumers are confident about their jobs and their future incomes then this might encourage them to spend more now, perhaps even to borrow money to buy a house, a new car or other expensive items. However, income and employment can change over the economic cycle. If consumers think they may become unemployed or suffer falling income during an economic recession then this may persuade them to save more rather than spend. ➤ **6.3**

Interest rates

If interest rates are high people may save more of their disposable income because it pays them to do so. However, if interest rates are low people may spend more, and may even borrow more because loan repayments will be less.

Spending, saving and borrowing

ACTIVITY 3.16

Spending patterns

▼ Household expenditure as a % of total household expenditure, by lowest and highest gross income households, UK 2009

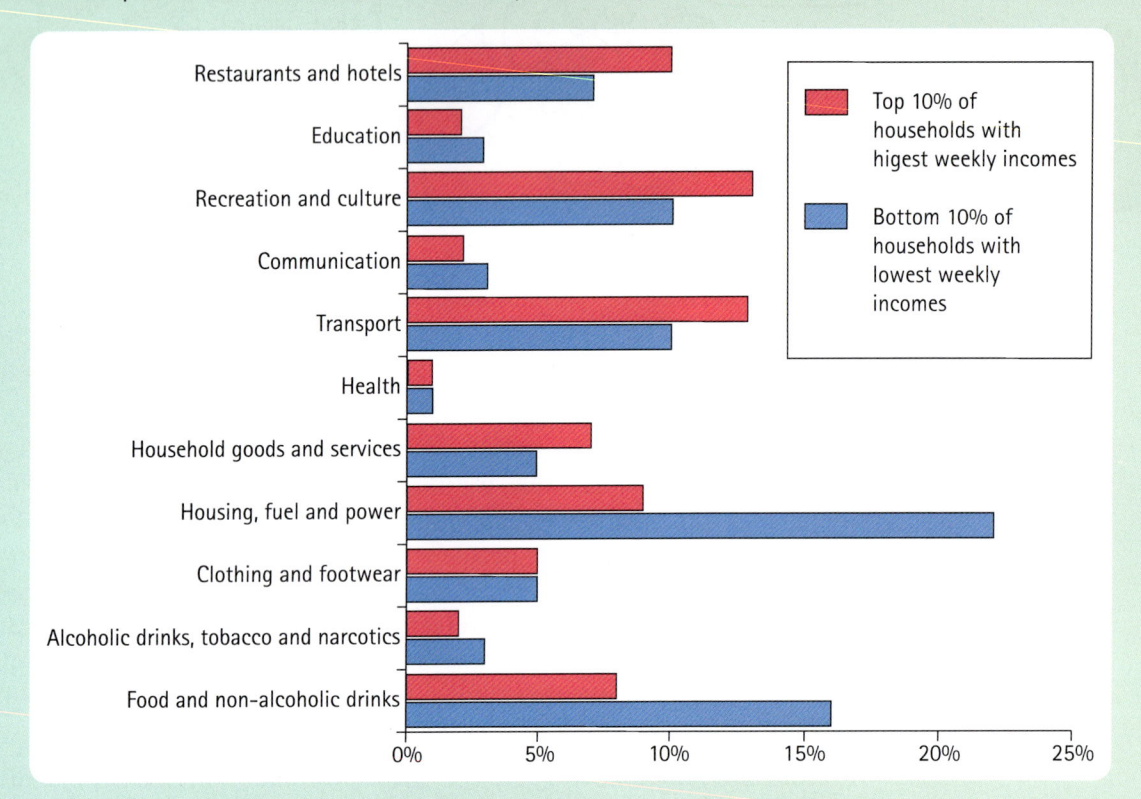

Category	Top 10%	Bottom 10%
Restaurants and hotels	~10%	~7%
Education	~2%	~3%
Recreation and culture	~13%	~10%
Communication	~2%	~3%
Transport	~13%	~10%
Health	~1%	~1%
Household goods and services	~7%	~5%
Housing, fuel and power	~9%	~22%
Clothing and footwear	~5%	~5%
Alcoholic drinks, tobacco and narcotics	~2%	~3%
Food and non-alcoholic drinks	~8%	~16%

Legend:
- Top 10% of households with higest weekly incomes
- Bottom 10% of households with lowest weekly incomes

Source: *Family Spending 2009*, UK Office for National Statistics

Look at the chart comparing how the average low-income household and average high-income household in the UK divide up their weekly spending between different goods and services.

1 Which type of household spent the highest proportion of their total spending on the following categories?:
   ▶ Food and non-alcoholic drinks
   ▶ Housing, fuel and power
   ▶ Recreation and culture
   ▶ Alcohol and tobacco
   ▶ Transport
   ▶ Restaurants and hotels

2 What do you think explains these different expenditure patterns?

Consumption patterns and trends

The proportion of disposable income individuals spend, known as their propensity to consume, and what they spend it on, varies greatly across populations. We can examine consumption patterns by income group, gender and age, and also over time. Firms find this information useful because it allows them to target the goods and services they produce and advertise at particular groups of consumers they want to attract to buy those products.

People on lower incomes tend to spend all of their money to meet basic needs for food, clothing, housing and heating, and if possible to satisfy a few wants from time to time. People on high incomes may spend far more, and on luxury

The individual as producer, consumer and borrower

items, leisure activities and other goods and services to satisfy their wants, but overall will tend to spend a lower proportion of their total disposable income.

What we buy tends to change as we get older. For example, young people may spend more on fashionable clothes, going out to clubs and bars, and music CDs than older people, who will tend to spend more on household goods for their homes. ▶ 7.2

▼ Trends in US household expenditure, 1984–2009

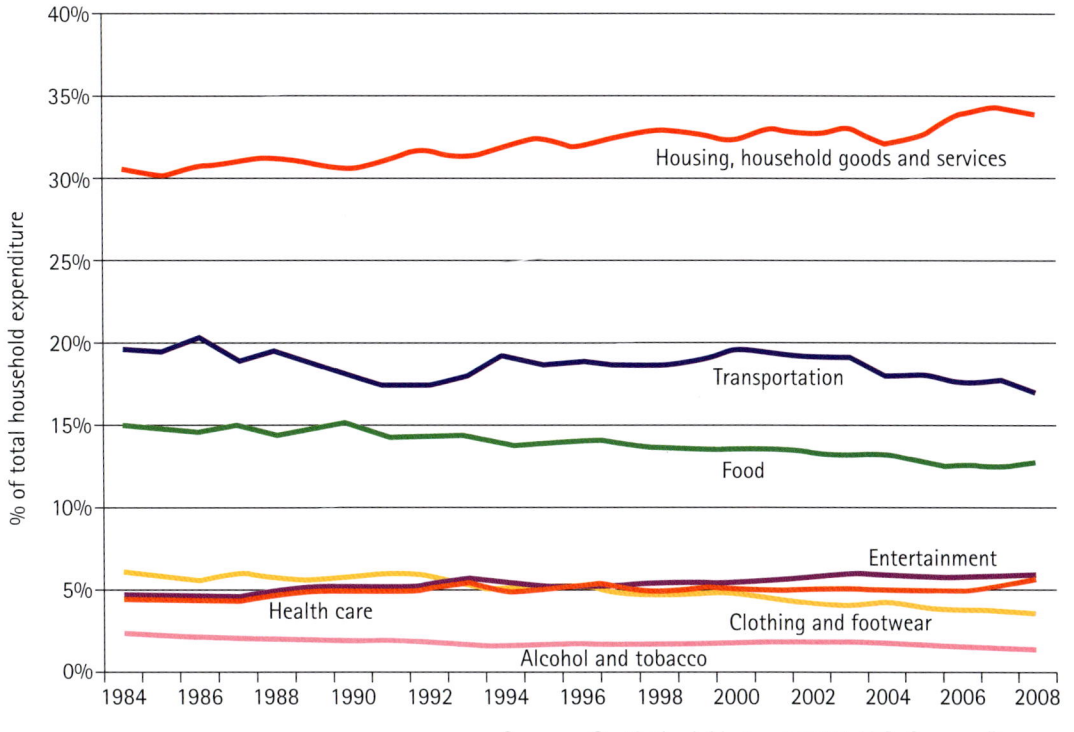

[Chart: Trends in US household expenditure 1984–2008, showing % of total household expenditure for: Housing, household goods and services (~30–34%); Transportation (~17–20%); Food (~13–15%); Entertainment (~5–6%); Health care (~4–6%); Clothing and footwear (~3–6%); Alcohol and tobacco (~1–2%)]

Source: *Statistical Abstract 2011*, U.S. Census Bureau

The chart opposite shows how household spending patterns have changed over time in the USA.

Spending by US households on food, alcoholic drink and tobacco as a proportion of their total spending has fallen and they are now devoting more of their expenditure to housing, household goods and services and to health care and entertainment.

The same consumption trends have been observed in many developed countries, and also now in some developing countries, and are the result of a number of factors:

- **Real incomes have risen**

More people are now better off. Higher incomes enable people to spend more on satisfying their wants. The increased use of credit cards to boost spending also reflects a change in attitudes over time towards borrowing and debt.

- **People work fewer hours than many years ago**

This has given people more leisure time, and increased spending on holidays, sporting activities, garden plants and equipment, and eating out in restaurants.

- **Social attitudes have changed**

More females are going out to work in many countries. This means they have less time to look after their families and has increased the demand for time-saving appliances such as microwave ovens and dishwashers.

Spending, saving and borrowing

- **Couples are marrying later in life and having fewer children**

Consumption patterns for different goods and services, and also savings patterns, are therefore changing over time as the average age of populations rises in many developed and rapidly developing countries due to a fall in their birth rates. It has also meant a growing number of single people and an increase in the number of households, but a fall in their average size. This has helped to increase the amount spent on housing and household goods and furnishings over time. Single people tend to spend more on going out and travel. ➤ **7.2**

- **People have become more health conscious**

Spending on sports activities, exercise equipment and gym membership has increased. Demand for healthier foods has also risen. ➤ **2.2**

- **Concern for the environment is growing**

This has increased the demand for products which release fewer harmful pollutants into the atmosphere when they are produced or consumed, can be recycled, and are not tested on animals.

- **Technology has advanced rapidly**

New products have become available and created new consumer wants. Spending on DVDs, computers, mobile phones, large-screen televisions, Internet services, games consoles and other advanced consumer products has increased.

EXAM PREPARATION 3.3

It was reported that in a country the poorest households spent 30% of their income on food while the richest households spent 13% on food.

a   Do these figures mean that the actual amount that the richest households spent on food is lower than that spent by the poorest households? Explain your answer. [4]

b   Ali has started his first job. Faizal is now in a senior position in her company. Describe how the expenditure pattern of these two people might be different. [4]

c   Analyse the motives that might cause a person to save rather than to spend. [6]

d   What might be the result of a general increase in the level of consumers' spending in an economy? [6]

Cambridge IGCSE Economics 0455/04 Q6 May/June 2004

ACTIVITY 3.17

Shop 'til they drop

1. What patterns and trends in consumer spending patterns can you identify in the charts below?
2. Suggest possible reasons for the patterns and trends you have identified.
3. Do you think these trends will continue in future? Give reasons for your views.
4. How might private sector firms and government organizations use this information and why?
5. How do these trends compare to consumption patterns and trends in your own country? Suggest and explain reasons for any similarities or differences.

Global ICT developments, 1998–2009

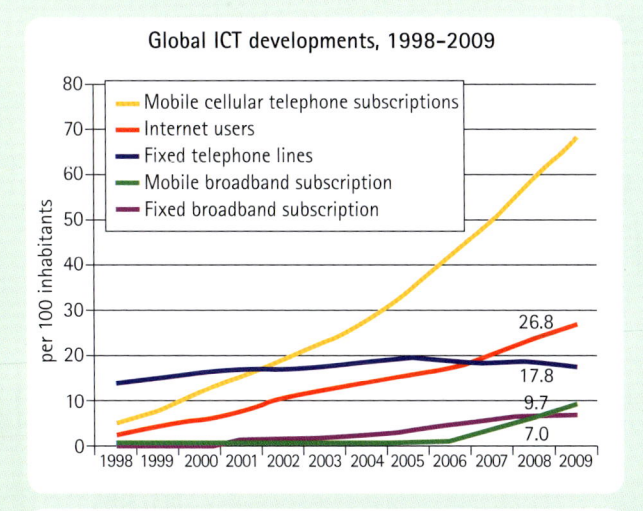

Sales of new motor vehicles, Australia

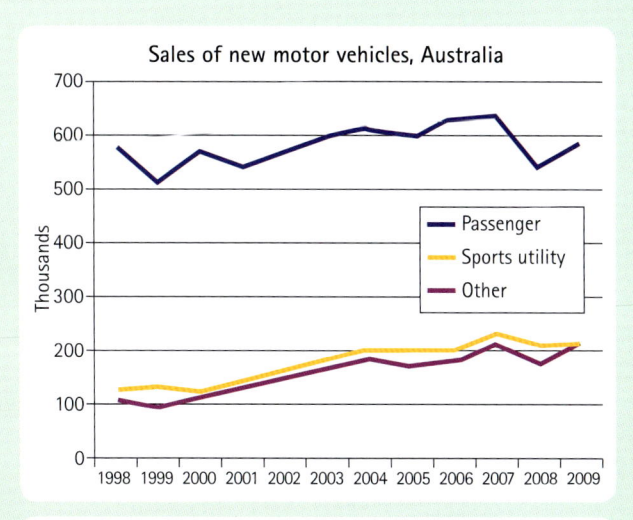

Home ownership of selected consumer durables/services (%)

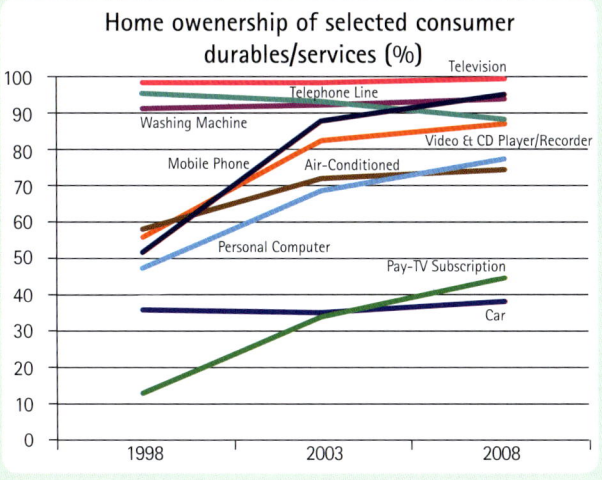

Food consumption by selected foods
United Kingdom
Grams per person per week

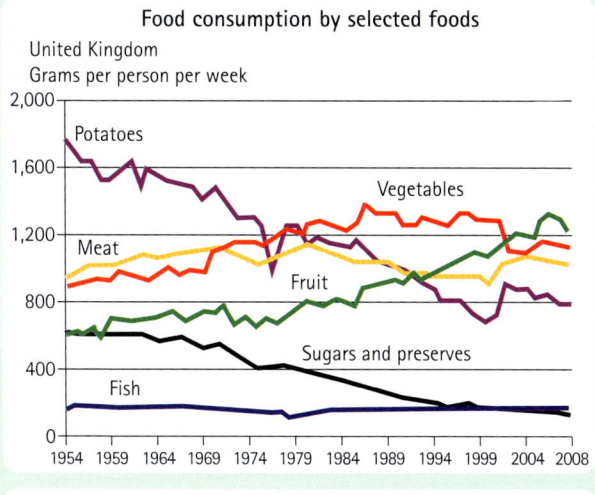

Prevalence of adult cigarette smoking, USA

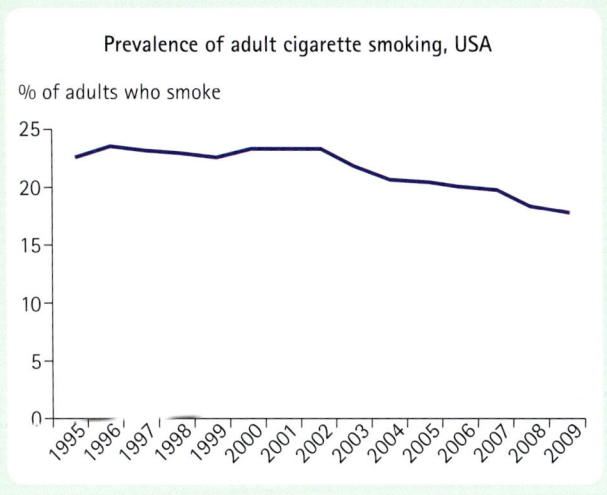

Global health and wellness tourism market 2002–2008

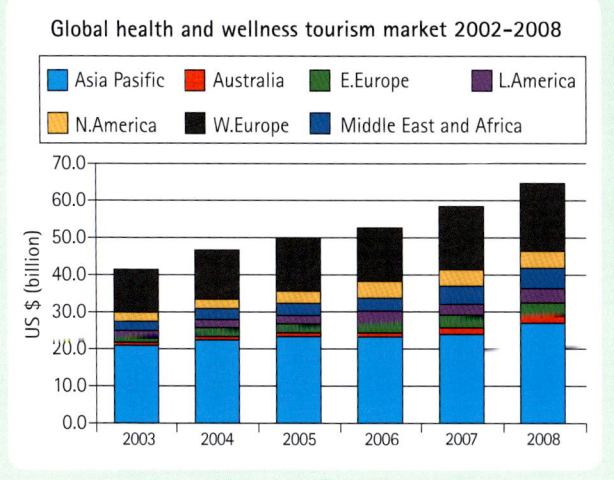

Spending, saving and borrowing 167

SECTION 2

Saving

What determines savings?

Saving involves people delaying consumption until some later time when they withdraw and spend their savings plus any interest. Just as with consumer spending, the more disposable income individuals have the more they will be able to save. So, as income rises, total savings tend to rise. But the relationship is not so straightforward.

▼ US savings ratio: personal savings as a percentage of disposable income

Source: US Bureau of Economic Analysis

The **savings ratio** measures the proportion of the total disposable income saved in an economy. The chart above shows the savings ratio for the US economy between 1970 and 2010. It has varied a lot, from a peak of 14.6% in May 1975 to a low point of 0.8% in April 2005. However, the trend over time has been very clearly downwards despite rising real incomes.

The savings ratios in many other countries also tend to vary widely as a proportion of their incomes over time. This suggests the amount of savings in an economy depends on many other factors. For example, increases in the US savings ratio in the above chart have been closely associated with economic recessions in the US economy, notably in 1975, the early 1980s and most recently between 2008 and 2010.

Why do people save?

Just like the consumption of goods and services, saving money and feeling wealthier also gives people utility. But the amount people choose to spend will depend on a number of factors.

Saving for consumption

This might seem odd at first but people often save money in order to make bigger purchases later on, for example, the purchase of a new car, or for a deposit on an apartment or house. They may also save money to spend on

168 The individual as producer, consumer and borrower

goods and services when they get older and only have a pension to live on. Many people save money in pension schemes. Recall from 3.1 how a good money will be a store of value and means of making deferred payments.

Interest rates

Interest is the return to saving, or the opportunity cost of consuming what could have been saved instead. The higher the rate of interest the more return people can earn by saving their incomes, or the more they will forego if they spend their incomes on goods and services. If interest rates are low, and especially if price inflation is higher, people may choose to save less and consume more. This is because the value of any savings in terms of their purchasing power, or real value, will be eroded by price inflation faster than interest can add to the value of savings. ➤ **6.1**

Consumer confidence

How confident people feel about their financial situation now and in the future can affect consumption and savings behaviour. Many people save as a precaution in case their circumstances change. If people think they could be made unemployed in the future then they may start saving more so they can draw on their savings if and when they lose their jobs and have little or no income. Similarly, if people think inflation will rise in future they may save more now so that they can afford to pay the higher prices of goods and services later on. They may also increase their savings during periods of rising price inflation in order to protect the overall value of their wealth.

Availability of saving schemes

The more ways people can save, the more they might be tempted to do so. Banks and other financial institutions now offer a wide variety of savings schemes with different terms and conditions to suit different people. ➤ **3.1**

The more people are willing to save, and the longer they are willing to save without withdrawing their money, the higher the rate of interest they can normally get. Similarly, there are schemes that offer returns that are tax-free, linked to stock market performance, or a mark-up over the rate of price inflation. Some governments even offer national savings schemes that do not pay interest but enter people's savings certificates into a draw each month to win prize money. A national savings scheme is a way of borrowing money from savers by a government. ➤ **5.1**

Savings patterns

Not everyone wants to save money, even if they could. Our desire and ability to save tends to vary according to our income, age and family circumstances.

In general, the higher a person's income the more the individual tends to save. Young people also tend to save less of their incomes than middle-aged people, and people with children tend to save more to help pay for their children's education later in life. However, people on low incomes with children, especially single-parent families, often find it very difficult to save. Similarly, older people also tend to save less in general because they face greater financial hardships and lower incomes from pensions in their old age. They may also withdraw or spend savings they have accumulated over time to help meet their living expenses. This is known as **dissaving**.

ECONOMICS IN ACTION

What impact did deflation have on consumer spending and borrowing decisions in Japan? Why did these decisions simply cause further deflation?

Deflation in Japan

Deflation refers to a general decline in prices in an economy. This happened in Japan in the early 1990s and prices continued to fall for many years. It began following a collapse in Japanese stock market and house prices after they had risen dramatically in the late 1980s. Many banks had loaned money to companies and individuals to buy real estate but when house values dropped, these loans could not be repaid or recovered in full from the sale of the property. These factors triggered a fall in spending by consumers and, as a result, firms cut their prices. As prices fell, consumers delayed their spending, expecting prices to fall further so they could buy for cheaper later on.

As Japanese consumers delayed spending, firms reduced their prices further in an attempt to encourage greater demand. Revenues fell and Japanese firms were forced to cut wages and lay off workers. The fear of unemployment caused many Japanese workers to save more and the downward deflationary spiral continued.

In an attempt to boost borrowing and spending the Japanese government cut interest rates to zero. However, this policy did not work because consumers still expected prices to fall and as they did the real value of debts increased so borrowing was not worthwhile.

Savings behaviour can also vary due to differences in culture. For example, people in China tend to save a far higher proportion of their incomes than people in many other countries. A recent study found that the average person in China saves around 25% of their disposable income despite returns on savings being relatively low. The household saving rate in Japan is also relatively high. Similarly, another study found savings rates in Germany were relatively high and stable over time compared to those in many other countries, with saving for old age being a big motive.

SECTION 3

Why do people borrow money?

Borrowing money

Consumers may borrow money to increase their expenditure on goods and services, usually for a particular good or service they want, such as a new car or overseas holiday, that is expensive relative to their weekly or monthly earnings. They can then make loan repayments over time from their future earnings. However, some people on very low incomes may borrow simply to pay everyday bills such as electricity and phone charges.

One of the biggest purchases a person or family can make is to buy a house or apartment to live in. Loans to buy property are called **mortgages** and may take many years to pay off. However, property is an asset and will add to the stock of wealth a person has. It can therefore be considered to be a form of saving. For most people their home is their biggest asset. Some people may also borrow money to buy other assets, such as shares in companies, hoping the share dividends and appreciation in the value of shares will be more than enough to repay the loan and leave them with a nice profit. ➤ 3.1

Small business owners may also borrow money to help set up their business and will repay the loan from future revenues. Similarly, self-employed workers may borrow money to buy tools that will help them do their job. For example, a builder may need to buy a van and power tools.

A person may also borrow moncy to finance a training or education course that will help improve his or her skills and qualifications so that they can get a better-paid job in the future. For example, low-interest government loans to students are common in many countries to help them finance studies at university. They are able to repay their loans from their future earnings, with the amount repaid per month often depending on how much they earn. So, if their earnings are low they may not be required to make any repayments.

Personal debt

The total stock of accumulated borrowing by a person or a household is called their **personal debt**. So, for example, if a person borrows $100,000 to buy a house, another $15,000 to buy a car, and $5,000 to go on a luxury holiday their personal debt will be $120,000. If the interest rate is 10% per year on all these loans then that person will have to pay $1,200 in interest in the first year even before he or she is able to pay off some of the debt. Even if that person could repay $20,000 of the loan in the following year interest charges would still add up to $1,000.

What determines the level of borrowing?

You will not be surprised to learn that the main reasons are very much the same as those that determine consumption and savings, but by far the most important is the interest rate.

Interest rates

Interest is the cost of borrowing money. Often the larger the amount a person borrows, the longer the loan takes to repay, and the more risk it involves, then the higher the interest rate that will be charged by the financial institution granting the loan.

The base rate of interest in an economy is determined by the central bank and this is the rate at which it will lend money to the entire banking system. Commercial banks and other financial institutions will therefore charge their customers interest rates at or above the base rate. A rise in the base rate of interest in an economy will therefore mean all other interest rates rise, and rising interest rates make borrowing more expensive so demand for loans is likely to fall. Low interest rates, however, will tend to increase the demand for loans. ➤ 3.1

Spending, saving and borrowing

Wealth

A wealthy person may be more willing to take out a loan because he or she will be confident of being able to repay it by selling off some assets if need be. Further, a bank or other lender may be more willing to lend money to a wealthy person, and at lower interest rate, because there is less risk that person will **default** on the loan. To default means to fail to repay. In some cases a loan may be taken out against an asset, for example a mortgage against a house. Then if the person defaults the house has to be sold to repay the loan. In this way, a house or other valuable assets will offer the lender security, or **collateral**, against the loan. This means if a person defaults on the loan the bank will have an asset to sell to recover its funds.

Consumer confidence

How confident people feel about their financial situation in the future may affect their decision to borrow money. If people think they could be made unemployed then they may decide against taking out a loan because they may not be able to repay it should they lose their jobs. Similarly, if people think inflation will rise rapidly in future they may borrow now to make their purchases before prices rise.

Ways of borrowing and the availability of credit

The easier it is to borrow money, that is the greater the availability of credit, the more inclined people may be to borrow. These days it is possible for many more people to arrange credit and in so many more and different ways than ever before. People can arrange overdrafts, loans and mortgages with banks, simply over the Internet. They can use credit and charge cards issued by banks, credit card companies or even retail shopping chains. They can also buy goods on hire purchase in easy monthly instalments over time.

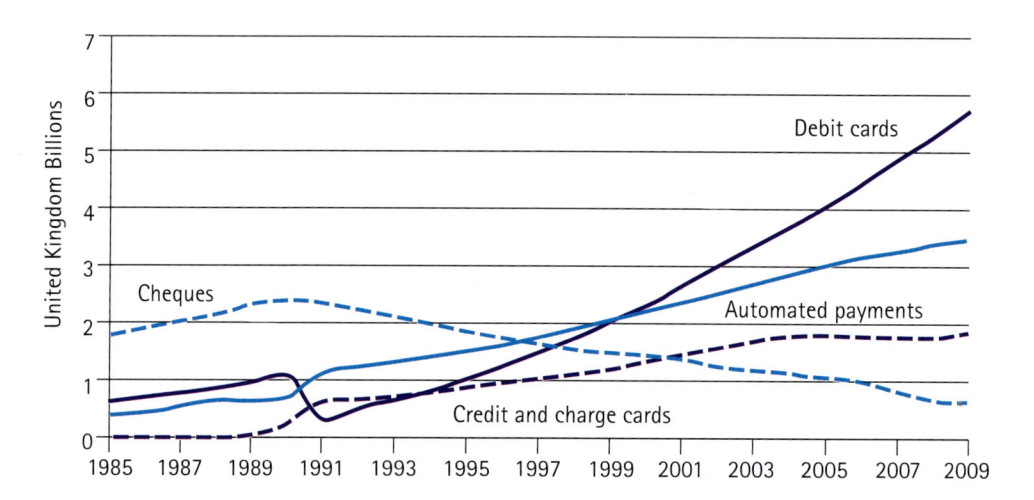

▼ Non-cash transactions: by method of payment

Source: Social Trends 41 UK Office for National Statistics

The chart on the previous page shows how use of plastic cards as a method of payment has increased rapidly over time in the UK. The same is true in many countries.

However, using credit cards and Internet banking can involve risks. Card and Internet fraud is on the increase. It involves criminals hacking into personal bank accounts and stealing credit card details. These criminals can then use this information to make fraudulent purchases and applications for loans.

Problems with borrowing

Borrowing money is not a problem as long as you can afford to repay the loan with interest. If your income rises each year then loan and interest repayments become easier. However, people will quickly run into problems if they keep on borrowing so that repayments rise more quickly than their income, or if their income falls and they cannot continue to make repayments, perhaps because they have become unemployed or their business has been forced to close down.

People unable to repay their personal debts will be declared bankrupt or **insolvent** by a law court. They may even have property and other goods they have bought with loans, credit cards or on hire purchase repossessed by their lenders or creditors. Or they may be forced to sell their assets to repay the money they owe.

Personal borrowing and debt levels increased significantly in a number of developed and other economies during the last decade. This raised concerns that borrowing money had become too easy and that some people did not consider the implications, especially if interest rates increased and/or their incomes fell in future. Much of the borrowing was in the form of large mortgages to finance purchases of land and property and the construction of new properties. Even a small rise in interest rates would mean monthly repayments would go up significantly. For example, if a person had borrowed $100,000 a rise in interest rates from 5% to 6% would have increased the annual interest payment, on top of any loan repayment, from $5,000 to $6,000. In addition, a fall in house prices due to an economic downturn can mean the person ends up owing more money than the value of the house, and this is what happened to many people following the global financial crash in 2008.

The global financial crisis in 2008 was triggered by increasing default rates on mortgages, notably in the US economy, which in turn led to a fall in US house prices and falling confidence in the ability of US banks to recover their debts and to survive. These fears soon spread to other economies as house prices tumbled around the world.

A number of large financial institutions with too many loans against property were unable to raise enough cash to meet withdrawals by their depositors or to repay their creditors and they subsequently collapsed. Many other banks had to be saved from collapse by their national governments. Banks stopped lending so much money to people and businesses. This, combined with the fall in property values and therefore the wealth of many people, caused a worldwide slump in consumer demand.

The prices of company stocks on the world stock market also collapsed as investors sold off their shares because of fears that the slump would damage profits and cause the collapse of many other businesses. Indeed, many firms were forced into bankruptcy because of the fall in demand for their products and because they were unable to borrow money to pay their bills.

▼ From boom to bust: increasing insolvencies in the UK and many other economies followed the rapid expansion of personal debt in the last decade

Net lending to individuals

United Kingdom £ billion per quarter at 2009 prices

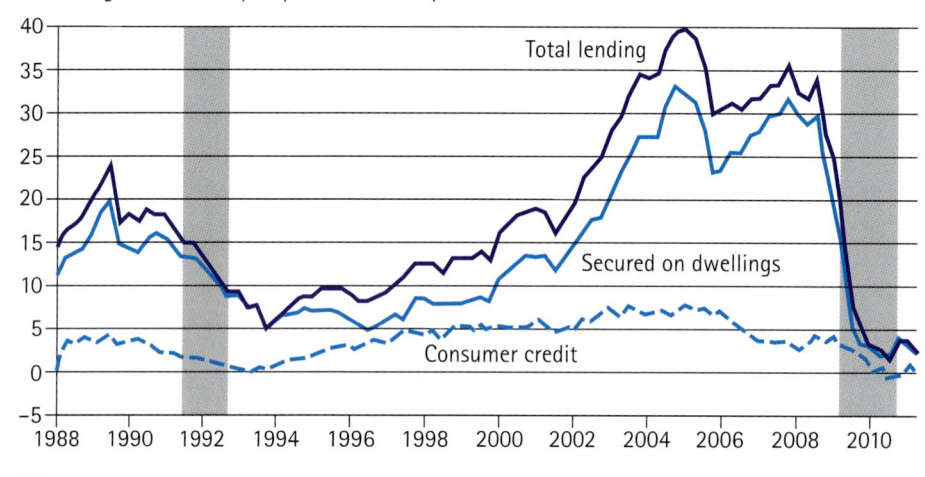

Quarters when economy was in recession

Individual insolvencies

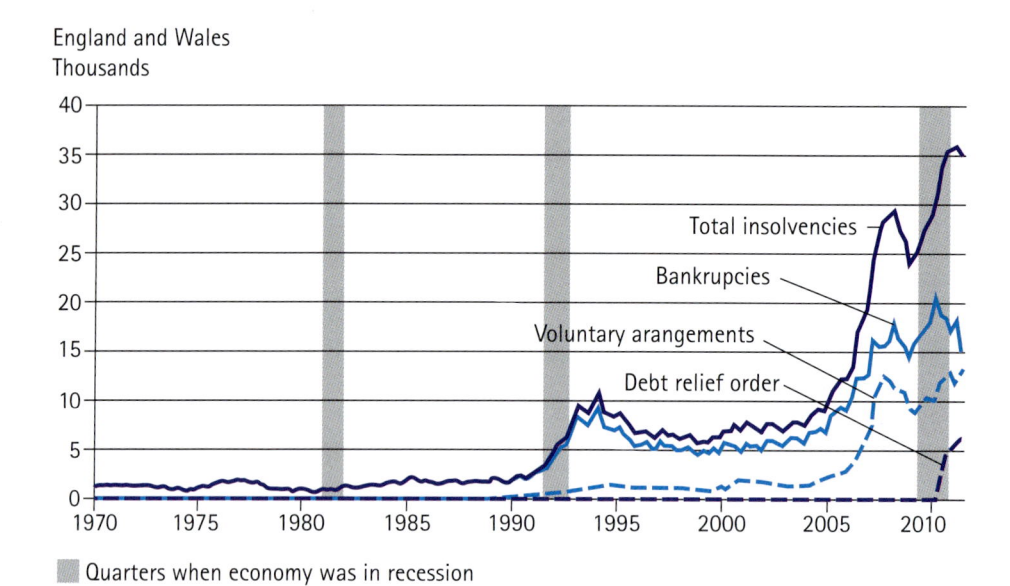

England and Wales
Thousands

Quarters when economy was in recession

Source: Social Trends 41 UK Office for National Statistics

The individual as producer, consumer and borrower

ACTIVITY 3.18

'If I owe you a pound, I have a problem; but if I owe you a million, the problem is yours'
John Maynard Keynes (1883–1946), English economist

SERI says household debt poses problems

Households could face greater debt risks if interest rates rise and stock market prices fall, according to a report by the Samsung Economic Research Institute (SERI) released yesterday.

It noted that household debt levels in South Korea have increased during and after the global financial crisis, encouraged by low interest rates and a strong stock market that had increased personal wealth.

But households are exposed to dangers since many of their loans are short-term and have variable interest rates rather than fixed rates, which means their repayments will rise when there is an increase in interest rates.

SERI said that household debt has steadily increased. In 2010, the average Korean household had debts of 143% of their disposable income compared to 87.4% just nine years earlier. Their disposable income to debt ratio was one of the highest in the world, even exceeding that of the USA, whose ratio was 128%.

Mortgages are the main component of household debt. Mortgage loans by banks have increased by 27% over the last 23 months to 281.8 trillion Korean Won. SERI said that mortgages had increased due to the abnormally low interest rates of the last few years following the global financial crisis.

SERI did not foresee an immediate household debt crisis since incomes and assets are also rising because of the bullish stock market. But a rise in interest rates would increase the debt burden. 'If household debts increase, consumer spending will drop and hurt economic growth,' said Lee Eun-mi, a senior analyst of SERI.

1. Describe two factors that, according to the article, have increased consumer debt.
2. What problems for a household are highlighted in the article concerning high levels of debt?
3. Suggest two ways a government could reduce consumer demand for borrowing.
4. Describe how and why consumer spending, savings and borrowing patterns may differ between the following types of household in a developed economy such as South Korea: young, unmarried university graduate; married couple with young children; retired couple receiving a pension.
5. Explain why 'if household debts increase, consumer spending will drop and hurt economic growth'.

WEBSITES

Take a look at the following websites to learn more about consumption, savings and borrowing:

- www.tutor2u.net/economics/content/topics/consumption/savings_ratio.htm
- www.tutor2u.net/economics/gcse/revision_notes/money_interest_rates.htm
- www.wikipedia.org/wiki/Financial_crisis

KEYWORDS

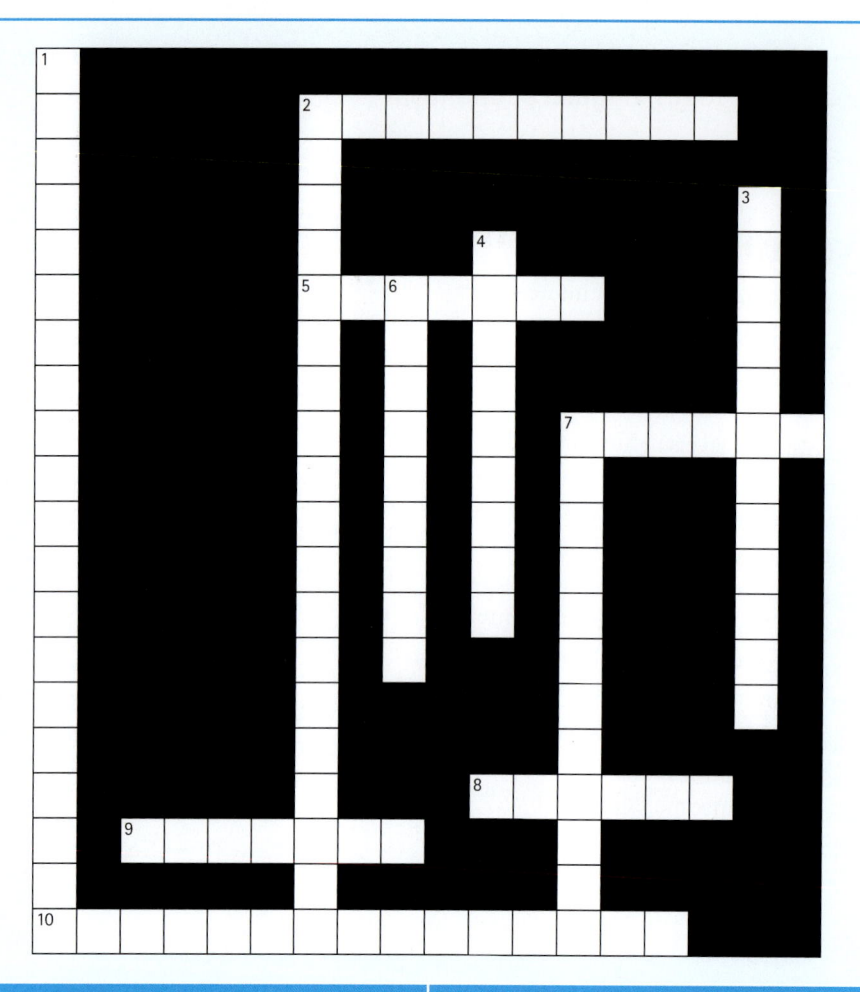

Clues across

2. Security against a loan, such a valuable asset that a bank can sell if the loan is not repaid (10)
5. The satisfaction a person gains from consuming a good or service (7)
7. Delayed consumption to accumulate wealth (6)
8. The stock of assets a person or a household owns that have monetary value (5)
9. A term used to describe a situation when a person fails to meet loan repayments on time (7)
10. Products for which it is difficult to judge how much we will enjoy them until we consume them (10, 5)

Clues down

1. Personal income remaining after income-related taxes have been deducted and after allowing for the effect of inflation reducing its purchasing power, that a person can choose to spend or save (4, 10, 6)
2. The amount spent on goods and services for final consumption (8, 11)
3. The stock of total borrowing accumulated by a person (8, 4)
4. Withdrawing or spending from savings, for example to meet living expenses when income is insufficient (9)
6. A person or organization will be this if they are unable to raise enough cash to pay off their debts (9)
7. Savings as a percentage of total disposable income (7, 5)

The individual as producer, consumer and borrower

Assessment exercises

Multiple choice

1. The wages of carpenters will tend to rise if:
   - A The supply of carpenters falls
   - B Their productivity rises
   - C The price of wooden products falls
   - D Demand for plastic products rises

2. The best explanation for the rise in demand from Dn to Dn1 is:

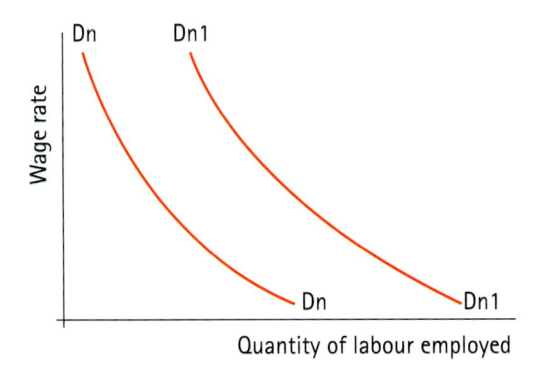

   - A A fall in wages
   - B A fall in the price of the product they produce
   - C An increase in unemployment
   - D Increasing productivity of labour

3. Disposable income is:
   - A Gross income before tax
   - B Personal income
   - C Taxable income
   - D Personal income after taxes on income are deducted

4. Which of the following factors is most likely to lead to a fall in the savings ratio?
   - A An increase in taxes
   - B A cut in interest rates
   - C A cut in borrowing
   - D A fall in people's propensity to consume

5. The supply curve above shows that:
   - A Wages fall as the amount of labour increases
   - B A rise in wages reduces the size of the working population
   - C After a certain level of wages labour chooses more leisure than work
   - D Supply rises as wages fall

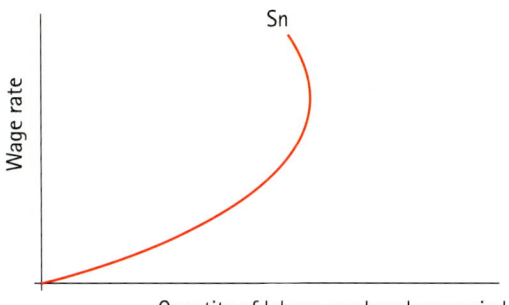

6. The supply of labour to an occupation will tend to rise when:
   - A Promotion prospects improve
   - B There are fewer perks
   - C Holiday entitlement is cut
   - D Unemployment benefit rises

7. Which one of the following is the least likely explanation for the observed increase in consumer spending on leisure goods and services over time in many countries?
   - A Increasing real disposable income per head
   - B Consumers want healthier lifestyles
   - C Increasing levels of personal debt
   - D Increased wealth

8. In general the supply of money in a modern economy is best defined as:
   - A Coins, notes and bank deposits
   - B All items of legal tender
   - C Coins, notes and bank loans
   - D Notes and coins

9. All the following are important characteristics of a good money except:
   - A It is durable
   - B It is in unlimited supply
   - C It is generally accepted
   - D It is carried easily

10. A single union agreement can have the following advantages for an employer except:
    - A It reduces time spent negotiating with unions
    - B It can increase union bargaining power
    - C It can protect the skills of the union workers
    - D Union members may agree to increase their productivity

Assessment

11 Which type of union would best describe a union of musicians?
  A Labour union
  B Craft union
  C Industrial union
  D General union

12 Collective bargaining involves:
  A Negotiations between employers and union representatives
  B Negotiations between individual workers and their employers
  C Negotiations between employers and government representatives
  D Negotiations between different employers

13 The stock market is a market for:
  A New issues of shares
  B Stocks of goods and services
  C Financial products
  D New and second-hand shares

14 Which of the following is NOT a function of a central bank?
  A Making personal loans
  B Managing the national debt
  C Controlling the money supply
  D Supervising the banking system

Questions 15–17 refer to the financial products:
  A Ordinary shares
  B Loan stocks
  C Bank loans
  D Mortgages

15 These can be issued by a government

16 These shares have voting rights at annual general meetings

17 These are long-term finance used to buy property

18 Which one of the following types of household is most likely to spend the highest proportion of its disposable income?
  A High income, middle-aged with no children
  B Low income, young single parent with young children
  C Middle income, young single person with no children
  D High income, middle-aged couple with two grown-up children

19 Which of the following is a non-economic reason why women may earn less than male employees for the same job?
  A They may be discriminated against
  B They undertake more part-time work
  C Married women may be less mobile than men
  D They take more career breaks to raise children

20 What has happened in the diagram to the equilibrium wage and employment?
  A Wages and employment have risen
  B Wages and employment have fallen
  C Wages have risen; employment has fallen
  D Wages have fallen; employment has risen

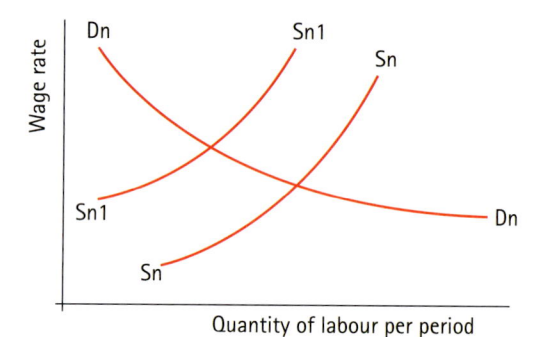

21 Personal borrowing has increased in many countries. Which one of the following factors is the most likely explanation?
  A Higher real interest rates
  B Reduced personal wealth
  C Increased availability of credit
  D Increased public sector borrowing

22 Disposable income will tend to rise if:
  A Indirect taxes are reduced
  B Interest rates are cut
  C Price inflation falls
  D Direct taxes are reduced

23 The savings ratio in an economy measures:
  A Deposits in banks as proportion of total savings
  B Total savings as proportion of gross household income
  C Long-term savings relative to total savings
  D Total savings as proportion of total disposable income

24 Which of the following changes is most likely to attract an increased supply of labour to engineering professions?

  A An increase in training requirements
  B An increase in holiday entitlements
  C An increase in contracted hours of work
  D An increase in income taxes

25 Why might a family increase the proportion of its income that it spends on food?

  A Some of the children start work
  B The government increases the benefits it pays to families
  C The number of children in the family increases
  D The second parent becomes employed

Structured questions

1 Saving in South Africa

In South Africa, between 1995 and 1998, savers were able to benefit from higher interest rates and reduced inflation. Moreover, they did not have to pay income tax on some of their income from savings. However, between 1990 and 1998 the amount of income from savings that was exempt from income tax (the 'tax allowance') remained unchanged.

The level of personal savings in South Africa in 1998 was thought to be low and meant that less than 10% of the people were able to retire financially independent.

An economist at the Industrial Development Corporation (IDC) in South Africa suggested that an increase in the level that was exempt from tax would encourage people to save. In 2002 this level was raised from R4000 to R6000. (R = rand, the currency of South Africa).

Changes in taxes can, however, have other effects. There is no guarantee that an increase in the amount of income exempt from tax will result in increased savings. Lower taxes do increase disposable income but this might result in extra spending rather than extra savings.

  a Explain how savers can benefit from:
   (i) high interest rates [1]
   (ii) reduced inflation [3]
  b Using information in the article, comment on the effect that changes in tax allowances might have on total savings in an economy. [5]
  c The article says that not many people will be financially independent when they retire. Why might this be a concern for the government? [5]
  d (i) What is meant by the expression 'disposable income'? [2]
   (ii) You are asked to investigate the differences in the spending and savings patterns of people with low disposable income and those with high disposable income. What do you think you would discover? [9]

Cambridge IGCSE Economics 0455/06 Q1 October/November 2003

2 Some workers work long hours but earn little because the rate they receive for each hour worked is very low.

  a Why do you think a worker would be prepared to work for very low wages? [5]
  b What reasons might make a worker decide to move to another job at the same rate of pay? [5]
  c Some workers belong to a trade union. Explain how membership of a trade union might be beneficial to a worker. [5]
  d An older skilled worker's pattern of spending and saving is likely to be different from that of a younger unskilled worker. Discuss why. [5]

Cambridge IGCSE Economics 0455/04 Q4 May/June 2005
Cambridge O Level Economics 2281/02 Q4 May/June 2005

3   People often have an account with a commercial bank in which they deposit some of their money and from which they can pay their bills.
   a   Describe the functions of money. [6]
   b   Identify and explain **three** functions of a central bank which differ from the functions of a commercial bank. [6]
   c   Sometimes the value of money is decreased because of inflation. Discuss the main causes of inflation. [8]

   Cambridge IGCSE Economics 0455/21 Q7 May/June 2010
   Cambridge O Level Economics 2281/21 Q7 May/June 2010

4   After studying for your Economics qualification you have to decide whether to leave school and find a job or enrol at a college for more specialised training.
   a   What factors might you consider when making your decision? [5]
   b   Is it always an advantage for an individual to have a specialised job? [5]
   c   Explain how an individual's earnings might change over time. [4]
   d   Analyse why different income groups have different spending patterns. [6]

   Cambridge IGCSE Economics 0455/02 Q3 October/November 2009
   Cambridge O Level Economics 2281/02 Q3 October/November 2009

5   a   Explain how the principle of opportunity cost might be relevant when a person chooses a new job. [3]
   b   Some service sector occupations pay very well, others have low rates of pay. Discuss why this might be so. [7]

   People often borrow by using a credit card. This notice was issued by a credit card company: 'For the next four months the interest rate charged on outstanding amounts has been reduced to the equivalent of 1.9 % per year.'

   c   Explain what motives people have for saving rather than spending. [4]
   d   How might a reduction in interest rates on credit card borrowing affect the way that people choose to save or spend? [6]

   Cambridge IGCSE Economics 0455/02 Q3 October/November 2007
   Cambridge O Level Economics 2281/02, Q3 October/November 2007

6   a   Explain what is meant by a trade union and describe its functions. [5]
   b   Trade unions are not often found in small enterprises. How significant might this be as a factor which influences someone in choosing to work for a small enterprise? [5]
   c   Why do small enterprises continue to exist as an economy develops and expands? [4]
   d   Discuss the effect that the activities of a trade union might have on an economy. [6]

   Cambridge IGCSE Economics 0455/04 Q2 May/June 2008
   Cambridge O Level Economics 2281/02 Q2 May/June 2008

4 The private firm as producer and employer

4.1	Types of business organization
4.2	Organizing production
4.3	The growth of firms
4.4	Competition
Assessment	Multiple choice
	Structured questions

Entrepreneurs will combine land, labour and capital into firms to produce goods and services. Most private sector firms aim to maximize their profit by combining these factor inputs in the most productive way possible. An increase in the productivity of labour and capital will therefore tend to increase demand for these resources from firms. This is because an increase in their productivity means more output can be produced from the same amount of input. A firm will be able to lower its costs and increase its profits by increasing the productivity of its resources.

The difference between the total cost of producing goods and services and the total revenue from their sale to consumers is profit. Total costs of production include variable costs that vary with the amount of output produced, such as wages of production workers and the purchase of components, and fixed costs such as rents, loan repayments and other overheads unrelated to output. A firm will break-even when its total revenues just cover its total fixed and variable costs.

A firm may take a number of legal forms according to how it is owned, controlled and financed. A sole trader is a small, one-person business. In a partnership, ownership, control and finance of the firm is shared between the partners. However, in order to finance significant growth an entrepreneur will wish to consider forming a limited company.

An entrepreneur will share the ownership of a limited company with other shareholders. Limited companies are therefore also known as joint-stock companies because they can sell stocks to finance their expansion. By increasing their scale of production, large firms can enjoy cost advantages over smaller firms. These are known as economies of scale. However, a firm that grows too large may experience diseconomies of scale, or rising average costs, often due to management and coordination problems.

The production of goods and services by firms involves a chain of activity, from primary production of natural resources, right through to the sale of finished goods and services to consumers. Secondary production involves processing natural resources to produce machinery and components for other manufacturers, as well as finished goods for consumers. Tertiary industries provide services such as banking, insurance and retailing services for other firms and individual consumers.

Private sector firms in every stage of production will compete with each other for sales and profits. Vigorous price and non-price competition between rival firms is a key feature of a competitive market. However, in some markets one or a handful of dominant firms may have sufficient market power to restrict competition, market supply and consumer choice. As a result, product prices may be higher and quality lower than in a competitive market.

Unit 4.1   Types of business organization

AIMS

By the end of this unit you should be able to:

▶ describe the **types of business organization** in the public and private sectors: **sole traders**, **partnerships**, **private companies**, **public companies**, **multinationals**, **cooperatives**, **public corporations**

- understand the concepts of **financial risk**, **ownership** and **liability**
- distinguish between different types of business organization according to how they are owned, controlled and financed
- understand the differences between **unincorporated businesses** and **joint-stock companies**
- evaluate the costs and benefits to an economy of hosting a **multinational** corporation
- describe the role of a **public corporation** and how public corporations are controlled

▶ describe and evaluate the effects of changes in the structure of organizations.

SECTION 1

Organizing firms

Starting a business

To produce goods and services, land, labour and capital are needed. However, these resources on their own will not satisfy consumer wants. For example, if we want football boots, it is no use just buying leather and hiring workers and a factory. Resources need to be organized and financed, and decisions need to be taken in order to manage and control the resources from day to day. The person who makes these decisions is called an **entrepreneur**. ➤ **1.1**

An entrepreneur combines and organizes resources in a **firm** for the purpose of carrying out productive activity or business. Firms are therefore also known as **business organizations**.

In a modern, mixed economy a firm may take a number of legal forms according to how it is owned, controlled and financed. For example, a small firm with just one owner will be very different in the way it is controlled and financed from a large firm which may have many thousands of owners who play little or no role in the day-to-day management of the organization.

Before starting a new business organization or expanding an existing organization, an entrepreneur needs to consider what type of organization they want. This will largely depend on how much money they will need to start or grow their business, if they want to continue managing it alone, how much risk they are willing to take, and whether or not they want to share the ownership and therefore the profits with others.

In the following sections we will trace the growth of a firm from a **sole trader**, owned by just one person, to a large **public limited company** owned and financed by a large number of shareholders. ➤ **3.1**

Serge Buchar is an unemployed school-leaver. Serge is good at carpentry and has decided to open a small hardware shop selling tools and supplies for building and decorating. Like every entrepreneur, Serge must first consider four key questions. The answers to these questions will help him decide what type of business organization is best for him.

Question 1: Do I have enough money?

To start a business an entrepreneur needs **capital**. Money invested in long-lived man-made resources such as premises, machinery and other equipment is called **fixed capital**. Money in a firm tied up in stocks of finished and unfinished products and used to pay day-to-day running costs, including wages and bills for electricity and telephones, is called **working capital**.

Some business organizations need more capital than others. If Serge does not have enough savings of his own to start his business, or is unable to raise the money he needs from friends and family or from a bank loan, then he may need to find investors who are willing to provide additional capital in return for a say in the running of the business and a share of any profits. Serge may therefore need to consider starting a **partnership** or a **limited company** and share the ownership of his business.

Types of business organization

▲ Fixed capital

▲ Working capital

Question 2: Can I manage my business alone?

All promising entrepreneurs, including Serge, must decide whether or not they can manage their business alone. Running a business can often mean trying to do everything yourself, working very long hours and going without holidays.

For example, to manage his business Serge will need to place orders for tools and building supplies with other producers, ensure that his premises comply with planning regulations, make payments, keep accounts, develop a marketing strategy and, if necessary, recruit and manage staff, be familiar with employment, minimum wage and health and safety laws, and much more.

Starting a business with others can therefore spread this heavy workload and also bring people with different skills into the business, for example in business law, accounting, purchasing, production, marketing and human resource management.

Question 3: Do I want to share ownership and profits?

If Serge's answer to this question is no then he should start his business alone and be a **sole trader**. However, if he doesn't have enough money to start up his business and doesn't have the skills, time or energy to manage it alone then he will need to find other investors to help him. This means Serge will not be able to make all the business decisions. He will first need to consult other owners who have a share in his business. He will also need to share any profits the business makes with them.

Question 4: Am I prepared to risk everything I own?

If Serge goes it alone he could end up having to repay all the debts of his business if it fails. His liability for business debts would be unlimited. He may have to use up all his savings or sell his house, car and other possessions to pay off his business debts.

Having **unlimited liability** means Serge can be taken to court and declared bankrupt if bills are unpaid. This is because he will not have a **separate legal identity** from his business. The business and Serge are the same under the law.

However, if Serge does not want to risk losing everything he owns he will need to consider other types of organization that will limit his liability to repay

184   The private firm as producer and employer

business debts. In a limited partnership or limited company most, if not all, of the owners have **limited liability** and their businesses are considered to be legally separate from them. This means in the event of business failure they will only lose the amount of money or capital they invested in their businesses. They cannot personally be held responsible for any business debts.

Similarly, it will be the business organization and not Serge or the other owners that will be liable for any injury caused to a third party as a result of the activities of the business, for example if a customer or employee slips on a wet floor in the place of business and seeks compensation for injury. In these ways, having limited liability reduces the risk of running a business and therefore helps to encourage entrepreneurship and new business start-ups in an economy.

ACTIVITY 4.1

The sole trader

Read the following article and identify the advantages and disadvantages of owning and running a business alone.

Want to do-it-yourself? Then BBS can help

Serge Buchar is now the proud owner of Buchar Building Supplies in the town centre. We asked Serge why he decided to open his own shop.

'Following the collapse of the construction boom I became unemployed. But by running my own business I have a full-time job, I am my own boss and I keep all the profits I make. Not that I have made any yet' he laughed. 'I have to work every hour I can to keep the shop going, whether it is ordering supplies, serving customers, cleaning up and even keeping the accounts. If I had the time and money I would hire some employees to help me!'

Starting your own business can be expensive and risky, as Serge soon discovered. 'Banks would not lend me any money. They all said there was too much competition and my business could be at risk'. Instead Serge had to invest all his own savings to buy equipment and pay the deposit on his shop premises.

'Monthly bills for rent, insurance, phone and electricity are also high' he said. 'I must earn at least $600 in revenue each month just to break even. I'd love to take a few days off but I wouldn't make any money'. 'Then, of course, if the business fails I will have to repay any business debts even if it means selling my possessions to do so! But I plan to make the business a success and so far, so good!'

BBS opened its doors last week and is offering special price reductions for the first month on many of the tools, paints, wallpaper and other products the shop offers. If you cannot get what you want, Serge is willing to order your requirements.

Shoppers can look forward to a personal and friendly atmosphere in the shop. Most local residents already know Serge and he promises that he will be making tea at regular intervals throughout the day for the benefit of his customers.

Types of business organization

SECTION 2

Ownership and control

The sole trader

Serge Buchar decides he has enough money to start up his own business and will be able to manage it without help. He knows he risks losing all his savings or more if the business fails but, as his friends keep saying, 'Nothing ventured means nothing gained.' Serge's new business, like many other small business organizations that run shops or provide personal services, such as hairdressing, plumbing, window cleaning and vehicle repairs, is a sole trader.

A **sole trader** or sole proprietorship is a business organization owned and contolled by one person. A sole trader may employ other people to work in the business, but it will only ever have one owner.

The sole trader is the oldest and most popular type of business in the world. In fact, many of today's largest and most successful businesses started out as sole traders many years ago.

Advantages of the sole trader

1 A sole trader business organization is easy to set up

Most sole traders need very little capital to start up with, so it is fairly easy for one person to set up a business alone. There are also usually very few legal formalities involved in starting up and running a sole proprietorship. For example, the business is not required to publish financial accounts.

Modern technology has reduced the cost of starting up and running many new small businesses. Many sole traders can run their businesses from home today using the Internet to keep in contact with their customers and suppliers.

2 The sole trader business is a very personal one

The owner of the business will have personal contact with customers and staff. The owner will be able to find out quickly what people want and then change what the business sells to suit what customers wish to buy. Furthermore, because anybody dealing with the firm deals with the owner personally this can encourage customer loyalty to the business.

3 The sole trader has full control over the business

The owner of a sole proprietorship is his or her own boss and has full control over the business. This means the person can make decisions quickly, such as deciding whether or not to expand the business, what jobs to do, when to employ staff and who to employ.

4 The sole trader receives all the profits

Being your own boss and not having to share any business profits are important advantages to many entrepreneurs and this, in part, explains why the sole trader is such a popular form of business organization.

Disadvantages of the sole trader

1 A sole trader has unlimited liability

Unlimited liability means that the sole trader could lose all his or her possessions to pay off any business debts in the event of bankruptcy.

Unlimited liability exists because, in the eyes of the law, the sole trader business and its owner are the same legal entity. So if the business owes money, its owner must pay.

2 A sole trader has full responsibility for managing the business

The owner of a sole proprietorship has full responsibility for running the business from day to day. For example, this can mean the owner needs to keep accounts, plan and undertake his or her own advertising, recruit and manage staff, deal directly with customers and suppliers, and carry out all manner of other tasks necessary to operate the business successfully. This often means that sole traders have to work very long hours and if they are ever ill they will lose revenue and profit because they may have no one to take over the running of the business.

3 Sole traders lack capital

If Serge's business is successful he may wish to expand into a larger or second outlet. The problem is that expanding the scale of a business requires money and sole traders like Serge have often used up all their savings starting up in business and are often unable to raise debt finance.

Most sole traders finance their business from their personal savings, borrowing from friends and family or from a bank loan. However, banks are often unwilling to lend to sole traders because they are considered risky enterprises. They can face considerable competition from larger businesses and other small businesses, and many close down within their first few years of operation.

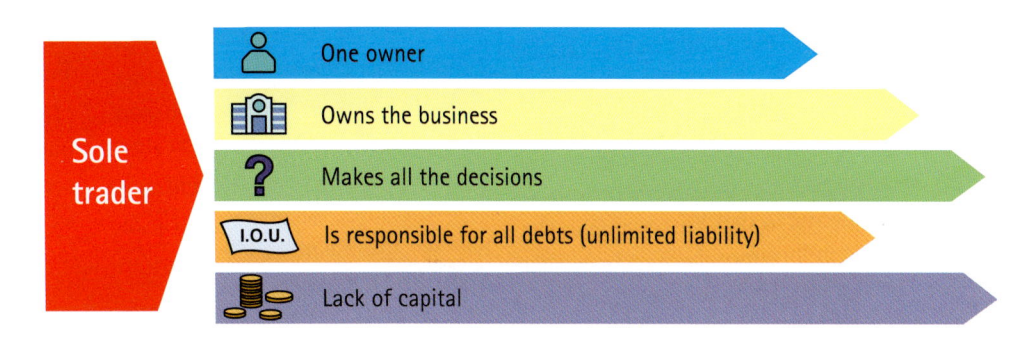

Sole trader
- One owner
- Owns the business
- Makes all the decisions
- Is responsible for all debts (unlimited liability)
- Lack of capital

SECTION 3

Partnerships

If Serge wants to expand the organization he may need to share the ownership of his business. Other owners can provide finance for expansion and help run the enlarged business. He can do this by forming a partnership.

A **partnership** is a legal agreement between two or more people, usually no more than 20, to own, finance and run a business jointly, and to share any profits. Most are small, local businesses. Partnerships are popular business organizations among professionals including solicitors, doctors, accountants and veterinary surgeons.

Most partners are **general partners** who share unlimited liability. However, it is also possible to have some **limited partners** with limited liability. A **silent partner** or **sleeping partner** will provide money to the partnership in return for a share of the profits, but will not be involved in the management of the organization.

In a **limited liability partnership (LLP)** some or all the partners can have limited liability, although laws governing this vary between different countries and often different regions within large countries. LLPs in which all partners have limited liability are therefore very similar to limited companies except that partners retain an automatic right to manage their business directly. Shareholders in limited companies do not.

ACTIVITY 4.2

Building a partnership

Read the article below and list the advantages and disadvantages of forming a partnership.

The Local Informer
BBS Builds on Success

Today Serge Buchar of Buchar Building Supplies celebrates over one year's successful trading with the opening of a new store. So what is secret of his success?

'There is growing demand from people to take on home improvement projects themselves,' he said. 'Our customers like the friendly atmosphere and personal service we offer at BBS. As a result they come back again and again and I always try to help them out with their home improvement problems if I can.'

But the banks are still not convinced. They have been unwilling to lend the business money to expand, suggesting the market remains too competitive.

'Sure it is' Serge agreed, 'but it just means you have to work harder to be the best! We have proved the banks wrong and that's exactly what attracted my new partners' to the business'.

Koji Mao and Prema Mangesh have joined Serge to form the BBS partnership. They have invested enough money to buy and equip a new, larger store.

'Not only that, they have brought some key skills into BBS and will help me manage the business. Koji is a former marketing executive and Prema is a qualified accountant.'

'I will have to share the profits with my partners but at least I can take some time off at last,' Serge joked.

So why did Prema want to risk investing her savings into an expanded BBS. 'It's a good business model' she explained.

'Of course, if it fails I will lose my investment and have to repay the debts, but we have exciting plans for BBS?'

'These plans include more and larger outlets across the country, and sponsoring some community building projects, but raising the money we need for this may take some time.'

We asked Koji if the new partners foresee any other problems. 'Only when Serge takes that time off!' he laughed. 'And we all disagreed about the layout of the new store but we eventually reached a good compromise. We're all friends really!'

The private firm as producer and employer

Advantages of partnerships

1 Partnerships are relatively easy to set up

There are few legal requirements involved in drawing up a partnership agreement or deed of partnership. Most partnerships are also not required by law to publish annual financial accounts.

2 Partners can bring new skills and ideas to a business

Serge has taken on Koji and Prema as partners because they have skills that his business needs. They can also participate in decision making and managing the business from day to day.

3 Partners invest new capital into the business to finance expansion

If other people want to share in the ownership and control of a private sector organization then they must buy their way in. New partners therefore provide capital that can be used to finance business expansion in return for a share of the profits. Because partners share the profits of their business they are motivated to work hard.

Disadvantages of partnerships

1 Partners can disagree

Discussions between partners can also slow down decision making and the more partners there are, the more likely are disagreements. If Serge, Koji and Prema find they cannot agree on important decisions the business may suffer.

Problems can also arise if one or more partners are lazy, inefficient or even dishonest. There may be arguments, the business may lose money and other partners will have to work harder

2 General partners have joint unlimited liability

Like a sole trader, general partners could lose all their possessions of value if the partnership fails or is negligent and causes injury to a third party. Furthermore, each partner can be held responsible for the actions of other partners. In contrast, silent or sleeping partners have limited liability.

3 Partnerships lack capital

Because many countries place a limit on the number of partners allowed in each partnership, raising additional capital to finance further business expansion can be difficult.

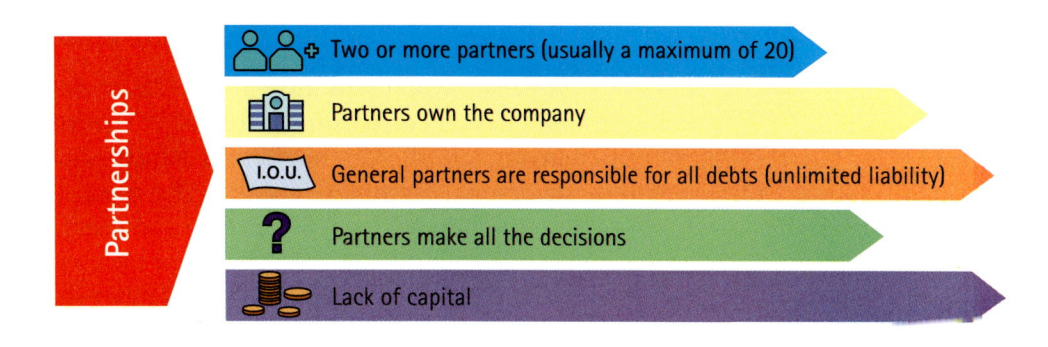

Partnerships
- Two or more partners (usually a maximum of 20)
- Partners own the company
- General partners are responsible for all debts (unlimited liability)
- Partners make all the decisions
- Lack of capital

Types of business organization

As a result, very few large businesses in the world are partnerships. This is simply because it is difficult for partnerships to raise the necessary capital to expand into a large enterprise. Therefore, if Serge wants to expand his business further he may need to consider forming a joint-stock company.

SECTION 4

Ownership and control

Joint-stock companies

Joint-stock companies are also known as **limited companies** or corporations in many countries because their owners have limited liability.

Joint-stock companies sell **stocks** (also known as **shares**) to raise capital. The people and organizations who invest in shares become the owners or shareholders of joint-stock companies. A joint-stock company is therefore jointly owned by the investors who have bought its stock. ➤ **3.1**

Each share purchased in a company receives a share of its profit after any taxes on profits have been paid. This payment is called a dividend. Therefore, the more shares a shareholder holds the greater the share of the company that person owns and the more dividends he or she will receive from any profits.

For example, imagine BBS wants to raise $500,000 to expand the organization by selling 50,000 shares at $10 each. The people who buy these shares will become **shareholders** in BBS. The more shares a person owns the more of BBS that person will own and the bigger will be his or her share of any profits each year. Imagine now that BBS makes enough profit to pay $2 for every share held. This payment is known as a share **dividend**. A person who holds 100 shares in BBS will therefore receive a total dividend of $200 from profits, while a person who owns 3,000 shares will receive a dividend of $6,000.

Because some large limited companies have so many thousands of shareholders they may be required to hold an annual general meeting (AGM) that shareholders can attend if they choose. An AGM allows shareholders to be kept informed about the performance of their company and company decisions. At an AGM shareholders will also be asked to accept the financial accounts of the company, elect directors to manage the business and vote on major strategic decisions.

Shareholders will elect a **board of directors** with valuable financial and business skills to manage and run their company from day to day. In small companies the directors are often the most important or largest shareholders in the company. However, company directors need not be shareholders.

A person who owns more than 50% of the value of shares issued in a company will have a **controlling interest** in that company. This means they will be able to out vote all shareholders on company issues and the election of directors and therefore control the business. The more shares a person holds the more votes they will have. So, if Serge, Koji and Prema, the original partners in BBS, want to maintain overall control of their business and remain directors they will want to hold more shares than all other shareholders in BBS.

190 The private firm as producer and employer

Legal status

There are two main types of limited or joint-stock company:

- A **private limited company** has one or more shareholders but can only sell shares to people known to the existing shareholders.
- A **public limited company** has at least two shareholders and can sell shares to any individual or organization on the stock market through a stock exchange or bourse. ➤ **3.1**

In many countries, but not all, limited companies are incorporated businesses or corporations. A **corporation** is a separate legal body from its owners. This means:

- all the business owners (shareholders) have limited liability
- the business can own assets, buy shares in other companies and borrow money in its own right
- the business can be taken to court and held responsible for any harm or injury suffered by an employee, customer or anyone else as a result of the activities of the business
- the business can be taxed on its revenues or profits and must produce separate financial accounts.

▼ Company abbreviations around the world

Country	Public limited company	Private limited company or equivalent
France	S.A	S.A.R.L
Germany	A.G	Gmbh
Greece	A.E	e.p.e
India	LTD	Pvt Ltd.
Malaysia	Bhd	Sdn Bhd
Spain	S.A	S.L; S.L.N.E; S.R.L
South Africa	Plc	Pty. Ltd.
UK	Plc	Ltd.
US	Corp. ; Inc.	LLC; LC; Ltd Co.

You can often tell where a company is registered from the letters used after its name. For example, the letters S.A after a company name, for example Telefónica S.A means anonymous company or share company in many languages. However, different abbreviations are used around the world to denote corporate status. The legal status of corporations can also vary between different countries.

Public limited companies are some of the largest and most successful business organizations in the world. For example, in 2009 Royal Dutch Shell was the world's biggest company with annual revenue of over $458 billion. Other large public corporations include such multinational giants as Wal-Mart Stores, Exxon Mobil, BP, Chevron, ING Group and Toyota Motors.

There are more private limited companies in the world than public limited companies, but they tend to be much smaller in size than most public limited companies. Nevertheless, there are a number of very large privately held corporations, notably Koch Industries, Inc., IKEA and Cargill, Inc. Koch is involved in activities ranging from petroleum and chemicals, to ranching, securities and finance. IKEA is a global home furnishings and furniture retailer while Cargill's business activities include the purchase, processing and distribution of grain and other agricultural commodities.

ACTIVITY 4.3

Expanding privately

From the article below find and make a note of the answers to the following questions.

- How do private limited companies raise capital?
- What encourages people to buy shares in the ownership of a company?
- Who decides who will manage the company?
- What are the main advantages and disadvantages of a private limited company?

Local Business News

BBS builds for the future

The BBS partnership, owners of the chain of home improvement stores, has become a private limited company following a private issue of shares. The sale of shares has raised $500,000 in new capital to finance expansion.

Head of Sales and Marketing, Koji Mao, explained the attraction. 'We are a growing and profitable business. The more profit we make the more dividends our shareholders will receive. The only downside is they could lose their investment if the business fails, but they have no responsibility for business debts.'

Serge Buchar will hold 51 per cent of the new shares in BBS and will continue as Managing Director, but all shareholders will be able to vote on major company decisions and the election of other members of the Board of Directors to run the company.

Finance Director, Prema Mangesh, has been busy preparing all the legal documents required to form a limited company.

Founding owner Serge Buchar, and now Managing Director of BBS Ltd., explained his plans to expand the number and size of stores, and to develop the country's first zero carbon housing development.

'This all requires significant new capital' he said, 'and we did not want to take on an expensive bank loan. So we decided to incorporate and to invite friends, family, our employees and our suppliers to buy shares in the company.'

'It has been a difficult process at times' Prema explained. 'We have spent a lot of time and money getting the legal and financial advice we need to incorporate and sell shares.'

Limited companies are also required to keep and publish detailed annual accounts of their revenues and profits, capital, business loans and director's salaries.

'Yes, quite a list,' she sighed.

Advantages of a private limited company

1 They are a popular form of organization for sole traders or partnerships seeking to raise additional capital

The sale of shares can help small business owners raise **permanent capital** that never has to be repaid to the original investors. This is because shareholders who buys shares will have to sell their shares to other investors to get their money back. The sale of shares is therefore a much cheaper form of finance for business owners than loans from banks that have to repaid with interest. ▶ 3.1

2 Company shareholders have limited liability

This means any individuals or other organizations that own shares in a private limited company are only putting the amount of money they invested in those shares at risk if the company fails and leaves debts. Far fewer people and other organizations would invest in shares if they had an unlimited liability to repay any business debts and therefore many companies would be unable to raise capital to expand their scale of production.

3 Shareholders have no management responsibilities

Shareholders will elect directors to manage their company on their behalf. Shareholders can vote for directors at an AGM.

4 A company has a separate legal identity from its owners

In the eyes of the law a private limited company and its owners are treated as separate legal bodies. As a result, if the company owes money, the company can be sued and taken to court, but the owners cannot. The company can be forced to pay its debts or pay compensation out of company funds, but the owners are not considered responsible.

Disadvantages of a private limited company

1 Limited companies may be required to disclose financial information

In some countries, private limited companies are required by law to publish details of their financial performance in annual accounts.

These accounts give details of the profits made in the past year, total sales, the money the company owes and the people and institutions that it owes it to. Clearly it is an advantage for shareholders to have information about their company but the writing, printing and postage of such details can be very expensive. In addition, publishing such details allows competing companies to learn some of the company secrets.

However, private limited companies generally have fewer or less comprehensive reporting requirements than publicly traded companies.

2 Private limited companies cannot sell their shares publicly

Shares in private limited companies can only be sold privately and only with the agreement of all other shareholders. This is a big disadvantage because it is possible to raise far more money by selling shares to the general public on the stock market. This means that private limited companies are often confined to being small to medium-sized firms, unable to raise money to expand their scale of production significantly.

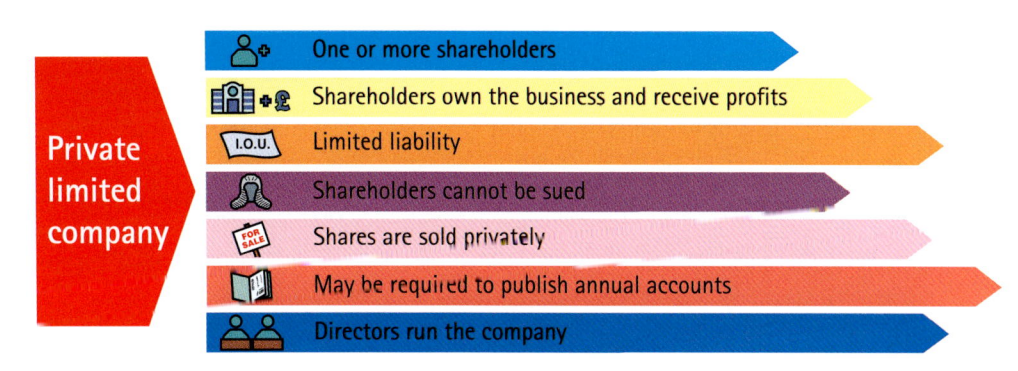

Private limited company
- One or more shareholders
- Shareholders own the business and receive profits
- Limited liability
- Shareholders cannot be sued
- Shares are sold privately
- May be required to publish annual accounts
- Directors run the company

ACTIVITY 4.4

Going public

From the article below find and make a note of the answers to the following questions.

- Why is it likely to be easier for a public limited company to raise capital than a private limited company?
- How much share capital does BBS plan to raise from the sale of new shares?
- Why are the original owners of BBS now more at risk of losing overall control of their company?
- What are the main advantages and disadvantages of a public limited company?

Global Times

BBS cements its position on stock market

Home improvement expert BBS has gone from strength to strength since owner Serge Buchar started the retail chain just four years ago. But today's announcement that it has received the green light to issue shares for sale to the public paints a bright future for the company.

'We plan to expand into all major cities nationwide and open our first superstore in Europe' explained founding owner Serge Buchar. 'This of course requires a significant injection of new capital, but our projections for future growth and profitability are very healthy. We have already received a lot of interest from new investors.'

The new issue of 1,500,000 shares with a face value of $10 each will raise $15 million in permanent capital for the business. 'Our business model is to keep bank debt as low as possible' explained Serge. 'Loan repayments and interest charges reduce profits. Share capital provides a low-cost source of finance that we never have to repay.'

Obtaining a listing on a stock exchange to sell shares publicly can, however, be a very involved and expensive business.

'We have worked closely with the governing body of the stock exchange to ensure that we have a sound business model and sufficient financial strength to attract new investors' said Finance Director, Prema Mangesh. 'Full information about the company and how to apply for shares is contained in a detailed prospectus.'

'We plan to issue this next week along with our annual accounts, and also publish it in all major national newspapers.'

However, Prema's position could be at risk if powerful new shareholders want to elect new board members to key positions such as Finance.

'That doesn't worry me' she said. 'All shareholders including me will want the most highly skilled, motivated and honest people in key board roles. I have a strong record of achievement with the company but if there is someone better then so be it.'

Much of course will depend on who Serge Buchar wants on his board. He will remain the majority shareholder in BBS plc. Combined with the shareholdings of original owners Prema Mangesh and Koji Mao, he will retain the controlling interest in the company.

194 The private firm as producer and employer

Forming a public limited company

A public limited company must have a minimum of two shareholders. Shares are normally issued for sale to the general public on the stock market. Hence the term 'going public' is often used to describe a company that obtains a full or **public listing** to sell shares through a stock exchange or bourse. ➤ **3.1**

Before a limited company can offer its shares for sale through a stock exchange the governing body of the exchange will investigate the company to ensure that it is a trustworthy and well-run business, and meets agreed standards of practice and size. If a company meets these requirements then it will be allowed to sell its shares through the exchange. The public listing and sale of new shares in a company is called a **flotation**.

Advantages of a public limited company

The public limited company business structure has all the same advantages of the private limited company but some important additional features.

1 Public limited companies can sell shares publicly

A company that is able to sell its shares to members of the public and other companies through a stock exchange can potentially raise far more money to finance its business operations than any other type of business organization.

2 Public limited companies can advertise their shares

A public limited company is able to advertise the sale of its shares through a **prospectus** informing would-be shareholders about the business, its activities and earnings, the current directors, and the number and price of the shares being issued. This can also be published in newspapers and magazines. Advertising a share issue helps to create interest in the sale and can attract many more investors than might otherwise be the case.

Disadvantages of a public limited company

A public limited company shares many of the same disadvantages as a private limited company but, because of these companies' size and the way they raise finance through sales of shares to the public and other companies, they can suffer additional problems.

1 It can be expensive to form a public limited company

Many legal documents and company investigations are needed before a company can be listed on a stock exchange to sell shares. Developing and advertising an issue of shares in a prospectus can also be expensive.

2 Public limited companies are required by law to publish detailed annual reports and accounts

Public limited companies are legally required to keep and publish detailed annual accounts of their revenues and profits, fixed and working capital, loans and other liabilities, shareholdings, dividend payments and directors' salaries.

3 Public limited companies must hold AGMs

All shareholders must be invited to an AGM with company directors. These can be expensive and time consuming to set up, especially if there are many thousands of shareholders all over the world.

An AGM allows shareholders to be kept informed about the performance of their company and company decisions. At an AGM shareholders will be asked to accept the financial accounts of the company, elect directors to manage the business and vote on major strategic decisions.

4 Management diseconomies

Some companies may become so large that they become difficult to manage effectively. There may be communication problems between different parts of the business and between different layers of management. Decision making can be slow and disagreements between managers and owners can occur. ➤ **4.3**

5 Some public limited companies may be vulnerable to takeovers

Because shares in public limited companies are traded publicly on the stock market the original owners may also lose control of their company if it is taken over by another. A takeover or acquisition occurs when one company buys enough shares in the ownership of another company to gain control of that firm.

6 There can be a divorce of ownership from control

The owners or shareholders of a large public company can lose control of their company in a number of ways:

- because banks and other creditors can withdraw finance
- because the board of directors control company decisions
- because large shareholders can out vote shareholders with minority interests.

For example, the Curzon Group lost money on two major contracts when, because of delays, it ran out of cash. The company's main activity was decorating and fitting out hotels and offices for other businesses to make them ready for occupation. Although the company was profitable, because of the delays on the contracts it had no revenue to draw on to pay its usual bills. Costs were rising but the company would only receive revenue once it had completed the contracts. The company therefore had to borrow more money from its bank overdraft. However, the bank was concerned about the growing size of the overdraft, which had increased to $11 million, and the ability of the management team at Curzon to complete the projects in good time to repay it. As a result, the bank closed the overdraft facility and asked for immediate repayment, forcing the company into bankruptcy and to sell off assets to pay its debt.

When a company owner sells shares or takes out a bank loan to raise finance for expansion he or she will lose some control of the business. Other shareholders can exercise their voting rights and providers of loans often have some control (or security) over of the assets of the business, such as valuable machinery and equipment or unsold stocks of goods. They may not agree with the original owners on how best to run their company or who to elect to the board of directors. If a bank is seriously worried about the ability of the managers of a company to run it successfully it may withdraw its loans, forcing the company to sell off its assets and even to close down, regardless of the interests of the company shareholders.

Similarly, as an organization grows, more managers are employed to run a company on a day-to-day basis but many of them may not be shareholders, especially in larger companies. They may not own a part of the company or directly share any of its profits. Because of this, managers and shareholders may have different objectives. For example, directors in a large company may award themselves and their senior managers large pay rises and annual bonuses even if company performance and profitability have been poor. Large pay awards reduce profits available to shareholders.

Directors may also spend a lot of money buying luxury company cars and having their offices lavishly decorated. This again will reduce company profits. They may also agree to expansion plans that may be considered too risky by shareholders. Running a larger company can increase the status of its directors and may justify higher salaries. Directors may be willing to take more risks because unlike shareholders they may not have invested money in the business.

If directors pay themselves large sums of money, spend wildly or take too many risks, shareholders may be able to vote to replace them at an AGM. Shareholders can also try to influence important company decisions taken by the directors, for example on whether or not to merge with another business organization.

However, many public limited companies have many thousands of shareholders, many of whom will be unable or unwilling to attend AGMs. This may be especially true of individual shareholders who only hold a limited number of shares, and therefore have limited voting power. Only a handful of shareholders, often the largest ones, may actually use their votes and so directors, once elected, can often act very much on their own from day to day and may pursue business strategies that are in their interests far more than in the interests of their shareholders. For this reason the majority of shareholders tend to lose control of the companies they own. This is known as the divorce of ownership from control.

Another problem for the small shareholder is the fact that large financial institutions, including major banks, insurance companies and pension fund operators, have substantial shareholdings in many other companies and may often have controlling interests in some companies. As such they can easily out vote small shareholders on company policy and who should be on the board of directors.

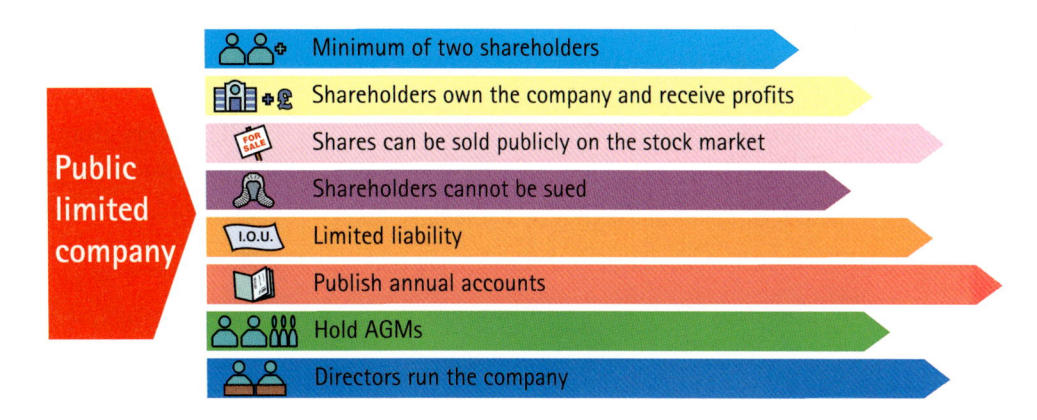

Public limited company
- Minimum of two shareholders
- Shareholders own the company and receive profits
- Shares can be sold publicly on the stock market
- Shareholders cannot be sued
- Limited liability
- Publish annual accounts
- Hold AGMs
- Directors run the company

Types of business organization

ECONOMICS IN ACTION

How do these articles illustrate the divorce of ownership from control in large publicly traded companies?

Disney's Eisner Rebuked in Shareholder Vote

Despite a shareholder revolt that led him to lose the chairmanship of The Walt Disney Co., Michael Eisner vows that he will stay on as CEO through to the end of his term.

Earlier today, 43 per cent of shareholders who voted at the company's annual meeting withheld their support for Eisner. The number of shareholders who withheld their support was higher than many had been expecting.

Shareholders blast Qantas over payouts

Shareholders at Wednesday's annual general meeting for Qantas Airlines again expressed their anger over big payouts to executives.

The central issue was the final payment to chief executive Geoff Dixon, who left last year. Mr Dixon pocketed nearly $11 million despite lower share values, employee lay-offs and mid-air incidents.

ACTIVITY 4.5

Types of business organization

Below is a table listing the advantages and disadvantages of a sole trader organization.

Advantages of operating as a sole trader	Disadvantages of operating as a sole trader
• Sole trader organizations are easy to set up. There are usually few legal requirements involved in business registration. • They can often be set up with little capital. • The owner is his or her own boss and has full control over the business. • The owner receives all profits after tax and therefore has an incentive to work hard. • Personal contact with customers can increase customer loyalty. • Separate accounts are not required for the business.	• The owner has full responsibility for running the business from day to day. This may mean working very long hours and going without holidays. • The business may lose revenues and profits if the owner is off sick or on holiday and cannot manage the business. • The owner has unlimited liability to repay any business debts. • Sole traders often lack capital to buy new equipment or to expand. • Sole traders often lack all the skills they need to run their businesses successfully.

Complete similar tables of advantages and disadvantages for partnerships, private limited companies and public limited companies.

SECTION 5

Multinational corporations

What is a multinational?

A **multinational** is a firm that has business operations in more than one country but will usually have its headquarters based in its country of origin.

▼ The first multinational on the Moon?

Multinationals are some of the largest joint stock companies in the world, often selling many billions of dollars' worth of goods and services, and employing many thousands of workers globally.

Many of the biggest multinational businesses in the world are US-owned corporations with interests in oil and gas exploration and petroleum.

In 2009 the largest multinational company was Royal Dutch Shell. Its total revenue that year was just over US$458 billon. The company is Dutch and British in origin and has business units in over 140 countries. However, the most profitable multinational was US owned Exxon Mobil with profits in 2009 of over US$45 billion and operations in over 200 countries.

▼ World's 10 largest multinationals by revenue, 2009

Company name	Main sectors	Total revenue (US$ billion)	Employees	Country of origin
Royal Dutch Shell plc	Oil and gas	$458.4	102,000	Netherlands, UK
Exxon Mobil Corp.	Oil and gas	$445.7	79,900	USA
Wal-Mart Stores Inc.	Retailing	$405.6	2,100,000	USA
BP plc	Oil and gas	$361.2	92,000	UK
Toyota Motor Corp.	Automotive	$263.4	320,808	Japan
Chevron Corp.	Oil and gas	$255.1	65,000	USA
ConocoPhillips	Oil and gas	$225.4	33,800	USA
Total S.A	Oil and gas	$223.2	96,959	France
ING Groep N.V	Insurance	$214.0	124,661	Netherlands
General Electric Co.	Various	$182.5	323,000	USA

▼ Royal Dutch Shell and Wal-Mart – two of the largest publicly traded companies in the world

Types of business organization

Of the world's largest 100 economic entities in 2009 in terms of total income, 51 were corporations and 49 were national economies. Royal Dutch Shell, Exxon Mobil, Wal-Mart and Toyota Motors, among others, all ranked above countries such as Indonesia, Saudi Arabia, Norway, Poland, South Africa and Greece in terms of their total annual income. Multinational companies are also responsible for around two thirds of total world trade and global industries can be dominated by a handful of these global giants.

ACTIVITY 4.6

Global giants

The following table lists a number of multinational companies. Try to find out their country of origin and their main activities to complete the table. The first one has been completed for you.

Company	Country of origin	Main business acivities
Volkswagen	Germany	Automotive
Carrefour		
General Electric		
Siemens		
Sinopec		
Samsung		
Nestlé		
HSBC Holdings		
ArcelorMittal		

Advantages of being a multinational

The global presence and size of many multinational companies gives these organizations a number of key advantages. A multinational can:

- reach many more consumers globally and sell far more than other types of business
- avoid trade barriers by setting up operations in countries that apply tariffs and quotas to imports from businesses located overseas ➤ **8.1**
- minimize transport costs by locating plants in different countries to be near to sources of materials or key overseas consumer markets
- minimize its wage costs by locating operations in countries with low wages
- raise significant amounts of new capital for business expansion, research and development (R&D), and to employ workers and managers with the highest skills
- reduce the average cost of producing each unit of output below the average costs of smaller firms because of its large scale of production. ➤ **4.3**

The economic impacts of multinationals

National governments will often compete with each other to attract multinationals to locate operations in their countries for these reasons:

- They increase investment in new business premises, modern equipment and cutting edge technologies. This is called **direct inward investment**.
- They provide jobs and incomes for local workers.

The private firm as producer and employer

- They bring new knowledge and skills into a country which can help domestic firms improve their own productivity.
- They can pay taxes on their profits which boosts government revenues.
- They can increase export earnings through international trade. ➤ 8.1

However, multinationals are big powerful companies and may create problems in their host countries. Here are some examples of problems:

- **Some multinationals may exploit workers in low-wage economies**, for example by paying workers in these economies far less to do the same or even more work than employees in more-developed economies. Health and safety standards may also be lower in less-developed economies and employment laws weaker.

- **Natural resources can be exploited and the environment damaged by some multinationals.** Laws and regulations to protect the natural environment may be weak or not enforced in some developing and less-developed countries.

- **Profits may be switched between countries so that multinationals avoid paying taxes.** Multinationals will often move or 'repatriate' their profits from their business units in different countries to those countries with the lowest taxes. They may also avoid taxes altogether in some less-developed economies with poor tax-collection and legal systems.

ECONOMICS IN ACTION

Should developing countries encourage multinationals to locate in their economies?

Alleged human rights violations against Coca-Cola

In the late 1990s, Coca-Cola was accused of bringing in paramilitaries to intimidate, kidnap, torture and then ultimately murder trade union leaders who were trying to improve working conditions for employees at their bottling plant in Columbia. Many other US multinational companies with factories in Columbia, including Occidental Petroleum and food producer Del Monte, were accused of similar offences by the Permanent People's Tribunal in Columbia which included professors, human rights commissioners, doctors, judges and social workers from Argentina, Australia, Belgium, Brazil, Chile and a number of other countries.

Toyota boosts car production in Indonesia

Toyota Motor Corp and subsidiary Daihatsu are to build a new small, low-cost car in Indonesia aimed at consumers there and in neighbouring countries.

Mini-vehicle specialist Daihatsu, 51 per cent owned by Toyota, will invest around $250 million in a new high-tech factory able to build 100,000 cars annually in Indonesia, 70 per cent of which it will supply to its parent company.

A spokesperson for Toyota and Daihatsu said the project will contribute to Indonesian society in the area of motorization. At the same time, it will help develop local parts and supply businesses and create jobs.

Toyota aims to make Indonesia its second big production base in Southeast Asia after Thailand.

- **Some multinationals may use their power to obtain generous subsidies and tax advantages from host governments.** Multinationals can move their production to the most profitable and advantageous locations anywhere in the world. Because multinationals provide jobs and incomes many governments provide incentives to encourage them to locate and stay in their national economies, including generous grants to pay for new factories and tax concessions on imports and their profits.

- **Local competition may be forced out of business by multinationals.** Because of their size and market power multinationals can often restrict competition by forcing smaller local firms to close down in the countries in which they operate.

- **Some multinationals may interfere in government.** Some commentators have suggested that some large powerful multinational companies have used subversive and illegal activities to try to influence a government of a country in order to promote and protect their own interests.

SECTION 6

Cooperatives

Cooperatives are business organizations that are owned and controlled by a group of people, to undertake an economic activity to their mutual benefit. That is, a cooperative provides benefits for its members. Anyone can usually become a member and, in turn, each member of a cooperative has an equal share in the ownership and control of the organization, regardless of how much money that person may have invested in the business; that is, cooperatives operate a strict policy of one member, one vote.

There are two main types of cooperative. **Worker cooperatives** are owned and controlled by their workers. **Consumer cooperatives** are retail enterprises owned and controlled by their customers. They can aim to make a profit or be non-profit-making organizations. ➤ 4.2

Cooperatives that aim to make a profit usually return any profit to their members either in the form of a dividend on their shareholdings, or as bonuses, or as lower prices in retail cooperatives.

Other common types of cooperative include the following:

- **Housing cooperatives** allow residents to share in the ownership or have occupancy rights in the property they live in together, such as an apartment block.

- **Building cooperatives** are cooperatives in which people pool their resources, usually using their own labour, to build houses they can live in.

- **Utility cooperatives** are a type of consumer cooperative set up by their customers to provide members usually in remote areas with utilities such as electric power.

- **Farming cooperatives** are groups of farm owners who cooperate to grow, market and sell crops and farm animals. They are popular forms of business enterprise in many developing and less-developed countries.

- **Credit unions** and **cooperative savings banks** provide financial and banking services to their members. Many developed, particularly in Europe, to help lend money to farming cooperatives.

It is estimated that over 800 million people worldwide are members of cooperatives and that cooperatives provide some 100 million jobs.

▲ Canadian maple sugar cooperatives produce 35% of the world's maple sugar

▲ In Cyprus, cooperative banks have a 30% market share in banking services

Worker cooperatives

These are organizations owned by their workers, such as in a farming cooperative. They pool their money to buy equipment and share equally in decision making and any business profits.

Worker cooperatives can employ people who are not members. Membership is not compulsory, but only employees can become members.

Worker cooperatives are relatively commonplace in Europe, especially in Italy, Spain and France. One of the largest and most successful is the Mondragón Cooperative Corporation in the Basque country of Spain. It consists of a group of manufacturing and retail companies across Spain and overseas.

Advantages of worker cooperatives

1. Worker cooperatives are popular with workers because they themselves are in charge and everyone has an equal say. They are also likely to work harder because they can take part in making decisions about how to run the business.

2. The workers receive the profits they make. Profits are paid out as dividends either on the basis of each worker getting an equal share, or according to how much money each put into the enterprise.

Disadvantages of worker cooperatives

1. One of the main reasons why worker cooperatives may not be successful is because they find it difficult to raise money. They must rely on borrowing from banks, workers and local councils. Their lack of capital means that worker cooperatives cannot expand easily and so tend to remain small businesses.

2. Worker cooperatives may be badly run simply because the workers making the decisions may have little business experience or entrepreneurial ability.

Retail cooperatives

These are retailing businesses run for the benefit of their customers. The first retail cooperative society was formed in the UK in 1844 when a group of workers fed up with low pay and high food prices joined together to buy food direct from wholesalers. Because they were able to buy food in bulk, suppliers would often give them discounts. Today, any profits made by retail cooperatives are given back to their consumers as dividends or credits they can use against further purchases, or by subsidising prices to keep them low.

Types of business organization

The world's largest consumer cooperative is the Co-operative Group in the UK, which has a variety of retail and financial services. It is owned in part by other cooperatives as well as by members. Japan also has well-established consumer cooperatives with over 14 million members.

The principles of modern consumer cooperatives are unchanged since they were first formed:

- Modern cooperatives are owned by their members.
- Any person can become a member by buying a share for as little as $1.
- Members elect a board of directors to run the cooperative.
- Each member has one vote regardless of the number of shares held.
- Profits are shared between members.

Today many of the smaller cooperative shops have closed because of competition from large supermarkets. To compete, a number of cooperatives have formed into larger superstores selling a wide variety of goods and services, normally located on large sites outside of town centres.

The cooperative movement has also successfully expanded into other retail activities such as banking, insurance, travel agents, funeral direction and bakeries.

Worker cooperative	Retail cooperative
▶ Workers own all the shares	▶ Owned by its members
▶ Managed by its workers	▶ Managers run the organization
▶ Workers have limited liability	▶ Owners have limited liability
▶ Workers share any profits	▶ Members receive profits

ACTIVITY 4.7

The ownership, control and finance of different firms

Below is a table listing how different types of business organizations are owned, controlled, raise finance and distribute their profits. Copy and complete the table by filling in the blank spaces.

	Type of business organization					
	Sole trader	Partnership	Private limited company	Public limited company	Worker cooperative	Consumer cooperative
Ownership						Owned by its members (customers)
Control	Owner manages and makes decisions					
Main sources of finance				Public sales of shares on stock market		
Distribution of profits						Profits shared by customers, as dividends or through price discounts

204 The private firm as producer and employer

SECTION 7

Public sector organizations

Indian Railways is the state-owned railway company of India, which owns and operates most of the country's rail transport.

Each year the government allocates Indian Railways a budget to operate rail services and to invest in the new and replacement tracks and rolling stock it needs.

Pradesh Verma, a regional manager, explained that all the railway managers are accountable to the Indian Parliament. 'We are entrusted by government to spend public money efficiently' he said, 'and to meet performance targets for punctuality, safety, passenger and freight traffic and more.'

'Ticket prices are kept low to enable people on low incomes to use the rail service and to carry freight to rural areas where there may be no other way of getting goods to people who need them. However, the company is still expected to generate an operating surplus or profit each year for the government.'

XIAN-LI IS THE CHIEF EXECUTIVE of one of Hong Kong's public hospitals funded by the government. Her job is to ensure that the objectives of the hospital and the government's health care policy are met.

'The hospital is not required to make a profit from the provision of health care' she explained, 'but it does have to meet targets including for patient care and satisfaction, treatment waiting times, hospital cleanliness, and surgical and running costs.'

Unlike private sector firms owned and run by private individuals, the two organizations above are owned and controlled by their governments. They are part of the public sector in the economies of Hong Kong and India and they have very different objectives from many private sector organizations.

Many public sector organizations employ resources to deliver essential public services. These are considered to be services that are in the best interests of public welfare or the economy to make widely available, such as street lighting, health care and education.

Some of these services may be provided free of charge or at a low cost to people and organizations that need them the most. They do not aim to make a profit. Instead many public sector organizations aim to provide cost-effective public services that are funded from taxes paid by private sector businesses and individuals. ▶ 5.1

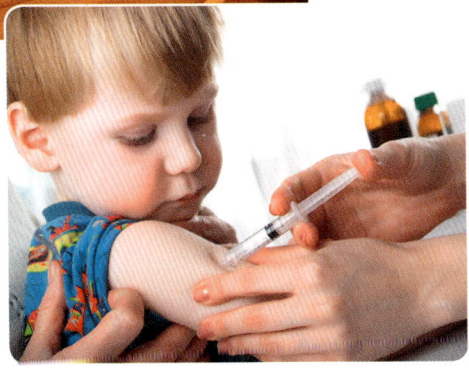

▲ Many public services may be provided for no direct charge

Types of business organization 205

Types of public sector organization

The public sector is a major employer, producer and consumer in many modern economies. For example, public sector organizations in the UK employ 21% of the workforce. There are four main types of public sector organizations.

1 Central government authorities

Central government is responsible for making decisions on political, economic and other issues of national importance. For example, these can include matters of national security and defence, levels of interest rates and taxes, laws and regulations, education, and building hospitals and major roads. Responsibility for making decisions and implementing actions is usually given to different government departments or ministries, or their agencies, for example a Ministry of Defence, a Department of Health and a Ministry of Finance. Names and responsibilities will vary by country. Civil servants are employed in these bodies.

The main decision-making body in central government is a cabinet made up of government ministers. The Premier, Prime Minister or equivalent, as the head of government, appoints each minister to take responsibility for the activities of a particular department or ministry.

2 Local government authorities

Local government organizations will often be given responsibilities by central government to implement its national policies at the regional, local or municipal level. However, they will also usually have the responsibility to make decisions on economic and other issues of local importance, such as the maintenance of local roads and parking enforcement, planning issues for new housing and retail developments, refuse collection and running parks and local leisure facilities such as libraries and swimming baths.

3 Government agencies

These are non-elected organizations given the responsibility for the oversight and administration of specific government functions, such as an intelligence agency, statistical agency or a food standards agency.

4 Public corporations

Public corporations are business-like organizations created to carry out particular public sector functions or to operate under governmental control, such as a municipal water company, a public health service or a central bank.

Public corporations

Some public corporations are trading bodies. This means, like Indian Railways, they produce and sell goods and services to earn revenues. For example, they may sell rail or bus services, electricity and water supplies.

In addition to providing these and other public services, many public sector trading bodies may aim to make a profit from their activities just like many private sector business organizations. Others may simply aim to cover their costs. Their objectives and the amount of profit they aim to make each year will often be set by government ministers and officials.

Any profits made by public corporations can be re-invested in improving their public services or they can be used by the government to fund other public sector spending. However, any losses will be funded from taxes and other government revenues. ➤ **5.2**

Public corporations are responsible for the day-to-day running of nationalized industries.

Nationalized industries (or state-owned industries) are entire industries owned and controlled by a national government. This means the national government is responsible for the productive activities of these industries and for setting their objectives.

Nationalization is the transfer of ownership of an entire industry from the private sector to the public sector. Nationalization allows a government to take control of entire industries or in some cases large firms, for political, social or economic reasons.

▲ Postal services are provided by public corporations in many countries

Why are some industries nationalized?

- Nationalization is carried out to control large powerful firms, especially those providing essential services for consumers such as electricity, gas and water supplies.
- Some industries are nationalized to protect employment in large firms which may be forced to close down by private sector owners if they fail to make a profit.
- Nationalization can be carried out for national security. For example, some industries such as nuclear energy are thought to be too dangerous to be controlled by private entrepreneurs.
- Some industries are nationalized because they are considered too important to the economy in terms of national output and income to be under private sector control.
- Some industries are nationalized to protect public services. Nationalized industries can continue to provide essential services even if they make a loss, such as many postal and rail services in rural areas.
- Nationalization may be carried out for political reasons. The governments of some countries believe they should control the vast majority of resources and industries rather than the private sector.

There are many examples of nationalized industries around the world. For example, the US government owns Amtrak, the national passenger train operator, and the United States Postal Service.

The oil and gas industries in many countries including Libya, Kuwait, Mexico, Nigeria, Saudi Arabia and Venezuela are also nationalized.

Many banks across many different countries were also taken into public ownership during the banking crisis and global economic recession in 2008 to stop them failing.

Types of business organization

Key features of public corporations

Ownership and control	▸	A board of directors runs a public corporation
	▸	The government establishes policy, and ensures that directors perform their functions properly
	▸	The relevant government minister can influence the choice of a public corporation's board and chairperson. If serious problems arise, the minister is questioned in parliament, and is ultimately responsible
	▸	Parliamentary select committees and consultative committees may be set up to monitor and investigate any irregularities or complaints about public corporations
Legal status	▸	A public corporation has a legal identity separate from its board of directors and from government
Finance	▸	Much of the financing for public corporations comes from central government, from taxes or grants
	▸	The public corporations that do make a profit may be self-financing and may be allowed by government to plough these profits back into improving services
	▸	Alternatively, any profits may be used by central or local government to finance other public services or to reduce taxes

Public corporations
- Government ownership
- Government receives any profits
- Government is responsible for debts
- Corporation can be sued. Government cannot be sued
- Corporation is accountable to a government minister
- Board of directors can be chosen by a government minister

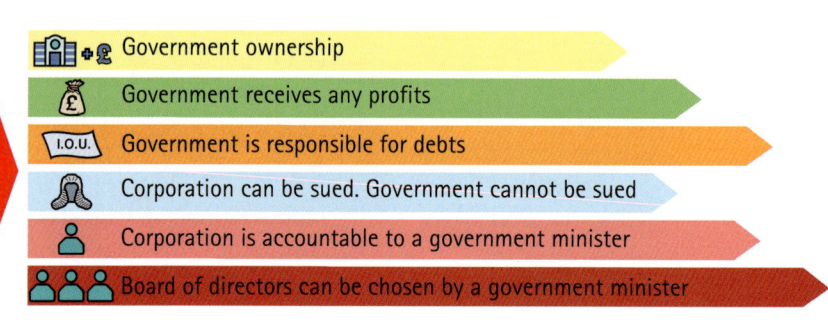

WEBSITES

Some useful web-based resources on types of business organizations are:
- Fortune magazine on-line *money.cnn.com/magazines/fortune/global500*
- *www.business.gov/register/incorporation/sole-proprietorship/*
- International Co-operative Alliance *www.ica.coop/al-ica/*
- Co-operatives UK *https://offline.cooperatives-uk.coop/live/cme0.htm*
- *www.wikipedia.org/wiki/Corporation*

KEYWORDS

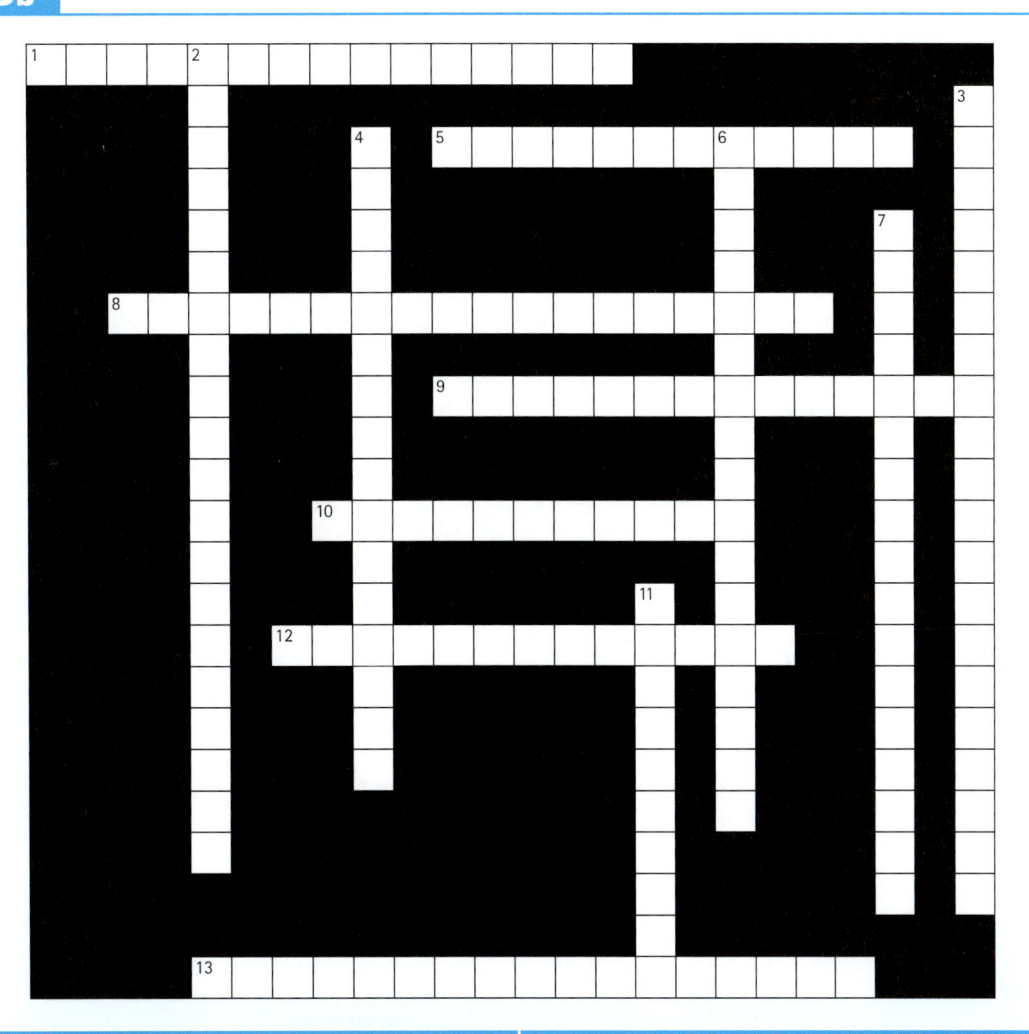

Clues across

1. A person who invests money into a partnership, but who is not involved in the day-to-day running of the business (8, 7)
5. Money invested in long-lived productive assets including factories, offices, machinery and vehicles (5, 7)
8. The legal responsibility of a business owner or owners to repay all the debts of their business in the event it fails (9, 9)
9. Money tied up in a firm in stocks of finished and unfinished products, and used to pay for day to day running costs (7, 7)
10. A legal agreement between two or more people, usually no more than 20, to jointly own, finance and run a business, and to share any profits (11)
12. A business organization with plant and operations in more than one country (13)
13. A business organization owned and managed by its employees (6, 11)

Clues down

2. A business organization able to raise permanent capital from the sale of shares to the general public through a stock exchange (6, 7, 7)
3. An industry in an economy owned and controlled entirely by the government (12, 8)
4. Legal term to describe the financial obligation of a firm's owners in the event it fails being no more than the amount of capital they invested in the enterprise (7, 9)
6. A business organization created to perform a public sector function or to operate under government control, such as a municipal water company, public hospital or central bank (6, 11)
7. A business organization owned jointly by its shareholders. Also known as a limited company (5-5, 7)
11. A business organization owned and usually controlled by one person (4, 6)

Types of business organization

Unit 4.2   Organization of production

AIMS

By the end of this unit you should be able to:

- describe what determines the demand for factors of production
- define productivity and recognize the difference between **productivity** and **production**
  - identify factors that increase **productivity**
  - understand **factor substitution** and analyse why firms may substitute one factor of production for another
- distinguish between **capital-intensive** and **labour-intensive production**
- define **total and average cost**, **fixed and variable cost** and perform simple calculations
- analyse particular situations to show changes in total and average costs as output changes
- define **total and average revenue** and perform simple calculations
  - calculate profit or loss as the difference between total revenue and total cost
  - identify and explain the **break-even level of output**
- describe the principle of **profit maximization** and recognize that business organizations may have different goals.

210   The private firm as producer and employer

SECTION 1 — Production

Adding value

Goods and services are produced in order to satisfy consumer wants. The **production** of goods and services is organized by entrepreneurs in firms. A firm combines scarce resources of land, labour and capital (**inputs**) to make goods and services (**outputs**). ➤ 1.1

A firm may own one or more plants where resources are employed and productive activity is carried out. A **plant** is simply a workplace and includes premises such as a warehouse, retail outlet, office or factory.

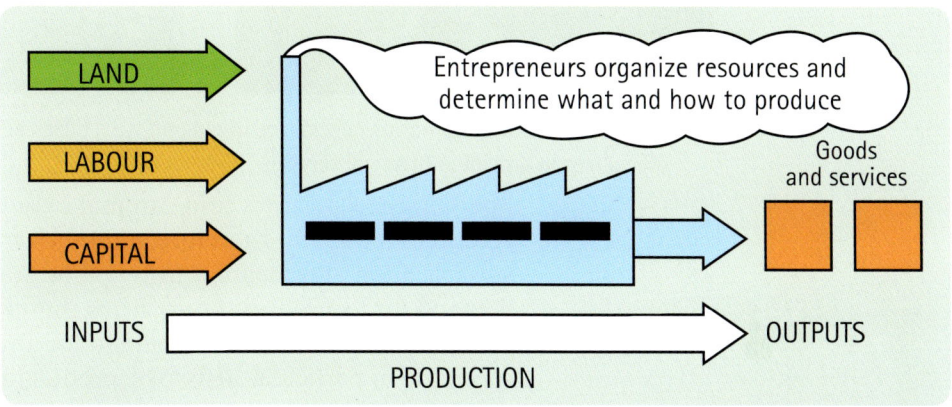

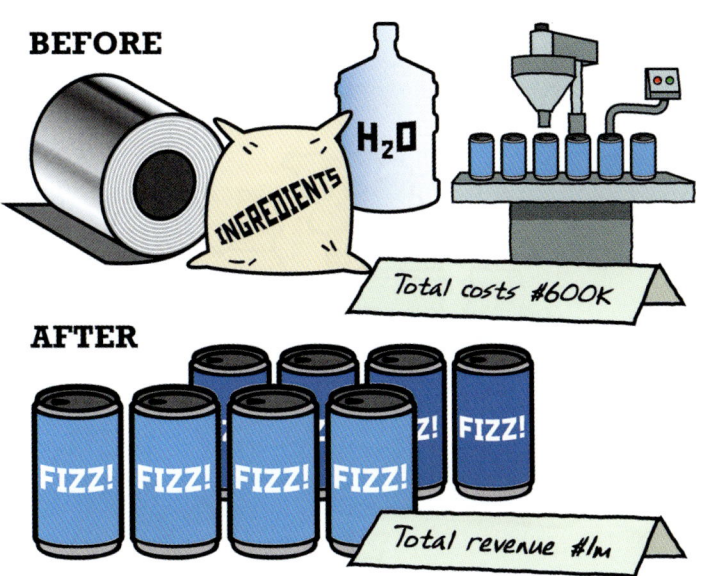

Given that the aim of production is to satisfy consumer wants, the process is not complete until the goods and services actually reach the people and other organizations who want them. Warehouses and shops that sell goods and services to consumers, as well as all those people and machines involved in transportation, insurance and many other tasks, are all part of the production process.

By combining resource inputs to produce outputs consumers want and are willing and able to buy, productive activity adds value to those resources. For example, a firm that produces 1 million cans of fizzy drink which are sold for $1 each but cost only $600,000 to produce has added $400,000 to the value of the resources used in their production, including labour, water, aluminum, machinery, vehicles and electricity.

▲ How production adds value to resources

Value added in production is the difference between the market price paid for a product by a consumer and the cost of the natural and man-made materials, components and resources used to make it. Value added is therefore equal to the wages paid to labour to produce the product and the profit received by the owners of the firm that organized the production of the product.

Specialization in production by firms

Imagine you set up a firm and try to produce lots of different products to sell, from light bulbs and garden tools, to designer clothes and bus services. You are unlikely to be successful at all these activities. This is because you and the people you employ would be trying to do too many things at the same time.

It would be far more sensible for you and your employees to concentrate on producing what they are best at. This is called **specialization**. ➤ 3.1

Organization of production 211

▲ The Toyota Motor Corporation specializes in making cars, buses and commercial vehicles and HSBC specializes in providing financial services

Specialization means a firm can make the best possible use of the skills and resources it has and therefore add much more value to them. However, specialization also means a firm will be at greater risk from a fall in consumer demand for its product. Some firms therefore produce a range of different products in case consumer demand for any one of them falls. Because firms specialize in particular activities, production will normally involve a **chain of productive activity**.

ACTIVITY 4.8

Dough!

1. The jumble of cartoons and numbered descriptions that follow on the next page together describe how bread is produced. Match each picture to a description. Write down the descriptions to form a chain of the productive activities involved in bread production, right through to final sale to consumers. Some descriptions may be used more than once.

The private firm as producer and employer

1. Wheat, water, yeast and other ingredients are mixed together to produce dough
2. Coal and oil are used to power electricity stations for use by firms and households
3. Farms plant seeds to grow wheat
4. Supermarkets and other shops sell bread to consumers
5. Road haulage service providers transport harvested wheat and finished breads
6. Consumers buy bread
7. Wheat is harvested
8. Insurance firms provide insurance to protect firms from risk of damage or theft
9. Dough is poured into baking pans and placed in ovens to cook
10. Sealed packets for the bread are produced and labelled in printing machines
11. Consumers make sandwiches or toast to consume
12. Finished loaves of bread are sealed in plastic packaging
13. Commercial banks provide loans and payment services to firms
14. Food inspectors check the quality and hygiene of the breads and the bakery

2 Investigate and list the chain of productive activities involved in the production and sale of the following products:

- a new computer game
- sweets
- hairdressing
- fresh orange juice
- washing powders
- a good or service of your choice

Each chain of productive activity will link together many different firms and activities – from those producing natural resources such as coal, corn and oil, to those that use these materials to make component parts and finished goods and services for consumers, and finally to those businesses that operate warehouses, transport services and shops to distribute and sell products to customers.

Industrial sectors

Similar firms and productive activities are grouped together into industries. It is therefore useful to classify or group firms into industrial sectors.

An **industrial sector** or **industry** is a group of firms specializing in similar goods and services, or using similar production processes. An industry will include small, local firms employing very few workers and large, national or even multinational firms employing many thousands of workers and selling products all over the world.

For example, the automotive manufacturing industry consists of all firms making and supplying vehicles and engines, tyres, body parts and components. Similarly, the air transport industry includes all firms providing air passenger and airfreight transport services and facilities, including airports and airlines.

Primary industries

The production or extraction of natural resources is the first stage of production for most goods and services.

Industries in the **primary sector** in an economy specialize in the production or extraction of natural resources by growing crops, managing forests, mining coal and other minerals, and extracting oils and gases.

Primary sector industries

- Crop and animal production
- Forestry and logging
- Fishing
- Mining
- Quarrying
- Oil and gas extraction

Secondary industries

Turning unprocessed natural resources and other unfinished products into other goods is a process called **manufacturing** and firms that engage in this activity belong to the manufacturing or **secondary sector**. For example, oil is used in plastics, glass is made from sand, and paper is made from pulped wood. Many electrical products are made from metals and plastics.

Construction firms using materials to build homes, offices, roads and other infrastructure, and firms processing oil, gas and other fuels to supply electricity are also part of the secondary sector of an economy.

Some secondary sector industries

- Food processing
- Textiles
- Paper, pulp and paperboard
- Chemicals
- Oil and gas refining
- Pharmaceuticals
- Rubber and plastic products
- Fabricated metals
- Computer, electronic and optical products
- Water collection, treatment and supply
- Electric power generation, transmission and distribution
- Construction

Tertiary or service industries

Firms that provide services are part of the **tertiary sector** in an economy. The distribution and sale of manufactured goods and the provision of services to consumers is the final stage in their production. Firms in the wholesale and retailing industries specialize in these activities.

However, there are many businesses providing services that are used at every stage of production, such as banking, insurance and transport. Some firms also provide personal services such as hairdressing, decorating, health care and personal training.

214 The private firm as producer and employer

Some tertiary sector industries

- Wholesaling, retailing and repairs
- Transportation and storage
- Accommodation and food services
- Publishing and broadcasting
- Telecommunications
- Banking and insurance
- Real estate
- Public administration
- Defence services
- Education
- Arts and entertainment
- Health care
- Legal services

ACTIVITY 4.9

Which stage of production?

1. Go back to Activity 4.8. Look again at the activities being carried out in each picture and state which are primary, secondary or tertiary.

2. Under three column headings sort the following list of industries into primary, secondary and tertiary industries.

Television broadcasting	Health service	Advertising
Film making	Farming	Shipbuilding
Shipping	Banking	Universities
Decorating	Hotels	Motor cars
Construction	Furniture	Mining
Fishing	Retailing	Chemicals
Forestry	Engineering	Restaurants

SECTION 2

The aims of production

The aim or objective of most private sector firms is to make as much **profit** as possible from the production and sale of their goods or services. This means generating more in revenue from the sale of goods and services than it costs to produce them.

Profit is a reward for enterprise. Without it people would not bother to start up and own business organizations. People who invest money in productive activities stand to lose their money if their businesses fail. Enterprise therefore involves risk taking and high risk normally requires a high reward. Without such rewards for enterprise there would be far less production, fewer jobs, lower incomes and fewer goods and services to buy. ➤ 4.1

For example, entrepreneurs will not know in advance how much of a particular product consumers will buy and how much they will be willing and able to pay for it. Even so, entrepreneurs must pay in advance for the services of land, labour and capital in order to make their chosen product. In some cases, there may be a very long time between first designing and making a product and selling that product. For example, designing, making and testing a new aircraft takes many years and may cost many billions of dollars before the manufacturer is ready to start making the aircraft for sale to airlines.

Profit maximization can therefore be difficult to achieve. A firm that is unable to cover its costs with enough sales revenue will make a loss and could be forced to close down if losses continue. A firm may make a loss if it fails to make a product consumers want, at the price or quality they want, or provides a poor customer service. A firm may also make a loss if it is unable to produce products at the same or lower cost than rival firms. It is therefore important for firms to be efficient and continually try to increase their sales and reduce their costs of production to remain competitive. However, a firm that increases its prices too much or cuts its costs too deeply may fail to its boost profits. Consumers may not want to pay high prices for products especially if they have also fallen in quality because production costs have been cut back so much.

In contrast, some business owners may not aim to maximize profits. They may instead aim for a satisfactory level of profits that provides them with enough income to buy and enjoy the goods and services they want without having to work long hours or pay too much in tax.

Other objectives

▼ Charities do not aim to make profits

Not all organizations aim to maximize profits, for example:

- **Charities** aim to help people or animals in need, or to protect the natural environment. They rely on donations or gifts of money to pay for their costs.

- **Not-for-profit organizations**, such as many cooperatives and mutual societies that are run by or on behalf of their members and use any surplus of revenue over costs to re-invest in the business or to lower prices. These organizations may also include local social or sports clubs organized and run by their members who pay a small membership fee to cover the costs of newsletters and the hire of venues ➤ 4.1

- Government organizations may provide **public services** free of charge, including free health care and bus travel for elderly people and people on low incomes. The cost of their provision is funded from tax revenues. ➤ 5.2

216　The private firm as producer and employer

SECTION 3

Productivity and factor demand

What is factor productivity?

Productivity measures the amount of output (goods and services) that can be produced from a given amount of input (land, labour and capital resources).

For example, a business that uses 10 units of resources to produce 40 units of output per week is twice as productive as a business that uses 10 units of the same resources to produce just 20 units of output per week.

The aim of any business will be to combine its resources in the most efficient way. That is, it will aim to produce as much output as it can with the least amount of resources it can, and therefore at the lowest cost possible.

For example, farms in Pakistan obtain 33 million tonnes of milk from 20 million milking animals, compared with over 37 million tonnes obtained by Chinese farms from 15 million animals and 84 million tonnes of milk produced in the USA by 9.1 million cows.

▼ How productivity in dairy farming differs around the world

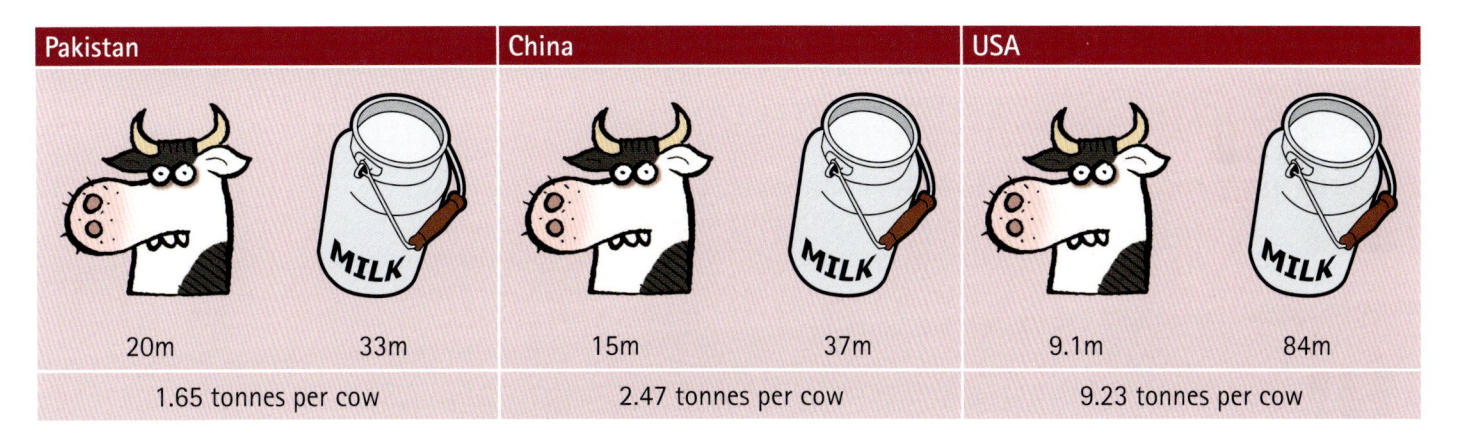

Pakistan	China	USA
20m　33m	15m　37m	9.1m　84m
1.65 tonnes per cow	2.47 tonnes per cow	9.23 tonnes per cow

Although the combined farms in Pakistan are the fourth largest producer of milk in the world after farms in India, the USA and China, the productivity of milking animals in Pakistan is clearly much lower than that of US or Chinese cows.

Low milk yields increase the cost of production of milk. For example, US farmers feed one cow to obtain the same quantity of milk that a Pakistani farmer obtains by feeding 4.5 cows.

According to livestock experts, milk yields of diary herds in Pakistan could be increased by around 600 litres per animal by providing them with adequate clean drinking water. Feeding them a balanced diet and improving hygiene could lead to an increase of another 600 litres of milk per animal.

Productivity therefore measures how efficiently resources are being used in production.

In general, productivity in a business will have increased if:

- more output or revenue is produced from the same amount of resources
- the same output or revenue can be produced using fewer resources.

Resources cost money to buy or hire. For example, materials must be purchased from suppliers, wages must be paid to hire labour, machinery and equipment must be purchased outright or leased, and premises must be rented. Therefore,

Organization of production

if the same amount of labour, land and capital can produce more output for the same total cost, then the cost of producing each unit of output (or average cost) will have fallen. Increasing the productivity of resources can therefore reduce production costs, make a firm more competitive, and increase profits.

▲ Productive

▲ More productive

A firm that fails to increase the productivity of its resources or factors of production at the same pace or at a faster rate than rival firms will have higher production costs and therefore lower profits than its competitors.

Measuring productivity

Labour productivity is the most common measure of factor productivity. It is calculated by dividing total output over a given period of time, for example a day, week or month, by the number of workers employed. This gives a measure of the average productivity per worker per period.

$$\text{Average product of labour} = \frac{\text{total output per period}}{\text{number of employees}}$$

The average productivity of labour is a useful measure of how efficient workers are and how efficiently they use other resources. For example, if a company employs 10 workers who produce 200 plant pots each day, the average product per employee per day is 20 pots. If daily output is able to rise to 220 pots per day without employing additional workers then productivity will have increased to 22 pots per worker per day.

Productivity in business organizations producing services can be more difficult to measure. For example, a hair salon could measure the number of customers or hair treatments per day per employee, but not all employees in the salon will be hairdressers. Some may be office staff and cleaners. So how can we measure their productivity?

A better measure of overall productivity is the average revenue per worker per period.

$$\text{Average revenue product of labour} = \frac{\text{total revenue per period}}{\text{number of employees}}$$

Productivity is also difficult to measure in organizations that do not produce a physical output or earn revenue, for example government-funded hospitals or schools, government departments or a police force. Other performance measures, such as time spent waiting for an operation, meeting deadlines, numbers of students passing qualifications and numbers of arrests, will often be used instead.

Another problem with productivity measures is that they take no account of the quality of work. Increasing productivity is also about improving product quality because consumers demand, and are often willing to pay a premium for, better quality goods and services

The division of labour

Increased labour productivity in many firms over time has been the result of the **division of labour**, whereby each worker specializes in carrying out one particular task or operation in a production process.

Many hundreds of years ago different groups of workers were identified according to the type of good or service they produced. Workers skilled in making the same good or providing the same service formed guilds to protect their trades and provide training to new apprentices. For example, there were guilds for bakers, engineers, blacksmiths, butchers, carpenters, tailors and many more. However, since then, modern production processes have become broken down into a series of separate operations, each one performed by a different employee or group of employees. ➤ 3.2

For example, in the early days of the motor car industry one employee would put together an entire engine. Then Henry Ford decided to divide up the work involved into 84 varied operations, so that 84 employees were needed to build a whole engine instead of just one person. However, it meant many more engines could be built each day.

ECONOMICS IN ACTION

How did the division of labour benefit the Ford Motor Car Company and Ford assembly line workers?

The Ford Model T

Work on the famous Model T began in 1907, and the production began two years later in 1910 at the company's new plant in Highland Park, Michigan.

As simple as the Model T was, there remained the problem of volume production. Each car was practically hand-built. To boost production Mr Ford and his associates began sub-dividing jobs, bringing parts to workers and scheduling parts to arrive at the right spot at the right time in the production process.

Finally, they devised the moving assembly line, which, with later refinements, pointed the way to mass production. In the beginning it took 12 hours and 28 minutes to assemble a Model T. The time was cut to 5 hours and 28 minutes, then to 93 minutes. Mr Ford set a goal of a car a minute, but eventually Model Ts were rolling off the assembly line at the rate of one every ten seconds during each working day. With increased production, the price of cars came down and the pay of workers went up.

Advantages of the division of labour

The organization of labour into a number of separate and specialist tasks has brought significant gains in labour productivity in many firms for the following reasons.

1 More goods and services can be produced

When workers specialize, repetition of the same operation increases the skill and speed of the worker and, as a result, more is produced.

2 Full use is made of employees' abilities

With the division of labour there is a greater chance that people will be able to do those things at which they are best and which interest them the most.

3 Time is saved

If a person had to do many different tasks or operations then too much time would be wasted switching from one task to another. Time can also be saved when training people. It would take a great many years to train someone to be able to build a complete car, but a person can be trained quickly to fulfill one operation in the production process.

4 It allows the use of machinery

As labour is divided up into specialist tasks it becomes worthwhile to use machinery that allows further savings in time and effort. For example, today cars are painted by robots instead of by hand.

The disadvantages of the division of labour

1 Work may become boring

A worker who performs the same operation each and every day is likely to become very bored.

2 Workers may feel alienated

Workers may feel undervalued and lose pride in their work because they can no longer see the final result of their efforts. Boredom and alienation among workers may also cause industrial disputes. ➤ 3.3

3 Products become too standardized

Whether this is a disadvantage is a matter of people's own opinion. For example, there is probably enough variation in the colour and design of cars and clothes to please most people. However, it is not possible to please everyone because in most factories it would be difficult and expensive to change the production process to suit individual tastes. This is because many large, modern manufacturers practice **mass production**. This term is used to describe a production process that aims to use the fewest workers to produce the greatest number of goods at the lowest cost possible.

Other ways firms can increase labour productivity

Although the division of labour has increased labour productivity significantly over time, there is a limit to how many gains in productivity can be achieved in this way, especially if it results in some of the problems above. Firms may therefore combine other ways to improve labour productivity, such as:

- training workers to improve their existing skills and learn new skills
- rewarding increased productivity with performance-related pay and bonus payments
- encouraging employees to buy shares in their organization – improved productivity will help to raise profits and pay higher dividends on shares
- increasing job satisfaction, for example by improving the working environment, making jobs more interesting, introducing more team working, involving workers in business decision making and giving regular feedback on performance
- replacing old plant and machinery with new, more efficient machines and tools for workers to use
- introducing new production processes and working practices designed to continually reduce waste, increase speed, improve quality and raise output in all areas of a firm. This is known as **lean manufacturing** but its principles can equally apply to the production of services.

Many of the above initiatives will tend to raise the cost of employing labour in the short run. However, if productivity improves, the average cost of producing each unit of output will fall and profits will tend to rise. Lower costs can be passed on to consumers as lower prices in an attempt to increase consumer demand and generate more sales revenues. If consumer demand expands, then the demand for labour may also increase.

Combining factors of production

Firms will attempt to combine factors of production in the most productive and efficient way possible to maximize output and minimize production costs. For example, a **labour-intensive** organization will employ more labour than capital machinery and equipment. In contrast, a **capital-intensive** firm is one that has invested heavily in capital equipment and machinery and employs relatively few workers. Most production will be automated.

▲ Labour-intensive production

▲ Capital-intensive production

Organization of production

The amount of labour or capital demanded by a firm will depend on a number of factors.

1 The amount of goods and services consumers demand

The more goods and services consumers want and are willing and able to buy, the more factors of production firms will tend to employ. That is, demand for factors of production is a **derived demand**. The demand for labour and capital in a firm depends on there being sufficient demand for the goods and services they produce.

2 The market prices of labour and capital

Just like the demand for other goods and services, the demand for factors of production by firms is related to their price. For example, as the wage rate increases, the demand for labour by firms will tend to contract. Similarly, if the cost of buying or hiring capital equipment increases then demand for capital will also tend to contract. It follows that if wages rise while the cost of capital equipment falls, then a firm might consider reducing the number of workers it employs and using more machinery instead. However, crucially it also depends on how productive labour is relative to capital.

3 The productivity of labour and capital

In general, a profit-maximizing firm will only employ extra labour or capital if the addition to production costs is less than or at least no more than the value of the additional output produced. For example, if the cost of employing an extra worker is an additional $100 in wages per week, but that extra worker will only produce an extra $90 worth of output each week, then he or she is not worth employing.

Imagine a firm producing table lamps. Each lamp sells for $10. At present, four units of labour (that is, four employees) are employed producing a total output of 300 lamps each week. The firm wants to increase output but doesn't know how many extra workers to employ. To help the firm decide, it estimates how much more output each additional worker is likely to produce.

▼ Table lamp production

Number of workers	Total output per week	Extra output per worker per week	Value of extra output (quantity × price)
4	300	–	–
5	350	50	$500
6	390	40	$400
7	420	30	$300
8	440	20	$200
9	450	10	$100

The firm has estimated that adding a fifth worker would raise total output by 50 lamps each week. When these extra lamps are sold, the firm's revenue will increase by $500. The revenue productivity of the fifth worker is therefore $500 per week.

If the wage rate is $300 per week, it is worth employing the fifth worker as well as a sixth worker. A seventh worker will add $300 to the value of total output each week, and costs $300 in wages to employ. In a profit-maximizing firm this worker is worth employing because each one of the extra lamps produced will be adding to profit. However, if the firm attempted to employ an eighth worker it would gain only $200 in extra output but lose $300 in extra wage costs. Profits would fall by $100. The only way the firm would extend its demand for labour to eight workers would be if wages fell to $200 each week. The firm's demand curve for labour therefore slopes downwards. ➤ 3.2

Alternatively, our table lamp manufacturer could attempt to increase the productivity of all its workers. It estimates that if it trains new and existing employees in more productive techniques each worker could produce a further 10 lamps worth an additional $100 each week.

So now, a fifth worker would increase output by 60 lamps each week, worth $600 in extra revenue. A sixth worker would increase output by another 50 lamps, worth $500 in revenue, and so on. This has the impact of shifting the demand curve for labour to the right at every possible wage rate (from DnDn to Dn1Dn1 in the diagram below). If the weekly wage rate remains at $300 per employee, then clearly it is now worth employing up to eight workers, since the eighth worker will now add as much to revenue as he or she will cost to employ.

▼ Demand for table lamp makers

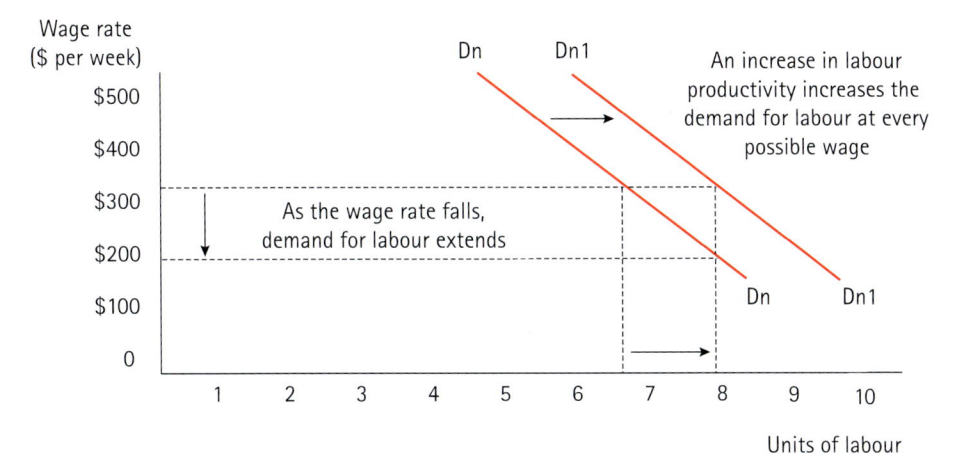

Exactly the same will apply to a decision to increase the amount of capital employed in the table lamp firm if it could employ computerized machinery to make the lamps instead of extra workers. If the productivity of capital rises, and/or the cost of capital falls, firms will tend to expand their demand for capital.

A firm will want to combine its resources in the most efficient way to maximize overall productivity for the minimum of costs. It will therefore compare the costs and productivity of labour with capital and will tend to employ more of the most productive factor. It follows that if wages rise or the productivity of capital rises, a firm will tend to replace labour with more capital. This is known as **factor substitution.**

Factor substitution

Factor substitution involves replacing labour in a production process with new capital equipment and machinery. The substitution of labour with capital has occurred in many modern industries in many countries. Technological advance has greatly lowered the cost of new equipment and machinery and has increased their productivity relative to labour. For example, the work of once skilled typesetters and compositors in the printing industry has now been replaced by desktop publishing software on computers operated by writers and journalists. Intelligent robots controlled by computer have taken over human tasks in manufacturing processes such as car assembly and food packaging. This is known as **computer aided manufacture (CAM)**.

Organization of production

However, labour and capital are not perfect substitutes. The ability of a firm to substitute capital for labour will very much depend on the type of product and the production process used. For example, automated mass production processes are used to produce many thousands or millions of very similar products, such as newspapers, cars, paints and computer discs. However, machines cannot replicate the work of a doctor, solicitor, hairdresser or other workers providing personalized care and services. Similarly, some consumers want personalized jewellery or furniture made for them. This production is usually by hand, and involves many hours of labour.

The costs of installing and maintaining new machinery and other equipment can also be very expensive and will affect the decision by a firm to employ more capital at the expense of labour, even if the new capital is more productive. Short-term production costs may also rise, as workers may need to be re-trained to use new machinery and equipment.

Substituting capital for labour may also cause bitter labour disputes between trade unions and their employers over possible job losses. Strikes by workers and redundancy payments for those forced to leave can be very expensive for a firm. ▶ 3.3

ACTIVITY 4.10

March of the robots

India Steps Up to Robotics

With the Indian manufacturing sector booming, the robotics industry is gearing up for sharp growth. At India's biggest auto manufacturer, Tata Motors, the workforce has been reduced by 20 per cent, while the company's turnover has increased 2.5 times. Its Pune plant alone has invested in 100 robots.

At the same time the country's top government scientists are at work on robot and artificial intelligence (AI) technologies for use in everything from border patrols to the deployment of 'robot armies' to replace human soldiers.

'The use of robots is growing extremely fast in India' say industry analysts. 'Robots can be expensive to buy and implement but they save labour and help companies raise their productivity and quality, to meet the demands of international competition. Customers in India are also beginning to understand how useful robots are in production: they not only save costs, but are a safer and a healthier option.'

1. What do you think are some of the advantages of employing robots in business?
2. Why do you think industrial robots are described as labour-saving technology?
3. How can the use of robots in business affect workers and consumers?
4. What do you think may be some of the main obstacles to employing more robots in firms in your economy and other national economies?

SECTION 4 — Calculating costs and revenues

ACTIVITY 4.11

Bear Necessities

Sue Brennan used to make toys when she was a young girl at school. Her friends and relatives thought that they were so good that they asked her to make some for them to give as presents to others. This gave Sue an idea for the future.

When she left school she went to work in a local furniture-making factory for two years where she gained experience of using cloth to make seat covers. She saved some money and asked her bank to lend her some more so that she could start up her own firm under the name of 'Bear Necessities'.

Sue rented a small factory unit on a new industrial estate. The cost of the building including fittings is $100 per week. She also hired some machinery at a cost of $45 per week. Sue employs her two brothers to help her to make toy bears. Sue pays herself and her brothers a piece rate of $1 for each bear they complete.

Since she started, Sue's toy bears have become very popular and she has many orders for them. She must, however, rely on regular custom from other firms and shops for her bears and so she must try and keep quality high and prices low. The average price she charges for her bears is $10 each.

The costs of Bear Necessities

In running her toy-making business Sue has a number of things she has to pay for. These are her costs. Some things have to be paid for each and every week no matter how many bears Sue makes and sells. These are her **fixed costs** that do not vary with the number of bears she produces. On the other hand, **variable costs** change with the number of bears produced. The more Sue produces the more fabric and foam she needs. Wages paid to herself and her brothers also rise.

Fixed costs per week ($)		Variable costs per bear ($)	
Factory rent	100.00	Fabric	6.00
Machinery hire charges	45.00	Foam	1.00
Electricity supply	5.00	Wages	1.00
Bank loan repayments	50.00		8.00
	200.00		

Sue keeps any **profit** that is left after she has taken away her costs from the money or **revenue** she earns from selling bears.

Answer the following questions.

1. Write a definition of fixed costs and give two examples.
2. If Sue produced 100 bears in a week, how much would her fixed costs be that week?
3. If Sue produced 1,000 bears in a week, how much would her fixed costs be that week?
4. Write a definition of variable costs and give two examples.
5. If Sue produced 100 bears, how much would her variable costs be?
6. If Sue produced 1,000 bears, how much would her variable costs be?
7. The **total cost** of producing a given number of bears each week is found by adding together all the fixed costs (total fixed costs) and all the variable costs (total variable costs).

    Total cost (TC) = total fixed costs + total variable costs

    a. If Sue produced 100 bears in a week, what would her total cost be?

    b. If Sue produced 1,000 bears in a week, what would her total cost be?

Organization of production

8 Copy the table below and work out the fixed, variable and total costs of producing different numbers of toy bears in a week. The costs of producing 400 bears and 500 bears have already been done for you. We will then plot all this information on a graph (Do not complete the final column in the table for now.)

Bears produced per week	Total fixed costs $	Total variable costs $	Total cost $	Average cost per bear $
0				
50				
100				
200				
300				
400	200	3,200	3,400	8.5
500	200	4,000	4,200	8.4
600				
700				
800				
900				
1,000				

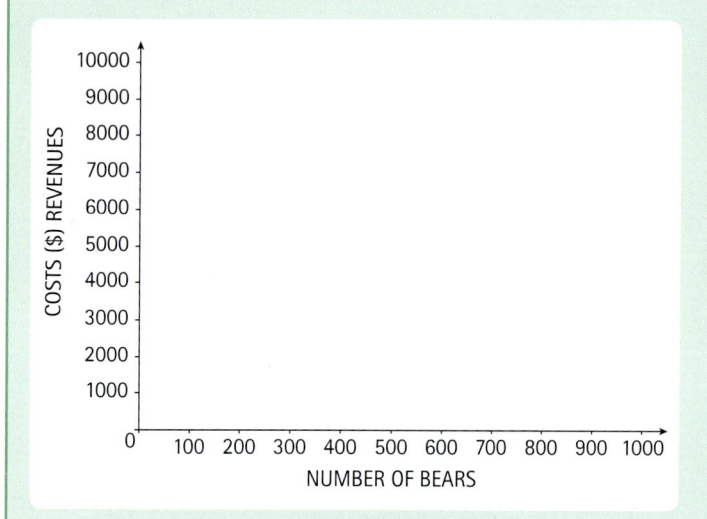

9 Now draw a pair of axes for a graph like the one above on a large piece of graph paper. Use your calculations to plot the total fixed cost curve, total variable cost curve and total cost curve to show how costs change with the number of bears produced. Do not forget to label each line you plot with its correct name.

10 What is the price charged for each bear?

11 How much money or revenue does Sue receive from the sale of each bear?

You will notice that your answers to questions 10 and 11 are the same.

Clearly if Sue sold five bears for $10 each, the revenue per bear is $10, while her **total revenue** is $50. Total sales revenue is also known as **turnover**.

Total revenue (TR) = price per bear × number of bears sold

If the total revenue from the sale of five bears is $50, then the average revenue for each of those bears is $10, which is the same as the price of each bear.

$$\text{Average revenue (AR)} = \frac{\text{total revenue}}{\text{number of bears sold}}$$

12 If Sue sold 100 bears what would her total revenue be?

13 If Sue sold 1,000 bears what would her total revenue be?

14 Draw the table below and calculate the total revenue from the number of bears sold. Again, this has already been done for 400 and 500 bears sold.

15 Now look back at the graph you drew earlier and on it plot your figures for total revenue in a different colour and label this line total revenue.

Bears produced and sold per week	Total revenue $	Total cost $	Profit or loss $
0			
50			
100			
200			
300			
400	4,000	3,400	600
500	5,000	4,200	800
600			
700			
800			
900			
1,000			

226 The private firm as producer and employer

16 To calculate the total **profit** or **loss** Sue makes from producing and selling bears we take away her total costs (TC) from her total revenue (TR). If her total costs are greater than her total revenue, Sue will make a loss. If she is successful, her total revenue will exceed her total costs and she will make a profit.

Profit (or loss) = TR − TC

On the table you copied in question 14, write in the total costs of producing the different number of bears and calculate the profit or loss. We assume Sue sells all the bears she makes.

On your graph the area between the total revenue and the total cost curves represents the profit or loss. Where the total cost curve is above the total revenue curve the area in between them represents loss. Label this area and shade in one colour. Where the total cost curve lies below the total revenue curve the area in between represents profit. Label this area and shade in another colour.

Where the two curves cross, no profit or loss is made. This level of output and sales is known as the **break-even level of output**. This means that if Sue manages to sell all the bears she makes at this point, she will just cover her costs and be able to remain in business. You should find from your tables and graphs that to do this Sue must make and sell at least 100 toy bears each week.

Break-even level of output occurs where TR = TC, i.e. profit or loss is zero.

17 Now look again at the total costs of producing a different amount of bears each week. We now wish to calculate for Sue just how much it costs on average to make one bear. This is known as the **average cost** or **unit cost** of production.

We found in question 8 that when Sue produced 400 bears per week her total costs were $3,400. Clearly then if 400 bears cost $3,400 to make then one bear costs $8.50 to make (i.e. $3,400/400).

Average cost (AC) = $\dfrac{\text{total cost}}{\text{number of bears produced}}$

Go back to the table you drew in question 8 and, in the final column, calculate the average cost of producing each bear if 50, 100, 200 and so on bears were made.

18 We will now plot the average cost curve on another graph with the number of bears produced along the horizontal axis and cost ($) on the vertical axis. You will need your cost axis to go up to at least $12. When you have done this write down what you notice about the slope of the curve; that is, what happens to the average costs of production as more and more bears are produced? Can you suggest reasons for this? (Hint: Even if no bears or 1,000 bears are produced what costs does Sue have to pay?)

Well done! By completing the activity about Bear Necessities you have learnt all about costs and revenues associated with production in a firm, how to calculate them and what they mean for profit. The rest of this unit will now help you to understand these important business and economic concepts fully, and to apply your knowledge to other examples.

Just like the Bear Necessities toy-making firm in Activity 4.11, most private sector firms aim to make as much profit as possible. Profit is calculated as the difference between what it costs a firm to produce its goods or services and the revenue it earns from their sale. That is,

profit = total revenue − total cost

Organization of production

To maximize profit a firm will aim to raise as much revenue as it can, for example by using advertising to boost demand and pricing strategies to attract consumers from rival firms, and it will also aim to minimize costs. Controlling costs is also very important in non-profit making organizations such as charities. However, to control costs a firm must be able to identify and measure the costs of all the factors of production it employs and uses up in production. These are the cost of wages for labour, payments for capital goods, components and materials, and the costs of many other goods and services supplied by other producers, including banking and insurance services, telecommunications, energy, legal services, transportation and much more.

Fixed costs

Before a firm can begin production and make goods and services for sale it will need to buy or hire many items. It may need premises, vehicles, computers and other equipment, stationery and it may need to undertake market research. These are start-up costs. Starting a business or developing a new product can be expensive and there will be no revenue to cover these start-up costs until production begins and products are sold.

Fixed costs, such as mortgage payments or rents for premises, interest charges on bank loans, leasing charges for machinery, telephone bills, cleaning costs and insurance premiums, will continue to be paid once production has started, no matter how much a firm produces and sells. That is, fixed costs do not vary with the level of output.

We can plot the total of fixed costs for a firm on a graph just like the one you drew for Bear Necessities in Activity 4.11. You will have noticed from your graph that the total fixed cost curve is flat because fixed costs do not vary with the level of output. However, this is only true up to the point at which a firm is operating at full capacity. This is because when a firm has no more space or equipment to raise output further it will need to hire or buy more equipment and possibly invest in larger premises to expand its scale of production.

The graph below plots total fixed costs for an imaginary firm producing motor vehicles. It is a large manufacturing organization that can produce up to 10,000 cars each month and has fixed costs of $10 million each month whether it produces 10,000 cars or not. If it wants to increase its scale of production up to, say, 20,000 cars each month it will need to hire or buy a new, bigger factory and more equipment.

▼ Total fixed costs for car production

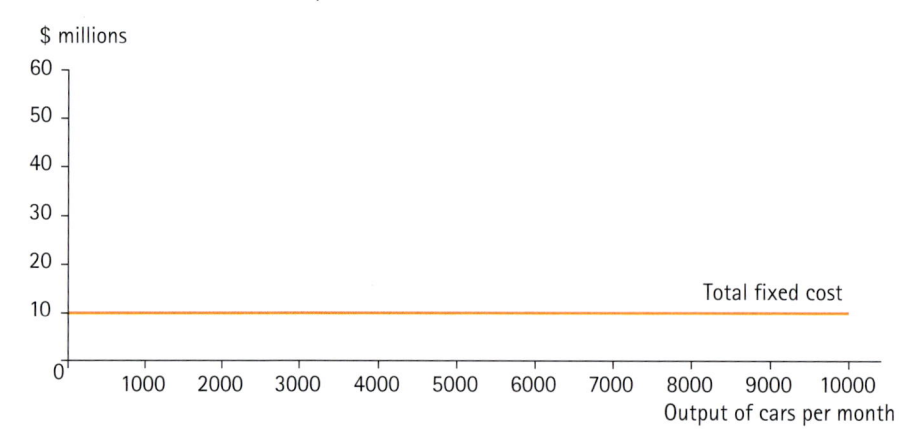

The private firm as producer and employer

Variable costs

To increase output a firm will need more materials or component parts. Similarly, more electricity may be needed to power machines and computers, and to heat and light premises, over longer periods of time. The firm may also need to employ more workers or pay its existing workers overtime to work more hours.

If we plot the total variable costs for a firm on a graph the variable cost curve will slope upwards. This is because **variable costs** vary directly with the level of output. For example, our car manufacturing firm can produce up to 10,000 cars per month with its existing factory and equipment. The total cost of materials and other variable items per car is $2,000. So, if the variable cost of producing one car is $2,000, then the total variable cost of producing 10,000 cars will be $20 million.

▼ Total variable costs for car production

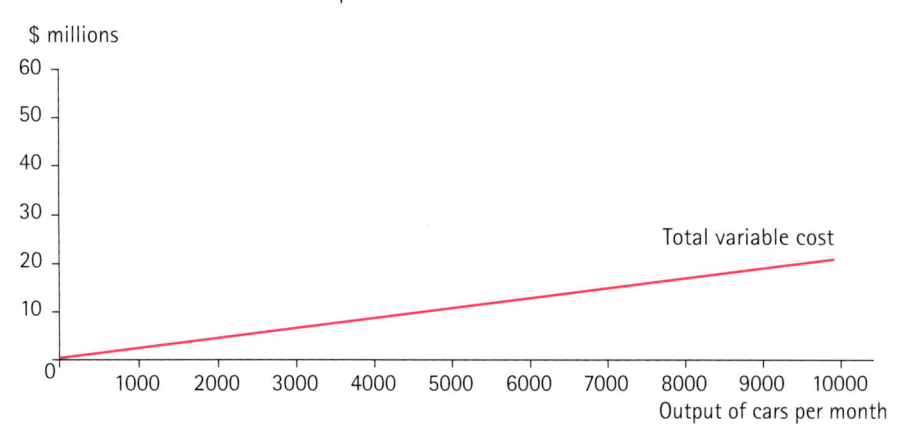

In general, therefore, the total variable cost of a given level of output is calculated as follows.

Total variable cost = variable cost per unit × quantity produced

If we add together all the fixed and variable costs of production of a firm we can calculate the total cost of producing each level of output.

Total cost = total fixed cost + total variable cost

If a firm produces no goods or services its total costs will be equal to its total fixed costs. Adding total variable costs to fixed costs means total costs will also increase as output rises, so the total cost curve will be upward sloping.

In our car firm the total cost of producing no cars will therefore be the fixed costs it will have to continue paying for at $10 million per month, while the total cost of producing 10,000 cars each month will be $30 million of fixed costs plus variable costs.

▼ Total cost for car production

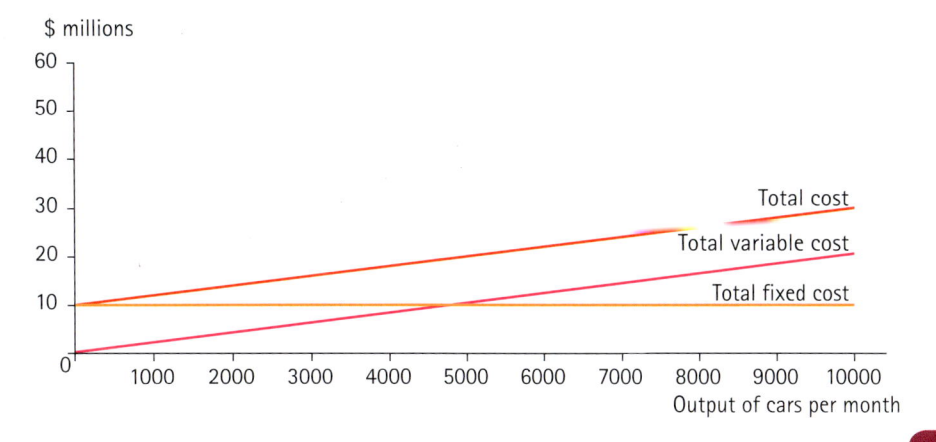

Organization of production

Average costs

If the total cost of producing 10,000 cars each month is $30 million, then the **average cost** of producing each car, or cost per unit of output, is $3,000. We can calculate the average cost per unit of output using the following equation:

$$\text{Average cost per unit} = \frac{\text{total cost}}{\text{total output}}$$

To make a profit the car company must therefore sell each car for more than $3,000 to make enough revenue to cover its costs and leave a surplus. But the car company must be careful not to charge too high a price for each car, otherwise consumers may not buy them, especially if demand for cars is highly price elastic. ➤ **2.2**

A firm can calculate the average cost per unit of providing a service in exactly the same way. For example, the average cost of one hour of labour from a car mechanic, the average cost of one mile of journey on a train, or the average cost of treating one patient at a hospital. All a firm needs to know are the fixed and variable costs of providing its service. So, if it costs a passenger rail company a total of $20,000 each day to run a train service over 1,000 kilometres then the average cost per kilometre travelled is $20.

From Activity 4.11 you will have discovered how the average cost of producing a toy bear fell as the number of bears produced by Bear Necessities increased.

At a production rate of 400 bears per week each bear cost $8.50 to produce. The unit cost per bear fell to $8.20 as output was raised to 1,000 bears each week. Similarly, if our car firm produces only 500 cars each month the average cost would be a massive $22,000 per car, which is unlikely to be a profitable level of production.

In general, therefore, the average cost of each unit of a good or service will tend to fall with the volume produced, simply because fixed costs remain the same but their burden is spread over a much larger output. However, after a point, average costs may start to rise again because it can become more difficult and expensive to increase output further.

For example, imagine the Bear Necessities business in Activity 4.11 attempts to increase output to 1,100 bears each week. However, the producer supplying synthetic fur fabric and foam to Bear Necessities is unable to increase the amount it supplies. The owner of Bear Necessities, Sue Brennan, may then have to buy the extra fabric and foam she needs from another supplier where prices are higher. In addition, Sue may have to employ more people to work in the firm and may have to increase wages to attract a supply of labour. ➤ **3.2**

Sue pays herself and her two brothers $100 each week regardless of how many bears they produce. Her total wage bill per week is $300. If she employs another three workers to produce more bears, wage costs will double to $600 or may more than double if she has to increase wages. However, as more labour is added, output will rise but may only do so at a diminishing rate as the average productivity of labour falls. So, while wage costs double, the output of bears may not double. Therefore, the average cost of producing each bear will begin to increase. ➤ **4.3**

▼ Average cost curve

[Graph: U-shaped AVERAGE COST curve, with COST PER UNIT ($) on y-axis and TOTAL OUTPUT on x-axis, showing MINIMUM AVERAGE COST marked at point x.]

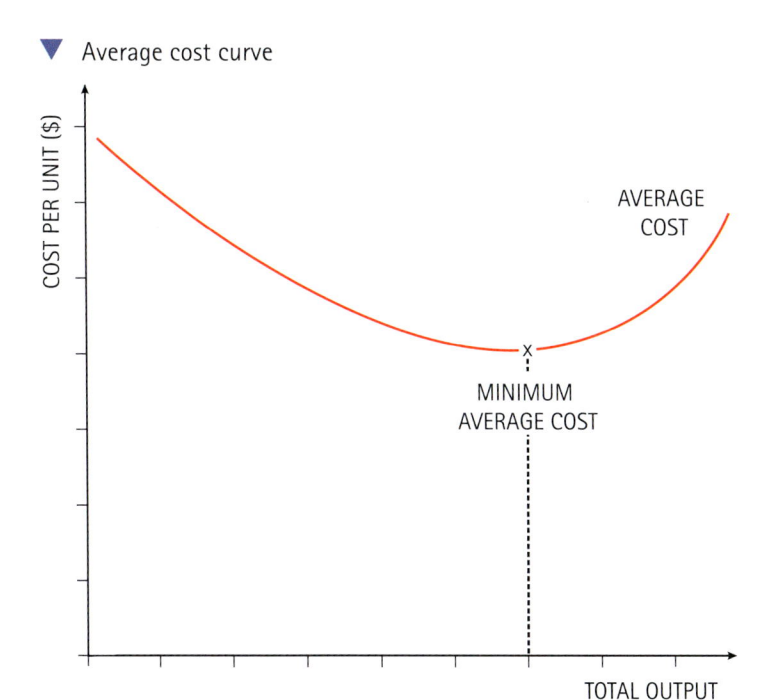

If we plot the average cost of production on a graph it will appear as a U-shaped curve for many firms, showing that as output rises, average costs fall up to a point and may then begin to increase slowly as output is raised yet further.

Similarly, our car manufacturer may find that there is a shortage of the skilled manufacturing workers it needs to increase output from, say, 8,000 cars per month up to full capacity of 10,000 cars per month. It may have to hire unskilled workers and spend more money training them, or it will have to increase wages to attract skilled workers away from other manufacturing firms. It too will find, therefore, that its average cost curve is U shaped, with the average cost of producing each car falling at first but then rising after output increases beyond 8,000 cars per month.

Revenue

Firms earn revenue from the sale of their goods and services to consumers. **Total revenue** is therefore the total amount sold multiplied by the price per unit sold.

Total revenue = price per unit × quantity sold

Revenue from sales is also known as **turnover**.

What happens if a firm sells its goods or services to different consumers at different prices? For example, in Activity 4.11 Bear Necessities charged a price of $10 per bear. Now imagine that the firm wants to expand into overseas markets, but to do so the bears will have to be sold at a lower price than $10 each in order to attract overseas consumers to buy them. For example, if the firm sells 1,000 bears at $10 each and another 500 overseas at $7 each then total revenue will be $13,500, and the average revenue per bear sold will be $9 as follows:

Total revenue = ($10 × 1,000 bears) + ($7 × 500 bears) = $13,500

Average revenue per bear sold = $\dfrac{\$13{,}500}{1{,}500}$ = $9

A firm can calculate the average revenue or average price per unit of output sold using the following equation:

Average revenue per unit = $\dfrac{\text{total revenue}}{\text{total units sold}}$

Average revenue will often fall as output and sales rise. This is because demand tends to expand as price falls and to sell more output firms will therefore need to lower their prices. We also know that as the market supply of a product increases so market price will tend to fall. ➤ **2.2**

A firm entering a new market may also price low to attract demand. This pricing strategy is known as penetration pricing. ➤ **4.4**

Organization of production

> **EXAM PREPARATION 4.1**
>
> British Gas is a large profit-making public company in the UK. A publicity leaflet from the company stated that the number of customers it served had increased. It also said that the company was more willing to pay compensation to customers for failure to meet required standards of service.
>
> a   Explain what is meant by the principle of profit maximisation. [4]
>
> b   Discuss what might have happened to profits as a result of each of the changes mentioned in the leaflet. [6]
>
> c   Describe briefly the main types of business organisation and consider which of them is likely to be the most significant in a developed economy. [10]
>
> *Cambridge IGCSE Economics 0455/04 Q7 October/November 2003*
> *Cambridge O Level Economics 2281/02 Q7 October/November 2003*

SECTION 5

Profit and loss

Profit, loss or break-even

Any firm will want to closely monitor its total revenue and average revenue so that it can calculate whether it is making a profit or a loss. Profit or loss is calculated as the difference between total revenue and total cost at each level of output. If total revenue exceeds total cost a firm will make a profit. But, if total revenue does not cover total costs, a firm will make a loss. If this continues the firm will go out of business and its resources will move to more profitable uses.

Profit (or loss) = total revenue − total cost

We can identify profit and loss from a graph of total revenue and total cost just as you did in Activity 4.11 for the Bear Necessities firm.

If we return to the example of the car manufacturer, let us assume each car sells for $6,000. Total revenue therefore appears as an upward sloping curve, from zero when no cars are sold to $60 million when 10,000 are sold. The car firm makes a loss on all sales up to 2,500 cars per month, and a profit on all sales over and above this level of output.

▶ Total revenue, total cost, profit and loss for car production

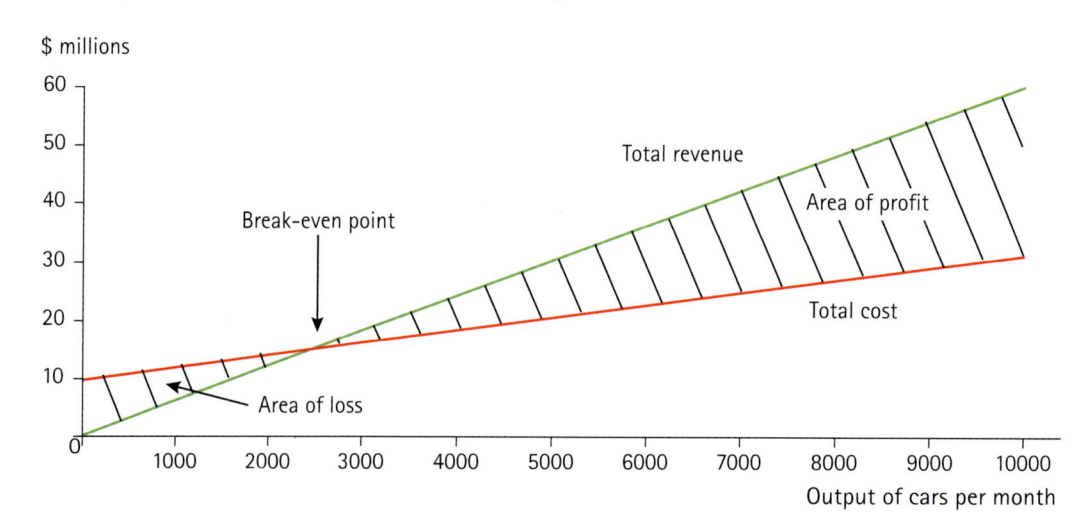

232 The private firm as producer and employer

It is also useful to know how much profit or loss is made from every unit of output sold by calculating the difference between average revenue and average cost.

Profit (or loss) per unit = average revenue – average cost

This is particularly informative for a firm planning to expand production. We already know that average cost per unit may start to rise after a certain level of output is reached because extra wages may have to be paid to attract more workers or there may be supply problems with component parts and other materials. We also know that average revenue may start to fall after a certain level of sales is reached, as prices may need to be cut to attract additional demand or when entering new markets. It follows, therefore, that a firm may find it unprofitable to expand output too much if its average revenue falls below its average cost.

Breaking-even

The **break-even level of output** is that level of output, which if sold, will generate a total revenue that will exactly equal total cost. At the break-even level of output a firm will neither make a profit or a loss. That is, break-even occurs where

total revenue = total cost

or where

total revenue – total cost = 0

For example, Bear Necessities broke even when output and sales reached 100 bears per month. Sales below this level of output made a loss, while sales above it earned a profit. Similarly, the car manufacturer has a break-even level of output of 2,500 cars per month.

The break-even level of output can be found graphically where the total revenue line crosses the total cost curve. At break-even a firm is able to cover all its costs and so can remain in business, although clearly if it wants to make a profit it must either increase revenue and/or lower costs otherwise it might as well stop production and move its resources to more profitable uses.

How to calculate the break-even level of output for a firm without using a graph

If you want to it is easy to calculate the level of output a firm needs to sell to break even using the equation below. All you need to know is the price at which the good or service is to be sold and its fixed and variable costs:

$$\text{Break-even level of output} = \frac{\text{total fixed cost}}{\text{price per unit} - \text{variable cost per unit}}$$

Let's quickly calculate break-even this way for Bear Necessities and our car firm example.

From Activity 4.11 we know the fixed costs of bear production were $200 per month, variable costs were $8 per bear and the final price per bear sold was $10. So, the break-even point is:

$200/($10 – $8) = $200 / $2 = 100 bears per month.

Our car firm has fixed costs of $10 million per month, variable costs of $2,000 per car, and sells its cars for $6,000 each. So, the level of output and sales needed to break even is:

$10,000,000/($6,000 – $2,000) = $10,000,000/$4,000 = 2,500 cars per month.

Organization of production

ACTIVITY 4.12

A calculated issue

1 Below are different levels of output of a new rock and pop magazine. The producer of the magazine intends to price each copy for sale at $5 each. The cost of hiring printing machinery is $2,400 per month and the print factory costs $1,600 per month to rent. The cost of materials and wages per magazine is $3. There are no other costs in this simple example. Use a calculator or a spreadsheet to complete the table with costs, revenue and profit or loss.

Magazines per month	Total fixed costs	Total variable costs	Total cost	Average cost	Total revenue	Profit or loss
0	$4,000	0	$4,000	–	0	–$4,000
1,000						
2,000						
3,000						
4,000						
5,000	$4,000	$15,000	$19,000	$3.80	$25,000	$6,000
6,000						
7,000						
8,000						

2 At what level of output will the magazine publisher break-even?

3 Plot and label the following curves on a graph with 'magazines per month' along the bottom axis and costs and revenues ($) in $1,000 intervals along the side axis. This needs to extend up to $40,000.

　a Total cost
　b Total revenue

4 Label those areas that represent profit and loss on your graph.

5 Investigate productive activities in a local small business. How is production organized?

Identify different costs incurred running the business as fixed and variable costs. How do costs vary with the scale of production or level of service provided (for example, if a shop opened longer hours or a hairdresser booked more appointments)? At what level of output per period does the business break-even at current prices and costs? Suggest potential advantages and disadvantages to the business from expanding its current level of output or service.

The private firm as producer and employer

ECONOMICS IN ACTION

The CEO of US car maker Chrysler reports that the company's break-even level of output has been reduced since November 2009. What has to have happened to the average revenue per car sold and/or total costs for this to have occurred?

Chrysler sales above break-even point

Chrysler Group is selling more vehicles than it needs to break-even, CEO Sergio Marchionne told investors today at a Deutsche Bank conference in Detroit.

'Due to better-than-expected performance, we estimate the profit break-even point has been lowered to about 1.5 million vehicles,' said Marchionne, who took over management of the company after the automaker shed debt in bankruptcy in 2009 and merged with Fiat SpA. Marchionne also is Fiat CEO.

In the five-year business plan made public in November 2009, Chrysler cited 1.65 million vehicles as its operating break-even point.

Chrysler sold almost 1.6 million vehicles globally in 2010, including 1.085 million in the USA.

WEBSITES

The following websites contain additional examples and explanations to help you learn more about the economics of production:

- www.bized.co.uk/search/node/costs and revenues
- www.wikipedia.org/wiki/Break_even_analysis
- www.answers.com/topic/productivity-economics
- www.bized.co.uk/reference/glossary/Productivity
- www.wikipedia.org/wiki/Category:Economics_of_production
- www.wikipedia.org/wiki/Productivity

KEYWORDS

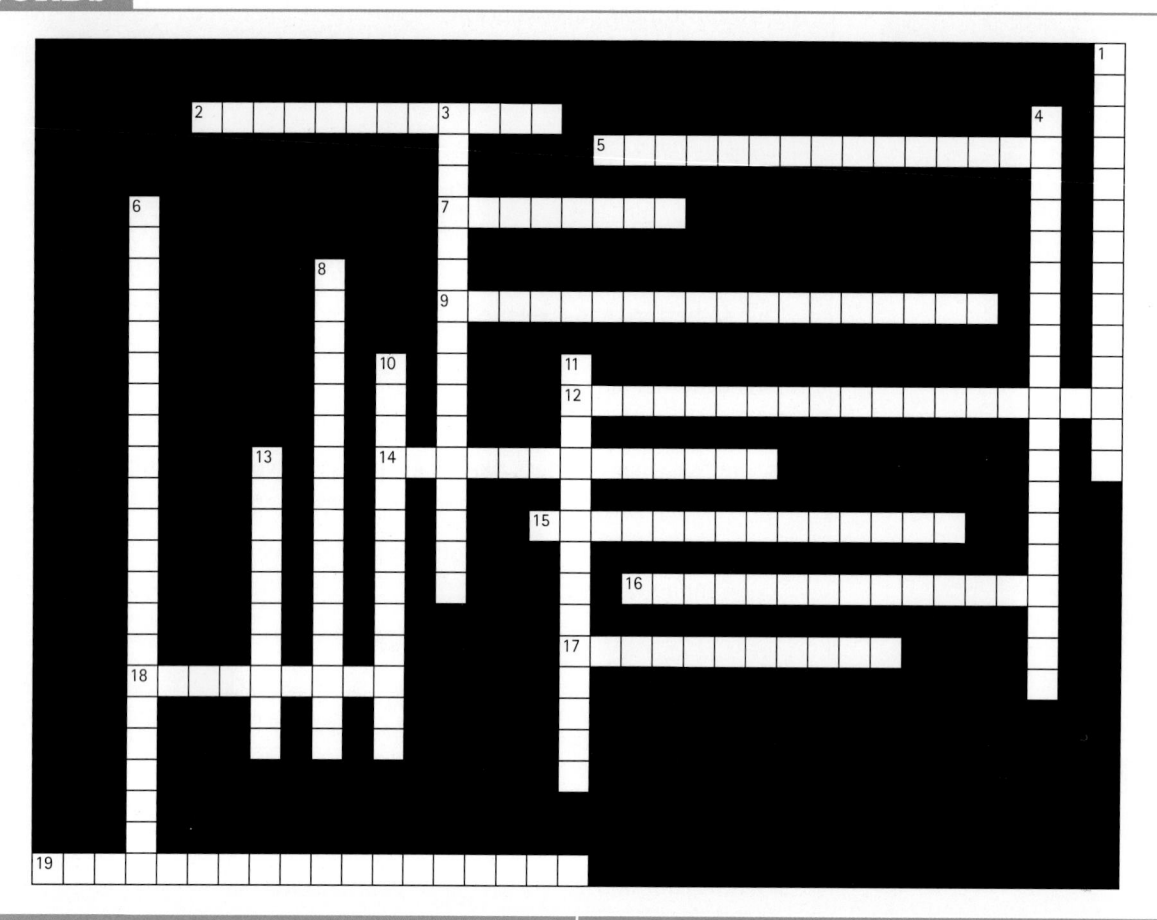

Clues across

2. A cost of production that varies directly with the level of output in a firm (8, 4)
5. A production process which uses a large amount of labour input relative to capital (6, 9)
7. The collective term used to describe a group of firms specializing in similar goods and services, or using similar production processes (8)
9. The average output or revenue per worker per period of time (6, 12)
12. This is the aim of most private sector organizations, to increase to the greatest possible extent their surplus of revenue over costs (6, 12)
14. Turning unprocessed natural resources and other unfinished products into other goods (13)
15. The production, usually in a continuous flow, of a large amount of standardized products (4, 10)
16. Service industries form this sector of an economy (8, 6)
17. The cost per unit of output, calculated by dividing the total cost of a given level of output by that total volume of output (7, 4)
18. A cost of production that does not vary with the level of output in a firm (5, 4)
19. Replacing one factor of production with another in a production process, for example, to make production more capital intensive (6, 12)

Clues down

1. The revenue per unit of output sold, found by dividing the total revenue from the sale of a given output by that volume of output (7, 7)
3. A production process which employs a significant amount of capital relative to labour (7, 9)
4. All manufacturing and construction firms (9, 10)
6. That volume of output which, if sold in full, would raise a total revenue exactly equal to the total cost of its production (5-4, 5, 2, 6)
8. The separation of a production process into a series of tasks, with each one completed by a different worker or group of employees (8, 2, 6)
10. All extractive industries or those producing natural resources (7, 6)
11. Production involving employees or organizations each concentrating their productive efforts on a limited range of tasks or products (15)
13. The increase in the 'value' of resources used up in production to make goods and services consumers are willing and able to buy. It is measured by the difference between the price paid for the product and the cost of resources used to make it (5, 5)

The private firm as producer and employer

Unit 4.3 The growth of firms

AIMS

By the end of this unit you should be able to:

▶ describe the main reasons for the different sizes of firms (size of market, capital, organization)
- explain why some firms remain small
- distinguish between **large-scale production** and **small-scale production**

▶ describe and evaluate **integration**, **economies** and **diseconomies of scale**
- explain reasons why firms seek to grow
- distinguish between **organic growth** in firm size and **external growth** through **merger** or **takeover**

- explain differences between **horizontal integration**, **vertical integration** and **lateral integration** between different firms and identify examples of each
- describe the problems connected with growth
- identify examples of **economies and diseconomies of scale**.

The growth of firms 237

> **SECTION 1**
>
> **Measuring and comparing the size of firms**

The size of firms

Wal-Mart Stores is one of the world's largest business organizations employing some 2.1 million people worldwide and with over $170 billion invested in buildings, computers, vehicles, forklift trucks and other capital assets.

China National Petroleum also ranks as one of the world's largest firms. It employs 500,000 fewer workers than Wal-Mart but has capital assets worth over $325 billion. So does this make China National Petroleum smaller or larger than Wal-Mart?

Of course both these giant organizations are huge compared to the many millions of other firms worldwide that serve small local markets, employ very few workers and have few capital assets.

It is useful to group firms together according to whether they are large enterprises or **small and medium-sized enterprises (SMEs)**. The size of firms can be measured in a number of ways and these also provide useful clues about the reasons why some firms grow into very large organizations while others remain small.

There are a number of ways to measure and compare the size of firms:

- how many workers they employ
- how they are organized
- how much capital they employ
- their market share.

Measure 1: number of employees

This is a straightforward measure. Firms with less than 50 employees are often classed as small. However, not all large firms employ many hundreds or thousands of workers.

Some large firms are capital intensive and employ relatively few workers. Instead they use a lot of machinery and computer-controlled equipment to automate their production processes in order to mass-produce large quantities of output. ▶ 4.2

Measure 2: organization

Larger firms are often divided up into different departments specializing in particular functions, such as purchasing, sales and marketing, finance and production. In smaller firms the owners and employees tend to carry out all the various functions between them. Larger firms may also have many different layers of management and different offices, factories and/or retail outlets spread across different locations, and in different countries if the firm is a multinational. The size of an organization can therefore be judged by how it is organized internally.

Measure 3: capital employed

Capital employed is money invested in those productive assets in a firm that help it generate revenue. They are assets used to produce and sell goods and services.

Assets used in production include machinery, factory and office buildings, stocks of materials and components and money held by a firm to pay wages and other costs.

The more capital employed in a firm the more it can produce and therefore the greater its size or scale of production. However, some large firms may be labour intensive. This means their production process requires the employment of a lot of workers but relatively little capital.

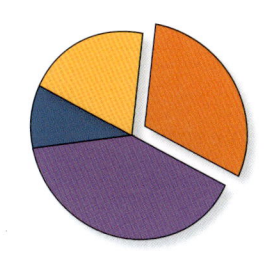

Measure 4: market share

The market for any good or service consists of all those consumers willing and able to buy it no matter where they might be located. ➤ **2.2**

The size of the market for a good or service is measured by the total amount spent by consumers on that product per week, month or year. The bigger the market demand for a particular good or service, the more scope there is for firms supplying that market to increase their scale of production. The share of the total market sales any one firm is able to capture is its **market share**.

The market share of a firm measures the proportion of total sales revenue or turnover that is attributable to that firm. For example, in 2008 global consumer spending on fizzy soft drinks was $146 billion. Coca-Cola sold the most, earning it almost $69 billion in revenue. This means it had a significant 47% share of the global fizzy soft drinks market.

But not all markets are so large. For example, a local hairdressing salon may be a very small business in terms of the number of people and amount of capital equipment it employs but it may have a very large share of the local market it serves because it is the only salon in a town where most local people can have their hair cut and styled.

ACTIVITY 4.13

Size matters

The table below contains information on four different business organizations.

▸ Which firm is the largest?

▸ Is it sensible to use only one measure of a firm's size?

▸ What are the problems with the individual measures used to determine a firm's size?

Name	Sector	Total employees	Capital employed ($ million)	Total output ($ million)	Global market share (% of revenues)
Google	Software and computers	20,222	21,795	31,768	67%
Exxon-Mobil	Oil and gas production	79,900	228,052	459,579	10%
GlaxoSmithKline	Pharmaceuticals	35,637	57,647	101,133	6%
Toyota Motors	Automobiles and parts	368,304	112,196	261,837	13%

The growth of firms 239

Because the size of markets for different goods and services varies considerably from huge global markets to small, localized markets, it is not very sensible to compare the volume of output or sales of firms in different industries. For example, a major ship building company may produce only one large warship or cruise liner each year while a small local bakery may produce and sell many thousands of bread and cake products each year.

SECTION 2

How firms grow in size

Entrepreneurs often want their firms to grow in size and increase the volume and value of their outputs. Producing more output means increasing the **scale of production** in a firm.

There are two main ways a firm can grow in size and expand its scale of production.

Internal growth

Internal growth or **organic growth** involves a firm expanding its scale of production through the purchase of additional equipment, increasing the size of its premises and hiring more labour if needed. This will increase its fixed costs.

To finance this growth the owners will need to use the profits of the firm, borrow money from banks and other lenders or sell shares in the ownership of their business to other investors. To sell shares a firm must become a joint-stock company. The new investors will become owners or shareholders in the company and be entitled to a share of any profits. ➤ **3.1**

External growth

External growth in the size of firms is more common. It involves one or more firms joining together to form a larger enterprise. This is known as **integration** through merger or takeover.

A **merger** occurs when the owners of one or more firms agree to join together to form a new, larger enterprise.

A **takeover** or **acquisition** occurs when one company buys enough shares in the ownership of another so it can take overall control. This may happen with or without the agreement of the owners of the other company.

In this way, the firm being taken over by another company often loses its own identity and becomes part of the other company.

Alternatively, an entirely new company may be formed for the sole purpose of buying up shares in the ownership of a number of other companies. This is known as a **holding company**. The companies acquired in this way may keep their own names and management but their overall policies are decided by their holding company. For example, HSBC Holdings plc is one of the largest UK companies and owns many other companies around the world in the financial services industry.

▼ Some well-known business mergers and takeovers

In 2007 India's Tata Steel won a $12 billion takeover battle for UK-based steel maker Corus. The acquisition immediately made Tata the fifth-biggest steelmaker in the world and allowed the company to cut its costs by $350 million a year.

ExxonMobil was formed in 1999 following an agreement by US companies Exxon and Mobil to merge their operations. The combined company is now one of the largest in the world and benefits from a large market share and significant economies of scale in oil and gas exploration, production and sales.

Types of integration

▼ Horizontal integration

There are three main types of integration between firms.

Horizontal integration involves a merger or takeover of firms engaged in the production of the same type of good or service. Most integration between firms is horizontal integration.

This type of integration may provide a number of economies of scale, for example the employment of more specialized machines and labour, the spreading of administration costs and bulk buying.

The major criticism of firms linking horizontally is that very large firms are formed which may be able to dominate their market. They may be able to raise prices and reduce competition by creating entry barriers for new firms. ➤ 4.4

Vertical integration occurs between firms at different stages of production. For example, a car manufacturer may combine with a chain of car retailers. This involves **forward integration**. In this way the car manufacturer can be certain it has showrooms at which it can promote and sell its cars.

Backward integration can also occur between firms. For example, a cheese maker may combine with a dairy farm so that it is guaranteed supplies of milk.

Lateral integration occurs between firms in different industries in the same stage or different stages of production.

▲ Vertical integration

▲ Horizontal integration

The growth of firms

Lateral integration is also called **conglomerate merger** and forms firms called **conglomerates** because they produce a wide range of different products. For example, Samsung is a major global business group well known for its televisions, mobile phones and other electronic products, but it also has business interests in shipbuilding, construction, chemicals, financial services and entertainment.

However, a firm producing a wide range of goods and services reduces the risk of falling consumer demand for any one of its products having a major impact on its business.

ACTIVITY 4.14

What type of integration?

Which of the following mergers or takeovers involve horizontal, vertical or lateral integrations?

Merger or takeover	Horizontal?	Vertical?	Lateral?
A chocolate maker takes over a cocoa plantation		✔	
A travel insurer merges with an online holiday company			
A clothing retailer takes over a clothes manufacturer			
A bus manufacturer merges with a car maker			
An investment bank takes over an electronics producer			
An aircraft maker merges with an aero-engine company			

SECTION 3

Internal economics of scale

Increasing the scale of production

The Reliance Group is India's largest private sector enterprise. It began as a small textile maker in the 1960s using imported polyester to make a range of garments under the brand name 'Vimal' which is now a household name in India. It soon began to manufacture its own polyester yarn and fibres and is now the world's largest producer of these synthetic materials. It went on to develop and merge with businesses involved in oil and gas exploration, petroleum refining, petrochemicals and also retail stores. In this way the business successfully controls its supply chain from the production of natural oils and gases which are used in the manufacture of petrochemicals needed to make polyester fibres for textile production, and retail outlets that sell its brand of clothing. The business has a saying: 'Growth is life'.

Through this growth in size the Reliance Group, like many other large firms, is able to enjoy a number of cost advantages over smaller firms. When a firm expands the scale of production it has a chance to become more efficient and lower its average costs of production. ➤ **4.2**

Average or unit costs can be reduced as a firm grows in scale because it gives the management or owners a chance to reorganize the way the firm is run and financed. Such decisions are taken within the firm and so the advantages or economies they bring are known as **internal economies of scale**. These are the cost savings that result from large-scale production.

ACTIVITY 4.15

Big is beautiful

Case 1: Cleaning up their act

A global detergent manufacturer has recently decided to invest in new equipment to expand its production. The new machines are very expensive but can produce twice as many soaps each hour as their existing machines.

A bank loan will be used to finance the expansion. Banks are willing to lend to the firm on very reasonable terms because it owns many valuable assets it is able to use as security or collateral against loans. Banks also recognize that because the firm produces a wide range of detergents for many different overseas markets any demand fluctuations are unlikely to seriously affect the firm's ability to repay its debts. Smaller competitors, however, will find it difficult to raise money for their modernization. Even if loans are made available, interest charges tend to be higher because smaller firms are often less financially secure than larger ones and therefore their risk of business failure is higher.

The large manufacturer has a new soap coming on to the market next week and it is planning a big advertising campaign to launch it. The cost of the campaign is around $1 million, but with an output of 10 million bars of soap per month, this only adds 10 cents to the cost of producing each unit of soap. If it was producing, say only 2 million soap bars a month, like many of its smaller rivals, the campaign would add 50 cents to the unit cost of each bar.

Case 2: Blasting off!

The large iron smelting company in Northern Ecoland has recently announced how pleased it is at having won a big overseas order as a result of it being able to offer a lower price than its main overseas rivals in Nomicia.

'Our specialist sales staff were a great help in winning the order,' enthused Mr Justin Time, the Company Director. 'Our Nomician competitors could not afford to employ such specialists.'

He went on to say how his company had managed to offer a lower price than Nomician producers. He explained that unit costs were much lower in Ecoland because its plant had managed to invest in a large blast furnace, while the smaller Nomician plants had to band together in certain areas to be able to afford such furnaces. Mr Time also added that some Nomician firms incurred higher transport costs as a result of their scale of operations being smaller. They have to use external road haulage services and therefore will be paying a profit margin in transport costs to these providers. The Ecoland Company, however, has its own fleet of juggernauts able to carry far more tons of iron than smaller trucks. Petrol costs per mile are lower and fewer drivers are also required.

Time also explained how his firm's average costs were lower because it is able to buy bulk quantities of iron ore. 'Because we buy 40 million tons of the stuff every year, our suppliers are willing to sell it for just $50 per ton,' he said, 'whereas the average Nomician firm only buys 10 million tons a year, but pays $60 per ton.'

The growth of firms 243

Internal economies of scale will reduce the average cost of producing each unit of output as the scale of production is expanded in a firm. There are five main types of economies of scale.

1 Purchasing economies

Large firms are often able to buy the materials, components and other supplies they need in bulk because of the large scale of their production. Suppliers will usually offer price discounts for bulk purchases because it is cheaper for them to make one large delivery than several smaller deliveries.

2 Marketing economies

Large businesses may buy or hire their own vehicles to distribute their goods and services rather than rely on other firms to do so. In this way a large firm can reduce its costs because it does not have to pay the profit margin of another supplier. It may also be able to increase the reliability and efficiency of its distribution. Similarly, the fixed costs of advertising in a newspaper or on television will be spread over a much larger output in a large firm than a small firm.

3 Financial economies

Larger firms can often borrow more money and at lower interest rates than smaller businesses. Bank managers and other lenders often consider lending to big organizations as less risky than lending to smaller ones. This is because large firms are usually more financially secure and can offer more assets, including property and other investments, they can use as collateral against loans. Banks can sell these assets in the event a firm fails and cannot repay its debts. Large public companies are also able to sell shares to raise permanent capital that never has to be repaid. ➤ **3.1**

4 Technical economies

Larger businesses often have the financial resources available to invest in specialized machinery and equipment, to train and recruit highly skilled workers, and to research and develop new products and processes to increase the efficiency of their production. Smaller firms may not be able to afford to do so.

5 Risk-bearing economies

A large firm may have more customers, sell into more markets at home and overseas and offer a larger range of products than a smaller business. In this way a large firm is able to reduce the risk to its business of losing a major customer, or a fall in demand for one its products in one of its markets. Producing a varied range of products and expanding into different consumer markets to reduce risk is called **diversification**. For example, Unilever is famous for its soap and detergent products but it also has interests in the production of food, paper, plastics, animal feeds, transport and tropical plantations.

External economics of scale

In addition to internal economies of scale, large firms may share **external economies of scale** with rival producers as a result of their entire industry being large. These may include the following:

- Large firms may have **access to a skilled workforce** because they can recruit workers trained by other firms in their industry.

- **Ancillary firms** develop and may locate nearby large firms in particular industries to provide them with the specialised equipment and services they require. In so doing they also gain from economies of scale so firms can buy their services more cheaply than providing them internally. For example, ancillary firms may provide specialist transport, equipment maintence, training and marketing services and develop and supply specialised machinery, computers and components for larger firms.

  Similarly, universities and colleges may offer courses to train engineers for firms in the aerospace and automotive industries and in banking and finance for major banks.

- There may be **joint marketing benefits**. For example, firms in the same industry co-locating together in an area well known for producing high-quality products may share an enhanced reputation.

- Firms may benefit from **shared infrastructure**. The growth of an industry may persuade firms in other industries to invest in new infrastructure such as new power stations, dock facilities and airports to meet increasing demand for these services, especially where firms are co-located or clustered together in an area. Similarly, a government may invest in new road and railway links to industrialized areas.

ECONOMICS IN ACTION

What evidence is there in these articles that large firms enjoy lower average costs than smaller firms producing the same or similar products?

Larger businesses fare better than smaller ones during recession

According to a new report larger businesses continue to enjoy many cost advantages over smaller businesses that has allowed them to discount their prices more heavily in the economic recession to maintain customer demand. Larger businesses also benefit from serving more than one market, many overseas, which has reduced their risk of falling demand at home.

Tech Group signs major contract to supply Hinshu

Tech Group, a leading supplier of engine cooling systems has signed a $1.5 billion contract to supply Hinshu Motors over the next 3 years.

Hinshu Motors is scaling up production of its successful range of automobiles. Delton Williams, Marketing Director at Hinshu, said the deal was a good one for both companies because 'Tech Group offers high-quality components, fast delivery times and substantial discounts for bulk orders to its largest business customers. It is cheaper for them to make one large delivery each week than several smaller deliveries over the same period.'

SECTION 4
Diseconomies of scale

Can firms grow too much?

The answer to this question is yes. This is exactly what happened when Mozambique's Mozal aluminium smelter wanted to expand its operations and increase output but was unable to do so because of a shortage of electricity in the country.

Similarly, the global US coffee shop chain Starbucks had to sell off 600 stores in the USA in 2008 because coffee sales and the value of the properties the business owned were falling. The business had expanded significantly in the 1990s and invested a lot of money in business properties. The fall in property prices and consumer spending during the economic downturn in 2008 had a big impact on the business. Starbucks also closed 61 of its 85 shops in Australia due to weak sales. The business had failed to attract consumers away from established cafés and coffee bars in Australia's main cities.

Many firms can experience problems if they try to expand their size and scale of production too much and too quickly. As a result, productivity may fall and average costs will rise. These problems are caused by **diseconomies of scale**.

- Managing a large firm can be difficult, especially if the firm has factories or offices spread over many different locations producing many different types of products, and with many different layers of management. This can cause communication breakdowns and disagreements between different managers in different parts of the organization and at different levels in the management hierarchy. Decision making will be slowed down, and it may take longer for decisions to be acted on by employees at the bottom of the organization. These are **management diseconomies**.

- Some very large firms may need vast quantities of materials, components or power for production. They may experience shortages and this may hold up production.

- Some large firms may be unable to attract enough workers with the right skills. They may have to spend more money on training their workers and increasing their wages to ensure that they do not leave to take jobs in other firms.

- Large firms may automate many production processes using computer-controlled equipment and machines. Workers operating the machinery may become bored undertaking repetitive tasks. They may become de-motivated and less cooperative. Disputes and strikes may occur if workers feel poorly treated. These are **labour diseconomies**.

- Large firms may also find it difficult to continually attract new customers because their products are too standardized and they have outgrown their market.

- To raise finance for business expansion the original owners of a firm may need to sell part of their ownership stake to other investors. The new owners may not always agree with the original owners or among themselves on how best to run the business. Disputes can occur which may harm the business.

- **Agglomeration diseconomies** can occur if a company takes over or merges with too many other firms producing different products at different stages of production. The business owners and managers may find it difficult to coordinate all the different activities of the merged firms.

Some consumers may also be badly treated by very large firms. For example, mergers and takeovers can form large powerful organizations able to control a large share of the market for the product they supply. This may discourage competition from smaller firms and enable a large firm to charge consumers higher prices. ➤ **4.4**

SECTION 5

The relationship between costs and productive scale

If a firm needs to increase output quickly or just temporarily to meet an increase in demand, then it can:

- reorganize its existing production processes to make them more efficient
- pay its existing labour to work overtime
- motivate its existing workforce to increase its productivity, for example by paying performance bonuses linked to increased output
- hire some additional labour on short-term contracts.

Reorganizing and employing more labour will help to increase output in the **short run**. In the short run economists assume capital is a fixed factor of production and cannot be varied. However, firms can increase the amount of capital they employ in the **long run** to expand the scale of their production. For some firms, this can take more time than others.

For example, a retail chain may be able to buy and decorate a new retail outlet in a matter of weeks while an electricity supply company may take several years to build new power stations.

We know that as the scale of production in a firm is expanded it may enjoy a reduction in its average cost per unit of output. However, for some firms average costs may be unchanged while others may experience diseconomies of scale. Activity 4.16 gives three examples of firms producing boxes of sweets. All three have expanded the scale of their production through investments in new factories and equipment and hiring more labour.

ACTIVITY 4.16

Chewing over a problem

The following three manufacturing firms make identical boxes of sweets. They have all expanded the scale of their production in year 2. All three firms have doubled their inputs of factors of production. But what has happened to their total output of boxes of sweets?

The ACE company	The BOOM company	The CRIKEY company
Year 1		
Labour input 50	Labour input 40	Labour input 60
Number of machines 10	Number of machines 15	Number of machines 5
Number of factories 1	Number of factories 1	Number of factories 1
Total output 10,000	Total output 12,000	Total output 9,000
Year 2		
Labour input 100	Labour input 80	Labour input 120
Number of machines 20	Number of machines 30	Number of machines 10
Number of factories 2	Number of factories 2	Number of factories 2
Total output 25,000	Total output 20,000	Total output 18,000

A firm that doubles all its inputs and is able to more than double its output of goods or services as a result is said to be experiencing **increasing returns to scale**. This is what happened in the Ace company in Activity 4.16.

The Boom Company, however, doubled its factor inputs but failed to double its output of boxes of sweets. Firms like this are said to be experiencing **decreasing** or **diminishing returns to scale**.

On the other hand, the Crikey company experienced **constant returns to scale** because as it doubled its inputs it also doubled its output.

The growth of firms | 247

ACTIVITY 4.17

Chewing it over some more

The three sweet manufacturing companies have doubled all their inputs and have therefore doubled their total costs. However, only one firm managed to more than double its output. The others experienced either constant or decreasing returns to scale. Calculate what has happened to the average cost of producing boxes of sweets as a result.

The ACE company		The BOOM company		The CRIKEY company	
Year 1					
Total costs	$10,000	Total costs	$12,000	Total costs	$9,000
Total output	10,000	Total output	12,000	Total output	9,000
Average cost	$1	Average cost	$1	Average cost	$1
Year 1					
Total costs	$20,000	Total costs	$24,000	Total costs	$18,000
Total output	25,000	Total output	20,000	Total output	18,000
Average cost	?	Average cost	?	Average cost	?

Which of the firms above has doubled all its inputs in the long run and experienced:
1. Falling average costs?
2. Rising average costs?
3. No change to average costs?

In the above activity, the Ace company has enjoyed a significant reduction in its average cost of producing each box of sweets from $1 to just 80 cents per box. This is because it doubled its scale of production and total costs but more than doubled its outputs. That is, it has enjoyed economies from large-scale production.

However, the Boom company and Crikey company were not so fortunate. The Crikey company was able to double its inputs, costs and outputs leaving its average costs of production unchanged. In contrast, the Boom company suffered a fall in average costs from $1 per box of sweets to $1.20 after it had doubled all its inputs because it experienced decreasing returns to scale. It was therefore an unwise decision by the Boom company to expand the scale of its production by so much.

Clearly the best size or **optimum size** for a firm is where it can reduce its average costs to their lowest point in the long run, that is at that level of output that corresponds with the lowest point on its U-shaped average cost curve in the long run. ➤ 4.2

SECTION 6

Why some firms remain small

ACTIVITY 4.18

Staying small

Most firms are small and remain small. Make a list of all the reasons given in the quotes below from owners of small businesses against expanding their businesses

> 'I can't be bothered to run a larger business. It would be too stressful and take up too much of my time. I am happy being small. I make enough profit and I get to keep it all! My business taxes are also low because I run a small business.'

> 'I own and run a small restaurant serving a small, local market. There is no point growing larger. I know all my customers and can offer them a good personalized service. Large restaurant chains can't provide this.'

> 'I work from my home designing and building websites for major business customers all over the world. I don't need to be big. I only need a computer and access to high-speed Internet.'

> 'We make exclusive and luxury designer knitwear. All our garments are hand-made and sell for between $500 and $1,000 each. Our market is therefore quite limited. Most of our customers are high net-worth individuals, including film, TV and music industry celebrities.'

> 'My bank wouldn't lend me enough money to finance the purchase of the new premises and equipment I need.'

Not all firms can or should grow into much larger enterprises. A firm that grows beyond its optimum size will suffer rising average costs and this will reduce profits.

Most firms are small. Most firms start small. Some may grow over time into large national or even multinational organizations but the vast majority remain small for sound economic reasons.

1 The size of their market is small

The most efficient size for a firm is closely related to the size of its market. If there are only a relatively small number of consumers willing and able to buy a product there is no point in a firm supplying that market expanding in scale significantly.

There are many examples of sectors in which small firms thrive because the markets they serve tend to be quite local. For example, hairdressers, restaurants and cafés, window cleaners, decorators and many hotels, taxi services and shops only supply the villages and towns they are located in. They are also able to offer their customers a more personalized service than many large firms that mass produce goods or provide standardized services across all their business locations. For example, tailors can make made-to-measure suits and carpenters can make furniture to order.

Similarly, firms that produce luxury items may have relatively small or niche markets. Only consumers with very high incomes may be willing and able to pay high prices for 'exclusive' products such as designer clothing and jewellery, sports cars and luxury holidays.

The growth of firms 249

2 Access to capital is limited

Sole traders often have to use up all their personal savings to start up in business. Banks are not normally willing to lend money to small, untested business propositions. This is because small businesses usually lack collateral to offer against loans, face fierce competition from larger rivals and may not be able to make enough revenue each month to repay a loan.

Recognizing that lack of capital is a problem for small firms, many governments encourage business start-up by providing grants to cover the costs of premises and equipment, or by subsidizing wages and other costs. They may also benefit from lower rates of tax on their profits, and can often seek help and advice on business issues from specialist advisers employed by government agencies. Governments do this because small firms are often very innovative: they invent new products that help to boost trade and new processes that other firms can eventually use to increase their productivity. Some small firms will also eventually grow into much larger firms that help to create wealth in an economy through additional employment and profits.

3 New technology has reduced the scale of production needed

The size and cost of new technology has fallen significantly over time. Most small businesses now have access to computers and other modern equipment. Many years ago they would not have been able to afford such equipment. Also, through the Internet many small businesses can now reach suppliers and consumers all over the world.

4 Some business owners may simply choose to stay small

Some entrepreneurs may simply decide they do not want to increase the size of their firm as long as they continue to make a reasonable profit after tax. Running a larger enterprise can also be very time consuming and stressful. Some entrepreneurs may lack the skills they need to manage and run larger firms employing many more people and much more capital.

▲ Smaller firms can often provide more personalized goods and services than many larger firms

EXAM PREPARATION 4.2

Sometimes in an industry a firm buys a smaller competitor that uses similar factors of production. At other times a firm buys another firm that supplies it with the raw materials and other inputs for its production.

a Explain what is meant by the factors of production. [4]
b Discuss the reasons why some firms remain small. [6]
c Identify the types of integration in the two situations described above. [3]
d Discuss whether such integration is always beneficial. [7]

Cambridge IGCSE Economics 0455/04 Q2 May/June 2006
Cambridge O Level Economics 2281/02 Q2 May/June 2006

WEBSITES

Here are just some of the useful websites on the growth of firms:
- *www.tutor2u.net/economics/revision-notes/a2-micro-growth-of-firms.html*
- *www.wikipedia.org/wiki/Economies_of_scale*
- *www.tutor2u.net/business/gcse/production_economies_of_scale.htm*

KEYWORDS

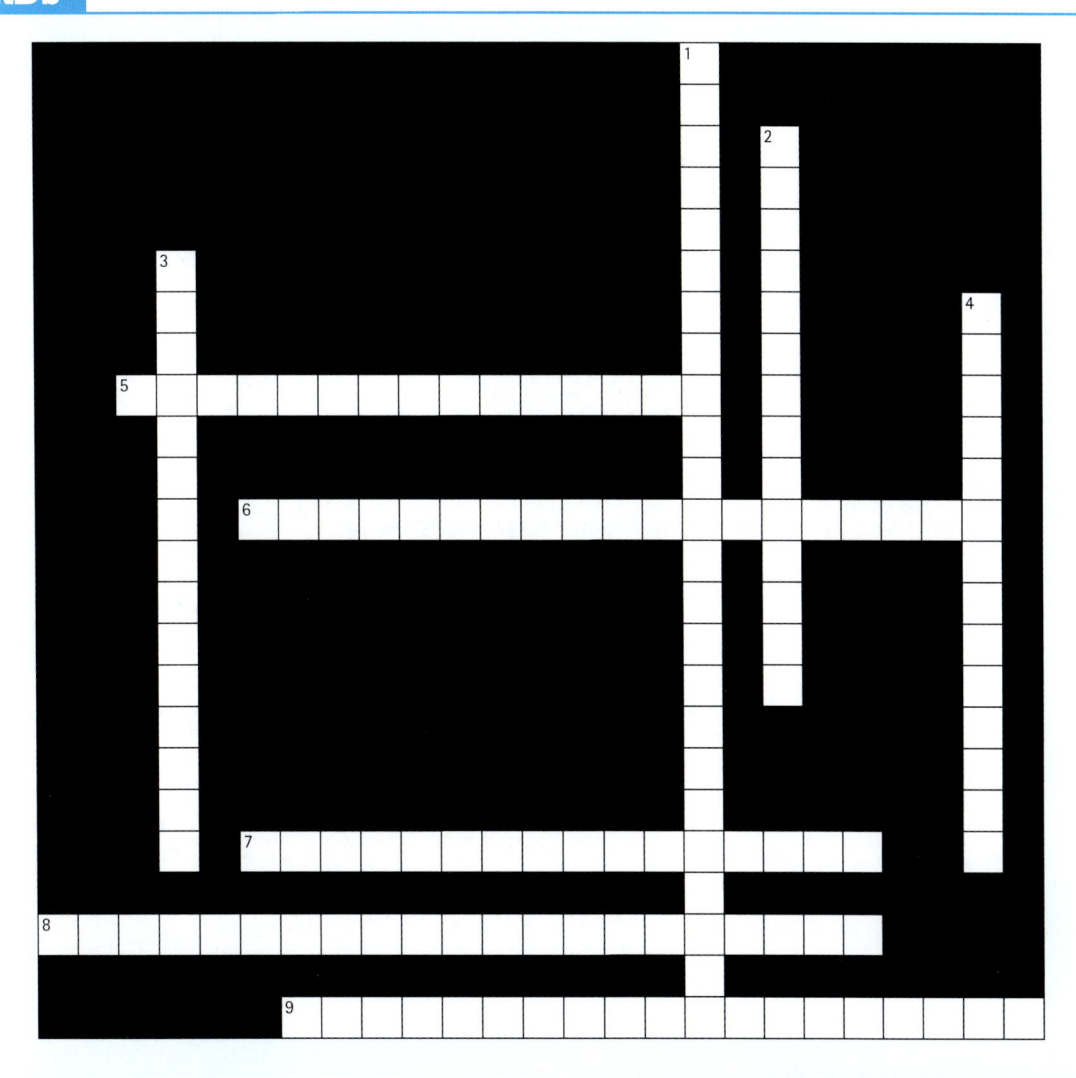

Clues across

5. Producing a range of different products for different markets to spread market risks (15)
6. A merger between two or more firms at different stages of production of the same product, such as between a farm and a food processing company (8, 11)
7. Factors that result in falling unit costs or production as the scale of production is increased (9, 2, 5)
8. This occurs when two or more firms producing similar goods or services at the same stage of production combine to form a larger enterprise (10, 11)
9. Problems that cause unit costs to rise as a firm expands beyond its optimum size (12, 2, 5)

Clues down

1. A firm that increases its inputs by 10% but expands output by more than 10% will enjoy these returns (10, 7, 2, 5)
2. An 'organic' increase in the scale of production in a firm through the employment of additional factors of production (8, 6)
3. Money invested in or tied up in productive assets in a firm that enable it to carry out production and generate revenue (7, 8)
4. An increase in the size of a firm through the takeover of, or merger with, another enterprise (8, 6)

The growth of firms

Unit 4.4 — Competition

AIMS

By the end of this unit you should be able to:

▶ describe the characteristics of **perfect competition** and **monopoly**
  • understand why markets can have different **market structures**
▶ describe the **pricing and output policies** in **perfect competition** and **monopoly**
  • distinguish between **price competition** and **non-price competition**
▶ discuss the advantages and disadvantages of **monopoly**
  • distinguish between **pure monopoly** and **oligopoly**
  • distinguish between and identify examples of **natural and artificial barriers to entry** that may restrict competition

SECTION 1
Competing for the market

Why do firms compete?

Competition between firms is, in most cases, good for the consumer. Competition encourages firms to use their resources efficiently to reduce their costs, lower their prices and develop new and better products and product features for consumers to choose from. Firms that do not are unlikely to survive in a competitive business environment.

For example, Hollywood Video once owned and managed thousands of DVD video rental stores in the USA but all its stores were eventually closed down and the company liquidated because consumers were instead downloading movies from rival suppliers over the Internet or renting DVD movies from companies who would post them in the mail. These alternative ways of renting movies saved consumers time, offered them more choice and were cheaper than renting discs over the counter from a local store. Hollywood Video had failed to change its service, prices and marketing in the face of competition from new technology and competition from rival video rental providers.

Firms will therefore compete for a market for a number of reasons.

1. **To increase their customer base:** firms will compete with each other in the same market on prices, product quality and through promotional strategies to increase the number of people or other firms buying their products. More customers should mean more revenue and, if the costs of increased competition do not rise as fast, it will also boost profits.

2. **To increase sales:** firms will not only aim to increase the number of consumers buying their products but will also hope that existing customers will buy more and provide repeat custom. Cutting prices can increase sales revenues from products for which demand is price elastic. Advertising and other promotions, such as free gifts, can help to expand sales, possibly without the need for price cuts. Promotional strategies can also create a brand image for a product and encourage customer loyalty.

3. **To expand market share:** the market share of a firm is calculated as its proportion of the total market volume or value of sales. For example, in the last quarter of 2010, sales of the Google Android phone reached 33.3 million units, accounting for just under 33% of the 101.2 million smartphones sold around the world. One year earlier the Google Android accounted for just 8.7% of the total volume of smartphones sold. Many organizations will aim to increase their share of total market sales. The larger a firm's market share, and the more widely established its product, the more able it will be to withstand new competition from new products and firms.

4. **To achieve product superiority.** This has two meanings. On one hand it refers to making a product that is clearly better than rival products for reasons of prestige and profit. A superior product will help a firm to achieve objectives of generating sales and expanding market share. However, product superiority also means the product dominates a market by outselling all others, which is not necessarily because it is the best product on the market.

5. **To enhance image:** a firm will also compete to improve its organizational image. Consumers' perceptions of an organization will tend to be reflected in sales. A poor image will reduce sales; a good image will help to expand sales and market share.

6. **To maximize profits:** ultimately the achievement of all the above objectives of competition should help increase the total profits of a firm that is successful.

Types of competition

Firms can compete with each other in a number of ways:

- **Price competition** involves competing to offer consumers the lowest or best possible prices for rival products. Cutting price below that of rival products is one way a firm can try to boost its sales and market shares at the expense of competing firms. However, the ability of a firm to undercut rivals will be constrained by market conditions and its production costs. If demand is price inelastic, cutting price may not boost sales and it will also reduce the profit margin between price and average cost.

- **Non-price competition** involves competing on all other product features other than price. It can involve new product development, product placements in different retail outlets and at trade fairs, providing after-sales care and promotional campaigns including advertising, attractive in-store displays, running competitions and issuing consumer loyalty cards. Non-price competition is important because consumers do not just compare product prices. They are also looking for the best value for money in terms of the quality of the good or service, ease of purchase, levels of customer service and whether or not there is good after-sales care should anything go wrong and they want to exchange their product.

▶ Price and non-price competition

The power of advertising

Firms can communicate the prices, availability and key features of their goods and services to consumers using advertisements. **Advertising** is the commercial promotion of goods, services, companies and ideas and each year many billions of dollars are spent by firms on these promotions. This is because good advertising can create a consumer want for a product and increase sales. If sales revenue increases enough it will not only cover the costs of advertising but also increase business profits.

There are two main types of advertising:

- **Informative advertising** provides information about a product to a consumer. Some examples include bus and train timetables, menus, technical specifications for computers, and the ingredients of foodstuffs. Informative advertisements can also increase product credibility and generate a good reputation for a business. Government organizations and agencies often use informative advertising to tell people about new regulations or to increase awareness of personal health and safety issues.

- **Persuasive advertising** is designed to create a consumer want and boost sales of a particular product, often at the expense of rival products. This is known as brand switching.

▲ Informative?

▲ Persuasive?

Advertising involves the creation of consumer wants

The main objective of persuasive advertising is to create and reinforce positive consumer perceptions about a product that will in turn create a consumer want for, and loyalty to, that product and the firm that produces it.

▼ The desired impact of advertising on consumer demand

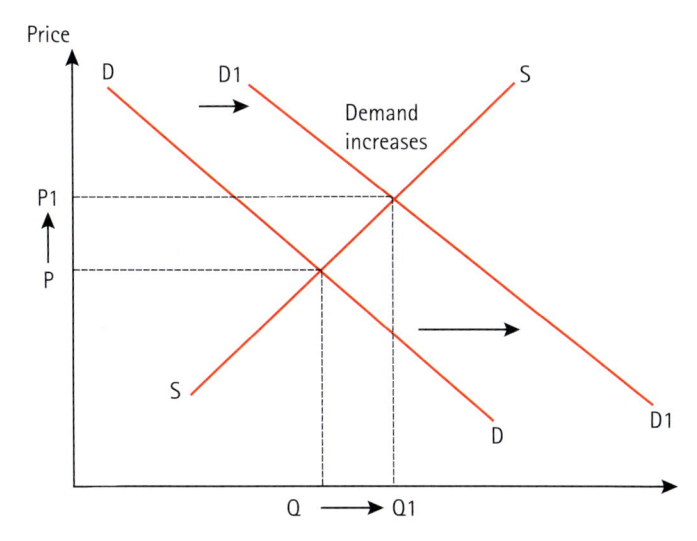

An increase in demand for a product will tend to push up the market price and quantity traded. The increase in demand desired by a firm for its product may be achieved by advertisements that convince consumers that their product is new, or that it is somehow better than rival products, or that the consumer will benefit from buying the product, either through the features of the product or by 'buying into' the image created for the product.

Advertising can create powerful brand images and customer loyalties

Competition between firms through advertising is significant. Advertising can be designed to persuade consumers to buy a product they would not otherwise choose to buy by changing their attitudes, opinions and perceptions of that product and towards the firms that make and sell it. In so doing firms that advertise their products can expand market demand and capture a larger share of total market sales from competing firms.

Competition 255

Creating a brand image can change consumers' perceptions of a product. A distinctive name, logo, humorous catchphrase or exciting visual treatment for a product can make it more attractive than its close substitutes. That is, a firm will differentiate its product from similar competing products to encourage consumers to buy it. This is called **product differentiation**.

Of course, it does not really matter whether the product really is very different – what matters is whether consumers think it is. For example, most washing detergents are very similar, yet individual manufacturers of detergents often spend vast sums of money attempting to persuade consumers that their product is more powerful, smells better, or leaves clothes softer or whiter than other detergents. In this way they try to create **customer brand loyalty** to their product.

Brand loyalty has the following benefits for a business:

- Repeat purchases from loyal customers provide a steady stream of revenue.
- It helps to protect the sales and market share of the firm from competition.
- Customers may pay a higher price for the brand.
- Customers continue to buy the brand even if the producer increases its price or the prices of rival products fall.

In these ways brand loyalty helps to reduce the price elasticity of consumer demand for the product. Increasing the price of the brand will have little effect on sales and will increase revenue.

Advertising can reduce competition

Creating a powerful brand image and spending a large amount of money on big advertising campaigns can create a barrier to the entry into that product market by new competing firms. A rival producer seeking to supply a similar product could be deterred by the need to spend equally large amounts of money on similar advertising campaigns, especially if it needs to reduce consumer loyalty to the leading product in the market. This may be especially difficult for new, and therefore unknown, small firms attempting to enter the market.

As a result, advertising may actually restrict competition. This may have a number of disadvantages for consumers, including less choice and possibly higher prices if one or a small number of firms are able to dominate the market supply as a result.

Is competition wasteful?

Although competition is usually good for the consumer in that it increases product variety and lowers prices, some people argue it can also be wasteful. For example, advertising is a cost of production and can use up significant resources. Unless producers pass on this cost to consumers, advertising expenditure will reduce profits. Some people argue using up resources to make advertisements is wasteful. The same resources could be used to produce more goods and services to benefit consumers and lower product prices.

Similarly, product development by rival firms can often result in duplicated effort and use of resources. For example, competing pharmaceutical and cosmetic companies are accused of running many unnecessary and harmful tests of their new products on animals in an effort simply to produce very similar drugs and cosmetic products.

SECTION 2

The pricing decision of a firm

Pricing strategies

Setting the price of a good or service is a difficult decision. For example, when Apple announced a steep price cut for its new iPhone just 10 weeks after it was launched, it angered many of the early adopters who had bought their handsets at a premium price shortly after it came on the market. This anger could mean future new product launches may not attract so many consumers who will instead buy rival products or wait for prices to be cut.

If a firm sets the price of a product too high consumers may be unwilling to buy the product. If on the other hand price is set too low it may not cover its costs of production. Setting the right price for a product is therefore an important element in any competitive strategy.

The amount of competition or rivalry in a market is also a major factor in price setting. If there is a lot of competition prices will need to be low enough to compete with rival products. If there are no or very few substitutes for consumers to buy they may be willing to pay a higher price to buy the available product. ➤ 2.2

Three major factors will therefore influence the pricing decisions of different firms in any market:

- the level and strength of consumer demand
- the amount of competition from rival producers to supply a market
- the costs of production and level of profit required.

Because costs, sales and the degree of market competition vary over the commercial life of a product, pricing strategies will also need to change over time. For example, when a new product is launched prices may have to be set low to build sales and fight off competition but this can cause a business to lose money. In the longer term, a business must be able to recover its costs if it is to survive.

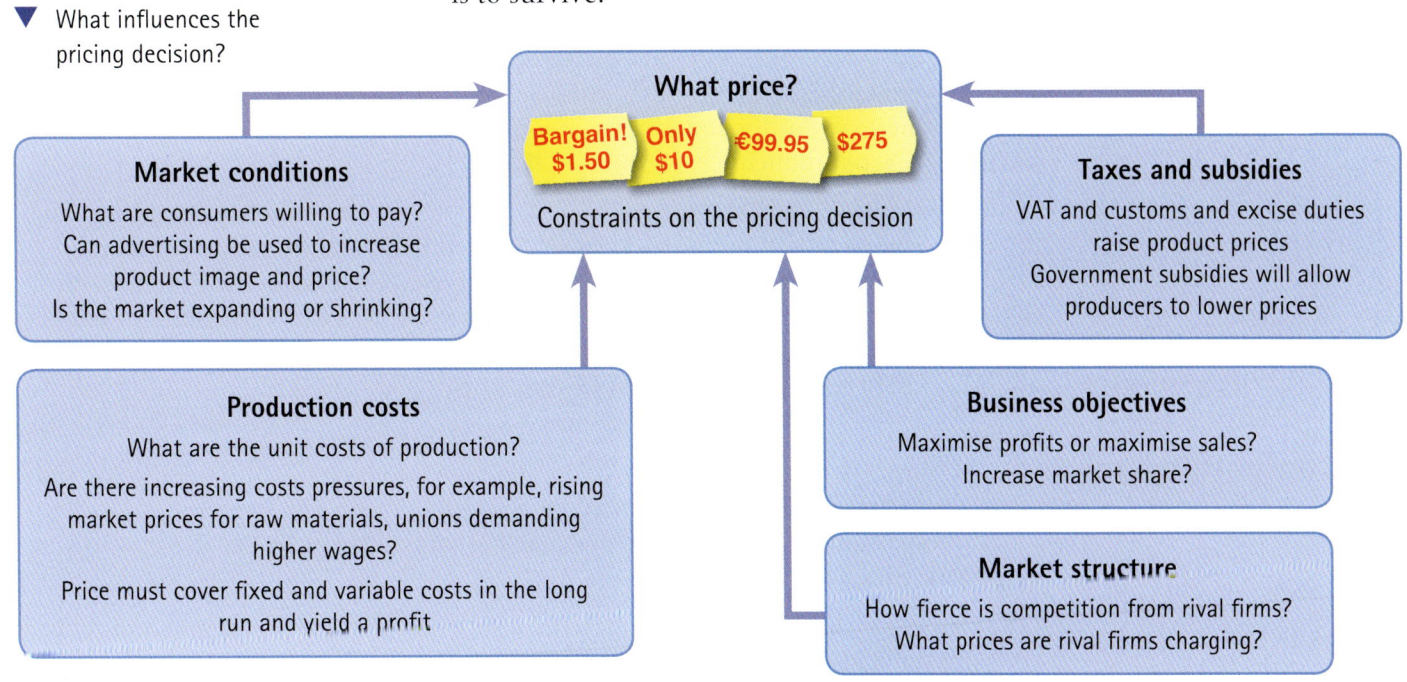

▼ What influences the pricing decision?

What price?
Bargain! $1.50   Only $10   €99.95 $275
Constraints on the pricing decision

Market conditions
What are consumers willing to pay?
Can advertising be used to increase product image and price?
Is the market expanding or shrinking?

Taxes and subsidies
VAT and customs and excise duties raise product prices
Government subsidies will allow producers to lower prices

Production costs
What are the unit costs of production?
Are there increasing costs pressures, for example, rising market prices for raw materials, unions demanding higher wages?
Price must cover fixed and variable costs in the long run and yield a profit

Business objectives
Maximise profits or maximise sales?
Increase market share?

Market structure
How fierce is competition from rival firms?
What prices are rival firms charging?

Competition

Governments can also affect the final market prices consumers will pay for different products in shops and online. Any tariffs, excise duties, sales taxes or value added taxes will raise the final retail prices of products. In contrast, subsidies paid to producers to reduce their total costs will allow them to lower the prices they charge. Firms will need to take account of the impact taxes or subsidies will have on their prices in their strategies. ➤ **2.2**

Demand-based pricing strategies

Demand-based pricing strategies involve setting price at 'what the market will bear'. That is, setting price according to how much consumers are willing to pay. Producers will therefore tend to price high when consumer demand is high and price low when consumer demand is low. Similarly, a firm that faces little or no competition will be able to price high 'at what the market will bear' because consumers will have few alternatives. The following are examples of pricing strategies:

- **Price skimming** is a pricing strategy that is often used when there is little competition in a market for a new or improved product. It involves charging a high price to recover development costs and to yield a high initial profit from those consumers who are willing to pay more because the product is new or unique. As rival products are introduced, prices are lowered to increase sales and to protect market share.

  Price skimming is a strategy often observed in the market for new technologically advanced products such as computers, televisions and music and video disc players. For example, the first large flat-screen televisions, DVD players, and more recently high definition blu-ray disc players, launched onto the consumer electronics market were priced very high. Some consumers were willing to pay these high prices because they wanted to be the first to purchase these new advanced products. These consumers are known as early adopters.

- **Penetration pricing** involves setting price low to encourage consumers to try a new product to expand sales and increase loyalty. In this way a new product is able to 'penetrate' a market. It is an important strategy if the product and the firm are new to a market and if there are already well-established rival products and firms. As demand expands, a firm can increase output and enjoy economies of scale that will lower the average cost of producing each unit. ➤ **4.3**

  However, penetration pricing can be high risk and only large firms may be able to afford to use this strategy. It may involve setting price below the average cost of producing each product so a firm makes a loss. If sales do not increase rapidly the firm may not be able to survive. Further, in markets that are very competitive penetration pricing by a new entrant to a market could start a **price war** with rival firms.

Competitive pricing strategies

In markets where there is fierce competition between rival firms for sales and market share, firms will often adopt aggressive competitive pricing strategies. These usually involve setting prices at the same level or below the prices of rival products.

For example, when existing electricity supplier Airtricity in Ireland announced it would also start supplying gas it said it would undercut the prices of the established gas supplier, Board Gais, by 10% saving the average family up to €200 a year.

There are many other similar examples of aggressive pricing strategies, especially in mobile telecommunications markets around the world that have seen both consumer demand and the number of competing suppliers expand rapidly.

- **Destruction pricing** (or **predatory pricing**) is like penetration pricing but involves much deeper cuts in prices, often below costs, in order to 'destroy' the sales of a new or existing competitor. If a firm is successful at removing the competition it can then raise prices again and recover its losses.

- **Price wars** may develop in markets that are very competitive if one or more firms cuts their prices or if the market shares of established firms are threatened by a new entrant. Prices may be cut drastically to force the new firm out of the market.

  Prices wars involve competing firms continually trying to undercut each other's prices. They occur frequently but are not popular because all firms usually end up losing money by trying to out compete each other on price.

- **Price leadership** may be used to avoid price wars because firms engaged in them all tend to lose money. Instead firms will charge very similar prices and will raise them or lower them together at the same time to avoid price competition. The firm with the largest market share will usually be the price leader. If the price leader raises or lower its prices other firms in the market will do the same.

ECONOMICS IN ACTION

Why do you think markets for modern telecommunications are prone to price wars? (Hint: what is happening to the cost of the technologies; growth in market size and productive scale; the number of new market entrants?)

Indian telecom market crowded by new entrants

Uninor, controlled by Norwegian telecom company Telenor, is the 14th player to enter India's cellular market.

But after soaring growth in customer numbers to almost 17 million, industry revenues are flattening as rivals slug it out in a savage price battle.

Price war heats up in New Zealand telecoms

2degrees launched an aggressive calling plan yesterday that will challenge the prices of Vodafone and Telecom.

The mobile carrier has dropped the cost of calls between networks by nearly a third, in a bid to increase its market share.

Cost-based pricing

If a firm is to survive in the long run it must be able to cover its costs of production and earn a profit. If revenues fail to match costs a firm will make a loss. ► **4.2**

Cost-plus pricing involves calculating the average cost of producing each item or unit of output, and then adding a mark-up for profit.

For example, if a firm produces 10,000 packets of biscuits at a total cost of $10,000, the average cost per packet is $1. A 40% mark-up for profit will mean each packet is priced for sale at $1.40.

Price = (total cost/total output) + mark-up for profit

The problem with cost-plus pricing is that it is does not take into account what consumers may or may not be willing to pay or how much competition there is to supply the market.

In the example above, if a rival producer can produce and supply the same biscuits at a lower average cost, say at 80 cents a packet, then that rival will be able to add a mark-up of 50 cents and still price below the other firm.

ACTIVITY 4.19

All washed up

1. What is a price war?
2. What motives do you think P&G had for cutting its prices?
3. What impact has the price war had on the profits of the two companies?
4. Explain why Hindustan Unilever's 'much larger size, market share and product portfolio should enable it to continue aggressive pricing strategies more than the smaller P&G'.
5. Do you think demand for detergents is price elastic or inelastic? Explain.
6. What other pricing strategies could the two companies have used to avoid a price war?

Will Hindustan Unilever tide over price war?

Shares in Hindustan Unilever have fallen in price amid concerns about a renewed price war emerging in the detergents category.

The previous such turf war in 2004 had led to profit margins for both main players taking a substantial hit, though Hindustan Unilever (HUL) did manage to hold on to its market share by matching Procter & Gamble's moves.

The renewed concerns about a price war with HUL's arch rival (P&G) have been triggered by a series of events. Selling prices of detergents in the mass-market category have been heading down for several months now but the battle for market share entered a fresh chapter recently with aggressive television advertisements pitting HUL's Rin brand against P&G's Tide Naturals.

Reports now suggest that P&G has increased volumes for its Tide Naturals by 25 per cent, without changing prices. This translates into a 20 per cent reduction in effective prices for the brand.

HUL's much larger size, market share and product portfolio should enable it to continue aggressive pricing strategies more than the smaller P&G. This suggests that the company may be able eventually to ward off this new threat to its market share. However, for investors in HUL this could mean a loss of pricing power and profits in one of HUL's key product categories for some time to come.

SECTION 3

Market structures

What is market structure?

In economics, **market structure** refers to the characteristics of a market, usually on the supply side, including how many firms compete for the market, the degree of competition or collusion between them, the extent of their product differentiation, and the ease with which new firms can enter the market to compete with them.

Competition between firms encourages them to make the best use of scarce resources, because in order to maximize profits they must produce outputs at the lowest possible cost that give consumers the best value for money to satisfy their wants. Any restriction on competition may therefore result in a misallocation of scarce resources with costs and prices higher than they would otherwise be and with fewer wants being satisfied. This is why economists will examine market structures and the degree of competition between firms. It is also a reason why governments often intervene in markets to ensure that sufficient competition takes place.

We can examine the amount of competition in a market for a particular good or service by looking at the following features:

- the amount of control a firm or group of firms has over the total market supply or output
- the amount of influence a firm or group of firms have over market price
- the freedom new suppliers have to enter the market.

Perfect competition

Economists have developed the concept of **perfect competition** in order to compare different market structures. In a perfectly competitive market there will be a large number of different firms competing to supply an identical product and an equally large number of consumers wanting to buy it. As such, all producers and consumers will exchange at the equilibrium market price.

In a perfectly competitive market therefore no one firm or consumer will have any power to influence the market price. That is, they are all **price takers**. If a firm did try to raise its price above the market price it would lose custom to rival producers and soon go out of business. Similarly, a firm would be unable to lower its price below the market price without losing money unless it was able to produce much more cheaply than others. Even if it did, it could not do so for long, as other firms would soon find out how this was done and use the same methods to lower their own production costs. Subsequently, market price would fall.

Perfect competition therefore doesn't really involve any competition at all – since the products are identical, all firms have the same average costs and have to accept the same market price. It is an extreme and limiting concept used by economists only as a comparator for all other market structures. Not surprisingly, most markets are in reality not 'perfect'.

However, while there are few examples of perfect competition there are many examples of highly competitive markets.

A competitive market will display many of the following features:

- There will be vigorous price competition and non-price competition between firms supplying similar goods and services.
- Firms will pursue different pricing strategies depending on the type and amount of competition they face from new and existing competitors.
- Product features and brand images will be highly differentiated, and the range of product designs available, the quality of after-sales services and product prices will tend to change frequently as firms develop new ones they hope will attract consumer demand away from other products.
- The market shares and profits of competing businesses will vary over time as new businesses enter the market and inefficient firms are forced to close.

However, some firms in competitive markets may be tempted to mislead customers, for example by making misleading or exaggerated claims about their products in order to increase their sales and boost their profits at the expense of their competitors. Some firms may also cut product quality in an attempt to reduce their costs.

Large powerful firms may use destruction pricing strategies to force smaller rivals out of business in order to protect their market positions. Competition in some markets may therefore be short lived and result in the formation of monopolies.

For economists there is **imperfect competition** in markets in which one or more competing firms have a degree of control over price setting and can influence demand, for example through advertising and product differentiation. The more control a firm has over setting the market price the more imperfect the market is.

ACTIVITY 4.20

Market concentrations

The table below provides data on the share of total output of the five largest producers in a number of UK industries in 2004. For example, it shows that the five largest firms in the UK sugar industry accounted for 99% of the total industry output by value.

▼ UK industry concentrations, 2004 (% share of total output of the five largest firms)

Industry	% share	Industry	% share
Sugar	99%	Metal forging, pressing, etc.	4%
Tobacco products	99%	Plastic products	4%
Gas distribution	82%	Furniture	5%
Confectionery	81%	Construction	5%
Man-made fibres	79%	Structural metal products	6%
Soft drinks and mineral waters	75%	Wholesale distribution	6%
Pesticides	75%	General purpose machinery	8%
Weapons and ammunition	77%	Wood and wood products	9%

Source: 'Input-Output: Concentration ratios for businesses by industry in 2004', UK Office for National Statistics 2005, www.statistics.gov.uk

1. Which UK industry was the most concentrated and which industry was the least concentrated in 2004?

2. What do the figures suggest about the market structure and degree of competition in these different industries?

3. What other information would you require to make a proper assessment of the degree of competition between producers in individual markets? For example: what about competition from foreign firms? Do market prices suggest there is a lack of price competition in these markets? Are the top five firms in each industry necessarily the same five each year? Investigate possible sources of data to provide answers to these and other questions about how to measure the degree of competition in markets.

The private firm as producer and employer

SECTION 4

Monopoly and opportunistic behaviour

What is a monopoly?

In some markets one or a handful of dominant firms may have sufficient market power to restrict competition and influence the price and quantity traded to their favour. A firm or group of firms acting in this way is called a **monopoly**.

The opposite extreme in economics of a perfectly competitive market is a **pure monopoly**. A firm is a pure monopoly if it is the only supplier of a good or service wanted by consumers. For example, until 1998 British Gas supplied 100% of households connected to the national gas supply network in the UK. In fact, many public utilities around the world supplying gas and electric power remain pure monopolies.

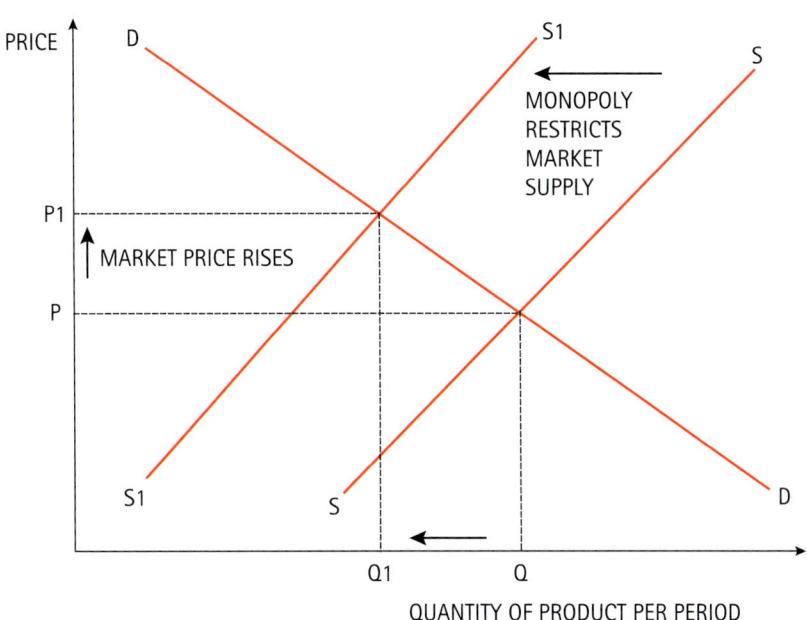

In a pure monopoly the single firm controls the total supply of the whole industry and may use this power to behave opportunistically. This means the monopoly can restrict market supply to force up the market price and earn **excess profits** or **abnormal profits** over and above what it could earn if it had to compete to supply the market with other firms.

Because a monopoly may use its market power to restrict supply and increase the market price, a monopoly is a **price maker**.

▼ The impact of a monopoly on market supply and price

The disadvantages of monopoly

Any firm able to exert influence and control over the market supply and price of a product will have a number of disadvantages for consumers, governments and economies over more competitive markets.

1 Less consumer choice

By restricting competition from rival producers and products a monopoly offers the consumer less choice than would occur in a competitive market.

2 Lower output and higher prices

A monopoly can restrict market supply to set a higher market price than would otherwise occur in a competitive market. Total output and employment in an economy will be lower. Consumers faced with few alternative choices may simply have to continue buying the product of the monopoly or go without. If consumer demand is relatively price inelastic, particularly if the product is an essential product, then demand will not contract by much and the monopoly will increase its revenue and profit. ➤ **2.2**

3 Lower product quality

Faced with little or no competition, a monopoly has no great incentive to increase the quality of the good or service it supplies. On the contrary, a monopoly may reduce quality in order to cut its production costs to increase its profit margins.

Competition 263

4 X inefficiency

Because a monopoly has little or no competition and earns abnormal profits it may make less effort than a competitive firm to ensure that its resources are used in the most efficient way. This means a monopoly may be managed inefficiently and production costs may be higher than they would otherwise be in a competitive firm. This **x-inefficiency** is caused by organizational slack due to a lack of competition.

5 The need for regulation

Many governments around the world have introduced laws and regulations to control monopolies that act against the public interest. Governments must therefore employ scarce resources paid for from tax revenues to monitor and regulate monopoly behaviour. These scarce resources could have been put to other more productive uses instead.

There are very few pure monopolies but many firms still have significant market power and may behave opportunistically.

Most markets can be described as 'oligopolistic'. An **oligopoly** exists if a small number of firms dominate the supply of a particular good or service to a market. The oil extraction and petroleum market, commercial banking, the manufacture of soaps and detergents, and the manufacture of large passenger aircraft are all example of oligopolies.

Sometimes firms in an oligopoly will collude to influence the market price by restricting supply and new competition, in effect forming a pure or near pure monopoly. As such, under the law of many countries oligopolies are deemed to be monopolies and are watched closely to ensure that they do not abuse their dominant market power.

A **cartel** is a formal agreement between firms to regulate market supply and price. The best-known cartel is OPEC (Organization of Petroleum Exporting Countries), which attempts to manage the world supply of crude oil to determine its market price.

Cartels and **price collusion** between firms to fix prices at artificially high levels are outlawed in many countries because they are deemed to be against the public interest. Instead, **price leadership** and vigorous **non-price competition** are key features of many oligopolistic markets. For example, despite the existence of numerous branded products the detergent market is supplied, primarily, by two very large producers (a **duopoly**) – Unilever and Procter & Gamble. Their competition concentrates on the creation of strong brand images and customer product loyalty through heavy advertising. Similarly, Boeing and Airbus are a duopoly in the manufacture and supply of large passenger aircraft.

▲ Oil extraction and petroleum refining is an example of an oligopoly

How monopolies may restrict competition

If a large monopoly or group of firms acting together to dominate a market wish to protect their market power and abnormal profits they must prevent new firms from entering the market to compete. Any increase in supply from new firms will force market prices and profits down.

New firms may face many obstacles that make it difficult for them to introduce their products into existing markets. These obstacles are called **barriers to entry**. There are two main types of barrier to market entry:

- **Natural barriers to entry** occur when being a large firm is more efficient than being small.

- **Artificial barriers to entry** are those created by a powerful monopoly or oligopoly purposefully to restrict competition.

Natural barriers to entry

Natural barriers to entry are not necessarily bad. They occur because large-scale production is often more efficient and smaller firms may be unable to compete with larger firms on costs and revenues.

1 Economies of scale

By increasing in size a firm may be able to reduce the average cost of producing each unit of output below the costs of smaller organizations. If a single firm is able to produce the entire market supply of a product at a lower average cost than a number of smaller competing firms together then it has a **natural monopoly**. Pipelines and grids for the supply of gas, electricity and water and therefore the companies that operate them are examples of natural monopolies. This is because it does not make economic sense to have more than one set of gas or water pipes or electricity cables supplying each house, office or factory in a country. Product duplication in these cases will be an example of **wasteful competition**.

2 Capital size

The supply of a product may involve the input of such a vast amount of capital equipment that new, smaller competing firms will find it difficult to raise enough finance to buy or hire their own. For example, consider the amount of capital a firm would need to produce electricity from building a new nuclear power station or wind farm.

3 Historical reasons

A business may have a monopoly because it was the first to enter the market for a product and has built up an established and loyal customer base. For example, Lloyds of London dominates the world shipping insurance market primarily because of its established expertise dating back to the eighteenth century.

4 Legal considerations

The development of new production methods and products can be expensive but can be encouraged by granting innovative producers **patents** or copyright to protect them from other firms copying their ideas and thereby reducing their potential sales and profits. In this way a government can create a **legal monopoly** with the sole right to supply a new and innovative good or service.

Artificial barriers to entry

Some powerful firms may introduce pricing, output and marketing strategies purposefully to restrict new competition from eroding their market power and profits. These are artificial barriers to entry. Complete Activity 4.21 to discover what these barriers might be and how they work.

1 Restrictions on supplies

New firms will only be able to enter a market if they can obtain supplies of the materials, components and business services they need to begin production. Existing firms in the same market with a dominant share can threaten their suppliers that if they supply any new firms, the existing firms will take their custom to other suppliers. This is likely to work if there are only a few suppliers and if these suppliers rely heavily on the dominant firms for business. For example, in the case of the Big Sell Supermarket in Activity 4.21, the store could threaten their wholesaler that if it supplies any new shops in the area it will lose its largest customer.

ACTIVITY 4.21

Creating barriers

Divide into groups. Each group should consider one of the following cases based on imaginary firms. You play the role of company directors of different monopolies and your task is to find barriers to entry to stop competition from other firms. You will report your findings to your shareholders (the rest of the class) who will then vote on whether or not to allow the directors to continue to manage the company depending on how well you have protected profits.

Big Sell Supermarket plc

You are the board of directors of the large Big Sell Supermarket in a town. There are very few other food shops in the town apart from some very small stores. The supermarket is supplied by a nearby wholesaler and your supermarket is its single most important customer.

Your monopoly position ensures that the supermarket continues to earn high profits. However, other firms know this and want to set up large shops in the same area to compete. The owners of Big Sell are worried about losing trade and profits to these new stores. They have asked you to find barriers to prevent new shops from setting up nearby.

You must report on what you plan to do before the next AGM, at which the shareholders will decide whether or not to re-elect you as directors.

Flyhigh Airlines

You are the directors of a large airline flying to countries all over the world.

A new airline company, Cut Price Atlantic, is about to enter the market with two scheduled flights per week on your most profitable route between the USA and Spain. Cut Price Atlantic intends to undercut your $150 fare by $40 for a one-way flight between the two countries.

Your shareholders in Flyhigh Airlines are very anxious. Because demand is price elastic they fear that the new low-cost airline will make large sales on the route across the Atlantic and will be able to use its profits to buy more planes in order to start up cut-price flights on other routes as well.

Your task as directors is to stop the new airline from taking away custom from your company by devising barriers to entry. (Hint: Flyhigh operates many profitable routes throughout the world, so what can you afford to do to try and force Cut Price Airlines out of business? Remember, your failure to do so could mean your rejection as directors by shareholders at their next meeting.)

Spreadwell Limited

You are the board of directors of Spreadwell Limited. You have a dominant share of the market for margarine, producing nearly all of the well-known brands on sale.

Spreadwell Limited relies heavily on television advertising to sell its products and will often help chains of supermarkets to publicize the sale of their margarines. Supermarkets benefit from the additional customers they attract as a result.

Because of your monopoly position, Spreadwell earns high profits and shareholders are keen to protect them from new firms who wish to produce margarine.

As the board of directors you need to limit any new competition. Try to decide how you can set up barriers to entry. Your report must prove favourable to your shareholders.

The private firm as producer and employer

2 Predatory pricing

In the Flyhigh Airlines example, the company has routes all over the world and makes many millions of dollars in profits each year. A smaller competitor could not afford to operate so many routes. In fact, Cut Price Airlines can only afford to operate two flights per week on just one route.

The new company has offered fares $40 cheaper than Flyhigh Airlines. To compete Flyhigh can afford to cut its fares on the Atlantic route by more. This will capture the market and should force Cut Price out of business. Flyhigh will lose money on the route by offering such low fares but it can afford to cover these losses from profits on other routes. Once Cut Price has been forced to close, Flyhigh can raise its fares again.

This is an example of predatory or destruction pricing. It occurs when a large firm cuts its prices, even if it means losing money in the short run, in order to force new and smaller competing firms out of business. Once the new competitor has been removed, the dominant firm can raise its prices again.

3 Exclusive dealing

This involves a monopoly preventing retailers from stocking the products of competing firms. This method of restricting competition is particularly effective if the product supplied by the dominant firm is very popular with consumers and therefore retailers and where retailers would lose too much trade if they did not sell it. In the example of Spreadwell Limited, the firm was the main supplier of popular margarines to supermarkets and other retailers who were able to attract consumers into their shops as a result of offering Spreadwell products. Spreadwell can use this brand power to threaten to stop supplying retailers if they stock competing margarines. Spreadwell's significant advertising effort will also be an entry barrier to many smaller firms.

4 Full line forcing

This is similar to exclusive dealing. It means a large multi-product firm will only supply a retailer if it stocks and sells the firm's full range of products. For example, Spreadwell could insist supermarkets either stocked all its products or these shops would risk losing an attractive and well-recognized brand.

EXAM PREPARATION 4.3

Firms employ factors of production to produce goods and services in order to make profits.

a What is meant by the term factors of production? [4]

b How do the characteristics of a monopoly differ from those of perfect competition? [6]

c Discuss how firms might become large and evaluate whether monopolies are necessarily advantageous. [10]

Cambridge IGCSE Economics 0455/21 Q6 May/June 2010
Cambridge O Level Economics 2281/21 Q6 May/June 2010

SECTION 5 — Controlling monopolies and regulating competition

Competition policy

Because of the disadvantages of monopoly many governments try to control or regulate the market power of dominant firms and have also introduced laws to protect consumers from exploitation.

It is therefore useful at this point to summarize and compare the key features of different market structures in economics ranging from a perfectly competitive market to pure monopoly. In this way the disadvantages of monopoly over more competitive market structures should be clear.

Market structure	Number of suppliers	What pricing strategies are usually observed?	Do firms engage in non-price competition?	Are there barriers to entry?
Perfect competition	Many	All firms are price takers and trade at the market price	No	No
Competitive market	Many	Penetration pricing	Yes, producers differentiate their products from rivals in terms of quality, after-sales care and through use of promotions	Few. A firm may enjoy a small degree of monopoly power by differentiating its product and brand
Oligopoly	Few	Price leadership; price collusion; price wars; predatory pricing	Yes, there is fierce competition on product image, quality and promotions	Yes
Pure monopoly	One or a group of firms acting together	Price maker because it has control over market supply	There is no competition, so this is not necessary but may be used to expand demand	Yes

Competition policy refers to measures that can be used by a government to control the behaviour of firms thought to be acting anti-competitively and against the interests of consumers. There are three main measures.

Competition policy in action

(1) Imposing fines on firms that abuse their market power

In August 2010 South Africa's Competition Commission found petrochemicals group Sasol had charged excessive prices for polypropylene and propylene to its local customers compared with prices for overseas customers. It proposed to fine Sasol 10% of its annual turnover of Rand 138 billion.

(2) Breaking up monopolies into smaller competing firms

In 2008 the UK competition Commission recommended that BAA Ltd., owner and operator of six of the UK's International airports, should be forced to sell off three of its airports to increase competition in the provision of UK airport services for passengers and airlines.

(3) Regulating the prices and service levels of monopolies

In March 2010 competition authorities in Germany were given powers to regulate the prices charged by German water companies.

Water prices charged in Germany are some of the highest in Europe.

Some private sector monopolies may even be nationalized; that is, taken into public sector ownership. For example, the generation and supply of electricity, passenger railway services and postal services are nationalized industries in a number of countries because they are natural monopolies and provide necessary public services. Running them in the public sector means their prices and service levels can be controlled directly. ➤ 4.1

Consumer protection laws are designed to protect consumers from exploitation and harmful business activities. For example, in many countries it is an offence to sell goods or services which are unsafe or in an unsatisfactory condition and to mislead consumers about prices and product features.

But are all monopolies bad?

It would be wrong to think all large monopoly firms will try to restrict competition and exploit consumers. For example, Boeing in the USA and Airbus in Europe dominate the global market supply of large passenger aircraft but nevertheless compete vigorously against each other for market share.

Some monopolies, because of their size and ability to earn high profits, can benefit consumers. Here are some examples:

- A monopoly may be more efficient than smaller firms supplying the same market because of its scale of production.

- A monopoly may still face competition from firms overseas or from firms selling products that can satisfy similar wants. For example, a monopoly provider of air or railway services could still face competition on some routes from providers of bus, coach or boat services.

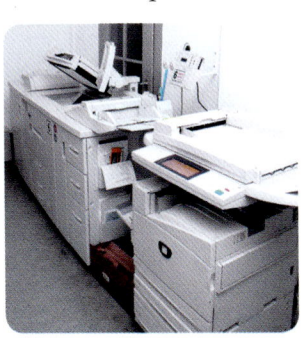

- A monopoly may still charge low competitive prices and offer high-quality products because it fears new firms would otherwise be attracted by much higher prices to enter the market it dominates and will compete for its sales. A market is a **contestable market** if barriers to entry are low and new firms can enter a market easily to compete.

- A monopoly business may re-invest some of its profits in new inventions and better products because the profits it could earn from these will not be competed away.

▲ Some revolutionary products, like the jumbo jet and photocopier, may never have been developed if the business organizations that invented them were unable to enjoy monopoly profits. Abnormal profits were a reward for their significant investment risks

WEBSITES

Some helpful websites on competition and market structure include:

- www.competition-commission.org.uk
- www.europa.eu/comm/competition/index_en.html
- biz/ed online service www.bized.co.uk/search/node/market structure
- www.wikipedia.org/wiki/Competition_policy

KEYWORDS

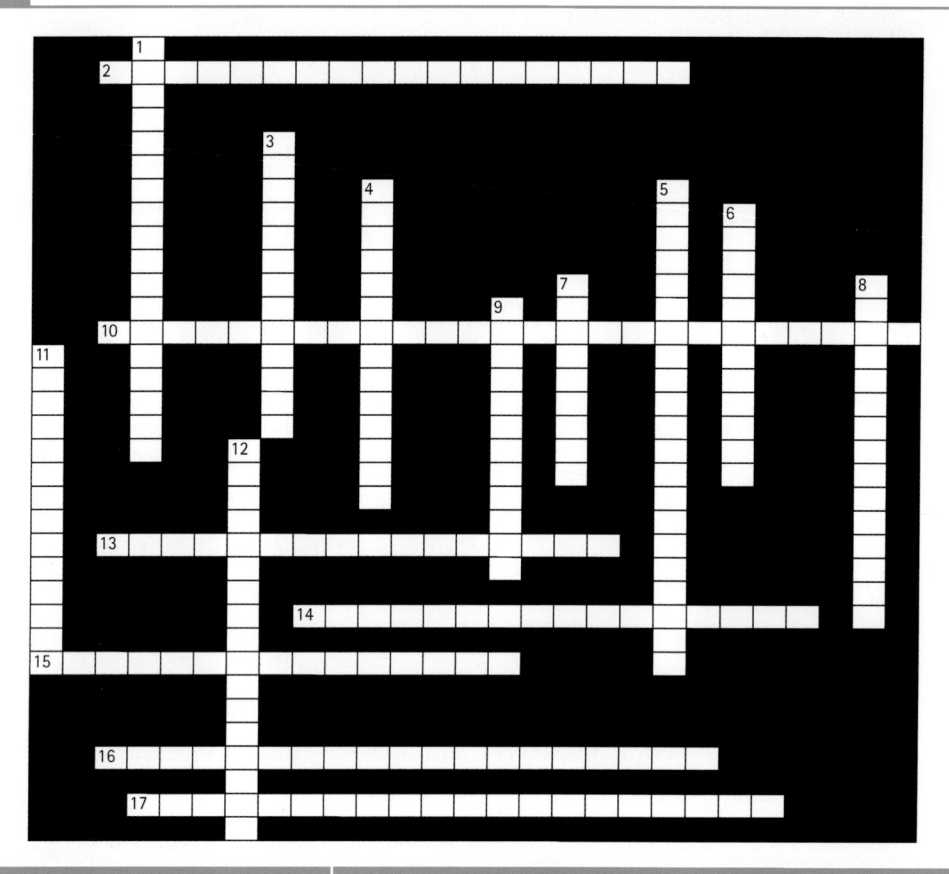

Clues across

2. A theoretical market structure in which there are many firms supplying identical products to an equally large number of consumers such that no individual firm has any influence over market price (7, 11)
10. Obstacles created by a powerful monopoly or oligopoly purposefully to restrict competition (10, 8, 2, 5)
13. Rivalry between firms supplying the same market based on reducing prices or offering discounts for customers (5, 11)
14. A pricing strategy involving deep cuts to prices that is often used by an established and dominant firm in a market to deter or destroy new competition (9, 7)
15. A market structure in which there is a single firm controlling the entire market supply of a product because it has an overwhelming cost advantage over any other potential market structure involving more than one firm (7, 8)
16. Rivalry between firms supplying the same market through advertising and product differentiation strategies (3-5, 11)
17. Less than perfectly competitive market structures in which firms have some degree of influence over market supply and prices (9, 11)

Clues down

1. A price strategy that might be adopted by a firm seeking to gain market entry and expand sales (11, 7)
3. Higher costs resulting from organizational slack in a monopoly that is protected from competition (1, 12)
4. The surplus of revenue over costs enjoyed by a monopoly that is in excess of the surplus it might expect to earn in a more competitive market (8, 5)
5. Television, radio, newspaper and other commercial promotions designed to create or influence consumer wants for a product (9, 11)
6. A single firm that controls 100% of the supply of a product to a market (4, 8)
7. A market structure in which a handful of large firms dominate the market supply (9)
8. The characteristics of a market, usually on the supply side, including how many firms compete for the market, the degree of competition or collusion between them, the extent of their product differentiation, and the ease with which new firms can enter the market to compete with them (6, 9)
9. The extent of the faithfulness of consumers to the product or products of a particular firm, expressed through their repeat purchases and irrespective of changes in the prices and promotions of competing products from rival firms (5, 7)
11. A group of firms acting together to determine or influence the market price of their product through their joint control over market supply (5, 9)
12. A market in which a monopoly prices and acts competitively because there are low entry barriers so new firms can enter the market easily (11, 6)

The private firm as producer and employer

Assessment exercises

Multiple choice

1. What distinguishes a multinational company from other companies?
   - A It has agents in other countries
   - B It produces in other countries
   - C It takes part in international trade
   - D It uses raw materials and components from more than one country

2. The table shows the value of output for some parts of an economy.

	$ billion
Fishing	25.0
Mining	23.0
Manufacturing	130.5
Financial services	100.3
Other services	170.0

   Which conclusion may be drawn from these statistics?
   - A The tertiary sector was the most valuable
   - B The value of the primary sector was $ 25.0 billion
   - C The value of the secondary sector was $ 153.5 billion
   - D The value of the secondary sector was worth less than the value of the primary sector

3. The table shows the total cost of a firm. It can sell the units for $4 each.

quantity produced (units)	5	6	7	8
total cost $	17	18	21	23

   How many units will the firm produce to maximize profits?
   - A 5 B 6 C 7 D 8

4. Which of the following is not a private sector business organization?
   - A Public limited company
   - B Partnership
   - C Public corporation
   - D Consumer cooperative

5. If a business owner has unlimited liability, this means:
   - A The business cannot go bankrupt
   - B The owner must meet all business debts
   - C The business has sold shares
   - D The business is only small

6. Which of the following best describes a public limited company?
   - A A company owned by a government
   - B A multinational corporation
   - C A company owned by its workers
   - D A company that is listed on a stock exchange

7. One of the main disadvantages of a large limited company is that:
   - A Owners of the company may lose control to the company directors
   - B Specialization is not possible
   - C There are no organized markets where shares in the company can be purchased
   - D There is a lack of capital

8. Which of the following is an advantage to a country of hosting multinational companies?
   - A They may force local firms out of business
   - B They may exploit cheap labour
   - C They may switch profits between countries.
   - D They may spread their advanced technical knowledge to local suppliers and employees

9. A furniture maker produces to order expensive, hand-made pieces of wooden furniture. In which type of business organization is the furniture maker most likely to work?
   - A A private limited company
   - B A retail cooperative
   - C A sole trader
   - D A public limited company

10. Which of the following mergers between two firms is an example of vertical integration?
    - A A bank and an insurance company
    - B A car rental firm and a carmaker
    - C A tin mine and a coal mine
    - D A restaurant and a hot food take-away

11 Cadbury Schweppes, the confectionery business, is reported to want to reduce the number of its offices in an attempt to decrease its general and administrative costs. Which type of cost does Cadbury Schweppes hope to decrease?
   A Average variable cost
   B Social cost
   C Total fixed cost
   D Total variable cost

12 A firm employs 25 full-time employees. They produce 500 shirts each week. What is average labour productivity?
   A 25
   B 500
   C 20
   D 12,500

Questions 13–15 are based on the following table of costs and revenues for a firm producing clocks.

	Output per week	Total cost ($)	Total revenue ($)
A	1,000	10,000	13,000
B	2,000	16,000	30,000
C	3,000	18,000	42,000
D	4,000	28,000	54,000

13 At what level of output is average cost at a minimum?

14 At which level of output is average revenue at a maximum?

15 At what level of output is profit maximized?

16 Which of the following is a variable cost of production?
   A Purchases of component parts
   B Insurance premiums
   C Loan repayments
   D Computer repair costs

17 A firm expands its scale of production by investing in additional factory space and machinery. What is the most likely impact of this decision on costs?
   A Variable costs will fall
   B Fixed costs will rise
   C Total cost will be unchanged
   D Average costs will rise

18 A firm that doubles all its inputs of factors of production and more than doubles its output as a result has experienced:
   A Constant returns to scale
   B Rising profits
   C Decreasing returns to scale
   D Increasing returns to scale

19 In the graph below at which level of output does the firm break even?

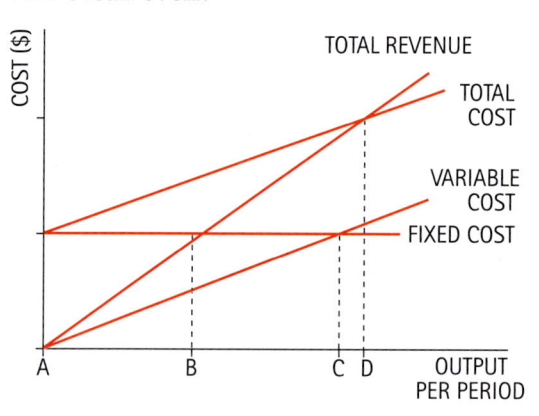

Questions 20–23 are based on the following table.

Total output of plastic boxes	Total costs $
0	100
100	800
200	1,500
300	2,200
400	2,900
500	3,600
600	4,300

20 The average cost of producing 200 boxes is:
   A $7   B $70   C $7.50   D $1,500

21 The total fixed cost of production is:
   A $1   B $10   C $100   D $800

22 The variable cost of producing each box is:
   A $7   B $8   C $7.50   D $5

23 If the company produces 500 boxes discs and wants to make a $1,400 profit from their sale, the price of each box sold must be:
   A $5   B $10   C $2.80   D $7.20

24 Which one of the following pricing strategies is most likely to be used by a dominant firm trying to undercut new competition?

- A   Penetration pricing
- B   Cost-plus pricing
- C   Price skimming
- D   Destruction pricing

25 Prices tend to be lower in a competitive industry than in a monopoly. Why is this?

- A   A monopoly has less influence on the market
- B   Competitive industry has more economies of scale
- C   New firms are free to enter the competitive industry
- D   Profits are lower in a monopoly

26 A market dominated by one or a handful of firms may be highly contestable if:

- A   Artificial barriers to entry are significant
- B   There are no natural barriers to entry
- C   Barriers to entry are low
- D   Existing firms have legal monopolies

27 If a pure monopoly restricts market supply of a product, the most likely outcome will be:

- A   A fall in demand
- B   A price war with rival producers
- C   A fall in profit
- D   A rise in market price

28 A market dominated by just two suppliers is known as:

- A   A pure monopoly
- B   A contestable market
- C   A competitive market
- D   A duopoly

29 Which of the following is an artificial barrier to entry that may be used by a monopoly to restrict competition?

- A   Economies of scale in production
- B   A predatory pricing strategy
- C   Development of new products
- D   Its significant capital size

30 India is experiencing rapid growth in air travel. The number and size of airlines is increasing every year.

Which effect arising from this growth is an external economy of scale?

- A   Banks are more prepared to lend to large airlines than to small airlines
- B   Fuel suppliers charge lower prices to airlines that buy in bulk
- C   Institutions are established to train flight crew
- D   Larger airlines operate aircraft which can carry more passengers

Structured questions

1 German television advertising

In 2003 a German TV broadcasting company has reduced its costs by 13%. The measures that it took included spending less on TV programmes, merging departments within its organisation and decreasing its workforce by 4%. These measures helped the company compensate for a decrease in advertising revenue, which generated approximately 90% of the company's total revenue. The company had lost nearly 20% of its advertising revenue in the previous two years.

- **a**   Identify the reason why the television company needed to cut costs. [1]
- **b**   Costs can be classed as fixed costs or variable costs. Explain which of the company's costs mentioned are fixed and which are variable. [6]
- **c**   Calculate the percentage of total revenue that the company lost. [1]
- **d**   Describe the possible benefits of advertising to producers and consumers. [5]
- **e**   The directors of the company wish to know how the company could improve its profit levels. If you had to report to the directors what would you need to investigate? [7]

Cambridge IGCSE Economics 0455/06 Q1 October/November 2005

2 The computer games industry

The United Kingdom is Europe's largest video game market and the third largest in the world in terms of developer success and sales of hardware and software by country alone but fourth behind Canada in terms of people employed.

According to a 2012 report by Newzoo, the UK games market generated US $5.2 billion of revenues in 2012, more than any other entertainment sector in the UK including books. Around 62 percent of the UK industry turnover is generated from exports, notably to the US, Canada, Japan and many European countries.

TIGA, the trade association for the UK games industry, reports there are around 300 design studios in the UK employing over 9,000 highly skilled staff. Directly and indirectly the industry is estimated to support the employment of around 100,000 people in the UK and contributes approximately £1 billion to UK Gross Domestic Product per annum.

   a Identify **three** ways of measuring whether an industry in a country is large or small. [3]
   b Discuss whether you would classify the size of the UK computer games industry as large or small. [4]
   c Explain what is meant by specialisation. [3]
   d Explain whether there is any example of specialisation in the article. [2]
   e Are specialisation and large company size advantageous for a producer? [8]

Adapted from Cambridge IGCSE Economics 0455/ 04 Q1 May/June 2002
Adapted from Cambridge O Level Economics 2281/02 Q1 May/June 2002

3 In the same industry there are often firms of different sizes. Sometimes a firm integrates with another firm.
   a What is the difference between horizontal and vertical integration? [4]
   b Contrast the characteristics of **two** types of business organisation. [6]
   c Discuss whether the growth of a firm is advantageous for both the firm and consumers. [10]

Cambridge IGCSE Economics 0455/02 Q4 May/June 2009
Cambridge O Level Economics 2281/02 Q4 May/June 2009

4 The American airline United Airlines cancelled thousands of flights between April and August 2000 because of crew shortages, bad weather and technical problems with aircraft. There was also a 3% reduction in flights because pilots refused to work overtime.
   a Explain the difference between a fixed cost and a variable cost. [4]
   b Discuss whether the cancellation of a flight would have affected the fixed and variable costs of United Airlines. [6]
   c What is meant by 'the principle of profit maximisation'? [3]
   d Analyse what might have happened to the level of profits for United Airlines as a result of the problems stated. [7]

Cambridge IGCSE Economics 0455/04 Q4 May/June 2002
Cambridge O Level Economics 2281/02 Q4 May/June 2002

5 Role of government in an economy

5.1	Government economic policy
5.2	Taxation
Assessment	Multiple choice
	Structured questions

In many mixed economies the government is a major consumer of goods and services as well as providing jobs and incomes for many people. Government spending, or public expenditure, therefore accounts for a large share of total spending in many economies. Public expenditures are financed mostly from taxes on incomes, wealth and the private expenditures of individuals and firms.

Most governments have four main macroeconomic objectives:

- low and stable inflation in the general level of prices
- high and stable employment
- economic growth in the national output
- a stable balance of international trade and transactions.

A government may also have additional objectives aimed at improving social and economic welfare through poverty reduction and environmental protection.

To achieve its macroeconomic objectives a government will attempt to influence total or aggregate demand and supply in its economy. For example, an economy may overheat if growth in aggregate demand exceeds growth in the aggregate supply of goods and services causing the general level of prices to rise at an accelerating rate. Demand-side policies may be used to influence aggregate demand while supply-side policies can help to expand total output in an economy.

A government may cut its own public expenditure or raise taxes to reduce disposable incomes and therefore the level of aggregate demand in the economy if it is overheating. This is known as contractionary fiscal policy. A government may also raise interest rates using monetary policy to encourage more saving and less borrowing.

In contrast, expansionary fiscal and monetary policies – increasing public spending and cutting taxes and interest rates – may be used to boost aggregate demand during an economic recession when unemployment is high to create jobs and to grow output. However, this may cause inflationary pressures.

Expanding the supply-side of an economy will also help to create additional employment opportunities and boost aggregate supply thereby reducing inflationary pressures caused by rising aggregate demand. Supply-side policies aim to remove or reduce any barriers to growth in the productive potential of the economy. For example, supply-side policy instruments can include reducing the burden of taxes on incentives to work and enterprise, removing costly and burdensome regulations on firms, and legislation to control monopolies and outlaw unfair competition.

Taxes are the main way of financing public sector expenditure as well as being a key policy tool in economic management. Direct taxes are levied directly on incomes and wealth. They include personal income taxes and corporation taxes on company profits. Indirect taxes are taxes, such as a sales tax or ad valorem tax, added to the prices of goods or services and collected from consumers by producers.

Unit 5.1   Government economic policy

AIMS

By the end of this unit you should be able to:

- describe the government as a producer of goods and services and as an employer
- describe the aims of government policies, such as **full employment, price stability, economic growth**, redistribution of income and **balance of payments** stability
- explain **fiscal, monetary** and **supply-side policies**
  - distinguish between **demand-side policies** that aim to manage **aggregate demand** in an economy and **supply-side policies** that aim to expand the productive capacity of an economy
  - describe the instruments of **fiscal policy** and **monetary policy** and analyse the possible impact of changes in these policies on an economy
  - describe different supply-side policies, including **tax policy, competition policy, privatization** and **deregulation**, and explain how changes in these policies can affect output and employment in an economy
- analyse the use of fiscal, monetary and supply-side policies
- discuss the possible conflicts between government aims
- discuss the government's influence (**regulation, subsidies, taxes**) on private producers.

SECTION 1

The role of government in a mixed economy

The government as an employer

The public sector is a major producer, employer and consumer in many modern economies. For example, the public sector in France employs 22% of the French workforce and is responsible for around 55% of total expenditure in the French economy. ➤ **2.1**

Public sector organizations include:

- national, regional and local government authorities and their administrative departments and offices
- government agencies that are responsible for the delivery of public services such as a food standards agency, health authority or law enforcement agency
- public corporations. ➤ **4.2**

Governments often employ many civil servants or public servants to work in government departments and agencies to develop and deliver government policies and services.

▲ In addition to civil servants, public sector employees will usually include members of the armed forces, the police and judiciary, teachers, doctors and nurses

To pay the running costs of public sector organizations, including the wages of public sector employees, and for the goods and services government organizations consume, the public sector must raise revenue. Taxes on income, wealth, or spending are the main sources of public sector revenue in most countries. ➤ **5.2**

The government as a consumer and producer

In many countries the government is a major consumer of goods and services as well as providing jobs and incomes for many people. Government spending or **public expenditure** therefore accounts for a large share of total spending in many economies. ➤ **2.1**

Current expenditure is recurring spending on goods and services consumed in the current financial year. These include the wages and salaries of public sector workers, state pensions and welfare payments, consumables, such as pens and paper, and the running costs of government offices.

Government economic policy

Capital expenditures are investments in long-lived assets such as computer equipment, roads, dams, schools, and hospitals. Capital expenditure has a lasting impact on an economy and can help to expand its productive capacity. ➤ **6.3**

Governments will use their spending to achieve a number of objectives:

- **To provide goods and services that are in the public interest**. These are **public goods**, such as street lighting and national parks, and **merit goods** including education, healthcare, and affordable housing for people on low incomes to rent. ➤ **1.1**

- **To invest in national infrastructure** such as roads and railway networks, universities, and other public buildings.

- **To support agriculture and key industries** by providing financial assistance or **subsidies** to firms to reduce their costs of production and make investments in staff training, new machinery, and the research and development (R&D) of new products, processes and materials.

- **To manage the macroeconomy**. Increasing public spending during an economic recession can boost total demand and reduce unemployment. In contrast, a government may cut its expenditure to control rapid and unstable price inflation. ➤ **6.1**

- **To reduce inequalities in incomes and help vulnerable people**, for example by providing income support and other welfare payments for people and families in need or on low incomes. Financial payments that a government gives to individuals, usually through a social welfare programme such as disability allowances, child support payments, old-age pensions and unemployment compensation, are known as **transfer payments**. They are transfer payments because a government is simply transferring money collected through taxes from people in work to those who are not able to be economically active.

▲ Public expenditures will benefit many private sector firms

Many private sector firms therefore benefit directly from different public expenditures or indirectly from their impact on consumer demand. Here are some examples.

- Construction firms benefit from contracts to build schools and other buildings.

- Office equipment manufacturers benefit from spending on equipping public offices.
- Farms may benefit from agricultural subsidies to increase their production of food.
- Power companies earn revenue from electricity supplied for street lights.
- The defence industry benefits from orders for defence equipment.
- Public sector workers use their incomes to buy goods and services from businesses.

Cutting or raising public expenditure can therefore have a big impact on consumers, employees and the activities and profitability of many private sector firms, as we will discover in the following sections.

SECTION 2

What is the macroeconomy?

Macroeconomic objectives

Macroeconomics is the study of how a national economy works. It involves understanding the interaction between changes in total demand and output and national income, employment and price inflation in an economy. In contrast, **microeconomics** analyses the market behaviours of individual consumers and producers and how markets work. ➤ **2.2**

Macroeconomics and microeconomics are closely related. A **macroeconomy** consists of all the different markets for goods and services, labour, money, foreign exchange and all other traded items. Changes in the behaviours of different producers and consumers in individual markets can therefore affect the distribution of incomes, total output and overall level of prices, employment and trade in a macroeconomy.

In fact it is useful to think of a macroeconomy as one big market consisting of the total demand for all goods and services available in the economy and the total supply of all those goods and services. It follows that rising total demand or falling total supply will tend to cause price inflation by pushing up market prices in the economy. ➤ **2.2**

However, a fall in the total supply of goods and services will tend to reduce prices and economic growth as less output is produced. Similarly, falling total demand will help lower price inflation but could result in higher unemployment as firms cut back production in response to lower demand for their goods and services.

The very simple diagram on the next page represents a macroeconomy. The total value of all final goods and services produced in a macroeconomy in a given year is its **gross domestic product (GDP)**. The total output or GDP is paid for by the total expenditure of consumers, firms and government. Workers and owners of land and capital supply their resources to private firms and public sector organizations to produce those goods and services. In return they are paid income; their total income is therefore the national income. ➤ **6.3**

▼ Total demand and supply in a simple macroeconomy

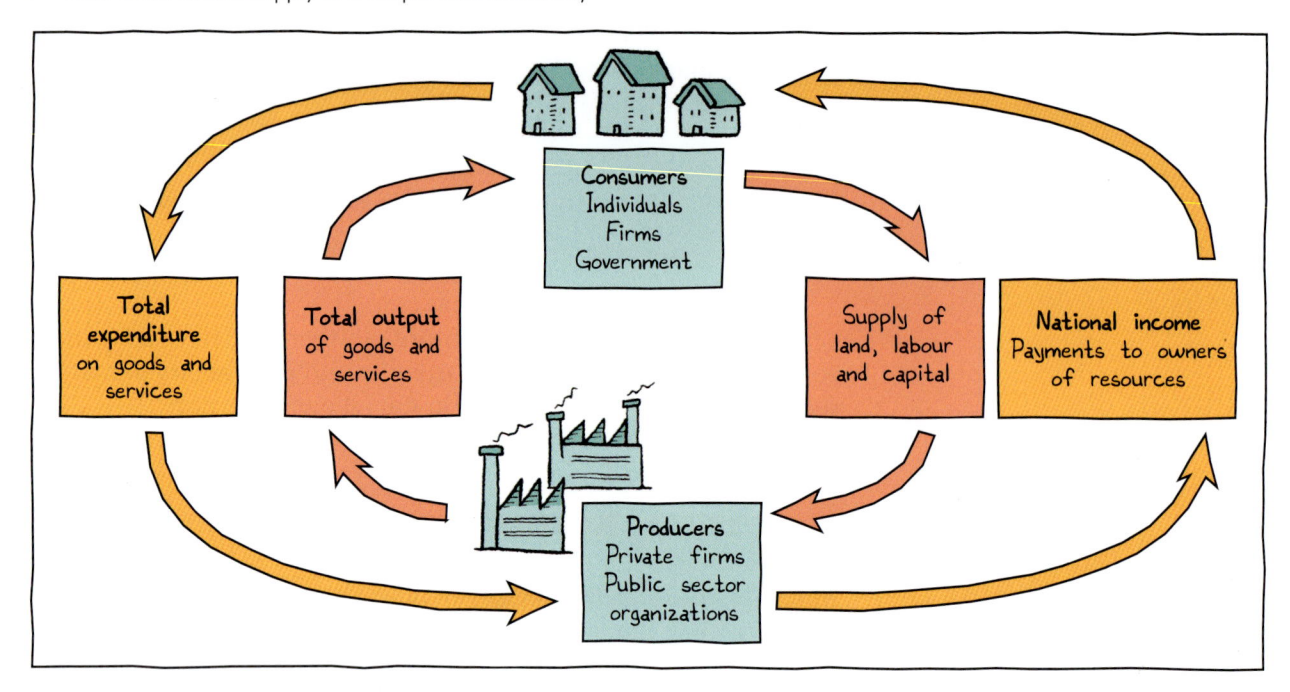

Total expenditure or **aggregate demand** in a macroeconomy is therefore the sum of:

- **consumer expenditure** on goods and services
- **investment expenditure** by firms on productive assets such as new machinery and working vehicles
- **public expenditure** on capital and current items
- **exports** or expenditure by overseas residents on goods and services produced in the macroeconomy.

The total expenditure in an economy is therefore spent on the total or **aggregate supply** of all goods and services in that economy. This is the sum of all goods and services provided by private firms and public sector organizations in the economy. ➤ 4.1

Government macroeconomics objectives

Most national governments have four main economic objectives for their macroeconomies. These are:

- a low and stable rate of **inflation** in the general level of prices ➤ 6.1
- a high and stable level of **employment**, and therefore a low level of unemployment ➤ 6.2
- **economic** growth in total output (i.e. the GDP) and increased standards of living ➤ 6.3
- a stable **balance of international trade and payments**. ➤ 8.2

A government may also have additional objectives which aim to improve the economic and social welfare of people in the economy, including:

- to reduce poverty and reduce inequalities in income and wealth

Role of government in an economy

- to reduce pollution and waste, protect the natural environment and therefore encourage more sustainable economic growth.

If a government can achieve these macroeconomic objectives it will create a favourable economic climate for business development and improve people's living standards.

Low and stable price inflation

Inflation is a continuous rise in the average level of prices. If prices rise too quickly it can be bad for business and an economy because:

- it reduces the purchasing power of people's incomes
- it causes hardship for people on low incomes
- it increases business costs, especially if workers demand higher wages
- it makes goods and services produced in the economy more expensive to buy than those purchased from other countries with lower rates of inflation.

Low and stable price inflation therefore makes it easier for private sector firms to manage their costs, for exporters to sell their products overseas and for consumers, especially those on low incomes, to afford goods and services.

High and stable employment

People who want to work but are unable to find a job will be unemployed. The following may happen if **unemployment** rises:

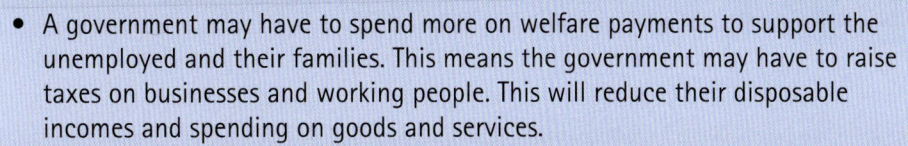

- The total national output is likely to fall.
- A government may have to spend more on welfare payments to support the unemployed and their families. This means the government may have to raise taxes on businesses and working people. This will reduce their disposable incomes and spending on goods and services.

If people remain unemployed for a long time they may lose the skills they need to work in new industrial sectors. High levels of employment therefore help to increase output, incomes, consumer demand and living standards.

Economic growth in national output

Economic growth will boost output and incomes. This will help to raise living standards. Without economic growth or, worse still, if output falls over time, an economy will suffer because

- employment, incomes and living standards will fall
- government tax revenues will fall and government spending will have to be cut
- the revenues and profits of firms will fall
- entrepreneurs will not invest in new firms.

Government economic policy

A stable balance of international trade and payments

Many countries sell exports of goods and services to overseas residents and receive other incomes and investments from overseas. Inward investments by overseas firms and the sale of exports help to create new jobs and incomes in an economy.

At the same time, many countries buy imports from producers overseas and also make investments in other countries. Most countries seek to balance their inflows and outflows of income from international transactions. Sudden changes in the amount of money flowing into or out of an economy can be very disruptive to the banking system, firms and government.

For example, the following may happen if a country has a deficit on its **balance of payments** with the rest of the world:

- It may run out of foreign currency to buy imports.
- The value of its currency may fall against other foreign currencies and make imports more expensive to buy. This can cause an imported inflation.

In a macroeconomy the conditions of aggregate demand and aggregate supply will determine the equilibrium level of prices and total level of output and employment. A macroeconomy therefore has a demand side and a supply side. Governments will therefore use **policy instruments**, or quantities and actions it is able to control to influence or alter aggregate demand and supply in their economies, to help achieve their macro-economic objectives for inflation, employment, output and international trade.

Demand-side policies try to influence the level of aggregate demand in an economy using a number of different policy instruments. These are:

- total public expenditure
- the overall level of taxation
- the rate of interest.

These demand-side policy instruments can be effective for these reasons:

- The amount consumers have to spend on goods and services depends on their level of **disposable income** after income taxes have been deducted. ➤ 5.2
- Taxes on profits will affect the amount of money firms have to invest in new productive capacity and their demand for labour.
- Increasing public expenditure can boost total demand and, therefore, stimulate higher output and employment in an economy.
- As interest rates rise consumers may save more and/or borrow less to spend on consumer goods and services. This may also encourage investments from overseas. As interest rates fall firms may borrow more to invest. ➤ 3.1

Supply-side policies aim to boost the aggregate supply of goods and services in an economy. Boosting the supply of goods and services in an economy will help to raise the rate of economic growth and employment, increase the supply of exports and reduce inflationary pressures because more goods and services will be available to satisfy aggregate demand.

Role of government in an economy

ACTIVITY 5.1

Being instrumental

Read the news articles and headlines below. Use them to identify different objectives governments have for their economies and what they are doing to try to achieve them.

SWEDEN TO CUT TAXES AGAIN

Sweden's government said on Saturday it would cut income tax by a total of 10 billion Swedish crowns ($1.45 billion) from next year, a move it said would boost employment.

Higher taxes on car imports to curb trade deficit

The Vietnam Ministry of Industry and Trade has proposed a rise in import duties on cars and a new luxury tax on mobile phones to narrow its international trade deficit. Payments for imported goods exceeded earnings from exports sold overseas by a record $17.5 billion last year.

Venezuela to increase public spending to boost economy and cut unemployment

The Venezuelan government will increase public spending to boost economic growth and generate employment in response to the global crisis. The government will invest in houses, schools, hospitals, roads and other public works projects, the President told the Venezuelan state newspaper.

Taiwan cuts interest rates to boost exports

Taiwan announced an emergency cut in its interest rate yesterday after data showed exports falling at a record pace.

The central bank said the slump in exports was having a severe impact on the economy.

'Cutting interest rates will help to increase consumer spending,' it said. 'It will also help reduce borrowing costs for companies and help boost new investment.'

'Exports are a key economic driver and if exports are bad, then it will reduce investments, and force companies to cut their workforce' experts warned.

India Raises Interest Rate to 8% to Curb Inflation

India's central bank unexpectedly raised interest rates for the first time in 15 months to combat a surge in inflation sparked by rising food and energy costs.

China launches tax reforms to boost economic growth

China's government announced it would reduce the tax burden on companies by more than 120 billion yuan ($17.6 billion) next year.

The changes will enable companies to get deductions against the taxes they must pay from spending on fixed assets such as new machinery and equipment.

Value added taxes paid by small businesses and the self-employed were reduced to 3% from 6%.

The government said the reforms would help encourage technological upgrading at Chinese companies and boost domestic demand.

Germany wants a million electric vehicles plugged in by 2020

The German government unveiled plans Wednesday to get one million electric cars on the road by 2020, by offering grants to jump-start national giants like BMW and Volkswagen.

The government will provide grants totalling $162 million to examine how the cars could best be introduced. It also plans to grant about $240 million for research on the batteries that power electric cars and on making domestic production a priority.

Government economic policy

Supply-side policy instruments are used to reduce barriers to increased employment and higher levels of productivity in domestic and international markets and to create the right incentives for firms and workers to increase their output. Supply-side policy instruments will include:

- specific public expenditures, for example providing government subsidies to firms to encourage them to fund the R&D of new and more efficient production processes and products
- changes to individual taxes, for example reducing taxes on wages and profits to increase the reward from work and enterprise
- new regulations and reforms, for example introducing legislation to outlaw unfair and anti-competitive practices by large, powerful firms.

Supply-side policy instruments therefore target the behaviours of specific groups of consumers and producers in particular markets to achieve the economic objectives of government.

SECTION 3

Demand-side policies

What is fiscal policy?

Fiscal policy involves varying the overall level of public expenditure and/or taxation in an economy to manage aggregate demand and influence the level of economic activity.

▼ Fiscal policy instruments can be effective if

INFLATION IS CAUSED BY TOO MUCH AGGREGATE DEMAND AND RISING COSTS.

UNEMPLOYMENT IS CAUSED BY LACK OF DEMAND.

Expansionary fiscal policy

If a government wants to increase aggregate demand in the economy to boost employment and output it can increase its expenditure and/or reduce taxation. This is called a reflationary or **expansionary fiscal policy**.

Cutting taxes on profits may provide firms with an incentive to increase output and investments in new productive capacity. Cutting taxes on personal incomes may encourage more people to participate in the workforce and motivate employees to increase their productivity. It will increase the amount of disposable income people have to spend. However, there is a risk they will simply save this extra money or spend it on imported goods and services.

Governments will often implement an expansionary fiscal policy during an economic downturn or recession, when private sector demand for goods and services is low or falling and unemployment in the economy is high or rising as a result. ▶ 6.3

An expansionary fiscal policy usually means running or increasing a **budget deficit**. The budget refers to the amount a government has to spend each year relative to the amount of revenue it raises from taxation. If public expenditure exceeds total tax revenue the budget will be in deficit and the government will have to borrow money to finance it. ➤ 5.2

ACTIVITY 5.2

Can increased public expenditure create jobs?

The diagram below shows how the building of new hospitals by a government could help to increase economic activity. In your own words explain what is happening in the diagram and how an expansionary fiscal policy can boost aggregate demand, output and jobs in an economy. How might the impact of the policy on the economy and your explanation change if the increase in public expenditure is paid for by **a** raising taxes or **b** raising interest rates to encourage people and firms to lend money to the government?

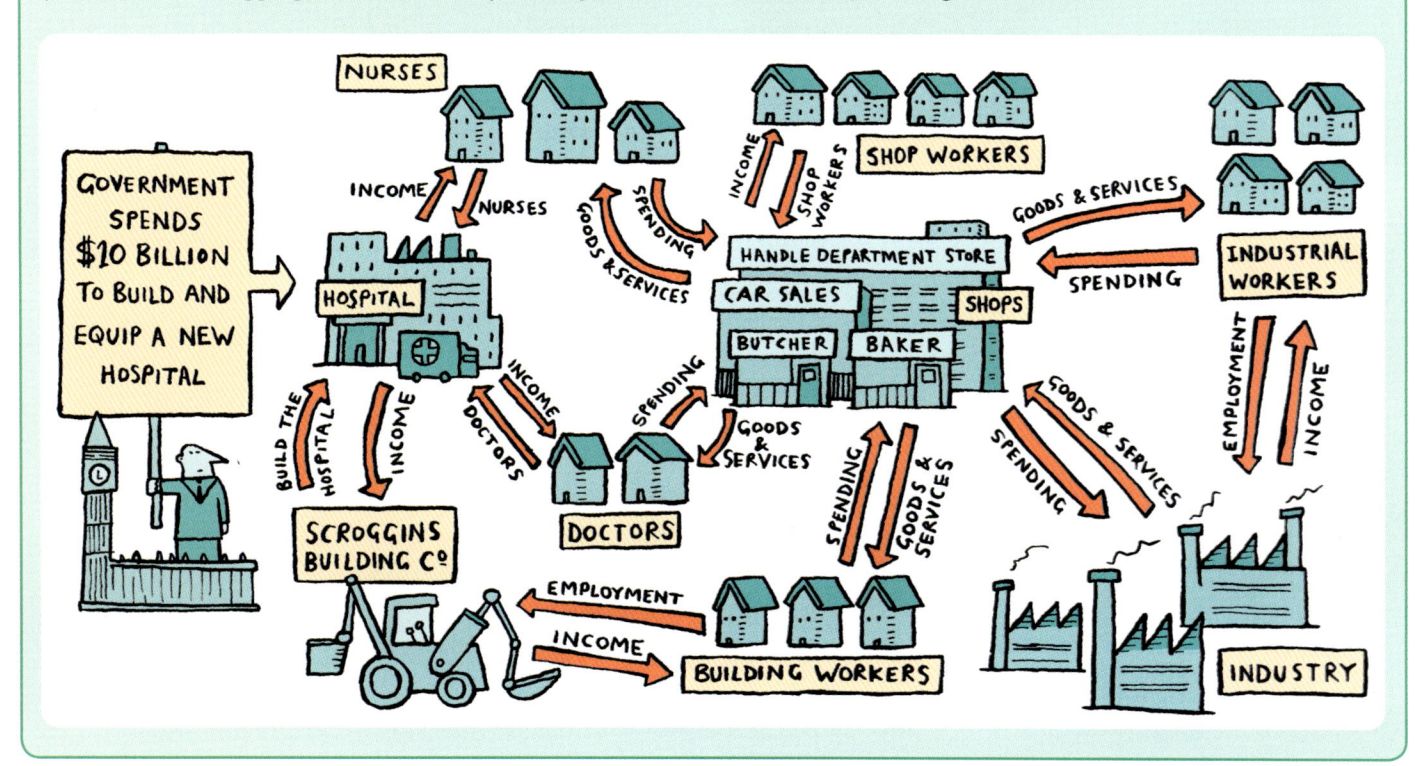

Contractionary fiscal policy

A deflationary or **contractionary fiscal policy** aims to reduce pressure on prices in the economy by cutting aggregate demand through a reduction in public expenditure and/or by raising total taxation. For example, cutting public sector wages and raising personal taxes will reduce total disposable income and consumer expenditure.

The budget deficit will be cut or may even go into surplus if tax revenues exceed public spending. However, a contractionary fiscal policy may reduce employment and growth in output.

Fiscal policy instruments can also affect the distribution of income

Fiscal policy instruments may also be used to redistribute incomes between rich and poor people in an economy. For example, income taxes may be increased on those with the highest incomes and the money raised used to finance more

Government economic policy 285

public services and increased welfare for people on the lowest incomes, or those unable to work because they are old, sick or unemployed. ➤ **5.2**

Taxing people on high incomes to provide income support to people on low incomes can also help to boost overall spending in the economy. This is because people on high incomes tend to save a large proportion of their incomes while people on low incomes tend to spend all or most of their incomes on the goods and services they need.

Problems with fiscal policy

Many economists have criticized the use of fiscal policy to influence the level of aggregate demand and economic activity in an economy. They argue there is not a clear trade-off between higher levels of inflation and lower levels of unemployment. For example, many countries have experienced high inflation and high unemployment at the same time and the overuse of fiscal policy has contributed to these conditions. ➤ **6.1**

1 Fiscal policy is cumbersome to use

It is difficult for a government to know precisely when and by how much to expand public spending or cut taxes by during an economic downturn. Boosting aggregate demand by increasing public spending and/or cutting taxes may cause an economy to 'overheat': the general level of prices will rise if aggregate demand expands faster than the aggregate supply of goods and services.

Similarly, if an economy is overheating, deep cuts in public expenditure or increases in taxes that are too severe may result in rising unemployment instead as the level of aggregate demand tumbles.

2 Increases in public expenditure crowds out private spending

To finance an increase in public spending and/or a cut in taxation a government may need to borrow the extra money it needs from the private sector. The more money the private sector lends to a government the less it has available to spend itself. This is called **crowding out**.

To encourage people, firms and the banking system to buy government stocks or bonds a government will raise interest rates. However, higher interest rates may discourage other people and firms from borrowing money to spend on consumption and investment. If firms invest less in new plant and machinery then their future productive potential, and therefore the rate of economic growth, will be reduced.

As the stock of government borrowing rises, the more a government must spend on interest payments for its debt. This will reduce the amount a government can spend on public sector wages, the construction of new roads, public health care or other public sector projects, or it will require an increase in taxes to cover the cost of additional interest payments. ➤ **5.2**

3 Increasing taxes on incomes and profits can reduce incentives to work and enterprise

If taxes are too high, people and firms may reduce their work effort. This will reduce labour productivity, total output and profits. As productivity falls the cost of production in many firms will increase and they will be less able to compete on product price and quality against more efficient producers overseas. As a result, demand for their goods and services may fall and unemployment may rise. ➤ **4.2**

4 An expansionary fiscal policy creates expectations of inflation

Consumers and producers in an economy may come to expect a future rise in inflation following an expansionary fiscal policy, especially if attempts by their government in the past to boost demand and economic activity have caused the economy to overheat. As a result, if their current government announces it will cut taxes and increase public spending to boost output and growth employees may push for higher wages now to protect them from an increase in their cost of living they fear will occur in the future. Rising wages will increase production costs and reduce the demand for labour. This in turn may cause a cost-push inflation and rising unemployment. ➤ 6.1

> ### Fiscal rules
>
> Problems with fiscal policy has led a number of countries to develop and follow a number of fiscal rules:
>
> - Current and capital public expenditures should be controlled separately. This is so that the costs and benefits of expenditures of long-term capital investments, for example in new roads, schools or advanced equipment, can be easily identified
> - The public sector should only borrow to pay for capital expenditures which will help to grow the economy: growing the national output and income will help to repay government borrowing and debt interest. Increasing current spending, for example on public sector wages, will not grow the economy
> - Public sector debt as a proportion of the national income should be kept low and at a stable level so that the burden of interest payments on the debt does not grow at the expense of other public expenditure or higher taxes.
>
> Fiscal rules can therefore help to keep public spending and borrowing under control so that interest rates and taxes can be kept reasonably low.

What is monetary policy?

Monetary policy involves changes in the money supply and/or interest rate in an economy to influence the level of aggregate demand and economic activity. It is also used by a government to influence the exchange rate of its national currency against other foreign currencies and, in so doing, to affect the level of international trade and transactions.

The main instrument of monetary policy is the minimum lending rate or rate of interest charged by the central bank to loan money to the banking system in an economy. Raising or lowering the interest rate will affect the rate banks then charge to their business and personal customers to borrow money and the rate of interest savers earn on their savings accounts. ➤ 3.1

However, a government may also directly increase or decrease the money supply in an economy to help achieve its economic objectives.

Expansionary monetary policy

This involves a cut in interest rates and/or expansion in the money supply to boost aggregate demand. These measures will often be taken when unemployment is rising and economic growth is falling or has turned negative during an economic recession. ➤ 6.3

If interest rates are reduced, people and firms will be able to borrow money more cheaply than before from banks or by using their credit cards. Lower interest rates can also make saving money less attractive. Therefore, reducing interest rates in an economy can help to raise consumer expenditure on goods and services and increase investment expenditure by private sector firms. This can help boost output and employment opportunities.

Increasing the money supply in the economy will give people and firms more money to spend on goods and services. A government may do this by printing more notes and coins to circulate or by something called **quantitative easing**. This involves the government using newly created money to buy up financial assets held by banks, such as government and corporate bonds. Investing in bonds ties up money for many years but banks are willing to buy bonds issued by the government and private companies because they pay out an attractive interest rate when they mature. By buying these financial assets back from banks a government can increase the quantity of money banks have available to lend to people and firms. ➤ 3.1

▼ Quantitative easing can boost the money supply and aggregate demand

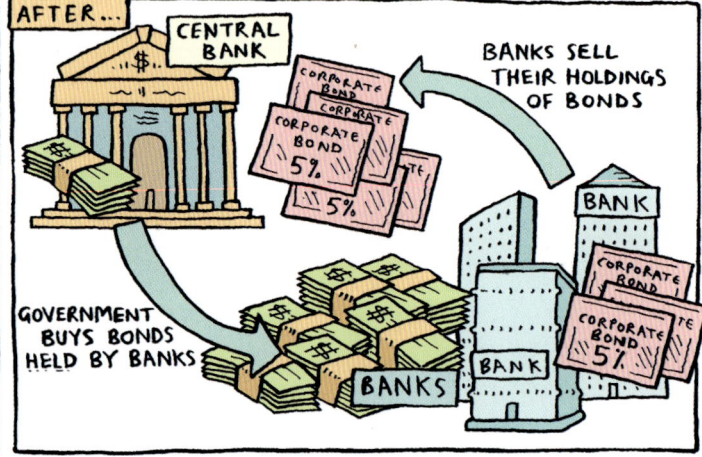

Many governments drastically cut their interest rates and used quantitative easing to try to boost activity in their economies following the global financial crisis in 2008 and deep economic recession that followed. ➤ 6.3

Contractionary monetary policy

This involves raising interest rates and/or cutting the money supply to reduce aggregate demand if the economy is overheating and inflationary pressures are rising. ➤ 6.1

Increasing interest rates will make borrowing more expensive. Reducing the quantity of money in the economy will also restrict the amount consumers and firms have to spend on goods and services. A government can do this by selling government bonds to banks at attractive interest rates. This will reduce the amount of money banks have available to lend.

However, falling aggregate demand may result in rising unemployment and if firms cut back their investment it can also hurt future economic growth.

Exchange rate policy

Changes in interest rates can be used to influence the exchange rate of a national currency. An exchange rate is the rate at which one currency can be exchanged for another on the foreign exchange market, for example how many Indian rupees can be exchanged for US dollars so residents of India can make payments in US dollars if they travel to the USA or import goods from US producers. That is, an exchange rate is the price of one currency in terms of another. ➤ **8.2**

If the exchange rate falls, for example if it costs more rupees to buy one US dollar, international transactions in US dollars for Indian residents will become more expensive. That is, the cost of goods imported from the USA will increase in India. This will have a negative impact on India's balance of international payments and its inflation rate. The Indian government may therefore increase the interest rate to raise the exchange rate of the rupee. As the interest rate in India rises relative to other countries wealthy residents from overseas may buy more rupees so they can save their money in Indian bank accounts. The increase in demand for rupees on the foreign exchange market will push up the price or exchange rate of the currency.

It follows that lowering the interest rate can reduce the exchange rate of a currency. This will reduce the cost to overseas residents of buying goods exported from that country. This can increase export earnings and boost output and employment.

ECONOMICS IN ACTION

What evidence is there that UK monetary policy between 2009 and 2011 was 'loose'? What was happening to UK fiscal policy at the same time and why? What risks do the articles raise about the policy mix being used by the UK government and why?

In May 2009 the Bank of England in the UK announced it was to introduce a series of measures aimed at increasing the supply of money in the economy.

Technically known as quantitative easing, the aim was to try to increase the amount of funds in the UK banking system. The hope was it would make it easier for the commercial banks to increase their lending levels.

At the same time the Bank also cut the interest rate to just 0.5%, the lowest it had been since the central bank was founded in 1694.

The Bank said increased quantitative easing was necessary as cutting rates would not be enough to help the UK economy out of recession.

In May 2011 the Monetary Policy Committee at the UK Bank of England voted to keep the official bank rate at just 0.5% and agreed it would continue to use quantitative easing to boost bank lending.

A number of economists argued that the UK economic policy mix was unbalanced. Fiscal policy was too tight and monetary policy was too loose. They were worried that the impact of deep cuts in public spending and increased taxes to reduce the budget deficit would harm the supply side of the economy while monetary policy was pumping too much money into the economy and could be inflationary.

> **EXAM PREPARATION 5.1**
>
> a Describe what is meant by a mixed economy. [4]
> b Explain **three** macro-economic aims a government might have. [6]
> c What is meant by a government's budget? [4]
> d Discuss how a government might finance its expenditure. [6]
>
> *Cambridge IGCSE Economics 0455/02 Q5 October/November 2009*
> *Cambridge O Level Economics 2281/02 Q5 October/November 2009*

SECTION 4 — Supply-side policies

ACTIVITY 5.3

A walk on the supply side

The articles below refer to some different supply-side policies. What are they and how do you think they can help to boost output and employment?

UK plans skills academies to close productivity gap

Workers are to be offered free vocational training as part of a huge government drive to tackle the chronic lack of basic skills among millions of adults, ministers are set to announce today.

The Pakistan Telecommunications Authority today found Mobilink, the country's leading cellular company, guilty of anti-competitive practices by overcharging its 'valued subscribers' for making calls to other cellular operators. The PTA has ordered Mobilink to make revisions to its tariffs.

Romania claims privatization in the energy sector was a step forward towards a healthy economy. New investors entering the energy market will bring substantial benefits to companies and the competition environment.

Milk market deregulation benefits Australian consumer

Six months after the deregulation of Australia's dairy industry, milk prices have fallen by as much as 40 cents a litre with the likelihood of further drops, said the Australian Competition and Consumer Commission (ACCC) this week.

New tax incentives finally approved

After months of back and forth, The European Commission has finally approved the UK's new film industry tax incentives. The new tax credit is expected to take effect from January 1st, and will benefit film-makers investing at least 25% of their budget in the UK.

Trade unions protest against anti-strike laws

Supply-side policies target economic growth: they are designed to the boost productive potential of an economy and increase the aggregate supply of goods and services. Expanding aggregate supply will help to reduce inflationary pressures on prices from rising aggregate demand, provide additional employment opportunities and boost the production of goods for exports. Over the long run, therefore, supply-side policies can help to achieve all the macroeconomic objectives of a government at the same time.

Supply-side policy instruments are used to influence the behaviours of different groups of consumers and producers, for example by increasing incentives to increase their effort and productivity, and to improve the efficiency of different markets by removing barriers to competition. ➤ **4.4**

Supply-side policy instruments

Supply-side policy instruments include the following.

Selective tax incentives

High rates of tax on personal incomes may reduce people's incentives to work hard or even to seek paid employment, expecially if they can expect more generous welfare payments if they are unemployed. Similarly, high rates of tax on profits can reduce the incentives of entrpreneurs to start new firms or to expand the scale of existing firms. Cutting taxes on earnings and profits can therefore have a positive impact on the productive efforts of workers and firms.

Granting reliefs from some taxes may also be used to encourage firms to invest in new plant and equipment to expand their productive potential. For example, many governments offer tax concessions against investments in the the research and development of new products and production processes, new technologically advanced equipment and in the provision of employee training. Firms that increase investments in these activties may be granted lower taxes on their profits and exemptions from import and other duties.

Selective subsidies

A **susbsidy** is a form of financial assistance paid to businesses or an economic sector by a government to help meet their costs. Subsidies can be used to expand output and reduce market price. For example, subsidies are often used to support farming, to fund investments in new technologies and to help small businesses to expand. Technological advance can increase the efficiency of production, lower costs and create new products to sell. ➤ **2.2**

Improving education and training

In order for firms to be successful when competing in international markets it is essential they have access to a highly trained and skilled workforce. Skill needs in industry are rising as the pace of change in global competition and technology increases. A well-educated and trained workforce can raise labour productivity and will be better able to adapt to new production methods and technologies. A government can assist firms by helping them design and finance training programmes, funding universities and providing access for more people to attend colleges and higher education.

Labour market reforms

Restrictions on the supply of labour to an occupation will force up the market wage and result in fewer jobs. Some governments have therefore introduced

▲ Tax incentives and subsidies can be used to encourage investments in productive capacity

Government economic policy | 291

laws and regulations to reduce the power of trade unions to take strike action and to demand unreasonable wage increases for their members. ➤ **3.3**

The payment of welfare benefits by a government to the unemployed may discourage some people from seeking paid employment. In some countries, benefits paid to the unemployed have therefore been reduced, are time limited and often linked to evidence that a person is actively seeking paid work or is in training. However, cutting payments to support people in unemployment may conflict with aims to reduce hardship and poverty that are often the result of long periods of joblessness. ➤ **6.2**

Some countries therefore also have laws on minimum wages to encourage more people into work. However, some firms argue that setting minimum wage levels too high will increase their costs and force them to cut jobs. ➤ **3.2**

Competition policy

Some firms may be large and powerful enough to control the market supply of a particular good or service. These firms are called monopolies. They may use their market power to restrict competition, charge high prices and earn excessive profits. Laws and regulations can be used to fine firms that are anti-competitive, to control their prices and even to force them to break up into smaller firms. ➤ **4.4**

Removing trade barriers

In much the same way as a monopoly, a national government may seek to protect its domestic firms and labour force from competition from producers overseas by using barriers against free trade. Some goods and services may be produced much more efficiently and at a far lower cost by firms overseas. However, a government may tax imports or simply restrict their entry into their country to protect domestic firms producing the same goods and services even if they do so at a higher cost. When these barriers to trade are removed, firms in other countries can expand by selling to many more consumers all over the world, and similarly those countries which previously restricted free trade can enjoy access to the cheapest and best sources of finished and unfinished goods, services, finance and new technologies from anywhere in the world. ➤ **8.1**

Privatization

Privatization involves the transfer of public sector activities, such as refuse collection, running a prison or public transport services, to private firms who may be able to provide them more efficiently because they have a motive to make a profit from these activities. If private firms can deliver public services at a lower cost and better quality than the public sector then consumers will benefit and taxes can be lowered. However, some people argue the profit motive of private sector firm's results in cuts in service levels and hikes in prices.

Regulation and deregulation

Regulations are rules and laws that restrict certain activities, such as shop opening hours and limits on noise and pollution levels, or set standards for products and for hygiene and safety in work places. ➤ **2.1**

For example, regulations are often used to:

- protect key industries and businesses from unfair competition
- protect employment and the rights of employees to fair treatment and to work in a healthy and safe environment
- protect consumers from misleading advertising, harmful products, powerful businesses and dishonest business practices
- protect the environment and reduce harmful emissions to limit climate change.

In some cases, new or toughened laws and regulations can increase production costs. For example, firms may have to employ additional staff and invest in new equipment, such as protective clothing, and install guards around machinery and filters to reduce dust and other pollutants to ensure that they comply with health and safety laws. These additional costs will reduce profits and a firm may offset them, for example, by cutting some jobs and production.

In contrast, some firms may benefit from new regulations. For example, global manufacturers of helmets for motorcycle riders, such as Arai Helmets of Japan, HJC in the USA and Zhejiang Jixiang Motorcycle Fittings Co. Ltd. in China, enjoyed increased sales following the introduction of laws in many countries making the wearing of crash helmets compulsory.

An increasing number of countries are also introducing targets for renewable energy. They want their power generating companies to generate more electricity from solar, wind and other forms of renewable energy installations than from coal and oil-fired power stations. This means they must change the way they produce electricity in future by investing in renewable energy installations, such as wind turbine farms. To do so, these companies may have to borrow more to invest which will increase their costs. However, manufacturers of wind turbines, such as Vestas Wind Systems in Denmark, now the market leader, Sinovel Wind Co. in China and Suzlon Ltd. in India, are enjoying rapid growth in their sales and profits and, as a result, are expanding their operations and creating more output and jobs in their economies.

Complying with regulations can be costly for firms and uses up management and employee time that could otherwise be put to more productive use. Public sector resources also need to be used up checking that firms are complying with regulations. **Deregulation** therefore helps to remove burdens on business, reduce production costs and free up resources by simplfying or removing old and unnecessary regulations. For example, reforms in some countries have included removing restrictions on shop opening hours, reducing requirements for product labelling and information and enabling firms to complete their tax returns, applications for patents and other paperwork required by government electronically over the Internet.

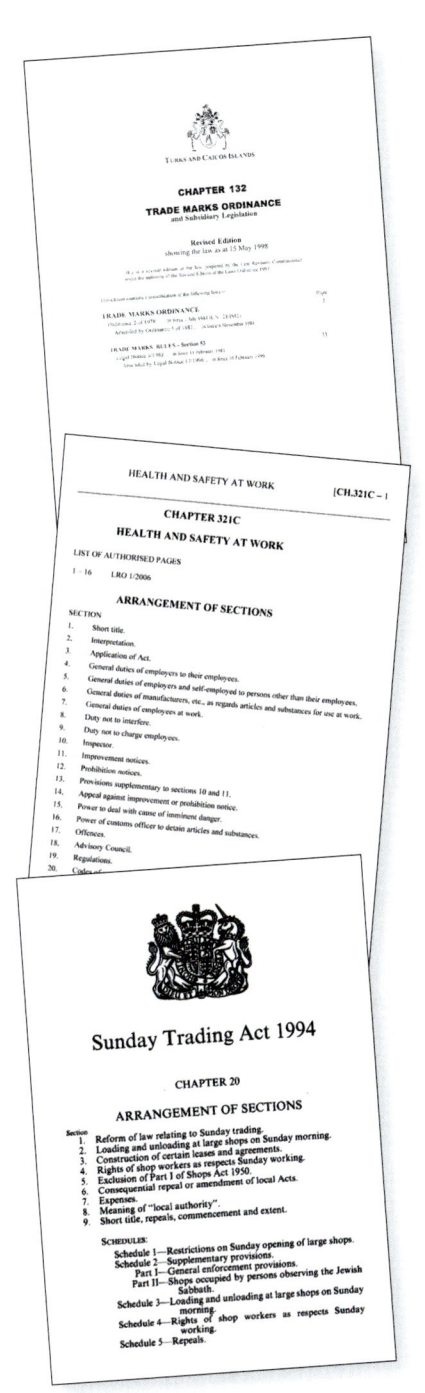

▲ Too much regulation is a burden on business. Simplifying or removing obsolete rules and laws is called deregulation

Government economic policy

ACTIVITY 5.4

Public or private provision?

Lee plans meeting on water-sewer privatization

There is to be a special informational meeting on the potential privatization of the town's sewer and water systems. Privatization means that the local government would hire a private company to take over the operation of its sewer and water systems.

The company would be under contract to the town of Lee, and would run the two systems under one company umbrella. The principal reason for such a move would be to save money and improve service levels. At this point, most town officials concede that it is unclear whether privatizing the sewer and water operation would be a money-saver. A consulting engineer would, in theory, be able to make that assessment.

However, many residents fear the principal task of the private sector firm would be making money for itself and have asked town officials how they would be able to ensure consistent quality service from a profit-making entity.

But perhaps the most controversial aspect of the plan is that the present workforce would all have to reapply for their jobs. Many workers have argued that there was no way to ensure they would get the same health and retirement benefits they currently do as public employees of Lee. In addition, the for-profit entity would not be bound to retain the workforce presently under contract to the town.

1. What is privatization?
2. How is the town of Lee planning to privatize its water and sewer systems?
3. What economic arguments does the article highlight for and against the privatization of Lee's water and sewer systems?
4. What are the likely implications and conflicts arising from the privatization for the employees, local residents and local taxpayers?
5. Investigate examples of privatization in your own country. What arguments have different groups of people used for and against these privatizations? What impact, if any, has privatization had on you and your family?

SECTION 5

Slower inflation or lower employment?

Policy conflicts

The macroeconomic objectives of a government can prove difficult to achieve all at once. In some cases policy aims might conflict. For example, some policy measures to reduce unemployment and boost economic growth may result in higher rates of price inflation.

Measures to increase aggregate demand during an economic recession might raise output and employment in an economy but may boost consumer demand for imports and therefore make the balance of international payments less favourable. Faster economic growth in the national output may also create more pollution and waste, possibly conflicting with any environmental objectives.

Similarly, raising taxes or interest rates, and cutting public expenditure to reduce price inflation by lowering total demand, may result in lower output and more unemployment. The impact of higher taxes and lower public spending may also fall heavily on people on lower incomes in the economy, especially if welfare benefits to people who are unemployed or on low incomes are cut back.

Who should pay higher taxes?

In the same way, policies that directly aim to redistribute income may also cause conflict between different groups in society. For example, taxes on high-income households may be raised and the tax revenues used to pay for increased benefits to very low-income families. Alternatively, taxes on business profits could be raised but this may conflict with an objective to encourage more people to start their own firms and an aim to attract overseas firms to invest in the economy.

Do policy objectives have to conflict?

However, not all economists accept there will always be trade-offs between government objectives. That is, they see no reason why low taxes, low rates of unemployment and high economic growth can only be achieved at the expense of low price inflation, a favourable international trade balance and reduced poverty in society. Government policies, they argue, can and should be designed to achieve all these aims at the same time by combining sound fiscal management of public spending and taxes with sensible supply-side policies.

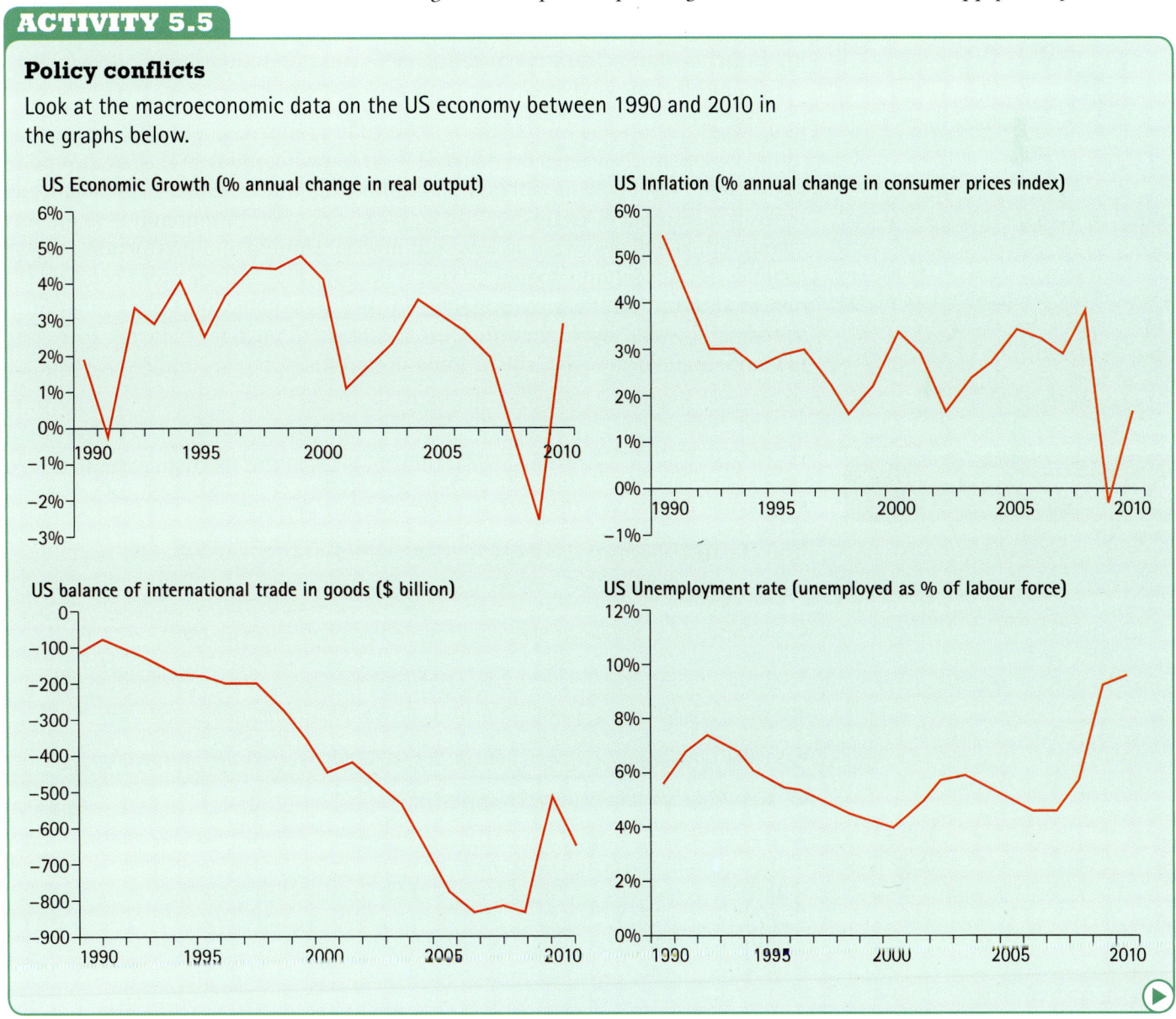

ACTIVITY 5.5

Policy conflicts

Look at the macroeconomic data on the US economy between 1990 and 2010 in the graphs below.

US Economic Growth (% annual change in real output)

US Inflation (% annual change in consumer prices index)

US balance of international trade in goods ($ billion)

US Unemployment rate (unemployed as % of labour force)

Government economic policy

1. How successful do you think US governments have been over time in achieving the four main macroeconomic objectives?
2. What evidence is there, if any, from the US economic experience to support the view that economic policy objectives may conflict?
3. Compare and contrast the US economic experience with that of your country over the same period. How successful do you think the national government in your country has been in achieving its macroeconomic aims, and why?

If price inflation can be reduced to a low and stable rate then more employment, faster economic growth and a favourable balance of payments can be achieved. Rising national income and employment also means people will become better off, thereby helping to reduce poverty. Rising incomes will also mean tax revenues collected by the government from wages and profits will be increasing and can be used to fund higher welfare payments, investments in new infrastructure such as roads and schools, and other public expenditures that will benefit the economy and growth.

Reducing inflation will help make domestically produced goods and services more competitive. As a result, demand for them will tend to rise at home and in overseas markets. This will help to improve the international trade balance. Firms will respond to rising demand by increasing their output and demand for labour. Firms will also want to invest in new machinery and production facilities as the economy expands. This is because they will be more confident of a good return on their investments. Further, if people expect price inflation to remain low and stable then they are less likely to push for big wage increases to compensate. If they did, this would raise production costs and reduce profits.

WEBSITES

Learn more about government economic policies at the following websites:

- www.britannica.com/EBchecked/topic/208363/fiscal-policy
- www.economicshelp.org/macroeconomics/fiscal-policy/fiscal_policy.html
- www.en.wikipedia.org/wiki/Monetary_policy
- www.bized.co.uk/learn/economics/govpol/macropolicies/index.htm
- www.tutor2u.net/economics/content/topics/macroeconomy/macroeconomics.htm
- www.tutor2u.net/economics/content/topics/supplyside/labour_policies.htm
- www.tutor2u.net/economics/content/topics/supplyside/product_markets.htm
- http://rru.worldbank.org/privatization

KEYWORDS

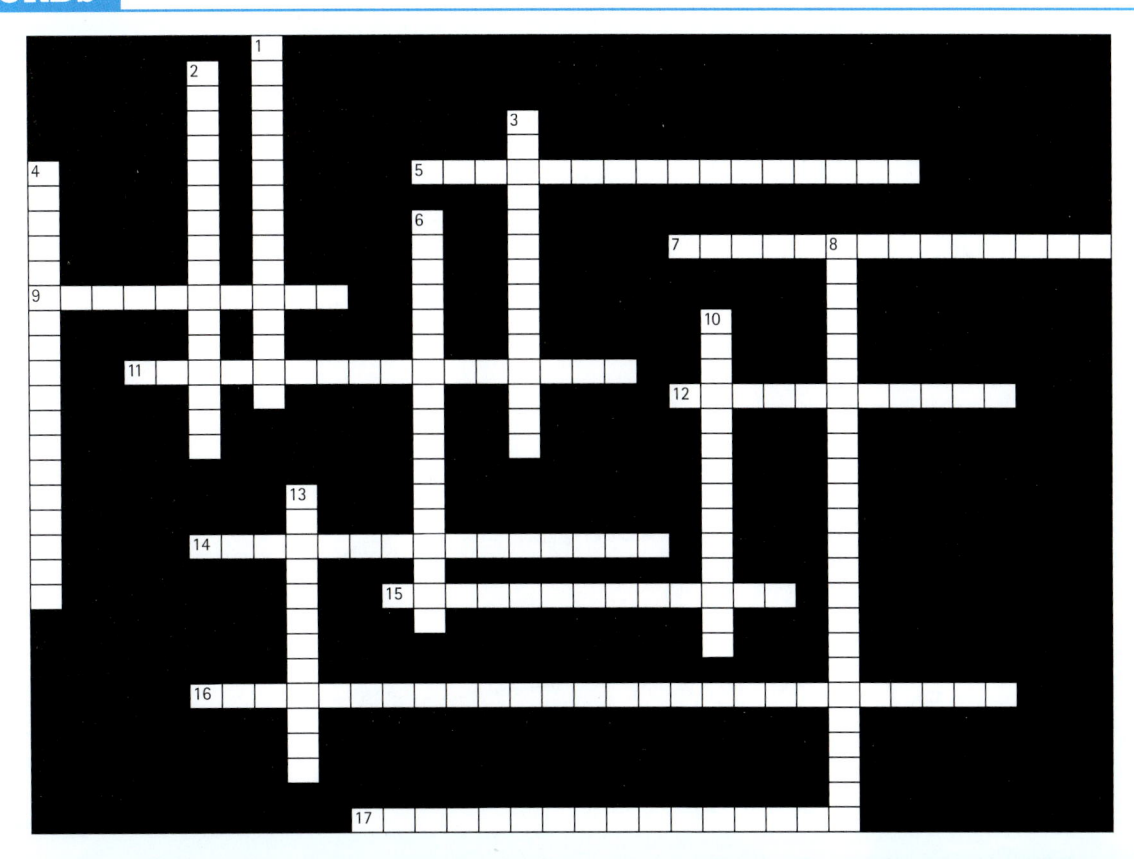

Clues across

5. Money that a government gives to individuals, usually through a social welfare programme, for example, disability allowances and old-age pensions (8, 8)
7. The study of how a national economy works. It involves understanding the interactions between total demand and output and national income, employment and price inflation (14)
9. The purchase of productive assets by firms (10)
11. A government policy designed to manage aggregate demand in the economy in order to control the level of price inflation, employment and output (6, 4, 6)
12. The displacement of private sector borrowing and therefore expenditure by increased public sector borrowing and spending. This is because the interest rate is increased as government borrowing rises (8, 3)
14. The total output or supply of all goods and services in an economy that all producers are willing and able to supply (9, 6)
15. A policy of transferring public sector activities to private sector firms who, because they have a profit motive, may be able to provide them more efficiently than public sector organizations (13)
16. A government policy that involves cutting public expenditure and/or increasing total taxation to reduce aggregate demand if the general level of prices is rising rapidly in the economy (12, 6, 6)
17. A government policy designed to improve the productive capacity of an economy (6, 4, 6)

Clues down

1. The total demand for goods and services in an economy. It is determined by consumer spending, investment, public expenditure and spending by overseas residents on exports (9, 6)
2. A tool a government can use, such as public expenditure, tax, the interest rate or a regulation, to help achieve its economic objectives (6, 10)
3. A government demand-side policy that involves changes in the interest rate or supply of money in an economy to manage the overall level of economic activity (8, 6)
4. A monetary policy action designed to boost the quantity of money held by banks during an economic downturn so they can boost their lending. It involves the central bank buying financial assets from banks (12, 6)
6. The amount of money spent in total by government organizations. It includes spending on recurrent items such as public sector wages and capital items, including investments in public infrastructure such as roads (6, 11)
8. A government policy that involves expanding public expenditure and/or cutting total taxation to boost aggregate demand during downturn in economic activity (12, 6, 6)
10. The study of the market behaviour of individual producers and consumers and therefore how different markets work (14)
13. The reform or removal of complex, old or even unnecessary regulations to reduce burdens on business (12)

Government economic policy

Unit 5.2   Taxation

AIMS

By the end of this unit you should be able to:

▶ describe the types of taxation (**direct**, **indirect**, **progressive**, **regressive**, **proportional**) and the impact of taxation

- access the impact and incidence of different taxes
- understand how taxes are used to finance public expenditures, redistribute income and influence the behaviours of consumers and producers in different markets to achieve a range of microeconomic objectives.

SECTION 1

Sources of public sector revenue

Financing public expenditure

Public spending as proportion of total final expenditure in many economies has risen over time. However, there is wide variation between countries. For example, in 2011 government spending in Zimbabwe was over 97% of total expenditure in the Zimbabwean economy while in Burma, the government was accountable for just 8% of Burmese total expenditure.

The chart below shows how public spending as a proportion of total expenditure on total output, or GDP, has varied over time in the 34 major economies that are members of the Organization for Economic Cooperation and Development (OECD). Public expenditure as a proportion of the GDP of these economies fell during the 1990s to a low of around 39% in 1999. During this period many economies were enjoying healthy economic growth. However, the proportion of total spending attributable to the public sector grew rapidly between 2007 and 2009 as many governments employed expansionary fiscal policies in an attempt to boost demand, employment and output in their economies during the global financial crisis and economic downturn. ▶ **6.3**

▼ Public expenditure as a percentage of GDP, OECD average 1993–2011

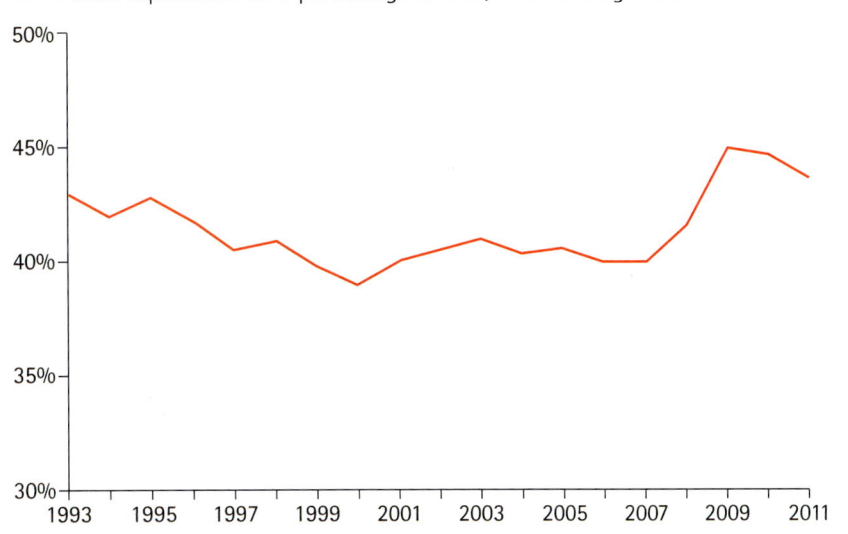

Source: 'Public expenditure as a percentage of GDP, OECD average 1993-2011', reproduced from OECD Statistics, www.oecd.org, copyright © OECD 2011

As public expenditure rises a government must raise more revenue to pay for it. This can be done in a number of ways, for example through:

- borrowing money from the private sector
- interest payments on government loans to private sector firms and overseas governments
- rents from publicly owned buildings and land rented to the private sector and any admission charges, for example from public museums and national monuments
- revenues from government agencies and public corporations that sell goods or services, such as postal services and public transport
- proceeds from the sale (or privatization) of government-owned industries and other publicly owned assets, such as land and public buildings
- taxes on incomes, wealth and expenditures.

Taxation

The tax burden

Taxes are by far the most important source of public sector revenue. Not surprisingly, therefore, as public expenditures around the world have risen over time as the proportion of total expenditure so too has the tax burden.

▼ Total taxation as a percentage of GDP, selected countries 2010

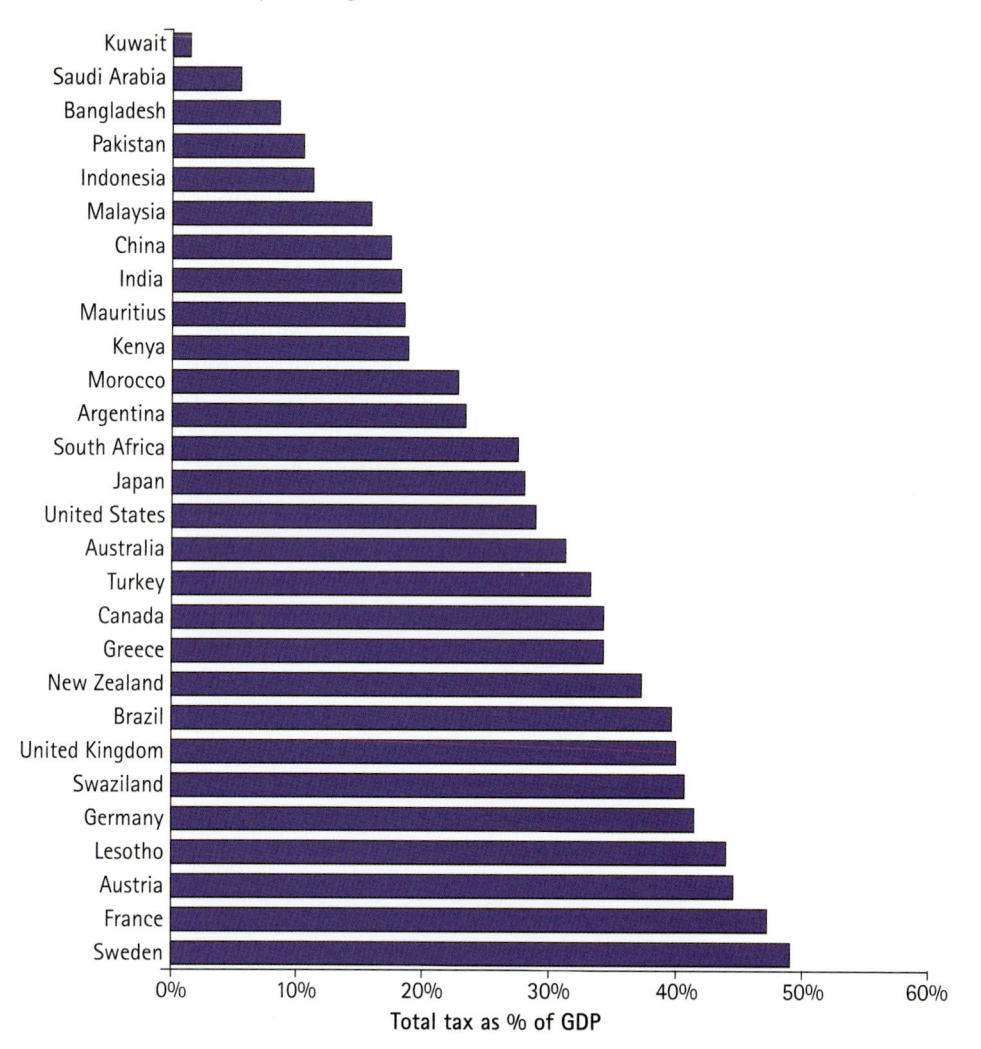

Country	Total tax as % of GDP
Kuwait	~1%
Saudi Arabia	~5%
Bangladesh	~8%
Pakistan	~10%
Indonesia	~11%
Malaysia	~15%
China	~17%
India	~18%
Mauritius	~18%
Kenya	~19%
Morocco	~22%
Argentina	~23%
South Africa	~27%
Japan	~28%
United States	~29%
Australia	~31%
Turkey	~33%
Canada	~34%
Greece	~34%
New Zealand	~37%
Brazil	~39%
United Kingdom	~40%
Swaziland	~40%
Germany	~41%
Lesotho	~43%
Austria	~44%
France	~47%
Sweden	~49%

Source: Heritage Foundation

The proportion of tax taken from the national income of an economy measures the total **tax burden** in that national economy. Individuals and firms also have personal or corporate tax burdens measured by the amount of tax they each have to pay as a proportion of their incomes. Tax burdens can vary greatly between different individuals, firms and countries depending on the design of their tax systems.

Tax evasion and avoidance

Taxes are compulsory payments backed by laws. Non-payment of tax, or tax evasion, is a punishable offence.

Some taxes can, however, be avoided legally. For example, taxes on cars or petroleum can be avoided by not owning or driving a car. Taxes on cigarettes can be avoided by not smoking. Similarly, wealthy people and multinational companies can avoid taxes in one country by moving their wealth to countries with lower tax rates.

ACTIVITY 5.6

Why have taxes?

For each of the images below suggest reasons why a government might impose taxes. What impacts could such taxes have on economic activity?

Many taxes were first introduced many hundreds of years ago by kings or governments to pay for wars. For example, the US federal government in 1862 introduced an income tax for the first time to pay for the Civil War. It was 3% of incomes above $600, rising to 5% of incomes above $10,000. Today, the reasons for taxes are far more complex.

- **Taxes raise revenue to fund public expenditures.** Taxes are the main way of raising money to finance public sector spending in most economies.

- **Taxes are used to manage the macroeconomy.** For example, a contractionary fiscal policy involves raising taxes to reduce aggregate demand and therefore inflationary pressures in an economy. Cutting taxes during an economic recession can help boost aggregate demand, and therefore output and employment. ➤ **5.1**

America's soft drinks industry battles proposals to tax sugary sodas

'Increasing taxes on drinks with high sugar content is the most effective way to reduce consumption' argue researchers at Yale University. They estimate a new tax would reduce the medical costs of treating obesity and dental problems by $50 billion and raise $150 billion in tax revenue in a decade.

However, powerful drinks manufacturers have argued their products should not be singled out over other food products with high sugar content. 'Taxing our industry more will simply harm jobs and people's livelihoods', argued a spokesperson for the industry.

- **Taxes can reduce inequalities in income.** High incomes can be taxed more than lower ones to reduce inequalities between after-tax incomes.

- **Taxes can discourage spending on imported goods.** A tax or tariff on the prices of goods purchased from producers overseas can encourage consumers to buy domestically produced goods instead. This will reduce a balance of payments deficit and boost indigenous output and employment. ➤ **8.1**

- **Taxes can discourage the consumption and production of harmful products.** For example, taxes are used to raise the prices of products such as alcohol and tobacco so that demand for them contracts. ➤ **2.1**

Taxation

India introduces carbon tax on coal producers

A tax of 50 rupees a metric ton will apply to coal to increase the cost of coal-fired electricity generation relative to other, cleaner energy sources.

The European Union, South Korea and Japan also have plans to tax harmful carbon-dioxide emissions from burning fuels such as coal and oil to slow down climate change.

- **Taxes can be used to protect the environment.** Increased taxes on productive activities that create pollution or harm the natural environment will reduce the profits associated with these activities. For example, taxes on landfill can encourage firms to recycle more of their waste by making dumping waste in landfill sites more expensive. Similarly, taxes on products that pollute or harm the environment can deter consumption of them. For example, many countries tax petrol to cut car use and harmful exhaust emissions. ➤ 2.3

ACTIVITY 5.7

When is a tax a good tax?

Look at the imaginary taxes proposed below. For each one consider whether or not it is a good tax or a bad tax from the point of view of:

▶ the taxpayer
▶ the government
▶ the economy.

- Overtime to be taxed at 95 per cent of earnings.
- New tax office set up at an annual cost of $15 million to administer tax on pet cats. The government expects its cat tax to raise $7 million in revenue each year.
- Tax system to be simplified! All taxes to be abolished and to be replaced by equal tax payment of $2 000 per person per year over the age of 18 years.
- Pay-as-you-earn income tax to be abolished. Tax-payers will receive bills every two years.
- Height tax to be introduced on all people under 5 feet and over 6 feet tall, says Minister of Finance, who is 5 feet 6 inches, in his Budget speech.

What is a good tax?

A good tax should designed with the following principles in mind.

1 Equity

This means taxes should be fair and tax taxpayers with similar characteristics, such as firms with similar levels of profits in the same industry or people earning the same incomes, in broadly the same way. This could also mean taxing people and firms according to their ability to pay. If most people think that a tax is unfair, they are unlikely to pay it. For example, a tax based on height would be very unfair.

2 Non-distortionary

As far as possible, taxes used to raise revenue should not affect or distort sensible economic behaviour. For example, taxes on incomes and profits should not be set so high as to discourage enterprise or people from working.

3 Certainty

People and firms should know when a tax should be paid and how much they should pay. Tax rates should also be relatively stable from year to year and should not be subject to sudden fluctuations. This allows people and firms to know broadly how much tax they will need to pay in the future and to plan their finances accordingly.

ACTIVITY 5.8

Window tax: daylight robbery or a smashing idea?

Government proposes new tax

Only a month after the last budget, the Government last night announced plans to once again broaden the existing tax base in the economy. Such plans include imposing a flat rate tax on the number and size of windows in a property.

Speaking at a meeting of industrialists, the Finance Minister told delegates that the issue of reducing the amount of Government borrowing must not be 'glazed over' and that if the public wished for public sector provision to remain at a high level then they must be prepared to provide the necessary funds.

Raising taxes on income and expenditure would only further reduce demand and output in the economy as work incentives and consumption plans would be damaged.

Business owners speculating that double glazed windows may be subject to a higher rate of tax have argued that such a move may seriously damage this particular growth area. The Government was, however, quick to reject such fears.

A study of the feasibility of the tax should be ready in time for next year's budget that already promises to provide the economy with a major tax shake up.

Divide into groups of three or four. Imagine you have been appointed to research and report on the feasibility of the proposed window tax. You are to write your report assessing the tax on the following grounds:

a Fairness
b The effect on consumption expenditure, output and employment
c The cost of collection
d The ease with which the tax payable can be calculated.

Your completed reports can form the basis of a class discussion. (You may be surprised to learn that a window tax did exist in the UK many years ago but has long since been abolished.)

4 Convenience

It must be simple and easy for people and firms to pay the taxes they owe on a regular basis. For example, income taxes are often collected by employers every month from the wages and salaries of their employees. People and firms can now also pay their taxes online in many countries using their debit or credit card, or electronic bank account transfers. A government will also need to receive tax revenues on a regular basis to pay for its recurrent expenditures.

5 Simplicity

Taxes should be easy to understand. If they are too complex people and firms may find it difficult to calculate how much tax they owe and could keep getting it wrong.

6 Administrative efficiency

Taxes should be cheap and easy to collect. There is little point introducing a tax if it costs more money to collect than it earns in revenue. For example, a tax costing $10 million to collect but only bringing in $3 million in revenue would be pointless and a waste of public money.

SECTION 2

Designing a tax system

Tax systems

All of the taxes in a country are together called its tax system. Governments must decide whether they want a progressive, regressive or proportional tax system. Each type of system will affect people and firms differently.

In a **progressive tax** system the proportion of income taken in tax rises as income increases. This means people or firms with higher incomes pay a higher proportion of their income in tax than those on lower incomes. Governments use progressive taxation because they feel those on higher incomes can afford to pay a larger proportion of their incomes in tax and to reduce income inequality after tax.

▼ An example of a progressive tax system

Annual income	% tax rate	Tax paid
$20,000	20%	$4,000
$50,000	40%	$20,000
$80,000	60%	$48,000

In a **regressive tax** system the proportion of income paid in tax falls as income rises. It may be considered unfair to people or firms with low incomes because a much larger fraction of their income is taken as tax although they will in total pay less tax than those on higher incomes.

▼ An example of a regressive tax system

Annual income	% tax rate	Tax paid
$20,000	50%	$10,000
$50,000	40%	$20,000
$80,000	30%	$24,000

A **proportional tax** takes the same proportion of income whatever the level of income. For example, a tax of 20% on all income is an example of a proportional tax. For this reason a proportional tax may also be referred to as a flat tax.

ACTIVITY 5.9

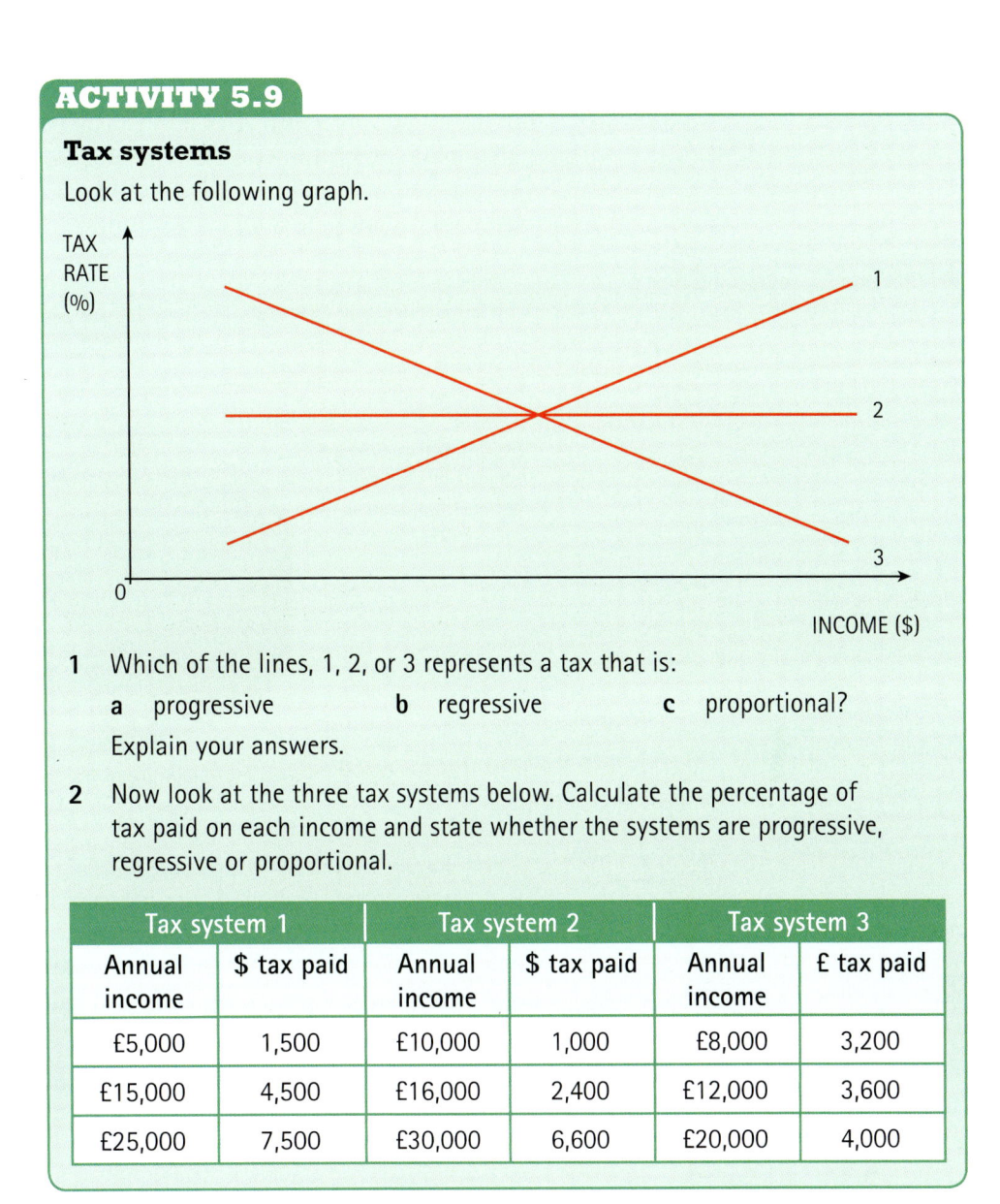

Tax systems

Look at the following graph.

1. Which of the lines, 1, 2, or 3 represents a tax that is:

   a progressive   b regressive   c proportional?

   Explain your answers.

2. Now look at the three tax systems below. Calculate the percentage of tax paid on each income and state whether the systems are progressive, regressive or proportional.

Tax system 1		Tax system 2		Tax system 3	
Annual income	$ tax paid	Annual income	$ tax paid	Annual income	£ tax paid
£5,000	1,500	£10,000	1,000	£8,000	3,200
£15,000	4,500	£16,000	2,400	£12,000	3,600
£25,000	7,500	£30,000	6,600	£20,000	4,000

Direct and indirect taxation

In economics there are two main types of taxes: direct taxes and indirect taxes. Their meaning in law in different countries can differ from how we define these taxes in economics.

Direct taxes are taken directly from individuals or firms and their incomes or wealth. That is, the burden of a direct tax falls on the person or firm responsible for paying it. Direct taxes include income taxes, corporation taxes on company profits, capital gains taxes on property and other valuable assets, and inheritance taxes.

Indirect taxes are taxes taken only indirectly from incomes when they are spent on goods and services. Indirect taxes are therefore sometimes called expenditure or outlay taxes. They include sales taxes, ad valorem taxes, and tariffs and excise duties added to the price of goods and services.

An indirect tax will normally be imposed on producers but they will pass on as much of the burden of the tax as possible to consumers through higher prices.

An indirect tax will increase a firms variable costs of production and therefore cause an upward shift in the firms supply curve. This means less will be supplied at each price and market price will rise. ▶ 2.2

Taxation

The chart below shows what proportion of total tax revenue was raised from different taxes in South Africa in the 2010–11 financial year. Direct taxes on personal incomes and corporate profits raised the most revenue followed by value added tax (VAT) on goods and services. The same pattern can be observed in many developed economies.

▶ Revenue by source and type of tax, South Africa 2010–11

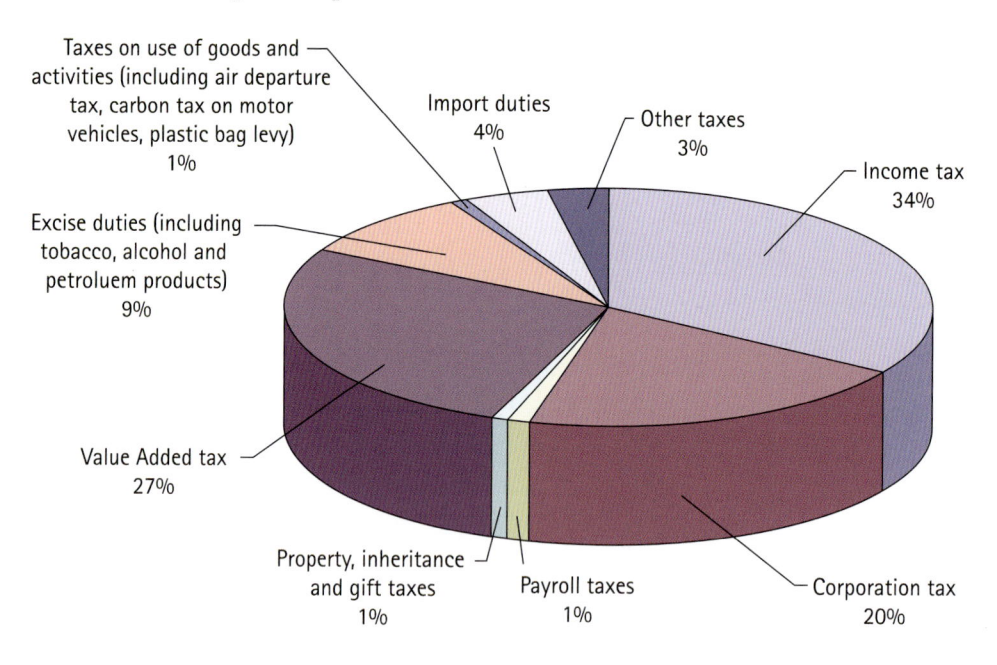

- Taxes on use of goods and activities (including air departure tax, carbon tax on motor vehicles, plastic bag levy) 1%
- Import duties 4%
- Other taxes 3%
- Income tax 34%
- Excise duties (including tobacco, alcohol and petroleum products) 9%
- Value Added tax 27%
- Property, inheritance and gift taxes 1%
- Payroll taxes 1%
- Corporation tax 20%

Most taxes are set, or levied, as a percentage (the **tax rate**) of a certain value (the **tax base**). Tax rates can vary significantly from country to country. The table below compares rates of income tax on personal earnings, corporation tax rates on large company profits and value added tax on the prices of many goods and services in a number of different countries.

Notice how similar the corporation tax rates are in many countries. This is because many large companies today are internationally mobile and can relocate their production facilities quite easily anywhere in the world. A country which taxes profits too highly risks losing companies to countries that offer much lower tax rates on profits. Some countries such as Ireland, Romania and Serbia, among others, clearly offer low corporation taxes to attract foreign multinational companies to locate in them. ▶ **4.1**

Personal income tax rates vary rather more, and often rise progressively with income, in Austria and the UK up to 50% of additional income. In contrast, personal incomes, including all forms of salary and capital gains, are not subject to tax in any of the United Arab Emirates.

Similarly, corporation taxes on profits are zero rated in the United Arab Emirates except those for foreign banks. In 2011, foreign banks were taxed at 20% of their taxable income in the Emirates of Abu Dhabi, Dubai, Sharjah and Fujairah. The tax is restricted to the taxable income that is earned in each Emirate. Oil companies also pay tax of 55% on their operating profits.

Role of government in an economy

▼ Main corporate, income and VAT rates, selected countries 2010–11

Country	Corporation tax rate %	Personal income tax rate%	VAT (or sales tax) rate %
Austria	25	0–50	20
Brazil	34	7.5–27.5	17–25
China	25	5–45	17
Croatia	20	15–45	23
Finland	26	6.5–30	23
France	33.33	5.5–40	19.6
Greece	23	0–40	23
India	30–40	10–30	12.5
Ireland	12.5	20–41	21
Kenya	30	10–30	16
Malta	35	15–35	18
Romania	16	16	24
Serbia	10	10–20	18
Spain	30	24–45	18
Turkey	20	15–35	18
United Kingdom	28	0–50	20
United Arab Emirates	0	0	0

Source: www.worldwide-tax.com

National and local taxes

Most taxes are levied by national governments to pay for public expenditures and to help control the macroeconomy. However, regional and local government authorities also spend money to provide local public services. Many receive the bulk of their money in grants from their national governments but some countries also allow local governments to levy their own taxes to raise revenue from local residents and businesses.

There are many examples of local tax systems in the world. For example, in Sweden municipal and county governments can raise money from local income taxes. Tax rates can vary by area and are paid in addition to the national income tax.

Similarly, in the USA each state has its own tax system in addition to national taxes. Local taxes usually include taxes on property, income taxes and sales taxes on the prices of goods and services. Some states, including Alaska, New Hampshire, Florida and Washington, do not levy local income taxes. US cities and counties may also levy additional taxes, for instance to pay directly for the upkeep of parks or schools, or for a police and fire service, local roads and other services. Local taxes on hotel rooms are also common.

Local governments in China can also impose local taxes, including taxes on property, taxes on business turnover and even a slaughter tax on the value of meat from slaughtered animals.

Taxation

▲ Occupied farm land, the use of rare earth minerals and banquets, among many other items and activities, are taxable in China

EXAM PREPARATION 5.2

a   Using examples, describe the difference between direct and indirect taxes. [4]

b   How might a reduction in taxation help any **two** macro-economic aims of a government? [6]

c   Why might a government wish to increase employment opportunities? [5]

d   Discuss what might be the consequences of unemployment. [5]

Cambridge IGCSE Economics 0455/04 Q5 May/June 2008
Cambridge O Level Economics 2281/02 Q5 May/June 2008

SECTION 3

Personal income tax

Direct taxes

Personal **income tax** is a tax payable from an individual's earnings usually on a pay-as-you-earn basis. Most countries allow people to earn a certain amount of income that is tax free, usually known as a personal allowance. For example, in the UK in 2011–12 a single person could earn up to £7,475 each year, up to £9,940 if aged between 65 and 74, or £10,090 if over 75 years old, before having to pay any tax on their income above these thresholds.

Exactly how much tax a person pays in income tax will depend on how much they earn and in some cases their personal circumstances, for example whether they are single, married, with or without children, old and retired. Income tax in many countries is a progressive tax. That is, higher **marginal tax rates** are applied to progressively higher slices or parts of a person's income. A marginal tax rate is therefore the percentage taken from the next dollar of taxable income above a pre-defined income threshold. The rate may differ for different groups of people. For example, tax free allowances and marginal rates of tax tend to be more generous for old people and for people with children so that they pay less tax overall than a person who earns the same amount but is single and has no children.

It is useful to distinguish between the average tax rate a person pays and their marginal tax rate. The average tax rate is the total amount of tax paid by a person divided by their total income. The marginal tax rate is the rate of tax paid on an additional slice of income. A person could therefore pay many different marginal rates of tax on their income, especially if they earn a high income. By adding up the amount of tax paid on each additional slide of income the average tax rate can be calculated.

Role of government in an economy

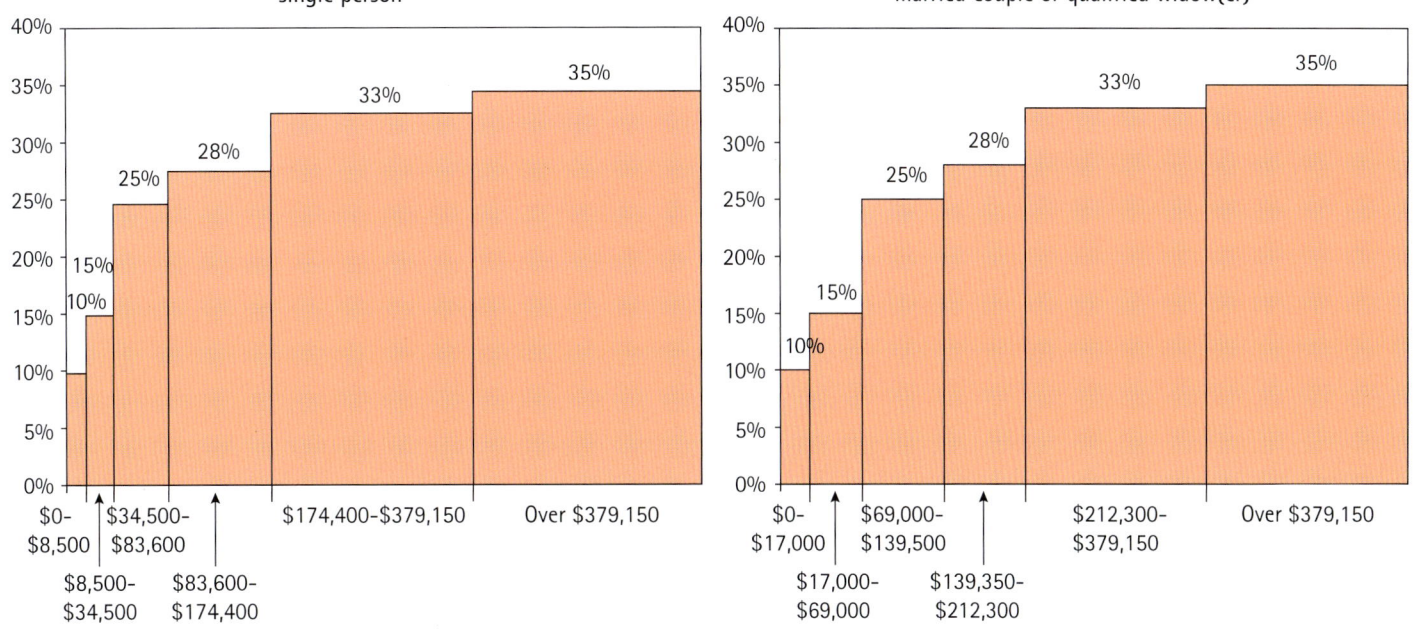

▲ US national income tax structure, 2011–12

For example, the diagram above shows the US federal income tax system in 2011–12. It had six marginal tax rates, rising from 10% to 35%, applied to six different income tax bands. The highest marginal tax rate of 35% applied only to that part of a single person's or married couple's annual income over and above $379,150.

So, a single person living in the USA earning $50,000 a year will pay a marginal rate of tax of 25% on the top slice of their income over $34,500, but overall will pay an average rate of tax of 17.45%. This is calculated as follows.

▼ US marginal and average income tax rates for a single person earning $100,000 per year

Slices of income up to $100,000 per year	Marginal tax rate % (A)	Amount of income marginal tax rate is applied to (B)	Amount of tax paid $ (A × B)
$0–$8,500	10	$8,550	850
$8,500.01–$34,500	15	$25,999.99	3,900
$34,500.01–$83,600	25	$15,499.99	3,875
Average tax rate % = $\frac{\$8,725}{\$50,000} \times 100 = 17.45\%$		Total income: $50,000	Total tax: $8,725

Income tax is a payroll tax that employers are required to withhold from the wages of salaries of their employees each week or month. Employees will therefore receive their wages or salaries net of tax deducted. Employers will then pay the income tax they have collected to the government's tax authority. People who are self-employed must provide evidence of their annual earnings and will pay their income tax direct to the government usually in a lump sum once or twice each year.

Employer payroll taxes

Other payroll taxes exist in many countries, for example social security contributions to meet the cost of welfare benefits and old-age pensions provided by government, levies to pay for public health care and unemployment insurance to pay towards unemployment benefits. These payroll taxes are often based on an individual's earnings but may be payable from an employer's own funds as well as by an employee. Payroll taxes that have to be paid from an employer's own funds are often called employment taxes because they increase the cost of employing workers.

International comparisons of personal tax burdens

Each year the Organization for Economic Cooperation and Development (OECD) adds together income taxes and social security contributions payable in different countries to make international comparisons of personal tax burdens on wage income. The charts show that average tax rates paid by people with children are generally lower worldwide than average tax rates paid by single people on the same level of income. However, average tax rates vary widely. The average tax rate for single people in Belgium in 2009–10 was over 41% of their average earnings, while a single person in Mexico paid just over 5%. A married person with two children on average earnings in the USA paid just over 5% on average in income tax and social security contributions compared to over 30% in Austria.

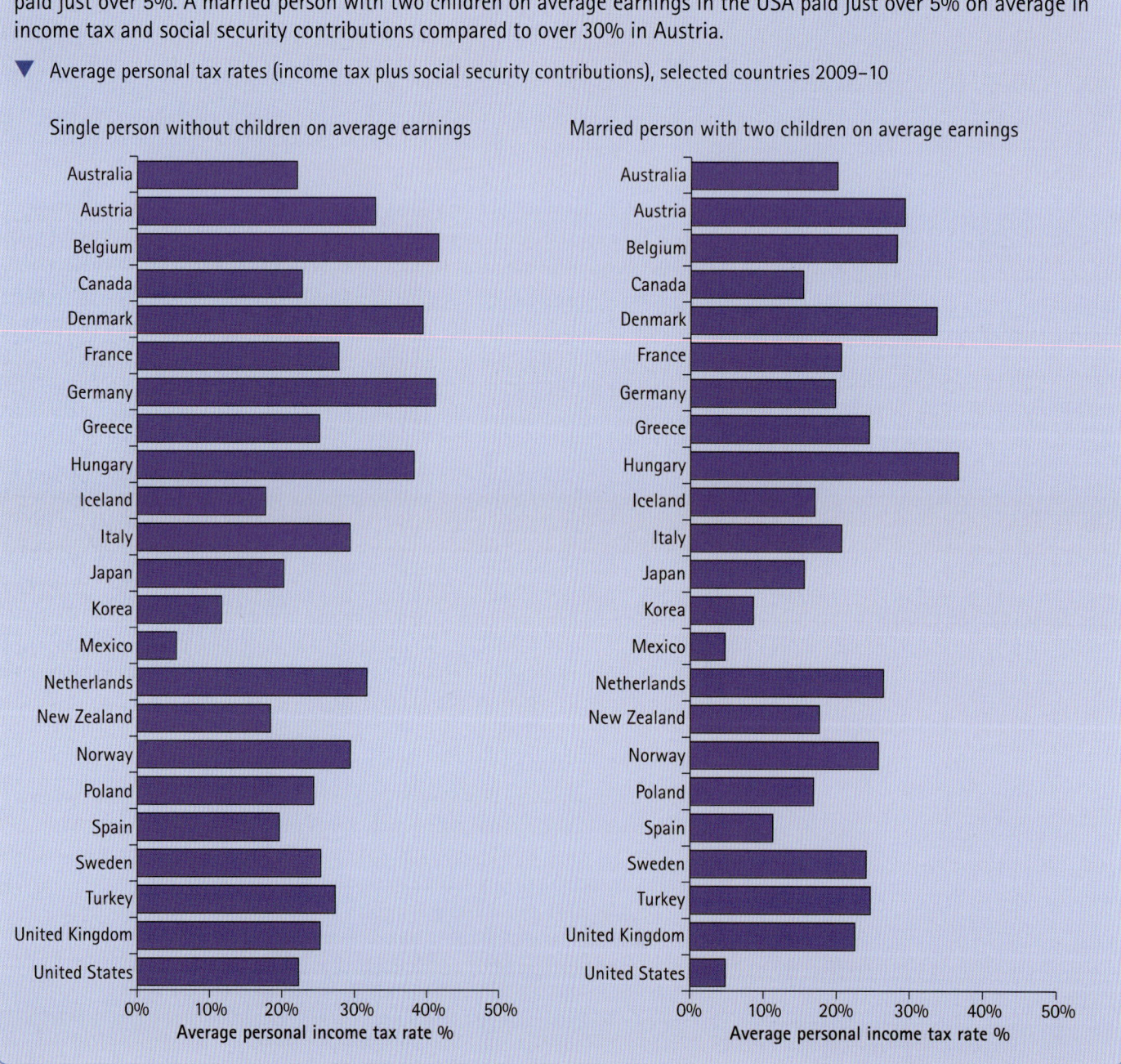

▼ Average personal tax rates (income tax plus social security contributions), selected countries 2009–10

Source: 'All-in personal tax rates' Table 1.6 updated with 2010 information, reproduced from www.oecd.org/ctp/taxingwages *Taxing Wages* (OECD, 11 May 2011), copyright © OECD 2011

> ### ACTIVITY 5.10
>
> **Taxing USA**
>
> 1 Use the information on page 309 on marginal income tax rates in the USA in 2011–12. For each of the following people determine the highest marginal tax rate the individual will pay on his or her income and the individual's average tax rate:
>
> ▸ single person with annual income **a** $20,000 **b** $500,000
>
> ▸ married person with annual income **c** $150,000 **d** $800,000.
>
> 2 How progressive do you think the US income tax system is? For example, how do average tax rates compare for people on middle to high incomes? Explain your answer.

Corporation tax

Corporation tax is levied on the profits of limited companies or corporations and may also be called a profits tax if applied to unincorporated businesses, notably sole traders and partnerships. Sometimes a government may also impose a one-off windfall tax on the profits of a company either thought to be a monopoly and making very significant profits, or benefiting from world events that boosted its profits. For example, the UK has from time to time imposed a windfall tax on the profits of oil companies when they have enjoyed a significant increase in their profits simply as a result of a rise in world oil prices over which they have no direct control.

To encourage new businesses to start up, corporate tax rates on the profits of smaller firms are often set at a low or zero rate in some countries. Corporation tax rates often rise progressively with the scale of profits.

Capital gains tax

It is possible to make a profit from the sale of shares, famous paintings, jewellery, property and other valuable assets that have increased in value over time. Profits made in this way are called capital gains and may be taxed by a government. Sometimes allowances are made, for example for the length of time someone has held an asset – the longer someone has held it the lower the tax the person pays. For example, in Canada, only 50% of a capital gain is classed as taxable income.

Wealth taxes

Wealth taxes can include taxes on the value of residential and commercial land and property. Wealth taxes can also include inheritance taxes on the transfer of wealth from one person to another upon their death. When an individual dies and leaves his or her house, savings and/or other valuable possessions to someone else, inheritance tax might be payable on the total value inherited.

Advantages of direct taxes

1 High revenue yield

The big advantage of direct taxes, like income tax and corporation tax, is that they have a high yield of revenue compared to their cost of collection. The total amount of money collected can be estimated with reasonable accuracy in advance, which is of great help to a government when planning how much it can afford to spend.

2 They can be used to reduce inequalities in incomes and wealth

The progressive nature of many direct taxes means that wealthier members of society are taxed more heavily than poorer groups, to help reduce inequality.

3 They are based on ability to pay

A direct tax will usually be based on a person's or firm's ability to pay the tax. Family commitments and dependants can also be taken into consideration and a system of tax allowances can be used to reflect these responsibilities.

Disadvantages of direct tax

1 They can reduce work incentives

Some people may prefer to remain unemployed if high taxes on incomes reduce the return from employment. Similarly, people in work may reduce their productive effort, stop working overtime or developing their skills to seek promotion because the more they earn the greater the proportion of their income they will have to pay in tax if the tax system is highly progressive.

2 They can reduce enterprise incentives

Private sector firms have a profit motive. Corporation tax on profits can therefore reduce the incentive for entrepreneurs to start up new firms or expand existing ones. A firm will have less profit after tax to reinvest in new productive assets.

3 Tax evasion

High tax rates increase the advantages of evading taxes and finding loopholes in tax laws. As a result, revenues are lower and a government will need to use up more resources trying to catch those who evade.

SECTION 4

Indirect taxes

Indirect taxes are added to the prices of goods and services and are therefore collected from transactions made by people and organizations. An indirect tax may be a fixed percentage of a price or value or it may be a fixed amount.

The collection and payment of indirect taxes to government is normally the responsibility of producers who will then pass on as much of each tax as they can to consumers through raised prices. This means the incidence of an indirect tax, i.e. who bears the cost of it, will often be shared between a producer of a product and the consumers of that product. For example, in a highly competitive market for a product for which consumer demand is highly price sensitive, producers may be unable to increase their prices to cover the indirect tax. If they do, demand for their product and therefore their revenues may fall significantly. ▶ 2.2

Ad valorem taxes

Ad valorem taxes such as **VAT** and other sales taxes are levied as a percentage of the selling price of goods and services or on sales revenues. Some necessities, such as many foods and medicines, may be exempt from these taxes or zero-rated. Raising VAT will increase the cost of buying goods and services for many consumers.

Unlike a sales tax a VAT is levied not just on finished goods and services but also on semi-finished components and materials bought by producers. VAT is therefore added at every stage of production. However, a firm can recover the

VAT it has had to pay on inputs of materials, components and services it has purchased from the VAT it collects on the sale of its output. In this way VAT only taxes the value each firm adds at each stage of production.

Excise duties

Excise duties are applied to specific goods, such as alcohol, cigarettes, vehicles and petrol. They are normally fixed charges based on the amount sold, such as $1 on a litre of petrol or $2 on a bottle of wine. For example, some countries have introduced vehicle duties on larger cars that are greater than duties on smaller cars. This is to encourage consumers to buy smaller vehicles that burn less petrol and produce lower engine emissions. In response to increasing demand, car manufacturers have increased production of smaller cars with more efficient engines.

Import tariffs

Tariffs are custom duties on the value of imported goods entering a country. Tariffs may be used to raise the prices of certain imported products to protect domestic firms from overseas competition. Domestic firms producing products that compete with overseas imports should benefit from increased consumer demand for their products. However, domestic firms that rely on imported materials, components and finished products to use in production or sell will face increased costs as a result. ➤ **8.1**

User charges

User charges are taxes or charges linked to the use of specific goods or activities. For example, they include toll charges to use major bridges or roads and pay for their upkeep. London and other major cities around the world have also introduced congestion charges that charge vehicle drivers a fixed amount to enter these cities during peak periods. Some of the revenue raised from these charges is used to fund improvements in public transport.

▲ Indirect taxes include ad valorem taxes, excise duties, user charges and import tariffs

A tax on a specific good or activity used to raise revenue for a specific purpose, such as paying for road or public transport improvements, is called a **hypothecated tax**.

Advantages of indirect taxes

1 They are cost effective

Indirect taxes are relatively cheap and easy to collect. The administrative burden of collecting indirect taxes lies mainly with the manufacturers, wholesalers and retailers collecting VAT and with importers paying custom and excise duties.

2 They expand the tax base

Indirect taxes are paid by young, old, employed and unemployed alike when they buy goods and services, not just by people in work with earned incomes. As a result, the effects of indirect taxes are spread more widely across all industrial sectors and groups in a society.

3 They can be used to target specific products and activities

Indirect taxes can be used to achieve specific government aims. For example, taxes on cigarettes and alcohol can discourage their consumption to promote healthier lifestyles and to reduce the cost to the government of public health treatment for smoking- and alcohol-related problems. Taxes on oil can help to conserve a valuable non-renewable resource and also help reduce pollution from the burning of oil in energy production and vehicle use.

4 They are flexible

It is often quicker and easier for a government to alter tax rates for VAT and excise duties than to make changes to income tax and other direct taxes. As such, the effect of these changes on consumption patterns and the macroeconomy is more immediate.

Disadvantages of indirect taxes

1 They are inflationary

Raising indirect taxes will increase the prices of many goods and services and reduce the real incomes of consumers. As a result, their demand for many goods and services will fall. However, some firms selling cheaper products may benefit from increasing sales as consumers switch their demand away from more expensive items.

2 They are regressive

Indirect taxes tend to be regressive in nature. That is, their burden as a proportion of income is greater on people with low incomes than it is on people with high incomes.

For example, consider the purchase of a pair shoes for $48 inclusive of VAT at 20% or $8. This amount of tax will take 8% from an income of $100 compared with just 1.6% from an income of $500. Many basic foodstuffs and other essential items, such as medicines, educational books and baby clothes, are exempt from VAT in many countries to reduce the regressiveness of the tax.

3 Revenues are less certain and predictable

It is can be difficult for a government to predict accurately how much consumers will spend on goods and services, and therefore revenues from indirect taxes. This makes planning future public expenditure based on likely tax revenues difficult. Employment, earnings and profits tend to be less variable than consumer expenditures over time and so direct tax revenues tend to be more predictable.

4 They can encourage tax evasion

For example, high tariffs on imported goods and excise duties may encourage the illegal smuggling of untaxed or lower taxed items from overseas. As a result governments may have to use up more resources to patrol ports and other entry points to catch smugglers.

ACTIVITY 5.11

A taxing problem

What type of tax is most likely to be applied to the following?

SECTION 5

Balancing the budget

What is the budget?

> The Spanish government has approved an austerity budget, including a tax rise for the rich and 8% spending cuts

> Australia plans US$3.8 billion budget surplus in two years

> Dubai Finance Chief expects budget surplus

> Greek crisis worsens as budget deficit grows

Every organization will normally prepare a budget each year. A budget is simply a forecast of its spending and revenue over the next 6 to 12 months made so that it can plan and manage its finances sensibly. An organization will use its budget forecast to monitor actual expenditures and revenues as they occur to look at how similar or how different they are from the forecast and why.

In exactly the same way, a government will set out in its budget its plans for public spending and raising tax and other revenues at the start of each financial year. In most countries it is so important it is simply called '**the budget**'.

In the budget a government may change tax rates, announce new taxes or even abolish old ones. The budget is also used to announce how the government intends to spend public revenues on different current and capital expenditure items. ➤ **5.1**

Sometimes governments will announce spending cuts in the budget that may be unpopular. However, high tax burdens to pay for high public spending can be equally unpopular and can also damage economic growth.

A government that budgets for a deficit plans to spend more than it expects to earn from public revenues. A **budget deficit** is normally associated with an expansionary fiscal policy whereby a government seeks to increase aggregate demand during an economic downturn to boost employment and output. There will be an actual budget deficit if actual spending exceeds actual revenues. ➤ **5.1**

In contrast, a government may plan to reduce its budget deficit compared with that of previous years or even budget for surplus by cutting public expenditure and/or raising taxes or other sources of revenue. A government that budgets for a surplus will expect to raise more public revenue than it will spend in total over the coming financial year.

The budget is therefore balanced if a government plans to spend no more in any one financial year than it expects to raise in revenue.

Public sector borrowing

If the public sector spends more than it raises in tax and all other revenues the government will need to finance the shortfall with loans. The amount of money the public sector in an economy needs in order to balance its spending is normally called the **public sector borrowing requirement** or similar.

Governments usually borrow money from the private sector by selling loan stocks or securities, such as government bonds. Short-term debt is generally

316 Role of government in an economy

10 years or more. Medium-term debt reaches maturity somewhere in between these periods. At maturity the government will repay each bond with interest to the bondholder. Government bonds can be bought and sold on the stock market through a stock exchange. ➤ 3.1

Government debt can be internal debt, owed to private individuals, firms and the banking system within its economy, and external debt owed to overseas banks, residents, governments or international organizations such as the World Bank and International Monetary Fund.

A country with a public sector that is unable to meet its loan and interest repayments will face bankruptcy.

ACTIVITY 5.12

Greece lightning

1. What is a budget deficit?
2. Why has the Greek budget deficit increased so much over time?
3. What was the impact of these successive budget deficits on public sector borrowing in Greece?
4. Why did Greece require financial help from the EU and IMF?
5. Why are the EU and IMF insisting Greece cut its public spending and raises taxes? What impact could this have on the Greek economy?
6. What could be the likely impact on government finances and the economy of Greece if it fails to reduce its budget deficit?

WORLD NEWS — May 2010

Greece faces three years of recession – as it tries to slash its budget deficit

Greece has been living well beyond its means in recent years, and its rising level of debt has placed a huge strain on the country's economy as it tries to meet spiralling debt interest charges and loan repayments.

The Greek government borrowed heavily and went on something of a spending spree during the past decade. Public spending soared and public sector wages practically doubled during that time. There was also widespread tax evasion.

The government now owes about 300 billion euros ($400 billion) and has to pay off part of it this month but does not have enough revenue to do so. Greece's high levels of debt mean investors are wary of lending it more money.

To assist the country the European Union (EU) and International Monetary Fund (IMF) have announced a bail-out package – the biggest in recent history.

They are offering 110 billion euros ($146.2 billion) spread over three years – but on condition that Greece slashes its public spending and increases taxes.

National debt

Each year a government must sell enough debt or secure loans to finance its borrowing requirement. However, every year in which a government borrows more money it will add to its total stock of debt. The total amount of money borrowed by the public sector of a country over time that has yet to be repaid is called the public sector debt or **national debt**.

The national debt is money owed by all levels of government: central, regional, local or municipal government. As the government of a country represents its people and borrows money to finance public spending on their behalf, the national debt is indirectly the debt of taxpayers.

Taxation

The US national debt was a staggering $14.5 trillion in May 2011, equivalent to around 97% of the US national income. It has risen significantly over time. In 1980 it was $2.8 trillion or around 33% of the US national income.

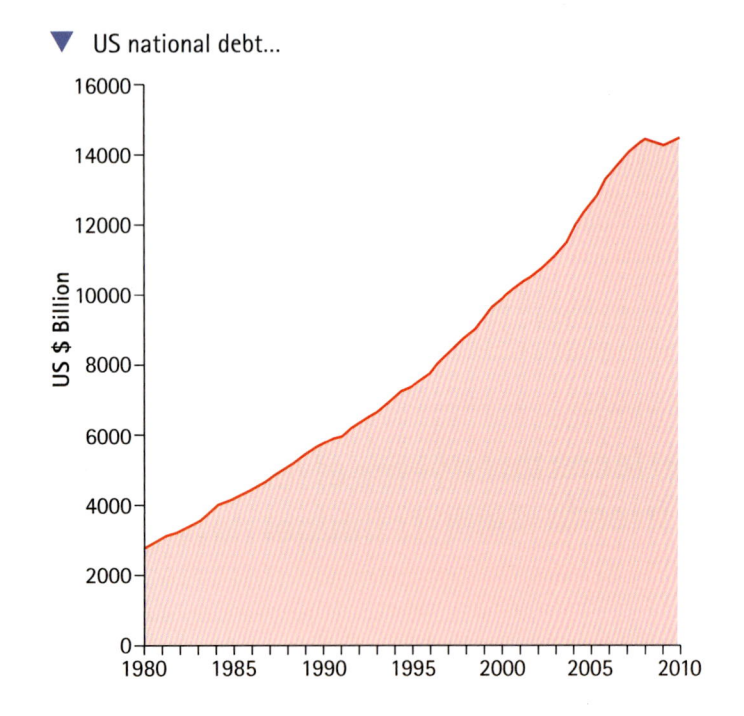

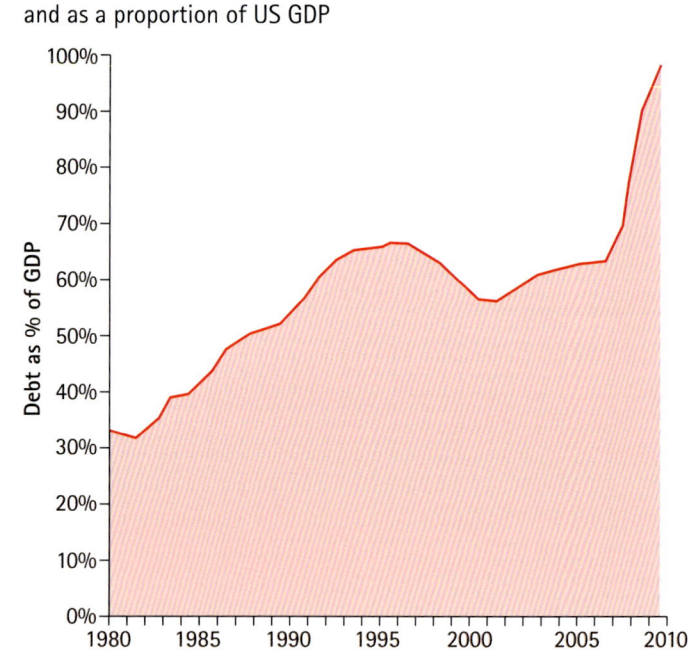

▼ US national debt... and as a proportion of US GDP

Source: www.usgovernmentspending.com

It is useful to compare the national debt of an economy to its national income or GDP because this tells us about the ability of that economy to manage and repay its debts. The table below lists the 10 countries with highest national debt to GDP ratios and the 10 countries with the lowest. You will note that Japan had a national debt in 2010 over twice the size of its national income while countries such as Libya, Oman and Chile had relatively little debt compared to their national incomes.

▼ Countries with the highest and lowest ratios of national debt to GDP, 2010

Country	National debt (as % of GDP)	Country	National debt (as % of GDP)
Japan	234.1	Azerbaijan	12.3
St Kitts and Nevis	204.9	Uzbekistan	11.7
Greece	139.3	Saudi Arabia	11.0
Lebanon	137.5	Equatorial Guinea	10.7
Jamaica	131.6	Kuwait	10.7
Eritrea	125.0	Estonia	7.8
Italy	119.7	Chile	6.9
Grenada	116.3	Oman	4.3
Barbados	113.3	Hong Kong	0.6
Iceland	107.8	Libya	0.0

Source: IMF

Role of government in an economy

As the national debt of a country rises, both in absolute terms and especially as a proportion of its national income, the burden of paying debt interest rises. This burden will increase if the stock of national debt increases at a faster rate than GDP. If economic growth in GDP is slower then debt payments will be rising faster than tax revenues are growing. Taxes will have to increase or public expenditures diverted from other uses to pay the rising interest charges.

However, rising public sector debt and rising interest payments need not be a bad thing as long as the national income or GDP of a country rises faster than the total debt. As income grows, tax revenues will grow by more than enough to meet rising interest charges for the debt. The burden of debt as a proportion of GDP will also be falling. This is just the same for individuals who borrow money from a bank. The burden of their debt and interest payments will fall as their income and ability to pay back their loan rises.

Some politicians and people still claim the national debt is a burden on a country. This is because a government must raise extra money in tax from people and firms to pay interest payments. However, if the extra taxes pay for interest on internal debt held by people and firms in the same country then all the government will be doing is raising taxes from some to pay interest to others. That is, interest payments made to people and firms in the same country are simply a transfer from one group of taxpayers to another, and overall the economy is no worse off. Yet, clearly, if taxes have to be very high to pay significant interest charges then people and firms may not have the incentive to work so hard and this may damage economic growth.

Interest payments on debt held by overseas residents are, however, a drain on an economy. This is because extra tax revenue will have to be raised simply to pay interest to lenders overseas, and the country will be worse off as a result.

WEBSITES

Some useful websites on public finance and taxation are:

- www.en.wikipedia.org/wiki/Tax
- www.en.wikipedia.org/wiki/Government_debt
- www.tutor2u.net/economics/gcse/revision_notes/tools_taxation.htm
- www.taxworld.org/History/TaxHistory.htm

KEYWORDS

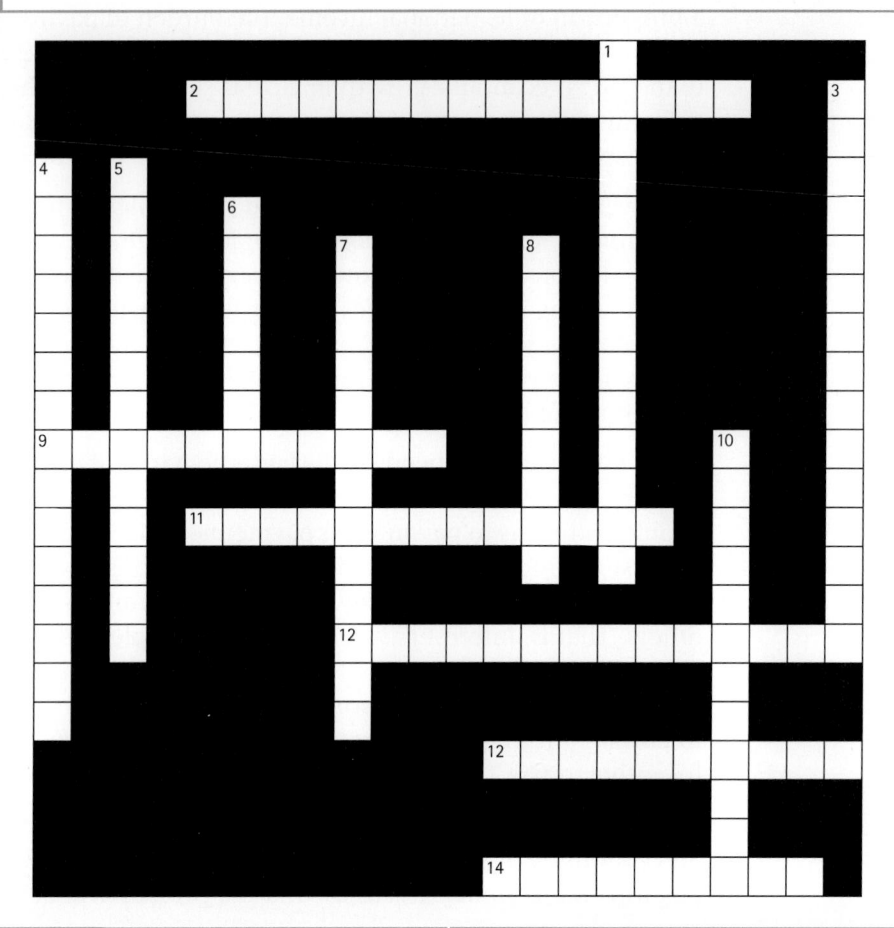

Clues across

2. Economic term used to describe a tax rate applied to each additional dollar of taxable income above a pre-defined income threshold (8, 3, 4)
9. A tax on expenditure on goods or services that is collected by producers but usually paid for by their consumers in the form of higher prices (8, 3)
11. A tax designed to take proportionally less in tax from a high income than a low income (10, 3)
12. A tax on company profits (11, 3)
13. A tax or charge applied to certain goods and services based on their quantity and not their value (6, 4)
14. A tax levied on the incomes or wealth of individuals or firms that must be paid from their own funds and cannot be passed on to others to pay (6, 3)

Clues down

1. A tax designed to take proportionally more in tax from a higher income than a low income (11, 3)
3. Term used to describe a tax on a specific good or activity used to raise revenue for a specific purpose, such as paying for road or public transport improvements, rather than financing general public spending (12, 3)
4. A flat tax that takes the same proportion of income in tax from all incomes (12, 3)
5. A tax added as a percentage of the value of goods and services at each stage of their production. Because firms can deduct the tax they pay on the purchase of inputs from the tax they collect from the sale of their outputs the tax only taxes the additional value they add during production (5, 6, 3)
6. The assessed value of income, wealth or expenditure that is then made subject to taxation (3, 4)
7. This financial situation occurs if a government plans to spend more than it earns in tax revenues over the coming financial year (6, 7)
8. This measures total tax revenue as a proportion of the national income of an economy (3, 6)
10. The total outstanding stock of public sector borrowing accumulated over time to finance shortfalls of public revenues below public spending (8, 4)

Role of government in an economy

Assessment exercises

Multiple choice

1. What would cause disposable incomes to become less equal?

   A Increased employment
   B Increased welfare benefits
   C More progressive taxes
   D More regressive taxes

2. The table shows earnings and total income tax paid per annum.

earnings $	total income tax paid $
5000	1000
8000	2000
9000	3000

   Which type of tax system does this illustrate?

   A Indirect
   B Progressive
   C Proportional
   D Regressive

3. A country has different rates of income tax depending on the level of income earned.

   The highest rate of income tax is cut from 35% to 30%.

   From this statement it can be deduced that taxation will become:

   A Less indirect
   B Less progressive
   C Less regressive
   D More difficult to evade

4. The government pays a subsidy for each worker employed by a firm in an area of high unemployment.

   When would this policy be most successful in reducing unemployment?

   A When the firm is capital-intensive
   B When the firm is labour-intensive, requiring mainly unskilled labour
   C When the firm provides professional services
   D When the firm requires mainly specialist, skilled labour

5. The Central Bank of Swaziland increases its interest rate from 5% to 6%.

   Which effect is this likely to have on producers and consumers?

	producers	consumers
A	borrow less	save more
B	borrow less	spend more
C	invest more	save more
D	invest more	spend more

6. What is most likely to conflict with a government's aim of keeping price inflation low and stable?

   A Higher direct tax rates
   B Higher government spending
   C Higher interest rates
   D Higher unemployment

7. What can a government do to increase aggregate demand in its economy?

   A Budget for a surplus
   B Cut taxes
   C Encourage savings
   D Reduce its expenditure

8. Government advisers have suggested the following policies to reduce youth unemployment.

   Which would not increase public expenditure?

   A Cutting the minimum wage paid to young people
   B Raising the school-leaving age
   C Giving a subsidy to employers to recruit young people
   D Introducing national military service for all

9. A government wishes to help people with very low incomes.

   Which policy would achieve this?

   A Increasing housing subsidies
   B Increasing income tax
   C Increasing indirect taxation
   D Increasing inheritance tax

10 What might a government decrease if it wished to slow down the rate of growth in an economy?
   A Expenditure on defence
   B Tax on goods and services (for example VAT)
   C Interest rates
   D The rate of income tax

11 What is most likely to cause the government to have a budget surplus?
   A A decrease in government spending
   B A decrease in private sector investment
   C An increase in unemployment
   D An increase in the wages of public sector employees

12 Which aim of government policy is most likely to be achieved by an increase in interest rates?
   A Economic growth
   B Greater equality of income
   C Full employment
   D Price stability

13 What may a government change when it uses monetary policy?
   A Budget deficit
   B Minimum lending rate
   C Regional assistance
   D Rate of income tax

14 When is a tax progressive?
   A When some goods have a higher tax than others
   B When the tax is on incomes rather than on goods or services
   C When the marginal rate of tax increases as income increases
   D When the tax is linked to the rate of inflation

15 Which of the following is not a government macroeconomic objective?
   A A balance of payments deficit
   B Economic growth
   C Full employment
   D Price stability

16 When is the budget described as balanced?
   A When direct taxes and indirect taxes are equal
   B When exports and imports are equal
   C When government spending and government revenue are equal
   D When the demand for money and the supply of money are equal

17 What would be most likely to encourage saving?
   A A rise in the exchange rate
   B A rise in the goods and services tax rate
   C A rise in the income tax rate
   D A rise in the interest rate

18 Expansionary fiscal policy to increase aggregate demand involves:
   A Increasing public spending and taxes
   B Reducing public spending and taxes
   C Reducing interest rates and the money supply
   D Increasing public spending and reducing taxes

19 Which of the following is a direct tax?
   A VAT
   B Air passenger duty
   C Import duties
   D Corporation tax

20 When is there a budget surplus?
   A When public expenditure is greater than public sector revenue
   B When public sector revenue is greater than public expenditure
   C When imports are greater than exports
   D When exports are greater than imports

Structured questions

1 Public finances in Sweden

In 2011 the government of Sweden forecast it would have a growing budget surplus over the next four years and planned to cut taxes for a sixth consecutive year as other nations such as the UK were attempting to reduce their deficits. The Swedish economy grew 5.5% in 2010 as exports recovered from the global financial crisis.

The public sector in Sweden is a major producer of goods and services in the economy. For example, Sweden has an extensive child-care system that guarantees a place for all young children aged two through six in a public day-care facility. It also benefits from an extensive social welfare system, which provides childcare and maternity and paternity leave, a cap on personal health care costs and generous old-age pensions, among other benefits.

Public expenditure in Sweden accounted for over 50% of all spending in the economy in 2011, higher than in many other European economies. The total tax burden in Sweden, at just under 50% of GDP, was also high.

a What measures can a government take to reduce a budget deficit? [2]
b Explain the difference between public expenditure and private expenditure, giving one example of each. [3]
c How might a reduction in taxation help any **two** macroeconomic aims of the Swedish government? [6]
d Discuss how some aims of government policy might conflict with each other. [6]
e When might it be desirable for a government to act as a producer of goods or services? [6]
f Sometimes a government does not act as a producer of goods and services but still influences the behaviour of private producers. Explain how it might do this. [9]

2
a Distinguish with the use of examples between
   (i) direct and indirect taxes, [3]
   (ii) progressive and regressive taxes. [3]
b Explain why governments impose taxes. [6]
c Discuss what might happen in an economy if a government increases income tax rates. [8]

Cambridge IGCSE Economics 0455/04 Q6 October/November 2006
Cambridge O Level Economics 2281/02 Q6 October/November 2006

3 It was reported in 2002 that people in Germany were expecting tax rises and an increase in unemployment.

a Distinguish between a direct tax and an indirect tax. Give an example of each. [4]
b Identify **three** types of unemployment and explain how they are caused. [6]
c Describe **four** main aims of government macro-economic policy. [4]
d Discuss whether a rise in taxes can help to achieve any of these aims. [6]

Cambridge IGCSE Economics 0455/04 Q3 October/November 2004
Cambridge O Level Economics 2281/02 Q3 October/November 2004

4 a Using examples, contrast a direct tax with an indirect tax. [4]
  b Discuss how a government might use taxation to affect the distribution of income. [6]
  c Explain the concept of price elasticity of demand. Choose **two** goods and explain why they might have different price elasticities of demand. [6]
  d Use the concept of elasticity to discuss how indirect taxes may be used by a government to
   (i) increase its revenue,
   (ii) decrease imports. [4]

Cambridge IGCSE Economics 0455/04 Q3 October/November 2005
Cambridge O Level Economics 2281/02 Q3 October/November 2005

5 a Describe what is meant by a mixed economy. [4]
  b Explain **three** macro-economic aims a government might have. [6]
  c What is meant by a government's budget? [4]
  d Discuss how a government might finance its expenditure. [6]

Cambridge IGCSE Economics 0455/02 Q5 October/November 2009
Cambridge O Level Economics 2281/02 Q5 October/November 2009

6 Economic indicators

6.1	Price inflation
6.2	Employment and unemployment
6.3	Output and growth
Assessment	Multiple choice
	Structured questions

Government macroeconomic objectives seek to keep price inflation low and stable, a high and stable level of employment and maintain healthy economic growth in national output and income. To measure progress towards these objectives a government will collect and analyse data on them.

High and rising inflation, caused either by an excess demand for goods and services, rising production costs or rising import prices, is a concern because it erodes the value of money and can cause hardship for many people, particularly those on low and fixed incomes. It can also make export prices uncompetitive overseas and lead to a fall in business confidence. The rate of inflation is normally measured by changes in a consumer or retail price index (CPI or RPI) calculated from the average prices of a 'typical' basket of consumed goods and services in an economy.

High unemployment can also cause hardship for those without paid employment but, importantly, it is also a waste of resources that could otherwise be used to produce goods and services. Changes in the industrial structure of an economy can also result in high unemployment over long periods of time, as redundant workers need to re-train in new skills required by new and growing industries. Globally, participation in the labour force, particularly among females, and employment, especially in services, have been rising. In contrast, male participation rates have been falling as the share of employment accounted for by agriculture and industry has reduced over time.

Rates of inflation and unemployment also tend to vary with the economic cycle in activity in an economy. During an economic recession, falling demand and incomes can lead to cyclical unemployment and disinflation as the rate at which prices are rising slows down. If a recession is particularly deep and prolonged economic activity may continue to shrink and result in deflation. During an economic boom, rising demand for goods and services can boost output and employment, but may also increase price inflation and suck in more imports from overseas causing an unfavourable balance of trade with the rest of the world.

Government policies not only try to reduce cyclical variations in economic activity but also try to raise the overall rate of growth in national income and output in their economies. Growth, through technical progress, investments in new plant and machinery and increased levels of productivity, and as measured by an increase in the real gross domestic product (GDP) of an economy, can help improve living standards and economic welfare. However, faster economic growth may use up scarce resources more quickly and can result in higher levels of pollution and waste. This may not be sustainable in the long term. Other measures of changes in living standards and economic welfare are therefore often used in addition to real GDP, including people's general health and life expectancy, access to education and the quality of their environment.

Unit 6.1   Price inflation

> **AIMS**

By the end of this unit you should be able to:

▸ describe how a **consumer price index**/**retail price index** is calculated
  - calculate a simple **weighted price index** series and evaluate how changes in different economic factors can affect the series
  - describe how price indices are used to measure and monitor inflation

▸ discuss the causes and consequences of **inflation**
  - explain and distinguish between **demand-pull inflation**, **cost-push inflation** and **imported inflation**
  - analyse the personal and economic consequences of inflation

▸ discuss the causes and consequences of **deflation**.

SECTION 1

What is inflation?

Many of the news headlines shown below express concern over how the prices of many goods and services are rising, or inflating, over time. However, not all prices rise at the same rate. The prices of some goods and services may even fall over time, perhaps because consumer demand has dropped or because there has been technical progress that has reduced unit costs. So what exactly is inflation, and why is it a cause for concern for consumers, workers, businesses and governments?

> **13% rise in house prices**
>
> ROW OVER FARES RISE
>
> Cheap food era 'over' as prices rise 10pc in supermarkets
>
> Finance Minister concerned about inflation
>
> Industry demands inquiry into surging gas bills
>
> **Price of petrol soars**
>
> **LCD prices fall; on weak PC sales**

Inflation refers to a general and sustained rise in the level of prices of goods and services. That is, prices of the vast majority of goods and services on sale to consumers just keep on rising and rising. Prices change over time so inflation is always expressed as a rate of change per period of time – per month or per year. For example, in 2010 the inflation rate in the UK was 4.7%. This meant, on average, that the prices of all goods and services rose by 4.7% for every pound during that year. However, this general increase in prices was relatively low compared to the inflation rate in 1975. In 1975 the inflation rate in the UK was at 25%: on average, a product that cost £100 at the start of 1975 would have cost £125 by the start of 1976.

But even this inflation rate is low in comparison with the increase in prices some countries have faced at different times in history. In the mid-1990s Brazil experienced a rise in prices by an average of 2,300% in one year while Bolivia faced an annual inflation rate of 20,000% during the 1980s! This type of runaway inflation during which prices rise at phenomenal rates and money becomes almost worthless is called **hyperinflation**. ▶ 3.1

Living with 24,000% inflation

Germany in the 1920s is often cited as the best example of so-called 'hyperinflation'. The Berlin government printed huge quantities of worthless paper money to pay off its debts after World War I. People needed a wheelbarrow full of money to buy one loaf of bread; the joke was that thieves would steal the wheelbarrow – and leave the pile of worthless money behind.

Price inflation 327

ACTIVITY 6.1

Price inflation in the UK

The graph below shows how the rate of price inflation in UK varied between 1960 and 2011. A similar historical pattern has been experienced in many other developed countries.

▼ UK price inflation 1960–2011 (% annual change in the retail prices index: RPI)

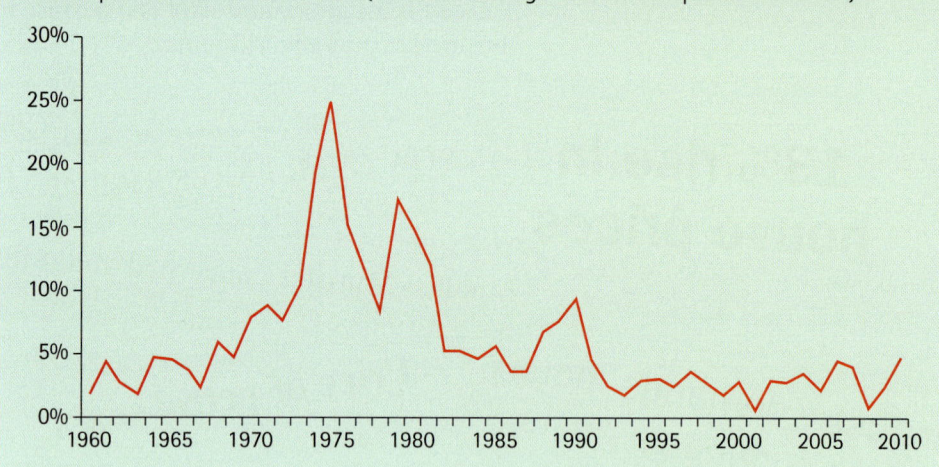

Source: Office for National Statistics, www.statistics.gov.uk

The UK inflation experience can be divided into three broad phases. During the 1960s the rate of price inflation was relatively low and stable, averaging just under 3.7% each year. Over the next 15 years from 1970, annual recorded price inflation increased significantly and became much more volatile, averaging 11.2% per year and peaking at almost 25% in 1975 following a dramatic increase in world oil prices in 1974. This means that between 1970 and the start of 1985 the general level of prices increased almost fivefold, reducing the purchasing power of £1 in 1970 to the equivalent of just 20 pence by 1985. The rapid rise in inflation during the 1970s was accompanied by rising unemployment. The term **stagflation** is used to describe the economic situation when prices and unemployment rise together.

Despite rising back to almost 10% per year in 1990, UK price inflation since the early 1990s has been relatively low and stable. From 1991 to 2011 it has averaged just 2.9% per year, falling as low as just 0.7% in early 2001 and to 0.9% in 2008 during periods of economic recession. By 2010 price inflation began to climb once more as food and energy prices began to rise rapidly around the world. Some economists predict the era of low inflation may be over once more.

1. From the graph, in which year was UK price inflation at its **a** highest **b** lowest?

2. Over which ten-year period was UK price inflation at its **a** highest **b** lowest?

3. Explain the statement 'between 1970 and the start of 1985 the general level of prices increased almost fivefold, reducing the purchasing power of £1 in 1970 to the equivalent of just 20 pence by 1985'. By 2010 the average price level observed in 1970 had increased by a factor of 12. How much would that same £1 in 1970 be worth in real terms in 2010?

SECTION 2

How to measure inflation

Consumer price indices

The rate of price inflation in an economy is measured by calculating the average percentage change in the prices of all goods and services, from one point in time to another, usually each month and year on year.

However, it is difficult to obtain up-to-date price information on all of the many millions of different goods and services exchanged in an economy, so most countries track the prices of a selection of goods and services. These goods and services will normally be those purchased by a 'typical' family or household. The prices of this typical 'basket' of goods and services will then be monitored at a small number of different retail outlets across the economy, including online retailers. This price information will then be used to compile a **consumer price index (CPI)** or a **retail price index (RPI)**. Both a CPI and RPI provide a measure of price inflation in an economy. The way they are calculated is the same: they differ only in terms of what goods and services and households they include (see page 333).

Most countries use a CPI as their main measure of price inflation affecting consumers. This is often considered to provide a cost-of-living index, although cost of living will vary by household according to which products they buy and in what quantities. The index simply indicates what we would need to spend in order to purchase the same things we bought in an earlier period.

A CPI will usually include any sales taxes and excise taxes paid by consumers on their purchases of goods and services, but exclude changes in income taxes and the prices of assets such as stocks and shares, life insurance and housing.

The prices of oil, electricity, gas and food may also be excluded from the calculation of a 'core' CPI used by some governments to set their inflation targets and monetary policies. This is because the prices of these products can be highly volatile, both up and then down again, due to relatively short-lived shortages caused by the weather, such as droughts or severe winters or cutbacks in oil production. These products are therefore excluded from a core CPI on the grounds they can distort measures of more 'usual' or underlying price inflation targeted by government policies. ➤ **5.1**

Calculating a price index

Index number series, or indices, are simply a way of expressing the change in the prices of a number of different products as a movement in just one single number. The average price of the 'basket' of products in the first year of calculation, or **base year**, is given the number 100. Then, if on average the prices of all the goods and services in the same 'basket' rise by 25% over the following year, the price index at the end of the second year will be 125. If in the next year prices rise on average by a further 10%, the price index will rise to 137.5 (that is, 125 × 1.10 = 137.5). This tells us consumer prices have risen on average by 37.5% over a two-year period.

Consider the following simple example to construct a CPI. Imagine there are just 100 households in our simple economy. In the table below, the weekly spending patterns of these households have been observed and recorded over a 12-month period: the base year. The average prices of the goods and services they buy have been calculated for each category of their spending from a sample of different shops.

Price inflation 329

▼ How to calculate a simple CPI: spending profile of households in base year

Types of goods and services	Proportion of weekly household expenditure spent on each category (%)	Average price ($) of goods and services purchased in each category	Weighted average price ($)
Clothing and footwear	25	$40	0.25 x $40 = $10
Household goods and services	15	$60	0.15 x $60 = $9
Food	40	$5	0.40 x $5 = $2
Travel	20	$20	0.20 x $20 = $4
Total	100%		Price of basket $25

The proportion of total household expenditure spent on each category is used to weight the average prices of each type of good and service to find their weighted average prices. These tell us how big an impact a change in the price of one particular type of good or service will have on the cost of living of our households. For example, from the table it should be clear that a 10% increase in the average price of clothing and footwear, from $40 to $44 per item, will matter more than a 10% increase in the prices of household goods and services, from $60 to $66, because our households spend proportionately more of their weekly expenditures on clothes and shoes. The weighted average price of clothing and footwear purchased is higher than the weighted average price of household products purchased.

Adding up the weighted average prices in the basket of goods and services in the table above sums to $25. We set this overall weighted average price in our base year equal to 100 to begin our CPI.

We now observe how prices and the weekly spending patterns of the same households change over time over the following year in order to recalculate weighted average prices and the CPI.

Notice how both the prices and the proportion of household expenditure spent on each category of goods and services have changed in the table below. The biggest increases in prices have been for food products and household goods and services, up by a significant 60% (from £5 to £8) and 50% (from $60 to $90) respectively. As a result, households are now spending proportionately more on food, up from 40% of total weekly expenditure to 50%, and proportionally less on households products and travel.

▼ How to calculate a simple CPI: spending profile of households in year 1

Types of goods and services	Proportion of weekly household expenditure spent on each category (%)	Average price ($) of goods and services purchased in each category	Weighted average price ($)
Clothing and footwear	25	$44	0.25 x $44 = $11
Household goods and services	10	$90	0.10 x $90 = $9
Food	50	$8	0.50 x $8 = $4
Travel	15	$20	0.15 x $20 = $3
Total	100%		Price of basket $27

Economic indicators

The overall weighted average price of the basket of goods and services at the end of year 1 is now $27. This represents an 8% increase in the price of the basket since the base year. That is, consumer price inflation has been 8% over the year since the base year. The consumer price index at the end of year 1 is therefore 108 and it is calculated as follows:

$$\text{CPI in year 1} = \frac{\text{weighted average price year 1}}{\text{weighted average price base year}} = \frac{\$27}{\$25} \times 100 = 108$$

Now imagine we repeat the entire exercise for a further year and calculate a weighted average price for the basket of goods and services of $30. The CPI at the end of year 2 will then be 120.

$$\text{CPI in year 2} = \frac{\text{weighted average price year 2}}{\text{weighted average price base year}} = \frac{\$30}{\$25} \times 100 = 120$$

This tells us that, on average, consumer prices have risen by 20% since the base year.

ACTIVITY 6.2

A calculated problem

1. Continuing the same example above, use the information on average prices and household spending patterns in the table below to calculate the weighted price of the basket of goods and services at the end of years 3 and 4.

Types of goods and services	Proportion of weekly household expenditure spent on each category		Average price ($) of goods and services purchased in each category	
	Year 3	Year 4	Year 3	Year 4
Clothing and footwear	25%	26%	50	55
Household goods and services	15%	14%	100	110
Food	45%	46%	9	10
Travel	15%	14%	22	25

2. Use the weighted average price of the basket at the end of each year to calculate the CPI.
3. Overall, by how much has the weighted average price of the basket of consumer goods and services risen by since the base year?
4. In which year was price inflation at its **a** highest **b** lowest?
5. Suggest why and how you might account for the following changes in the calculation of your consumer price index over time:

   ▸ changes in the number, structure and composition of households, for example due to inward migration and an ageing population

   ▸ changes in retailing, for example online retailing over the Internet

   ▸ changes in the quality of goods and services, for example the increased performance and efficiency of cars and household goods such as microwaves and ovens

   ▸ new goods and services not previously available, such as 3D flat-screen televisions and iPads.

Price inflation

Uses of price indices

There are three main uses of the CPI in most modern economies.

1 As an economic indicator

The CPI is a widely used as a measure of price inflation and therefore as a measure of changes in the cost of living. Governments try to control price inflation using their macroeconomic policies. The CPI in an economy will be used by workers to seek increases in their wages that match or exceed the increase in their cost of living. The CPI will also be used by entrepreneurs in making many business decisions concerning their purchases and the setting of wages and prices.

2 As a price deflator

Rising prices reduce the purchasing power, or real value, of money. Rising prices will therefore reduce the purchasing power of wages, profits, pensions, savings, tax revenues and a host of other economic variables of importance to different groups of people and decision makers. A CPI is therefore used to deflate various economic series to calculate their real or inflation-free values. For example, if annual earnings have risen by 10%, but price inflation increased by 15% over the same period, then the real value of earnings will have fallen by 5% because the purchasing power of those payments will have been reduced by inflation.

3 Indexation

Indexation involves tying certain payments to the rate of increase in price inflation to keep their real value constant. For example, public pensions paid to retired people by a government may be indexed so that they increase by the rate of inflation each year. Similarly, some savings may be index-linked, meaning that the interest rate on those savings is set equal to the official price index, thereby protecting the real value of those savings. Many workers may also be covered by collective bargaining agreements that tie their wage increases to changes in the CPI. A government may also index-link the threshold at which people start to pay tax or higher rates of tax on their incomes, otherwise people would end up paying more income tax simply due to price inflation even if their real incomes were unchanged each year. ▶ **5.2**

Is inflation eating into your savings?

...it doesn't have to with our...

Protected Capital Account Inflation linked 9

Early exit fees may apply

Find out more >>

Some problems with price indices

Over time the 'typical' household and the basket of goods and services it buys will tend to change. A CPI will need to take account of these changes but deciding how and when to make them can be difficult. For example, household expenditure patterns will tend to change over time due to:

- changes in tastes and fashion
- the introduction of new goods and services, such as mobile phones, flat-screen televisions and iPods
- the changing composition of the population and households, due to migration, changes in birth and death rates, and later marriages ▶ **7.2**

Similarly, a CPI will also need to take account of changes in the quality of goods and services over time, and how and where households buy goods and services, including the introduction of new shops, television shopping channels and the increasing use of online shopping using the Internet.

International comparisons of consumer price inflation are difficult to make because household composition and spending patterns can differ significantly by country.

Consumer price index (CPI) or retail price index (RPI)?

Some countries use an RPI to measure and monitor their price inflation, often in addition to a CPI.

The basic approach to the measurement of inflation adopted by both the CPI and RPI is the same. For example, in the UK both track the changing cost of a fixed basket of goods and services over time and both are produced by combining together around 180,000 individual prices of around 700 representative items.

The RPI and CPI differ only by what products they include and the types of consumer they cover. As a result they can provide different measures of inflation. For example, in the year to June 2011 the RPI recorded an increase in prices of 5% in the UK compared to 4.2% by the CPI. The measure of inflation by the RPI was higher mainly because of increases in mortgage charges, buildings insurance and local taxes not included in the CPI.

The UK introduced a CPI in 1996 because it provides a more internationally comparable measure of inflation.

	RPI	CPI
Products	The RPI covers a range of costs excluded from the CPI, including: ▶ mortgage interest payments ▶ buildings insurance ▶ house purchase costs ▶ television licence fees ▶ trade union subscriptions. It also includes a price index for cars based on used car prices.	The CPI covers certain charges and fees excluded from the RPI, including: ▶ stockbroker fees ▶ university accommodation ▶ foreign student tuition fees. The index for the purchase of new cars in the CPI is based on actual published prices for new cars.
Population base	Representative of the majority of private households but excludes highest earners and pensioner households dependent mainly on welfare benefits. It includes expenditure both within the UK and abroad by UK households.	Representative of the majority of private households including institutional households (for example nursing homes) and foreign visitors to the UK. Only expenditure within the UK is covered.

SECTION 3

What causes inflation?

Economists today tend to agree that the main cause of inflation is 'too much money chasing too few goods'. This means people are increasing their spending on goods and services at a faster rate than producers can expand the supply the goods and services, because the supply of money in the economy has increased. As a result, there is an excess of aggregate demand, or total demand, for goods and services and market prices are therefore forced to rise. ▶ **2.2**

A government can allow the supply of money to rise in an economy by issuing more notes and coins or by allowing the banking system to create more credit' that is, by lending more to people and firms to spend. ▶ **3.1**

A government may allow the money supply to expand:

- to increase total demand in the economy during an economic recession in an attempt to reduce unemployment
- in response to an increase in demand for goods and services from consumers and firms
- in response to workers' demands for higher wages, or a rise in the other costs of production.

If the money supply expands, people have more money to spend. As they spend this money the increase in demand drives up the prices of the goods and services they buy. To understand why increases in the rate of growth in the money supply cause inflation, let us consider a very simple example.

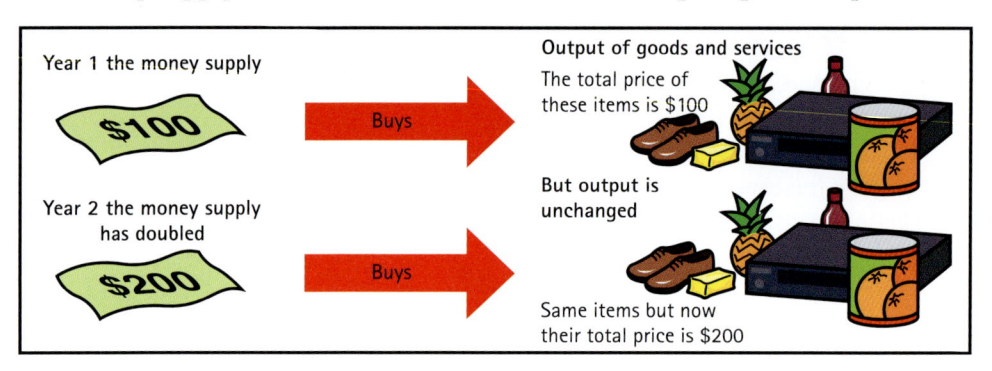

In year 1 the money supply stood at $100 and bought six items with a total price of $100. In the second year output has remained unchanged because there are no more resources available to make any more each year. Now imagine that the money supply doubles to $200. As consumers try to spend this money they find there are no extra goods and services to buy. With a fixed supply prices must rise. Indeed, they double. Inflation is 100%! Clearly, if output could have risen prices need not have gone up by so much, if at all.

A monetary rule

Economists argue that what is true in the simple example above is true for a highly complex economy. Any increase in the supply of money will cause inflation to accelerate if there is no growth in real output. Only if the output of goods and services rises should the money supply rise, so that people have enough money to buy these extra products.

This means there is a monetary rule a government can follow if it wants to keep inflation low and stable in its economy: it should only allow the supply of money to expand at the same rate as the increase in real output or real GDP over time. Increases in the money supply over and above increases in output are likely to cause prices to rise. However, this may take time. It may take a year or more before inflation increases following an expansion in the money supply. It takes time for consumers' spending to rise, for firms to realize demand has increased and for firms to raise their prices.

Some economists argue that different governments over time only have themselves to blame for the high inflation rates many countries experienced during the 1970s and 1980s. It was because they did not follow the monetary rule. Instead they allowed their money supplies to expand faster than output was growing in their economies in an effort to boost demand and reduce unemployment. For a time the increase in demand would reduce unemployment as firms took on more resources to increase the production of goods and services. However, inflation soon began to rise as aggregate demand grew faster than output. Eventually, the high inflation would reduce the purchasing power of people's incomes and demand for goods and services would begin to fall again. Workers would demand higher wages to keep pace with the rising cost of living, but as wages increased, firms reduced their demand for labour, and unemployment increased once more. As a result, government policy was responsible for **stagflation** – a situation when inflation and unemployment were both high and/or rising together.

Demand-pull inflation

Inflation caused by an increase in total demand is called a **demand-pull inflation**. Aggregate demand in an economy will rise if spending by governments, households and/or firms increases.

An increase in aggregate demand will cause market prices to increase and inflation to rise if firms are unable to increase the supply of goods and services at the same rate as demand.

To finance an increase in aggregate demand consumers and firms may borrow more from the banking system and/or the government can issue more notes and coins. Both these ways of financing an increase in demand involve increasing the supply of money in an economy.

Cost-push inflation

Inflation caused by rising production costs passed on by firms to consumers is a **cost-push inflation**. The cost of producing goods and services can rise because workers demand increases in wages not matched by increased productivity. Firms may raise their prices to cover these higher costs so that their profit margins are unchanged. However, as wages rise the demand for labour will tend to fall and workers could be made unemployed. To prevent a rise in unemployment the government may expand the supply of money to boost aggregate demand.

Continual increases in prices may occur if workers demand further increases in wages to compensate them for rising prices. This will cause a **wage–price** spiral. As prices rise, workers will demand higher wages to keep pace with inflation. However, wage increases will simply add to production costs and so prices will tend to rise even further prompting even higher wage demands, and so on.

Increases in the cost of materials, transport, energy and other costs of production can also place upward pressure in prices. For example, inflation rose rapidly in many economics in 1974 and 1979 following significant increases in the world price of oil. Today, rising food, fuel and energy costs are contributing to rising inflation rates around the world.

Price inflation

Imported inflation

Rising prices in one country may be 'exported' to other countries through international trade. Rising import prices can cause **imported inflation**. Similarly, a fall in the value of the national currency against the currencies of other countries will mean imports become more expensive in that country. For example, if value of the euro against the Indian rupee falls from €1 = 60 rupees to €1 = 30 rupees, then a product imported to Europe from India priced at 600 rupees will rise from €10 to €20. ➤ **8.1**

It has been argued that one of the main reasons why many economies enjoyed relatively low and stable price inflation during the 1990s and in the first decade of this century was because of low wage costs in China and the growth of exports from the Chinese manufacturing industry. However, by 2010 many economists were suggesting that this period had come to and end as wages began to rise rapidly in China. ➤ **3.2**

ECONOMICS IN ACTION

What factors have caused, and continue to drive, inflationary pressures in China and why is this worrying other countries?

The 800-Pound Inflation Gorilla

In 2011 China was the 2nd largest economy in the world and gaining rapidly on the U.S. Among other statistics, it's the world's largest importer of copper, steel, cotton, and soybeans, and the world's largest exporter of goods – to say nothing of being the world's largest provider of debt finance to the U.S.

Global inflation fears started to rise as China launched a massive $585 billion fiscal stimulus in the depths of the financial crisis in 2009. All that easy money chasing a limited supply of goods, properties, and investments caused China's economy and stock market to surge ahead.

But the problems began coming home to roost last year. Concern about its overheated economy and soaring real estate prices finally prompted the Chinese central bank to raise interest rates, but this did little to slow down demand.

The global spike-up in food and oil prices has not helped for sure. But China's inflation problems are not just confined to real estate and commodity prices.

China is in the stage of its economic development where it needs, and wants, to increase domestic demand for its products, and move away from a dependence on exports. To achieve that goal, wages and salaries must rise to move more of the population into the middle class. Already the minimum wage in China's major cities and ports has been raised an average of 10%. Meanwhile, the Chinese government is meeting this weekend to establish China's next 'Five-Year Plan'. An important feature of the plan is reportedly endorsement of higher wages and salaries across the economy

Wage-price inflation is the worst kind of inflation because it feeds on itself. As wages rise, companies have to increase the prices of their products. As prices rise further, workers demand still higher wages, and a difficult to stop inflationary spiral can get underway, as took place globally in the 1970s.

With China being the world's largest exporter, a potential wage-price spiral has serious implications for the rest of the world.

For example, Li & Fung Ltd., headquartered in Hong Kong, the largest supplier of products to Wal-Mart, predicted that the price of Chinese exports will increase as much as 15% this year. The second-largest retailer in Britain, Next Plc, said it expects higher labor costs in China will result in an 8% increase in its prices in the first half of this year.

SECTION 4

The benefits of low and stable inflation

The costs of inflation

Governments often aim to keep inflation in their economies at around 2–3% per year. Low inflation can be beneficial for an economy. It encourages consumers to buy goods and services sooner rather than later as delaying will mean they will have to pay more for the same product.

Low inflation also makes it more appealing to borrow money, since interest rates are also usually low during periods of low inflation. For example, if inflation and interest rates are low and stable, firms will be more optimistic and more confident to borrow money to invest in new plant and machinery, and this will enable higher rates of economic growth in the future. A low and stable demand-pull inflation will also tend to boost profits.

Also, if the government is committed to keeping inflation within a certain target it may result in expectations that inflation will be low, and this will help reduce demands for higher wages by workers and their representatives. In fact, if money wages rise by less than the inflation rate each year, the real cost of employing workers will fall for firms and may encourage them to increase their demand for labour.

ACTIVITY 6.3

How inflation can affect different households

The tables below shows how different income groups in a developed economy might allocate their spending to different goods and services.

LOW INCOME %age of spending
- Housing............15
- Leisure............13
- Fuel................7
- Food...............24
- Drink & Tobacco....7
- Clothes.............5
- Household Goods...13
- Transport & Services..11
- Miscellaneous.......5

MIDDLE INCOME %age of spending
- Housing............16
- Leisure............14
- Fuel................5
- Food...............20
- Drink & Tobacco....6
- Clothes.............6
- Household Goods...13
- Transport & Services..15
- Miscellaneous.......5

HIGH INCOME %age of spending
- Housing............13
- Leisure............13
- Fuel................3
- Food...............15
- Drink & Tobacco....5
- Clothes.............6
- Household Goods...14
- Transport & Services..16
- Miscellaneous.......5

1 How does inflation affect the amount of goods and services money can buy?

2 Which income group displayed above will be the most affected by a rise in the price of:
   a food, heating fuel and housing costs?   b household goods and transport?

3 Are people always worse off if prices rise? Explain your answer.

4 Which income groups above are probably the:
   a most able to raise their incomes at the same rate as inflation or higher?
   b least able to raise their incomes at the same rate as inflation?

Exports from a country that has lower price inflation than others will also become more competitive than rival products from overseas producers on international markets. This will help to boost demand for those exports, thereby creating additional incomes and employment opportunities in the low inflation country.

Maintaining low inflation is therefore an important goal for many governments and central banks because of the economic benefits. ➤ **5.1**

However, high and rising rates of inflation can cause significant problems for different groups of people and the economy they live in.

The personal costs of inflation

Inflation erodes the value or **purchasing power** of money. For example, if the price of a good today is $1 but it increases at the rate of 5% each year, its price rises to $1.05 next year, to $1.28 after 5 years and to $1.63 after 10 years. It follows that a dollar of currency exchanged for the good today will not be enough to purchase that same product in the future.

Looked at another way, $1 of currency today will only be able to purchase the equivalent of 95 cents one year from now, or 78 cents 5 years from now and 61 cents in 10 years time.

If inflation was 5% per year…

a dollar today will be worth…   78 cents in 5 years from now   61 cents in 10 years from now

If inflation was 10% each year, the purchasing power of the currency would be eroded much faster. After 5 years it would purchase the same as 62 cents will today and just 38 cents after 10 years of annual inflation at 10% per year.

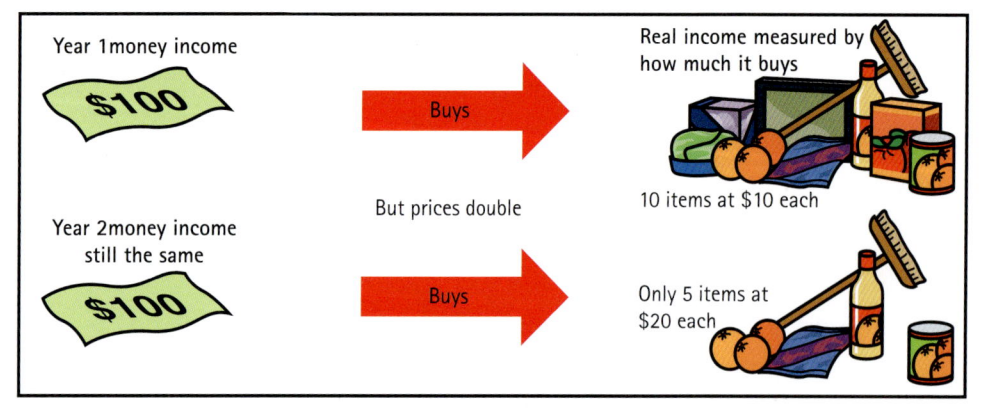

Year 1 money income $100 Buys 10 items at $10 each (Real income measured by how much it buys)

But prices double

Year 2 money income still the same $100 Buys Only 5 items at $20 each

Inflation therefore reduces the **real income** of every person in terms of what their income can buy over time. For example, if a person's **money income** (or **nominal income**) was $100 it could buy 10 products at $10 each. If each one of those products increases in price to $20 that person's money income of $100 will now only buy five of those products. That is, his or her real income has fallen. Clearly, if the person could increase his or her money income to $200, that person will be no worse off. However, many people will face hardship if they are unable to increase their money incomes at the same rate as price inflation.

338 Economic indicators

Old-age pensioners, the unemployed and other people who tend to be on fixed incomes and welfare payments are particularly vulnerable to high and rising inflation. If the prices of the goods and services they buy rise they will be unable to afford as much food, heating and other goods and services as they did before. Their real incomes and therefore their living standards will fall. For example, if the general level of prices rises by 10% in one year, real incomes will have fallen by 10%. Increasing pensions and other fixed incomes in line with inflation, known as indexation or index-linking, can help overcome this problem.

In contrast, skilled labour and workers with strong bargaining power will probably be able to secure wage or salary increases that protect their real wages and incomes. Indeed, they may be able to push for an increase in their money incomes that exceeds the rate of inflation. For example, if inflation is 10% in one year and their money incomes increase by 15%, then in real terms they will be 5% better off. However, many workers, especially the low paid and non-unionized workers, may have very little bargaining strength in wage negotiations. As prices rise their real incomes fall and they become worse off. Despite rising food and energy prices during the widespread recession in 2008 and 2009, many workers had their pay frozen or even cut as both governments and firms in many countries cut back their spending. ➤ **5.2**

People who save or lend money may also be badly affected by inflation. If the interest rate received on the money they have saved or loaned is lower than the rate of price inflation the real value of their money will fall. They will be worse off. In contrast, people who have borrowed money will benefit by repaying less in real terms than the amount they were originally loaned.

The costs of inflation to an economy

High and rising inflation can cause many problems in an economy:

- **It imposes additional costs on firms**

In a demand-pull inflation increased consumer spending tends to boost company profits. In contrast, in a cost-push inflation their profits are squeezed. However, all types of inflation can involve 'menu costs'. This is a general term used to describe all types of inconvenience that firms and individuals can face as prices continue to rise. For example, as prices increase firms will have to retype and print new price lists, change price labels, reprint menus and so on. Individual consumers may also face surcharges on products they have already paid for, such as additional charges for holidays to cover higher fuel costs for flights or voyages on cruise ships. Consumers may also have to spend more time searching around for the best bargains as the prices of the products they want continue to rise.

- **It reduces the competitiveness of exports**

If prices in an exporting country are rising at a faster rate than prices in rival countries then exports from that country will become less competitive on international markets. Demand for those exports from overseas consumers may fall. This will have a negative effect on the balance of payments and employment in exporting industries. ➤ **8.2**

- **It creates economic uncertainty**

If inflation is high or keeps rising, consumers, firms and governments may find it difficult to plan ahead. They may be uncertain about their costs in the future and the impact inflation may have on their incomes and revenues. Firms may become reluctant to invest in new plant and equipment and individual consumers may be reluctant to spend. Both of these factors could reduce employment and future economic growth.

If inflation is very volatile and becomes a **hyperinflation**, people may lose all confidence in their currency as a medium of exchange and store of value. ➤ **3.1**

It is not surprising therefore that many economists and the governments they advise argue that high and uncontrolled inflation is a cause of unemployment and low or falling economic growth in an economy, because of its impact on production costs, competitiveness and uncertainty.

> **EXAM PREPARATION 6.1**
>
> In 2004, economists were concerned about the inflationary impact of unusually high oil prices, which were caused by political uncertainty in the Middle East.
>
> a Explain how inflation is measured. [6]
> b Low inflation is one of the aims of government policy. Choose **two** other macro-economic aims of government and explain what they mean. [4]
> c Explain how high oil prices might cause inflation. [4]
> d Discuss the actions that a government might take to control inflation. [6]
>
> *Cambridge IGCSE Economics 0455/04 Q4 October/November 2006*
> *Cambridge O Level Economics 2281/02 Q4 October/November 2006*

SECTION 5

What is deflation?

Imagine you had saved up to buy a new computer, a pair of trainers or bicycle. Imagine also that over time the prices of these products had been falling and economists were predicting their prices would continue to fall over time. Would you buy them now or wait to buy them later? Clearly it would be better to wait until their prices had fallen further unless you really wanted one or more of these products so much that you just had to get them now.

Product prices can fall for a number of reasons, including when:

- their market supply has increased relative to demand
- competition between firms to supply them has increased
- labour productivity rises, increasing output and reducing average costs
- technological advance has reduced their costs of production
- market demand for them has fallen ➤ **2.2**

Increasing supply, competition, productivity and technological advance are good things for an economy and consumers and have reduced the prices of many products over time, such as mobile phones, televisions, cars, holidays and clothing, in many countries. However, when falling product prices become widespread and prolonged due to a slump in demand, the result is **deflation**. It is therefore the opposite of inflation and should not be confused with **disinflation** during which there is simply a slowdown in the rate at which prices are rising in general.

Deflation involves a continuous decline in the general level of prices in an economy. Many economies have suffered relatively short-lived deflations from time to time during economic downturns when aggregate demand tends to fall, causing many firms to compete more vigorously for available consumer spending.

However, longer periods of deflation do occur and can have very serious consequences. For example, there have been two significant periods of deflation in the world, between 1873 and 1896 following the American Civil War when prices fell in the USA on average by 1.7% a year, and in Britain by 0.8% a year, and during the Great Depression in the early 1930s when the rate of deflation in the USA was around 10% per year and unemployment reached 25% of the workforce. More recently, the worst case of deflation in consumer prices (with the exception of food and energy prices) has been experienced by Japan, starting in the early- to mid-1990s.

▼ Japanese inflation, 1970–2010 (% annual change in CPI)

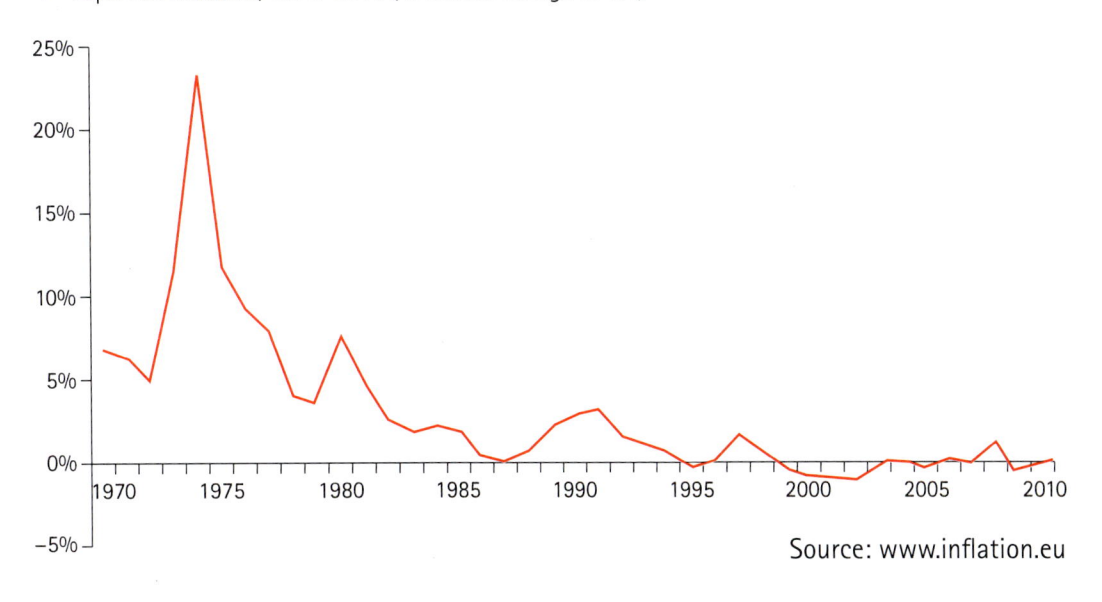

Source: www.inflation.eu

The consequences of deflation

The following changes will occur during a sustained or **malign deflation**:

- Consumers will delay many spending decisions as they wait for prices to fall further.
- Stocks of unsold goods accumulate so firms cut their prices and this reduces their profits and incentive to invest.
- Firms cut their production and reduce the size of their workforces.
- Household incomes fall as unemployment rises, further reducing demand for goods and services.
- The value of debts held by people and firms rise in real terms as prices fall and this increases the burden of making loan repayments.
- Firms stop investing in new plant and machinery as demand falls and the cost of borrowing rises. This will reduce future growth in the economy.
- The real cost of public spending rises but tax revenues fall as economic activity slumps. This means the government must borrow more money despite the rising real cost of doing so.
- Eventually the economy goes into a deep recession as demand, output, the demand for labour, and incomes continue to fall. Many firms may go out of business because they are unable to make any profit no matter how much they cut their prices by as consumers simply continue to delay their spending further.

Government policy and deflation

It is therefore hard to break out of the downward spiral that can occur in a malign deflation and it will require a major boost to consumer demand and confidence if it is to be achieved.

The first line of defence used by a government is usually to cut interest rates to a low level. However, if prices are falling this means real interest rates will be rising, even if the nominal interest rate is zero.

Imagine interest rates are zero but prices are falling by 5% each year. A woman borrows $1,000 that must be repaid in full after 12 months without interest. However, because of falling prices the real value of her debt has actually increased from $1,000 to $1,050. The real interest rate is effectively 5% even if the actual interest rate charged by a bank is zero.

ACTIVITY 6.4

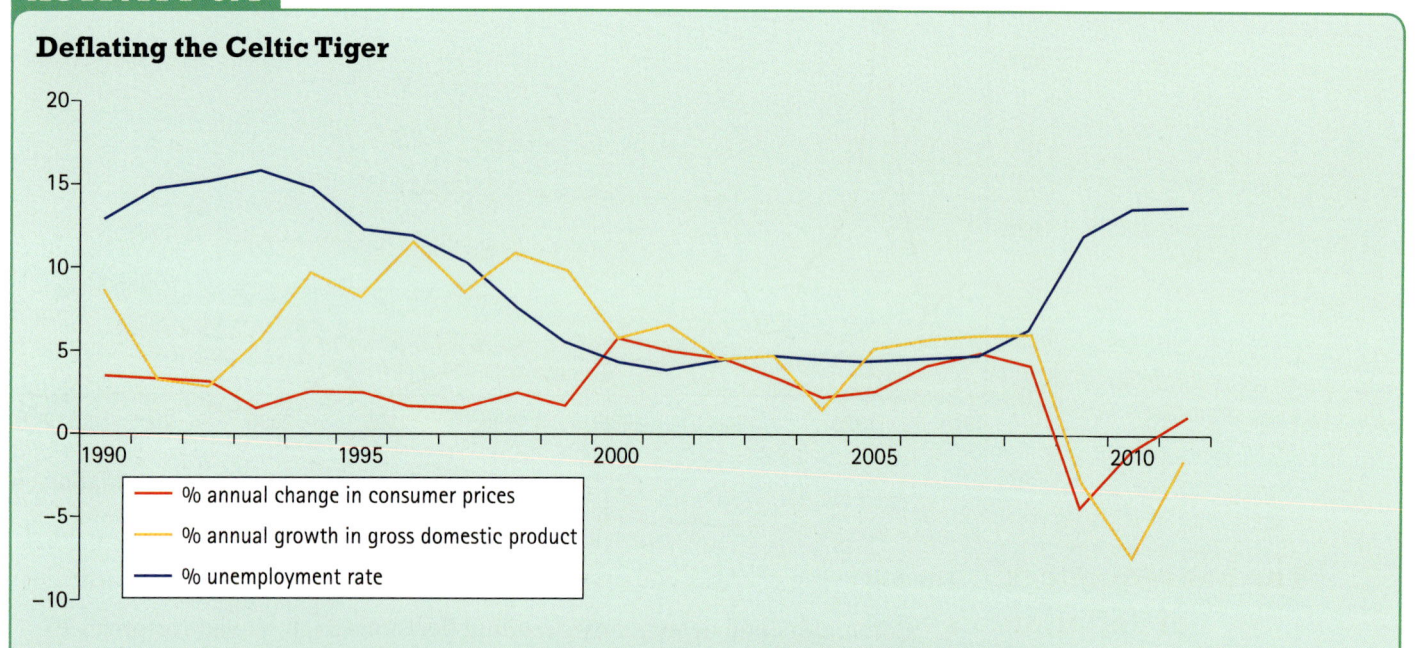

Deflating the Celtic Tiger

- % annual change in consumer prices
- % annual growth in gross domestic product
- % unemployment rate

Source: Central Statistics Office, Ireland, www.cso.ie

The chart above displays economic indicators for Ireland between 1990 and 2011.

The Irish economy was one of fastest growing economies in Europe during the 1990s and became known as the Celtic Tiger. However, boom turned to bust following the global financial crash and recession in 2008. As a result, both private sector and public sector debt increased sharply and the government had to seek financial assistance worth $113 billion from the European Union and International Monetary Fund (IMF) to help it reduce its debt and to support the fragile banking system in the country. The Irish banks had loaned heavily against land and property developments that had since fallen significantly in value due to the slump in demand. Many of their loans were in default as rising unemployment had meant many people could not continue their loan repayments.

1. Explain what each of the indicators in the chart measures
2. What trends can be identified in inflation, unemployment and output from the chart?
3. What evidence is there that there was deflation in the Irish economy towards the end of the period shown in the chart?
4. What evidence is there from the chart that deflation, unemployment and falling economic activity are closely related? Explain why.

A government may also print more currency to pump more money into the economy during a malign deflation but people and firms may not increase their own spending as a result if they expect most prices to continue falling. The additional money supply can however be used by the government to fund projects that will draw more people back into employment. An expansionary fiscal policy may also involve tax cuts on incomes and profits to boost demand.

However, all these policies have been tried in Japan yet the economy has continued to struggle with persistent deflation, slow growth and rising unemployment for many years. Japan's problems are being made more difficult by a shrinking and ageing population. This is also reducing demand for many goods and services in the Japanese economy. ➤ 7.2

WEBSITES

The following websites can help you learn more about inflation, price indices and deflation:

- *www.bized.co.uk/virtual/economy/policy/outcomes/inflation/inflth.htm*
- *www.wikipedia.org/wiki/Consumer_price_index*
- *http://economics.about.com/cs/economicsglossary/g/inflation.htm*
- *www.economicshelp.org/blog/inflation/difference-between-rpi-rpix-and-cpi/*
- *http://economics.about.com/cs/inflation/a/deflation.htm*
- *www.economywatch.com/inflation/deflation/effects.html*

KEYWORDS

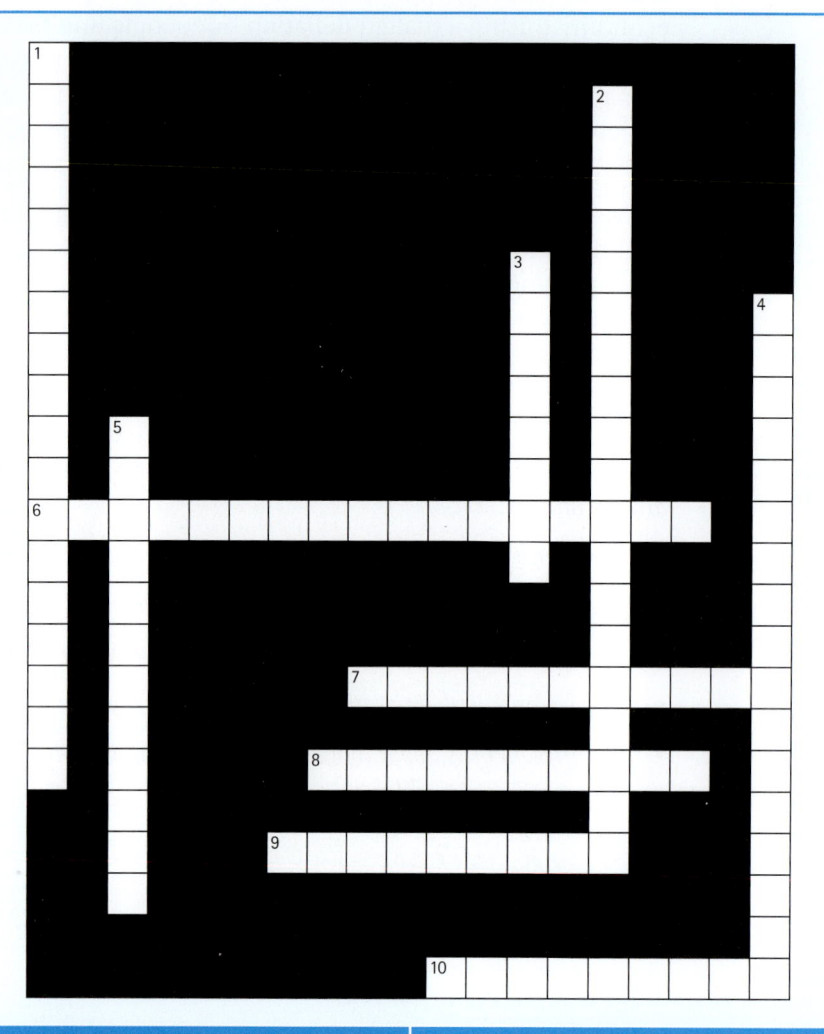

Clues across

6. Persistently rising general price levels caused by rising production costs (4,4,9)
7. An economic situation in which both price inflation and unemployment are rising (11)
8. The automatic adjustment of a monetary variable, such as wages, taxes or pension benefits, by the change in the consumer or retail price index, so that its value rises at the same rate as inflation (10)
9. A sustained decrease in the general level of prices in an economy (9)
10. A persistent rise in the general level of prices in an economy (9)

Clues down

1. An indicator of inflation that measures changes in the average price of a basket of goods and services purchased by a 'typical' hosuehold and expresses these average prices as an index number series (8,4,5)
2. A persistent increase in the general level of prices resulting from a continued excess of aggregate demand over supply (6,4,9)
3. The year used as the reference point or beginning of a consumer or retail price index in which the average price of the 'typical' basket of products is assigned the number 100 (4,4)
4. A sustained increase in the prices of products bought from overseas producers either resulting from their rising costs or a fall in the exchange rate against overseas currencies (8,9)
5. A slowdown in the rate at which the general price level is rising over time (12)

Economic indicators

Unit 6.2   Employment and unemployment

AIMS

By the end of this unit you should be able to:

▶ describe the changing patterns and levels of **employment**
- identify and discuss trends in **labour force participation rates** in different countries
- distinguish between **full-time**, **part-time** and **temporary employment** contracts

▶ discuss the causes and consequences of **unemployment**
- distinguish between **frictional**, **seasonal**, **cyclical** and **structural unemployment**
- define and calculate an **unemployment rate**
- understand how **labour market failures** can restrict employment.

SECTION 1

Employment trends

Most governments share an objective to maintain a high and stable level of employment in their economies, and a low level of unemployment. Employment provides people with incomes and wealth. In contrast, unemployment wastes productive resources.

Because of these objectives, governments and economists will be interested in keeping a close eye on the following employment trends.

▼ Key employment indicators

Labour force	The total number of people of working age in work or actively seeking work
Labour force participation rate	The labour force as a proportion of the total working-age population
Employment by industrial sector	How many people work in agriculture and manufacturing industries, relative to services
Employment status	The number of people employed full-time, part-time or in temporary work
Unemployment	The number of people registered as being without work, and as a proportion of the total labour force (the unemployment rate)

▼ Global employment and unemployment, 1999–2010

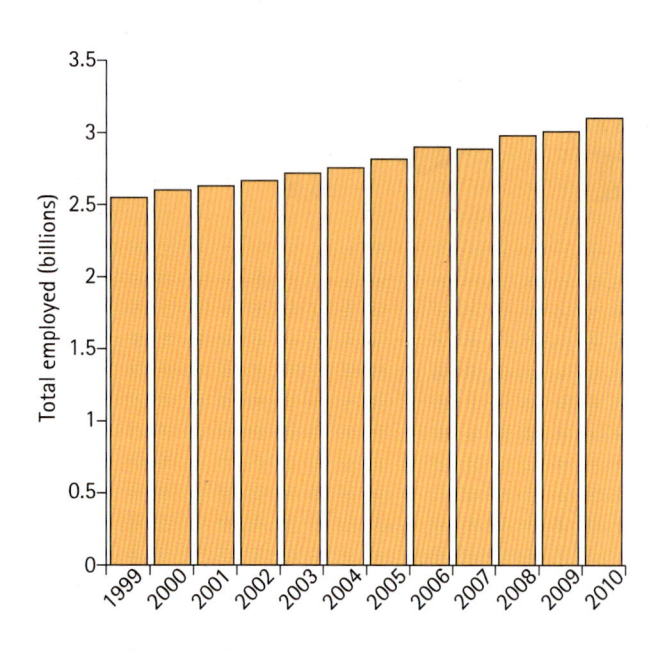

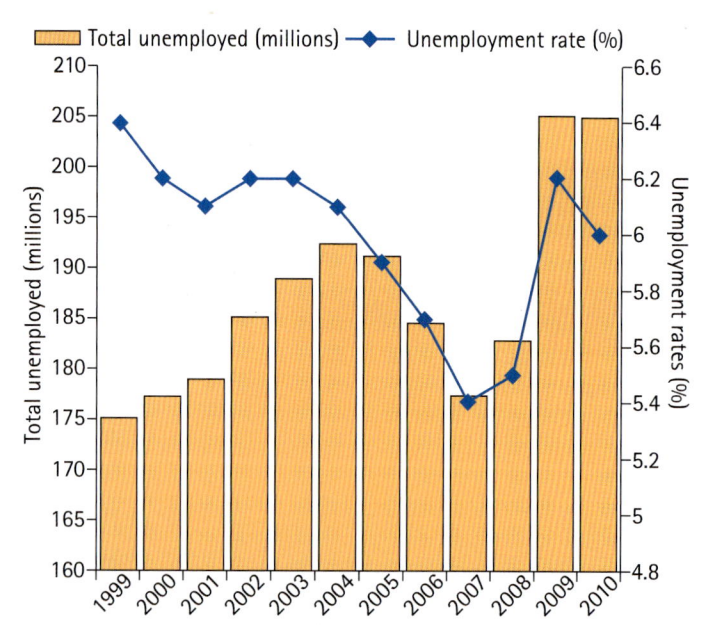

Source: 'Global employment and unemployment 1999-2010' reproduced from *Global Employment Trends 2011*, copyright © International Labour Organization, 2011.

Labour force participation

Between 1999 and 2010 the global labour force grew by around 550 million workers, to just over 3 billion. The **labour force** is the **working population** or **economically active population** of a country. It consists of all those people of working age who are both able and willing to work. That is, it forms the total supply of labour in a country and usually includes people who are employed by private sector firms and public sector organizations, the self-

346 Economic indicators

employed, the armed forces, those on work-related government training programmes and even people who are unemployed but looking for work.

People not counted as economically active in the labour force include students in education, retired people, stay-at-home parents, people in prisons or similar institutions, as well as people who simply do not want to work. These form the **dependent population** because they depend on the labour force to produce and supply the goods and services they need and want. ➤ **7.2**

▼ The working and dependent populations

The Young | Housewives | Schoolchildren and Students | The Employed | Self Employed | Armed Forces | The Unemployed | The Old and Severely Disabled

The **labour force participation rate** measures the percentage of the working-age population that is either in work or looking for work and therefore able to produce goods and services. Globally the labour force participation rate has fallen slightly over time, from 65.5% in 1999 to 64.7% over the 10-year period to 2010. This means around 65 people in every 100 in the global population of working age is in or seeking paid employment. Much of this decline in participation is explained by the increasing number of younger people in education worldwide and the growing number of old and retired people in many developed countries. ➤ **7.2**

However, not all countries have followed the global trend. Participation in the labour force has risen over time in a number of developing countries and especially among females, particularly in Latin America and the Caribbean, the Middle East and Africa. For example, around 23% of females of working age participated in the labour force in the Middle East in 1999. By 2009 this had increased to over 25% of females of working age.

There are a number of reasons for these patterns in participation rates. In less-developed countries, poverty has forced many people to seek paid employment rather than work on the land to grow the food they need and they hope will yield a surplus they can sell. But many workers in less-developed countries still earn very low wages. ➤ **7.1**

Increasing real wages in many countries have also attracted more females into work. The rising cost of living in many of these countries has also forced many into work to maintain the living standards of their families. This can explain why more mothers are returning to work after raising children, or younger women entering the labour market rather than starting a family. Social attitudes have also changed in many countries so that is it now more acceptable for wives and mothers to work. Many more part-time jobs have become available to them so they can balance their family and working commitments.

Employment and unemployment | 347

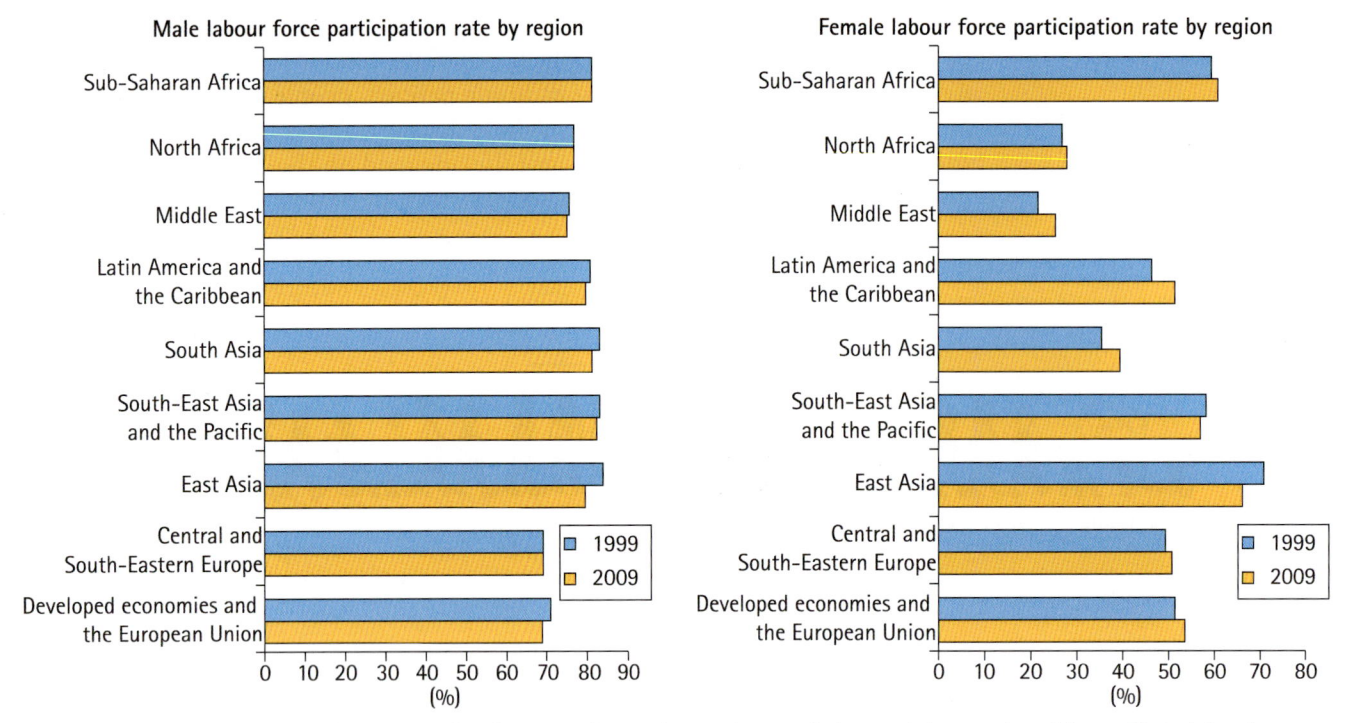

▼ How labour force participation rates have changed around the world

Male labour force participation rate by region (1999 blue, 2009 yellow), regions: Sub-Saharan Africa, North Africa, Middle East, Latin America and the Caribbean, South Asia, South-East Asia and the Pacific, East Asia, Central and South-Eastern Europe, Developed economies and the European Union. X-axis 0–90 (%).

Female labour force participation rate by region (1999 blue, 2009 yellow), same regions. X-axis 0–80 (%).

Source: 'How labour force participation rates have changed around the world' reproduced from *Global Employment Trends 2011*, copyright © International Labour Organization, 2011.

Employment by industrial sector

However, male participation rates have been falling. Globally, around 80 in every 100 males of working age was in work or seeking work in 1999. By 2009 this had fallen to around 78. This fall has been explained by the changing industrial structure in many developed economies, with traditionally male-dominated sectors such as mining and manufacturing industries shrinking over time as their tertiary sectors have expanded. But falling male participation rates have also been observed in many developing countries as female participation has increased.

In 2009, the agriculture sector employed around 35% of global employees, or just over 1 billion workers. This compared with 21.8% employed in mining, construction and manufacturing industries, and 43.2% in services.

However, there are big regional differences. In developed economies such as the USA and Europe, agriculture employed just 3.7% of their employees in 2009. The service sector dominates these economies, accounting for just under 73% of their total employment. In stark contrast, agriculture continues to dominate employment in economies in South Asia and Sub-Saharan Africa, employing over 53% of all employees in these economies. ► **7.2**

Many economies are experiencing the same broad trends. The share of employment accounted for by jobs in agriculture has been falling as the share of total employment in services has risen around the world. Globally, services employed just over 43 out of every 100 employees in 2009 compared with just over 39 out of every 100 in 1999. However, while employment in manufacturing and construction in many developed economies continues to decline, these industries are expanding rapidly in newly industrialized economies in regions such as South and East Asia, including China and India.

Changes in the industrial structure of economies have been a cause for some concern. The loss of jobs from agriculture, mining and manufacturing industries

▼ Shares of total employment by sector and region (%)

in many developed economies has increased unemployment in some cases, especially in economies in which these industries once dominated. Nearly 73 out of every 100 employees in developed economies are now employed in services.

Region	Agriculture 1999	Agriculture 2009	Industry 1999	Industry 2009	Services 1999	Services 2009
World	40.2	35.0	20.6	21.8	39.1	43.2
Developed economies and the European Union	5.6	3.7	27.6	23.4	66.9	72.8
Central and Eastern Europe	27.0	20.2	24.5	24.6	48.5	55.2
East Asia	47.9	36.9	23.8	27.8	28.3	35.3
South East Asia and the Pacific	49.3	44.3	15.9	17.8	34.8	38.0
South Asia	59.5	53.5	15.4	18.9	25.1	27.6
Latin America and the Caribbean	21.5	16.9	21.4	22.1	57.1	61.6
Middle East	22.1	19.1	25.9	26.1	52.1	54.8
North Africa	29.2	27.8	20.5	22.5	50.3	49.7
Sub-Saharan Africa	62.4	59.0	8.8	10.6	28.8	30.4

The decline of employment in agriculture and the expansion of jobs in industry and services have also meant that many people have moved from rural areas into urban areas in many developing countries. The rapid growth of densely populated urban areas and increasing demand for energy, rising car use and overcrowding are causing many problems. ➤ 2.3

Source: International Labour Organization (ILO), Global Employment Trends 2011

Employment status

Most workers, especially males, are in **full-time employment** contracts which for many means working Monday to Friday each week, for around seven to eight hours each day. However, hours of work vary greatly in different countries. For example, the average worker in France worked 38 hours each week in 2009, up slightly from 37.2 hours in 2000. This compared with an average in 2009 of 46.6 hours per worker per week on average in Korea and around 49.4 hours per week in Turkey.

Many countries follow an international standard that defines the working week as 40 hours from Monday to Friday, although clearly many people are employed to work weekends and overtime. The EU Working Time Directive regulates that workers cannot be forced to work for more than 48 hours per week on average, although the UK allows individual employees to opt out if they so choose. ➤ 3.2

In many countries, average hours worked per week have fallen over time as working conditions have improved, and as a result of more **part-time employment** opportunities.

There has been rapid growth in part-time employment in the last few decades and in Sunday working in many developed economies. These trends are related to the increase in the female participation rate, but also linked to growth in the services sector, and particularly in retailing. Hiring part-time workers allows firms greater flexibility to remain operational for more hours each day and to use more staff during busy periods.

Unemployment

People without work but who are actively looking for employment are considered to be unemployed. In 2010, over 205 million people were unemployed globally. There was an increase of almost 28 million in just three years since early 2008 following the global financial crisis and economic recession. ➤ 6.3

Almost half of the unemployed are young people. Young workers tend to be the least productive employees until they have developed the skills and experience they need. They are often therefore the first to be laid off when firms cut back staff to reduce their costs or during an economic recession when demand is falling.

Unemployment is usually measured by the number of people claiming welfare or unemployment benefits. However, in many countries benefits may only be paid for a short period of time, and some people who want to work may not receive any financial help from government. This group might include people who are old or disabled, mothers looking after children at home, students who want to work but instead continue with their education, and people who may only work a few hours each week but would like to work longer.

In practice, therefore, measuring the number of unemployed workers actually seeking work is very difficult and measures can vary by country. Some countries do not pay benefits to unemployed people and may not even count the number of people without paid work, so numbers are estimated where possible.

▼ Unemployment rate (%) by region

Region	2000	2010
World	6.3	6.1
Developed Economies and European Union	6.7	8.8
Central and Eastern Europe	10.8	9.5
East Asia	4.4	4.1
South East Asia and the Pacific	5.0	4.8
South Asia	4.4	3.9
Latin America and the Caribbean	8.6	7.2
Middle East	10.5	9.9
North Africa	13.6	9.6
Sub-Saharan Africa	9.2	8.2

Source: International Labour Organization, 2011

▼ Countries with the highest unemployment rates (%)

Country	Unemployment rate %, est.
Zimbabwe	95.0
Nauru	90.0
Liberia	85.0
Burkino Faso	77.0
Turkmenistan	60.0
Cocos (Keeling) Islands	60.0
Djibouti	59.0
Namibia	51.2
Zambia	50.0
Senegal	48.0

Source: *CIA World Factbook*, 2011

The **unemployment rate** in an economy is the percentage of people in its labour force that are without work and recorded as unemployed. Globally, the unemployment rate fell during the economic boom in the middle of the last decade from 6.4% in 1999 to 5.4% in 2007. However, unemployment rose sharply around the world between 2008 and 2010 as the boom came to end and many economies suffered from falling incomes and demand during the recession. By 2010 the unemployment rate had climbed back up to 6%. This meant 6 out of every 100 people of working age in the global labour force was without paid employment in 2010.

The global economic recession from 2008 to 2010 affected some regions far more than others. In some developed economies, including some in the European Union, the unemployment rate climbed from 12.4% in 2007 to over 18% in 2010 with countries such as Spain, Greece and Ireland particularly badly hit. In other regions the unemployment rate increased only slightly, while in the South and South East of Asia and the Pacific the unemployment rate continued to fall as many of these economies continued to expand.

ACTIVITY 6.6

Calculating unemployment rates

The table below presents data on the labour force and number of people unemployed in selected countries in 2005 and 2010. From these calculate the unemployment rate in each country for each year using the following formula.

$$\text{Unemployment rate (\%)} = \frac{\text{number unemployed}}{\text{labour force}} \times 100$$

Country	Labour force (000s) 2005	Labour force (000s) 2010	Unemployed (000s) 2005	Unemployed (000s) 2010
Czech Republic	5,174	5,287	410	352
France	28,123	28,694	2,462	2,603
Japan	66,500	66,170	2,940	3,360
Mexico	41,925	46,399	1,470	2,353
Spain	20,885	23,037	1,911	4,147
Turkey	25,065	21,791	2,388	3,471
USA	150,581	155,454	7,591	14,265

Source: OECD

The highest unemployment rates are observed in many of the least developed economies in the world where low levels of education and skills among the labour force and a lack of paid employment opportunities continue to cause problems for economic development. ➤ 6.3

EXAM PREPARATION 6.2

Unemployment in eurozone countries fell to a record low towards the end of 2006 as many European economies enjoyed an economic boom. As a result, there was concern that inflation could increase.

a Identify two possible advantages for an economy if unemployment falls. [2]
b Define inflation and briefly describe how it is calculated. [6]
c Identify **two** types of unemployment and explain how they are caused. [4]
d Discuss whether a reduction in unemployment should be the main aim of government policy [8]

SECTION 2 — The causes and consequences of unemployment

Casual and seasonal factors

There will always be some unemployment in an economy. **Frictional unemployment** occurs as workers leave one job and spend some time looking for a new one. Workers may become unemployed for relatively short periods as they leave jobs they dislike, move to higher paid jobs, move their homes, are made redundant or are sacked. People who are 'in between jobs' do not tend to remain unemployed for long.

Similarly, **seasonal unemployment** occurs because consumer demand for some goods and services is seasonal. For example, the number of jobs in the tourist industry tends to expand during the summer because that is when most people want to take holidays. However, during winter months many workers in hotels and holiday resorts are not required. Agriculture and construction activity also tend to be very seasonal.

Frictional and seasonal unemployment are not a big problem. Most governments, however, are concerned with unemployment that is long-lived and due to more serious problems in their economies.

ACTIVITY 6.6

What causes unemployment?

Look at the extracts below. What do they suggest causes unemployment? In groups, write a report for your government expressing a summary of your thoughts on the possible causes of unemployment and what actions you might take to reduce it.

Firms cut output as consumer spending falls

Government introduces minimum wage law: businesses warn demand for labour will fall

---

State council votes to increase unemployment tax

Starting January 1, employers will be hit with a 50 percent increase in the taxes they pay to fund unemployment benefits, the Nevada State Employment Security Council decided Tuesday.

Despite business leaders' protests, council members voted to increase the unemployment tax rate to an average of 2 percent on the first $26,600 of each employee's wages, up from the 1.33 percent rate.

The Las Vegas Chamber of Commerce had urged the council to keep the current rate since higher taxes will raise the cost of employing people and will force some businesses to lay off more workers.

The Council argued the tax increase is necessary to cover the increasing cost of providing public unemployment insurance. The unemployment rate in Nevada has increased over the last two years to over 21 percent.

Unemployed workers in Nevada receive weekly benefit checks that average $325. The taxes paid by Nevada employers cover the maximum 26 weeks of state benefits that some unemployed workers receive. Some business leaders have argued these benefits are too generous. They suggest a family man on or below average earnings will be better not working and receiving benefits.

---

700 Jobs lost in switch to new technology

At least one quarter of a major newspaper's workforce are to be made redundant this week in a plan to introduce new computerised typesetting and printing machines

---

Business experts call for help for manufacturing industries

A study by a group of business experts has found that the country's poor export performance and high import penetration is the result of low levels of investment in capital and workforce skills. This has caused a serious decline in the health of the manufacturing industry. The report argues government assistance is required to boost performance and jobs.

Falling aggregate demand

Falling aggregate demand for goods and services can have a downward multiplier effect on output, employment and incomes.

Demand-deficient unemployment or **cyclical unemployment** occurs when there is too little demand for goods and services in the economy during an economic recession. ▶ 6.3

Economic indicators

Falling demand during a downturn in an economic cycle will mean reduced spending on goods and services. Stocks of unsold products will accumulate and in response firms will cut their production and workers may become unemployed.

A change in aggregate demand whatever its source, be it consumption expenditure, investment by firms, government spending and/or spending on exports by overseas consumers, can have widespread effects in an economy. Once under way, a change in expenditure will tend to carry on. Why is this so?

ACTIVITY 6.7

The multiplier effect

A fall in total demand in an economy can have widespread effects. This is known as the multiplier effect.

Here is an example of how unemployment can spread following a fall in demand for automobiles.

Our simple example involves an imaginary car manufacturer called Fast Cars Inc. It has a plant in Malaysia that assembles cars from materials and components made by other companies in the country.

As demand for its cars falls Fast Cars Inc has no need to make so many. As a result, it reduces production and makes 400 of its workers redundant. Now consider how this might spread.

1. How many jobs are lost immediately as a result of the fall in demand for cars?
2. How many jobs are lost in Fast Cars Inc in total?
3. All the factories use electricity. As they now produce fewer cars they do not need to consume much electricity. What may happen to output and employment at power stations?
4. The power stations run on coal and oil. What will happen to the demand for coal and oil? What will happen to coal miners and oil drillers?
5. All the people who have lost their jobs now have less money to spend on clothes, entertainment, food, travel and many other things. What is likely to happen to the level of demand for these goods?

In Activity 6.7, the fall in demand for cars forced Fast Cars to reduce production and cut employment in many of its factories. Fast Cars buys component parts and uses power produced by other firms that also reduce their output as demand for their products falls. The workers who find themselves out of work have less money to spend. Shops suffer and have to reduce their orders from their suppliers. The fall in demand for goods and services becomes more widespread and causes many more firms to reduce their output and employment. As unemployment rises so aggregate demand falls. Firms cut back their demand for labour further. This is known as the **multiplier effect** whereby a relatively small change in total expenditure can cause much larger changes in income, output and employment

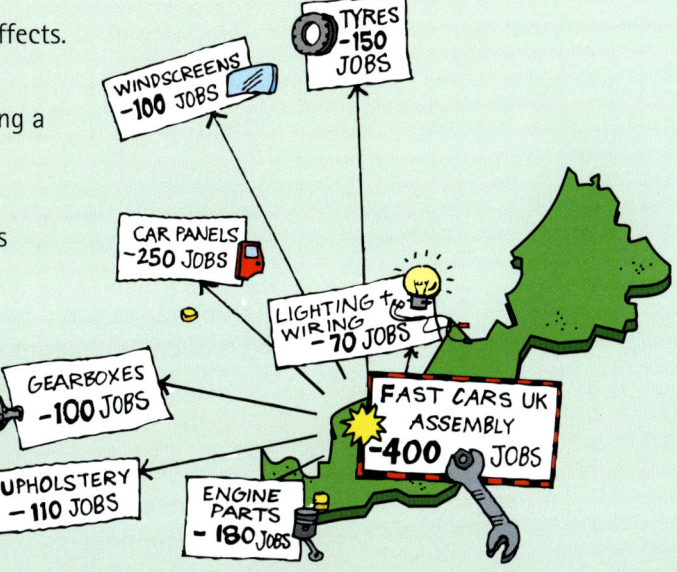

Structural change

If the fall in demand for some goods and services is permanent because of a change in people's tastes, for example in favour of new goods and services or cheaper sources of supply from overseas firms, the change in demand is called structural.

Structural unemployment arises from long-term changes in the structure of an economy as entire industries in an economy close down because of a lack of demand for the goods or services they produce or because production is moved to countries overseas able to produce at much lower average costs, often because their wages are lower. As a result, many workers are made unemployed and have skills that are no longer wanted. That is, they are occupationally immobile because they lack the skills modern industries want. Re-training them in new skills may help them become more mobile and find new jobs. ➤ 3.2

Structural change can cause prolonged **regional unemployment** if most of the firms in the affected industries are located in one particular area.

Changes in industrial structure is evident in many developed and developing economies. Many years ago far more people were employed in agriculture than in manufacturing industries. Manufacturing has also changed over time in many countries from labour-intensive production in industries such as shipbuilding, coal mining and textiles, to the high-tech capital-intensive production of computers, pharmaceuticals and electronic equipment. Nowadays most workers in developed countries are employed in services.

Technological change

Technological progress has had a major impact on the way many goods and services are produced and sold. Industrial robots and computerized machinery and equipment have been substituted for labour in many modern production processes, giving rise to what has been termed **technological unemployment**. For example, many banks and retailers are reducing the number of staff they employ as more people bank and shop online using the Internet. However, as economists we should consider the potential benefits of being able to reallocate these unemployed resources to other uses. For example, there has been a rapid growth in employment in technologically advanced industries such as electronics, biotechnology, renewable energy and mobile communications.

Imperfections in the labour market

Demand and supply conditions will determine the market wage rates for different occupations and how many workers are employed in a free labour market. However, labour markets in many countries have imperfections that can disrupt labour market outcomes and the efficient allocation of resources. ➤ 2.2

1 Powerful trade unions may force up wages

Trade unions may attempt to increase the wages of their members without also improving their labour productivity, for example by restricting the supply of labour to an industry or occupation by insisting all workers belong to the union or by threatening to take industrial action. As wages rise, employers may not be able to afford to employ as many workers and will contract their demand for labour. Reducing the bargaining power of trade unions, it is argued, may allow wages to fall and employment to rise. ➤ 3.3

2 Unemployment benefits may reduce the incentive to work

Some countries provide welfare or unemployment benefits to people who become unemployed. However, some people argue these can reduce people's incentive to seek paid employment, especially if these benefits are too generous.

People who decide not to work (**voluntary unemployment**) could be forced back to work if the benefits they receive are cut. However, this may be unfair to those people who are out of work through no fault of their own, for example because of a fall in the demand for the good or service they produce (**involuntary unemployment**).

3   Other employment costs can reduce the demand for labour

Firms that employ workers may have to pay more than just their wages to do so. As well as wages and salaries, total employment costs may include taxes and contributions to fund publicly provided unemployment and welfare benefits and non-wage costs including sickness, maternity and paternity costs, recruitment and training costs. If any of these additional costs increase, the demand for labour by firms may fall and unemployment will tend to rise. Cutting payroll taxes on employment may therefore increase the demand for labour.

4   A lack of information can prevent people from finding jobs

Unemployment may be higher and people may remain unemployed for longer periods than necessary if they have trouble finding jobs because of a lack of information on employment opportunities or because it costs too much time and money to search for the most suitable ones.

Workers who become unemployed may never be fully aware of all the various jobs that might be suitable for them and the wages, conditions and other factors involved in these jobs. They will spend time and effort looking for the best match for their skills and interests. This of course is beneficial for an economy since it results in a much better allocation of resources. However, if the cost of job search is too high, or if it takes people too long to find suitable jobs and so they make too many compromises by accepting less suitable jobs or by waiting for better jobs to become available, then an economy will suffer: the allocation of resources will not be as good as it could be, productivity will be lower and some work may even not get done.

Governments can help reduce search costs by providing advice and assistance to people looking for employment and by collecting information about job vacancies and providing it at government-funded employment offices and agencies.

5   Minimum wage legislation may reduce labour demand

Many countries have introduced laws that make it an offence for a firm to pay its workers less than a certain hourly, daily or monthly wage. The first national minimum wage laws were introduced by New Zealand in 1896. Minimum wages are designed to raise the market wage rates of the lowest paid workers. However, some employers argue they have been set too high in some countries and this has reduced their demand for labour, especially for low-skilled workers with low levels of productivity. ➤ **3.2**

6   Labour immobility prevents workers from finding new jobs

When economists talk of labour immobility they refer to the inability of workers to move easily into other jobs. When unemployed workers are immobile they will tend to remain out of work for longer periods of time.

Occupational immobility refers to the inability of workers to move easily between different occupations because of a lack of transferable skills. For example, an engineer will be unable to get a job as a doctor in a hospital without extensive re-training.

However, in some cases a trade union closed shop may prevent non-union members taking on a particular job. Professional associations of solicitors or architects, for example, may act in the same way and prevent people entering their occupation unless they have taken certain professional examinations.

Some employers may even refuse to employ some people because of their sex or colour, although this is illegal in many countries if it can be proved.

Other workers are immobile if they are unable or unwilling to move to another area to take up a job. In this case a worker is said to be **geographically immobile**. Regional differences in house prices, ties with family and friends, children's schooling and many other factors may prevent people from moving location in search of work. ➤ **3.2**

The costs of unemployment

Labour unemployment has been described as a 'drain on a nation' and 'a waste of resources'. In this section we will try to discover the consequences of labour unemployment.

Personal costs

Unemployment can have both economic and emotional costs. People who lose their jobs will lose their income and may have to rely on charity or government benefits. Unemployed people can also lose their working skills if they are unemployed for a long period of time and, without re-training, they may find it even harder to find work. They may become depressed, possibly even ill, and it may also put a strain on other family members and health-care services.

> The Jamaica Gleaner Youth Link usefully describes some of the personal and social costs of unemployment as follows:
>
> - Persons who are unemployed are unable to earn money to meet their financial obligations.
> - In many cases, unemployment results in failure to meet mortgage payments or rent. It may lead to homelessness through foreclosure or eviction.
> - Unemployment increases people's susceptibility to malnutrition, illness, mental stress and loss of self-esteem, leading to depression.
> - The combination of unemployment, lack of financial resources and social responsibilities may push unemployed workers to take jobs that do not fit their skills or allow them to use their talents.
> - Unemployment can cause underemployment, and fear of job loss can cause psychological anxiety.
> - During a long period of unemployment, workers can lose their skills, causing a loss of their human capital and future earning potential.
> - High levels of unemployment can increase crime and cause civil unrest.

ACTIVITY 6.8

A sorry tale to tell

UNEMPLOYED DROWN THEIR SORROWS

Beneath the national aggregates for disposable income and consumer durables, the country is fostering an underclass of unemployed and unskilled workers, afflicted by family breakdown and also alcoholism, according to recent data.

In recent years a network of advisory and counselling services have grown up, among them Alcoholics Anonymous, reflecting growing alcohol abuse in society and especially among the unemployed. In spite of the fact that the unemployed usually have less to spend on drink and everything else there is a considerably higher proportion of heavy drinkers among unemployed men.

In addition, divorce rates among couples where the man is jobless are noticeably high. There is also a link with chronic illness.

▼ Suicide and unemployment in Japan

1. What impact can unemployment have on government finances and the economy?
2. How do the articles suggest unemployment can affect families?
3. What other personal costs can an unemployed person face?
4. Ronald Reagan, the 40th president of the USA, once famously described unemployment benefits as 'a pre-paid vacation for freeloaders'. Using information from the articles and drawing on your own experience of people who have been or are unemployed, write a series of short letters of complaint to a national newspaper to express how you might feel about being out of work if you were:
   a a teenager living with parents who are unemployed
   b an unemployed person in their early thirties with children to support
   c a person in their late fifties who until recently has been in work all their life.

For each case, compare your views on how you might feel with the views of others in your class.

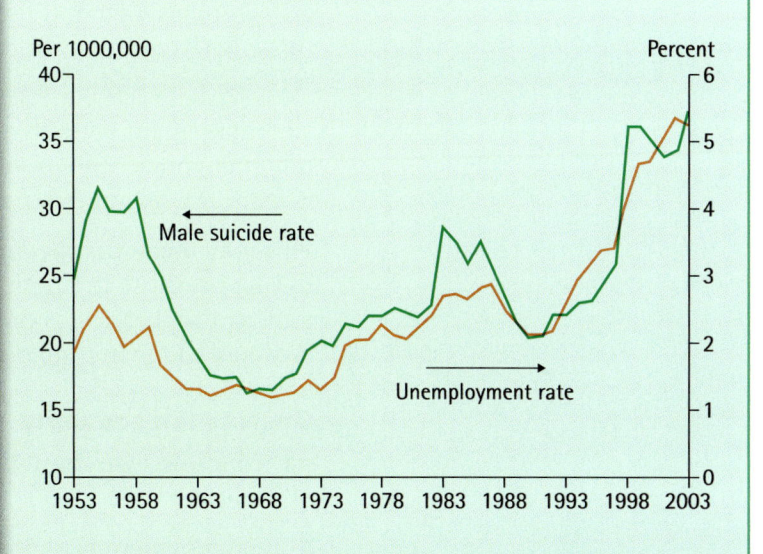

Is the REAL cost of unemployment £61 billion per year?

Unemployment costs the taxpayer a massive £61 billion a year, with more than five million who could work claiming benefits, a recent UK study has declared.

The analysis of official data takes into account not just the costs of benefits paid to the unemployed, but also the taxes they and their employers would have paid if they were in work.

Taking into account the potential tax revenue lost, the analysis shows the cost of unemployment in the UK is £61 billion a year. That works out as £2,810 for every household in Britain.

But it in no way measures the true cost in terms of lost opportunities. 'We need more imaginative ways of helping people back into work so that we can reduce the cost of unemployment to families, communities and the taxpayer' said the authors of the study.

Employment and unemployment

Fiscal costs

Governments in many countries pay benefits to people who are unemployed. In many cases the benefits paid may only be enough to pay for food and other necessities and for only a limited period of time. Unemployment benefits, also called unemployment insurance in some countries, are generally given only to those who register as unemployed and on condition that they are actively seeking work and do not currently have a job.

Unemployment benefits are paid from direct and indirect tax revenues. As unemployment rises, public expenditure on unemployment benefits tends to rise but tax revenues tend to fall as incomes and spending fall.

This may mean that people remaining in work may have to pay higher taxes to support those in unemployment. Other public expenditures may also have to be cut back, such as on schools, health care and roads. The disposable incomes and living standards of many more people may fall as a result.

Costs to the economy

As economists we should realize that leaving labour unemployed is a waste of resources.

If unemployment is high total output and income will be lower than they might otherwise be and people will have fewer goods and services to enjoy. That is, the opportunity cost of having so many workers unemployed is the goods and services they could have produced instead. In addition, there is the opportunity cost to taxpayers. The tax revenue used to pay for unemployment benefits could have been used to fund other beneficial projects in the economy, such as roads and new hospitals.

WEBSITES

The following websites can help you learn more about employment and unemployment and provide access to useful statistics;

- *www.bized.co.uk/virtual/economy/policy/outcomes/unemployment/unempth2.htm*
- International Labour Organization *www.ilo.org/stat*
- *www.tutor2u.net/economics/gcse/revision_notes/big_picture_unemployment_causes.htm*
- *www.wikipedia.org/wiki/Unemployment*

KEYWORDS

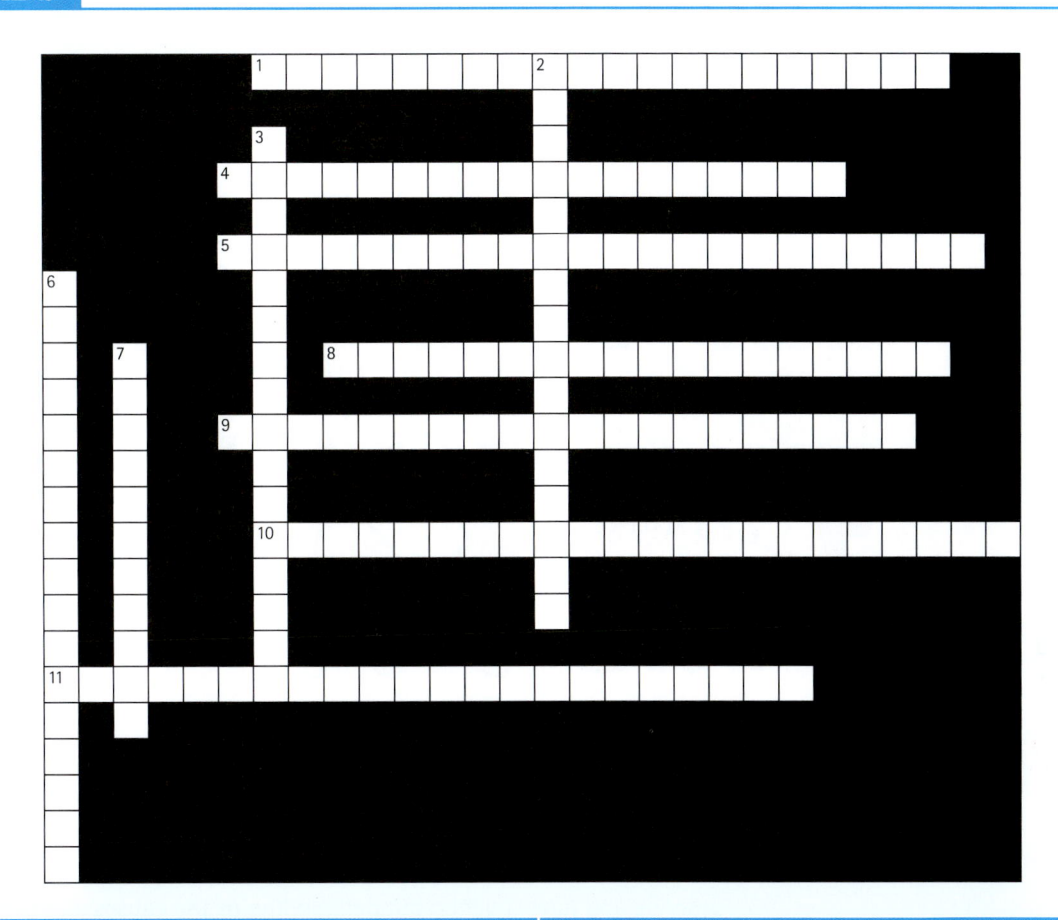

Clues across

1. Periods of joblessness caused by deficient demand during an economic downturn or recession (8, 12)
4. A contract for work that involves the employee working the full number of hours defined by his or her employer as a working week, which is normally around 40 hours each week between Monday to Friday (4-4,11)
5. Joblessness among workers because their skills are out of date and no longer wanted due to changes in demand patterns or technologies that have resulted in the decline of some established industries in an economy (10, 12)
8. A contract for work in which an employee's working time is substantially less than a full working week (4-4, 11)
9. An economic situation in which people on temporary employment contracts lose their jobs during seasonal downturns in activity in particular industries, such as tourism and construction (8, 12)
10. An economic situation in which people find themselves voluntarily out of work usually for short periods of time as they change their jobs (10, 12)
11. The inability of workers to move easily between different occupations because they lack of transferable skills. This can prolong structural unemployment (12, 10)

Clues down

2. The proportion of the labour force in an economy that is out of work (12, 4)
3. An effect in economics in which a change in spending produces a much larger change in output and income (10, 6)
6. The percentage of people of working age who choose to be economically active in the labour force (12, 4)
7. The total supply of labour or economically active population in an economy (6, 5)

Employment and unemployment

Unit 6.3   Output and growth

AIMS

By the end of this unit you should be able to:

▶ define **gross domestic product (GDP)**
  - distinguish between **real GDP** and **nominal GDP**
▶ describe and have a general understanding of the causes and consequences of **economic growth**
▶ define the term **recession**
  - define and describe the **economic cycle**
  - compare and contrast and **economic boom** with an economic slump
▶ describe and evaluate measures and **indicators of comparative living standards**, such as **GDP per head**, Human Development Index (HDI)

SECTION 1

An important economic relationship

Measuring output

Imagine a very simple and tiny economy with just three people and one $10 note between them. You are one of those people, the baker, and you hold the $10 note. This is the money supply in the economy. ➤ **3.1**

You use the $10 note to buy candles from the candlestick maker. This exchange involves the following three transactions:

- The candles are sold for $10 (output; that is, the value of the candles).
- You (the baker) pay $10 for the candles (expenditure).
- The candlestick maker receives $10 in payment for the candles (income).

360 Economic indicators

The candlestick maker now uses her income of $10 to buy meat from the butcher. In turn, the butcher uses his income of $10 from the sale of his meat to buy $10 of bread from your shop. The same $10 has now been circulated three times in the economy.

So, how much was the total value of output in the tiny economy? How much expenditure was there in total in the economy? And how much was the total amount of income earned by the three people in the tiny economy?

The answer to all these questions is $30. The butcher, you (the baker) and the candlestick maker each earned $10 in income from the sale of their output of meat, bread and candles, and they each spent $10 buying up this output from each other. This means there was a circular flow of income, expenditure and output in the tiny economy.

▼ A simple circular flow of income, expenditure and output

The circular flow of income in this tiny economy demonstrates an important relationship in macroeconomics: the value of output = expenditure = income.

The same relationship is true of all economies, no matter how large or complex they are:

national output = national income = national expenditure

Measuring economic activity

As economists, we would like to measure the total output of goods and services of a country, and monitor how it grows or changes over time. In a macroeconomy, the total value of output of goods and services produced is known as the **national output**.

Factors of production – land, labour and capital – are used to produce the national output. Firms pay workers, and the owners of natural resources and capital, for their use in production. These payments are a cost to firms but an income for labour and owners of factors of production. Similarly, owners of

Output and growth

firms will receive income in the form of profits if their businesses are successful. The total amount of income earned by factors of production, including entrepreneurs, in a macroeconomy is therefore its **national income**.

The value of the total or national output of an economy can be measured by how much people and organizations pay for all the goods and services it comprises. It follows that the total or national output should also be the same as the total or **national expenditure** in a macroeconomy. What people and organizations spend on goods and services provides income for the people and firms that produce and supply the goods and services.

Gross domestic product (GDP)

The total market value of all final goods and services produced within an economy by its factors of production in a given period of time is its **gross domestic product** or **GDP**.

There are, therefore, three ways of measuring the GDP or value of economic activity in an economy:

- the output method
- the income method
- the expenditure method.

Government experts and economists collect statistics on all three measures of the GDP of their economy. In practice, however, the values of the three measures do not always add up exactly to the same amount. This is because economic activity is complex. Flows of outputs, incomes and expenditures occur between many millions of different people, firms and governments, all over the world every day. It is also possible that some activities and their transactions are not recorded because people and firms may try to hide their incomes to avoid taxes.

The output method

This involves adding up the value of the output produced each period by every firm in every industry in an economy. However, only final outputs should be counted otherwise the double counting of the value of some outputs can occur. For example, cotton produced by farms is used as an input to the production of clothing and bed linens by the textile manufacturing industry. Similarly, the value of the output of the shipbuilding industry includes output produced by the steel and electronics industries. To avoid the problem of double counting, economists will only add up the value added by each firm at each stage of production. ▶ **4.2**

Economic activity involves organizing and combining resources to make final outputs that are more desirable to consumers. In this way a business adds value to the resources it uses. The **gross value added (GVA)** by each firm is the market value of its output of goods or services less the value of the inputs used in the production if outputs. GDP is therefore a measure of the total value added to resources in an economy through the production of goods and services.

The income method

This measures the total income earned from the production of goods and services within the economy. The figures provided break down this income into, for example, profits earned by companies and other business organizations and the wages and salaries of employees and the self-employed.

Value added = $300

However, **transfer payments**, such as welfare payments, unemployment benefits and pensions, from a government to individuals are excluded because they are unearned incomes: there is no corresponding productive activity by the people who receive them. ➤ **5.2**

The expenditure method

Most goods and services produced are sold. The value of output can therefore be measured by adding up the total amount spent on all final goods and services produced in an economy. This includes spending by individual households, firms and government organizations. Spending on exports by overseas consumers is also included in this total but spending on imported goods and services must be deducted. This is because imports have been produced in other economies and therefore do not earn profits or other incomes for domestic firms and residents.

▲ Gross domestic expenditure includes consumer expenditure, investment, government expenditure and exports but excludes spending on imports

Real versus nominal GDP

This distinction is very important if we want to determine by how much national output has grown or changed over time. This is because GDP is measured in monetary values. That is, the value of output, income and expenditure in an economy are all measured at their current market values or prices. These measure the **money GDP** or **nominal GDP**. However, these values will rise over time as prices increase due to inflation.

This means that the value of the national output, expenditure and income may increase simply because prices have risen but people may be no better off. Indeed, they may even be worse off if at the same time the total amount of goods and services available in the economy has fallen because real output has decreased.

Nominal GDP can therefore be a misleading indicator of what is happening to the total output of an economy, so economists adjust nominal GDP to exclude the impact of inflation on monetary values. **Real GDP** therefore measures changes in total output assuming prices are unchanged over time. That is, GDP in constant prices provides a measure of the real output of an economy.

For example, in the last year the nominal GDP of a country was $100 billion. In the current year this has increased to $110 billion. However, price inflation was 10% over the same period. This means all of the increase in the nominal GDP is explained by the rise in general level of prices. There was no increase in real GDP.

If price inflation had been, say, 7% over the same 12-month period then $7 billion of the increase in nominal GDP would have been simply due to rising prices. The other $3 billion therefore would have been due to an increase in the real output of firms in the economy. That is, people in the economy enjoyed an increase in the amount of goods and services available to them to satisfy their wants.

Using GDP statistics

Many years ago no one was very interested in collecting national income and output figures. However, during the Second World War many governments realized there was a need to know how much food and ammunition their nations could produce because it was difficult for many to import the essential goods and services they needed during the war. Since then, governments all over the world have collected and published figures on their national output, incomes and expenditures.

GDP statistics can help governments and economists in a number of ways.

1. If a government is better informed about the allocation of resources in its economy and how much they are producing, it can make better decisions on economic policies and how they may affect the resource allocation and production. For example, if a government thinks its economy is producing too many consumer goods and too few capital goods, it may try to encourage the production of capital equipment through higher taxes on consumer goods and lowering taxes on the profits of machinery and equipment manufacturers.

2. It allows comparison to be made of the standard of living in one year compared with the next. If the amount of goods and services produced in an economy has increased over time we might assume many people are better off.

3. The figures allow us to compare the standard of living in different countries or even in different areas of the same country. Dividing GDP by the population gives an indication of the average income of each person.

SECTION 2

Economic growth

What is economic growth?

Economic growth means there has been an increase in the real GDP of an economy. An increase in output one year compared with previous years can improve the living standards of people by providing them with more goods and services and incomes to enjoy.

If the total supply of goods and services can increase over time in line with rising demand then they can be enjoyed without an increase in their prices. Economic growth can therefore help to keep price inflation low and stable in an economy.

Economic growth in an economy can be represented on a production possibility curve (PPC) by an outward shift in the frontier. In the following PPC diagram, the economy is able to produce more consumer and capital goods with its available resources because there has been economic growth in its productive capability. That is, before economic growth the economy produced the combination of consumer and capital goods at point X in the diagram but output of both consumer and capital goods has since expanded to point Y. ▶ **1.1**

▼ Economic growth in the productive potential of an economy

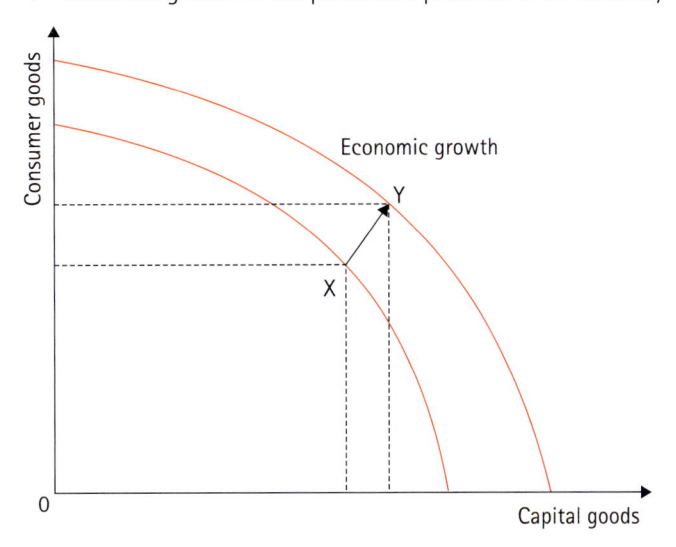

How economies grow

Demand for increased living standards means many governments have a macroeconomic objective to improve their long-term rate of economic growth. Economists measure the rate of economic growth by how much the real GDP has increased each year in an economy.

As economists we want scarce resources to be as fully employed as possible, in the most efficient ways possible, to produce as many goods and services as possible. This will satisfy the most wants.

If resources are unused; that is, if some labour is left unemployed, land disused or capital lying idle; then an increase in the amount of goods and services can be achieved simply by using these available resources more fully. However, it is clearly more difficult for an economy to grow if all its available resources are fully employed. Other changes are therefore required to achieve growth.

1 The discovery of more natural resources

The discovery of gas and oil has given a number of countries the ability to grow rapidly. Indeed, the discovery of more natural resources, including mineral deposits, such as coal and iron ore or even new varieties of fruit or cereals, can help any economy to increase output. Searching for new natural resources, however, costs a lot of money and some countries, particularly those in the developing world, lack the funds to do this.

2 Investment in new capital and infrastructure

Investment by private sector firms involves spending on capital goods such as new machinery, buildings and technology so that they can expand their scale of production, lower their average costs and produce more goods and services in the future. Similarly, investments in modern infrastructure such as road networks, airports and ports by governments can improve access and communications to expand the productive potential of the economy.

By lowering interest rates, a government can make it less costly for private sector firms to borrow money for investment.

Output and growth

3 Technical progress

New inventions and production processes can increase the productivity of existing resources and produce new materials and products. Technical progress is a major driver of economic growth.

Technological advances made in one industrial sector can often 'spill over' into other sectors. For example, fibreglass was originally invented for use as insulation material but is now used in the production of bows and crossbows, roofing panels, automobile and aircraft bodies, surfboards, artificial limbs and many more products. Similarly, the Internet is based on a system originally developed by the US Defense Advanced Research Projects Agency to enable communications between military computers to withstand nuclear attack.

Governments can support investments in the research and development (R&D) of new products and processes, either directly through public funding of firms and universities or by providing tax breaks for firms that undertake R&D. They can also encourage R&D by protecting new inventions from copy or theft through the issue of patents. ➤ 4.4

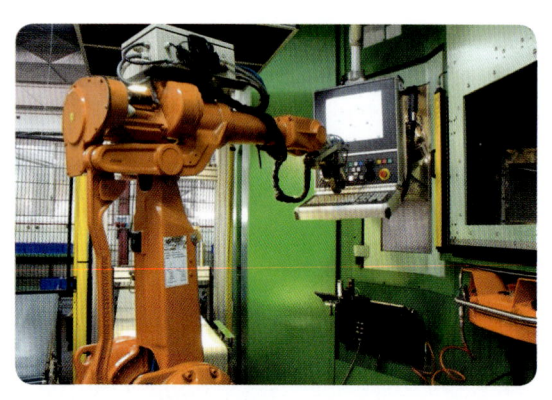

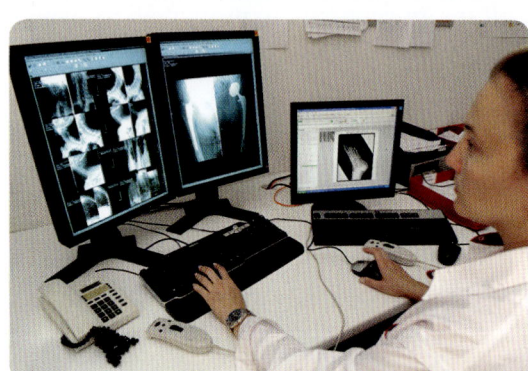

▼ Major advances in technology have revolutionised many production processes and the way firms operate

Time line	Major innovations
1785	Water power
	Textiles
	Iron
1845	Steam power
	Railways
	Steel
	Telephones
1900	Refrigeration
	Plastics
	Electricity
	Chemicals
	Internal combustion engine
1950	Petrochemicals
	Jet engines and aviation
	Electronics
1990	Digital cameras
	Mobile phones
	Computer software
	Biotechnology
2000	Wind, wave and solar power
	Electric cars
	Social networking
2010 +	?

4 Increasing the amount and quality of human resources

A larger and more productive work force can boost economic growth. Education and training are often called 'investments in 'human capital' and will help create a better skilled, knowledgeable and more productive workforce. ➤ **4.2**

Improvements in health care and medicines can also improve the health and productivity of the workforce and reduce the number of days they are sick and unproductive.

Expanding the work force may require policies to encourage more people into work, for example cutting income taxes and unemployment benefits, and increasing the age at which people can retire and receive a pension from the government. The working population of a country can also be expanded through the inward migration of skilled labour and, in the longer term, through an increase in the birth rate. ➤ **7.2**

5 Reallocating resources

An inefficient allocation of resources will constrain economic growth. Moving resources from less-productive uses to more-productive uses will boost output and growth. Similarly, moving some resources from the production of consumer goods and services into the production of capital goods will help increase the productive potential of an economy.

Negative growth

The rate of economic growth is a measure of how quickly or slowly real output rises over time. For example, in 2011 real output in India grew rapidly by 8.3% over 2010. In comparison, the US economy grew by only 2.7% over the same period.

The rate of economic growth in an economy, like any economic variable, can vary over time but while it remains above zero that economy will continue to expand: real output will be increasing each year. A fall in the growth rate, say from 5% to 2% each year, will mean real output is rising more slowly than in the past. In contrast, an increase in the growth rate of an economy, from say 5% to 7% each year means its real output is expanding at a faster rate than in the past.

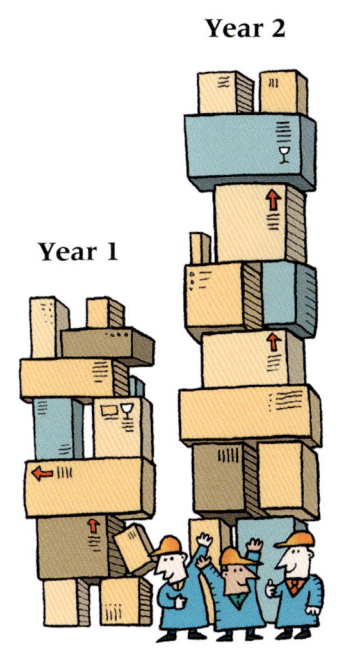

Rapid economic growth

Slow economic growth

Negative economic growth

Output and growth

However, sometimes economies can experience negative growth. This means real output is shrinking. Fewer goods and services are being produced over time, incomes will be falling and the living standards of many people may be deteriorating. Economic growth may be negative for a relatively short period of time during an economic recession. However, prolonged negative growth can be very painful for an economy, its firms and citizens.

▼ Economic growth in Zimbabwe, % annual growth in real GDP

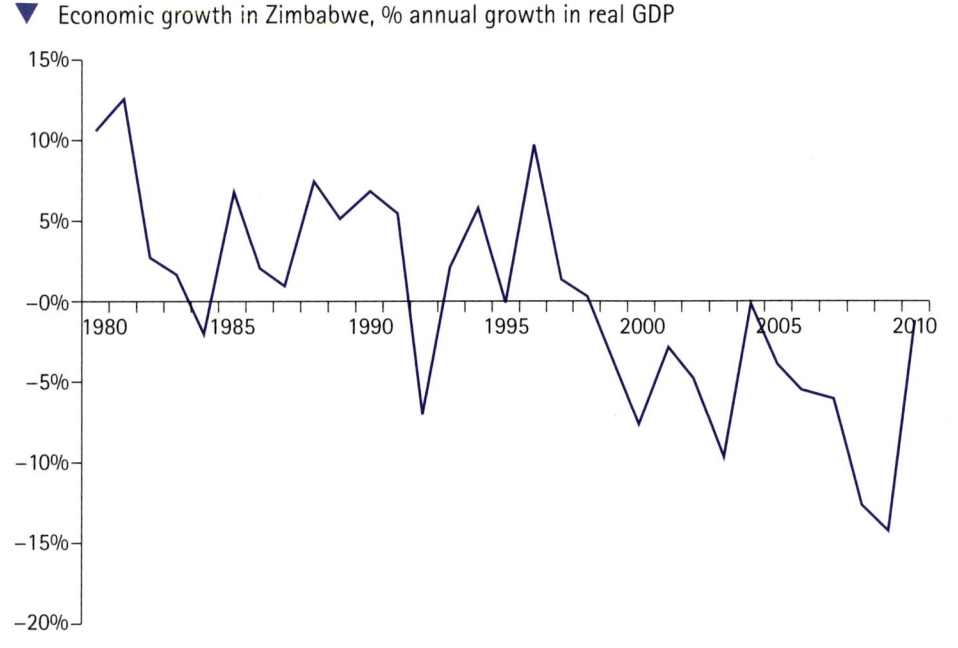

Source: United Nations Conference on Trade and Development, www.unctad.org

The chart plots the annual rate of economic growth in Zimbabwe since 1980. It shows how the growth rate has bounced up and down over time. Until 1998 annual growth in the real output of the economy was mostly positive: the amount of goods and services it produced was expanding in most years, by as much as 12.5% in 1981 and 9.7% in 1996.

However, since 1999 the economy of Zimbabwe has shrunk considerably. There was year-on-year negative economic growth between 1999 and 2010, resulting in widespread unemployment and poverty. By 2010 the economy was producing 55% fewer goods and services than it did in 1998. That is, the size of the economy had more than halved since 1998. Hyperinflation has also been a major problem in Zimbabwe due to lack of supply of even many basic goods and services. ➤ **6.1**

ACTIVITY 6.9

Really growing?

The table below shows annual average growth rates in the value of real output or real GDP, in a number of countries between 2005 and 2011.

▼ GDP in constant prices, % annual average growth rate selected countries 2005–2011

Country	% annual growth rate	Country	% annual growth rate
Belgium	1.47	Malaysia	4.84
China	10.04	Portugal	0.41
Dominican Republic	6.17	Spain	1.59
Hungary	1.19	Thailand	4.03
India	7.99	United Arab Emirates	5.46
Qatar	10.60	Zimbabwe	-5.30

Source: www.indexmundi.com

1 Which country experienced the fastest rate of economic growth between 2005 and 2011?
2 Which country had the slowest growing economy?
3 Which country had a shrinking economy?

Economic indicators

SECTION 3

What is the economic cycle?

Growth cycles

Most governments want to achieve long-term stable economic growth in the real GDP of their economies. Plotted on a graph over time this should look like a steadily rising line. However, in practice the annual rate of growth in real GDP often varies considerably in the short run.

The business cycle or **economic cycle** refers to the pattern of recurrent ups and downs (or cyclical fluctuations) observed in real GDP growth over time in many economies. Most economies go through a fairly predictable economic cycle of changes in their rate of economic growth every 5–10 years, some more severe than others.

▼ The economic cycle

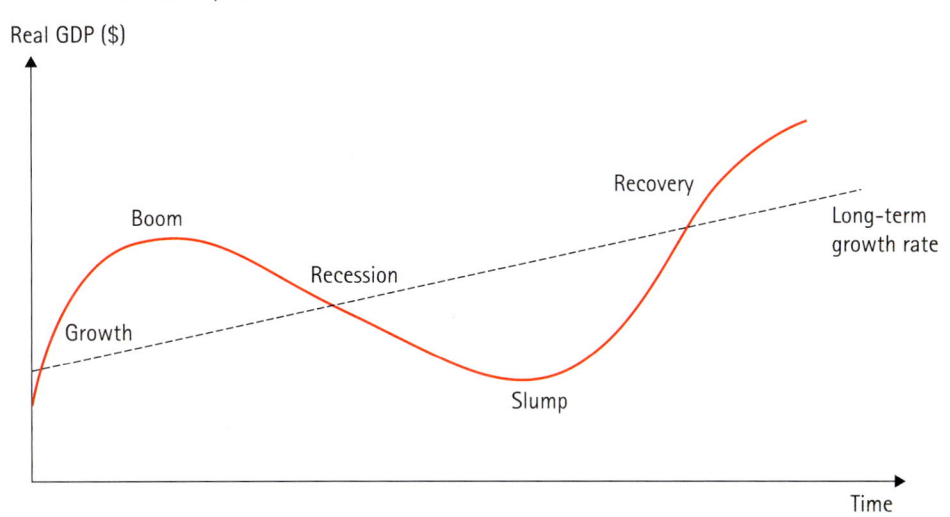

Typically, an economy passes through four distinct phases during one complete economic cycle:

- **Growth (or expansion)**

Economic activity is expanding rapidly. Many firms enjoy increased sales and profits. New business organizations are formed. Output, incomes and employment are all growing.

- **Economic boom (or peak)**

Aggregate demand, sales and profits peak. There may be rapid inflation as prices rise quickly because demand exceeds the amount of goods and services firms can produce and supply. The economy 'overheats'. Shortages of materials, parts and equipment will increase business costs. There is a shortage of labour. Unemployment is low and wages rise as firms compete to employ skilled workers. The government may raise interest rates to control rising inflation. Consumer confidence and spending may begin to decline as inflation and interest rates rise.

- **Economic recession (or downturn)**

There is a general slowdown in economic activity following an economic peak. Economic growth may even turn negative. Demand for many goods and services begins to fall. Sales and profits decline. Firms cut back their production and workers are made redundant. Unemployment rises and incomes start to

Output and growth

fall, causing consumer spending to fall further. Many firms reduce their investment in new plant and machinery and cut back their demand for materials, parts and equipment. Competition between rival firms increases as they fight to survive. There is disinflation as the rate of inflation declines.

Many countries around the world entered economic recession following the global crash in the financial and property markets in 2008. These sectors had been growing rapidly in the years prior to the crash. Banks and other financial institutions drastically cut back their lending, especially against residential and commercial properties, causing a collapse in the global construction industry and resulting in growing unemployment around the world. ➤ **6.2**

The government may increase public spending, cut taxes and reduce interest rates to encourage consumer borrowing and spending during a recession. ➤ **5.2**

A recession that is deep and prolonged may become an economic slump or depression during which economic activity shrinks and unemployment remains high. There may be deflation as a result. ➤ **6.1**

- **Economic recovery (or upturn)**

Business and consumer confidence starts to recover. Spending on goods and services begins to rise. Sales and profits begin to rise. Firms increase their output and employ more workers. New businesses are formed. Unemployment falls and incomes rise, boosting consumer spending further. The economy starts to expand again.

The 'shape' of economic recessions

Economists often talk about and compare the shape of different economic recessions. This refers to what the plot of real GDP growth during a recession look likes over time on a graph.

A U-shaped recession is a prolonged slump. In contrast, a V-shaped recession refers to a short-lived contraction in the economy followed by rapid and sustained economic recovery.

In official statistics, an economy is normally declared to be in recession if it has experienced negative growth in its GDP for more than two successive three-month periods.

In the USA, the National Bureau of Economic Research (NBER) defines an economic recession as 'a significant decline in economic activity spread across the country, lasting more than a few months, normally visible in falling real GDP growth, real personal income, employment, industrial production, and wholesale-retail sales'.

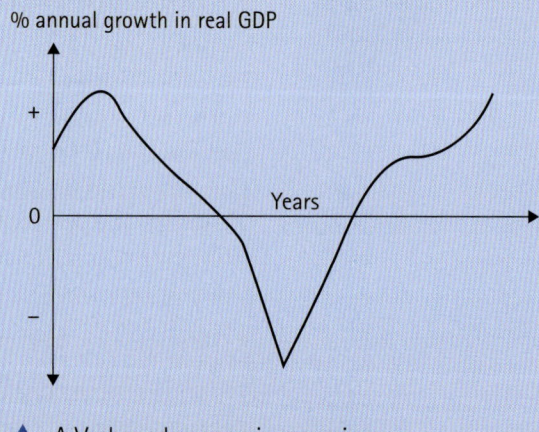

▲ A U-shaped economic recession

▲ A V-shaped economic recession

ACTIVITY 6.10

Boom or bust?

The charts below show cyclical changes or fluctuations in economic growth in the Maltese and South African economies between 1991 and 2011.

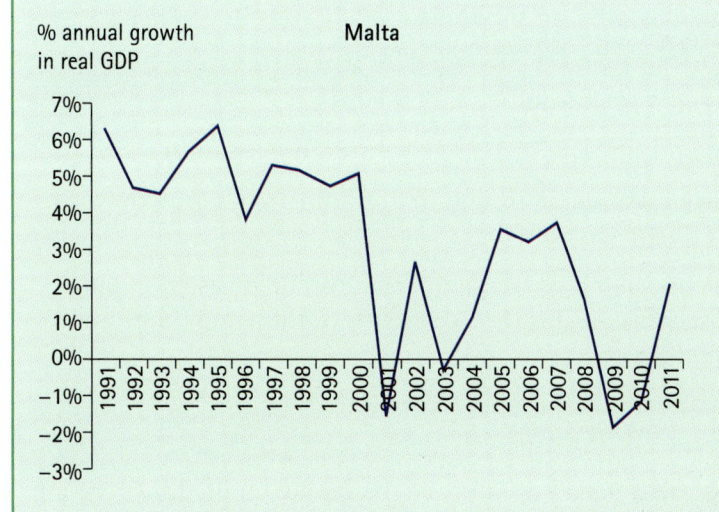

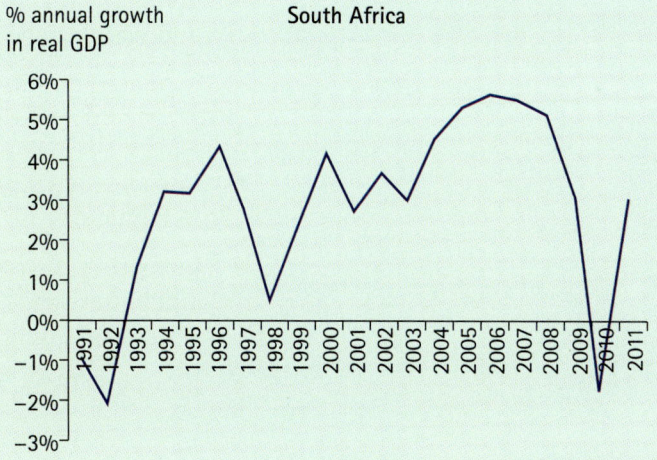

% annual growth in real GDP — Malta

% annual growth in real GDP — South Africa

1. What is the economic cycle?
2. What evidence is there from the charts that Malta and South Africa have economic cycles?
3. In which years did Malta and South Africa experience economic booms?
4. In which years did Malta and South Africa experience economic recessions?
5. Describe what might be happening to consumer expenditure, investment, employment and government revenues during these periods of recession.

ECONOMICS IN ACTION

According to the article, what is a double-dip recession?

Why did this occur in Finland?

How do you think, or try to find out, how economists might describe a double-dip recession in terms of a letter to represent its 'shape'.

Finland suffers double-dip

Finland has become the first European Union country to suffer a double-dip recession after its economy contracted again in the first quarter of 2010, hit by a port strike in March and a colder than usual winter.

Despite a brief recovery during the last quarter of 2009 data yesterday showed January–March 2010 gross domestic product (GDP) had fallen 0.4% since the end of 2009.

Export-dependent Finland had one of the deepest recessions in the European Union in 2009, with GDP plummeting 7.8% as the global downturn hit demand for its main exports of mobile phones, paper and machines.

A recovery is expected to be slow, with growth of just 1.25% in 2010 and 2% in 2011 forecast.

Output and growth

SECTION 4

Economic growth or economic welfare?

The benefits of growth

Sustained economic growth can bring widespread benefits to an economy, its people, firms and government, for example:

- greater availability of goods and services to satisfy consumers' needs and wants
- increased employment opportunities and incomes
- increased sales and profits, and increased business opportunities
- low and stable price inflation, if growth in output matches growth in demand
- increasing tax revenues for a government, that can be invested in more and better roads, schools, health care, crime prevention and other merit goods and public services
- improved living standards and economic welfare.

Growth and welfare

However, economic growth need not improve the quality of life for everyone. While some people may become rich many others may remain poor and have a low standard of living. The distribution of income and wealth in many countries is very unequal and may become more so if the benefits of growth are concentrated among relatively few people.

In addition, economic growth can have other negative impacts:

- Technical progress may replace workers with machines so more people become unemployed for long periods of time.
- Growth might only be achieved by producing more capital goods at the expense of consumer goods. However, are people necessarily better off if growth is achieved, for example, by producing more weapons, cigarettes or coal-fired power stations? Equally, are people better off simply because they have more cars, televisions and computer games?
- Economic growth may mean we use up scarce resources at a faster rate. Oil, coal, metals and other natural resources are limited and may soon run out. Forests may be cut down and green space used up at a increasing rate to build more houses, roads, factories, offices and shops.
- Increasing production and energy use may increase noise, air, water and scenic pollution. Marine and wildlife habitats may be destroyed killing many creatures and plants. People may also suffer from more health problems as a result. ▶ **2.3**

Economic growth can therefore involve a significant opportunity cost in terms of its social and environmental impacts. Because of this, governments around the world are increasingly concerned with achieving **sustainable growth**.

Sustainable economic growth involves reducing the rate at which we use up natural resources, reducing waste in production and consumption and reducing harmful emissions by changing the way we produce and consume goods and services.

▲ Progress at any price?

For governments this means using policies to minimize the costs and harmful effects of economic growth – for example, by encouraging investments in renewable energies, recycling and more efficient production methods, placing restrictions on emissions of harmful pollutants from power stations and vehicle exhausts, raising taxes on petrol to reduce car use, and so on.

ACTIVITY 6.11

Economic boom, environmental bust

China's spectacular economic growth – averaging 8% or more annually over the past two decades – has produced an impressive increase in the standard of living for hundreds of millions of Chinese citizens. At the same time, this economic development has had severe ramifications for the natural environment.

There has been a dramatic increase in the demand for natural resources of all kinds, including water, land and energy. Forest resources have been depleted, triggering a range of devastating secondary impacts such as desertification, flooding and species loss. Moreover, poorly regulated industrial and household emissions and waste have caused levels of water and air pollution to skyrocket. China's development and environment practices have also made the country one of the world's leading contributors to regional and global environmental problems, including acid rain, ozone depletion, global climate change and biodiversity loss.

China's environmental crisis is evident everywhere. The country's air quality is among the worst in the world: According to the World Bank, 16 of the world's 20 most polluted cities are on the mainland, and acid rain affects one third of China's agricultural land. The country is already one quarter desert, and that desert is advancing at a rate of 1,300 square miles per year.

It is the dramatic effect the country's environmental problems are having on Chinese economic productivity, however, that is finally making Beijing take notice. All told, according to the World Bank, environmental degradation and pollution cost the Chinese economy the equivalent of 8% to 12% of GDP annually due to crop and fishery losses, factory closings and increased medical care.

The Chinese government could make real headway by taking three steps. First, increase its investment in environmental protection from 1.2% of GDP to at least 2.2%, the amount that experts have said is necessary just to keep the situation from deteriorating further.

Second, raise the price of scarce natural resources such as water, now grossly undervalued in many regions of the country. This would alleviate some of the scarcity and pollution issues by promoting conservation and encouraging waste-water treatment.

Third, enforcement of existing policies must be strengthened. Often, environmental-protection officials are overruled by powerful local interests who have a political or financial stake in the operation of a polluting activity, no matter what the long-term costs are.

1. What is economic growth?
2. By how much has the Chinese economy grown on average each year recently?
3. What have been the likely benefits of this growth to Chinese people?
4. According to the article, is the fast pace of economic growth in China sustainable?
5. From the article identify social and environmental costs of economic growth in China.
6. In groups discuss the possible impacts the policy measures suggested in the article could have on firms, consumers, employees and the economy in China, and globally.

Output and growth

Measuring welfare

Simply measuring and monitoring the rate at which real output grows over time therefore reveals very little about how standards of living are changing, if growth is sustainable and whether our economic welfare is improving or deteriorating.

In addition to real GDP, therefore, a number of other indicators are used to examine our living standards and economic welfare and how these are changing over time.

GDP per capita

GDP per capita measures average income per head or per person. So, for example, if the GDP of a country is $100 million and the population is 5,000, GDP per capita will be $20,000.

Changes in GDP per capita are a better measure of growth in living standards than the annual increase in GDP because it also takes account of changes in the population. If the population of a country grows faster than GDP grows then the average income per person will be falling. In the example above if the GDP increases to $108 million but the population expands to 6,000, then GDP per capita will have fallen to $18,000. Falling average incomes suggests people are becoming worse off. ➤ **7.1**

However, as we now know, using nominal GDP takes no account of the impact on inflation on real value of incomes and living standards. For example, if annual inflation in the above example had been 8% then real GDP would have been unchanged from $100 million and the real average income per head would have been $16,667 (that is, $100 million/6,000 or $18,000/1.08). **Real GDP per capita** or **real national income per head** is therefore the best and most readily available measure of living standards in most countries.

However, real GDP per capita still provides a relatively poor indicator of people's overall welfare and living standards because of the following:

- It takes no account of what people can buy with their income. People in a country with a relatively high average income may be no better off than people in another country with a lower average income if there are far fewer products they can choose from and average prices are much higher.

- The distribution of income is very unequal in many countries. Some people may be very rich while most of the population remain poor and lack access to good-quality health care, education, water and housing.

- Real GDP per capita excludes unpaid work people do for charities or voluntary organizations, or which they carry out for themselves, their families or friends. As a result it understates total output and well-being.

- It takes no account of the impact of growth on the environment.

Human Development Index

The **Human Development Index (HDI)** provides a wider measure of living standards and economic welfare than GDP per capita and is used by the United Nations to make comparisons between different countries. It combines three different measures into a single index with a value between 0 and 1. These are:

- having a decent standard of living, measured by the average gross national incomes per person adjusted for differences in exchange rates and prices in different countries

- level of education, measured by how many years on average a person aged 25 will have spent in education and how many years a young child entering school now can be expected to spend in education during his or her life.
- access to health care and having a healthy lifestyle, measured by life expectancy.

Human Development Index (HDI)	
Gross national income per capita measures average income per person	People's incomes are unequal in many countries. For example, economic growth in China increased the number of millionaires in the country to 477,000 by 2010, but over one third of the population still had to survive on less than $2 a day.
Education measured by expected years of schooling and average years in schooling	Most adults in the most developed countries have spent between 7.5 and 12.5 years in education while children entering education for the first time in 2010 can be expected to spend up to 16 years in education over their lifetime. In contrast, people in the least developed economies in the world may have received only 3.7 years of schooling although children starting school for the first time can now be expected to spend 8 years receiving education during their lifetimes.
Health measured by life expectancy at birth	People in developed countries tend to live longer than people in developing countries because they have better living standards and access to good food and health care. Malnutrition, poor sanitation and a lack of health care reduce life expectancy in many less-developed countries.
	On average, a baby born in one of the most developed countries in 2010 could expect to live to 79 years of age, while a baby born in a less-developed country could expect to live around 54 years. However, in some of the poorest countries in Africa, average life expectancy from birth is less than 42 years.

Countries can be ranked by their HDI. In 2010, Norway had the highest HDI of 0.938 and Zimbabwe the lowest at just 0.140. Countries with an HDI equal to or greater than 0.800 are generally thought to have high human development, while those with an index value less than 0.500 are considered to have low human development.

▼ Human Development Index rankings, 2010

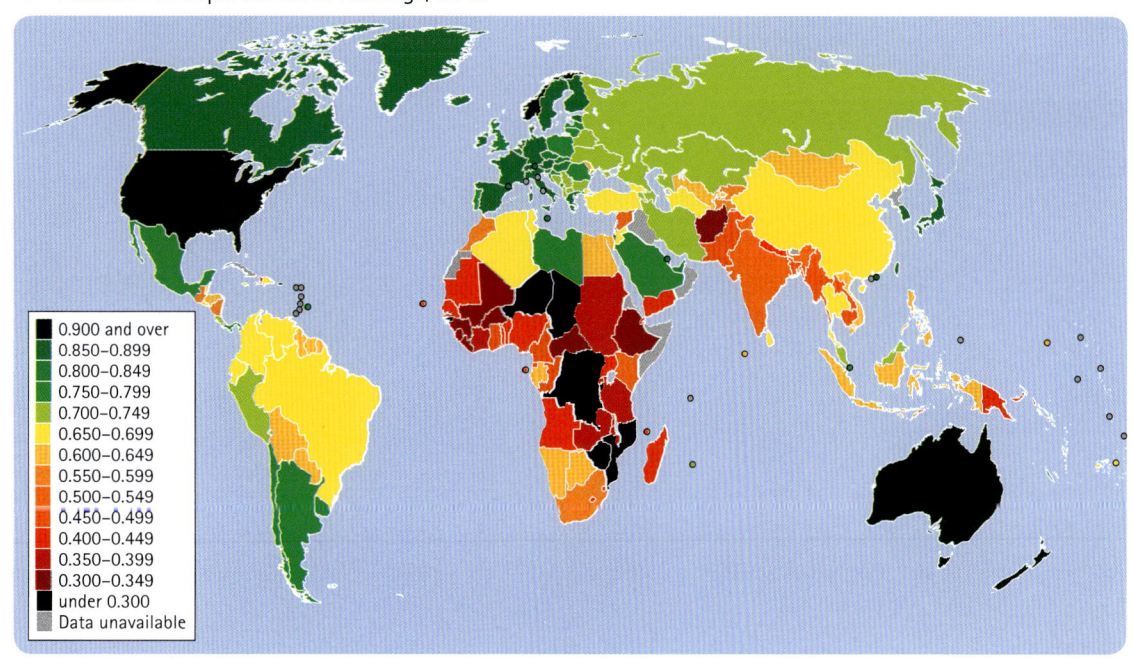

Source: *Human Development Index* rankings (UNDP, 2010)

▼ Countries with the highest HDI values

1	Norway	0.938
2	Australia	0.937
3	New Zealand	0.907
4	United States	0.902
5	Ireland	0.895
6	Liechtenstein	0.891
7	Netherlands	0.890
8	Canada	0.888
9	Sweden	0.885
10	Germany	0.885

▼ Countries with the lowest HDI values

160	Mali	0.309
161	Burkina Faso	0.305
162	Liberia	0.300
163	Chad	0.295
164	Guinea-Bissau	0.289
165	Mozambique	0.284
166	Burundi	0.282
167	Niger	0.261
168	Congo (Democratic Republic of the)	0.239
169	Zimbabwe	0.140

The main problem with the HDI is the fact that it is a composite index that covers a range of separate indicators. So, for example, it is possible for a country to have relatively high HDI if average income is high and people have good literacy skills but many people are nevertheless poor and have low life expectancy, perhaps due to wars, poor working conditions and/or high levels of smoking.

The HDI has also been criticized for failing to take into account other factors that affect living standards including environmental quality, political freedoms and crime rates.

Genuine progress indicator

The genuine progress indicator, first devised in 1989, is an attempt to capture as many different aspects as possible of economic well-being and happiness in one indicator of human and economic development and growth. It incorporates a wide range of measures and information from surveys including:

- average income, levels of consumer debt and changes in the distribution of incomes
- measures of pollution, noise and traffic levels
- physical health metrics, such as people with severe illnesses
- measures of mental health, including use of antidepressants and the number of psychotherapy patients
- social metrics such as crime rates, discrimination, divorce rates and domestic conflicts
- changes in workplace accidents, complaints and lawsuits
- measures of political, religious and individual freedoms.

However, the indicator series suffers from many problems, again because it is composite index and is trying to measure too much all at once. Many of the measures also depend on individuals' opinions and international comparisons are therefore difficult to make.

WEBSITES

Learn more about economic growth and find statistics at:

- www.wikipedia.org/wiki/Economic_growth
- www.wikipedia.org/wiki/Gross_domestic_product
- Human Development Index rankings http://hdr.undp.org/en/statistics/
- hdr.undp.org/en/data/explorer
- www.unctad.org/Templates/Page.asp?intItemID=2364&lang=1
- www.economicshelp.org/blog/economics/genuine-progress-indicator-gpi-v-gdp/

KEYWORDS

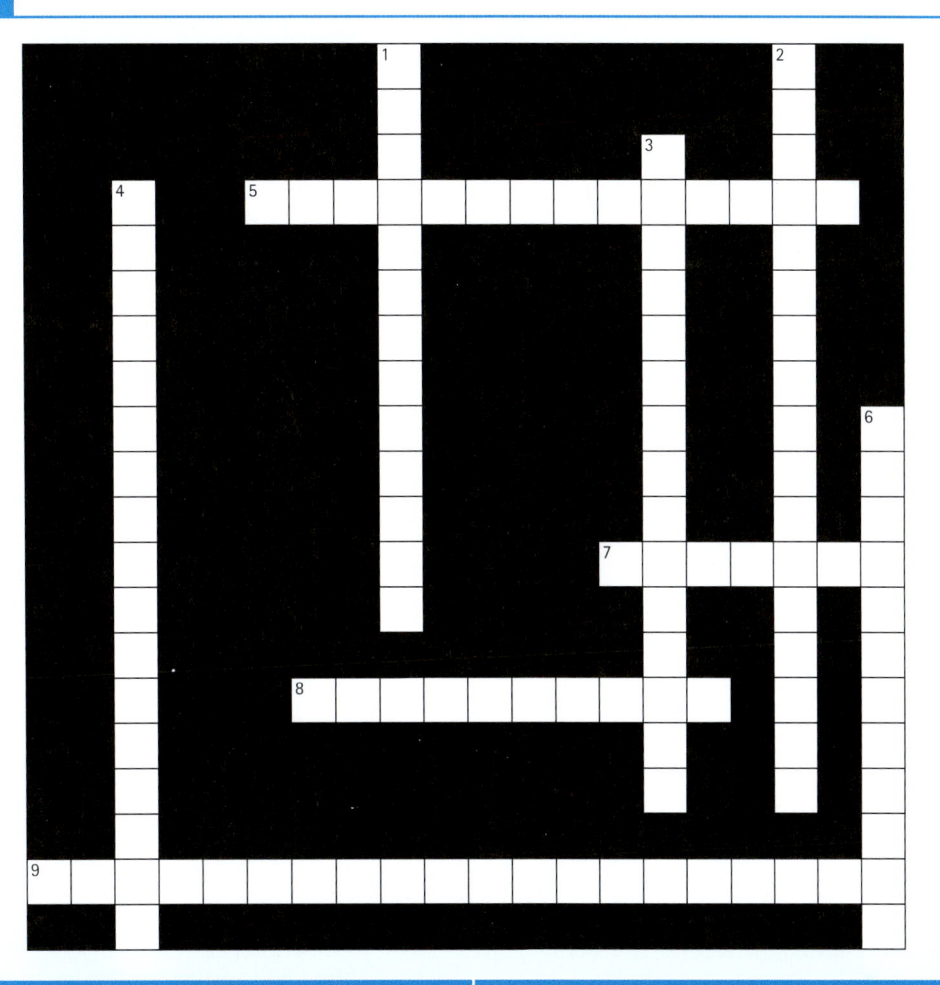

Clues across

5. An increase in the real GDP of an economy (8, 5)
7. The value of the total output of an economy after adjusting for changes in prices over time. It is a measure of GDP at constant prices (4, 1, 1, 1)
8. The money value of the GDP of an economy (7, 1, 1, 1)
9. The total market value of all final goods and services produced within an economy by its factors of production in a given period of time (5, 8, 7)

Clues down

1. The recurrent pattern of fairly predictable fluctuations in the growth rate of real GDP over time that can be observed in many economies (8, 5)
2. Stable growth in real output without depleting natural resources or harming the natural environment (11, 5)
3. The difference between the market value of an output and the cost of inputs used in its production (5, 5, 5)
4. A general slowdown in the rate of economic growth in an economy following an economic boom or peak. Officially, it is usually associated with negative growth in real GDP (8, 9)
6. Average income per head (1, 1, 1, 3, 6)

Output and growth

Assessment exercises

Multiple choice

1. The diagram shows the annual rate of inflation for a country over a five-year period.

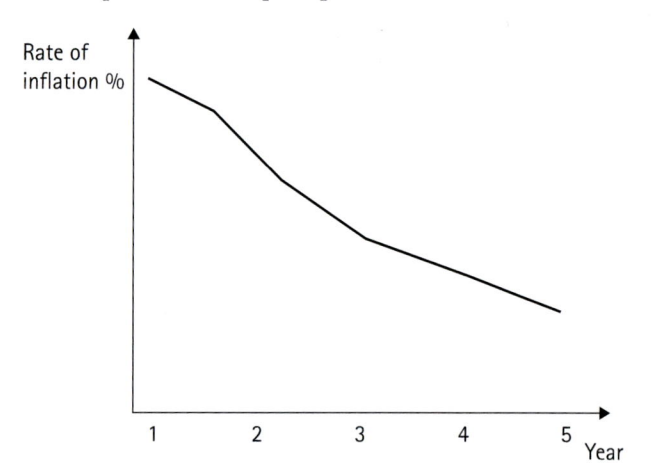

   Which statement is true of the period displayed?

   A The cost of living was unchanged
   B The price level increased
   C The retail price index fell
   D The value of money increased

2. The table shows some data about an economy.

	Year 1	Year 2
Rate of inflation	4%	6%
Personal incomes	+4%	+5%

   What happened between Year 1 and Year 2?

   A Both prices and real incomes fell
   B Both prices and real incomes rose
   C Prices rose but real incomes fell
   D Prices fell but real incomes rose

3. Many fishermen have become unemployed after new laws to conserve fish stocks in the North Sea were introduced.

   What type of unemployment is this?

   A Demand-deficient
   B Frictional
   C Seasonal
   D Structural

4. The graph shows the labour force of a country from 2003–2015.

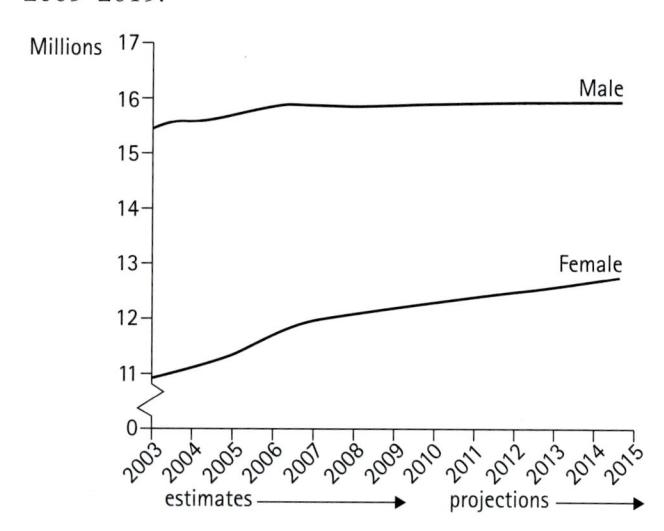

   What may be concluded from the graph?

   A Between 2003 and 2015, the proportion of females in the labour force will have increased
   B The labour force in 2015 will be around 16 million people
   C More girls than boys are forecast to be born
   D The total population of the country in 2010-2011 was approximately 28 million

5. Economic growth can be defined as:

   A A reduction in unemployment
   B An increase in a country's population
   C An increase in the productive capacity of an economy
   D A reduction in inflation

6. During the recent recession, demand for many goods fell, resulting in many workers losing their jobs due to cutbacks in production by firms.

   What type of unemployment does this describe?

   A Cyclical   C Seasonal
   B Frictional   D Structural

7. What is likely to lead to a decrease in structural unemployment?

   A Reducing the interest rate
   B Increasing the rate of unemployment benefit
   C Reducing the rate of income tax
   D Increasing labour mobility

8 Changes in the standard of living of a country are best measured by changes in:
   A National income
   B National income per head
   C Real national income
   D Real national income per head

9 Which of the following groups are most likely to benefit from an inflation?
   A Pensioners   C Savers
   B Borrowers   D Consumers

10 From the following table what is the weighted price index for all items?

Item	Price index	Weight
Food	120	50
Housing	130	40
Services	110	10

All items = 100

   A 360   C 120
   B 123   D 100

11 Which of the following is least likely to contribute to economic growth?
   A An increase in technical progress
   B An increase in training
   C An increase in investment
   D An increase in tax rates on profits

12 Which of the following provides the best measure of economic growth over time?
   A The change in national income
   B The change in total expenditure
   C The change in nominal GDP
   D The change in real GDP per head

13 The wages of foreign workers living and working in France have been increasing rapidly and, as a result, French firms have been increasing their prices to maintain their profit margins. What type of inflation does this represent?
   A Imported inflation
   B Cost-push inflation
   C Demand-pull inflation
   D Hyperinflation

14 What is most likely to cause demand-pull inflation?
   A An increase in saving
   B An increase in consumer spending
   C An increase in interest rates
   D An increase in taxes

15 Labour force participation has risen in many countries. What is the most likely reason for this trend?
   A Unemployment has fallen
   B More females have entered employment
   C The working population has increased
   D More people are retiring earlier

16 Which type of unemployment is most likely to occur when aggregate demand in an economy falls during an economic recession?
   A Seasonal   C Structural
   B Voluntary   D Cyclical

17 Look at the labour market data below.

	Millions
Working population	30
People employed	18
People unemployed	6

What are the unemployment rate and the labour force participation rate?

	Unemployment rate %	Participation rate %
A	60	40
B	80	20
C	20	60
D	40	60

18 Which of the following best describes the economic cycle in an economy?
   A Successive booms and busts in consumer spending
   B Recurrent cyclical changes in the rate of growth of real GDP around its trend growth rate
   C Cyclical changes in price inflation
   D Seasonal fluctuations in total national expenditure

Structured questions

1 Inflation in Namibia

Namibia's inflation rate in January 2001, measured as an annual percentage change in the Consumer Price Index (Retail Price Index), was estimated at 10.6%. Examples of some of the annual increases in prices of the major components that make up the weighted price index were household goods (4.2%), imported goods (10.6%), food (11.7%), housing, fuel and power (12.2%), transport and communications (13.8%).

Examples of increases in prices of some of the minor items in the index were tobacco (9%), recreation and entertainment (4.7%), medical care and health services (20%).

a	What is meant by inflation?	[2]
b	The information above relates inflation to a weighted consumer price index. How do researchers calculate the rate of inflation?	[7]
c	Study the information above and assess whether it might be a source of concern for the Namibian government.	[6]

Cambridge IGCSE Economics 0455/06 Q2 May/June 2003

2 Australia's unemployment rate fell to 5.5% in May 2004, the lowest for 23 years. At the same time total employment decreased to 9.6 million. Full-time jobs decreased by 42 600 but part-time employment rose by 1500. The shift from employment in agriculture and manufacturing to services has continued.

a	Calculate the change in total employment. (Show your working).	[2]
b	Explain why the pattern of employment might change.	[8]
c	The above extract says that the unemployment rate fell yet the numbers employed decreased. Explain how these statements can both be true at the same time.	[3]
d	Discuss the economic consequences of unemployment.	[7]

Cambridge IGCSE Economics 0455/04 Q4 May/June 2006
Cambridge O Level Economics 2281/02 Q4 May/June 2006

3
a	Describe what is meant by economic growth and explain how it might be measured.	[5]
b	If there is economic growth, unemployment often declines. Identify **three** types of unemployment and explain their causes.	[6]
c	Discuss how **(i)** consumers **(ii)** firms and **(iii)** the government might benefit if there is economic growth.	[9]

Cambridge O Level Economics 2281/21 Q5 May/June 2010

4 Investment spending is undertaken by both the private sector and the public sector.

a	Use examples to distinguish between private sector and public sector investment spending.	[4]
b	Explain why investment spending is important for an economy.	[6]
c	What is the difference between a mixed economy and a market economy?	[4]
d	Explain how economic growth might change the relative importance of the primary, secondary and service sectors.	[6]

Cambridge IGCSE Economics 0455/04 Q5 October/November 2008
Cambridge O Level Economics 2281/02 Q5 October/November 2008

7 Developed and developing economies: trends in production, population and living standards

7.1	Developed and less-developed economies
7.2	Population
Assessment	Multiple choice
	Structured questions

Economic development involves growth in the productive scale and wealth of an economy. Government policy in many countries generally aims for continuous and sustained economic growth, so that national economies expand, generate more output and incomes, and become more developed.

A less-developed economy has a relatively low level of economic development. Almost 90% of the world's population lives in less-developed economies. Some newly industrializing economies, such as those in South-East Asia, are developing rapidly but have yet to achieve the same high levels of economic and human development characteristic of many modern developed economies.

The level of economic and human development in different economies can be measured and compared using a range of indicators. Gross domestic product per capita, a measure of average income per person, is a commonly used indicator of levels of wealth or poverty but it does not take account of living standards, including the availability of health care, education and clean water supplies. Income is also distributed very unequally in many countries. Other development indicators are also used, therefore, such as the adult literacy rate, life expectancy at birth and the number of people earning less than $1 per day.

Many less-developed countries lack the capital required to invest in modern infrastructure, such as road and communication networks, and they also lack the consumer demand required to stimulate investments in an industrial base and services sector. Instead, less-developed countries tend to depend heavily on agriculture for employment and incomes. Rapid population growth is also a feature of many less-developed economies and places further pressure on their scarce resources.

The natural rate of increase in a population is the difference between its birth rate and death rate. Populations in a number of developed countries are shrinking and their average age increasing as birth rates have fallen significantly and below death rates. It is estimated that one in every three people in developed countries will be over 60 by 2050. In contrast, more than a third of the population of less-developed countries is under the age of 15.

Around half the world's population now lives in urban areas, and this is expected to rise as more people move from rural areas to cities in search of work and higher incomes. The number and size of cities is expanding rapidly, especially in many emerging economies. However, increasing urbanization has increased the consumption of scarce natural resources such as trees, open space and water, as more homes, factories, offices, shops and roads are built. Increased energy and car use in cities has also increased pollution, reduced air and water quality, and increased health risks.

Unit 7.1 Developed and less-developed economies

AIMS

By the end of this unit you should be able to:

▶ describe why some countries are classified as developed and others are not
  • distinguish between **developed economies** and **developing economies** and evaluate reasons for their different stages of development
▶ describe the difference between **absolute** and **relative poverty**
▶ recognize and discuss policies to alleviate poverty
▶ discuss differences in standards of living within countries and between countries, both developed and developing
  • describe simple measures and indicators of comparative living standards.

SECTION 1

Economic development in different economies

Economic development involves an increase in the economic welfare or well-being of people through growth in the productive scale and wealth of an economy. Government policies in different countries generally aim for continuous and sustained economic growth, so that their national economies expand from **developing economies** into more **developed economies**.

Development objectives therefore tend to include increasing the output and quality of essential goods, including food and shelter and making sure they reach more people in need, improving standards of education and health care, investing in better roads and communications, and generally expanding economic and social choice.

However, different countries and even different regions within the same countries in the world today are at very different stages of economic development. Almost every day on the television or in newspapers we learn about the problems many people have living in many less-developed or developing economies.

> **ACTIVITY 7.1**
>
> **The characteristics of developed and less-developed economies**
> These pictures depict typical scenes from less-developed economies and developed economies. In pairs compare and contrast the pictures and then list what you consider to be key characteristics of a less-developed economy and a developed economy, and how they differ.

Developed economies

A **developed economy** is generally thought of as having large modern efficient farms, a wide range of industries with firms of different sizes producing and selling a wide variety of goods and services, a well-developed road and rail network, modern communication systems, stable government and a relatively healthy, wealthy and educated population. Developed economies are also sometimes called industrialized nations, but this is despite the great majority of their output, income and employment now being created by their service sectors rather than manufacturing industries. ➤ **6.2**

Developed and less-developed economies

Despite these characteristics there is no general rule for designating regions or countries as developed or developing. Nevertheless, it is commonly accepted that countries such as Canada and the USA in North America, Australia and New Zealand in Oceania, Japan in Asia and many countries in Europe are considered to be developed economies.

Less-developed economies

A **less-developed economy** has a relatively low level of economic development. Farming methods tend to be poor, sometimes providing scarcely enough food for a rapidly growing population to eat. There are few industries and very few firms producing and selling good-quality goods and services. Road, rail and communication networks are underdeveloped and many people are poor. Many live in poor housing conditions with poor sanitation, receive little or no education, have a low life expectancy and may even lack access to clean water. Many countries in Africa are considered less developed.

Less-developed countries are also called **developing economies**, suggesting that over time they are becoming more prosperous, that their industrial structure is expanding and fewer people suffer the extremes of poverty. However, not all less-developed countries are developing. Some are, in fact, experiencing negative economic growth, meaning that incomes are falling and levels of poverty, malnutrition and disease are rising. For example, between 2002 and 2010 the real GDP of Zimbabwe halved. ➤ **6.3**

In contrast, some countries are developing rapidly, such as India, China and Malaysia in Asia, Poland in Eastern Europe, Brazil and Chile in South America and other countries such as the United Arab Emirates, Turkey and South Africa. These rapidly developing economies or **newly industrialized economies** are undergoing significant growth in their industries and infrastructure but are yet to display the full range of characteristics of modern developed economies.

In recent years new terms have been introduced to describe, for example, the largest and fastest developing economies, Brazil, Russia, India and China, which have been labelled the BRIC countries. Variations on BRIC include BRICK, which recognizes South Korea as a rapidly developing economy, and BRICKS with the addition of South Africa.

Reasons for low economic development

There are many reasons why some countries remain less developed compared with others:

- **An over-dependence on agriculture to provide jobs and incomes**

More people in less-developed economies work in farming than in manufacturing industries and services compared with developed nations. Many produce only enough food for themselves and their families to live on and very little surplus they could sell to earn money. In some areas there has been over-farming so the land is no longer any good for growing crops. The failure of rain to arrive in some areas due to global climate change has also meant that crop yields have fallen.

- **Domination of international trade by developed nations**

It is argued that rich developed economies have exploited many poorer countries by buying up their natural resources and the food crops they produce at very low prices. They then use these resources to produce goods and services which they export back to the same less-developed countries at much higher prices. Further, many rich countries have protected their own mining and agricultural industries by paying them subsidies. These subsidies have increased the global supply of these products and forced down world prices. Producers in less-developed countries have not been able to compete and, as a result, they have lost sales, incomes and jobs.

- **Lack of capital**

Because incomes remain so low in many less-developed countries, there are insufficient funds to invest in building factories and the purchase of machinery and equipment to develop an industrial base. Without these capital goods, less-developed countries will not be able to produce more of the goods and services they need and could also export to earn money from overseas trade.

- **Insufficient investment in education, skills and health care**

Many people in many less-developed countries do not have access to basic education, training or health care which can help them become healthier, more productive and more innovative workers. Better education about family planning may also help reduce birth rates and improve living standards.

- **Low levels of investment in infrastructure**

Road, rail and communication networks are often poor in many less-developed countries. This makes travel and access to rural areas, and the sharing of information, very difficult.

- **Lack of an efficient production and distribution system for goods and services**

Many less-developed countries lack industries and services. If incomes are low there is little incentive for firms to set up different shops and retail centres. If transport is difficult outside of cities then people from rural areas cannot travel to cities, and it is also difficult to take goods and services to rural communities. If workers are uneducated and lack skills then industry may be unable to employ them. All of these factors combined make production and trade difficult. Costs of production will be higher and revenue potential lower than in locations in more-developed economies.

- **High population growth**

Many less-developed countries have rapidly expanding populations because birth rates remain high. This means the supply of goods and services has to be shared between more and more people over time. ➤ **7.2**

- **Other factors**

Unstable and corrupt governments, and wars with neighbouring nations or between different tribes or religious groups, have often blighted the development of some less-developed countries. Money that could have been used to invest in economic development has in some cases been misused by corrupt officials or squandered on buying arms and fighting wars.

ECONOMICS IN ACTION

Do you think the actions described below will help or hinder the development of less-developed and newly industrializing economies in Africa and elsewhere?

The food rush: rising demand in China and West sparks African land grab

A million Chinese farmers have joined the rush to Africa, according to one estimate, underlining concerns that an unchecked 'land grab' not seen since the 19th century is under way.

Some of the world's richest countries are buying or leasing land in some of the world's poorest to satisfy their insatiable appetites for food and fuel. In the new scramble for Africa, nearly 2.5 million hectares (6.2 million acres) of farmland in just five sub-Saharan countries have been bought or rented in the past five years at a total cost of $920 million, research shows.

'Lands that only a short time ago seemed of little outside interest are now being sought by international investors to the tune of hundreds of thousands of hectares,' said a recent report by the International Fund for Agricultural Development (IFAD) and UN Food and Agriculture Organisation (FAO).

The report said farmland purchases are being driven by food security concerns, rising demand and changing dietary habits, expanded biofuel production and interest in what is, in theory, an improved investment climate in some African countries.

Beijing's billions buy up resources

China is pouring another $7 billion (£4.4 billion) into Brazil's oil industry, reigniting fears of a global 'land grab' for natural resources.

The agreement follows many similar deals across the world. While much of the developed world is struggling with debts in the aftermath of the financial crisis, China has continued a global spending spree of unprecedented proportions, snapping up everything from oil and gas reserves to mining concessions to agricultural land, with vast reserves of US dollars.

This year alone, Chinese companies have laid out billions of dollars buying up stakes in Canada's oil sands, a Guinean iron ore mine, oil fields in Angola and Uganda, an Argentinian oil company and a major Australian coal-bed methane gas company.

'China is rich in people but short of resources, and it wants to have stable supplies of its own rather than having to buy on the open market,' Jonathan Fenby, China expert and Director of research group Trusted Resources, said.

SECTION 2

UN millennium development goals

Development indicators

In 2000, a total of 189 different nations belonging to the United Nations (UN) agreed to a set of **millennium development goals** comprising eight anti-poverty goals with a target date of 2015 for their achievement.

United Nation goals:
- Eradicate extreme poverty and hunger
- Achieve universal primary education
- Promote gender equality and empower women
- Reduce child mortality
- Improve maternal health
- Combat HIV/AIDS, malaria and other diseases
- Ensure environmental sustainability
- Develop a global partnership for development

For all these goals the UN has given member nations a set of ambitious targets, including halving between 1990 and 2015 the number of people whose income is less than $1 per day, halting or reversing the spread of HIV/AIDS by 2015, and providing access for developing countries to affordable, essential medicines. Progress towards achieving all these goals and targets is monitored using a range of different statistical measures and indicators.

ACTIVITY 7.2

Developing measures

In groups discuss indicators or measures the UN could use to monitor each millennium development goal listed above. Try to think of at least three measures or indicators for each goal. Compare your ideas with other groups in your class and together compile a full list of measures and indicators for each development goal.

If possible, compare your lists to those actually used by the UN in its *Millennium Development Goals Report 2010*, available online at www.unfpa.org/public/home/publications/pid/6090.

Measures of poverty

The UN uses around 50 different measures and indicators to monitor progress towards its millennium development goals. They combine both absolute and relative measures. This is because there is no single way to measure economic development or living standards and therefore poverty:

- **Absolute poverty** is the inability to afford basic necessities needed to successfully live, such as food, water, education, health care and shelter. The extent of absolute poverty is usually measured by the number of people living below a certain income threshold.

Determining the level of income below which people suffer absolute poverty is usually done by finding the total cost of all the essential resources that an average human adult needs to consume to survive. The common international absolute poverty threshold has in the past been around $1 a day.

However, absolute poverty is not just about income. According to the UN absolute poverty is 'a condition characterized by severe deprivation of basic human needs, including food, safe drinking water, sanitation facilities, health, shelter, education and information. It depends not only on income but also on access to services.'

▲ Poor

Developed and less-developed economies | 387

▲ Relatively poor

- **Relative poverty** is a condition of having fewer resources than others in the same society. It is usually measured by the extent to which a person's or household's financial resources fall below the average income level in the economy.

Despite incomes and standards of living rising in many countries, gains in income and welfare are often not shared equally across the population. This means despite everyone becoming better off over time, some people remain relatively poor compared with many others. For example, around 44 million were measured to be in poverty in the USA in 2009 out of total population of 307 million people.

Relative poverty is therefore a comparative measure and similar to measuring income inequality, but it also takes account of access to essential and other services such as education, health care and travel, and ownership of consumer durables such as washing machines, freezers and even television. People without all or some of these goods may be considered relatively poor in many developed economies although they are considerably better off than many people in less-developed countries who survive on less than $1 per day, have no shelter and lack access to clean water and sanitation.

While cases of absolute poverty are rare in developed economies, relative poverty can be significant if there are a large number people enjoying much higher incomes than others, and may even increase even if these economies are growing and incomes and living standards are generally rising.

Perversely, relative poverty will be cut in developed economies if the incomes and living standards of the vast majority of people fall because it will reduce the gap between low and high incomes.

Development indicators

Below are some of the most commonly used measures and indicators of economic development and living standards in different countries.

Gross domestic product (GDP) per capita

GDP per capita, or average income per person, is the most commonly used comparative measure of development. Developed countries tend to have a relatively high GDP per capita.

▼ Countries with highest and lowest GDP per capita, 2010

Country	GDP per capita ($)	Country	GDP per capita ($)
Luxembourg	104,390	Eritrea	423
Norway	84,543	Guinea	420
Qatar	74,422	Madagascar	391
Switzerland	67,074	Niger	383
Denmark	55,113	Ethiopia	364
Australia	54,869	Malawi	354
Sweden	47,667	Sierra Leone	325
United Arab Emirates	47,406	Liberia	226
USA	47,132	Democratic Republic of Congo	188
Netherlands	46,418	Burundi	177

Source: IMF

According to the International Monetary Fund, Luxembourg had the highest annual GDP per person in 2010 at $104,390 and Burundi, in Eastern Africa, the lowest at just $177.

However, GDP is a narrow measure of economic development or economic welfare in a country. For example, it does not take account of what and how much people can buy with their incomes, their access to healthcare and education, or other non-economic aspects such as the amount of political and cultural freedom people have, the quality of their environment or the level of security against crime and violence. ➤ **6.3**

Calculating average GDP per person also tells us nothing about how incomes are distributed between populations. For example, consider China. Rapid economic growth had increased the number of millionaires in the country to over 477,000 by 2010, but still around 36% of the Chinese population had to survive on less than $2 a day, with 16% on less than $1.25 each day. Similarly, Saudi Arabia has a reasonably high income per head, around $16,641 in 2010, but most of the wealth in the country is held by less than 3% of the population. Even within highly developed countries such as the USA there are still big disparities between rich and poor people. For example, in 2009 around 7% of US households had an annual income of $10,000 or less compared with 2% of households with $250,000 or more.

Other countries such as Equatorial Guinea, Brunei, and Trinidad and Tobago also have relatively high average incomes but are generally not considered developed countries because their economies depend so much on the production of oil. These countries also have very unequal distributions of incomes. For example, in 2010 average income in Trinidad and Tobago was $16,167 but 13% of the population lived on less than $2 per day and 21% were considered below the national poverty threshold.

▼ Population below $1 per day, selected countries 2009

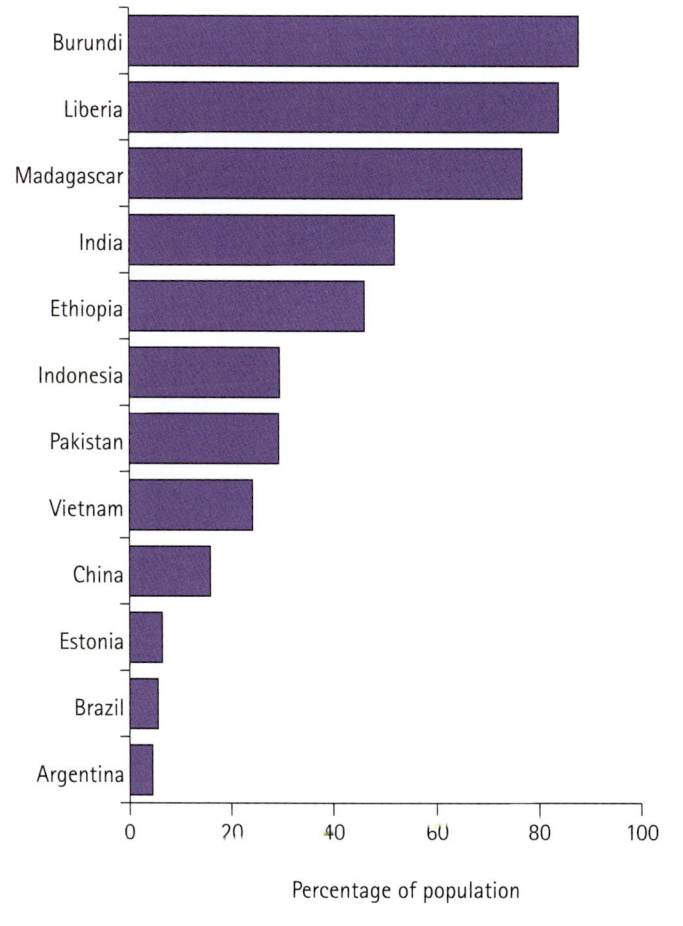

Population on less than $1 per day

A widely used measure of the absolute level of poverty in a country is the proportion of people living on very low incomes, usually $1 (extreme poverty) or $2 per day (moderate poverty). In 2009 around 31% of employed people in developing economies were estimated to be living on less than $1 per day, down from 41% in 1999.

Other indicators of poverty include levels of malnutrition, numbers of underweight children, levels of unemployment and numbers of people living in slums.

Life expectancy at birth

People in developed countries tend to live longer than people in less-developed countries because they have better standards of living and access to good food and health care. In contrast, malnutrition, poor sanitation, lack of access to health care, wars and famines mean that many people in less-developed regions do not live to old age.

Life expectancy from birth is therefore a good measure of economic development in a country or region. On average, a baby born in the developed world in 2005 could expect to live to 75 years of age, while a baby born in the less-developed world could expect to live around 66 years. However, in some of the poorest countries in Africa, average life expectancy from birth is less than 42 years. ➤ **7.2**

Developed and less-developed economies

Other health-related indicators of economic development include baby and mother mortality rates, the proportion of children and adults receiving inoculations against diseases and death rates from various diseases including tuberculosis and HIV/AIDS. For example, in 2008 around 65 out of every 1,000 children under the age of five died in developing regions of the world compared with just 6 out of every 1,000 in developed regions.

Adult literacy rate

A good measure of education provision in an economy is the proportion of the adult population that is able to read and write. For example, most adults can read and write in developed countries such as the USA, Canada, Japan and those in Europe. In contrast, in 2008 only around one in three adults living in developing countries in Sub-Saharan Africa such as Chad, Equatorial Guinea, Niger and Sierra Leone could read and write.

Other education-related indicators include school and college enrolment and completion rates among children and young people.

Access to safe water supplies and sanitation

Clean water is a necessity and safe, clean sanitation can help stop the spread of disease. These are generally available services to most people living and working in developed countries. Yet only just over half of all people in developing regions had access to good sanitation in 2008, and just 80% to a safe and sustainable water source. Access to improved sanitation is particularly poor in rural areas in the least-developed countries with only 31% of rural populations having access compared with 50% living in cities and urban areas.

Ownership of consumer goods

Low incomes and the lack of an efficient production and distribution system for goods and services in many less-developed economies means ownership of consumer goods such as washing machines, cars, telephones and personal computers is low compared with ownership in many developed countries.

For example, in 2008 the number of personal computers and Internet users in every 100 people was 67.7 in developed regions compared with 15.1 in developing regions of the global economy. Similarly, the number of mobile phone subscribers in every 100 people was just 48.8 in developing economies, although up significantly from just 5.5% in 2000. This compared with 104.6 in developed regions where some have two mobile phones, one for personal use and one for work. Fast and efficient communications are a necessary factor in the development of an economy.

Proportion of workers in agriculture compared to industry and services

Relatively high incomes in developed economies mean that people have money to spend in shops, eating at restaurants and on leisure activities. They also want banks, insurance, public transport, holidays and many other services. The large number of firms located in developed economies also requires a range of business services. As a result, most employed people in developed countries work in services while, in contrast, most employees in less-developed countries work in agriculture. ➤ **6.2**

However, unemployment can be very high in many less-developed countries because there is little paid employment available. Many people instead try to be self-sufficient and produce from subsistence farming the food their families need. Any surplus can be sold at local markets to earn some money or exchanged for other goods and services through barter. ➤ **3.1**

ACTIVITY 7.3

Rich or poor?

Look at the table of different development indicators below for three countries. Which country do you think is developed? Which is a newly industrialized economy? Which is a less-developed economy? Is the choice clear-cut in each case? Suggest why the measures and indicator values given may sometimes appear misleading and contradict each other.

Indicator	Country A	Country B	Country C
▸ Life expectancy at birth (years)	68	45	75
▸ Adult literacy rate (%)	71.9	83.2	99.6
▸ GDP per capita (US$)	22,214	5,135	69,841
▸ Population using an improved drinking water source (%)	76	49	100
▸ Prevalence of underweight children under 5 (%)	6	27	less than 5
▸ Share of women in wage employment in non-agricultural sector (%)	44.0	32.4	46.8
▸ Patients successfully treated for tuberculosis (%)	82	46	92
▸ Ratio of land protected to maintain biological diversity to total territorial area (%)	6.4	11.7	13.6
▸ Total carbon dioxide emissions (tons per capita)	7.7	0.9	12.2
▸ Employment to population rate (%)	60	64.9	55.3

Source: Selected values from *Millennium Development Goals, Targets and Indicators, Statistical Annex* 2010

Human poverty index

To make international comparisons of economic development and poverty a little easier the UN compiles two key statistical series combining a number of measures and indicators. These are:

- **the human development index (HDI)** which combines measures of GDP per capita, years of schooling and life expectancy into one simple indicator ➤ **6.3**

- **the human poverty index (HPI)** which combines a range of measures of economic hardship.

The HPI is used to compare and rank the scale and extent of poverty in developing and developed countries. To do this there is an index (HPI-1) compiled for developing economies and an index (HPI-2) for developed economies.

Developed and less-developed economies

HPI-1 Developing economies Indicators include:	HPI-2 Developed economies Indicators include:
▸ probability at birth of dying before the age of 40 ▸ percentage of people unable to read or write ▸ population below income poverty line ▸ population without sustainable access to an improved water source ▸ proportion of underweight children	▸ probability at birth of dying before the age of 60 ▸ percentage of people unable to read or write very well ▸ population with less than 50% of average income ▸ proportion of people unemployed for 12 months or more

In 2007–08, the Scandinavian countries of Sweden, Norway and the Netherlands had the lowest poverty values of the 22 developed countries included in the comparison. The UK, Ireland, Italy and the USA had the highest values, and therefore scored the worst in terms of the poverty measure for developed economies.

SECTION 3

Poverty reduction measures

Measures to reduce international poverty

Governments often intervene in their economies in an attempt to reduce absolute and relative poverty in a number of ways:

- They may introduce measures to **reduce unemployment**, which is a major cause of poverty in many societies. These may include expansionary fiscal and monetary policies to increase total demand in an economy, but also government training programmes to teach unemployed workers new skills.

- **Progressive taxation** applied to personal incomes can reduce income inequality and therefore relative poverty because people on higher incomes will pay a greater overall percentage of their incomes in tax. ➤ **5.2**

- Money raised from taxes can fund **welfare services** and provide **income support** to people on very low incomes. For example, elderly people, single parents and disabled people may be unable to work and may have insufficient incomes or savings to afford essential goods and services.

- Tax revenues can also be used to subsidize the building of free or **low-cost homes** for poor families to live in, and to provide them with free health care and travel.

- Governments may introduce **minimum wage laws** to raise the wages of the lowest paid employees. ➤ **3.2**

- The **quantity and quality of education** available to children may be improved to increase their job prospects and earning potential once they leave school or college.

- Governments may attract **inward investment** from overseas firms to provide jobs and incomes and teach employees new, more advanced skills.

Types of overseas aid

However, governments in less-developed economies will often lack the resources to reduce poverty in their countries. Some may also lack the will to do so. As a result, governments and aid agencies from more-developed economies will often provide help to less-developed economies to improve the living standards and economic welfare of their populations. Such **overseas aid** can take a number of forms.

1 Food aid

The EU and the USA often produce far more food than they need. Overproduction of basic foodstuffs such as wheat, butter and meat resulting in huge surpluses have been common in Europe in the past.

The cost of storing all of this food is very high and the food is sometimes given away to less-developed countries as food aid.

While food aid is necessary when people are starving, it is not always a good thing. If free food is given to an underdeveloped country, people may not need to buy the produce of farmers in that country. If their farmers cannot make a living they may leave farming to find work in the cities. This means that in future the country will have even fewer farmers and may need even more food aid.

2 Financial aid

Financial aid may be given to developing countries but will often be governed by a number of conditions to ensure that it is spent wisely, for example, on a major project such an airport or a dam, on training public servants to improve their efficiency, or on implementing new taxes and spending programmes to ensure that the countries do not have to continue relying on overseas aid in future. Sometimes overseas governments will demand the money is used to employ companies from their countries, for example to construct new infrastructure projects and to enter into trade agreements to buy exports from their countries.

3 Technological aid

To improve living standards aid is often given to developing countries in the form of modern technologies, for example by building modern power plants and providing advanced machinery. The problem with technological aid is that people in developing countries will need to be trained to use the new methods and machines. Overseas experts must also therefore be provided to educate and train local people.

Developed and less-developed economies

Even if people can be trained quickly, modern machinery may employ only a small number of workers. Technological aid should therefore be simple, for example providing instruction on how to use land better to grow more food using labour, or on how to start and run a small business.

4 Loans

In addition to financial aid, many less-developed and developing countries have borrowed significant amounts of money from multinational banks, governments of other countries, the International Monetary Fund (IMF) and the World Bank.

However, some countries borrowed so much that they became unable to repay their external debts. This was the case for Mexico during the 1980s and Argentina in 2001, causing economic crises in these countries.

Some very poor countries even struggle just to pay their annual interest charges. Countries classified as developing by the World Bank owed over $345 billion in debt in 2010 of which the lowest income countries owed $135 billion.

5 Debt relief

Because of the problems debt is causing in many less-developed countries, a number of poor countries have received partial or full cancellation of their loans from foreign governments, the IMF and World Bank.

For example, the **Highly Indebted Poor Countries (HIPC)** programme was initiated by the IMF and the World Bank in 1996. It provides debt relief and low-interest loans to cancel or reduce external debt repayments in 40 of world's least-developed countries with the highest levels of poverty and external debts.

> **EXAM PREPARATION 7.1**
>
> a In developing countries the standard of living is often lower than the standard of living in developed countries. Identify **four** indicators that might confirm this. [4]
>
> b Sometimes there is much poverty in developing countries. Discuss reasons why this might be so. [6]
>
> c Discuss how the standard of living in a developing country might be improved. [10]
>
> *Cambridge IGCSE Economics 0455/04 Q7 May/June 2005*
> *Cambridge O Level Economics 2281/02 Q7 May/June 2005*

Arguments against overseas aid

Of the 40 countries classified as HIPCs 29 are in Sub-Saharan Africa. By the end of 2009 the stock debt held by the HIPCs had been reduced by 80%.

Overseas aid to less-developed countries can provide food and help them invest in the schools, hospitals, health care and technology they need to care for their populations and help their economies grow. In time their economies should expand to generate enough jobs and incomes so they will no longer need aid. However, some economists argue that overseas aid has not worked. Many of the poorest countries that receive overseas aid remain poor and, for some, economic growth is negative, meaning they are getting poorer. ▶ **6.3**

ACTIVITY 7.4

Aiding or abetting?

Read the articles below, then as a class group discuss whether or not you think developed economies should provide financial aid to less-developed countries.

Tens of millions in foreign aid wasted on salaries and commissions

AUSTRALIA'S foreign aid programme is under siege after revelations tens of millions of dollars are being wasted on huge salaries for consultants and rich contracts for private firms.

An extensive investigation has uncovered a lucrative foreign aid 'industry', raising questions about the Rudd Government's decision to double annual spending to more than $8 billion.

And a high-level review has slammed the $414 million programme in Papua New Guinea, claiming $100 million is being paid to a handful of firms – but delivering little.

Overseas aid is funding human rights abuses

OVERSEAS aid to Ethiopia is being used to shore up the power of an authoritarian regime and marginalize its opponents, according to a new report by the respected organization Human Rights Watch.

While the aid provided by western governments is passed on to regional and village administrations in Ethiopia, the human rights group says it has found evidence of systematic discrimination in its administration. Government supporters were favoured in the distribution of seeds and the allocation of land, and trade union members were discriminated against in schools, which were also used for the indoctrination of children with the ruling party ideology.

The group also found widespread problems with the administration of a food-for-work scheme funded by Ireland and other donors. In every area visited by the group, the programme was being used to target opponents of the regime.

Millions in overseas aid to Africa embezzled

The true scale of the theft of overseas aid money by corrupt foreign regimes is disclosed in leaked documents obtained by *The Daily Telegraph*. Tens of millions of pounds of taxpayers' money has been pocketed by their ministers and officials, much of it used to buy luxury goods. In one of the worst cases, £1.2 million given to Sierra Leone by the Department for International Development (DfID) to 'support peacekeeping' was stolen by the country's 'top brass' and spent on plasma television sets, hunting rifles and other consumer items.

Other examples include £16.5 million allegedly stolen by ministers in Uganda and £800,000 intended for schools in Kenya stolen by education ministers.

Many economists argue that aid alone cannot reduce poverty in many less-developed countries. Their governments must do more themselves to expand their own economies and reduce poverty through investment and international trade. ➤ 8.1

Instead, some economists argue, overseas aid is either wasted or diverted away from those people who need it the most, for the following reasons.

1. Aid budgets are often used up employing expensive overseas firms and consultants rather than being spent locally to alleviate poverty.

2. Many less-developed countries are poorly managed or do not have the skills they need to invest financial aid wisely in projects that will help their economies grow. Aid providers also find it difficult to monitor how well the money is being used.

3. Some governments of less-developed countries are corrupt and overseas aid is misused to fund lavish lifestyles for government officials.

4. Some less-developed countries are ruled by ruthless dictators. They have used financial aid to fund armies to suppress people who oppose them. In some cases, it is these dictators who have caused debt problems in their countries by borrowing so much. Giving them debt relief may mean they will simply get richer: it may not be used to help the poorest people in their countries. For example, in 2005 the then president of Nigeria estimated that 'corrupt African leaders have stolen at least $140 billion from their people in the four decades since independence'.

WEBSITES

There are a great many excellent websites providing a wealth of data and information on economic development and developing economies. Here are just a few:

- CIA World Factbook www.cia.gov/cia/publications/factbook/index.html
- United Nations Statistics Division https://unstats.un.org/unsd/default.htm
- UN Millennium Development Goals www.un.org/millenniumgoals/
- World Bank Development data and statistics www.worldbank.org/data
- www.globalissues.org/TradeRelated/Poverty/Hunger.asp
- www.bized.co.uk/learn/economics/development/indicators/index.htm
- www.wikipedia.org/wiki/Developing_countries

KEYWORDS

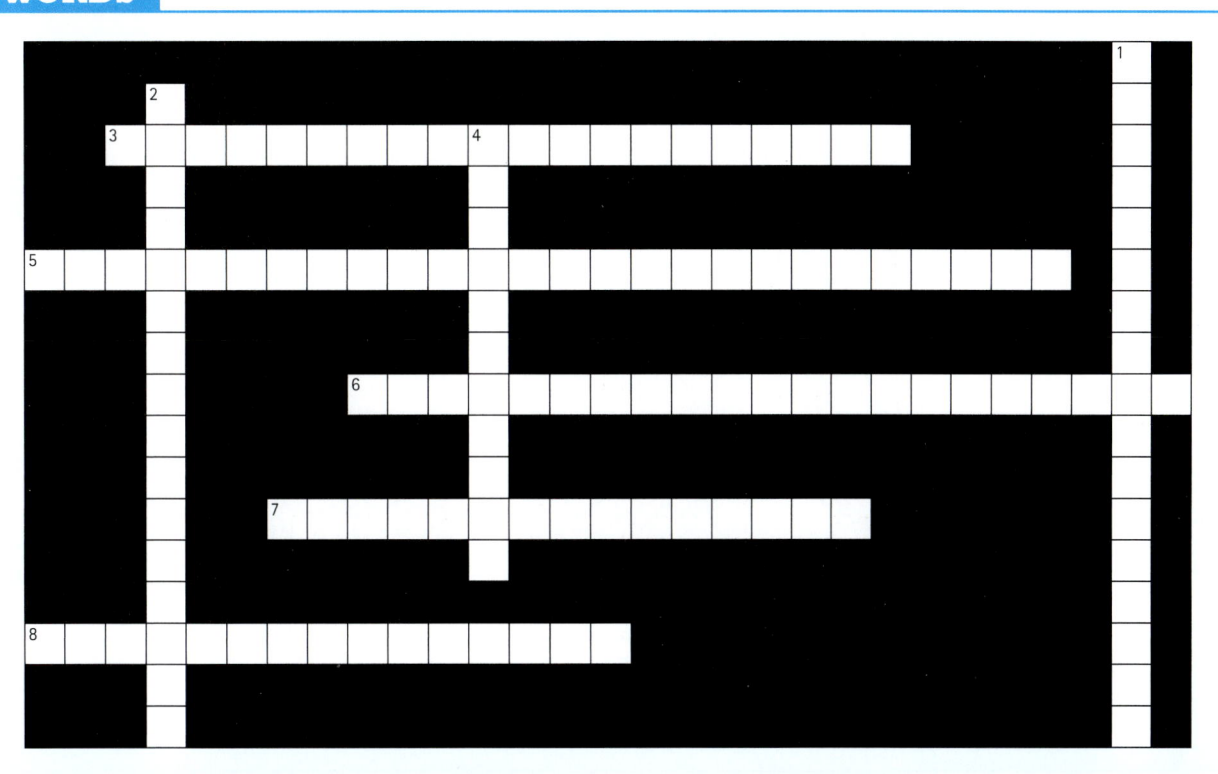

Clues across

3. A country with a relatively low level of economic development (4, 9, 7)
5. A term used to describe a country that is undergoing significant growth in its industries and infrastructure but is yet to display the full range of characteristics of a modern developed economy (5, 14, 7)
6. A statistical measure complied from different development indicators by the United Nations to measure and contrast economic development in different countries (5, 11, 5)
7. An economic condition of having fewer resources than others in the same society, usually measured by the extent to which a person's or household's financial resources fall below the average income level of others in their economy (8, 7)
8. An economic condition of lacking both money and basic necessities needed to live successfully, such as food, water, education, health care, and shelter (8, 7)

Clues down

1. A measure of the number of people of working age as a proportion of the total population in a country who can read and write (5, 8, 4)
2. A country with a high level of economic development, including high average incomes; good-quality housing, legal and education systems; modern infrastructure and a wide range of industries (9, 7)
4. The voluntary transfer of resources from one country to the benefit of another, for example to help it reduce poverty and improve its level of economic development. This help may be in the form of financial or technological assistance, food supplies and debt relief (8, 3)

Developed and less-developed economies

Unit 7.2 Population

AIMS

By the end of this unit you should be able to:

▶ describe the factors that affect **population growth** (**birth rate**, **death rate**, **fertility rate**, **net migration**)

▶ discuss reasons for the different rates of growth in different countries

- distinguish between the **natural rate of population growth** in a country and net migration

▶ analyse the problems and consequences of these population changes for countries at different stages of development

- understand what is meant by a population **dependency ratio** and calculate ratios for different countries

▶ describe the effects of changing size and structure of population on an economy

- compare and contrast the **age distribution**, **geographic distribution** and **occupational distribution** of populations in different countries
- explain why populations are ageing in some countries.

SECTION 1

The global population

Since the 18th century the world has experienced a population explosion, and it is still increasing faster than ever before. While there is potential for the production of more goods and services, natural resources are limited, and, as fast as goods and services are produced, so the needs and wants of an ever-increasing world population grow. The population of the world is increasing by over 70 million people each year, or 200,000 a day. Imagine a city the size of Madrid in Spain being added every month, and the people in those new cities being on average only four to five weeks old!

The population explosion started in Europe after the Industrial Revolution in the 18th century. Improvements in housing, sanitation and medicine reduced the number of deaths and helped increase the number of births. The population of Europe rose by over 300% in a 160-year period after 1750. Many of these Europeans moved overseas.

▼ World population, annual average growth rates by major region, 1800–2050 (UNPD)

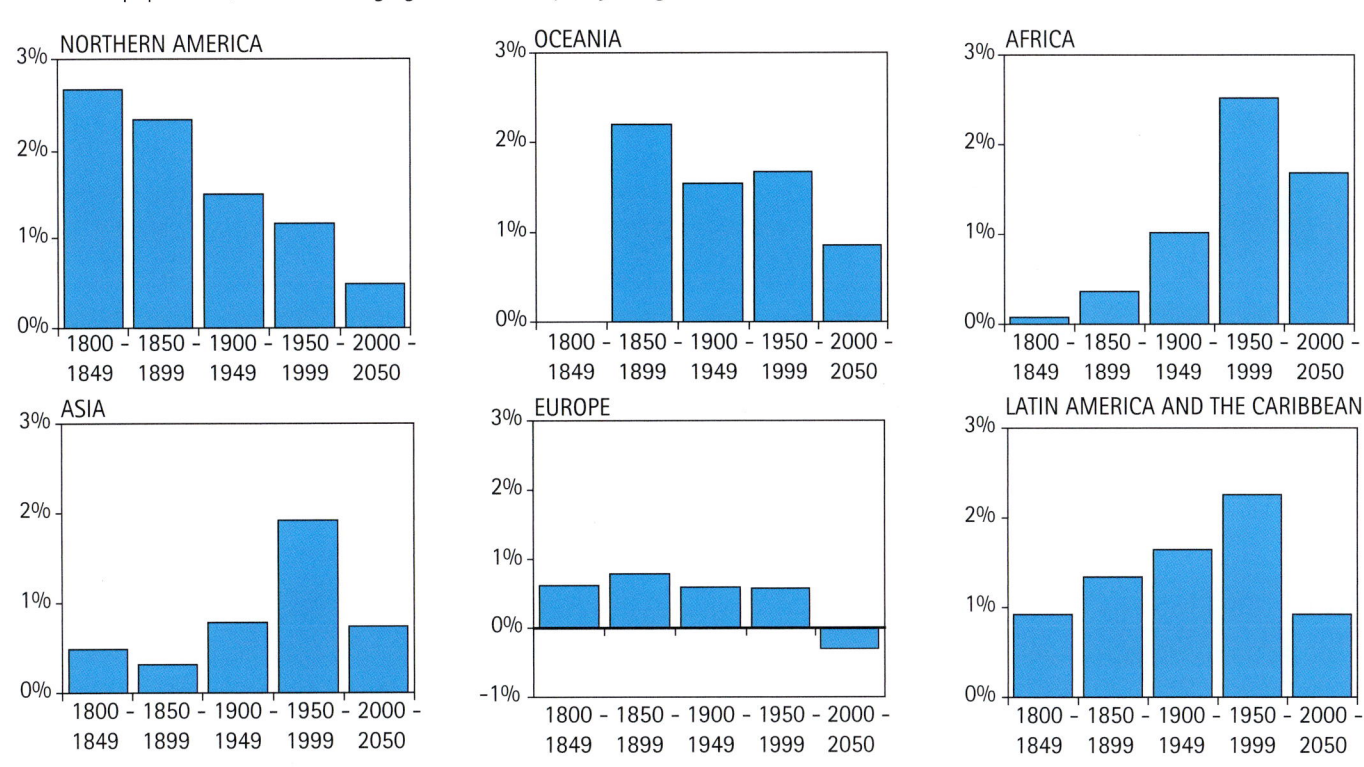

Source: 'World population, annual average growth rates per major region, 1800-2050' (UNPD)

In the 20th century population growth in Europe and many developed countries has slowed down. In some European countries recently there has even been negative population growth as people have been moving overseas and birth rates have fallen to low levels.

The new population explosion is in developing countries, particularly in Asia and Africa. Around 4 billion people, over 60% of the world population, currently live in Asia. The two largest countries by population, China and India, together account for around 37% of the world's population. Africa follows with 1 billion people, 15% of the world's population while Europe has 733 million inhabitants, around 11% of the world's population.

Population 399

The populations of Asia and Africa are forecast to continue growing rapidly, from around 5 billion people in 2010 to over 7 billion by 2050 – an increase of 60%. In contrast, the population of Europe is expected to fall from 733 million to around 690 million people.

The world population is expected to reach 9 billion by 2050. Just under 90% of all these people will live in countries currently considered as developing. ▶ **7.1**

ACTIVITY 7.5

Explosion!

The world population reached 1 billion around 1804. The second billion was added 123 years later in 1927, the third billion just 33 years later in 1960. It then took just 14 years for the world population to grow by another 1 billion people to reach 4 billion.

The graph below illustrates this population explosion. By 2010 the world population had reached almost 7 billion and is expected to grow to 9 billion by 2050.

▼ The world population explosion

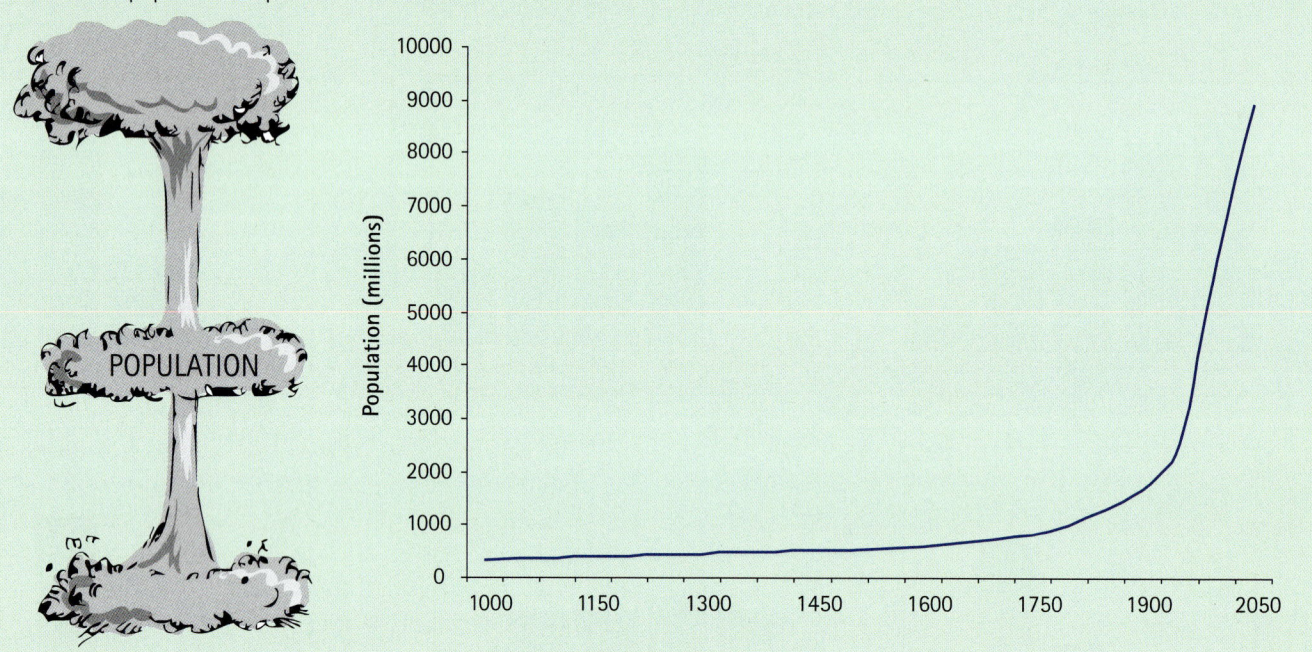

1. As the world population increases, what will happen to the total of needs and wants in the world?

2. If resources are scarce, such as oil, coal, metals, fertile soils and clean air, what will happen to the rate at which we use them up?

3. The population of the world rises as fewer people die and live to an old age, and as more babies are born. What is likely to happen to the demand for the following?

   ▶ Food   ▶ Education   ▶ Housing
   ▶ Consumer goods ▶ Health care   ▶ Transport

4. If one country is unable to produce enough goods and services for the needs and wants of its population how should it try to obtain more of these products?

   ▶ What is likely to happen to the country's balance of international trade?
   ▶ If it is unable to obtain more goods and services what is likely to happen to prices in the country?

Is population growth a cause for concern?

In 1798 the Reverend Thomas Malthus wrote about population growth in the UK. At the time of writing, the UK population was growing fast and this seemed to support his view that increasing numbers of people would only bring misery. There would be too many people and too few resources. That is, there would be **overpopulation**. As a result, people would start to starve and there would be famines and plagues as people lacked the strength to fight off disease. Wars would start as countries tried to take over each other's resources to support their own populations. Population growth would eventually be stopped.

However, Malthus was proved wrong in the UK. Although the population increased four times over during the 19th century, technology and productivity increased sufficiently to meet the needs of a growing population. Output of food increased and new methods of transport allowed food to be brought to Britain from the vast agricultural lands of the USA. More houses were needed and the building of these provided work and incomes for people. Increasing numbers of people meant more consumers. This increase in demand expanded the markets for goods and services, stimulating investment in new capital equipment to produce them and creating employment for many more people. Economic growth occurred, and, despite the costs of increased congestion in growing cities and increasing pollution from factories, living standards rose.

Nevertheless, many people still believe Malthus will eventually be proved right. Rapid population growth in many developing countries is increasing pressure on scarce resources, particularly natural resources, as more and more people, farms and factories compete for land and access to safe drinking water. Cutting down trees to make way for intensively farmed land can cause it to become depleted of soil and nutrients, increasing the risk of famine.

Among many experts expressing concerns over continued population growth, the UK chief scientist, Professor John Beddington warned changing conditions could create a 'perfect storm' by 2030. Rising populations, food shortages, insufficient water and energy resources may unleash public unrest, cross-border conflicts and mass migration from the worst-affected regions.

Beddington said food reserves are at a 50-year low but the world will need 50% more energy, food, and water by 2030. Similarly, the United Nations' Food and Agriculture Organization (FAO) has warned that the world will have to produce 70% more food by 2050 to feed a projected extra 2 billion people.

ECONOMICS IN ACTION

Do you agree with the predictions made? How does the article illustrate the concept of opportunity cost? Should countries allocate more scarce resources to developing new technologies and equipment and less to the production of consumer goods? Do you think governments should introduce population controls?

World faces 'perfect storm' of problems by 2030

In a major speech to environmental groups and politicians, Professor John Beddington, who took up the position of UK chief scientific adviser in 2008, will say that the world is heading for major upheavals which are due to come to a head in 2030.

He will tell the government's Sustainable Development UK conference that growing populations and success in alleviating poverty in developing countries will trigger a surge in demand for food, water and energy over the next two decades, at a time when governments must also make major progress in combating climate change.

'We head into a perfect storm in 2030, because all of these things are operating on the same time frame,' he said. 'If we don't address this, we can expect major destabilisation, an increase in rioting and potentially significant problems with international migration, as people move out to avoid food and water shortages,' he added.

Beddington said a major technological push is needed to develop renewable energy supplies, boost crop yields and better utilise existing water supplies.

Looming water shortages in China have already prompted officials to build 59 new reservoirs to catch meltwater from mountain glaciers, which will be circulated into the water supply.

The dependent population

Imagine there are five people living in your home: your mother and father, your sister and a grandparent. Your mother is the only person at work. She earns $150 per week, which is used to provide food, clothing and shelter as well as the other goods and services for five people including herself. That is, your father, you and your sister and a grandparent all depend on your mother going to work. Clearly, if there was just your mother and father their standard of living would be much higher. They would have more money to spend on themselves. If, on the other hand, they had more children, all the family would have a lower standard of living as the mother's income and the goods and services it buys would have to be shared out between more people. As the number of dependants rise, everybody will be worse off unless the productivity of scarce resources also rises. The same applies to the population as a whole.

People in work produce goods and services not only for themselves but also for people not in work. For example, in South Africa there are approximately 49 million people, of which 17 million people make up the working population or labour force. The rest of the population of about 32 million people rely on the labour force to produce the goods and services they need and want. These 32 million people are therefore the **dependent population**: that part of a population that does not work and relies on others for the goods and services they consume.

From these figures we can calculate the **dependency ratio** in South Africa. This ratio compares the number of people in the dependent population of a country with the working population in the same country.

$$\text{Dependency ratio} = \frac{\text{dependent population}}{\text{working population}}$$

Using the figures for South Africa the dependency ratio is 1.9 (32 million/ 17 million). That is, every person in the labour force not only supports himself or herself but also 1.9 other people.

The dependent population of a country includes the very young, schoolchildren, students, housewives and old-age pensioners. Any increase in these groups of people will increase the dependency ratio in a country. The higher the ratio the greater the burden on the working population, and therefore the entire economy, of supporting people not in employment.

▼ The dependent population includes both young and old

More resources, and expenditure on them, will have to be devoted to education for the young, and medical and welfare services for young and old alike. In a country such as Sweden, where many essential services and merit goods are provided by the government using tax-payers' money, this means working people will have to pay more tax to support dependants. In addition, if people in work cannot produce enough goods and services to satisfy the needs and wants of a growing dependent population, the country will have to use some of its income to purchase more and more imported goods from abroad. Its balance of international trade may become unfavourable. ▶ 8.2

The dependency ratio has increased in many countries for a number of reasons; the school leaving age has been increased over time; more young people are encouraged to stay on in full-time education after leaving school; people are living longer and the number of elderly people has increased; and an increasing number of people have taken early retirement. To offset this in part, many governments have increased the age at which people can officially retire from their jobs and receive a basic pension from the government. Some governments have also introduced compulsory pension savings schemes and have transferred many care services for the elderly to the private sector to encourage greater and more efficient provision.

However, many less-developed countries face some of the biggest problems. Improvements in health care have reduced child mortality rates and increased life expectancies. As a result, their already large dependent populations are increasing further, placing more strain on their scarce resources.

Population

ECONOMICS IN ACTION

What impact will the changes below have on dependent populations? What are the economic costs and benefits of countries such as France, Australia and many others in raising state retirement ages and school leaving ages?

France to raise retirement age from 60 to 62

France is to raise the retirement age from 60 to 62 in 2018 in an effort to get the country's spiraling public finances under control, the labour minister said Wednesday.

The French government's budget deficit was 7.5 per cent of gross domestic product last year. The government aims to reduce it to under 3 per cent by 2013.

The labour minister said the reform will bring France more into line with other European countries, including the UK, Germany and Greece, which have also raised retirement ages and taken other measures to slash budget deficits. 'We cannot at the same time work less long and continue to increase pensions' he said.

However, the French measure is still not as drastic as some changes elsewhere in Europe. Germany, for example, is to gradually raise its retirement age over time from 65 to 67, starting from 2012.

Minimum school leaving age jumps to 17 in Australia

Students will be forced to spend an additional two years in school or go into a vocational training program under a government plan to raise the minimum leaving age to 17.

The 60-year-old laws allowing students to finish school at 15 will be changed to ensure that all students complete their year 10 School Certificate. After that, students will not be able to leave unless they are enrolled in a vocational training programme.

'It will mean over the course of your lifetime, you're much less likely to be unemployed, over the course of your working life, you're much more likely to earn a better income, and there are also are additional health benefits and so on,' said the Australian premier in support of the changes.

What is an optimum population?

A country will be considered underpopulated if it does not have enough human resources to make the best use of its other natural and man-made resources. That is, there is not enough labour to maximize the amount of output of goods and services that can be produced for people to enjoy. In this case a government may provide help to families to have more children, for example by providing income support, free child care and employment policies that allow parents more time off work to look after children. A government may also encourage the immigration of skilled labour.

ACTIVITY 7.6

Someone to depend on

Below is a table of figures showing the total population and labour force in a number of countries in 2011.

Country	Total population	Labour force
China	1,336,718,015	819,500,000
India	1,189,172,906	478,300,000
USA	313,232,044	154,900,000
Indonesia	245,613,043	116,500,000
Brazil	203,429,773	103,600,000
Pakistan	187,342,721	55,770,000
Bangladesh	158,570,535	73,870,000
Nigeria	155,215,573	48,330,000
Russia	138,739,892	75,550,000
Japan	126,475,664	65,700,000

Source: *CIA World Factbook*

1 For each country calculate:
   a the size of the dependent population
   b the dependency ratio

2 Which countries have:
   a the highest dependency ratio?
   b the lowest dependency ratio?

3 What effect would the following have on the dependency ratio of a country?
   a A fall in the number of people in employment.
   b An increase in the number of old people.
   c An increase in the number of births.
   d An increase in employment.
   e A decrease in the number of births.
   f Net inward migration by people of working age

4 Of the above factors in question 3, which are characteristic of:
   • developing economies?
   • developed economies?
   • both types of economies?

5 a What is meant by overpopulation?
   b Can Japan be considered overpopulated? Explain.

In contrast, a country will be overpopulated, as Malthus envisaged, if there are too many people and too few resources to support them. Unless a government can increase the productivity of resources through new technologies or working practices it may have to seek ways to limit further population growth and even encourage people to move overseas to reduce the overall population.

Population

The optimum size of a population will therefore be that which will allow a country to maximize output per head of the population from its existing resources. However, because technologies and the quality and quantity of labour skills and other resources can change over time it is difficult to identify what an optimum population should be at any point. The concept also fails to take account of any social costs or issues different populations and levels of production may create. ▶ 2.3

SECTION 2

Causes of population change

There are three ways in which a country's population can increase.

1. The number of babies being born increases.
2. The number of people dying falls.
3. More people arrive from overseas to become residents of a country (**immigration**) than there are people leaving the same country to live overseas (**emigration**).

▼ Population size and components of growth, by major area 2000–2010

Region	Population 2010 (thousands)	Births	Deaths	Net migration	Total growth
		(annual average growth from 2000, thousands)			
World total	6,908,688	135,014	311,432	0	79,332
More-developed regions	1,237,228	13,551	12,293	2,968	4,226
Less-developed regions	5,761,460	121,437	43,388	-2,943	75,106
Africa	1,033,043	33,753	11,874	-521	21,358
Asia	4,166,741	77,338	27,208	-3,285	46,845
Europe	732,759	7,530	8,416	1,505	619
Latin America and Caribbean	588,649	11,152	3,320	-1,090	6,742
North America	351,659	4,641	2,627	1,286	3,300
Oceania	35,838	589	236	115	468

Source: United Nations Population Division

The **natural rate of increase in a population** is the difference between the birth rate and death rate. In most countries birth rates exceed death rates so populations are growing. For example, over the period 2000 to 2010 births exceeded deaths by 793 million in the world. Most of these births occurred in less-developed countries. For example, around 237 babies were born every minute on average in less-developed countries in 2009 compared to just 83 deaths per minute – an increase in the population by 154 each minute. In contrast, there were only 27 babies born every minute in more-developed countries that year and just 23 deaths. This means the natural rate of population growth in more developed countries averaged just four new people every minute.

In contrast, the natural rate of change in population in many European countries has recently been negative because birth rates have fallen below death rates. Over the period 2000 to 2010 deaths in European countries exceeded births by around 886,000 each year. The population of Europe only expanded by just over 6 million people over the decade due to **net inward migration**, notably from countries in Africa and Asia. However, within Europe itself many Eastern European countries were losing population to Western European countries such as the UK and France. Birth rates fell below death rates as many younger people from countries such as Bulgaria, Belarus and the Czech Republic have migrated overseas. This is called **net outward migration**.

Births

In some countries more babies are born than in others. The average number of children born in a country each year compared to the total population is known as the **birth rate**, which is normally expressed as the number of births for every 1,000 people in the population. The birth rate in Germany in 2011 was 8.3 births for every 1,000 German citizens but it used to be much higher. In the early 1900s the birth rate was over 35 per 1,000. Falling birth rates have been observed in many developed countries.

▼ Countries with highest and lowest birth rates, 2011

Country/Area	Highest birth rates (births per 1,000 of population)	Country/Area	Lowest birth rates (births per 1,000 of population)
Niger	50.54	Slovenia	8.85
Uganda	47.49	Czech Republic	8.70
Mali	45.62	Austria	8.67
Zambia	44.08	South Korea	8.55
Burkina Faso	43.59	Singapore	8.50
Ethiopia	42.99	Saint Pierre & Miquelon	8.32
Angola	42.91	Germany	8.30
Somalia	42.71	Hong Kong	7.49
Burundi	41.01	Japan	7.31
Malawi	40.85	Monaco	6.94

Source: *CIA World Factbook*

All the countries with the highest birth rates in 2011 were in Africa. In many of these countries there are on average six or more children for every adult female in the population. In contrast, many countries with low birth rates are in the Far East and Eastern Europe. In all these countries there is on average fewer than two children per adult female. The overall world birth rate in 2011 was just over 19 births per 1,000 people.

There are a number of reasons for differences in birth rates between countries, and changing birth rates over time.

1 Living standards

Improvements in the quality and availability of food, housing, clean water, sanitation and medical care result in fewer babies dying. Many years ago many children would die before they could go to work and earn money to help their families. As a result, people often had large families in case some of their children died. As living standards improved in many developed countries, fewer babies died and so people did not have as many children.

In less-developed countries birth rates remain high because many children still die, and people want large families so that the children can work to produce food and earn incomes.

Average number of children per adult female

Countries with 6 or more children born per woman

Niger Uganda Mali

Somalia Burundi

Bukino Faso Ethiopia

Countries with less than 1.25 children born per woman

Macau Hong Kong

Singapore Taiwan Japan

South Korea Lithuania

Source: CIA World Factbook

2 Contraception

The increased use of contraception and abortion has dramatically reduced birth rates in developed countries. The contraceptive pill for women was first introduced in the 1960s and has a 99% success rate in preventing pregnancy. However, because of a lack of sex education in some less-developed countries, many people are unaware of birth control. Perhaps they should learn from Japan's success in reducing it's birth rate from 36 births per 1,000 people to 17 per 1,000 people in just 15 years after the introduction of contraception.

3 Custom and religion

Many people, particularly in less-developed countries, hold religious beliefs that will not allow them to use contraception. The Roman Catholic religion is one such belief. But customs are changing. In developed countries it has become less fashionable and less socially acceptable to have large families so birth rates have fallen.

4 Changes in female employment

In developed countries, many women are in full-time or part-time employment. Working women may not wish to break their careers to bring up children. Children are also expensive to raise. Not only will the mother have to give up work for a while, but she may also have to pay a baby-sitter to look after her children if she returns to work. Female participation in the workforce is also rising in many developing countries. ➤ 6.2

5 Marriage

Most people have children when they are married. In many developed countries people are tending to marry later in life and this has reduced birth rates. For example, in the UK the average age of a new mother at all births increased from 26 years of age in 1971 to over 29 years of age in 2010.

Deaths

If people start to live longer it increases the size of the population. The number of people who die each year compared to every 1,000 people measures the **death rate**. The overall world death rate in 2010 was just under nine deaths for every 1,000 people. The countries with the highest death rates in 2011, of over 15 deaths per 1,000, included many in Africa. These death rates are similar to the death rate in the UK and many other developed countries over 100 years ago. The UK death rate is now just over nine per 1,000 of population. In contrast, many of the countries with the very lowest death rates in 2011, of less than three deaths per 1,000, were in the Middle East.

▼ Countries with highest and lowest death rates, 2011

Country/Area	Highest death rates (deaths per 1,000 of population)	Country/Area	Lowest death rates (deaths per 1,000 of population)
Angola	23.40	Gaza Strip	3.29
Afghanistan	17.39	Northern Mariana Islands	3.28
South Africa	17.09	Sint Maarten	3.00
Nigeria	16.06	Turks and Caicos Islands	2.99
Russia	16.04	Jordan	2.69
Ukraine	15.74	Bahrain	2.61
Chad	15.47	Mayotte	2.60
Guinea-Bissau	15.27	Qatar	2.43
Lesotho	15.19	Kuwait	2.11
Central African Republic	15.01	United Arab Emirates	2.06

Source: *CIA World Factbook*

A number of factors affect death rates and help to explain differences between countries.

1 Living standards

Better-quality food, clothing, sanitation and shelter, and an increased emphasis on cleanliness, have all helped improve health and life expectancy in developed countries. In the less-developed world a lack of the right types of food to provide vitamins and proteins has meant some people in these areas continue to die of malnutrition. However, in developed countries many people smoke and eat fatty foods, causing cancers and heart disease. These health problems occur very little in less-developed countries.

2 Medical advances and health care

Advances in medicine and health care in many countries have reduced the number of deaths from diseases. For example, killer diseases such as smallpox, cholera and tuberculosis can be prevented or even cured by modern medicines.

However, life expectancy at birth still remains low in many less-developed countries. Other diseases such as HIV/AIDS and malaria are widespread and increasing in many areas, particularly across Africa, and causing the death of many young people and adults. In fact, in some African countries general life expectancy has fallen on average by 10 years since the 1990s with some affected more than others. For example, average life expectancy in Botswana fell from 64 years in 1990 to 49 years by 2002, largely due to the spread of HIV/AIDs, but has since improved to 53 years.

▼ Average life expectancy at birth, 2011

Highest	Years	Lowest	Years
Monaco	89.73	Somalia	50.40
Macau	84.41	Central African Republic	50.07
San Marino	83.01	Zimbabwe	49.64
Andorra	82.43	South Africa	49.33
Japan	82.25	Guinea-Bissau	48.70
Guernsey	82.16	Swaziland	48.66
Singapore	82.14	Chad	48.33
Hong Kong	82.04	Nigeria	47.56
Australia	81.81	Afghanistan	45.02
Italy	81.77	Angola	38.76

Source: *CIA World Factbook*

3 Natural disasters and wars

Natural disasters such as hurricanes, floods and earthquakes, famines due to lack of rain and poor harvests, and wars and criminal violence can also have a significant effect on death rates and life expectancy over time in some countries.

▲ The Japanese tsunami on 10 March 2011 claimed over 70,000 lives due to devastating flooding

▲ Estimates of casualties resulting from conflict in Iraq between March 2003 and 2010 range from 150,000 to over 1 million

Migration

Net migration measures the difference between immigration and emigration to and from a country. Between 2000 and 2010 almost 3 million more people each year emigrated from less-developed countries to more-developed countries than migrated in the opposite direction. Net migration from Asian countries accounted for much of this. On average, net outward migration from Asia was 3.2 million people per year over the same period. In contrast, net inward migration to Europe was 1.5 million people per year, more than offsetting a natural population decline.

Such international migration has economic, social and political implications. Increasing numbers of migrants from less-developed countries to more-developed countries have helped to boost their working populations, but has also increased the demand for housing, education and welfare. This has placed pressure on government finances. In some cases, tensions can occur between different ethnic groups as a result. But countries that lose people to immigration can also face problems caused by a loss of skilled workers leaving to find higher-paid work overseas, such as nurses and doctors, engineers and entrepreneurs.

EXAM PREPARATION 7.2

a What determines the rate of growth of a population? [3]

b Contrast the expected age structure of the population of a developing country with that of a developed country. [7]

c In some developing countries life expectancy has been declining in recent years. This has been largely due to the spread of HIV/AIDS. Governments have allocated large amounts of expenditure to developing new hospitals and to providing health education programmes.

Discuss in what ways this policy might affect other major government economic policies. [10]

Cambridge IGCSE Economics 0455/04 Q6 October/November 2005
Cambridge O Level Economics 2281/02 Q6 October/November 2005

SECTION 3: The structure of populations

Demography involves studying the characteristics of and changes in population. This includes examining and comparing the structure of populations in different countries and considering how changes in structure can affect economies. The following characteristics of populations are relevant:

- age distribution: how many people there are in different age groups
- sex distribution: the balance of males and females
- geographic distribution: where people live
- occupational distribution: where people work.

Young or old?

The **age distribution** of a population refers to the number of people, or percentage of the population, in each age group. With falling birth and death rates in many developed countries, the average age of their populations is rising: there are a growing number of middle-aged and elderly people. For example, in 2011 in Italy, Greece, Germany and Japan, over one quarter of their populations were over 60 years of age, while 15% or less were under 15 years of age.

In contrast, in many developing countries more than one third of their population is under the age of 15, with some countries having almost half their populations made up of children. For example, in Uganda in 2010 half the population was under 15 and just 2.3% over 65 years of age.

Similarly, in Niger, Mali, Congo, Ethiopia and Burkino Faso, children made up 46% or more of their populations. This means that a large proportion of these countries' populations is too young to work and will have to depend on those who can, at least until they too are old enough to work.

▼ Youngest and oldest populations, 2010

Youngest countries	Under 15 years of age	Over 65 years and over	Oldest countries	Under 15 years of age	Over 65 years and over
Uganda	50.0	2.1	Japan	13.3	22.6
Niger	49.7	2.3	Germany	13.5	20.4
Mali	47.5	3.0	Italy	13.4	20.3
Congo	46.7	2.5	Sweden	15.4	19.7
Ethiopia	46.2	2.7	Greece	14.2	19.5
Burkino Faso	46.0	2.5	Spain	14.5	18.4
Malawi	45.3	2.7	Bulgaria	13.9	18.2
Mozambique	44.1	2.9	Belgium	15.9	18.0
Yemen	43.5	2.6	Latvia	13.5	16.9
Madagascar	43.3	3.0	Switzerland	15.2	16.9

Source: *U.S. Census Bureau*

In 1950, just 8% of the world population was aged 60 years or over. By 2010 that proportion had risen to 11% and it is expected to reach 22%, or 2 billion people, in 2050. One in every three people in developed countries will be over 65 by this time.

As the number of elderly people grows in many countries it will increase pressure on their working populations to support more non-working people. In 1950, there were 12 people of working age for every person aged 65 or older. By 2010, that number had shrunk to 9. By 2050, this elderly support ratio is projected to fall to just 4. These changes will also affect the allocation of resources in these economies. More resources will be needed to produce the goods and services older people want and need, such as more health care, pensions and leisure facilities. However, falling birth rates may mean less resources will be needed for maternity clinics, nurseries and schools.

Males and females

The ratio of males to females in a population reflects its **sex distribution**. Like most other species the human sex ratio is around 1:1. the sex ratio of the entire world population is estimated to be around 101 males for every 100 females.

The sex ratio tends to vary naturally by age but can also be affected by such factors as war and also influenced or even controlled by governments. Slightly more male babies tend to be born than females but the ratio of females to males tends to even out by adulthood. However, because females tend to live longer than males in many countries there are more females to males on average in older age groups. For example, in India there were 1.1 females for every male in the age group 65 and over in 2011. In the 85 years or over age group the ratio of females to males was 1.5. The same pattern can be observed in most countries.

Gender imbalance, an excess of males or females, has been observed in a number of countries and can occur for a number of reasons:

- Wars result in many deaths among young adult male populations.

- Violence towards females observed in some developing countries is creating an excess of males. For example, honour killings of females by their family members take place in some societies in the Middle East and Asia if, for example, a female member is thought to have shamed her family by going out with a male from another religious group, refusing to enter into an arranged marriage or having an affair with another man outside of her marriage.

- Gender imbalance can result from sex selection through abortion or even gender-based infanticide (selective killing of children of the same sex). In some less-developed countries, male children are often considered more productive and capable of work than females. Government policies and religious beliefs may also reinforce these views. For example, the extremist group Taliban which ruled large parts of Afghanistan from 1996 until 2001 banned females from receiving education during this period.

- Sex-specific inward migration to a country, often by male guest workers brought in by companies to work in construction and other industries, can cause gender imbalance. For example, according to the Ministry of Health in the Maldives, the island has a large, mainly male population of labour immigrants, especially in low-paid jobs that Maldivian people find unattractive. This has swelled the male to female sex ratio to 1.44. Similarly, a large number of male expatriates in the population of Qatar working in its petrochemical industry has resulted in a highly skewed sex ratio in the country of almost two males to every female.

High sex ratios at birth in some Asian countries are now attributed to sex-selective abortion and infanticide due to a strong preference for sons. This will affect future marriage patterns and fertility patterns resulting in fewer births in future and an ageing population. Eventually, it could cause unrest among young adult males who are unable to find female partners.

China facing major gender imbalance

China will have 30 million more men of marriageable age than women in less than 15 years as a gender imbalance resulting from the country's tough one-child policy becomes more pronounced, state media reported Friday.

China imposed strict population controls in the 1970s to limit growth of its huge population, but one side effect has been a jump in gender selection of babies. Traditional preferences for a son mean some women abort their baby if early tests show it is a girl.

Some families also abandon female babies to die soon after birth or transfer them for adoption to overseas families.

Sex-selective abortion is prohibited but the government says the practice remains widespread, especially in rural areas.

The report, carried in the newspaper, said China's sex ratio for newborn babies in 2005 was 118 boys to 100 girls, a huge jump from 110 to 100 in 2000.

In some regions such as the southern provinces of Guangdong and Hainan, the ratio has ballooned to 130 boys to 100 girls, the newspaper said.

The report predicted that by 2020 the imbalance would mean men of marriageable age – especially those with low income or little education – would find it difficult to find wives, resulting in possible social problems including more prostitution, alcoholism and violence. The ability of the population to reproduce will also be harmed.

China Daily said one way to solve the problem would be to create a proper social security system so rural couples would not feel they needed a son to depend on when they get old.

It has been reported that acute gender imbalance in countries such as China and also India, which has an estimated 32 million more males than females, is contributing to social and economic problems such as increasing prostitution, alcoholism, HIV/AIDS, and violence and the kidnapping and sale of women for forced marriage or into the sex trade.

Population pyramids

The age and sex distribution of a population can be displayed on a **population pyramid**. The pyramids in Activity 7.7 compare the age and sex distribution of the population of a developed country with the population of a less-developed country. Along the bottom axis is the number or percentage of males to the left of the vertical axis, and to the right the number or percentage of females. The vertical axis shows age in ascending ranges. The pyramid for the developed country bulges in the middle due to their ageing populations as birth and death rates remain low.

In contrast, many of the least-developed countries have pyramids with wide bases and narrow tops because birth rates are high and life expectancy is low.

Where do people live?

The **geographic distribution** or regional distribution of a population refers to where people live. Most people, almost 90% of the world population, live in developing countries. This places significant pressure on scarce resources in these countries.

ACTIVITY 7.7

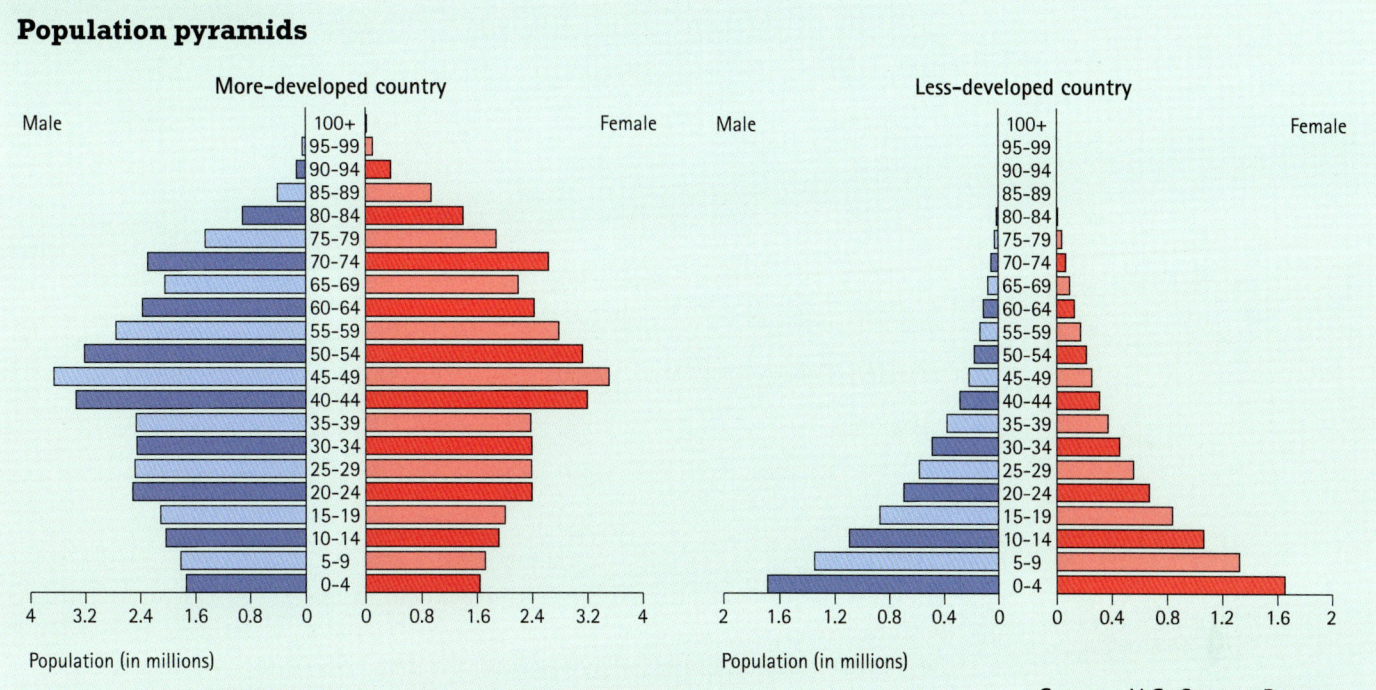

Population pyramids

More-developed country (Male / Female, Population in millions, age groups 0-4 to 100+)

Less-developed country (Male / Female, Population in millions, age groups 0-4 to 100+)

Source: U.S. Census Bureau

1. Looking at the pyramids, which group of countries have the highest dependency ratios for:
   a. those under 15 years of age?
   b. those over 60 years of age?

2. Which group of countries has the highest birth rate?

3. Which group of countries has the highest life expectancy?

4. List 10 countries that individually are likely to have similar population structures to those shown by the pyramids.

5. What is an 'ageing population'? Which group of countries has an ageing population? Describe likely impacts this will have on their economies.

▼ Most densely populated countries and areas, 2009

Country/Area	Population	Area (km²)	Density (People per km²)
Macau	541,200	29.2	18,534
Monaco	33,000	1.95	16,923
Singapore	5,076,700	710.2	7,148
Hong Kong	7,003,700	1104	6,349
Gibraltar	31,000	6.8	4,559
Vatican City	826	0.44	1,877
Malta	416,333	316	1,318
Bermuda	65,000	53	1,226
Bangladesh	162,221,000	143,988	1,127
Sint Maarten	37,429	34	1,101

Population

▼ Least densely populated countries and areas, 2009

Country/Area	Population	Area (km²)	Density (People per km²)
Mauritania	3,291,000	1,025,520	3.200
Suriname	520,000	163,820	3.200
Iceland	318,452	103,000	3.100
Australia	22,648,720	7,682,300	2.900
Namibia	2,171,000	824,292	2.600
French Guiana	187,056	90,000	2.100
Western Sahara	513,000	266,000	1.900
Mongolia	2,671,000	1,564,116	1.700
Falkland Islands	3,140	12,173	0.260
Greenland	57,000	2,175,600	0.026

The most densely populated place in the world in 2009 was Macau in China with just over 18,500 people per km². The principality of Monaco in Europe is next with 33,000 people living together on just 1.95 square kilometres of land. The world average is 51 people per square kilometre of the earth's surface. The least populated country is Greenland with an average density of just one person for every 38.1 km², or 0.026 people per km², largely because much of Greenland is frozen over all year round.

Within countries the geographic distribution of population can also vary widely and has changed significantly over time. Around half the world's population today lives in urban areas, and this is expected to rise to around 60%, or 5 billion people, by 2030. The movement of people from rural areas to urban areas has helped increase production of goods and services, and raised living standards.

However, increasing urbanization has also resulted in the increased consumption of scarce natural resources such as trees, open space and water as more homes, factories, offices, shops and roads have been built. Increased energy and car use in cities has increased pollution, reduced air and water quality, and increased health risks. The rapid growth of cities in many countries, but particularly in newly industrialized countries, is therefore some cause for concern.

For example, Serampore, Pateros and Dehli in India all have between 29,000 and 33,600 people per km². However, Manila in the Philippines is the most densely populated city with over 43,000 people per km².

The number of mega-cities or agglomerations in the world with over 10 million residents has also increased from just five in the late 1960s to 18 in 2000 and numbered 26 by 2011. Tokyo in Japan was the largest with 34.2 million residents. Guangzhou in China, Seoul in South Korea, Dehli and Mumbai in India. Mexico City, New York, São Paulo in Brazil and Manila all had over 20 million residents in 2011.

▲ Manila, Philippines: the world's most densely populated city in 2011

▼ World population density, population per km² in 2006

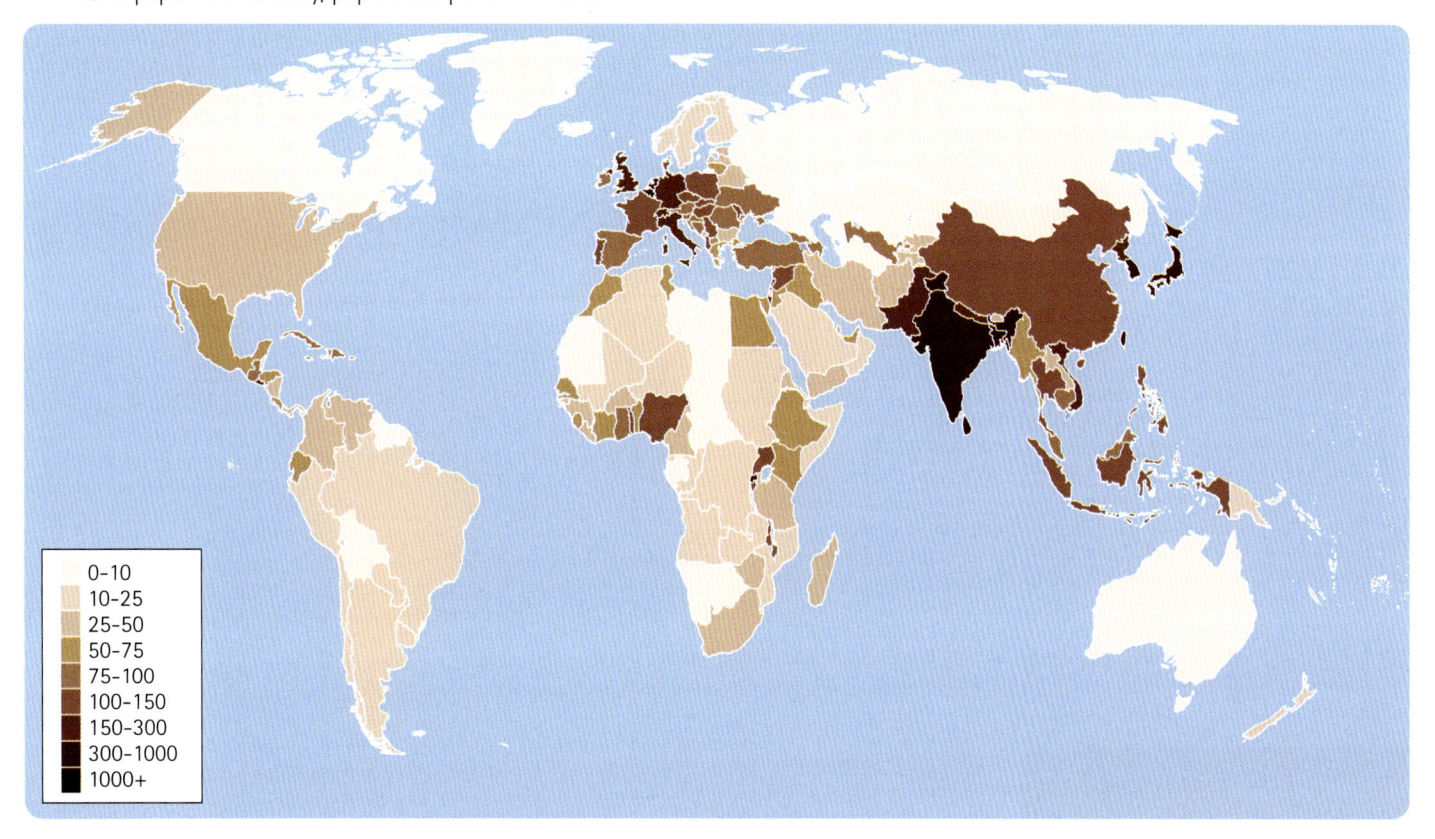

Legend:
- 0-10
- 10-25
- 25-50
- 50-75
- 75-100
- 100-150
- 150-300
- 300-1000
- 1000+

Where do people work?

The **occupational distribution** of a population refers to the types of jobs people do. In 2010 the total population of working age in the world was about 3.4 billion people. Of these around 37% worked in agriculture, 22% in industry and construction, and 41% in services. Most employed people in developed countries work in services while most employees in the least-developed countries work in agriculture. ➤ **6.2**

It is forecast that by 2020 India will be home to 28% of the world's working population. The trend in fast-developing economies, such as India and China, is for more and more people to move out of agriculture and other primary industries into employment in their rapidly expanding manufacturing and service industries.

Employment in services in many developed countries and also many small tourism-dependent countries is also expected to continue to rise. Female employment and self-employment is also growing in these and many other countries. For example, female participation rates in Sweden, Norway and Denmark are the highest in the world with over 77% of their female populations in employment or self-employment.

Population 417

▼ Employment by industry

Countries with highest proportion of employees in agricultural sector	Percentage of workforce in agriculture	Countries with highest proportion of employees In services sector	Percentage of workforce in services
Angola	85%	Andorra	81%
Burkina Faso	90%	Antigua & Barbuda	82%
Burundi	93%	Gaza strip	83%
Chad	93%	Israel	82%
Lesotho	93%	Luxembourg	81%
Malawi	86%	Netherlands	80%
Mali	80%	United Arab Emirates	80%
Mozambique	81%	UK	80%
Niger	90%	USA	79%
Rwanda	90%	Virgin Islands	80%

Source: *CIA World Factbook 2011*

WEBSITES

There is a wealth of information and statistics on population available from the following organizations and websites:

- CIA World Factbook *www.cia.gov/cia/publications/factbook*
- GeoHive *www.xist.org*
- Organisation for Economic Co-operation and development (OECD) *www.oecd.org (search For Demography and population statistics)*
- United Nations Population Division *www.un.org/esa/population/unpop.htm*
- United Nations Statistics *https://unstats.un.org/unsd/Demographic/default.htm*
- U.S. Census Bureau population division *www.census.gov/population/www/*
- *www.wikipedia.org/wiki/Population*
- World Bank *www.worldbank.org (search for Population)*
- World Bank *www.worldbank.org/depweb/english/modules/social/pgr/index.html*

KEYWORDS

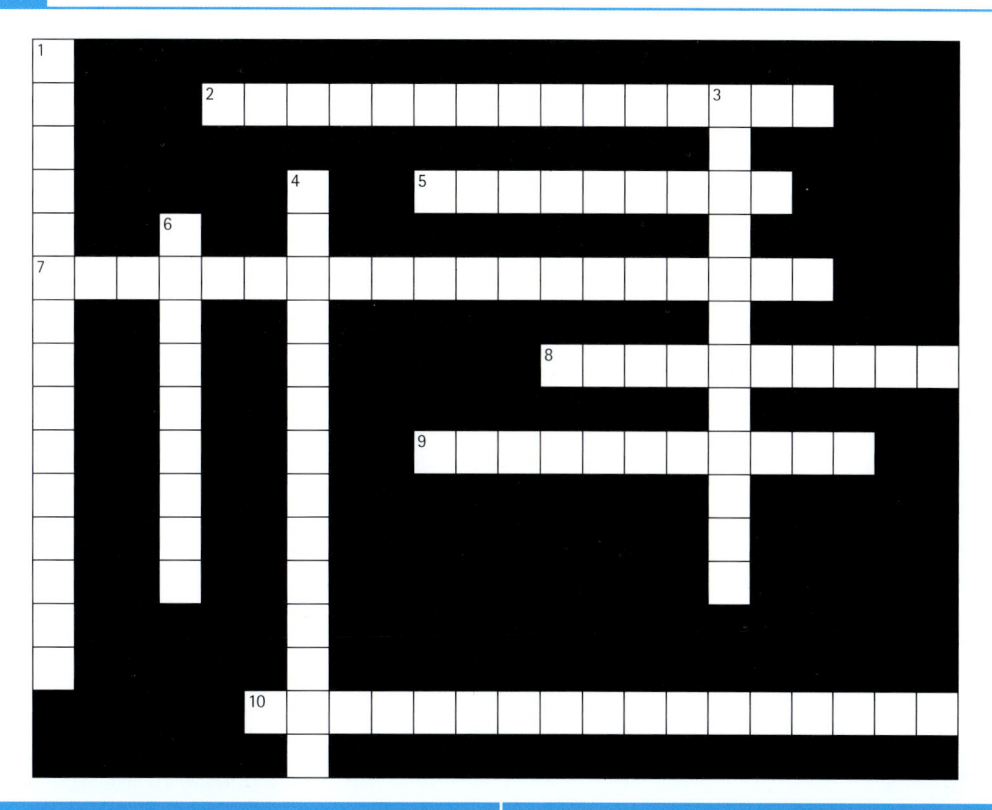

Clues across

2. An excess of males or females in a population, usually caused by factors other than nature, such as sex-selection bias, wars and male-dominated inward economic migration (6, 9)
5. A measure of the number of babies born per period per 1,000 people in a population (5, 4)
7. That part of a population that does not work and relies on others for the goods and services they consume (9, 10)
8. The act of leaving one's country to live overseas (10)
9. Inward migration: the introduction of people from overseas into the population of a country (11)
10. A graph that shows the distribution of males and females in various age groups in a human population (10, 7)

Clues down

1. A measure that contrasts the number of people in the dependent population of a country with the working population in the same country (10, 5)
3. The difference between immigrants and emigrants of a country per period of time (3, 9)
4. An economic condition in which there are too many people and too few resources (14)
6. A measure of the number of people who die per period per 1,000 people in a population (5, 4)

Assessment exercises

Multiple choice

1. Which factor is most likely to reduce the average age of a population in a developed country?
    A   A lower birth rate
    B   A lower death rate
    C   Emigration
    D   Immigration

2. What is most likely to be found in a typical developing country?
    A   A good education sector
    B   A small average family size
    C   A small percentage of very old people
    D   High spending on entertainment

3. The Chinese Government is concerned about two population problems – overpopulation and a gender imbalance, with males outnumbering females.

    In 2007 it reduced the number of babies that foreigners are allowed to adopt; almost all of the babies are girls.

    What effect might this have on the size of China's population and gender imbalance in the short run?

	size of population	gender imbalance
A	Increase	Increase
B	Increase	Reduce
C	Reduce	Increase
D	Reduce	Reduce

4. Changes in the standard of living of a country are best measured by changes in:
    A   National income
    B   National income per head
    C   Real national income
    D   Real national income per head

5. What might explain the high population growth in some developing countries?
    A   High birth rates and falling death rates
    B   High immigration and low emigration
    C   Falling birth rates and rising death rates
    D   Falling life expectancy

6. As a country develops, what is most likely to happen?
    A   A greater proportion of the workforce will be employed in the service sector
    B   The average age will decrease
    C   The birth rate will increase
    D   There will be reduced occupational mobility of labour

7. When must there be a rise in a country's population?
    A   When the birth rate is greater than death rate and there is net emigration
    B   When the birth rate is greater than death rate and there is no migration
    C   When the death rate is greater than birth rate and there is net immigration
    D   When the death rate is greater than birth rate and there is no migration

8. What is meant by overpopulation?
    A   Too many people to an area of land
    B   High population density
    C   Too many people and too few resources
    D   Rapid population growth

9. What is the dependency ratio of a country?
    A   The number of people not in work compared to the number of people in the labour force
    B   The number of old people compared to the total population
    C   The number of people over 16 years of age compared to the total population
    D   The number of children compared to the adult population

10. The death rate of a country is most likely to fall if:
    A   Housing conditions deteriorate
    B   More people smoke
    C   Health care deteriorates
    D   People's diets improve

11 Botswana has achieved high rates of economic growth.

What is most likely to have fallen as a result of this economic growth?

A   Employment
B   Income per head
C   Infant mortality rate
D   Literacy rates

12 Other things being equal, what will cause a population both to increase and to age?

A   A fall in the birth rate
B   A rise in both the birth rate and the death rate
C   A rise in the death rate and a fall in the birth rate
D   A fall in the death rate

13 Which of the following characteristics is most likely to be found in a developed economy?

A   Low infant mortality rate
B   Low investment rate
C   Low life expectancy
D   Low literacy rate

14 The table gives information on four countries. Which country is likely to be most developed?

	Population (m)	Gross domestic product (GDP) ($ billion)	Life expectancy (years)
A	100	800	51
B	1,000	1,600	63
C	60	600	48
D	150	6,000	63

15 What is likely to happen as a developing country becomes more developed?

A   A higher percentage of children will attend school
B   Infant mortality will rise
C   Life expectancy will fall
D   The agricultural sector will increase in importance

Structured questions

1   The charts below represent the proportion of people employed in different sectors in three different countries.

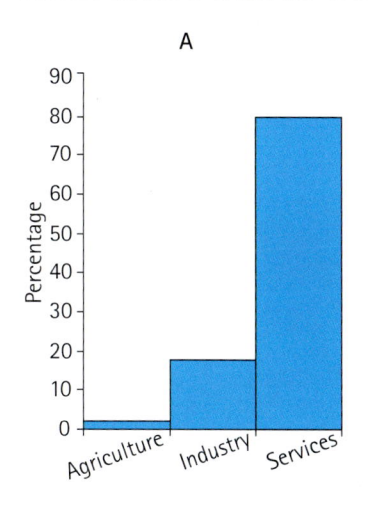

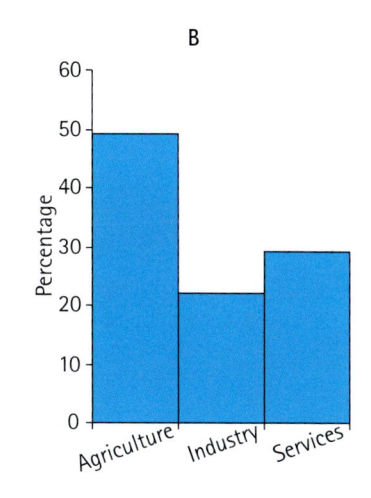

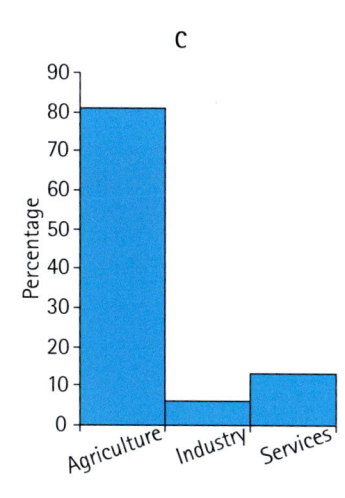

a   Which chart do you think represents:
    i   a country that is developing rapidly?
    ii a less-developed or low-income country?
    iii a developed or high-income country? [3]
b   Suggest how living standards might differ between the three different countries. [6]
c   Increasing numbers of females are entering employment in developed countries. How might this affect the birth rate in these countries? [5]
d   Suggest **three** other factors that have caused birth rates to fall in developed countries over the last 50 years or so. [6]

Assessment 421

2 a The rate of population growth in developed countries is often different from the rate of population growth in developing countries. Explain why this might be so. [5]

b Sometimes a government might try to limit the growth in the population of its country. Explain why it might want to do this. [4]

c As countries become more economically developed, there is a change in the relative importance of the different sectors of production. Describe what this change might be. [5]

d In many developed countries there will be a large increase in the proportion of older people during the next 10 to 15 years. Discuss how governments might deal with this situation. [6]

Cambridge IGCSE Economics 0455/04 Q7 May/June 2006
Cambridge O Level Economics 2281/02 Q7 May/June 2006

3 1 in 5 adults have not been educated to read or write; 98% of them live in developing countries and 66% of them are women.

a Explain **three** other differences that you might find between the population of a developed country and a developing country. [3]

b Another indicator of living standards, apart from education, is GDP. Discuss how useful this is in comparing the living standards between two countries. [7]

c Explain **two** reasons why education in a developing country is often provided by the public sector. [4]

d Discuss what effect investment in the education system might have in a developing country. [6]

Cambridge IGCSE Economics 0455/04 Q4 October/November 2007
Cambridge O Level Economics 2281/02 Q4 October/November 2007

4 Countries are categorised as less developed because of their poverty and low average incomes, their lack of good human resources and their low level of economic diversification.

a Explain what is meant by
  i 'their lack of good human resources' [3]
  ii 'their low level of economic diversification'. [3]

b Explain whether it can be concluded from the above statement that all people in less developed countries are poor. [4]

c Explain what is likely to be the occupational distribution of the population in a less developed country. [4]

d If a less developed country becomes classified as a developed country, what changes would probably have happened to the structure of its population and its occupational distribution? [8]

Cambridge IGCSE Economics 0455/04 Q4 October/November 2003
Cambridge O Level Economics 2281/02 Q4 October/November 2003

8 International aspects

8.1	International specialization and trade
8.2	Balancing international payments
Assessment	Multiple choice
	Structured questions

Resources are best allocated to those uses in an economy where there is an absolute or comparative cost advantage in production over other countries. Any surplus output can then be traded internationally with other countries that may be more efficient at producing other goods and services. Through international trade, countries can obtain a wider variety of goods and services at a lower cost than they could otherwise produce themselves. Global trade also allows firms and consumers to benefit from the biggest and cheapest sources of labour, raw materials and technologies from anywhere in the world.

However, growing international trade is increasing the rate at which natural resources are being depleted and the transportation of ever more people and goods across international borders has increased greenhouse gas emissions. Increasing trade with rapidly expanding economies is also threatening jobs in many developed economies and reducing opportunities for growth in less-developed economies. Established businesses may lose market share and may even be forced to close if they cannot compete with firms located in low-cost economies. Small businesses in less-developed economies may also be unable to grow if consumers in their countries are able to buy imported products far more cheaply than locally made products.

Some governments may try to protect their economies from the impact overseas competition can have on employment and incomes by using trade barriers. This can involve imposing taxes or 'tariffs' on the prices of goods imported from low-cost producers overseas or simply restricting the amount that can be imported. But trade barriers restrict free trade, consumer choice and economic growth.

International transactions between one country and the rest of the world are recorded in its balance of payments. Exports of goods and services to overseas consumers earn revenues. Imports require payments to overseas producers. International trade therefore also involves the exchange of national currencies. Currencies are exchanged on the global foreign exchange market. Changes in market demand and supply conditions for different foreign currencies can therefore affect their market value and, in turn, the prices of exports and imports.

An appreciation in the value of a national currency against other currencies will make exports from firms located in that country more expensive to buy in overseas markets. Demand for exports may fall as a result, reducing the sales and profits of exporting firms. However, import prices will rise causing imported inflation and increasing production costs for those firms that rely on imports of materials and components from overseas suppliers to produce their own finished products.

In contrast, a depreciation in the value of a national currency will make exports from firms located in that country cheaper to buy overseas. Demand for exports may rise, boosting revenues and employment opportunities. Import prices will increase and demand for them from domestic consumers is likely to contract. A depreciation in the value of a national currency on the foreign exchange market can therefore help to reduce a trade deficit by boosting demand for exports and reducing the demand for imports.

Unit 8.1 — International specialization and trade

AIMS

By the end of this unit you should be able to:

- describe the benefits and disadvantages of **specialization** at regional and national levels
  - demonstrate the application of **absolute advantage** and **comparative advantage** in international trade
- describe methods of **trade protection**
  - distinguish between **tariffs**, **subsidies**, **quotas** and **embargoes** as forms of **trade barrier**
- discuss the merits of **free trade** and protection
  - describe the gains from trade
  - explain and compare arguments for and against **protectionism** to safeguard **infant industries** and to prevent unemployment, **dumping** and **over-specialization**

SECTION 1

Globalization and trade

What is globalization?

People often joke about the world getting smaller. They are referring to the increasing ease at which people can travel around the world and the fact that our shops are full of a great variety of products from many different countries. In fact, this means the world is getting bigger. That is, the size of the global economy is growing as global travel and communications are becoming easier and cheaper and more goods and services are exchanged internationally between producers and consumers in different countries.

Tens of thousands protest at Summit in Seoul

Tens of thousands of anti-globalization activists have rallied in Seoul to protest a summit of the Group of 20 major economies.

The activists accuse the world's biggest economies of violating workers' rights and threatening social welfare programs by cutting public spending. South Korean police estimated the size of the rally at 20,000, while organizers said it drew 40,000 people.

The activists also oppose a proposed free trade agreement between the United States and South Korea.

Politicians, business and trade union leaders, environmental groups, consumers and the media frequently talk about the impact this 'globalization' is having on our economies and daily lives. For example, they may welcome inward investment from overseas companies, access to a greater variety of goods from other countries and the growing ease of overseas travel. But they also raise concerns about increasing numbers of firms moving production to low-wage economies and the effect this is having on jobs, and the dangers of global climate change caused by increasing pollution. Sometimes these concerns have caused many thousands of people to protest against increasing globalization.

Globalization can mean different things to different people. This is because it is a wide term used to describe economic, social, technological, cultural and political changes that are increasing interdependence and interaction between people, firms and entire economies all across the globe.

An economist will be interested the most in the following economic aspects of globalization:

- the increasing reliance of economies on each other through **international trade** for an increasing variety of goods and services
- opportunities for firms to buy and sell products in any country in the world
- increasing opportunities for labour and capital to move anywhere in the world
- the growth of global financial markets
- the impact all these changes are having on the amount and allocation of scarce resources, the balance of international payments, economic growth and living standards in different countries.

International specialization and trade 425

▼ Globalization involves increasing economic interdependence

More Filipino workers moving to Europe as demand for manpower continues to rise

Vietnam spends billions of dollars to import farm produce
Free trade agreements between South East Asian countries have made import products cheaper and more favourable for consumers.

Surging exports spur Thailand's economic growth

Dubai hit hard by global financial crisis

Turkish exporters creating new jobs
Turkish companies have successfully penetrated new markets across the Middle East. Iran, Syria and Iraq are becoming key markets for Turkish exports.

China loans Angola US $15 billion

Many of these changes have been happening for a long time so globalization is not really new but the reason why we are so much more interested in it and using the term more and more today is because the pace of these changes has increased.

Rapid globalization is the result of increasing wealth, the development of new technologies and faster and cheaper communications, allowing people to order goods and services and make payments via the Internet or over a telephone from anywhere in the world. Also, the transition of many former planned economies to free market economies has reduced barriers to international trade and allowed people and finance to move more freely between countries. As a result, many of these economies are now growing rapidly. But their rapid growth has also meant that scarce resources are being used up even faster and external costs, in terms of pollution and destruction of the environment, are rising. ➤ 2.3

Rapid globalization is also affecting the relative importance of different countries in the global economy. For many years, the USA has been the largest economy in the world. In recent years, however, the US share of the global economy has shrunk to approximately 25% from a peak of 33% in 1985, and will continue that trend as the economies of many newly industrialized countries, such as China and India, continue to grow rapidly. China became the world's second largest economy in 2010 after overtaking Japan.

SECTION 2

International specialization

Globalization for economists is about worldwide specialization through expansion of the division of labour. In Unit 3.1 we discovered how people have specialized in particular skills and occupations. This has allowed people to become more productive by enabling them to produce those goods and services they are best able to. This in turn has allowed whole economies to produce more goods and services more efficiently with their scarce resources. However, in some cases it has made jobs boring and repetitive, and it also means people must rely on each other to produce and exchange the range of goods and services they need and want. Specialization involves the need to trade and requires a generally accepted medium of exchange – money. ► 3.1

For the same reasons entire countries and regions have specialized in the production of particular goods and services and exchange them internationally with other countries. For example, many countries in the Middle East specialize in the production of oil because they are located over vast natural oil reserves. Similarly, Japanese industries became world leaders in the design and manufacture of many electronic products and cars because their workers became highly skilled in these activities.

China is now a major producer of low-cost electronic equipment and is also the world's largest manufacturer of wind turbines for renewable energy generation, recently overtaking Denmark and Germany.

Economies specialize in the production of those goods and services they are best able to produce because they have the natural, human or man-made resources to do so. Specialization allows them to produce a greater volume of their goods and services more efficiently than industries in other countries.

For example, imagine if Iceland tried to produce oranges. It would need to build vast greenhouses and use up a lot of power heating them and creating artificial sunlight. Growing oranges in Iceland would therefore be very expensive. Much better therefore to buy them from Spain or another country that is able to grow them easily and cheaply because it has a warm and sunny climate.

Through international trade some countries have become famous for the goods and services they produce, even if in some cases other countries make the same or very similar products. This is because their industries have developed a reputation among consumers worldwide for making these products cheaper and/or better than anywhere else.

There are many examples, including Italian shoes and clothes, Belgian chocolates, German beers, Swiss watches, Scotch whisky, Cuban cigars, Spanish olive oil, US aircraft and military equipment, and many more.

US aircraft

Spanish olive oil

Italian shoes

▲ Some examples of international specialization

International specialization and trade

ACTIVITY 8.1

Something special

1. Try to identify and list five or more goods or services that are not produced in your country and have to be purchased from producers located overseas.
2. Try to identify and list at least 10 goods and services that are produced by firms in your country but are also imported from overseas.
3. Look at the countries and products listed below. Which product do you think each country is best known for?

Saudi Arabia	France	Fish	Beef
Iceland	India	Tea	Lamb
Norway	Jamaica	Timber	Wine
Germany	New Zealand	Oil	Coffee
Argentina	Kenya	Manufactured goods	Tourism

4. Suggest ways in which you and your family benefit from international specialization and trade.

Comparative advantage

The benefits of international specialization and trade can be explained by the economic theory of comparative advantage. In the simple exercise below we will discover how countries can increase their output and their standard of living through international specialization and trade.

Assume that the countries of Taiwan and Chile both produce just two products, wheat and personal music players. Each country we assume has 100 workers, half devoted to wheat production and half to the production of personal music players. The total output per year of both countries is shown below.

▼ Before specialization

	Music players produced by 50 workers	Wheat (tonnes) produced by 50 workers
Chile	400	35
Taiwan	500	30
Total output per period	900	65

In this example, Chile is better than Taiwan at producing wheat. With the same number of workers Chile can produce five more tonnes of wheat than Taiwan. That is, Chile has an absolute advantage over Taiwan in wheat production. A region or country that is able to produce a good or service at a lower average cost per unit than any other region or country is able to have an **absolute advantage** in the production of that product. In contrast, Taiwan has an absolute advantage over Chile in the manufacture of personal music players. If each country specialized Chile would produce only wheat and Taiwan only music players. Total output of both would rise as shown below.

428 International aspects

▼ After specialization

	Music players produced by 100 workers (in Taiwan only)	Wheat (tonnes) produced by 100 workers (in Chile only)
Chile	0	70
Taiwan	1,000	0
Total output per period	1,000	70

The example assumes average labour productivity is constant. This means 100 workers can produce twice as much as 50 workers. This, of course, may not always be the case, for example, if there are decreasing returns to scale. ➤ **4.3**

If Taiwan now agrees to trade 400 personal music players for 30 tonnes of wheat from Chile, each country after trade is better off than it was before specialization and trade.

▼ After specialization and trade

	Music players	Wheat (tonnes)
Chile	400	40
Taiwan	600	30
Total output per period	1,000	70

It still benefits countries to specialize and trade even if one does not have an absolute advantage in the production of a particular product. Look at the example of Germany and Japan below. We assume for simplicity that each country devotes half its 100-strong workforce to the production of cars and televisions.

	Cars	Television
Japan	100	400
Germany	80	160
Total output per period	180	560

Japan has an absolute advantage in both goods. However, in Japan they would need to give up four televisions to produce one extra car. In Germany only two televisions would have to be given up to produce one extra car. That is, the opportunity cost of producing cars in Germany is lower than in Japan. This means Germany is relatively better at producing cars than Japan: it has a **comparative advantage** in car manufacturing. While Germany is less efficient than Japan in producing both goods, it is least inefficient in car production.

By concentrating on the production of cars, a country such as Germany can export cars and import other goods like televisions with its export earnings. Japan should, in our example, concentrate on the production of televisions. Both countries can then gain from specialization and trade.

ACTIVITY 8.2

At an advantage

The table below displays the daily output of clocks and peanuts in two countries, A and B. Each country devotes half its workforce to the production of each product and there are constant returns to scale in the production of clocks and peanuts.

Country	Clocks	Peanuts (kg)
A	2	21
B	4	7

1. What is the total output of clocks and peanuts?
2. Which country has an absolute advantage in **a** clock production, **b** peanut production? Explain the reasons for your answer.
3. Draw a table to show the output of the two countries after they have specialized in what they are best able to produce.
4. What are the total output figures now? By how much have they increased?
5. If the countries now agree to trade three clocks for 12kg of peanuts, show in a new table what they have gained from this exchange.

SECTION 3

What is international trade?

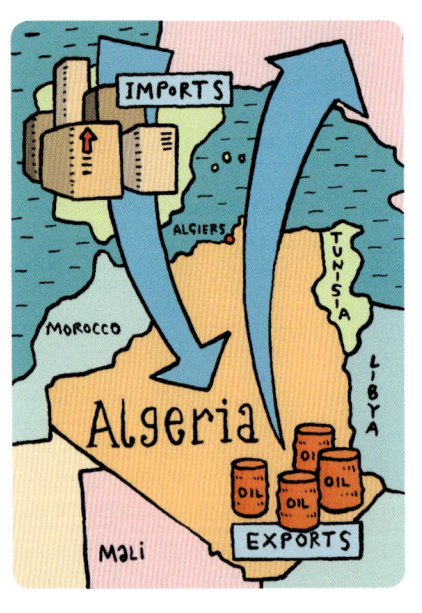

International trade patterns

No country is self-sufficient and able to produce all the goods and services it needs and wants. All countries therefore need to trade internationally in order to survive. For example, oil and gas production is the largest industry in Algeria in Northern Africa and accounts for around one third of its total national output each year. International trade therefore allows Algeria to benefit from specialization.

Because Algeria produces more natural oil and gas and petroleum products than the country needs it **exports** the surplus to consumers in other countries. It also exports some fruit and vegetables, animal products, iron ore and zinc. ▶ 8.2

The sale of exports earns the country revenues of around $75 billion each year that can be used to buy **imports** of goods and services from overseas that firms in Algeria are less able to produce using their resources. Imported products include farm machinery, many food and drink products and a wide range of clothes and other consumer goods.

National economies such as Algeria, in which industries specialize in the production of a relatively narrow range of goods or services, are therefore able to enjoy a much wider variety of products through international trade.

However, Algeria has also attracted inward investment from overseas companies, including in its oil and gas and financial services sector. For example, 12 of Algeria's banking groups are foreign owned. The country has also attracted skilled labour from overseas, notably from Egypt and China.

International trade therefore involves the movement and exchange of physical goods such as materials, component parts, equipment and finished products as well as services, ideas, money and labour across international borders.

How trade patterns are changing

For many years international trade flows between countries were dominated by raw materials such as iron ore, oil and wheat. Much of this trade was from less-developed countries in the southern hemisphere to the more-developed, industrialized economies in the northern hemisphere. However, global trade patterns have since changed significantly.

▼ Value of global trade in physical goods, 1960–2010

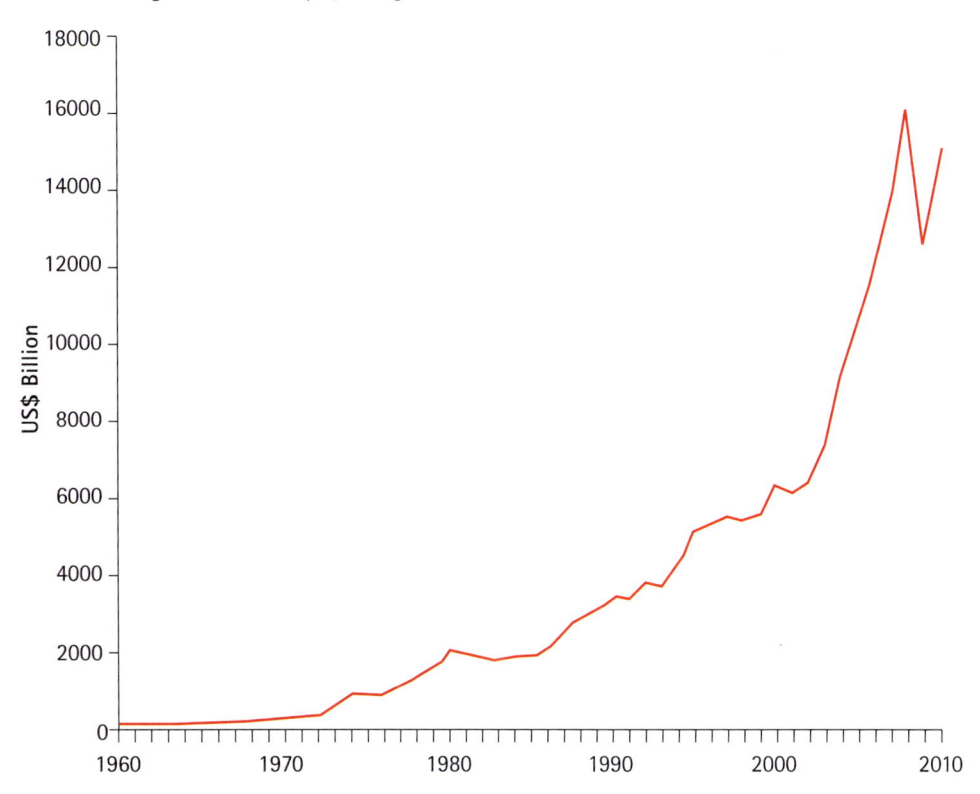

Source: 'Value of global trade in physical goods, 1960-2010', World Trade Organization

International trade is growing rapidly as more economies develop and incomes around the world rise. In 1963 the total global value of goods traded internationally was just under $160 billion with the USA, Germany and the United Kingdom accounting for 32% of total exports. By 2008 this had risen to $16.1 trillion before falling off again in 2009 (to $12.5 trillion) and 2010 (to $15.2 trillion) as many economies in the world experienced a slowdown in their economic activity. In 2009 the largest exporter in the world was China, followed by the USA and Germany. Together they accounted for almost 28% of global exported goods.

International specialization and trade

▼ Top 10 exporters of physical goods, 2009

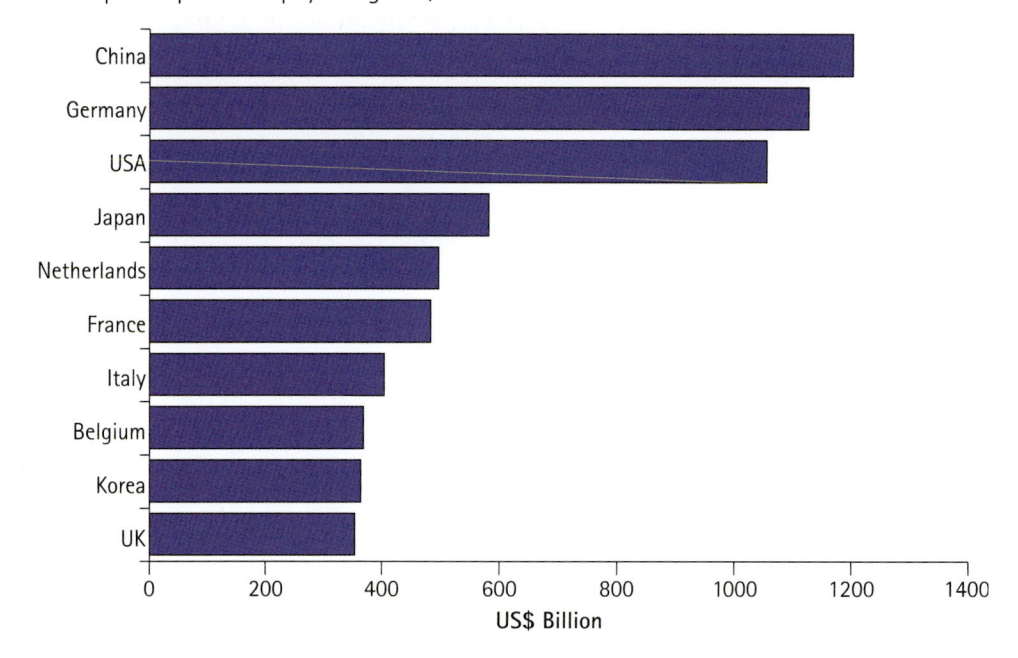

Source: 'Top 10 exporters of physical goods, 2009', World Trade Organization

Trade in manufactured goods has grown significantly. They accounted for over 50% of world exports in the early 1960s. By 2010 this share had climbed to 71%. The globalization of production has increased trade in manufactured goods while technological advances in transport, particularly containerization, have meant faster and more efficient handling of goods in bulk at ports.

▼ Global trade in physical goods, % share by major category

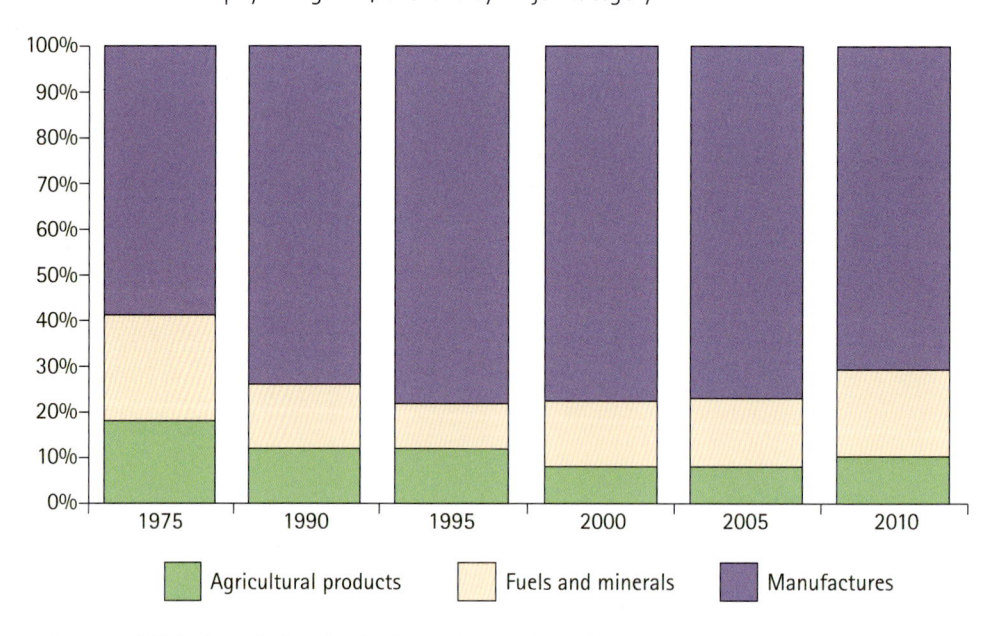

Source: 'Global trade in physical goods, % share by major category', 6 years shown', World Trade Organization

In contrast, the share of agricultural products in world trade has fallen, from around 28% in the early 1960s to just fewer than 10% in 2010. Processed food products have increased and now account for nearly half of agricultural trade.

432 International aspects

International trade in commercial services, including computer and information services, financial services, telecommunications, transportation and travel, has also increased rapidly, from just under $1.5 trillion in 2000 to almost $3.7 trillion in 2010. Services account for around 20% of world trade values.

Developed countries still accounted for three quarters of the global trade in 2000, but developing countries had seen their share climb to one third by 2010 and it continues to rise. Many industrial processes which initially took place in developed countries have relocated to countries offering lower production costs, namely from lower wages. As a result, global trade flows are now characterized by significant flows of goods from developing economies to developed ones.

Structural change in the global economy

An **open economy** is a national economy that engages freely in trade with other economies, and many national economies are becoming more open. This means they are trading more goods, services and capital investments internationally than ever before. This also means their firms are facing more competition from producers overseas.

Business expansion in rapidly expanding economies, including China, India and Brazil, is a growing competitive threat to many established firms in developed economies such as those in North America, Europe and the Far East. For example, China was the seventh largest exporter of physical goods in 2000. It had become the world's largest exporter by 2010.

Wages and salaries are still relatively low in newly industrialized economies. This enables many of their firms to produce goods and services far cheaper than those in more developed economies. They are also rapidly developing the workforce skills and technologies that will help their producers to remain competitive even as the wages of their workers begin to rise. ➤ **2.1**

At the same time rising incomes in these developing economies is increasing the number and spending power of their consumers. This is creating opportunities for firms in developed economies to sell more of their goods and services. An increasing number of business organizations are moving some or all of their business units to these countries to benefit from their low wages and their growing consumer markets. Many also offer lower taxes on profits on incomes. As a result, firms are closing in a number of developed economies to move their production overseas and jobs are being lost.

Less-developed economies also fear they will lose out in this global race. They are trying to develop their own manufacturing and service industries but cheap imports from rapidly developing economies could prevent them from doing so. This is because their consumers will prefer to buy cheap imports rather than goods or services produced locally, often at a higher cost and sometimes of poorer quality. Multinational companies are also locating in their economies attracted by the low wages of their workers and also low taxes in many cases. This again is creating more competition for local firms. ➤ **4.1**

Globalization is therefore creating economic conflict. As a result, some countries have introduced policies to restrict international trade and protect employment and production in their economies from overseas competition.

SECTION 4

The gains from free trade

Free trade or protectionism?

The concepts of absolute and comparative advantage in production explain the main advantages to countries from free and open international trade. These advantages are often referred to as the **gains from trade**.

1 International trade allows countries to benefit from specialization

If there was no international trade, countries would be forced to become self-sufficient by producing as many of the goods and services their citizens need and want themselves. Resources would be allocated to the production of a wide variety of goods and services rather than to their most efficient uses. This would mean total output was lower and costs higher than could otherwise be the case.

Instead, international trade enables economies to specialize in the production of those goods and services their natural, human and man-made resources are best able to produce, and then trade their surplus outputs with other countries to obtain the other goods and services they need and want. Through specialization and trade therefore, output, incomes and living standards will be much higher.

2 International trade increases consumer choice

Consumers can enjoy a greater variety of goods and services from different countries all over the world. For example, they can choose to buy clothes from France, or clothes from Italy, Spain, China or the USA. Take a quick look around your own home to see how many goods were produced by business organizations overseas.

3 International trade increases competition and efficiency

Through international trade, firms will have to compete with goods and services imported from overseas. This helps them to become more efficient and increase their sales. Consumers will also benefit from lower prices. For example, Algerian farms producing cereals and animal products such as wool will have to produce these products for a similar price and quality as imported cereals and wool otherwise Algerian consumers will simply buy them from producers overseas.

4 International trade creates additional business opportunities

A firm may be unable to expand in its home country because the size of the consumer market is relatively small. However, growing consumer markets overseas create additional opportunities for sales and business growth. Through international trade, a firm can expand its sales and scale of production because it is able to sell its products to a much larger number of consumers globally. This will allow a firm to lower its production costs, increase revenues and earn more profit. ▶ **4.3**

5 Free trade enables firms to benefit from the best workforces, resources and technologies from anywhere in the world

Having access to international markets allows a business to find the best and lowest cost sources of materials and components from different producers in other countries. For example, the Airbus 380, the largest passenger aircraft in the world, is assembled in Toulouse in France by the European company Airbus using components from over 500 suppliers in Spain, Germany, Japan, the UK, the USA, China, India, Romania, the United Arab Emirates and many other countries. Wages and material costs are lower in countries such as China and India than in Europe. As a result, Airbus is buying an increasing number of components for the Airbus 380 and other aircraft it manufactures from businesses overseas for it factories in Europe. Airbus also has a joint venture in China to manufacture its Airbus 320 aircraft. Employment and incomes are consequently rising in many overseas firms.

A firm can also import the latest equipment and ideas developed in other countries, borrow money from banks overseas offering the lowest interest rates and advertise for foreign workers with the skills it needs if these are lacking in its own country.

6 International trade increases economic interdependency and therefore reduces the potential for conflict

A further argument used in favour of free trade is that it helps to promote more international cooperation and peace. If economies are more dependent upon one another for goods and services then wars and armed conflicts could be less likely.

The disadvantages of uncontrolled trade

Despite the many gains from trade, increasing international trade may also be causing some problems.

1 International trade with low-cost economies is threatening jobs in many developed economies and reducing opportunities for growth in less-developed economies

Increasing global trade and competition, especially from rapidly growing economies, is threatening many established businesses in developed economies and new, small businesses trying to grow in many less-developed economies. Established businesses may lose market share and may even be forced to close if they cannot compete with larger overseas businesses or new businesses in low-cost economies. Small businesses in less-developed economies may also be unable to grow if consumers in their countries are able to buy imported products far more cheaply than locally made products.

2 International trade is contributing to rapid resource depletion and climate change

The rate at which we are using up the earth's natural resources is increasing because international trade has increased access to a greater number and variety of products for us to consume. In addition, increasing travel and the increased transportation of ever more goods across international borders by road, rail, ship or airfreight is polluting the atmosphere with more and more greenhouse gases. This is contributing to global climate change that may have a disastrous, long-term and irreversible effect on the planet. ► 2.3

3 International trade may increase the exploitation of workers and the environment

The free movement of capital internationally has made it easy for multinational firms to shift their production from countries where wages and other costs are high, to less-developed countries where wages, land prices and taxes on profits are lower. This shift, some people argue, has not only

International specialization and trade

increased the unemployment rate in many developed economies, but in some cases it has also led to the exploitation of workers in less-developed economies where health and safety laws may be more relaxed or easier to ignore. In some cases it has also resulted in environmental damage in less-developed countries where environmental protection laws are weak or their governments choose not to enforce them. ➤ 4.1

4 International trade may be increasing the gap between rich and poor countries

Some economists argue it will be free trade and not overseas aid that will help to lift the poorest countries out of poverty. By selling their goods and services overseas, less-developed countries can expand their industries, earn additional income and create jobs for their populations. ➤ 7.1

However, in direct contrast, some people argue that international trade has instead increased the gap between rich and poor countries. This is said to happen because multinational firms and consumers from many developed and rapidly developing economies dominate the global demand for many natural resources, including foodstuffs, timber, zinc, tin, copper and other ores, and use their purchasing power to force down global prices. This has reduced revenues for producers of natural resources in less-developed economies. For example, China, the USA, Japan and India consume over 50% of all the natural rubber produced in the world each year.

Barriers to trade

Economic conflict can arise from globalization because some developed countries fear they will lose jobs as it becomes cheaper to import goods and services from overseas than to produce them domestically, or if production is moved overseas to countries where costs, such as wages, land prices and taxes on profits, may be lower. This, in turn, can result in a loss of incomes, lower tax revenues, slower or even negative economic growth and falling welfare. As a result, some governments have introduced **trade barriers** to protect firms and jobs in their economies. This is called **protectionism**.

Protectionism involves the use of trade barriers by governments to restrict international market access and competition. The article below in Activity 8.3 highlights a number of examples.

1 Tariffs

These are indirect taxes on the prices of imported goods to make them more expensive to discourage domestic consumers from buying them. For example, the article in Activity 8.3 below reports that Russia has introduced tariffs on the price of imported poultry to protect its meat farmers from US farms who are able to supply these products at lower prices. The use of tariffs, however, can encourage retaliation from other countries.

Many neighbouring countries in different regions of the world have agreed to form **customs unions** to trade freely with each other but to impose a common tariff on all goods and services imported from non-member countries. Examples of customs unions include the European Union, the South African Customs Unions and MERCOSUR between a number of countries in Latin America.

ACTIVITY 8.3

Barricading the borders

From the article below identify:

- different barriers used by government to restrict international trade and competition
- reasons why governments use trade barriers
- the impact trade barriers could have on consumers, workers and businesses in different countries
- arguments against the use of trade barriers.

More Trade Restrictions as Global Slump Deepens

Just over a month ago world leaders agreed to reject trade protectionism and stick to free trade principles to fight the global economic slowdown. Yet an increasing number of countries are already breaking that promise.

For example, in a move designed to protect its battered manufacturers from foreign imports, Indonesia is slapping restrictions and quotas on another 500 products this month and demanding special licenses and new fees on imports. Russia is also increasing tariffs on imported poultry – a move that has angered US farmers: Russia is the single largest market for US poultry producers, which this year exported $740 million worth to Russian consumers.

France is launching a government fund to protect French companies from foreign takeovers while Argentina and Brazil are seeking to raise tariffs on products from leather goods and peaches to imported wine and textiles.

The list of countries making access to their markets harder also includes the United States. The US government's $17.4 billion bailout of the US auto industry has been branded an unfair subsidy by many because it places foreign competitors at a disadvantage. At the same time Russia, the largest car market in Europe, increased taxes on imported foreign cars by 35 per cent.

In hard times, analysts say, nations are more inclined to take steps that inhibit trade, often with dire consequences for consumers, businesses and entire economies.

'Because exporting firms face overseas competition they tend to be innovative, dynamic and capable of generating good job growth,' said a US professor of trade policy. 'If trade barriers shut these firms down, their suppliers shut down, job losses get worse, and you can quickly have an entire economy spiraling downward.'

2 Subsidies

These are grants paid to domestic producers to help reduce their production costs and sell their products at lower prices than imported products. For example, the USA is among a number of countries that have been accused by others of giving producers in their farming, steel and automotive industries unfair subsidies to lower their costs and prices. ➤ **4.2**

A disadvantage of subsidies is that to pay for them consumers and firms may have to pay higher taxes instead.

3 Quotas

A quota is a limit on the number of imports allowed into a country each month or year. Restricting the supply of imported products will push up their market prices relative to locally produced substitutes. ➤ **2.2**

International specialization and trade

> **EU trade ban will cause fruit shortage**
>
> British supermarkets face severe shortages of oranges, grapefruits and other citrus fruits this summer because of a highly contentious import ban on fruit from South Africa and South America. The ban will 'protect' European citrus plants from pests.

4 Embargo

An embargo is a ban on the importation of a particular product, or on all imports from a particular country. For example, embargoes are often used to control trade in weapons and other products with countries involved in conflicts or abuses of human rights. An embargo may be also used to stop the import of dangerous drugs or to exert political pressure on other countries.

However, embargoes may also be introduced on health grounds. For example, between 1996 and 2005 beef exports from the UK were banned in the European Union and many countries outside it because of fears about the spread of BSE ('mad cow disease') from UK herds to overseas cattle and possibly even to humans. Similarly, in 2011 a number of countries restricted imports of Japanese food produced on farms contaminated by radiation leaked from Japan's nuclear power stations at Fukushima. The nuclear plants were badly damaged following a huge tsunami in March 2011.

5 Excessive quality standards and bureaucracy

Countries can increase costs on exporters and slow down the flow of imports by introducing complex and unreasonable quality controls, standards and licensing requirements.

A government may set arbitrary and excessive quality standards on imported goods so many fail and can be rejected. Or it may keep changing product labelling and other regulations so that exporters are unable to keep up with new requirements.

An **import license** is a document issued by a government customs authority approving the importation of certain goods into its territory. They can be used as a barrier to trade if they are issued selectively against another country's goods in order to protect a domestic industry from foreign competition. Application forms can also be made time consuming and difficult to complete causing delays and uncertainty about whether or not goods will be allowed in to a country.

Subsidies, quotas, embargoes, licensing regulations and arbitrary standards are all examples of **non-tariff barriers**.

Arguments for trade barriers

1 To protect infant industries

Barriers to trade can be used to protect **infant industries**, also known as **sunrise industries**, such as those involving new technologies. This gives new firms the chance to develop, grow and become globally competitive.

New, small businesses in newly developing industries with the potential to provide many more jobs and incomes in the future, may not get the chance to develop and grow if they are quickly eliminated by competition from lower-cost economies overseas. Providing them with protection from overseas competition may allow them to grow to take advantage of economies of scale and become internationally competitive. The danger is that infant industries may continue to require protection from cheaper imports even when they have become established.

2 To protect sunset industries

Sunset industries are declining industries. They still employ many people in an economy and the closure of firms in these industries could result in high regional employment, especially if they are located together to benefit from external economies of scale. ➤ **4.3**

Many manufacturing industries in developed countries have been in decline for many years because of competition for newly industrialized economies.

To slow down the rate of their decline in these industries trade barriers may be used to protect them from cheaper overseas imports to allow employees to retrain or relocate for other jobs.

3 To protect strategic industries

Many governments seek to protect their agricultural, energy and defence industries so they are not entirely dependent on supplies from overseas. For example, vital supplies of food may be disrupted by natural disasters or even wars. Overseas suppliers may also use their market power to restrict supplies and to force up prices. ➤ **4.4**

4 To protect domestic firms from dumping

Dumping is a type of predatory pricing and unfair competition. It involves one country 'flooding' another with a product at a price significantly below its global market price to increase sales and force producers in the importing country out of business. Once this has happened and the overseas market has been 'captured', exporting firms can raise their prices.

Exporting firms are usually only able to price below average production costs if they are receiving generous subsidies from their own government. For example, Australia recently accused Indonesia and China of dumping glass on the Australian market to boost Indonesian and Chinese glass sales at the expense of Australian producers.

5 To limit over-specialization

Free trade encourages countries to specialize in the goods in which they have a comparative advantage. However, a country that specializes in the production of too narrow a range of products is at greater economic risk from a fall in global demand for one or more of them. Trade barriers can therefore help a country to maintain a wider range of different industries that would otherwise be threatened by overseas competition and thereby prevent over-specialization in production.

6 To correct a trade imbalance

A country that spends more on imports than it earns from the sale of its export will have a significant trade imbalance. Cutting spending on imports using tariff and non-tariff barriers can help to reduce a trade deficit. ➤ **8.2**

7 Because other countries use trade barriers

Before any country removes its barriers to trade on foreign goods it will want to be sure that other countries will remove barriers to trade in its exports. With so many countries engaged in international trade it is very difficult to get agreement on removal of barriers to trade.

Trade liberalization involves removing barriers to trade between different countries. The World Trade Organization (WTO) helps to negotiate reductions in trade barriers and to resolve trade disputes between member countries.

ECONOMICS IN ACTION

What is dumping in international trade? How can it benefit the USA? What is the likely impact on Chinese industry? If it was minded to, what possible non-tariff barriers could China impose on US imports?

US automakers accused of dumping vehicles

China has accused automakers in the United States of dumping sedans and sports utility vehicles with engines larger than 2.5 litres into the country.

The Ministry of Commerce said in a statement on its website that US subsidies for its automotive industry and dumping have caused substantial harm to the Chinese industry. However, the ministry said it will not levy temporary anti-dumping taxes or adopt other retaliatory measures.

The statement also said the ministry has given the relevant companies 10 days to submit written comments and evidence, and promises to examine further based on any new material.

The ministry began the anti-dumping investigation in November 2009. Five manufacturers, including General Motors, Chrysler and BMW, were listed in the ministry's statement. Dumping margins (the difference between the usual product price and the export price) range from 2 per cent to 21.5 per cent, and subsidy rates enjoyed by US automakers were up to 12.9 per cent of costs.

General Motors, which had the highest dumping margins and subsidy rates, said it was unaware of the statement, and declined to comment further.

Experts said the ministry's move is in accordance with World Trade Organization (WTO) rules, and the action will cause limited harm to the US automotive industry.

Arguments against trade barriers

The main argument against the use of trade barriers is that they reduce the gains from trade, notably the following.

1 They restrict consumer choice

Less international trade means consumers will have fewer goods and services to choose from and producers to purchase them from.

2 They restrict new revenue and employment opportunities

Trade barriers restrict the ability of firms to seek out new markets for their products overseas that will allow them to expand their scale of production and increase their demand for labour. Increasing the cost of imported materials and restricting their supply may harm domestic firms that use the materials in their production processes. Production costs will rise and production may also be disrupted due to supply shortages.

3 They protect inefficient domestic firms

If domestic firms are protected from overseas competition there is less pressure on them to improve their productivity and efficiency. Lack of competition can cause x-inefficiency. Production costs and consumer prices will be higher than they might otherwise be and product quality could also be lower as a result. ➤ 4.4

4 Other countries may retaliate

If one country introduces trade barriers to restrict imports from other countries, those affected may introduce similar restrictions on trade with that country in retaliation. A trade war may develop. Fewer goods and services will be traded and prices will rise. This is clearly bad for consumers but if it continues it can also mean higher unemployment and slower economic growth as firms are forced out of business.

For example, in 2010 Brazil threatened to increase tariffs on 102 products imported from the USA unless the US government reduced the subsidies it paid to US cotton producers. Sales of cheap US cotton were increasing and harming cotton farmers in Brazil. Although the action would have increased many prices for Brazilian consumers it was intended to reduce sales of imported US cotton and to put pressure on the US government.

> **EXAM PREPARATION 8.1**
>
> 'The most effective support the industrialised countries could provide for the poorer nations would be to open their markets to the products of developing countries by having fewer trade restrictions.' (Trade and Industry Minister for Ghana, 2001)
>
> a What forms do trade restrictions often take? [3]
>
> b Discuss the immediate and the long-term changes that might occur in developing countries if trading restrictions were reduced. [7]
>
> c Discuss whether it is better for a country to produce many products and protect its markets from international trade or whether it is better to try to achieve specialisation in some products only. [10]
>
> *Cambridge IGCSE Economics 0455/04 Q5 October/November 2003*
> *Cambridge O Level Economics 2281/02 Q5 October/November 2003*

WEBSITES

Learn more about globalization and international trade at:

- http://economics.about.com/od/globalizationtrade/
- www.globalization101.org/
- http://en.wikipedia.org/wiki/Globalization
- www.bized.co.uk/learn/economics/international/advantage/index.htm
- www.bized.co.uk/learn/economics/international/benefits/index.htm
- World Trade Organization www.wto.org/english/res_e/statis_e/statis_e.htm

KEYWORDS

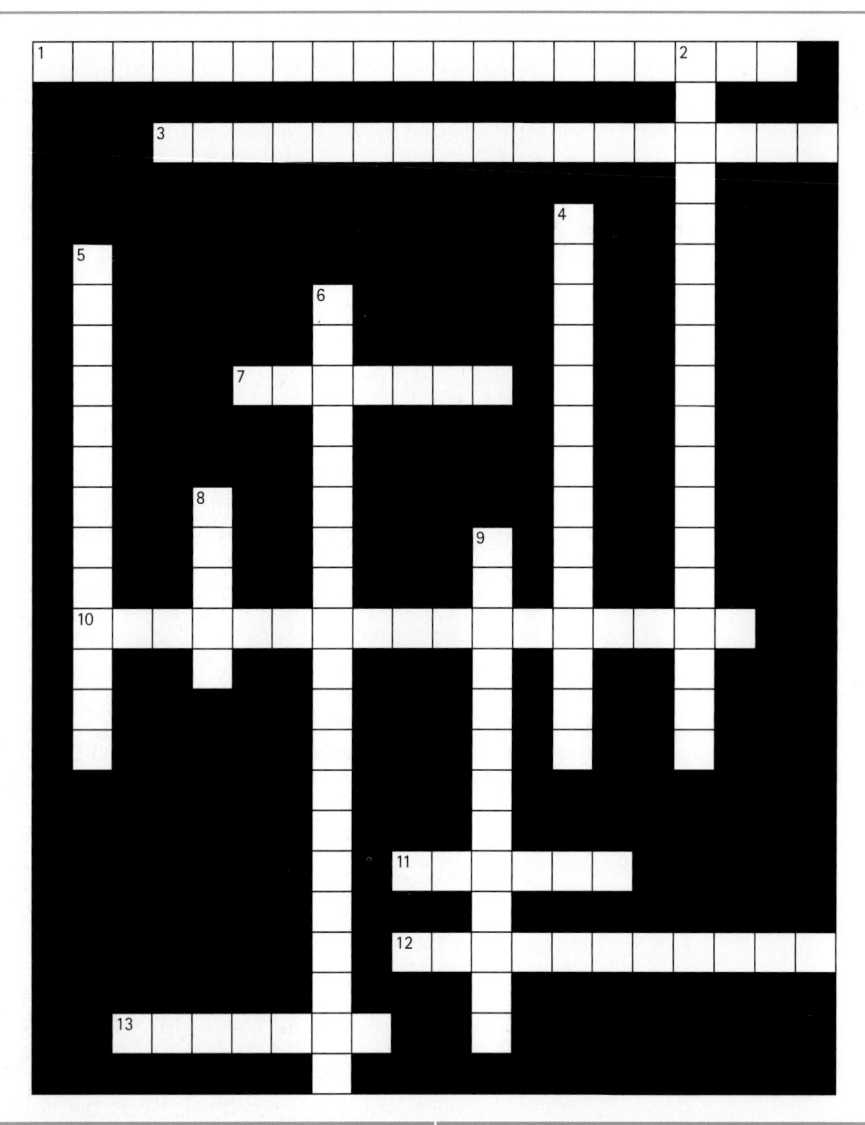

Clues across

1. The removal of or reduction in trade barriers between countries (4, 14)
3. The term used to describe the ability of a country or region to produce a good or service at a lower average cost per unit than any other country or region is able to (8, 9)
7. A form of international predatory pricing and unfair competition used by overseas producers to flood another country with cheap products to force its firms out of business (7)
10. A term used to describe subsidies, quotas, and embargoes, licensing regulations, arbitrary standards and all other non-tax trade restrictions (3-5, 8)
11. A tax levied on the price of an imported product to contract domestic demand for it (6)
12. A national economy that engages in free international trade (4, 7)
13. A ban introduced by one or more countries on the importation of a specific product or all products from another country (7)

Clues down

2. The movement and exchange of physical goods such as materials, component parts, equipment and finished products as well as services, ideas, currencies and labour across international borders (13, 5)
4. Another term used to describe the economic benefits from international specialization and trade (5, 4, 5)
5. The use of trade barriers by governments to protect their domestic industries and employment from global competition (13)
6. The term used to describe the ability of a region or country to produce a good or service at a lower opportunity cost than another (11, 9)
8. A restriction on the volume of an imported good allowed into a country (5)
9. Government measures designed to restrict international trade and competition (5, 7)

International aspects

Unit 8.2   Balancing international payments

AIMS

By the end of this unit you should be able to:

▶ describe the structure of the **current account** of the **balance of payments**
  - distinguish between trade in **visible** and **invisible imports and exports**
  - describe how different international transactions are recorded in the balance of payments on current account as the **balance of trade**, **balance on services**, **income balance** and **net current transfers**

▶ discuss the causes and consequences of **current account deficits and surpluses**
  - describe policies a government may use to correct a trade imbalance

▶ define **exchange rates**
  - explain why national currencies are traded on the **foreign exchange market**
  - distinguish between **fixed and floating exchange rates**

▶ discuss the causes and consequences of exchange rate fluctuations.

SECTION 1

Exports and imports

Every year countries such as the USA, China, Germany, Egypt and India produce and sell many billions of dollars' worth of goods and services to each other and to many other countries. Goods and services made by producers in one country and supplied to consumers in other countries are **exports**. An export from a country involves a flow of money back into that country as revenue from the sale of the export.

At the same time, these same countries buy many billions of dollars' worth of goods and services from each other and many other countries. Goods and services purchased by consumers in a country from producers located overseas are **imports**. An import into a country involves a flow of money leaving that country and going overseas in payment for the imported product.

Through international trade, consumers in all these countries enjoy a wider variety of goods and services than they would otherwise be able to. ➤ **8.1**

Visible trade

Visible trade involves trade in physical products, including natural resources such as crude oil and timber; parts and components for use in the production of goods; and finished products such as machinery, clothes, cars and processed foodstuffs. Trade in goods, or merchandise, is called **visible trade** simply because visible exports and imports can be seen, touched and weighed as they pass through ports and across borders.

▼ Visible exports

Oil   Machinery

When a country such as Japan sells **visible exports**, including machinery and other manufactured goods to other countries, it earns income. When Japan buys **visible imports** it involves spending money overseas. Imports therefore involve a leakage of money from an economy.

If Japan spends more on imported goods than it earns from the sale of its exports then it has a **trade deficit**. If, however, the value of Japan's exported goods exceeds the value of the goods it imports over the same period, then Japan will have a **trade surplus**.

The **balance of trade** records flows of income into and out of a country in payment for visible exports and imports.

Balance of trade = value of visible exports – value of visible imports

The balance of trade in Japan is calculated in terms of its currency, the yen (symbol ¥). For example, in 2010 Japan sold visible exports worth ¥63,922 billion and bought visible imports costing ¥55,943 billion: it had a trade surplus of ¥7,979 billion. Japan therefore had a **favourable trade balance** in 2010 because it was in surplus. If the balance of trade was in deficit, because visible imports exceeded visible exports in value, it would have had an **unfavourable trade balance**.

The balance of trade of many countries has changed over time as other countries have developed their manufacturing industries and have become more efficient at producing goods for export. For example, France is the second largest trading nation in Europe after Germany. Its main exports are aircraft and engines, beverages, electrical equipment, chemicals, cosmetics, luxury products and perfume. It had a modest trade surplus in most years during the 1990s. Its trade surplus reached $17.1 billion in 1997. However, since 2000 France has had a growing trade deficit as imports of manufactured goods increased at a faster rate than French exports. By 2008 the French trade deficit had reached almost $100 billion.

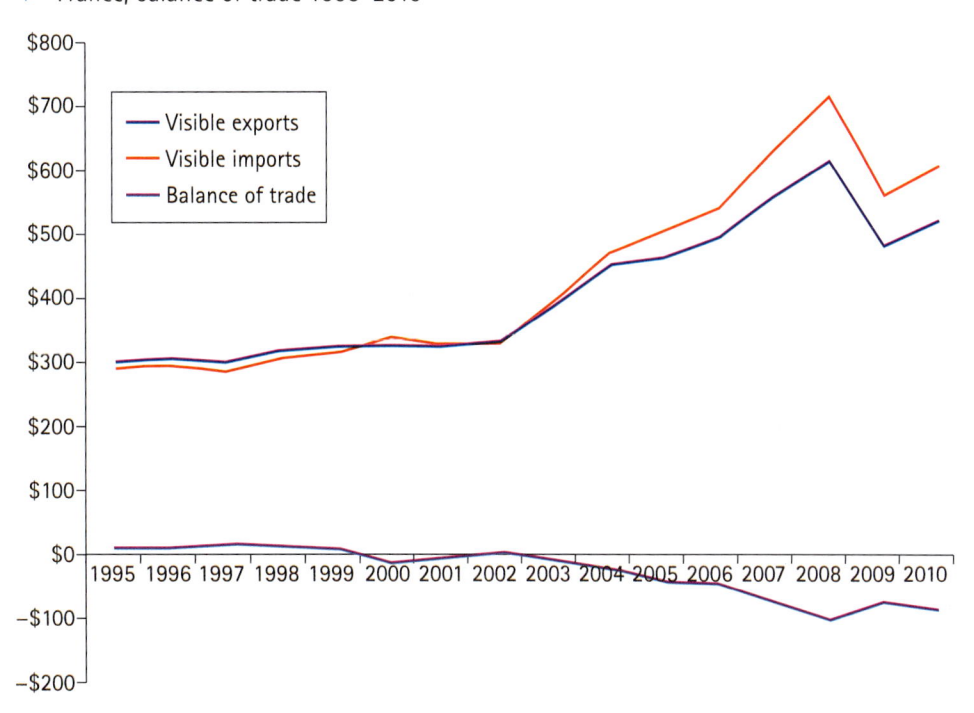

▼ France, balance of trade 1995–2010

Source: 'France, balance of trade 1995-2010', World Trade Organization

Invisible trade

Invisible trade involves international trade in services. Exports and imports of services, such as insurance, banking and tourism, cannot be seen or touched at ports or border crossings, hence the name invisible.

If a Japanese resident goes on holiday to Europe, he or she is paying for overseas services such as hotel accommodation, tickets for public transport and eating in European restaurants. The money spent by the Japanese tourist in Europe is an **invisible import** to Japan because it involves a debit of income from the Japanese economy to pay for services produced overseas.

Balancing international payments

If, on the other hand, a Kenyan resident buys insurance over the Internet from a Japanese insurance company, he or she is buying a Japanese service so the insurance premiums bring revenue into Japan. This credit to the Japanese economy is an **invisible export**.

If Japan spends more on imported services than it earns from invisible exports then its **balance on services** will be in deficit. If, however, the payments received for invisible exports exceeds the amount spent on invisible imports, then the Japanese balance on services will be in surplus.

The balance on services therefore records the flows of income into and out of a country in payments for invisible exports and imports.

Balance on services = value of invisible exports − value of invisible imports

ACTIVITY 8.4

Now you see them, now you don't

The following cartoons and descriptions describe international transactions between the UK and other countries. Which of the transactions represent visible and invisible imports and exports to and from the UK?

A. Wine bought from France
B. UK tourist takes holiday in the USA
C. Italian insures his ship in the UK
D. UK resident uses foreign bank
E. Foreign company uses UK advertising agency
F. UK car dealer buys Japanese cars

SECTION 2

The balance of payments

Visible and invisible exports and imports are accounted for by flows of money into and out of a national economy. However, there are also other flows of money into and out of an economy, including investments, loans, profits and dividends on shares. All such monetary transactions between the residents of a country and the rest of the world over a given period of time, usually every month and year, are recorded in the **balance of payments** for that country.

The balance of payments for a country is usually split into three main accounts: the current account, the capital account and the financial account.

We will look at the structure of the balance of payments of a country using the USA as an example.

The current account

Each month and year a government will collect statistics of the **balance of payments on current account** to monitor how well or how badly the national economy is doing in international trade in goods and services, and other flows of incomes and transfers to and from other countries.

The current account for the US economy therefore records the following:

- It records **visible trade** in goods.
- It records **invisible trade** in services.
- It records **income** received or made in payment for the use of factors of production.
    - Income debits include wages paid to overseas residents working in the USA, and any interest, profits and dividends (IPD) paid out to overseas residents and firms who have invested in the USA.
    - Income credits include wages paid to US residents working overseas, and interest and dividends earned by US residents and firms on investments they have in other countries.
- It records **current transfers**, which include payments between governments for international cooperation and other transactions that involve no direct payment for productive activity.

    Debits will include:
    - gifts of money, charitable donations and pension payments paid to the residents of other countries
    - taxes and excise duties paid by US residents on goods and services purchased overseas
    - overseas aid and other payments made by the US government to the governments of other countries
    - membership contributions to the budgets of international organizations such as the International Monetary Fund and World Trade Organization.

    Credits will include:
    - gifts, charitable donations and pension payments received from the residents of other countries
    - taxes and excise duties paid by residents of other countries on goods and services purchased in the USA

- overseas aid and other payments made by overseas governments to the US government
- any grants or refunds of contributions received from international organizations.

The balance of payments on current account therefore consists of the balance of trade, balance on services, balance on income and net current transfers. The current account will be in deficit when the value of all debit items exceeds credit items. It will be in surplus when credits exceed debits.

To illustrate, the US balance of payments on current account for 2000 and 2010 are summarized below.

▼ US balance of payments on current account

$ billion, current prices	2000	2010
Visible exports (X)	784.2	1,288.7
Visible imports (M)	1,230.4	1,935.7
Balance of trade (X − M = A)	−446.2	−647.0
Invisible exports (Xi)	286.4	545.5
Invisible imports (Mi)	219.9	−394.2
Balance on services (Xi − Mi = B)	66.5	−151.3
Balance on income (C)	21.0	163.0
Net current transfers (D)	−58.6	−137.5
Current account balance (A + B + C + D)	−417.3	−470.2

▼ US balance of payments on current account, 2000–2010

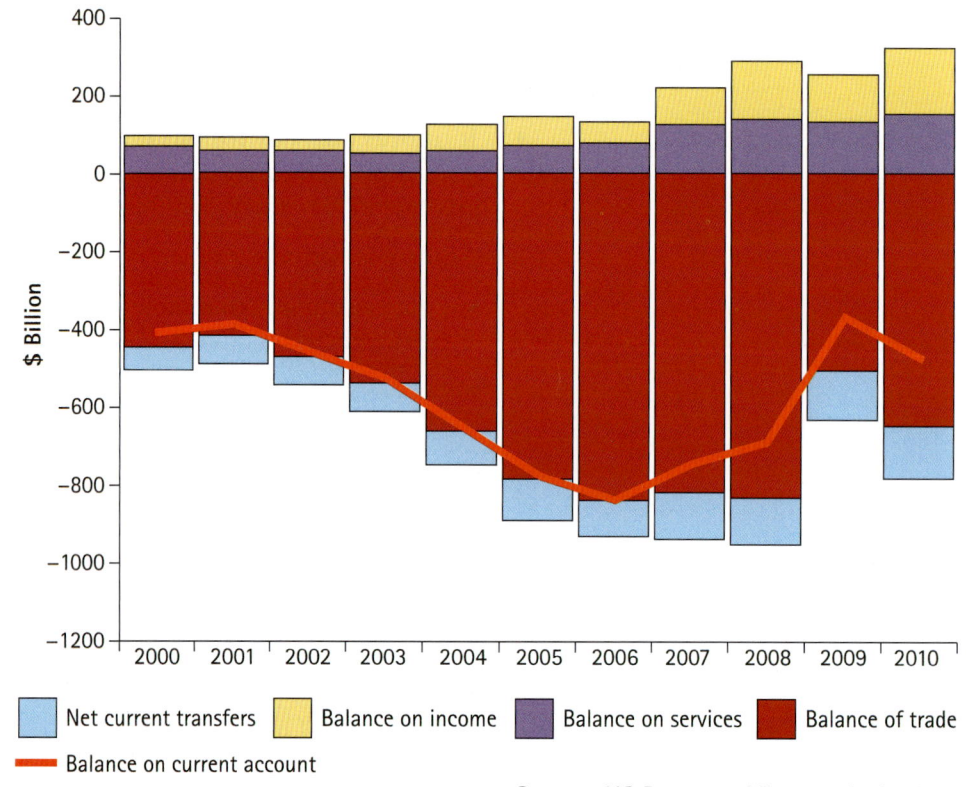

Source: US Bureau of Economic Analysis

448 International aspects

The US balance of payments on its current account has been in deficit for many years. This means more money was leaving the US economy each year to pay for imports, incomes and transfers overseas than it was earning from sales of its exports, or from incomes and transfers from overseas.

A large current account deficit can cause an economy a number of problems, as we shall investigate in Section 5 below.

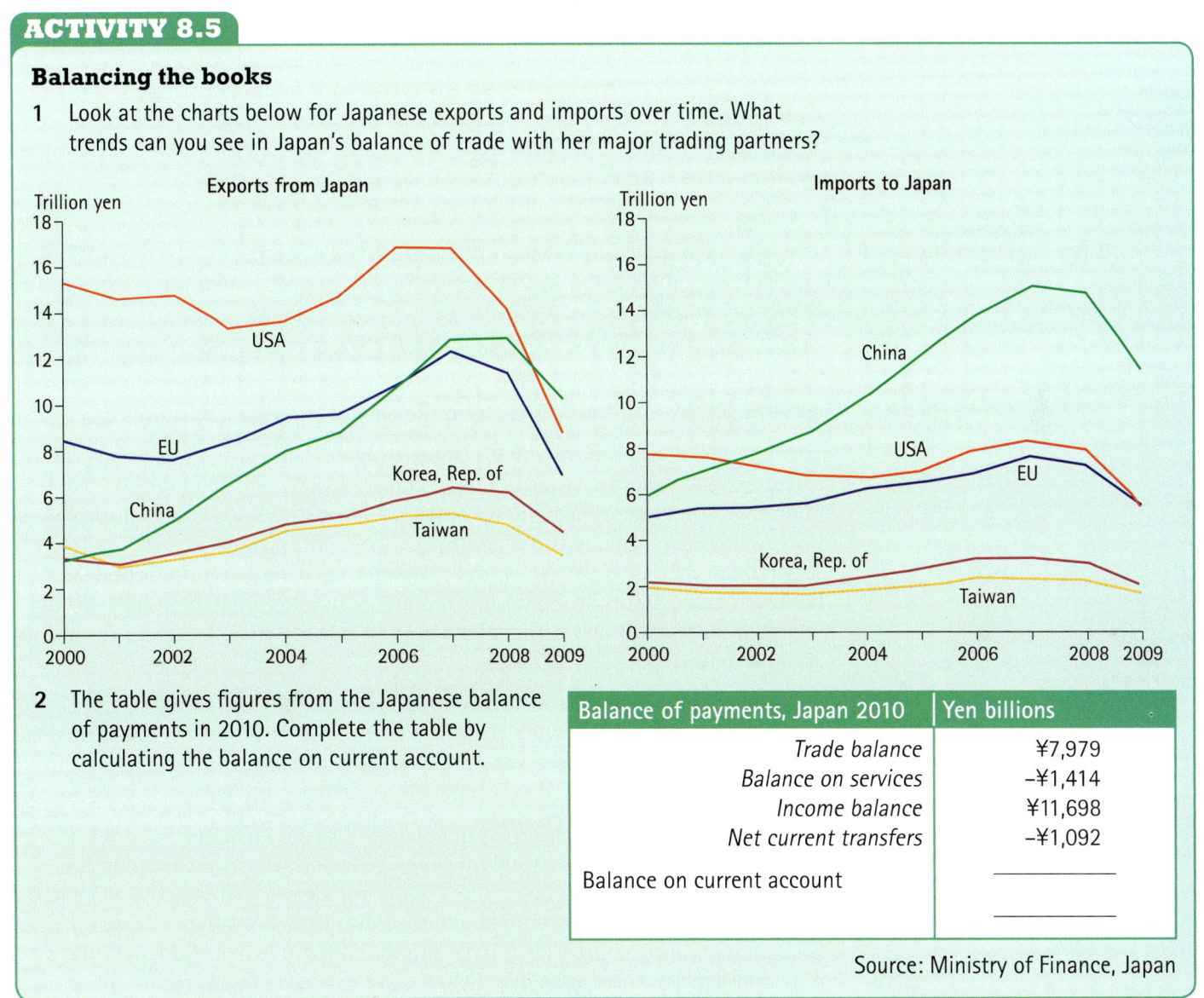

ACTIVITY 8.5

Balancing the books

1 Look at the charts below for Japanese exports and imports over time. What trends can you see in Japan's balance of trade with her major trading partners?

2 The table gives figures from the Japanese balance of payments in 2010. Complete the table by calculating the balance on current account.

Balance of payments, Japan 2010	Yen billions
Trade balance	¥7,979
Balance on services	–¥1,414
Income balance	¥11,698
Net current transfers	–¥1,092
Balance on current account	

Source: Ministry of Finance, Japan

The capital and financial accounts

Payments for goods, services, incomes and transfers are not the only international transactions recorded in a balance of payments.

The **capital account** of a country records international capital transfers for the acquisition, disposal or transfer of non-financial assets including land, factories, office buildings and machinery, between its residents and the rest of the world. It also records the cancellation of debts between countries, the transfer of goods and financial assets by migrants leaving or entering a country and any payments of gifts and inheritance taxes they may make.

Balancing international payments   449

In most countries, the size of capital account transactions is normally small compared to the current and financial accounts of the balance of payments.

In the **financial account**, international monetary flows related to investment in business, real estate, bonds, loan stocks and company shares are documented. Also included in the financial account are government-owned assets, notably reserves of gold and foreign currency. Any interest, profits and dividends (IPD) resulting from these investments are recorded as incomes in the current account.

A country receives **direct inward investment** whenever a foreign-owned firm sets up a factory, office or retail outlet in it. For example, the location of Japanese car manufacturers such as Nissan and Toyota in Mexico are examples of direct inward investments to the Mexican economy. ➤ **4.1**

The balancing act

The balance of payments of a country will always balance, such that total credits received from the rest of the world will exactly match total debits to the rest of the world.

This means a current account deficit should always be balanced against a combined surplus on the capital and financial accounts. Similarly, a current account surplus can fund a deficit on the capital and financial accounts.

For example, if an economy invests more overseas than it receives in inward investments from other countries its financial account will be in deficit. This is often the case when the balance of payments on current account is in surplus because the extra money the economy is earning from trade in goods and services can then be invested overseas. When the current account is in deficit, however, an economy will have less money to invest elsewhere. It may also try to attract more loans and investments from overseas to help balance the current account deficit.

A government will also draw down its reserves of gold and foreign currency to fund overseas payments when there is a current account deficit. In contrast, a surplus can be added to reserves or used to pay off loans from overseas. This will be recorded as a debit on the financial account.

In these ways changes in reserves of gold and foreign currencies should help to correct any imbalance in total international transactions recorded in the balance of payments. However, total credits and debits may not always match precisely because overseas trade and financial transactions figures are compiled from a great many sources by a large number of people over long periods of time and many transactions may be left out or recorded with error. These statistical discrepancies may be very large. A figure for **net errors and omissions** is therefore included in a balance of payments as a balancing item in order to balance the accounts. The table below shows these adjustments for the US balance of payments in 2000 and 2010.

▼ US balance of payments

$ billion, current prices	2000	2010
Current account balance (a)	−416.3	−470.2
Capital account balance (b)	0.0	−0.2
Net financial account (c)	−61.3	235.1
(a + b + c)	−477.6	−235.3
Net errors and omissions	477.6	235.3

SECTION 3

The foreign exchange market

Exchange rates

If you travel overseas on holiday you will need to have some notes and coins of the national currency of each country you visit in order to buy things. To obtain these notes and coins you will need to swap them for the money you use in your country. Every country has its own national currency and the amount you get in return for your own currency is called its **exchange rate**.

Similarly, business organizations involved in international trade must exchange different national currencies. This is true for any organization that:

IMPORTS	▶ buys materials, components or finished goods from firms overseas ▶ buys services from overseas suppliers
EXPORTS	▶ sells and ships materials, components or finished goods to business, government or individual consumers overseas ▶ sells services to business, government or individual consumers overseas
INVESTS	▶ buys shares in the ownership of overseas companies ▶ invests in premises and equipment to start and run business operations in other countries.

Payments for imports, exports and to make other payments overseas therefore require the exchange of different national currencies. This takes place on the global **foreign exchange market**.

Foreign currencies can be bought and sold just like any other product. The foreign exchange market consists of all those people, organizations and governments willing and able to buy or sell national currencies. It is the world's largest financial market and is sometimes simply referred to as the Forex or FX market.

For example, let us consider just some of the many reasons why there is an international demand for a currency such as the US dollar and why US dollars are supplied to satisfy that demand.

Balancing international payments

Why is there demand for US dollars?	Why are US dollars supplied?
▶ Consumers in other countries want to buy and import goods and services produced in the USA.	▶ US consumers want to buy and import goods and services produced in other countries.
▶ US-owned multinational firms with locations in other countries will want to send their profits back to their US headquarters	▶ Foreign-owned multinational firms with locations in the USA will exchange dollars for their own national currencies to repatriate their profits.
▶ Overseas firms located in the USA want to pay their US workers in dollars.	▶ US firms located in other countries will pay their overseas workers in their local currencies.
▶ Residents in other countries want to save money with US banks because they offer good interest rates.	▶ US residents want to save money with banks located overseas because they offer better interest rates.
▶ Currency speculators hold US dollars because they believe the dollar will rise in value against other currencies.	▶ Currency speculators sell their US dollars because they believe the dollar will fall in value against other currencies.
▶ People and firms overseas want to buy shares in US companies.	▶ US firms and individuals buy shares in foreign companies.
▶ A US resident working overseas sends a gift of money back to his or her family in the USA.	▶ A resident of another country working temporarily in the USA sends a gift of money back to his or her family overseas.
▶ Foreign-owned banks provide loans to US firms.	▶ US-owned banks provide loans to firm overseas.
▶ Overseas governments want to hold reserves of US dollars to settle international payments deficits.	▶ The US government draws on its reserves of US dollars to settle an international payments deficit.
▶ Overseas companies buy dollars to invest in business properties, equipment and other assets in the USA.	▶ US companies exchange dollars for other currencies to invest in business properties, equipment and other assets in other countries.
▶ Overseas governments lend money to the US government.	▶ The US government lends money to overseas governments.

What determines the exchange rate of a currency?

The equilibrium market price of one national currency in terms of another is its exchange rate. For example, an **exchange rate** of US$1 = 84 Kenyan shillings means that it will cost 84 Kenyan shillings to buy a US dollar, or one US dollar to buy 84 Kenyan shillings. Similarly, if US $1 = 3 Malaysian ringgits it means 3 ringgits can be exchanged for 1 US dollar. Every currency has an exchange rate in terms of every other national currency in the world.

For example, in the table and reading down each column, the price of one US dollar on 30 December 2011 was 0.77 euros, or 53.06 Indian rupees, or 3.67 UAE dirham and so on. Similarly, one rupee exchanged for 0.07 dirham that same day.

	US dollar US$	Indian rupee Rs	UAE dirham Dh	Argentine peso $	Egyptian pound £	Euro €
US dollar US$	US$1.00	Rs0.019	Dh0.27	$0.23	£0.17	€1.29
Indian rupee Rs	Rs53.06	Rs1.00	Dh14.45	$12.35	£8.80	€68.67
UAE dirham Dh	Dh3.67	Dh0.07	Dh1.00	$0.85	£0.61	€4.75
Argentine peso $	$4.30	$0.08	$1.17	$1.00	£0.71	€5.56
Egyptian pound £	£6.03	£0.11	£1.64	£1.40	£1.00	€7.79
Euro €	€0.77	€0.014	€0.21	€0.18	€0.13	€1.00

The exchange rate of each currency in terms of another will be determined by the market demand and supply conditions for each of those currencies. Just as for any other product demand for a particular currency will tend to contract as the price or exchange rate of that currency rises. In contrast, the market supply of the currency will tend to expand as its exchange rate rises. ➤ 2.2

The diagram below shows the demand for US dollars (DD) and the supply of US dollars (SS) on the foreign exchange market. The price of a dollar is given in Brazilian reals but it could be expressed in terms of any other foreign currency. US residents will supply dollars to buy reals in order to buy goods and services from Brazil. Brazilian residents will demand US dollars to make payments to US residents. They will sell reals in exchange for US dollars. Equilibrium in the market for US dollars is determined where the market demand for dollars is equal to their supply. In the diagram below this occurs at US $1 = 2 reals. So, for example, if a Brazilian consumer imports a car from a US manufacturer priced at $20,000, the equivalent price in Brazil will be 40,000 reals.

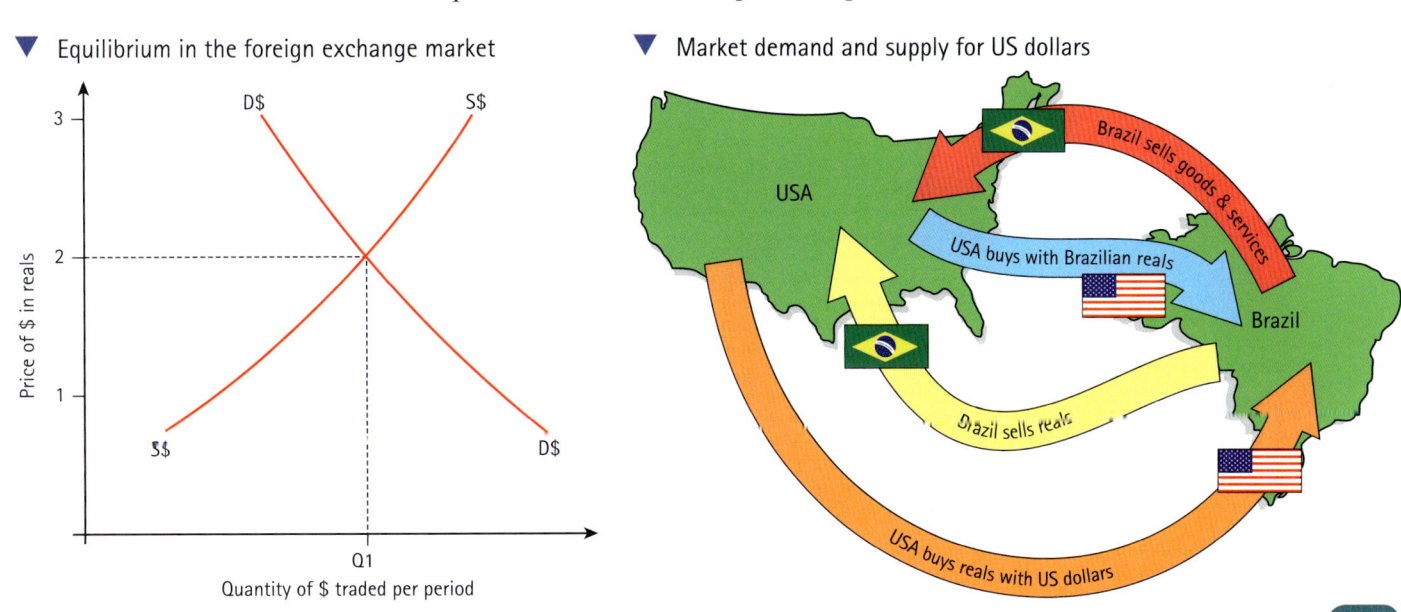

▼ Equilibrium in the foreign exchange market

▼ Market demand and supply for US dollars

Balancing international payments 453

Why do exchange rates fluctuate?

A **floating exchange rate** is one that is determined freely by market demand and supply conditions. As these conditions change, floating exchange rates will fluctuate.

An increase in the demand for a currency, for example because consumers are buying more goods and services from that country, will increase its exchange rate against other currencies. A rise in the value of one currency against others is referred to as an **appreciation** in the exchange rate.

▼ A appreciation in the $ following an increase in demand for the currency

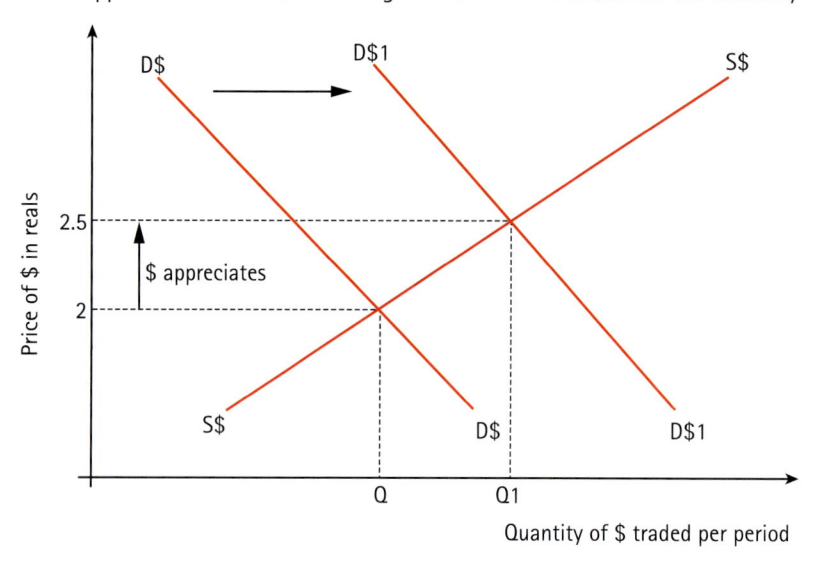

In contrast, if the global market supply of a currency rises, for example because firms are investing more overseas and therefore selling their national currency to buy foreign currencies, the exchange rate of that currency will fall. This is referred to as a **depreciation** in the exchange rate.

▼ A depreciation in the $ following an increase in supply of the currency

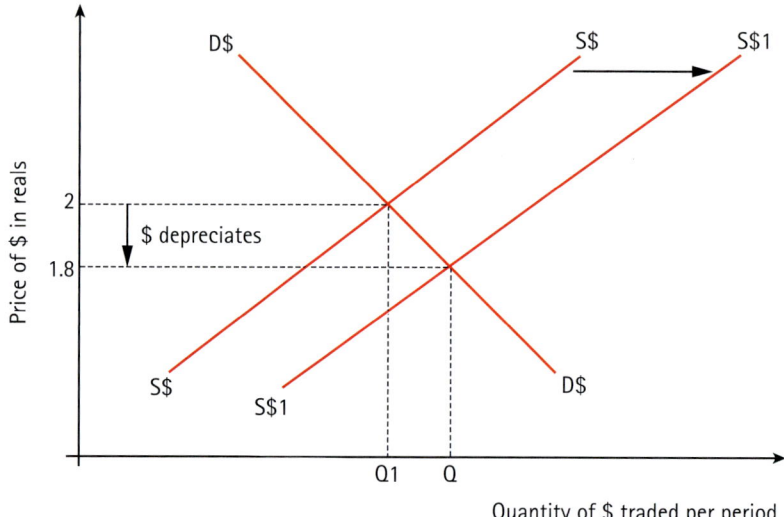

It follows that a fall in the market supply of dollars (from S$1S$1 to SS above) will therefore cause the $ exchange rate to appreciate (from $1 = 1.8 reals to $1 = 2 reals), while a fall in demand for $ (from D$1D$1 to DD in the first diagram) will cause a fall in its exchange rate (from $1 = 2.5 reals to $1 = 2 reals).

ACTIVITY 8.6

Activity 8.6 Floating around the world

The articles below describe changing economic conditions that could affect the exchange rate between the US dollar ($) and the euro (€), the currency used in eurozone countries, including France, Germany and Spain, within the European Union. For each article, complete the following tasks.

1. Identify how economic conditions are changing.
2. Suggest how the changed economic conditions might have affected **a** the demand for dollars, and/or **b** the supply of dollars.
3. Identify what has happened or could happen to the value of the US dollar on the foreign exchange market. Has or will the $ depreciate or appreciate against the €?
4. Copy the diagram of the foreign exchange market for the US dollar against the euro. Use your diagram to show how the demand for dollars or supply of dollars is likely to change based on your answers to question 2 and the impact this will have on the $ to € exchange rate.

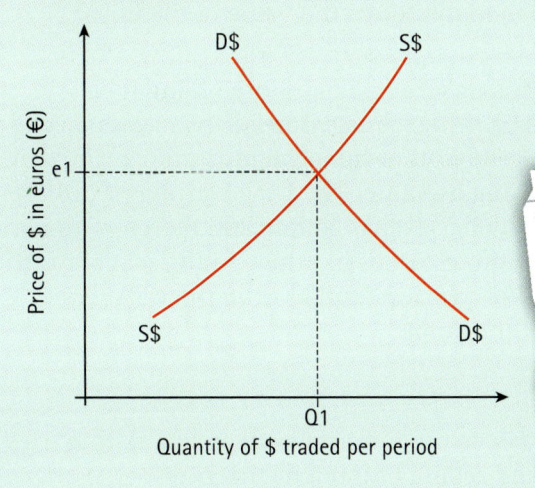

Libyan crisis pushes US dollar to record lows

The dollar fell Wednesday as traders pushed the US dollar down against European currencies on expectations of a rise in European interest rates and mounting tensions in North Africa and the Middle East.

The euro set a new four-month high against the dollar of $1.3900 as markets betted on the European Central Bank raising interest rates across Eurozone countries to combat growing inflation fears. Higher interest rates in Europe will increase demand for euro-based savings and investments and place more downward pressure on the US dollar exchange rate.

The escalating violence in Libya also sent the US dollar to record lows against other currencies, including the Swiss franc, viewed as safe havens by investors. They are worried about the impact surging oil prices and the potential for US and NATO forces to be dragged further into the Libyan conflict could have on the US economy and future growth prospects.

Euro falls on inflation news

The euro weakened yesterday against a basket of currencies after a report showed that Eurozone consumer prices rose last month.

The Consumer Prices Index rose 0.4 per cent last month as food and energy costs increased. Economists expect consumer prices, outside of food and energy, to increase this year as more companies pass on their rising costs to consumers. The jump in price inflation could make European goods less competitive on international markets.

US trade deficit increased by 33% in 2010

The US trade deficit ballooned in 2010 by the largest amount seen in a decade, new figures have revealed.

The trade deficit hit $497.8bn, up 32.8% on 2009, and the biggest annual percentage gain since 2000. Within this total the US trade deficit with China increased by over $47bn to $273bn. The US trade deficit with the European Union also widened from $61bn to $79bn.

A widening deficit, with a rising number of imports, is a sign that US consumers and businesses are spending more. However, it also means that more of their money is going overseas. This will reduce future US economic growth.

Balancing international payments 455

There are a number of reasons why the value of a currency changes or fluctuates on the foreign exchange market. Using the value of the US dollar as our example, these are the main factors.

1 Changes in the current account balance

If the USA imports a greater value of goods and services than it exports there will be a current account deficit. If the deficit increases it means the USA is buying more imports, or losing its export trade. As a result, more US dollars must be supplied to pay for the imports. At the same time demand for US dollars may be falling if overseas residents are spending less on US exports. As a result, the market price of the US dollar will depreciate.

If, on the other hand, the USA earns more from its exports than it pays for its imports its current account will be in surplus. More US dollars will be demanded by overseas residents to to pay for US exports. The value of the dollar will appreciate.

2 Inflation

If the US inflation rate is higher than that of other countries the price of US goods and services will be rising faster than the prices of overseas products. As a result, US goods will become less attractive. Demand for US exports, and therefore for US dollars, will fall. On the other hand, as the prices of imports become more competitive, US residents will spend more on imported goods and will therefore supply more US dollars in exchange for overseas currencies. High US inflation will therefore tend to reduce the value of the dollar.

3 Changes in interest rates

When US interest rates are high or rising, overseas residents may be keen to save or invest money in US banks and other financial institutions. The demand for the US dollar will rise, increasing its value. The US government can use interest rates to influence the US dollar exchange rate and therefore the price of exports and imports. A rise in interest rates in other countries relative to the USA may lead to the withdrawal of overseas capital from the USA with a depressing effect on the value of the dollar.

4 Speculation

A foreign currency speculator is a person or a firm such as a bank that tries to make a profit from the buying and selling of foreign currencies.

For example, if speculators think the value of the US dollar is likely to fall, perhaps because the US current account deficit is increasing or because of international instability that may negatively affect the US economy, they may sell their holdings of US dollars and buy other currencies. This increase in the supply of US dollars on the foreign exchange market will reduce their value. The speculators can then buy back US dollars at a lower exchange rate. The difference between the price they sold US dollars for and the price they later pay to buy back US dollars will be their profit.

The following diagram illustrates how speculators can gain from exchange rate fluctuations.

[Cartoon: Speculator with exchange rate $1 = €2 thinks dollar will fall in value, and so... sells $1000 for €2000. ONE WEEK LATER, exchange rate $1 = €1.6, sells €2000 for $1250. Success! I've made a profit of $250. (Speculation on the foreign exchange markets)]

If instead speculators speculate that the value of the US dollar will rise on the foreign exchange market, for example because they believe the US central bank is about to increase interest rates, they may buy US dollars now and sell them again later when they have risen in value. Of course the increase in demand for US dollars as a result will help to push up its exchange rate anyway while the increased sale of foreign currencies in exchange for dollars will tend to reduce the value of these currencies on the market.

How changes in exchange rates affect the prices of imports and exports

Imagine you are about to go on holiday to the USA. You have booked a hotel over the Internet for $60 per night for eight nights and will therefore be expected to pay the sum of $480 in US dollars at the end of your stay. Each unit of your national currency currently exchanges for 2 US dollars so you have calculated your eight-night stay will cost you just 240 units of your currency. However, imagine your horror when you come to pay your hotel bill at finding out the US dollar has appreciated considerably on the foreign exchange market since you booked your trip. A unit of your national currency can now only be exchanged for $1.50. This means you will now need to exchange 320 units of your currency to obtain $480 to pay your hotel bill – an increase in your cost by a further 80 units of your currency.

Before

[Cartoon: Woman at computer. HOTEL — 8 NIGHTS $480, EXCHANGE RATE 1 UNIT = $2, TOTAL COST = 240 UNITS]

After

[Cartoon: Woman at reception with hotel bill. HOTEL BILL $480 FOR 8 NIGHTS, EXCHANGE RATE $1.50 = 1 UNIT, TOTAL COST = 320 UNITS]

Balancing international payments

The same will be true for all other consumers in the world who buy goods or services from the USA if the US dollar has appreciated in value against their national currencies. They will have to pay more for US imports. For example, every year Egypt imports around $60 billion worth of goods from other countries, of which around $5 billion are imported from the USA. To pay for the US imports Egyptian importers must sell Egyptian pounds to buy US dollars. If the value of the Egyptian pound fell by 10% against the US dollar, the cost of the same imports from the US will therefore rise by 10% to $5.5 billion.

A rise in the value of the US dollar against other currencies could therefore be bad news for many US firms selling their products to consumers who live overseas. This is because overseas consumers now have to exchange more of their own currencies to obtain the same amount of dollars. This makes US exports more expensive for overseas consumers to buy and therefore less competitively priced compared to the same or similar products supplied by other non-US businesses. As a result, demand for US exports may contract and US firms will lose revenue from the sale of their exports.

▼ How a change in the exchange rate can affect the prices of imports

Exchange rate on 1 June $1 = E£6   **On 10 June US dollar appreciates $1 = E£8**

Changes in exchange rates can therefore greatly affect the prices we pay for many goods and services because they are imported from producers located overseas or have imported components that will affect their costs of production. A fall in the value of a national currency relative to other currencies will make imports to that country more expensive to buy. If a country relies heavily on imported goods this will cause imported inflation. ➤ **6.1**

However, a depreciation in the value of a national currency against other currencies can be beneficial for a country that relies heavily on sales of exports to provide jobs and incomes. Because the currency is cheaper to buy in terms of foreign currencies it will reduce the prices of exports from that country in international markets and make them more competitive. As a result, demand for its exports may expand.

458 International aspects

In contrast, an appreciation in the value of a national currency will make imports to that country cheaper but increase the prices of its exports on international markets. If, as a result, demand for imported products rises in the country while international demand for its exports falls this will move the balance of trade in an unfavourable direction.

> ### ACTIVITY 8.7
>
> **Appreciating the price impact**
>
> A clothing manufacturer located in Thailand makes and exports winter coats for the European market.
>
> Each coat is priced for sale to shops in Europe at 4,000 Thai Baht (THB)
>
> Today's exchange rate is 1 THB = 0.025 euros, or 40 THB = 1 euro. The price of each coat in euros is therefore 100 euros.
>
> 1 What would be the price of each coat if the euro depreciated against the baht to 1 euro = 32 THB?
>
> 2 What would be the price of each coat if the euro appreciated against the baht to 1 euro = 50 THB?
>
> 3 If the demand for winter coats in Europe is price elastic what is likely to happen to consumer demand for the coats and the sales revenue of the manufacturer in Thailand following each change in the exchange rate?

Managing floating exchange rates

Because of the impact changing exchange rates can have on imported inflation and export earnings and jobs, governments may intervene in the foreign exchange market to manage their floating exchange rates to stop them from fluctuating too wildly and causing economic uncertainty.

Typically, a government will do this by either buying or selling its own currency. This is called **managed floating** or dirty floating and is the main reason why governments keep reserves of gold and different currencies. ➤ **3.1**

A steep rise in the value of a national currency against other currencies will make its exports more expensive to buy overseas. As a result, export producers may experience a fall in sales and cut back their output and employment. In order to stop its currency value from rising too much and making exports uncompetitive a government may increase the supply of its currency to the foreign exchange market. It can do this by selling its reserves of the national currency. The increase in the supply of the currency should lower its market exchange rate. Alternatively, a government may cut interest rates to reduce overseas demand for its currency by reducing the incentive for overseas residents to save or invest in its country.

In contrast, a sharp fall in the value of a currency will make imports more expensive to buy because currency values overseas will have risen. To prevent imported inflation a government may use its gold and foreign currency reserves to buy up its own national currency on the foreign exchange market. This increase in the demand for its currency on the global foreign exchange market will help push up its market exchange rate. By selling reserves of foreign currencies this will also increase their market supply and thereby help to reduce their exchange rate. Alternatively, interest rates could be raised to curb domestic spending on imports and to stimulate demand for the currency from overseas investors looking for a high return on their money.

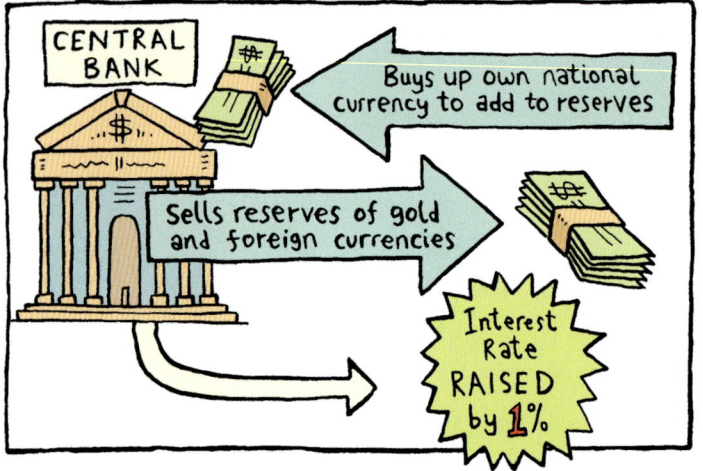

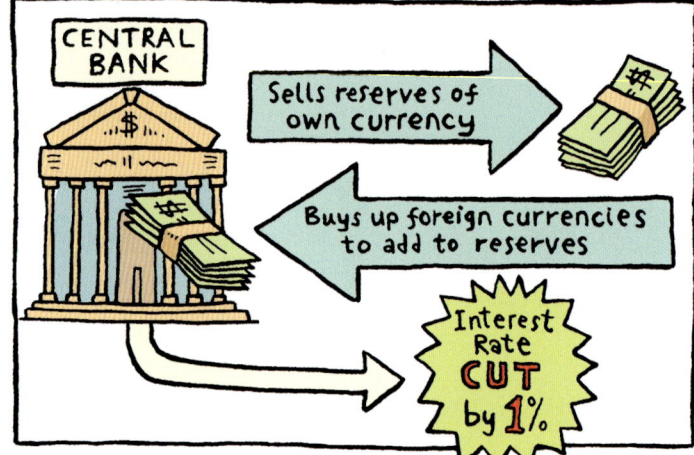

▲ To reduce imported inflation a government may aim to increase the value of its currency by buying up its national currency using its gold and foreign currency reserves and/or by raising interest rates to attract savings from overseas residents

▲ To boost demand for exports a government may seek to reduce the value of its currency by selling reserves of its national currency and/or cutting interest rates

Fixed exchange rates

In the same way as managed flexibility, a government can use its reserves of gold and foreign currency to buy or sell its currency on the foreign exchange market to stabilize or maintain a fixed value for its exchange rate against another currency or basket of foreign currencies.

This will mean buying up its national currency on the foreign exchange market when its value is low or falling below its desired value, and increasing its supply by selling off its reserves when its value is high or rising above its desired value.

In a **fixed exchange rate system**, a government or the central bank acting on the government's behalf will intervene in the above ways in the foreign exchange market so that the value of its currency remains the same or close to a desired exchange rate target.

Although very few countries now have fixed exchange rate systems many more countries have in the past fixed or 'pegged' their exchange rates often against the US dollar, given the scale and importance of the US economy and the US dollar in world trade for many years. Even the Chinese government, which had fixed its exchange rate for many years, announced in 2010 it will return to a managed floating system.

Many governments have fixed their exchange rates in the past to control the prices of exports and imports and thereby reduce uncertainty for exporters and importers that would otherwise be created by fluctuations in exchange rates.

In a fixed exchange rate system firms must also keep their costs under control so they can price their exports competitively in international markets. This is because their government will not allow the exchange rate of their currency to depreciate to help make exports cheaper overseas to boost demand for them. A fixed exchange rate will also keep imported inflation under control.

▼ How a fixed exchange rate system works

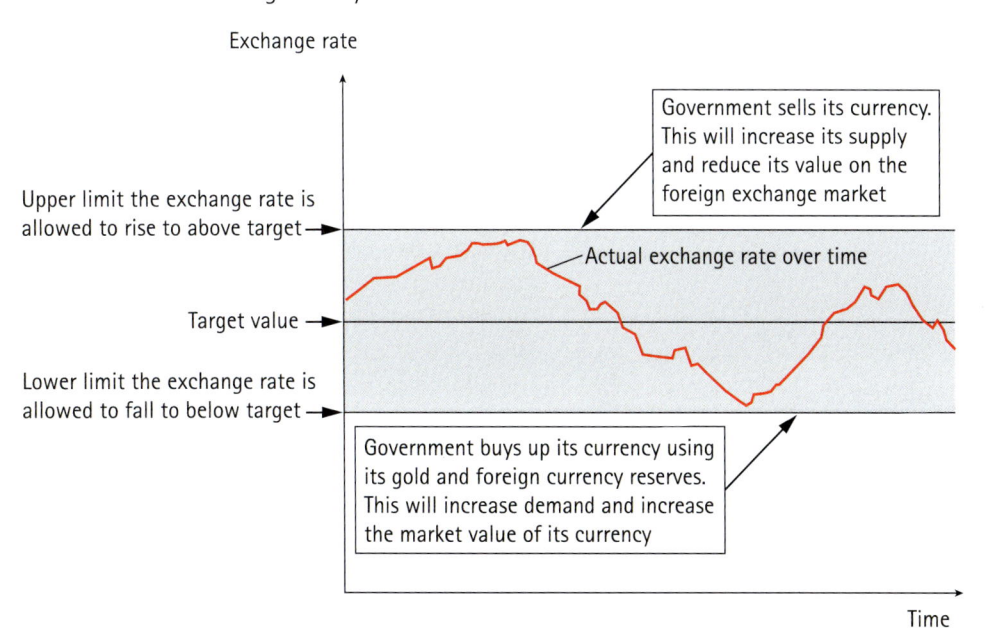

- Upper limit the exchange rate is allowed to rise to above target
- Target value
- Lower limit the exchange rate is allowed to fall to below target
- Actual exchange rate over time

Government sells its currency. This will increase its supply and reduce its value on the foreign exchange market

Government buys up its currency using its gold and foreign currency reserves. This will increase demand and increase the market value of its currency

EXAM PREPARATION 8.2

In February 2007 it was reported that the Japanese yen was gaining strength against the US dollar and that the Japanese exchange rate against other currencies was fluctuating less.

a Explain what the report means when it says that the 'exchange rate against other currencies was fluctuating less'. [5]

b Why do exchange rates fluctuate? [4]

c Discuss the consequences for an economy if its currency 'was gaining strength'. [5]

d A country has a deficit on its balance of payments on current account. Discuss **two** policies, other than exchange rate changes, that a government might use to try to achieve a surplus rather than a deficit. [6]

Balancing international payments

SECTION 4

Correcting a trade imbalance

From Section 2 you will recall how the balance of payments on current account of a country will be in deficit if more money is flowing out of its economy to make overseas payments than it receives from the sale of its exports or other credits from overseas. A country will have a current account surplus if the reverse is true.

By far the largest transactions recorded in a current account are revenues from the sale of visible exports and payments made overseas for the purchase of imports. That is, the current account position of most countries will be dependent on their balance of trade.

Large trade imbalances, whether a big trade deficit or a big trade surplus, can cause problems for a national economy. Consider a very simple example where there are just two countries in the world engaged in international trade with each other. Let's call these countries Surpland and Dearth. Surpland exports far more to Dearth than it buys from Dearth and therefore has a trade surplus. Dearth buys more imports from Surpland than she sells in exports and therefore has a trade deficit. Clearly, because Surpland has a trade surplus, it follows that Dearth must have a trade deficit. In fact, this will also be true in the real world. If one or more countries have a trade surplus, then one or more other countries must have a trade deficit equal in value to the total surplus of other countries.

462 International aspects

ECONOMICS IN ACTION

Is a trade deficit always bad news for an economy? Based on the article below, should the growing trade deficit worry the government of Bangladesh? What actions could it consider taking to correct it?

Bangladesh trade deficit widens

Bangladesh's trade deficit grew by $1.07 billion to $4.95 billion in the first half of the 2010/11 financial year compared to a year ago, due to a rising import bill as global food and oil prices hit record highs.

The jump reflected increased imports of food grains, industrial supplies and materials and capital goods as trade began to bounce back from the sharp fall caused by the global financial crisis.

Although imports to the country rose 36 per cent to $15.2 billion in the July–December period from a year earlier, exports grew strongly by 41 percent to $10.26 billion.

'Bangladesh typically runs a trade deficit but soaring global commodity prices and increased volumes are pushing the gap wider', said Mustafa K. Mujeri, Director General of the Bangladesh Institute of Development Studies.

'But it is also good for the economy as imports of capital goods and other industrial raw materials are rising on the back of economic recovery. This will help to boost economic growth.'

Is the US trade deficit really bad news?

One reason for a trade deficit can be that the deficit country is growing faster than its trading partners. Faster growth attracts new investment, which, along with rising incomes, allows the deficit country to buy more imports.

When Americans buy imports, foreigners must do something with the dollars they earn. They can either use the dollars to buy American exports or to invest in American assets, such as government bonds, company shares, real estate and factories, which offer the prospect of a better return than investments in their own countries. In the global economy, some countries, such as the United States, are therefore net importers of investment capital and thus always tend run a trade deficit. Inward investment in new capital goods can expand the productive capacity of the economy, creating more employment opportunities and wealth.

This also helps to explain why trade deficits have tended to expand in times of relative prosperity, and to contract in times of recession. During a recession people stop buying many imported goods and going on holidays overseas. When an economy is growing rapidly, people tend to spend more on all goods and services, including imports.

Problems with a trade deficit

A growing trade deficit may be a sign of economic expansion or recovery in an economy as people and firms increase their spending on all goods and services. Imports of capital goods can also help an economy to expand production in the long run.

However, a large and growing trade deficit may be a symptom of slow or negative economic growth and a declining industrial base, with fewer firms in the economy over time able to produce goods and services for export or to compete at home with imported products. This will reduce employment and incomes in the economy.

Governments therefore often worry that continuous and significant trade deficits could create difficult economic problems:

- If more money is paid out for imports than is earned from the sale of exports then this loss of money from the economy means less is available for residents to spend on domestic goods and services. Domestic firms that experience a fall in demand for their products may cut back production and reduce their demand for labour, resulting in higher unemployment.

- Because more currency is being supplied to pay for imports than overseas countries demand to buy exports, the value of the exchange rate will fall. As a result, imports will become more expensive for domestic consumers to buy. There will be imported inflation. If demand for imports is generally price inelastic then demand will not fall by very much and spending on imported products will rise at the expense of spending on domestically produced goods and services.

- To pay for annual deficits a country may need to borrow money from overseas. Total debt will rise and more income will have to be used each year to pay interest charges. This will increase the amount of money flowing out of the economy and reduce over time the amount of money it has to invest in new productive activities or spend on domestically produced products. This will harm economic growth. ➤ 6.3

A government may therefore try to correct a persistent and large trade deficit because of the economic problems it may cause. It can do so in the following ways.

1 Do nothing, because a floating exchange rate should correct it

Trade deficits should be self-correcting if the exchange rate is allowed to adjust freely. If there is trade deficit more of the national currency is being supplied internationally to pay for imports than is being demanded from overseas consumers to buy that country's exports. The value of the exchange rate will therefore fall. This will make imports more expensive to buy while reducing the prices of exports sold overseas. As a result, domestic demand for imports should fall and overseas demand for exports should rise until trade balance is restored at a new lower equilibrium exchange rate.

For example, Argentina has a large trade deficit with neighbouring Brazil in Latin America. Argentina's main export is soybeans. Because Argentina has a trade deficit with Brazil it means more Argentinean pesos must be used to buy Brazilian reals. As a result there will be downward pressure on the peso exchange rate against the real. As the peso falls in value soybean exports to Brazil will become cheaper to buy. For example, if the price of a ton of soybeans is 100 pesos and the exchange rate is 1 peso = 0.4 reals, then the imported price of Argentinean soybeans will be 250 reals in Brazil. If the peso falls in value to 1 peso = 0.5 reals then each ton of soybeans can now be imported at a price of 200 reals. If demand for soybeans from Brazilian consumers is price elastic then Argentinean producers of soybeans should enjoy an increase in demand and revenue for their exports thereby helping to close the country's trade deficit with Brazil. This is illustrated in the diagram below. ▶ **2.2**

▼ How a depreciation in the value of a currency can reduce a trade deficit

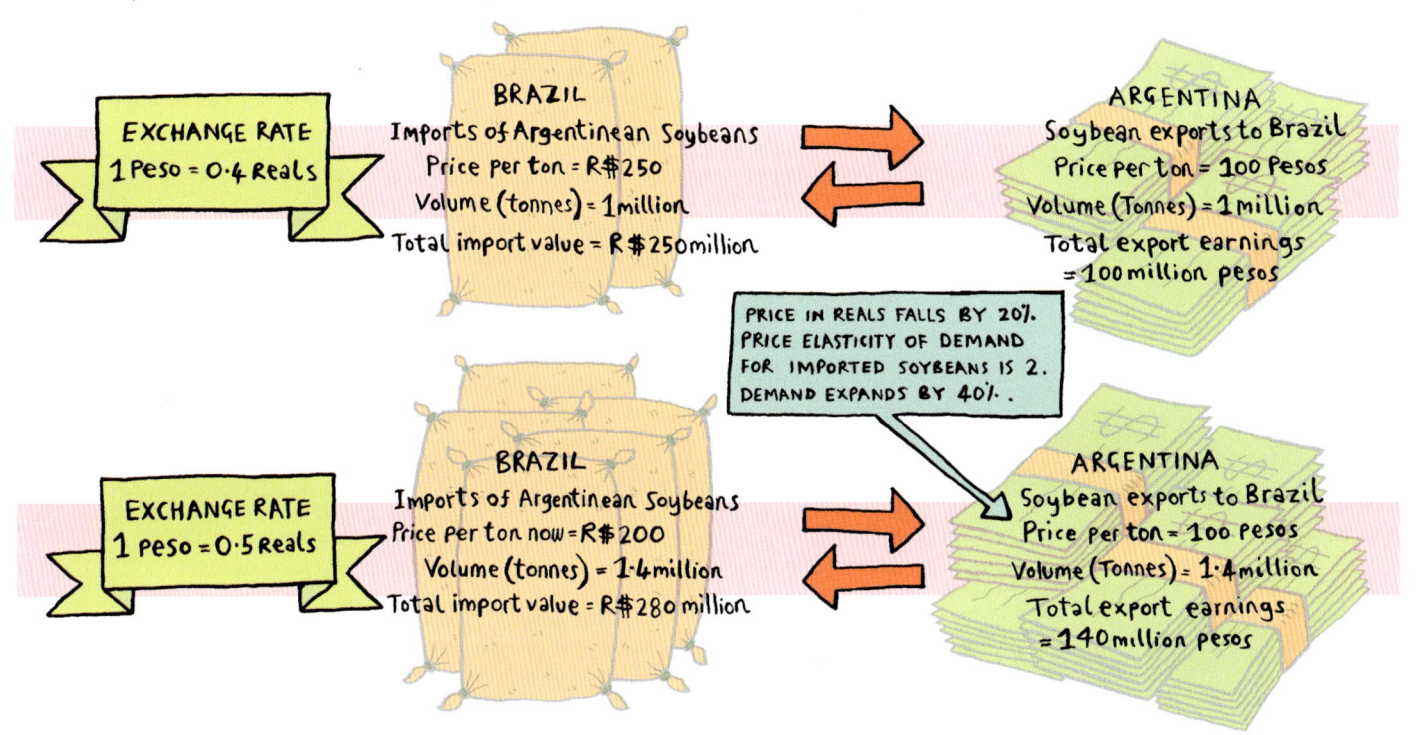

EXCHANGE RATE
1 Peso = 0.4 Reals

BRAZIL
Imports of Argentinean Soybeans
Price per ton = R$250
Volume (tonnes) = 1 million
Total import value = R$250 million

ARGENTINA
Soybean exports to Brazil
Price per ton = 100 Pesos
Volume (Tonnes) = 1 million
Total export earnings = 100 million pesos

PRICE IN REALS FALLS BY 20%. PRICE ELASTICITY OF DEMAND FOR IMPORTED SOYBEANS IS 2. DEMAND EXPANDS BY 40%.

EXCHANGE RATE
1 Peso = 0.5 Reals

BRAZIL
Imports of Argentinean Soybeans
Price per ton now = R$200
Volume (tonnes) = 1.4 million
Total import value = R$280 million

ARGENTINA
Soybean exports to Brazil
Price per ton = 100 Pesos
Volume (Tonnes) = 1.4 million
Total export earnings = 140 million pesos

2 Use contractionary fiscal policy

A government may cut public expenditure and raise taxes to reduce total demand in their economy so people have less to spend on imports. This will help to reduce a trade deficit. However, the fall in demand may also affect domestic firms who may cut output and employment in response. ▶ **5.1**

Balancing international payments

3 Raise interest rates

A government may attempt to attract more inward investment to help offset a trade deficit by raising interest rates. Higher interest rates will also make borrowing more expensive and reduce spending on imports. ➤ **3.1**

4 Introduce trade barriers

Trade barriers can make overseas products more expensive and difficult to import, for example by placing a tariff or excise duty on their imported price or by restricting the amount that can enter the country through a quota or embargo. If demand for the imports is price elastic, the increase in their prices will cause demand for them to fall significantly. ➤ **8.2**

A country may also subsidize the production of goods and services for export so they can be sold more cheaply overseas and provide employment opportunities at home. However, trade barriers restrict free trade and consumer choice, and often lead to other countries retaliating with trade barriers of their own.

Problems with a trade surplus

In contrast, it is not immediately obvious why having a trade surplus should be a problem. However, having a large and persistent trade surplus can also cause problems for an economy:

- There may be political and economic pressure on the government from other countries to reduce its trade surplus so they can reduce their trade deficits.

- Exporting firms enjoy significant and rising overseas revenues from the sale of their exports, but the increase in income from exports may cause demand-push inflation when it is spent in the domestic economy. ➤ **6.1**

- Because the trade balance is in surplus, demand for the national currency will exceed its supply and therefore the value of the currency will rise and stay high. This will increase the price of exports in international markets and could result in falling demand and therefore job losses.

- A persistent trade surplus may itself be a symptom of rapid industrial expansion of the economy through growth in exports and/or a government policy of maintaining an artificially low exchange rate to keep export prices low and import prices high. This will help create demand for domestically produced goods at home and overseas, thereby boosting output and employment.

International aspects

To correct a damaging trade surplus a government may take the following actions to increase spending on imports and/or reduce demand for exports:

1 Do nothing, because a floating exchange rate should correct it

If there is trade surplus, demand for the national currency overseas to pay for exports will exceed its supply in payment for imports. The value of the exchange rate will therefore rise. This will make imports cheaper to buy while increasing the prices of exports sold overseas. As a result, domestic demand for imports should rise and overseas demand for exports should fall until trade balance is restored at a new, higher equilibrium exchange rate.

2 Use expansionary fiscal policy

Increasing public spending and lowering taxes can boost total demand in an economy, including for imported goods and services.

3 Lower interest rates

Lowering interest rates can help to correct a trade surplus by lowering the cost of borrowing and thereby encouraging increased spending on imports. It will also lower the return overseas investors can expect from their inward investments in the economy. This may persuade some to invest elsewhere. In turn this will reduce demand for the currency and reduce upward pressure on the exchange rate.

4 Remove any trade barriers

Removing trade barriers can increase the flow of imports into an economy and reduce their prices, thereby encouraging increased spending on them.

WEBSITES

Some useful websites for data and more information include:

- *www.wikipedia.org/wiki/Balance_of_payments*
- *www.bized.co.uk/virtual/dc/trade/theory/th7.htm*
- *www.exchangerate.com/*
- *www.wikipedia.org/wiki/Exchange_rate*
- *www.tutor2u.net/economics/content/topics/exchangerates/forex_markets.htm*
- *www.economicsonline.co.uk/Global_economics/Trade_protectionism.html*

KEYWORDS

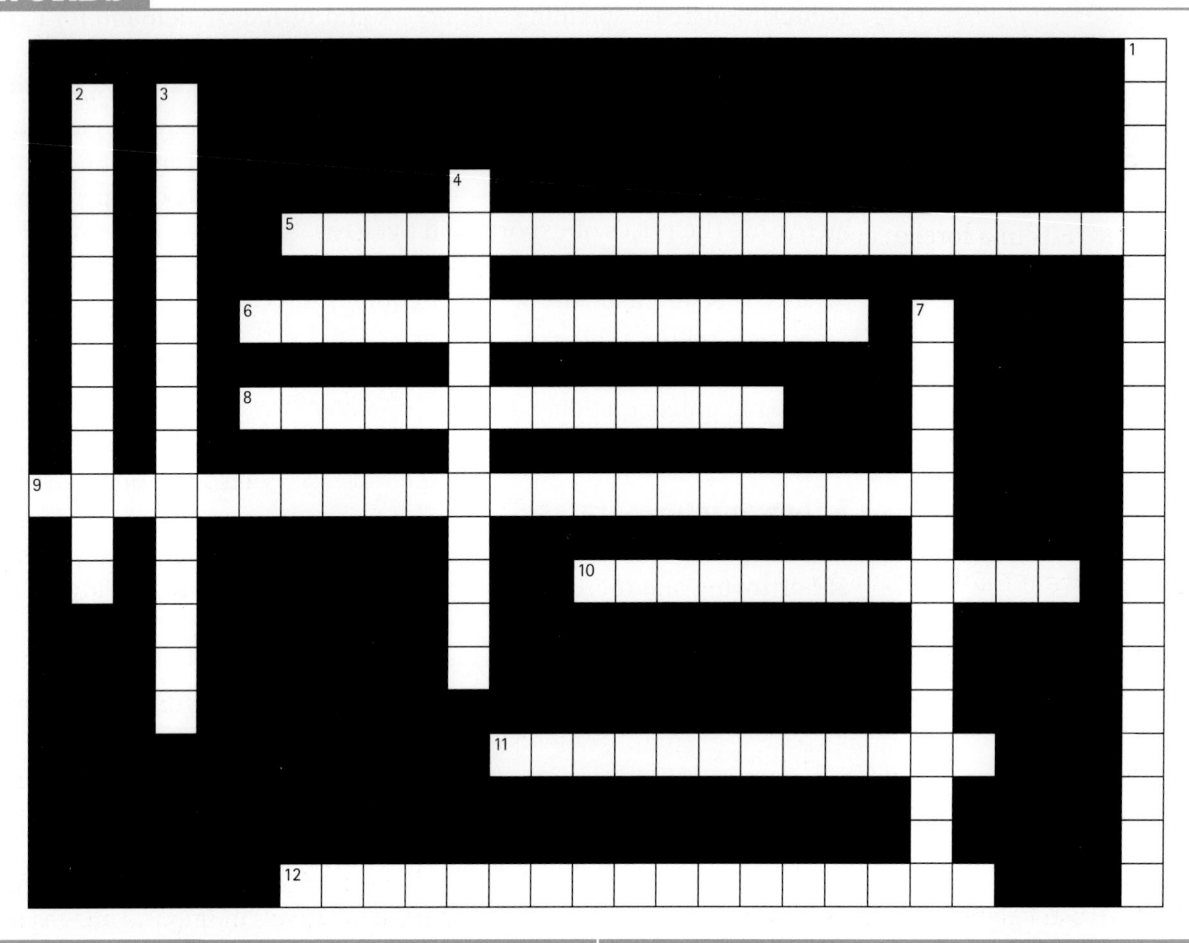

Clues across

5. The global market for the exchange of national currencies (7, 8, 6)
6. The sale of a service to an overseas resident. Payment received for the service will be credited to current account of the balance of payments of that country (9, 6)
8. A physical product purchased from a producer overseas. Payment for the product involves the transfer of money overseas and will be debited from the current account of the balance of payments of the country receiving the product (7, 6)
9. The term used to describe a situation in which a country has recorded more credits from the sale of visible exports overseas than debits for the purchase of visible imports from overseas suppliers in its record of international transactions (10, 5, 7)
10. A rise in the value of a floating exchange rate of a currency against another foreign currency (12)
11. A fall in the value of a floating exchange rate of a currency against another foreign currency (12)
12. An accounting record of all monetary transactions between a country and the rest of the world (7, 2, 8)

Clues down

1. The market price of a national currency against another currency that is determined on the foreign exchange market by the supply and demand for that particular currency (8, 8, 4)
2. The equilibrium market price of one national currency in terms of another currency determined through trade in currencies on the foreign exchange market (8, 4)
3. A floating exchange rate system that is partially controlled by government through the sale or purchase of its currency reserves to limit fluctuations in the value of its national currency (7, 11)
4. The movement and exchange of physical exports and imports across national borders (7, 5)
7. This section of the balance of payments of a country is used to record and monitor how well or how badly it is performing in international trade in goods and services, and other flows of incomes and transfers with other countries (7, 7)

468 International aspects

Assessment exercises

Multiple choice

1 What would increase a deficit on a country's balance of trade?
   - A A firm invests in a foreign country
   - B Foreign tourists visiting the country spend less money.
   - C People buy imported instead of home-produced cars.
   - D Teams of doctors are sent to a country that has experienced an earthquake

2 A newspaper reported that exports from Sweden remained low for five months as changes in the rate of exchange meant that Swedish goods became more expensive to buy abroad.

   What else would be likely to happen?
   - A Imported goods would become cheaper in Sweden.
   - B Swedish people would switch to buying domestically produced goods.
   - C The Swedish balance of payments would improve.
   - D The Swedish balance of trade would improve.

3 The USA decides to introduce a limit on the import of Japanese cars to 15 % of the total market volume.

   What is this policy instrument called?
   - A An embargo
   - B A quota
   - C A subsidy
   - D A tariff

4 What might encourage international specialization between countries?
   - A Free trade
   - B Inefficiencies in production
   - C Labour immobility
   - D Tariffs

5 The central area of a country produces coffee for which it has an ideal climate. The coastal area produces coconuts because its climate is different.

   Assuming there is no change in market conditions, what will happen if this country subsequently produces only coffee in both areas?

   - A It will increase its costs of production
   - B It will increase the productivity of its land
   - C It will increase its total income
   - D It will make the best use of its resources

6 The following is a headline from a newspaper.

   USA to impose tariffs of 40% on imported steel

   What is the most likely result of these tariffs?
   - A A fall in the cost of producing cars in the USA
   - B A fall in the exports of steel from the USA
   - C A rise in employment in the USA's steel industry
   - D A trade deficit for the USA

7 What would contribute to a fall in the value of the Egyptian pound?
   - A A fall in interest rates in other countries
   - B A rise in the number of foreign tourists visiting Egypt
   - C The removal of import tariffs by the USA
   - D The value of Egyptian imports increasing more than the value of Egyptian exports

8 What is meant by a depreciation in the value of a currency?
   - A A fall in its external value
   - B A fall in its internal value
   - C A rise in its external value
   - D A rise in its internal value

9 A country imports oil that is used in the production and distribution of goods. The country has also experienced a rise in incomes which has resulted in a large increase in the demand for goods, some of which it imports.

   What is likely to happen to the country's balance of trade in goods and to the price of oil?

	balance of trade in goods	price of oil
A	worsens	falls
B	improves	falls
C	worsens	rises
D	improves	rises

10 The introduction of a tariff on imported goods is likely to:
- **A** Ensure that the domestic industry becomes more efficient
- **B** Increase the demand for domestically produced goods
- **C** Reduce the price of domestically produced goods
- **D** Reduce the price of imported goods into a country

11 A country has a visible trade deficit of $5 billion and a surplus of invisible trade of $12 billion. This means the country has:
- **A** A balance of payments surplus
- **B** A surplus on capital account
- **C** A current account surplus
- **D** A favourable balance of trade

Questions 12–14 are based on the following answers:
- **A** Quota
- **B** Embargo
- **C** Tariff
- **D** Depreciation

Which of the above is:

12 A tax added to the price of an imported product?

13 A restriction placed on the import of a particular product?

14 A total ban on the importation of a specific good?

15 Which policy would best enable a government to encourage greater specialization in the use of its country's resources?
- **A** Encouraging diversification in industry
- **B** Protecting small businesses
- **C** Reducing tariffs on imports
- **D** Subsidizing job creation in rural areas

16 Which two items, as well as trade in goods and services, are included in the current account of the balance of payments?
- **A** Foreign reserves and international investment
- **B** Government spending and international borrowing
- **C** Incomes and current transfers
- **D** Taxation and foreign aid

17 Drinks producers in Brazil are resisting plans to remove tariffs on imported drinks. They claim that a reduction in tariffs would destroy the emerging drinks industry with large-scale imports of cheap drinks.

Which argument for protectionism are they putting forward?
- **A** The declining industry argument
- **B** The infant industry argument
- **C** The strategic industry argument
- **D** The sunset industry argument

18 What is an effect of trade protection?
- **A** It encourages home industries to be more efficient
- **B** It increases the demand for home-produced goods
- **C** It reduces the price of home-produced goods
- **D** It reduces the price of imports

19 Worldwide campaigns to reduce smoking will affect Tanzania, which has relied on tobacco for its main export earnings.

What is likely to happen if Tanzania is successful in replacing its earnings from tobacco by developing its tourist trade?
- **A** The number of jobs required in the service sector will decrease
- **B** The primary sector will become more significant in the economy
- **C** There will be greater expenditure on new roads and infrastructure
- **D** Visible earnings will decrease while invisible earnings will increase

20 Which of the following transactions is an invisible import to Pakistan?
- **A** A resident of Pakistan buys a car manufactured in Germany
- **B** A Chinese bank loans money to the government of Pakistan
- **C** A resident of Pakistan buys insurance from a UK company
- **D** A Japanese tourist spends money while on holiday in Pakistan

Structured questions

1. **South Africa imposes a quota on Chinese imports**

   In 2007, the South African Government imposed a quota on the imports of clothing and textiles from China. The aim was to try and reduce these imports and increase home production instead. In the first quarter of 2007, imports from China fell by 35% but some were replaced by imports from other countries, including unlikely sources such as Malawi and Zimbabwe which doubled their exports to South Africa. It was thought that China was exporting to South Africa via these countries. Overall, imports fell by only 13%.

   The hope of increased home production was not achieved as some South African companies could not obtain the imports of the necessary fabrics used as raw materials. Lack of raw materials forced one company to reduce its workforce by 8% despite previously investing heavily for a planned expansion.

   Other South African manufacturers did not have the capacity to meet demand so the quotas did not help create employment. The employers said that union power had also not helped. Unions wanted guaranteed employment but employers said, 'We run a business where fashion dictates what we buy and make. We do not know what our fabric requirements are years into the future and cannot promise future employment.'

   a   Where are clothing and textile imports recorded in the balance of payments? [2]
   b   Explain what effect the imposition of a quota by a government might have on an economy. [4]
   c   The graph shows imports of clothing and textiles from China. Suggest why imports took the path shown between 2006–2007. [2]

   d   Explain whether the existence of a union in an industry such as clothing manufacturing is always a benefit to the textile workers. [4]
   e   Consider whether there is evidence in the article to suggest that the quota system was a success. [8]

   Cambridge IGCSE Economics 0455/21 Q1 May/June 2010
   Cambridge O Level Economics 2281/21 Q1 May/June 2010

2. The mining and export of minerals and precious stones is a very important part of the Namibian economy. It was reported that despite a sharp decrease in the quantity of these exports between 1995 and 1999 the export value of the items rose in that period.

   a   Where would the minerals and precious stones be recorded in the Namibian balance of payments? [2]
   b   Discuss whether it is beneficial for a country to specialise in the production and export of a limited range of products. [8]
   c   The statement above says that the exports of minerals and precious stones decreased sharply yet the export value rose. How might this happen? [4]
   d   Discuss what measures a government might take to influence its country's balance of payments. [6]

   Cambridge IGCSE Economics 0455/04 Q5 May/June 2003
   Cambridge O Level Economics 2281/02 Q5 May/June 2003

3. a   Explain why specialisation in international trade might benefit a country. [6]
   b   Some countries use protective measures in international trade. Describe **two** types of protection a government can use in international trade. [4]
   c   Explain with the use of **one** example what is meant by a natural resource of a country. [3]
   d   For many countries international trade involves using their natural resources by selling them to other countries. Discuss whether it is wise for a country to exploit its natural resources rather than to conserve them. [7]

   Cambridge IGCSE Economics 0455/04 Q5
   October/November 2005
   Cambridge O Level Economics 2281/02 Q5
   October/November 2005

Assessment

Index

absolute and comparative advantage 424, 428, 430
advertising 195, 254, 255–6
age distribution 398, 411, 412
agglomeration diseconomies 246
AGMs (annual general meetings) 195
agriculture 381, 384, 390–1
annual reports and accounts 193, 195
arbitration 158
assets 112, 113

balance of payments 276, 280, 282, 443, 447–51, 456, 467, 468
    balance of trade 444–6
    capital account 449–50
    current account 443, 447–9, 456
    financial account 449–50
banks 113, 114–16, 117
    banking system 101, 102, 120
    central banks 101, 102, 119–21
    commercial banks 102, 117–18
    cooperative savings banks 202
    investment banks 118
    Islamic banks 118–19
barriers to trade 292, 436–41, 466, 467
barter 26, 104–5
basic economic problem 1–4, 11–12, 18, 19–20
benefits 75
    external benefits 75, 77, 79
    fringe benefits 131, 142
    joint marketing benefits 245
    private benefits 75, 76, 93, 97
    social benefits 75, 78–80, 93, 94
    welfare benefits 278, 354–5, 392
birth rates 398, 407–9
borrowing 161, 170–5
brand image 253, 255–6
break-even level of output 210, 227, 233–5
brokers 124
budget deficits 285, 316
bureaucracy 438
business organizations 157, 182, 183–5, 204, 208, 209, 434

capital 6, 183, 187, 189–90, 238, 250, 265, 365, 385
    capital employed 239
    capital expenditure 37, 278
    capital intensive production 138, 210, 221–3
    fixed capital 183
    permanent capital 122, 192
    share capital 102
    working capital 183
cartels 264
cash 112, 117
ceteris paribus assumption 43
charities 216
climate change 435
coins 110–11, 119
collateral 172
collective bargaining 150, 154–6
commercial return 81
companies 182
    holding companies 240
    joint stock companies 182, 190–1, 191–2, 192–3, 194–8
    limited companies 183, 190, 193
    private companies 182
    private limited companies 191, 192–3
    public companies 182
    public limited companies 183, 191, 194–8
competition 202, 252, 254, 269, 270, 434
    advertising 254–6
    barriers to entry 252, 264–6
    competing for the market 252–3

    government policy 268–9, 276, 292
    imperfect competition 262
    multinational corporations 202
    non-price competition 252, 254, 264
    perfect competition 252, 261–2
computer aided manufacture (CAM) 223–4
conglomerates 242
conservation 87–91,92–3
consumer expenditure 9, 161–4, 175, 176, 280
    patterns and trends 164–7
consumer price index (CPI) 326, 329–31, 332, 333
consumers 9, 21, 28, 30, 31, 32
    consumer confidence 161, 163, 172
    consumer demand 138
    consumer protection laws 269
    consumers' decisions 85–7
    government as consumer 277–9
consumption 9, 161–7
contraception 40
controlling interest 190
cooperatives 182, 202–4
corporations 191
    multinational corporations 182, 198–200, 200–2, 435–6
    public corporations 182, 206–8
costs
    average costs (AC) 210, 227, 230–1
    cost-push inflation 326, 335
    costs and productive scale 247–8
    employment costs 138, 355
    external costs 75, 76, 79
    fixed costs 210, 228
    private costs 75, 79, 93, 94
    social costs 75, 78–80, 93, 94
    total cost (TC) 210, 225, 227, 229, 232, 233
    unemployment costs 356–8
    variable costs 210, 229
credit 118, 161, 172–3
currency 119, 120, 423, 452–3
    foreign currency reserves 120
    managed (dirty) floating 459
current expenditure 37, 277
current transfers 447–8
custom 408–9
customers 253, 255–6
customs unions 436

death rates 398, 409–11
debt 171
    national debt 119, 317–19
    overseas aid 394
deflation 170, 326, 340–1, 342–3
demand 39–40, 74
    aggregate demand (AD) 276, 280, 352–3
    changes in demand conditions 47–8
    demand curves 39, 40–2, 42–3, 44–5, 64
    demand for labour 134–5, 138
    demand-pull inflation 326, 335
    demand-side policies 275, 282, 284–90
    derived demand 134, 222
    excess demand 55
    shift in demand 57
demographic changes 139, 166
dependency ratio 398, 403
depreciation 454
deregulation 276, 293
developing countries 381, 382, 384–6, 435
    multinational corporations 201–2, 435–6
    overseas aid 394–6
directors, board of 190
discrimination 142, 148
diseconomies of scale 237, 245–6
disequilibrium 56
disinflation 340

dissaving 169
diversification 244
dividends 122, 190
dumping 424, 439
duopoly 264

earnings 129, 131, 139–40, 142
economic cycle 360, 369
economic development 381, 382–3, 396, 397
economic growth 37, 276, 280, 281, 325, 360, 364, 372–3, 376, 377
    external growth 237, 240–1
    growth cycles 369–71
    how economies grow 365–7
    internal growth 240
    negative growth 367–8
    organic growth 237, 240
economic recovery 370
economic systems 21, 22, 24, 37, 38
    market economic systems 22, 25, 26–31, 31–2
    mixed economic systems 21, 22, 25, 31–2, 32–7, 275, 277–9
    planned economic systems 25, 35
economic uncertainty 304, 339–40
economic welfare 75, 372–6
economies 22–3, 244, 433
    developed economies 381, 382, 383–4
    developing and less developed economies 381, 383, 384–6
economies of scale 237, 265
education 139, 291, 385, 390, 392
embargoes 424, 438
emigration 406
employment 146, 280, 281, 294, 345, 349, 358, 359, 409
    employees 146, 238
    employment by industrial sector 348–9
    employment costs 138, 355
    employment trends 346–51
    full employment 276
    government as employer 277
    restrictive practices 146–7
    wage differentials 140–2
enterprises 6, 312
entrepreneurs 6, 181, 183
environmental concerns 166, 302, 373, 436
equilibrium price 39, 56
equilibrium wage rate 136–7
equity 302
exchange 9
exchange rates 104, 289, 443
    determinants 452–3
    fixed exchange rate systems 443, 460–1
    floating exchange rate systems 443, 454–5, 459–60, 464–5, 467
    fluctuations 454–7
    foreign exchange market 443, 451–2
excise duties 70, 313
exports 280, 339, 430, 443, 444–6, 457–9
externalities 75–7

factor substitution 133, 210, 223–4
factors of production 2, 4, 6, 53, 221–3
fertility rates 398
financial institutions and intermediaries 114
firms 6, 29–30, 31, 101, 181, 183, 204, 237, 250, 251
    ancillary firms 245
    business optimism and expectations 53–4
    competing for the market 252–3
    costs and productive scale 247–8
    customers 253, 255–6
    growth 240–1
    joint marketing benefits 245
    market share 239, 253

472 Index

optimum size 248–9
organization 238
products 253, 256
sales 253
size of firms 238–40
small firms 249–50
trade barriers 440–1
fiscal policy 276, 285–6, 286–7
   contractionary fiscal policy 275, 285, 465
   expansionary fiscal policy 275, 284–5, 287, 467
flotations 122

gender imbalance 413–14
gender pay gap 144
geographic distribution 398, 411, 415–16
globalization 26, 54, 425–6, 433
gold reserves 120
goods 1, 2, 4, 21, 23–4, 28, 29, 31, 181, 385
   capital goods 9–10
   complementary goods 47
   consumer goods 9, 390
   durable and non-durable goods 9
   experience goods 163
   free goods 7
   harmful goods 30, 32, 301
   inferior goods 47
   merit goods 10, 31, 278
   normal goods 47
   public goods 10, 31, 278
government interventions 22
   competition policy 268–9, 276, 292
   conflicts of interest 83–4
   deflation 342–3
   labour markets 101, 129, 146–8, 291–2
   mixed economic systems 32–7, 277–9
governments 206, 275, 296, 297
   budget 316–19
   central banks 119, 120
   economic policy 276
   government as consumer and producer 277–9
   government as employer 277
   policy conflicts 294–6
   stock 123
gross added value (GVA) 362
gross domestic product (GDP) 279, 360, 362–3
   nominal GDP 360, 363–4
   per capita GDP 360, 374, 388–9
   real GDP 360, 363–4

Heavily Indebted Poor Countries Initiative (HIPC) 394
Human Development Index (HDI) 360, 374–6, 391
Human Poverty Index (HPI) 391–2
human resources 5–6, 367
hyperinflation 327, 340

immigration 406
imports 301, 430, 443, 444–6
   exchange rates 457–9
   import licenses 438
   import tariffs 313
income 28, 47, 64, 101, 165, 285–6
   disposable income 47, 161–2, 282
   national income 362, 362–3, 374, 447
indexation 332
individuals 40, 101, 134
industrial disputes 150, 156–9
industry 213–15, 278, 348–9, 384
   industrial wage differentials 143–4
   infant (sunrise) industries 414, 438
   nationalized industries 207
   primary industries 213–14
   secondary industries 214
   service industries 214
   strategic industries 439
   sunset industries 439
   tertiary industries 214–15

inequality 278, 301, 312
inflation 106, 280, 281, 294, 314, 325, 326, 327–8, 343, 344, 456
   causes 333–6
   cost-push inflation 326, 335
   costs to economy 339–40
   demand-pull inflation 326, 335
   expansionary fiscal policy 287
   imported inflation 326, 336
   measuring inflation 329–33
   personal consequences of inflation 326, 338–9
information 140, 193, 195, 355
infrastructure 245, 278, 365, 381, 382
inputs 4, 211
insolvency 173
integration 237, 240, 241–2
interest rates 115, 161, 163, 169, 171, 456, 466, 467
international trade 280, 282, 423, 424, 425, 430–1, 441, 442
   barriers to trade 292, 436–8, 466, 467
   changing patterns 431–3
   developing countries 384–5, 435, 436
   free trade 424, 434–6
   protectionism 424, 436–40
investment 116, 118, 365
   direct inward investment 200, 392, 450
   investment expenditure 280

labour 5–6, 101, 148, 149
   demographic changes 139
   division of labour 104, 219–20
   labour diseconomies 246
   labour force 346–8
   labour force participation rate 345, 347
   labour immobility 141, 355–6
   labour intensive production 210, 221–3
   labour productivity 218, 221
   labour supply 129, 130, 135–6, 138–9, 142
labour markets 134–6, 354–6
   government interventions 101, 129, 146–8, 291–2, 345
land 5
laws 32, 82, 269
liability 182, 184, 185, 187, 188, 189
life expectancy 389–90, 410
literacy 390
living standards 360, 408, 409–10
loans 115, 117, 172, 394
local government 206
long run 247
loss 232–3

macroeconomics 279–80, 301
   macroeconomic objectives 275, 280–4, 325
management 187, 193
   management diseconomies 196, 246
manufacturing 214, 221, 223–4
markets 21, 22, 26, 39
   contestable markets 269
   market capitalization 122
   market concentrations 262
   market conditions 257
   market demand 40
   market demand curves 39, 42–3
   market economic systems 22, 25, 26–31, 31–2
   market failure 22, 29, 81–3
   market makers 124
   market price 28, 32, 55–9
   market share 239–40, 253
   market structures 252, 257, 260–2, 269, 270
   market supply 49
   market supply curves 39, 49, 50
   market wages 136–9
   money market 114–121
mergers 237, 240, 241, 242
microeconomics 279
millennium development goals 386–7

mixed economic systems 21, 22, 25, 31–2, 275
monetary policy 102, 120, 276, 287–8
money 101, 102, 103, 105–7, 112–13, 127, 128
   good money 108–10
   history of money 110–11
   money GDP 363
   money income 338–9
   money market 114–121
   money supply 112, 334
   velocity of circulation 113
monopoly 31, 32, 252, 263–4
   artificial barriers to entry 252, 264, 265–7
   government interventions 268–9
   natural barriers to entry 252, 264, 265
   pure monopoly 263
mortgages 117, 171
multinational corporations 182, 198–200, 435–6
   economic impacts 200–2
mutual societies 118

national expenditure 362, 363
natural resources 5, 88, 201, 365
needs 7–8
net migration 398, 407, 411
not-for-profit organizations 216
notes (currency) 111, 119

occupations 101, 129–30
   net advantages 138
   occupational distribution 398, 412, 417–18
   occupational mobility of labour 141, 356
   occupational specialization 133–4
   wage differentials 139–45
oligopoly 252, 264
opportunity cost 2, 10–12, 12–14, 14–15, 15–17, 84–5
outputs 4, 211, 230, 263, 360
   break-even level of output 210, 227, 233–5
   measuring economic activity 361–2
   national output 361
   output policies 252
overseas aid 392–6
ownership 182, 184
   loss of control 196–8

partnerships 182, 183, 187–90, 192
patents 265
planned economic systems 25, 35
plant 211
policy instruments 282
population 48, 385, 399–400, 418, 419
   dependency ratio 398, 403
   dependent population 347, 402–4
   labour force 346–8
   natural rate of increase 381, 398, 406–7
   optimum population 404–6
   population growth 398, 401–2
   population pyramids 414–15
   structure of populations 411–18
poverty 382, 387–8, 389, 391–2
   international poverty 392–6
price elasticity of demand (PED) 39, 59–61
   factors affecting PED 64–6
   measuring PED 61–2
   PED and total revenue 62–3
price elasticity of supply (PES) 39, 66–8
   factors affecting PES 68–70
price indices 329–31, 343, 344
   problems 332–3
   uses 332
   weighted price index 326
prices 47, 53
   price collusion 264
   price competition 252, 254
   price deflators 332
   price makers 263
   price mechanism 28, 40, 59
   price signals 32

price stability 276
price takers 261
wage-price spiral 335
pricing policies 252
pricing strategies 257–8
    competitive pricing strategies 258–9
    cost-based pricing strategies 259–60
    demand-based pricing strategies 258
    destruction pricing 259
    penetration pricing 258
    predatory pricing 259, 267
private expenditure 25, 35–7, 75, 286
privatization 276, 292
producers 4, 21, 31, 32
    government as producer 277–9
production 4, 23–4, 26, 28, 181, 210, 235, 236
    adding value 211
    aims of production 215–17
    capital intensive production 138, 210, 221–3
    chain of productive activity 212–13
    industrial sectors 213–15
    labour intensive production 210, 221–3
    large and small-scale production 237
    mass production 220
    production costs 12–14, 32, 257
    scale of production 240, 242–5
    specialization 211–13
production possibilities curves (PPCs) 2, 12–14
productivity 138, 210
    combining factors of production 221–3
    division of labour 219–20
    factor productivity 217–18
    labour productivity 218, 221
    measuring productivity 218–19
products 9, 28
    product differentiation 256
    product quality 263
    product superiority 253
professional associations 152
profit 26, 27–8, 29–30, 53, 184, 286
    abnormal profit 263
    aims of production 215–16
    excess profit 263
    mark-up for profit 259
    profit and loss 232–3
    profit maximisation 210, 216, 227–8, 253
protectionism 424, 436–40
public expenditure 277, 280, 319
    financing public expenditure 299–304
    job creation 285
    private sector 35–7, 75, 286
    sources of revenue 299, 301, 311, 315
public sector 25, 34, 205–6
    public sector borrowing requirement 316–17
purchasing power 338

quality standards 438
quantitative easing 288
quantity 40, 48, 229, 231
quotas 424, 437

recession 360, 369–70
regulations 32, 82, 264, 276, 293
religion 408–9
resource allocation 2, 22, 23, 367, 423
resources 1–4, 30, 69, 75
    economic and uneconomic use of resources 80–1
    human resources 5–6, 367
    man-made resources 6
    natural resources 5, 88, 201, 365
    non-renewable resources 88
    resource classification 5–6
    resource depletion 88, 435
retail price index (RPI) 326, 329, 333
returns to scale 247–8
revenues
    average revenue (AR) 210, 226, 231
    calculating revenues 225–32
    total revenue (TR) 210, 226, 227, 231, 232, 233
risk 182
robotics 224

saving 105, 161, 168–69
    savings accounts 117, 169
    savings patterns 169–70
    savings ratio 168
scale of production 240
    external economics of scale 244–5
    internal economics of scale 242–4
    returns to scale 247–8
scarcity 1–4, 10–11
self-sufficiency 103
separate legal identity 184, 193
services 1, 2, 4, 21, 23–4, 28, 29, 31, 181, 385
    consumer services 9
    public services 31, 216, 278
sex distribution 411, 413–14
shareholders 122, 190, 193
shares 122, 190
    private limited companies 193
    prospectuses 195
    public limited companies 195
    public listing 195
    share price indices 124–5
    speculating on share prices 125–6
short run 247
skills 143, 244, 385
sole traders 182, 183, 184, 185, 186–7, 192, 198
specialization 103–4, 109–10, 129, 211–13, 434
    international specialization 424, 426–30
    occupational specialization 133–4
    over-specialization 424, 439
speculation 125–6, 456–7
spending 161, 164–7
stagflation 334
statistics 364
stock 122–3, 190
stock exchanges 101, 102, 123–4
stock market 122–7
subsidies 37, 39, 72, 202, 276, 278, 424, 437
    influence on prices 257
    market failure 83
    selective subsidies 291
    subsidies and supply 72–3
substitutes 47, 64
supply 39, 49, 74
    aggregate supply (AS) 280
    aggregate supply 280
    excess supply 55
    restriction on supplies 265
    subsidies and supply 72–3
    tax and supply 70–2
supply curves 48–50
    fall in supply 51–2, 54
    increase in supply 51, 54
    infinitely price elastic supply 70
    market supply curves 39, 49, 50
    perfectly price inelastic supply 69
supply-side policies 275, 276, 282–4, 290–1
    policy instruments 291–4
sustainable growth 372

takeovers 196, 237, 240, 241
tariffs 313. 424, 436, 438
taxes 28, 32, 39, 47, 275, 276, 298, 319, 320
    ability to pay 312
    ad valorem (percentage) taxes 312–13
    capital gains tax 311
    collection 303–4
    corporation tax 311
    direct taxes 298, 305–7, 308–12
    employer payroll taxes 309–10
    hypothecated tax 314
    income tax 308–9, 311
    indirect taxes 70, 298, 305–7, 312–15
    national and local taxes 307
    progressive tax 298, 304, 392
    proportional tax 298, 304
    reasons for taxes 301-2
    regressive tax 298, 304, 314
    tax base 306, 314
    tax burden 300, 310
    tax evasion and avoidance 300, 315
    tax incentives 291
    tax rates 306, 308
    tax systems 304–8
    VAT 312
    wealth taxes 311
technology 53, 166, 250, 354, 366, 393–4
time 64, 68–9, 220
trade 384–5
    balance of trade 444–6
    invisible trade 445–6, 447
    trade deficit 444, 463, 464–6
    trade imbalance 439, 462
    trade liberalization 440
    trade surplus 444, 466–7
    visible trade 444–5, 447
    see also international trade
trade barriers 292, 436–8, 466, 467
trade unions 101, 150–1, 153–4, 159, 160, 354
    collective bargaining 150, 154–6
    functions 151–2
    industrial disputes 150, 156–9
    international cooperation 153–4
    national executive 153
    organization 153
    restrictive practices 146–7
    types 152
    union membership 154, 157
training 139, 291
transfer payments 37, 278, 363
turnover 226, 231

unemployment 148, 281, 325, 345, 349–51, 392
    casual and seasonal factors 351–2
    causes and consequences 351–8
    cyclical unemployment 345, 352
    falling aggregate demand 352–3
    frictional unemployment 345, 351
    imperfections in labour markets 354–6
    seasonal unemployment 345, 351
    structural unemployment 345, 354
    technological change 354
    unemployment costs 356–8
    unemployment rates 350–1
    voluntary and involuntary unemployment 355
urbanization 381
utility 162–3

wage differentials 139–45
    compensating differentials 140
    gender pay gap 144
    industrial wage differentials 143–4
    international wage differentials 145
    public-private sector pay gap 143
    skilled and unskilled workers 143
wages 101, 131, 354
    market wage 136–9
    minimum wages 147, 355, 392
    non-wage factors 129, 132
    wage differentials 139–41, 143–4, 145
    wage factors 129, 131
    wage rates 129, 131, 136–7
    wage-price spiral 335
wants 1–4, 7–10, 10–11
    double coincidence of wants 105
wealth 28, 163, 172

X inefficiency 264